Negation and Negative Dependencies

OXFORD STUDIES IN THEORETICAL LINGUISTICS

General Editors
David Adger and Hagit Borer, Queen Mary University of London

Advisory Editors
Stephen Anderson, Yale University; Daniel Büring, University of Vienna; Nomi Erteschik-Shir, Ben-Gurion University; Donka Farkas, University of California, Santa Cruz; Angelika Kratzer, University of Massachusetts, Amherst; Andrew Nevins, University College London; Christopher Potts, Stanford University; Barry Schein, University of Southern California; Peter Svenonius, University of Tromsø; Moira Yip, University College London

RECENT TITLES

66 **Parts of a Whole**
Distributivity as a Bridge between Aspect and Measurement
by Lucas Champollion

67 **Semantics and Morphosyntactic Variation**
Qualities and the Grammar of Property Concepts
by Itamar Francez and Andrew Koontz-Garboden

68 **The Structure of Words at the Interfaces**
edited by Heather Newell, Máire Noonan, Glyne Piggott, and Lisa deMena Travis

69 **Pragmatic Aspects of Scalar Modifiers**
The Semantics-Pragmatics Interface
by Osamu Sawada

70 **Encoding Events**
Functional Structure and Variation
by Xuhui Hu

71 **Gender and Noun Classification**
edited by Éric Mathieu, Myriam Dali, and Gita Zareikar

72 **The Grammar of Expressivity**
by Daniel Gutzmann

73 **The Grammar of Copulas Across Language**
edited by María J. Arche, Antonio Fábregas, and Rafael Marín

74 **The Roots of Verbal Meaning**
by John Beavers and Andrew Koontz-Garboden

75 **Contrast and Representations in Syntax**
edited by Bronwyn M. Bjorkman and Daniel Currie Hall

76 **Nominalization**
50 Years on from Chomsky's *Remarks*
edited by Artemis Alexiadou and Hagit Borer

77 **Majority Quantification and Quantity Superlatives**
A Crosslinguistic Analysis of *Most*
by Carmen Dobrovie-Sorin and Ion Giurgea

78 **The Grammar of the Utterance**
How to Do Things with Ibero-Romance
by Alice Corr

79 **The Derivational Timing of Ellipsis**
edited by Güliz Güneş and Anikó Lipták

80 **Negation and Negative Dependencies**
by Hedde Zeijlstra

For a complete list of titles published and in preparation for the series, see pp. 462–4.

Negation and Negative Dependencies

HEDDE ZEIJLSTRA

OXFORD
UNIVERSITY PRESS

Great Clarendon Street, Oxford, OX2 6DP,
United Kingdom

Oxford University Press is a department of the University of Oxford.
It furthers the University's objective of excellence in research, scholarship,
and education by publishing worldwide. Oxford is a registered trade mark of
Oxford University Press in the UK and in certain other countries

© Hedde Zeijlstra 2022

The moral rights of the author have been asserted

Impression: 1

All rights reserved. No part of this publication may be reproduced, stored in
a retrieval system, or transmitted, in any form or by any means, without the
prior permission in writing of Oxford University Press, or as expressly permitted
by law, by licence, or under terms agreed with the appropriate reprographics
rights organization. Enquiries concerning reproduction outside the scope of the
above should be sent to the Rights Department, Oxford University Press, at the
address above

You must not circulate this work in any other form
and you must impose this same condition on any acquirer

Published in the United States of America by Oxford University Press
198 Madison Avenue, New York, NY 10016, United States of America

British Library Cataloguing in Publication Data
Data available

Library of Congress Control Number: 2022930881

ISBN 978-0-19-883323-9

DOI: 10.1093/oso/9780198833239.001.0001

Printed and bound in the UK by Clays Ltd, Elcograf S.p.A.

Links to third party websites are provided by Oxford in good faith and
for information only. Oxford disclaims any responsibility for the materials
contained in any third party website referenced in this work.

Contents

Acknowledgements xii
General Preface xiii
List of Abbreviations xiv

I. INTRODUCTION AND OUTLINE

1. Introduction: Negation and negative dependencies 3
    1.1 Introduction 3
    1.2 The syntax of sentential negation 4
        1.2.1 Sentential and constituent negation 5
        1.2.2 Ways of expressing sentential negation 6
        1.2.3 On the syntactic status of negative markers 10
        1.2.4 On the syntactic position of negative markers 14
    1.3 Polarity-sensitivity 17
        1.3.1 The licenser question 18
        1.3.2 The licensee question 23
        1.3.3 The licensing question 26
    1.4 The landscape of negative dependencies 28
        1.4.1 Negative Concord 28
        1.4.2 Positive Polarity-sensitivity 31
    1.5 Conclusions 33

2. Outline: The pluriform landscape of negative dependencies 34
    2.1 The pluriform landscape of negative dependencies 34
    2.2 Outline 40
    2.3 Relation to earlier work 41

II. NEGATIVE CONCORD AND NEGATIVE QUANTIFIERS

3. Negative Concord is syntactic agreement 45
    3.1 Introduction: Negative Concord and neg-words 45
    3.2 The negative-quantifier approach 49
        3.2.1 Proposal 49
        3.2.2 Problems for the negative-quantifier approach 53
        3.2.3 Concluding remarks 58
    3.3 The Negative Polarity Item approach 58
        3.3.1 Proposal 58
        3.3.2 Challenges for the Negative Polarity Item approach 59

3.3.3 Concluding remarks	65
3.4 Negative Concord is syntactic agreement	66
3.4.1 Proposal	66
3.4.2 Application	69
3.4.3 Challenges for the syntactic-agreement approach	73
3.5 Conclusions	76
4. Types of Negative Concord systems	**77**
4.1 Variation on the domain of Negative Concord	77
4.2 Strict vs Non-strict Negative Concord languages	78
4.2.1 Strict vs Non-strict Negative Concord	78
4.2.2 Obligatoriness and optionality of Negative Concord	86
4.3 In search of a missing language: A closer look at Afrikaans	88
4.4 Partial and/or invisible Negative Concord	95
4.4.1 Negative Concord in French: Partial Negative Concord	95
4.4.2 Negative Concord in English: Invisible Negative Concord	100
4.4.3 Other invisible Negative Concord languages: Hindi and Punjabi	106
4.5 Conclusions	109
5. The flexibility of negative features	**111**
5.1 The nature of negative features	111
5.2 The Flexible Formal Feature Hypothesis	112
5.2.1 A universal set of formal features?	113
5.2.2 The algorithm	116
5.2.3 Consequences	118
5.3 Acquiring types of Negative Concord systems	121
5.3.1 Double Negation: Dutch	121
5.3.2 Non-strict Negative Concord: Italian	122
5.3.3 Strict Negative Concord: Czech	123
5.3.4 Negative Concord in Afrikaans Variety A	124
5.3.5 Optional Negative Concord: Catalan and West Flemish	125
5.3.6 Partial Negative Concord: French	128
5.3.7 Invisible Negative Concord: English and Hindi/Punjabi	129
5.3.8 Non-negative licensers of neg-words	131
5.4 Consequences in the domain of language variation, acquisition, and change	134
5.4.1 Types of Negative Concord systems: Language variation	134
5.4.2 Types of Negative Concord systems: Language acquisition	135
5.4.3 Consequences for language change	138
5.5 Conclusions	138

6. Diachronic developments in the domain of negation and Negative Concord — 140
  6.1 The nature of negative features — 140
  6.2 Jespersen's Cycle — 141
  6.3 The emergence of Negative Concord — 144
    6.3.1 The emergence of French Negative Concord — 145
    6.3.2 From Strict to Non-strict Negative Concord — 147
    6.3.3 The emergence of the Negative Concord system of Afrikaans A — 149
    6.3.4 The emergence of French partial Negative Concord — 150
    6.3.5 The emergence of English invisible Negative Concord — 151
  6.4 The disappearance of Negative Concord and the emergence of double negatives — 154
    6.4.1 En/ne-deletion in Dutch — 154
    6.4.2 Emphatic Multiple Negative Expressions in Dutch and German — 158
  6.5 Possible and impossible changes: The *NALL*-problem — 162
    6.5.1 Emerging negative indefinites — 162
    6.5.2 The *NALL*-problem — 163
    6.5.3 A diachronic solution — 166
  6.6 Conclusions — 170

7. Negative indefinites and split-scope readings — 171
  7.1 The problem — 171
  7.2 The phenomenon — 172
    7.2.1 Modal verbs — 173
    7.2.2 Object-intensional verbs — 175
    7.2.3 Idiomatic expressions — 176
    7.2.4 Concluding remarks — 177
  7.3 Proposal — 177
    7.3.1 Negative indefinites as pieces of syntactic structure — 177
    7.3.2 Deriving the split-scope readings: Modal verbs — 180
    7.3.3 Deriving the split-scope readings: Object-intensional verbs — 183
    7.3.4 Deriving the split-scope readings: Idiomatic expressions — 185
    7.3.5 Concluding remarks — 186
  7.4 Comparison with other accounts — 188
    7.4.1 Amalgamation and incorporation (Jacobs/Rullmann) — 189
    7.4.2 Quantification over abstract individuals (Geurts) — 191
    7.4.3 Higher-order quantification (De Swart) — 193
    7.4.4 Negative indefinites and choice-functions (Abels and Marti) — 194
    7.4.5 Negative indefinites are neg-words (Penka) — 196
  7.5 Conclusions — 198

8. Neg-raising — 199
  8.1 Introduction — 199
  8.2 Arguments in favour of the syntactic approach — 202
    8.2.1 Neg-raising and strict Negative Polarity Items — 203
    8.2.2 Neg-raising and Horn-clauses — 205
    8.2.3 Neg-raising and negative parentheticals — 208
    8.2.4 Summing up — 211
  8.3 Problems for CP14 — 212
    8.3.1 Horn-clauses and Cloud-of-Unknowing predicates — 212
    8.3.2 Phonologically deleted negations — 214
    8.3.3 Islands and Neg-raising — 219
    8.3.4 Summing up — 220
  8.4 Reinstalling the standard, pragma-semantic approach — 221
  8.5 Conclusions — 224

***

INTERMEZZO

9. Intermezzo. The landscape of polarity-sensitive elements: Convergence vs divergence — 226
  9.1 Neg-words and/or (other) Negative Polarity Items — 226
  9.2 Convergence vs divergence — 227
  9.3 Outline — 229

***

III. POLARITY-SENSITIVITY

10. Strong vs weak Negative Polarity Items — 233
  10.1 Introduction: Strong and weak Negative Polarity Items — 233
  10.2 Exhaustification approaches to NPI-hood and the strong–weak distinction — 234
    10.2.1 Exhaustification approaches to NPI-hood — 234
    10.2.2 The strong–weak distinction among Negative Polarity Items — 237
    10.2.3 Preliminary evidence for this treatment of the strong–weak distinction — 239
  10.3 Problems for the exhaustification approach and the strong–weak Negative Polarity Item distinction — 242
    10.3.1 Encoding weak and strong NPI-hood — 242
    10.3.2 Syntactic locality and the exhaustification approach — 243
  10.4 Syntactic vs pragmatic exhaustification — 245
  10.5 Negative Polarity Items and domain-wideners: A re-appreciation — 249
  10.6 Conclusions — 253

11. Other types of NPIs	254
11.1 Introduction: Superstrong, strong/weak, and superweak Negative Polarity Items	254
11.2 Strong/weak Negative Polarity Items	255
11.2.1 Distribution	255
11.2.2 Strong/weak Negative Polarity Items and split-scope constructions	259
11.2.3 The source of *need/hoeven/brauchen*'s NPI-hood	261
11.2.4 Acquiring *hoeven*	263
11.3 Superweak Negative Polarity Items	267
11.3.1 Non-veridicality	267
11.3.2 Negative Polarity Items and Free Choice Items	268
11.3.3 Chinese *shenme*: A superweak Negative Polarity Item	271
11.3.4 The Non-Entailment-of-Existence Condition and non-veridicality	274
11.3.5 Acquiring *shenme*	275
11.4 Acquiring weak Negative Polarity Items	276
11.5 Conclusions	278
12. Not a light negation	280
12.1 Introduction	280
12.2 Light negation (Schwarz and Bhatt)	286
12.3 Proposal	288
12.3.1 Negated indefinites	290
12.3.2 Negated definites	295
12.3.3 Negated disjunctions	297
12.4 Conclusions	298
13. Universal Quantifier PPIs	301
13.1 Introduction	301
13.1.1 Exhaustification approaches to Negative Polarity Items	301
13.1.2 Question: Universal Positive Polarity Items	303
13.1.3 Outline	305
13.2 Modal Positive Polarity Items	305
13.2.1 Modal auxiliaries and their scope with respect to negation	305
13.2.2 Metalinguistic/contrastive negation	308
13.2.3 Intervention effects	310
13.2.4 Clause-external negation	311
13.2.5 Variation among Positive Polarity Items	311
13.3 Why Positive Polarity Items?	316
13.3.1 Universal modal Positive Polarity Items as the mirror image of existential Negative Polarity Items	316
13.3.2 Universal Positive Polarity Items as self-interveners	319

x CONTENTS

13.4 Positive Polarity Items in the domain of universal quantifiers over individuals	323
13.5 Conclusions	327
14. The landscape of PPIs	**328**
14.1 Introduction	328
14.2 Strong vs weak Positive Polarity Items	329
14.3 Hybrid Polarity Items	334
14.3.1 Durative vs punctual *until*	335
14.3.2 Durative until *is* punctual until	338
14.3.3 Deriving the inferences	342
14.4 Existential Polarity Items	343
14.4.1 Existential Negative Polarity Items and Positive Polarity Items	343
14.4.2 Modal existential Positive Polarity Items	347
14.5 Conclusions	349
15. Negation and clause types	**351**
15.1 Introduction: Two phenomena	351
15.1.1 The ban on True Negative Imperatives	351
15.1.2 The ban on single negative markers in sentence-initial position in V2 languages	353
15.1.3 Outline	355
15.2 The ban on True Negative Imperatives	355
15.2.1 Previous analyses	356
15.2.2 Explaining the ban on True Negative Imperatives	362
15.2.3 Additional evidence	367
15.3 The ban on single negative markers in sentence-initial position in V-to-C languages	370
15.3.1 Previous analysis: Barbiers (2002)	370
15.3.2 Account	372
15.4 Conclusions	376

IV. CONCLUSIONS, OPEN QUESTIONS, AND AVENUES FOR FURTHER RESEARCH

16. Conclusions and open questions	**381**
16.1 Outline	381
16.2 Conclusions concerning Negative Concord, and negative quantifiers and their internal complexity	381
16.2.1 Negative Concord	381
16.2.2 Negative quantifiers and their internal complexity	384
16.3 Conclusions and open questions concerning the landscapes of Negative Polarity Items and Positive Polarity Items	385

	16.3.1 The landscape of Negative Polarity Items	385
	16.3.2 The landscape of Positive Polarity Items	387
16.4	Open questions	389
	16.4.1 Open questions concerning Negative Concord	389
	16.4.2 Open questions concerning negative quantifiers and their internal complexity	391
	16.4.3 Open questions concerning the landscape of Negative Polarity Items	394
	16.4.4 Open questions concerning the landscape of Positive Polarity Items	397
16.5	Final remarks	400
17. Avenues for further research		**402**
17.1	Outline	402
17.2	Upward Agree, the FFFH, and the derivational behaviour of formal features	403
	17.2.1 Upward Agree	403
	17.2.2 The FFFH and the derivational behaviour of formal features	407
17.3	Uninterpretable features, Positive Polarity Items, and the nature of V-to-I movement	412
	17.3.1 The Rich Agreement Hypothesis	412
	17.3.2 Alleged V-to-I movement in Korean	417
17.4	Other types of syntactic dependencies	422
	17.4.1 Sequence of Tense	422
	17.4.2 Pro-drop	426
	17.4.3 Modal Concord	430
17.5	Finally	433

References 435
Index 462

Acknowledgements

The current monograph is the result of an investigation into the syntax and semantics of negation and negative dependencies that started out more than 20 years ago when I worked on my PhD thesis at the University of Amsterdam. Ever since – during the two years as a postdoc in Tübingen, as assistant professor at the University of Amsterdam from 2006-2013, at my stay at MIT's Linguistics and Philosophy department in 2009 and now, at the University of Göttingen within the platform *Linguistics in Göttingen*, and more recently, the Research Training Group 2636 on form meaning mismatches – I have been able to work with many wonderful people who all in one way or the other have contributed to the work that lead to this monograph. Thanks to all of them for sharing their different perspectives.

It has made me very happy to have had the opportunity to collaborate with many co-authors, who have taught me so much and with whom it has been such a pleasure to work. I am grateful to all those with whom I could collaborate in a series of research projects. Of course, I also thank the funding agencies who made this all possible: Dutch NWO, German DFG and the Volkswagen Foundation, the latter who generously provided me with an *opus magnum* grant to work on this book and be replaced for three semesters.

Various parts of this work have been presented at invited talks, conference and/or workshop presentations, guest lectures and summer schools. I thank all the organizers for having made these events possible. This also holds for the journals and book series where earlier versions of the presented analyses have been published. Let me thank here all the editors and reviewers for the important work they have carried out.

I also wish to express my gratitude to the publishing team at Oxford University Press and Integra, and the anonymous reviewer who commented in detailed on an earlier version of the manuscript.

Finally I thank the one and only for everything.

General Preface

The theoretical focus of this series is on the interfaces between subcomponents of the human grammatical system and the closely related area of the interfaces between the different subdisciplines of linguistics. The notion of 'interface' has become central in grammatical theory (for instance, in Chomsky's Minimalist Program) and in linguistic practice: work on the interfaces between syntax and semantics, syntax and morphology, phonology and phonetics, etc. has led to a deeper understanding of particular linguistic phenomena and of the architecture of the linguistic component of the mind/brain.

The series covers interfaces between core components of grammar, including syntax/morphology, syntax/semantics, syntax/phonology, syntax/pragmatics, morphology/phonology, phonology/phonetics, phonetics/speech processing, semantics/pragmatics, and intonation/discourse structure, as well as issues in the way that the systems of grammar involving these interface areas are acquired and deployed in use (including language acquisition, language dysfunction, and language processing). It demonstrates, we hope, that proper understandings of particular linguistic phenomena, languages, language groups, or inter-language variations all require reference to interfaces.

The series is open to work by linguists of all theoretical persuasions and schools of thought. A main requirement is that authors should write so as to be understood by colleagues in related subfields of linguistics and by scholars in cognate disciplines.

Every human language has a means of expressing negation, but the linguistic behaviour of negation can be complex, both within a language and across languages, often involving multiple negative elements that enter into dependencies with each other. In this major new work, Hedde Zeijlstra investigates a wide range of such dependencies in human language. He shows that the full range of linguistic dependencies that are attested outside of the domain of negation also appear within that domain, and weaves syntactic, semantic, and pragmatic theories of such dependencies into a unified approach to the linguistics of negative concord, quantification, polarity, and scope.

David Adger
Hagit Borer

List of Abbreviations

AA	Anti-Additive
AI	actuality inference
b-s	backward-shifted interpretation
BEI	beyond-expectation inference
CP	Complementizer Phrase
DA	Downward Agree
DE	Downward-Entailing
DN	Double Negation
DP	Determiner Phrase
EMNE	Emphatic Multiple Negative Expression
EPP	Extended Projection Principle
EXH	Exhaustifier
FCI	Free Choice Item
FFFH	Flexible Formal Feature Hypothesis
FI	Full Interpretation
f-s	forward-shifted interpretation
GB	Government and Binding
GPSG	Generalized Phrase Structure Grammar
HMC	Head Movement Constraint
HPSG	Head-driven Phrase Structure Grammar
[iEXH]	interpretable exhaustifier feature
[iF]	interpretable formal feature
[iNEG]	interpretable negative feature
IP	Inflectional Phrase
ISC	Immediate Scope Constraint
LB	Left Boundary
MC	Modal Concord
NC	Negative Concord
NI	Negative Indefinite
NM	Negative Marker
NPI	Negative Polarity Item
NQ	Negative Quantifier
NSI	Negative-Sensitive Item
OS	Old Saxonian
PPI	Positive Polarity Item
PTS	Perfect Time Span
QR	Quantifier Raising
RAH	Rich Agreement Hypothesis

RB	Right Boundary
sim	simultaneous interpretation
SNI	Surrogate Negative Imperative
SoT	Sequence of Tense
ST	Situation Time
TNI	True Negative Imperative
TT	Topic Time
UA	Upward Agree
[uF]	uninterpretable feature
[uNEG]	uninterpretable negative feature
[uT]	uninterpretable Tense feature
UTS	time span introduced by *until*
[uWh]	uninterpretable *Wh*-feature
VISH	VP-Internal-Subject-Hypothesis
[iWh]	interpretable *Wh*-feature

PART I
INTRODUCTION AND OUTLINE

1
Introduction
Negation and negative dependencies

1.1 Introduction

This monograph deals with the question of how the variety of negative dependencies that have currently been attested can be explained, and what the repercussions of such an explanation are for the syntax and semantics of negative elements, negative dependencies, and related phenomena. The central hypothesis is that, to the extent applicable to negation, all possible ways to encode grammatical dependencies (at lexical, syntactic, semantic, and pragmatic levels) are attestable in the domain of negative dependencies, unless these are ruled out independently, e.g. on functional, formal, or learnability grounds.

However, before properly introducing the research questions and hypotheses of this monograph in detail, it makes sense to first introduce the empirical phenomena at stake, leaving the presentation of these research questions and hypotheses to the next chapter. In the current chapter, I therefore introduce the most important notions in the study to negation and negative dependencies. I start by discussing key areas in the syntax and semantics of negative elements, including the distinction between sentential and constituent negation, the syntactic status of negative markers (NMs), and the locus of negation in the clausal spine. Next, I introduce the notion of Negative Polarity Items (NPIs) and briefly discuss in what terms they have been studied over the past decades. What is their exact distribution? What makes them have these distributional restrictions? And what is the exact syntactic, semantic and/or pragmatic relation between an NPI and its licenser? I conclude by introducing two more types of negative dependencies: Negative Concord (NC) and so-called Positive Polarity Items (PPIs).

A universal property of natural language is that every language is able to express negation, i.e., every language has some device at its disposal to reverse the truth-value of the propositional contents of a sentence. However, languages may differ to quite a large extent as to how they express this negation. Not only do languages vary with respect to the form of negative elements, but the position of negative elements is also subject to cross-linguistic variation. Moreover, languages also differ in terms of the number of manifestations of negative morphemes: in some languages, negation is realized by a single word or morpheme, in other languages by multiple morphemes.

The syntax of negation is intrinsically connected to the phenomenon of negative dependencies. In short, and leaving the formal discussion for later, NPIs are items whose distribution is limited to a number of contexts which, in some sense, all count as negative. NPIs surface in various kinds and may also vary in terms of the restrictions they impose on their licensing contexts and the types of licensing relations. Therefore, studying NPIs does provides more insight not only into the nature of such context-sensitive elements, but also into the syntax and semantics of negation itself. NPIs may find their mirror image in PPIs—items that are banned from contexts which, in one way or the other, are negative.

The distinction between negative elements and NPIs is not always that clear-cut. In many languages, negative indefinites (NIs), quite often referred to as neg-words (or, previously, n-words, after Laka 1990), appear to be semantically negative in certain constructions, while exhibiting NPI-like behaviour in other configurations. The same may also apply to NMs in some languages. Of course, this raises questions regarding what negative elements are, what elements that are polarity-sensitive are, and where the boundaries between the two lie. What is negation and what are negative dependencies?

This book will aim at formulating answers to these questions, and several more. However, before outlining which questions in the domain of negation and negative dependencies are currently in need of explanation, in this chapter, I first provide a brief theoretical and empirical overview of the most important relevant notions and insights in this domain. This will set the stage for the next chapter, which introduces the research questions and hypotheses that I will entertain in this monograph.

Section 1.2 deals with the syntax and semantics of NMs; Section 1.3 discusses the syntax and semantics of NPIs. Section 1.4 then, extends the discussion on negative dependencies to NC—i.e. the phenomenon where multiple instances of morphosyntactic negation yield only one semantic negation—and PPIs. Section 5, finally, concludes.

1.2 The syntax of sentential negation

In this section, I provide a brief overview of the range of variation that the expression of (sentential) negation cross-linguistically exhibits and of what its underlying syntax is. First, in Subsection 1.2.1, I introduce the (non-dichotomous) distinction between sentential and constituent negation, after which I continue by describing the range of variation that is cross-linguistically attested with respect to the expression of sentential negation (Subsection 1.2.2). Subsection 1.2.3 deals with the syntactic status of NMs, and, finally, in Subsection 1.2.4, their syntactic position in the clausal spine is discussed.

1.2.1 Sentential and constituent negation

Before discussing the various ways in which sentences can be made negative, one important distinction needs to be made. Take the following minimal pair, dating back to similar examples since (at least) Jackendoff (1972).

(1) a. With no job is Kim happy
    b. With no job Kim is happy

Although both cases involve the same negative constituent (*with no job*), (1a) and (1b) crucially differ in their readings. Whereas (1a) denies Kim's happiness, (1b) entails it, albeit under special circumstances. Also syntactically, (1a) and (1b) are different, in the sense that (1a) triggers verbal movement to C°, whereas (1b) does not. Since, in (1a), the entire sentence is felt to be negative, and in (1b) only the PP *with no job*, it is said that (1a) constitutes an instance of *sentential negation*, whereas (1b) exhibits *constituent negation*.

Klima (1964) was the first to offer a number of diagnostics for sentential negation, such as (among others) continuations by positive question tags or *either*-phrases; sentences involving constituent negation, by contrast, can only be followed by negative question tags or *too*-phrases.

(2) a. With no job is Kim happy, is/*isn't she?
    b. With no job Kim is happy, isn't/*is she?

(3) a. With no job is Kim happy, and/or Mary either/*too
    b. With no job Kim is happy, and/or Mary too/*either

Klima's tests have invoked a number of criticisms. These criticisms initially concerned the diagnostics, though not the distinction between sentential and constituent negation itself. First, the criteria are language-specific and, therefore, do not naturally extend to other languages; second, Klima's tests also take semi-negative adverbs, such as *seldom* or *hardly*, to induce sentential negation (see (4)), even though inclusion of such elements does not reverse the polarity of the sentence: (4) does not deny that John drives a car.

(4) John seldom drives a car, does he?

Finally, sentential negation and constituent negation do not always appear mutually exclusive. Take, for instance, (5):

(5) Not every professor came to the party, did they?

Not every professor clearly forms a constituent (a negative DP). Although examples like (5) are often analysed as constituent negation (cf. Payne 1985; Cirillo 2009), the diagnostics point in the direction of sentential negation. It is, thus, a question whether exhibiting constituent negation is actually incompatible with expressing sentential negation. Rather, what seems to be the case is that sentential negation should be considered a scopal notion, rather than a notion purely in terms of syntactic structure. Then, (5) is simply an instance of constituent negation that is also able to express sentential negation.

Following a research tradition that essentially goes back to Jackendoff (1969, 1972), Lasnik (1975), and many others, Acquaviva (1997) argues that the notion of sentential negation should be defined in semantic rather than in syntactic terms (see also Penka 2011). Specifically, Acquaviva argues that sentential negation is the result of negating the quantifier that binds the event variable. In terms of neo-Davidsonian event semantics (Davidson 1967; Parsons 1990), representations of sentential negation must be represented along the lines of (6):

(6) John didn't drive
    $\neg \exists e[\text{drive}(e) \ \& \ \text{Agent}(j, e)]$

Currently, most scholars treat sentential negation à la Acquaviva (cf. Herburger 2001; Zeijlstra 2004; Penka 2007, 2011). Note, though, that adopting this kind of perspective on sentential negation does not necessarily preclude the validity of syntactic approaches to the analysis of sentential negation, as it is generally assumed that existential closure of a predicate containing an event variable takes place at the level of the vP boundary (cf. Diesing 1992; Ladusaw 1992; Herburger 2001; Zeijlstra 2004, 2008a; Penka 2007, 2011). This also means that sentential negation and constituent negation are not dichotomous; sentential negation results from a particular kind of constituent negation, namely negated constituents that at least involve the vP.

1.2.2 Ways of expressing sentential negation

The distinction between sentential and constituent negation paves the way for one of the central questions that this chapter is about: what are the syntactic properties of the expression of sentential negation, or, to be more precise, of the NMs that give rise to sentential negation?

Languages exhibit a fair amount of cross-linguistic variation with respect to the way sentential negation is expressed. However, closer inspection reveals some remarkable correspondences as well. Let me discuss two of them.

First, as has been noted by Horn (1989) in his seminal work on negation, the expression of a negative sentence is always marked in comparison to its affirmative counterpart. There is no language in the world in which affirmative sentences are marked and negative ones are not (see also Dahl 1979; Payne 1985). In this respect, negative and affirmative sentences are not symmetric in natural language, but rather asymmetric in nature (for a discussion on this asymmetric view on the positive–negative distinction, see also Ladusaw 1996).

Second, various strategies for expressing negation turn out to be universally absent. For instance, no language in the world is able to express negation solely by means of word order shift, a strategy that is often exploited to express other grammatical categories, such as interrogatives (cf. Horn 1989; Zeijlstra 2009).[1]

This leaves open a syntactically limited set of possible expression strategies: sentential negation must be expressed overtly (i.e., it cannot be left unspecified), and marking cannot occur as a result of mere remerge (visible due only to a word order shift). This means that every instance of sentential negation must be expressed by some negatively marked, overt element, with variation lying only in the type, position, and number of such markers.[2]

Elaborating on Zanuttini's (2001) state-of-the-art overview, three major classes of negative elements expressing sentential negation can be identified. The first class of strategies concerns negative verbs. In languages like Evenki (a Tungusic language spoken in Eastern Siberia), special auxiliaries can negate a sentence. Alternatively, in many Polynesian languages (e.g., Tongan), negative verbs even select an entire clause (in a way similar to the English *it is not the case that…*-construction). Examples are shown in (7).[3,4]

(7) a. Bi ə-ə-w dukuwūn-ma duku-ra (Evenki)
I NEG-PAST-1SG letter-OBJ write-PART
'I didn't write a letter'
b. Na'e *'ikai* [_CP_ ke 'alu 'a Siale] (Tongan)
ASP NEG [ASP go ABS Charlie]
'Charlie didn't go'

The second class of expression strategies is constituted by languages that make use of NMs which participate in the verbal inflectional morphology. An example is Turkish, where sentential negation is expressed by means of the negative morpheme *me*, which is located between the verbal stem and the temporal and personal inflectional affixes.

(8) John elmalari ser*me*di (Turkish[5])
John apples like.NEG.PAST.3SG
'John didn't like apples'

---

[1] Note, though, that this does not mean that the word order in an affirmative sentence is always the same as in a negatively marked sentence (see Laka 1990 for examples from Basque).
[2] There has been reported one type of exception in the literature. In Dravidian languages, negation can be marked through omission of a tense marker for affirmation, arguably an instance of an overt reflex (as a result of impoverishment) by the presence of a covert NM (see only Van der Auwera and Krasnoukhov 2020) for a discussion and literature overview of such cases.
[3] Data from (Payne 1985), cited in Zanuttini (2001).
[4] For many more examples of negative auxiliaries, see Miestamo (2005).
[5] Example from Ouhalla (1991), also cited in Zanuttini (2001).

The final class of expression strategies exploits negative particles to express sentential negation. Negative particles come about in different forms. Following Zanuttini (1997, 2001) and Zeijlstra (2007), one can distinguish the following two kinds of negative particles: NMs that attach to the finite verb, and those that do not.

The first type of these negative particles consists of NMs that, when expressing sentential negation, must be attached to the finite verb. This type of negative particle has been referred to by Zanuttini (1997) among others as *preverbal negative markers*, as these NMs generally left-attach to the finite verb. Czech *ne* and Italian *non* are two examples:

(9) a. Milan *nevolá* (Czech)
Milan NEG.calls
'Milan doesn't call'
b. Gianni *non* ha telefonato (Italian)
Gianni NEG has called
'Gianni didn't call'

In both examples, the NM shows up in a position to the immediate left of the finite verb (V_{fin}). It must be noted, though, that these markers exhibit different morphophonological behaviour. Italian *non* is a separate morphological word, which, for syntactic reasons, precedes the finite verb, whereas, in Czech, the NM seems to be affixed to V_{fin}. The examples in (9) thus show that this first class of these negative particles is not homogeneous.[6]

The second class of negative particles is characterized by the fact that, in contrast to those of the first class, their syntactic position does not depend on the surface position of the (finite) verb. Movement of V_{fin} does not trigger displacement of the NM. In this respect, the distributional position of these NMs is similar to that of aspectual adverbs, as is shown for German *nicht* ('not') and *oft* ('often') in (10) and (11).

(10) a. Hans kommt *nicht* (German)
Hans comes NEG
'Hans doesn't come'
b. ... dass Hans *nicht* kommt
... that Hans NEG comes
'... that Hans doesn't come'

---

[6] Cf. Zanuttini (1997) for a more fine-grained overview of different kinds of preverbal NMs based on a survey of Romance microvariation (mostly Northern Italian dialects), including a comparison between preverbal NMs and other clitics. See also Poletto (2008) for a further refinement.

(11) a. Hans kommt *oft* (German)
      Hans comes often
      'Hans often comes'
   b. ... dass Hans *oft* kommt
      ... that Hans often comes
      '... that Hans often comes'

A final remark needs to be made about the occurrence of multiple NMs. Many languages seem to allow more than one NM to appear in negative clauses. Catalan, for example, has, apart from its preverbal negative particle *no*, the possibility of including a second additional negative particle *pas* in negative expressions. In Standard French, the negative particle *pas* must even be accompanied by a preverbal negative particle *ne*.[7] In West Flemish, finally, the negative particle *nie* may optionally be joined by a negative particle *en* that attaches to the finite verb (12).[8]

(12) a. *No* serà (*pas*) facil (Catalan)
      NEG be.FUT.3SG NEG easy
      'It won't be easy'
   b. Jean *ne* mange *pas* (French)
      Jean NEG eats NEG
      'Jean doesn't eat'
   c. Valère (*en*) klaapt *nie* (West Flemish[9])
      Valère NEG talks NEG
      'Valère doesn't talk'

Jespersen (1917) observed that examples like the ones in (12) reflect a widespread cyclic development of languages. Languages like English, Dutch, Latin, and many others all went from a stage with only a clitic-like NM through intermediate stages as in (12a–c) to a stage in which negation is expressed only by means of a postverbal NM. This process is known as *Jespersen's Cycle* (after Dahl 1979) and has been formulated by Jespersen as follows:

> The history of negative expressions in various languages makes us witness the following curious fluctuation; the original negative adverb is first weakened, then found insufficient and therefore strengthened, generally through some additional word, and in its turn may be felt as the negative proper and may then in course of time be subject to the same development as the original word.
>
> (Jespersen 1917: 4)

---

[7] In colloquial French, though, this NM *ne* is often dropped.
[8] Another well-studied language that exploits multiple NMs to express sentential negation is Tamazight Berber (cf. Ouhalla 1991; Ouali 2005).
[9] Example taken from Haegeman (1995).

A number of analyses have been presented to account for the range of variation that is attested cross-linguistically (both synchronically and diachronically) with respect to the expression of sentential negation, a number of which will be discussed in this monograph as well (in Chapters 4 and 6). However, it must be noted that this range of variation is not unique to negation. It shows close resemblance to, for instance, the range of variation that tense, aspect, and mood markers exhibit, as well as their similar diachronic developments (cf. Hopper and Traugott 1993; Roberts and Roussou 2003; Van Gelderen 2009).

1.2.3 On the syntactic status of negative markers

The question now arises of what the exact syntactic status is of the different types of negative particles that have been discussed, and to what extent they can be analysed in formal syntactic terms.

Pollock (1989), basing himself on an intensive study of the distinction between French auxiliaries and lexical verbs, argues that negative particles, such as French *ne* and *pas*, are base-generated in a particular functional projection, dubbed NegP, that intervenes between TP and AgrSP. The finite verb, on its way to T°, then picks up the NM *ne*, leaving *pas* behind in its specifier position.

(13) [$_{TP}$ Jean ne-mange-s [$_{NegP}$ pas ~~ne-mange~~ [$_{AgrSP}$ ~~mange~~ [$_{VP}$ ~~mange~~]]]]

The idea that NMs are hosted in some functional projection in the clausal spine has strongly shaped the study of the syntactic status of NMs, the primary question being which particles may head such a negative phrase and which ones may not.

Zanuttini (1997, 2001) already applies a number of diagnostics to prove that those markers that always show up in the proximity of the finite verb are syntactic heads that have the entire vP in their complement. One such diagnostic concerns clitic climbing. In (14b), it can be seen that the presence of the French NM *ne* blocks movement of the clitic *la* from a position within an infinitival complement of a causative verb to a position adjoining the matrix auxiliary. The example in (14c) makes clear that this blocking effect is due to the intervening clitic-like NM *ne*, as clitic movement over *pas* is not illicit.[10]

---

[10] Zanuttini follows Kayne (1989) by arguing that this must be due to *ne* being an intervening head blocking antecedent government of the trace, although this analysis does not crucially rely on Kayne's explanation, as, in other frameworks, intervening heads are also taken to interfere with clitic movement as well (see Pollock 1989; Travis 1984).

(14) a. Jean la₁ fait manger t₁ à Paul (French[11])
 Jean it makes eat to Paul
 'Jean makes Paul eat it'
 b. *Jean l₁'a fait *ne pas* manger t₁ à l'enfant
 Jean it.has made NEG NEG eat to the child
 'Jean has made the child not eat it'
 c. Jean *ne* l₁'a *pas* fait manger t₁ à Paul
 Jean NEG it.has NEG made Paul eat it
 'Jean hasn't made Paul eat it'

Another diagnostic, presented in Zanuttini (1997), also concerns blocking of verb movement. Paduan, an Italian dialect from Veneto, requires the C° head to be overtly filled in yes/no interrogatives.[12] In positive interrogatives, the verb moves from V° to C°. As a consequence of the Head Movement Constraint (HMC) (Travis 1984), such movement would be illicit if another overtly filled head intervened. Hence, if the Paduan NM *no* is an intervening head, V-to-C movement is predicted to be excluded in Paduan yes/no interrogatives. This prediction is indeed borne out, as shown in (15).

(15) a. Vien-lo? (Paduan)
 comes-he?
 'Is he coming?'
 b. *Vien-lo *no*?
 comes-he NEG?
 'Isn't he coming?'

Zanuttini's account that those negative particles that attach to the finite verb must be heads of some functional projection in the clausal spine is further proved by Merchant (2006a), who developed another diagnostic: the so-called *why not* test. Merchant argues that the English *why not* construction must be analysed as a form of phrasal adjunction; therefore, it is predicted that this construction is allowed in only those languages in which the NM is phrasal as well, and thus forbidden for NMs that occupy a functional head in the clausal spine.

(16) [$_{XP}$ [$_{XP}$ why] [$_{YP}$ *not*]]

As Merchant shows, this prediction is borne out for many of the languages with a negative particle, illustrated by examples from Italian *non* and Greek *dhen* (17):

---

[11] Examples (14a–b) are from Kayne (1989), cited in Zanuttini (2001).
[12] Cf. Benincà and Vanelli (1982); Poletto (2000); Poletto and Pollock (2001).

(17) a. *Perche *non*? (Italian)
     b. *Giati *dhen*? (Greek)
        why NEG
        'Why not?'

In those languages, in order to express something meaning 'why not', a negative polar particle (like 'no' as in 'yes/no') must be used:

(18) a. Perche *no*? (Italian)
     b. Giati *oxi*? (Greek)
        why NEG
        'Why not?'

This observation holds for all languages where the NM itself is not taken to be phrasal, except for those languages where the NM is phonologically identical to the negative polar particle, as is the case in, for instance, Spanish and Czech.

(19) a. ¿Porqué *no*? (Spanish)
     b. Proč *ne*? (Czech)
        why NEG/no
        'Why not?'

The three discussed diagnostics all show that those negative particles that attach to the finite verb must be syntactic heads within the clausal spine.

It is only natural, then, to assume that those negative particles whose sentential position is in principle independent of the surface position of the verb should be taken as phrasal elements, i.e., not as elements occupying a head position in the clausal spine (leaving open the question whether these elements are then specifiers of NegP or not). This assumption indeed appears to be correct.

If negative adverbs are XPs, they should not block head movement and 'why not' constructions should be acceptable.[13] Both predictions are correct. V-to-C languages like Dutch, German, or Swedish exhibit V2 in main clauses. This implies that the verb has to move over the negative adverb to C° in a negative sentence, as is shown for Dutch and Swedish below and has been shown for German already in (10):

(20) a. ... om Jan *inte* köpte boken (Swedish)
        ... that Jan NEG bought books
        '... that John didn't buy books'
     b. Jan köpte *inte* boken
        Jan bought NEG books
        'Jan didn't buy books'

---

[13] Though it should be noted that these diagnostics are less straightforward under remnant movement approaches to verb movement (cf. Nilsen 2003; Müller 2004; Bentzen 2007), a result of the fact that remnant movement approaches in general are vulnerable to overgeneration.

(21) a. ... dat Jan *niet* liep (Dutch)
    ... that Jan NEG walked
    ... 'that Jan didn't walk'
  b. Jan liep *niet*
    Jan walked NEG
    'Jan didn't walk'

From these results, it follows that the negative adverbs in (20)–(21) behave like maximal projections. It is then also expected that these elements are allowed to adjoin to 'why' in the 'why not' constructions. This expectation is confirmed as well, as shown in (22), taking into account that, in these languages, negative polar particles (*no* in English, *nein* in German, *nee* in Dutch, *nej* in Swedish) are indeed different from NMs.

(22) a. Why *not*? (English)
  b. Warum *nicht*? (German)
  c. Waarom *niet*? (Dutch)
  d. Varför *inte*? (Swedish)
    why NEG?
    'Why not?'

To conclude, the distinction between the two types of negative particles can be naturally reduced to a distinction in syntactic phrasal status.

The next question to arise then is whether NMs that are instances of the verbal morphology—such as the Turkish NM *me*, which precedes tense, mood, and person affixes, and follows reflexive, causative, or passive affixes—are fundamentally different from markers that attach to V_{fin}. Can it be the case that they are both base-generated in some Neg° position in the clausal spine and differ only with respect to their morphophonological properties? This question is not restricted to the realm of NMs, but concerns the comparison between inflectional and non-inflectional morphemes in general. Traditionally, inflected verbs had been considered to be the result of a head movement process where the verb 'picks up' its affixes (cf. Baker 1985; Pollock 1989). In this sense, the underlying syntactic structure of sentences with a non-phrasal negative particle and an inflectional NM may be identical.

Such a view (present, for instance, in Pollock 1989) is, however, currently disputed, casting doubt on the idea that inflectional NMs are plain syntactic heads, and has been replaced by either lexicalist positions, where lexical items enter the derivation fully inflected (cf. Chomsky 1995a, et seq.), or distributed-morphology-based positions, where the formal features in the verbal tree are postsyntactically spelled out as either inflectional morphemes or separate words (cf. Halle and Marantz 1993, and subsequent work). Under lexicalist approaches, inflectional markers must be different from syntactic heads; other approaches refute the idea that inflectional markers are fundamentally different from syntactic heads: they are only the result of different mechanisms in the spell-out process. But even under lexicalist approaches, the presence of an inflectional morpheme is connected to a corresponding syntactic head to which the inflectional morpheme stands in an Agree relation. Thus, in principle, nothing stands in the way of a unified treatment of non-phrasal negative particles and inflectional NMs (i.e., all NMs whose sentential position is dependent on the position of the finite verb) in terms of elements occupying some head position in the clausal spine.

1.2.4 On the syntactic position of negative markers

The fact that NMs can be heads of a particular functional projection (known as NegP) leads to two further questions: (i) what is the syntactic position of this NegP with respect to other functional projections in the clausal spine; and (ii) is this negative projection also present in languages that lack an (overt) negative head, or do these phrasal NMs occupy specifier/adjunct positions of other projections?

Pollock (1989) proposed that NegP is located below TP and above Agr(S)P, but the exact position of negation within the clausal spine has been the subject of quite extensive discussion (cf. Belletti 1990; Laka 1990; Zanuttini 1991; Pollock 1993; Haegeman 1995, among many others).

Most of these proposals point out that nothing a priori forces the position of the negative projection to be universally fixed. Ouhalla (1991), for instance, shows that, in Turkish, negative affixes are in between the verb and tense affixes, whereas, in Berber, negation is in the outer layer of verbal morphology, as is shown in (23).[14]

(23) a. *Ur*-ad-y-xdel Mohand dudsha (Berber[15])
NEG.FUT.3MASC.arrive Mohand tomorrow
'Mohand will not arrive tomorrow'
b. John elmalar-i ser-*me*-di (Turkish)
John apples like.NEG.PAST.3SG
'John didn't like apples'.

Assuming that both inflectional NMs are hosted at Neg°, Ouhalla argues that the position occupied by NegP in the clause is subject to parametric variation along the lines of his *NEG Parameter* (24), which puts NegP either on top of TP or on top of VP.

(24) NEG Parameter
    a. NEG selects TP
    b. NEG selects VP

According to Ouhalla, the different values of this NEG Parameter are also reflected by the differences in the expression of sentential negation in Romance languages

---

[14] See also Ouali (2005) for a discussion of Berber negation.
[15] Example taken from Ouhalla (1991).

and Germanic languages. For him, in Romance languages, NegP dominates TP, while it does not do so in Germanic languages.[16]

The idea that the position of NegP is more flexible than initially suggested by Pollock (1989, 1993) was further adopted by Zanuttini (1991, 1997). She claims, much in line with the later cartographic approach initiated by Rizzi (1997) and Cinque (1999), and basing herself on various Italian dialect data, that different NMs in Romance varieties may occupy different positions in the sentential structure, and that, universally, at least four different NegPs are available (see also Benincà 2006; Poletto 2000, 2008; Manzini and Savoia 2005 for a discussion of negation in various Italian dialects):[17]

(25) [$_{NegP1}$ [$_{TP1}$ [$_{NegP2}$ [$_{TP2}$ [$_{NegP3}$ [$_{AspPperf}$ [$_{Aspgen/prog}$ [$_{NegP4}$]]]]]]]]

Zanuttini's proposal has met serious criticisms. While her proposal is essentially right in arguing that more positions should be available for NMs, she does not make clear why these positions have to be the result of a universal syntactic template. The fact that the distribution of negation appears to be richer than a fixed NegP position suggests does not necessarily constitute an argument in favour of an even more fine-grained fixed structure. It might just as well indicate that the syntactic distribution is relatively free and constrained only by independently motivated syntactic or semantic restrictions.

This is essentially the argument which I put forward in Zeijlstra (2004, 2013a) and which I will defend in this monograph. I argue that the minimal (semantic) requirement for an NM to express sentential negation is that it outscopes vP to ensure that sentential negation is yielded (see Section 2.1), and that this constraint determines the cross-linguistic range for variation. Similarly, Zeijlstra (2006, 2013a), following Han (2001), argue that negation may never be interpreted in a position at least as high as C° in main clauses (as, otherwise, negation would outscope operators with the illocutionary force of a speech act; see Chapter 15). These two assumptions thus require NMs to occupy a position somewhere in the syntactic middle field without alluding to any syntactic principle except the one after May (1977) that states that semantic scope reflects syntactic structure. Finally, I argue that semantic differences between different positions (or types) of NM should also follow from differences in scopal effects, i.e., the syntactic position of an NM is (relatively) free, but if the NM is included in different positions, different semantic effects are expected to arise (see also Ramchand 2004).

This line of reasoning is in line with a series of approaches put forward by (among others) Ernst (2001), Svenonius (2001), and Nilsen (2003), who argue that, generally, the fixed orders of adverbials, arguments, discourse particles, etc.

---

[16] Haegeman (1995), however, argues that, at least in West Flemish, NegP is located between AgrP and TP.

[17] It must be noted, though, that Cinque (1999) excludes negation from the adverbial hierarchy because of its freer distribution.

do not reflect a prefabricated syntactic template, but rather result from the fact that alternative orders would lead to semantic anomaly. Consequently, following the anti-cartographic nature of these approaches (mostly notably Nilsen 2003), while negative head markers must head a NegP of their own, negative specifiers do not necessarily do so. For languages like Dutch and German, I assume that their adverbial NMs (*niet* and *nicht*, respectively) occupy adjunct positions of vP, and that a negative projection NegP is altogether lacking in the clausal spine.

This more flexible analysis of the sentential locus of negation and NMs has been adopted by Penka (2007, 2011), Cirillo (2009), Breitbarth (2009), and also Haegeman and Lohndal (2010), who correctly argue that a serious consequence of this approach is that only NMs may occupy a Neg° position. As obvious as this may sound, closer inspection reveals that this has a serious consequence for the analysis of NMs that cannot express sentential negation without additional support by another NM, as illustrated in (12b–c) and repeated here as (26a–b).

(26) a. Jean *ne* mange *pas* (Standard French)
Jean NEG eats NEG
'Jean doesn't eat'

b. Valère (*en*) klaapt *nie* (West Flemish)
Valère NEG talks NEG
'Valère doesn't talk'

As Breitbarth and Haegeman and Lohndahl observe, West Flemish *en* is never able to render a sentence negative by itself.[18] It is only optionally available in sentences that have already been made negative by other overt negative elements. For that reason, *en*, strictly speaking, cannot be taken to carry some negative feature, which could, in turn, project Neg°. Instead, they argue that *en* carries a weak polarity feature that constitutes a Polarity Phrase (PolP). Similar arguments have been proposed for the Afrikaans sentence-final NM *nie* (Oosthuizen 1998; Biberauer 2008; Chapter 4 of this book) and French *ne* (Zeijlstra 2010a; see also Chapter 4). For the latter, Zeijlstra (2010a) argues, however, that French *ne*, being an element that may only survive in (semi-)negative contexts without contributing any semantic negation, should actually be considered a plain NPI and not the head of any PolP. One of the reasons for rejecting the existence of PolPs alongside NegPs is that negative clauses are always marked—the morphosyntax of negative and positive clauses is not the same (as would be the case with PolPs; see Horn 1989), and the scope of polarity always coincides with the surface position of the (highest) NM, not the alleged position of Pol°.

---

[18] Except for a small number of fixed constructions, such as '*k en weet* (I en know 'I don't know') in Ghent Dutch (cf. Haegeman 1995); see also Chapter 8 for similar cases involving French *ne*.

1.3 Polarity-sensitivity

The previous section has illustrated already that the expression of sentential negation is subject to a number of both syntactic and semantic constraints.

However, the syntax and semantics of negation is not restricted to the syntax of NMs and other negative elements only. As has already briefly been touched upon at the end of the previous section, some elements do not induce semantic negation by themselves, but rather only survive in contexts that, in one way or the other, are negative. Elements that form such negative dependencies are generally referred to as NPIs, although other names surface as well (e.g. Affective Items; cf. Giannakidou 1999).

The best-known examples of NPIs are formed by the English *any*-series, although many more can be given, e.g. English *yet, need, either,* or *lift a finger*:

(27) a. We *(didn't) read *any* books
 b. I have*(n't) been there *yet*
 c. I *need**(n't) do that
 d. I *(didn't) read the book, and John *(didn't) *either*
 e. Nobody/*somebody *lifted a finger*

NPI-hood is, however, not restricted to English. To the best of my knowledge, all languages have some NPIs at their disposal (see also Haspelmath 1997 for a non-exhaustive list of languages that display NPIs), and many languages exhibit a typology of NPIs, often at least as rich as that of English.

As has been pointed out by Giannakidou (1999), the term 'NPI', in the most literal sense, is actually a misnomer, as most NPIs are licensed in contexts that are, strictly speaking, not negative, such as restrictive clauses of universal quantifiers, yes/no questions, or contexts introduced by *at most N* constructions or semi-negative adverbs, such as *hardly*.

(28) a. Every student who knows *anything* about linguistics will join the event
 b. Do you want *any* cookies?
 c. At most three students did *any* homework
 d. Mary hardly likes *any* cookies

NPIs have received wide attention by scholars in syntax, semantics, and pragmatics, and they have constituted a fruitful and popular research area over the past 30 years. As Ladusaw (1996) points out in his seminal overview article, the study of the behaviour of NPIs has been dominated by four research questions: (i) the licenser question; (ii) the licensee (relation) question; (iii) the licensing (relation) question; and (iv) the status question.

The *licenser question* aims at determining what counts as a proper NPI licensing context. The *licensee question* seeks an answer to the question why certain elements are only allowed to occur in particular contexts and what distinguishes them from polarity-insensitive elements. The *licensing (relation) question* addresses the question of what kind of constraints the relation between the NPI licenser and its licensee is sensitive to. Finally, the *status question* addresses the status of sentences containing unlicensed NPIs: are such sentences bad for syntactic, semantic, and/or pragmatic reasons?

In Zeijlstra (2013b), I argued that this status question is tightly connected to the licensee question. If it is, for instance, a syntactic property of NPIs that they require a higher negative(-like) element, then a sentence containing an unlicensed NPI is syntactically ill-formed; on the other hand, if NPIs come along with a pragmatic effect that causes them to only be felicitously uttered in negative(-like) contexts, then, by contrast, a sentence containing an unlicensed NPI may still be grammatical. The four questions thus reduce to three core questions. In Subsections 1.3.1–3, I discuss these three questions, which have guided the study to negative dependencies over the past three decades, before addressing what questions are currently at stake.

1.3.1 The licenser question

As the examples (27)–(28) show, NPIs are licensed only in particular contexts, some truly negative, some not. The question thus arises as to what properties constitute NPI-licensing environments.

The first and still one of the most important and influential accounts that tries to reduce all NPI-licensing contexts to one single semantic property is Ladusaw's (1979) proposal, based on Fauconnier (1979), that all NPI licensers are Downward Entailing (DE), where DE is defined as follows (taken from von Fintel 1999):

(29) A function f of type $<\sigma, t>$ is Downward Entailing iff for all x, y of type σ such that $x \Rightarrow y$, $f(y) \Rightarrow f(x)$

To illustrate what is meant here, let us look at the examples in (30) and (31). In (30a), the first sentence entails the second one, but not the other way round (30b). This is due to the fact that the set of red shirts is a subset of the set of shirts. The entailment goes from a set to its supersets.

(30) a. Mary is wearing a red shirt $\Rightarrow$ Mary is wearing a shirt
 b. Mary is wearing a shirt $-/\Rightarrow$ Mary is wearing a red shirt

In DE contexts, entailment relations are reversed. This is shown for the negative contexts in (31), where the only valid inferences are now from a set to its subsets.

(31) a. Nobody is wearing a red shirt $-/\Rightarrow$ Nobody is wearing a shirt
 Nobody is wearing a shirt $\Rightarrow$ Nobody is wearing a red shirt
 b. John is not wearing a red shirt $-/\Rightarrow$ John is not wearing a shirt
 John is not wearing a shirt $\Rightarrow$ John is not wearing a red shirt

However, DE-ness is not restricted to negative contexts. Also, the first (but not the second) argument of a universal quantifier, semi-negatives such as *few*, and *at most N* constructions are DE and license NPIs.

(32) a. Every student went to bed ⇒ Every linguistics student went to bed
      b. Few people sing ⇒ Few people sing loudly
      c. At most three students left ⇒ At most three students left early

Although this proposal is to be considered a milestone in the study of NPIs, it faces several serious problems as well, as has often been addressed in the literature (see the following detailed discussions for references). The three most important ones are the following: (i) not every NPI is licensed in the same sets of DE contexts; (ii) some NPIs can be licensed in non-DE contexts as well; and (iii) successful NPI licensing does not necessarily depend only on the logico-semantic properties of the NPI-licensing context.

With respect to (i), it can be observed that some NPIs are subject to different licensing conditions from others. For instance, while English *any* terms seem to be fine in all DE contexts, the Dutch counterpart to *any*, i.e., *ook maar*, is ruled out in DE contexts like *niet iedereen* ('not everybody'):

(33) a. Nobody / not everybody ate *anything*

      b. {Niemand / *niet iedereen} heeft *ook maar iets* gegeten   (Dutch)
         nobody / not everybody has PRT something eaten
         'Nobody / not everybody ate anything'

Van der Wouden (1994), elaborating on Zwarts (1995), argues that DE should be thought of as some layer of a negative hierarchy, where the true negation (*not*), subject to all De Morgan laws, is Anti-Morphic, as defined in (34), and forms the highest layer of the negative hierarchy.

(34) A function f is Anti-Morphic iff $f(A \vee B) \Leftrightarrow (f(A) \wedge f(B))$ and $f(A \wedge B) \Leftrightarrow (f(A) \vee f(B))$.

English *not* is Anti-Morphic since *John doesn't dance or sing* means that John does not dance and John does not sing, and *John doesn't dance and sing* means that John does not dance or John does not sing. *No student*, by contrast, is not Anti-Morphic: if some students dance but do not sing, and if all other students sing but do not dance, it is still the case that no student sings and dances, but the second conjunct in (34) does not hold for *no student*.

No student belongs in the next layer of the negative hierarchy, which consists of so-called Anti-Additive (AA) elements, formally defined as in (35). These are elements like *nobody, nothing, no*.

(35) A function f is Anti-Additive iff $f(A \vee B) \Leftrightarrow (f(A) \wedge f(B))$.

No student is AA, since 'no student drinks or smokes' is truth-conditionally equivalent to 'no student drinks and no student smokes'. Note that 'not every' is not AA, as 'not everybody drinks and not everybody smokes' does not entail that not everybody drinks or smokes.

The next layer consists of DE elements (like *not everybody*). Note that every AA context is also DE (given (35)) and every Anti-Morphic context is also AA (given (34)). NPIs, then, differ with respect to which layer of negativity is qualified to license them. English *any* is licensed in DE contexts (and thus in all negative contexts), others only in AA contexts (such as Dutch *ook maar*), and some NPIs can be licensed by the Anti-Morphic sentential NM only. Generally, NPIs that are licensed in DE contexts are referred to as *weak NPIs*; NPIs that are only fine in AA contexts as *strong NPIs*; and NPIs that are fine in Anti-Morphic contexts only are called *superstrong NPIs*. An example of the latter category would be the Dutch idiom *voor de poes: zij is *(niet) voor de poes* (she is not for the cat 'she's pretty tough'); cf. Van der Wouden 1994; see also Chapter 11.

Although these observations are all empirically correct, it should be noted that even this classification should be subject to further modification. For instance, Hoeksema (1999a) shows that Dutch NPI *hoeven* cannot occur in the first argument of a universal quantifier, even though it can occur in non-AA DE contexts such as *weinig* ('few'):

(36) a. *Iedereen die *hoeft* te vertrekken, moet nu opstaan (Dutch)
everybody who needs to leave must now get.up
'Everybody who needs to leave, must get up now'
b. Weinig mensen *hoeven* te vertrekken
Few people need to leave
'Few people need to leave'

This already suggests that the distinction between superstrong, strong, and weak NPIs is not fine-grained enough.

With regard to (ii), Giannakidou (1998, 1999 et seq.) shows that, while DE-ness is not always a sufficient condition for NPI licensing, it is not always a necessary condition for it, either. For instance, yes/no questions are not DE, even though they license NPIs (see van Rooij 2003, though see Mayr 2013 and Nicolae 2015 for a different perspective), and similar observations have been made for *only* (cf. von Fintel 1999). *Only* is not DE, as the following does not hold:

(37) Only Mary has a car -/⇒ Only Mary has a BMW

Also, Greek *tipota* ('anything') can be licensed under modals meaning 'may' or 'want', or in subjunctive clauses (Giannakidou 1998, 1999, 2000). This may suggest that DE-ness does not seem to be the weakest layer of negativity; therefore, Giannakidou proposes, following Zwarts (1995), to further extend the hierarchy

1.3 POLARITY-SENSITIVITY

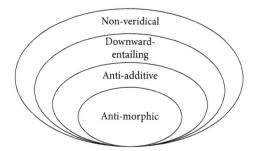

Fig. 1.1 The Negative Hierarchy (cf. Giannakidou and Zeijlstra 2017)

of negative contexts by another layer of negativity: non-veridicality (defined as in (38)).

(38) A propositional operator *F* is non-veridical if *Fp* does not entail or presuppose that *p* is true in some individual's epistemic model.[19]

To clarify this, *perhaps* (in (39a)) is a non-veridical operator, whereas *unfortunately* in (39b) is veridical since a speaker uttering (39a)a does not take the sentence *John is ill* to be necessarily true, whereas a speaker uttering (39b) does do so.

(39) a. Perhaps John is ill
      b. Unfortunately, John is ill

Non-veridicality can be seen as an additional layer of negativity (even weaker than DE-ness) and may account for those cases where NPIs, such as English *any* terms, may appear in non-DE contexts; see Zwarts (1995) for a proof that all DE contexts are non-veridical, as shown in Figure 1.1.

At the same time, however, NPIs like *any* may not appear in all non-veridical contexts, such as most modal contexts:

(40) *Perhaps John read *any* books

Note, though, that this does not mean that there cannot be 'superweak' NPIs that are licensed in all non-veridical contexts. Lin (2017) and Lin et al. (2014, 2015a) have argued that this is the case for Chinese *shenme* ('any/a') (see also Chapter 11), which, as (41) shows, are, for instance, fine in non-veridical contexts, but not in veridical ones (42):

(41) a. Yuehan   keneng   mai   le   shenme   shu   (Chinese)
        John   maybe   buy   PRF   a/some   books
        'Maybe John has bought a/some book(s)'

---

[19] After Giannakidou (1998, 1999, 2011).

b. Yuehan kending mai le *shenme* shu
John must buy PRF a/some book
'John must have bought a/some book(s)'

c. Mali zuotian haoxiang mai-le *shenme* shu
Mary yesterday probably buy-PRF a/some book
'Mary has probably bought a book yesterday'

(42) *Yuehan zuotian mai le *shenme* shu (Chinese)
John yesterday buy PRF a/some book
Intended: 'John has bought (a) book(s) yesterday'

Hence, the question arises whether classical weak NPIs like *any* or *ever*, and superweak NPIs like *shenme* should indeed be considered to be licensed in non-veridical contexts. An alternative would be to rethink DE-ness in such a way that it captures those cases of apparent non-DE contexts that allow NPIs in their scope.

This is what von Fintel (1999) proposed. He suggests to reformulate DE-ness into Strawson-DE-ness in the following way:

(43) A function f of type <σ, t> is Strawson Downward Entailing iff all x, y of type σ such that x ⇒ y, *and f(x) is defined*, f(y) ⇒ f(x)

Now, an element like *only* (which is defined if its prejacent is true) is Strawson DE. If it is given that Mary has a BMW, (37) holds again. Similarly, if Mayr (2013) and Nicolae (2015) are right in assuming that polar questions may contain something like a covert *only*, it also follows that polar questions are DE. Hence, it seems that DE-ness (thought of as Strawson DE-ness) remains a relevant and important characterization of the distribution of NPIs, albeit one that may not hold for every NPI.

In connection with (iii), we should note that all approaches to NPI licensing discussed so far are only dependent on the logico-semantic properties of the licensing context. This is, however, not always the case. For instance, conditionals only allow NPIs under particular pragmatic conditions, as discussed by Heim (1984) and von Fintel (1989). Ladusaw (1996), Linebarger (1980, 1987), and Giannakidou (1999) provide additional examples where contexts that are clearly non-DE or non-veridical still license NPIs if they come along with a particular negative implicature, as is shown below:

(44) Exactly four people in the room *budged an inch* when I asked for help[20]

The source of licensing in (44) cannot be reduced to the semantic properties of its position at LF, but seems to lie in the fact that, for the speaker, the number of assistants is smaller than expected/hoped for.

---

[20] Example taken from Ladusaw (1996).

The last example suggests that not only semantic but also pragmatic conditions apply to NPI licensing.

1.3.2 The licensee question

Perhaps even more important than the question of what licenses an NPI is the question of what property an NPI has, such that it can occur only in this particular type of context. It is exactly this question which has dominated the study of NPI licensing over the past 20–30 years.

Two types of approach have been formulated to address this question. For some scholars, NPI-hood reduces to some semantic and/or pragmatic requirement that ensures that NPIs can only be felicitously uttered in negative contexts of some sort (DE, AA, or non-veridical). For others, the answer should lie in syntax, i.e., NPIs come along with some syntactic feature that forces them to appear in negative environments only.

The first major contribution in the first direction is the *widening + strengthening* account by Kadmon and Landman (1993). Their account consists of two steps. First, they propose that NPI indefinites, such as English *any* terms, differ semantically from plain indefinites in the sense that these NPIs are domain wideners. Such domain-widening indefinites extend the domain of reference beyond the contextual restrictions that plain indefinites are subject to. Take (45), which contains Kadmon and Landman's original examples:

(45) a. I don't have potatoes
      b. I don't have any potatoes

Whereas (45a) entails that, in a particular domain, the speaker does not have potatoes, (45b) suggests that the speaker does not even have a single old potato in some corner in the kitchen.

The second step in Kadmon and Landman's line of reasoning is that they claim that sentences containing NPIs like *any* must be stronger than sentences containing a plain indefinite. (45b) is stronger than (45a): the set of situations where (45b) is true is a clear subset of the set of situations where (45a) is true—so, (45b) entails (45a). The strengthening requirement is thus met. However, the fact that (45b) is stronger than (45a) is due to the presence of the NM: given that negation is DE, removal of the negation in the examples in (45) would reverse the entailment relation. Therefore, without the presence of the negation, a sentence like (45b) would actually be weaker than the sentence without *any*. Uttering (45b) without the negation would thus violate the pragmatic strengthening condition. This is exactly what, for Kadmon and Landman, rules out sentences containing unlicensed NPIs.

The idea that NPIs come along with widening and strengthening effects, which makes sure that they can be felicitously uttered only in DE contexts, has been adopted and implemented in various ways. Krifka (1995), for instance, argues that the strengthening condition follows as an implicature, as sentences with a weak reading generally bring along an implicature that the stronger reading is ruled out. In this respect, he focuses on elements denoting minimal amounts and explains that especially those elements are prone to become NPIs.

Lahiri (1998) connects the NPI property to NPI *even*, arguing that the underlying structure of NPIs is something like 'even a(n) N', basing himself on data from Hindi, where the word for *even* is overtly present in indefinite NPIs:

(46) a. Koii bhii (Hindi[21])
 one even
 'Anybody'
 b. Koii bhii nahiiN aayaa
 one even NEG came
 'Nobody came'

One problem, already acknowledged by Krifka (1995) and also present in Giannakidou (2011) and Chierchia (2006, 2013), is that, under Kadmon and Landman's approach, NPIs pose strengthening restrictions on the contexts that they can appear in, without such restrictions being encoded in their lexical representations. Therefore, it remains unclear what enforces that sentences containing NPIs must be stronger than those with a plain indefinite.

In order to ensure that NPIs are always subject to a strengthening, Chierchia (2006, 2013) proposes that NPIs obligatorily introduce domain and scalar alternatives and additionally carry a syntactic feature that requires that they must appear under the direct scope of an abstract exhaustifier that renders any stronger domain and scalar alternatives of the sentence containing the NPI false.

This way, Chierchia argues, assertions containing an NPI always yield a semantic contradiction unless this NPI appears in DE contexts. The reason for that is that for Chierchia in non-DE contexts all stronger (or non-weaker) alternative propositions introduced by the NPI jointly entail the assertion. If as a result of exhaustification all those alternatives are to be negated, the assertion will be contradicted. In DE contexts, these alternatives become weaker and will thus no longer be negated under exhaustification. This way, it follows that NPIs are doomed in any other contexts than DE ones.

Naturally, this gives rise to various questions. For one, pragmatic infelicitousness and semantic contradictions are generally not judged as being ungrammatical. However, the judgements on unlicensed NPIs are much stronger: speakers generally feel them to be ungrammatical. Chierchia, following Gajewski

---

[21] Example taken from Lahiri (1998).

(2002), circumvents this problem by distinguishing two types of contradiction: logical contradictions and grammatical contradictions. Only logically contradictory expressions, they argue, are ungrammatical; not just any contradictory expression.[22]

By contrast, Giannakidou (2011, 2018) takes NPIs to be lexically deficient for referentiality. For instance, she assumes that NPIs like Greek *kanenas* ('anybody') can be uttered felicitously only when they do not have to refer to some entity in the real world. Therefore, these elements are expected to not appear in veridical contexts. But we also saw before that not every NPI is a superweak NPI.

Also problematic is that analyses like the ones I have outlined apply to indefinite NPIs only. Although most NPIs are indefinites, not all of them are. For instance, NPIs like *either* or *need* are not. Concerning the latter, as Iatridou and Zeijlstra (2010, 2013) and Homer (2015) have shown, deontic modal NPIs are actually always universal and not existential. This suggests that, though not necessarily on the wrong track, the original approach is insufficient: it is not the only way to explain why NPIs are banned from certain contexts. It should be noted, however, that most NPIs denote scalar end points, suggesting that scalarity still underlies NPI-hood.

Although, currently, many scholars assume that the ill-formedness of sentences containing unlicensed NPIs is due to pragmatic and/or semantic factors, others have argued that these are ungrammatical as a result of some syntactic constraint.

The tradition that takes NPIs to come along with a syntactic requirement that they be licensed by a (semi-)negative operator goes back to Klima (1964), and has been presented in more modern frameworks by Progovac (1992, 1993, 1994), who takes NPI licensing to be some special instance of syntactic binding, and by Laka (1990), who relates NPIs to the obligatory presence of an affective phrase (ΣP).

Postal (2004), followed by Szablocsi (2004) and Collins and Postal (2014), introduces a revival of Klima's theory and claims that NPIs, such as English *any*, underlyingly carry a negation, suggesting a syntactic representation of *any* as (47).

(47) *any*: [$_D$ NEG [SOME]]

In a negative sentence containing *any*, the negation moves out of *any* to a higher position where it is realized as an overt negator; in semi-negative sentences, this negation may incorporate in other elements.

Den Dikken (2006) adopts the essence of Postal's analysis, but modifies it in more minimalist terms by assuming that NPIs carry an uninterpretable negative feature that must be checked against a negative head in the clause. Independently,

---

[22] An expression is logically contradictory if and only if, under all significant rewritings of its non-logical parts, the contradiction remains, as is the case for unlicensed NPIs of the relevant kind. This is not the case for grammatical contradictions, such as *It rains and it doesn't rain*, since one could rephrase the second *rain* with *snow* and the contradiction disappears.

and for different reasons, Neeleman and Van de Koot (2002) and Herburger and Mauck (2007) reach this conclusion as well.

The main problem, however, for such purely syntactic approaches is that it is hard to understand why most types of NPI that are attested always denote some end point of a scale. In principle, if NPI licensing is an instance of syntactic feature checking, all kinds of element should be able to act as NPIs, whereas the distribution of most, if not all, NPIs seems to be restricted semantically.

Herburger and Mauck (2007), however, try to overcome this criticism by arguing that the scalar-end point property is a necessary, but not a sufficient condition for NPI licensing. For them, it is indeed a pragmatic and/or semantic property whether some element may be a candidate for becoming an NPI, but that it is only the presence of some uninterpretable negative feature that turns an element into an NPI.

1.3.3 The licensing question

Finally, all cases discussed so far show that all NPIs must stand in a particular relation to their licensers. Ladusaw (1979) suggests that, since the licensing requirement involves a scopal semantic property, this relation basically boils down to a scope requirement at LF: all NPIs must be within the scope of a DE operator at LF.

But as Ladusaw (1979) has already remarked, this constraint on the licensing relation may be a necessary, but not a sufficient condition. NPIs, generally speaking, may not precede their licenser, even if this licenser outscopes the NPI at LF. Hence, Ladusaw (1979) argues that the c-command relation must hold not only at LF, but also at surface structure. This now explains why (48) (taken from Ladusaw 1996) is ruled out.[23]

(48) *He read any of the stories to none of the children

However, Linebarger (1980) points out that the NPI-licensing relation must be more severely constrained. Concretely, she claims that NPIs must not only be outscoped by a DE operator at LF, but that no scope-taking element may intervene between the NPI and its licenser, either—a claim dubbed the *Immediate Scope Constraint* (ISC). Take the following minimal pair (again taken from Ladusaw 1996):

---

[23] However, as has been pointed out by Ross (1967), Linebarger (1980), and Uribe-Etxebarria (1996), NPIs sometimes appear outside the scope of their licenser at surface structure, as shown below. The example is from Linebarger (1980).

(i)   A doctor who knew anything about acupuncture wasn't available

(49) a. Sam didn't read every child a story   ¬>∃>∀; ¬>∀>∃
     b. Sam didn't read every child any story ¬>∃>∀; *¬>∀>∃

Although (49a) is ambiguous between a reading where the existential scopes over the universal and a reverse reading, this second reading is out in (49b). This directly follows from the ISC, as the NPI would then not be directly outscoped by a DE operator.[24]

However, as discussed in Section 3.1, NPIs are sometimes fine in non-DE contexts, as long as these contexts introduce some negative implicature. The relevant example was (44), repeated here as (50).

(50) Exactly four people in the room *budged an inch* when I asked for help

Obviously, the well-formedness of (50) does not follow under the above-sketched ISC analysis.

For Linebarger, examples such as (50) show that NPI licensing actually takes place indirectly. In short, she states that what is responsible for NPI licensing is that a sentence containing some NPI gives rise to an implicature that contains a negation directly outscoping this NPI. For sentences already containing a negation, this follows straightforwardly; for other DE operators, this implicature needs to be paraphrased in such a way that it contains a negation (e.g. *few N* implies *not many N*). For (50), the required negative implicature should contain a paraphrase such as *Not as many people as I expected*. Note that, as long as a formal computation procedure of such implicatures is lacking, this type of account cannot make exact predictions. In fact, the lack of a formal procedure for implicature computation makes this type of analysis extremely vulnerable to overgeneralization, as almost every sentence brings in negative implicatures (cf. Krifka 1995).

Giannakidou (1999, 2006a) occupies an intermediate position between Ladusaw's and Linebarger's proposals. She takes NPI licensing to be a relation which takes place at LF between an NPI and a non-veridical operator and which is subject to the ISC. But she also allows *NPI rescuing*, where a sentence containing an NPI that lacks a non-veridical licenser at LF may be rescued from ill-formedness if the sentence still gives rise to a negative implicature. This mechanism is close to Linebarger's account, with the difference that, for Linebarger, all NPI licensing functions in this way, whereas, for Giannakidou, it is a secondary mechanism: Giannakidou thus allows NPI licensing to take place at two distinct levels.[25]

---

[24] Interestingly enough, modals do not count as interveners between NPIs and their licensers (witness the well-formedness of *Nobody may read any book*) (cf. von Fintel and Iatridou 2007).
[25] In order to distinguish between licensing in the broad sense (all types of NPI licensing) and LF licensing of NPIs, Giannakidou refers to the former as NPI sanctioning.

1.4 The landscape of negative dependencies

On the basis of the previous discussion, two things ought to be kept in mind. First, it should be noted that the three questions I have outlined are not independent. If it turns out that some NPI has a particular distribution, for instance (Strawson-)Downward Entailment, the licensee question must address why this NPI has exactly that distribution, and why this requirement also imposes constraints on the structural relation between itself and its licenser. Second, these questions do not have to be answered in the same way for every NPI. If, as appears to be the case, various NPIs are subject to different licensing conditions, it may very well be that different kinds of NPIs are NPIs for different reasons, and therefore also require different types of licensing relations. In the following chapter, I will take this conjecture to heart and argue that a more pluriform approach to NPI-hood can better explain the attested landscape of negative dependencies.

The reason why a pluriform approach to NPI-hood seems necessary is not only because it has been attested that NPIs can be sensitive to different logico-semantic, syntactic, or pragmatic requirements. We already saw that there are NPIs that appear to be licensed in (Strawson-)DE contexts (often referred to as weak NPIs), and NPIs that are licensed in AA (strong NPIs) or Anti-Morphic contexts (superstrong NPIs). And, as it turns out, there are also NPIs, like Dutch *hoeven* ('need'), which are dubbed strong/weak NPIs, that are licensed only in a subset of DE contexts as well as NPIs that are licensed only in a superset of DE contexts, namely non-veridical contexts (so-called superweak NPIs).

But these five types of NPI do not jointly constitute the landscape of negative dependencies. There are two more phenomena that also form kinds of negative dependencies. The first phenomenon is known as Negative Concord, and involves elements that sometimes appear to behave like negative quantifiers (NQs) and sometimes more like NPIs. The second phenomenon concerns Positive Polarity Items, elements that are banned from negative contexts. I will discuss each in turn.

1.4.1 Negative Concord

Although the distinction between negative elements (as discussed in Section 1.2) and NPIs (as discussed in Section 1.3), at first sight, appears to be straightforward—negative elements are semantically negative, NPIs are not—it turns out that things are not always that clear. In this section, I present one such case. Take the following examples from Italian:

(51) a. Gianni *non* ha telefonato (Italian)
 Gianni NEG has called
 'Gianni didn't call'

b. *Nessuno* ha telefonato
NEG-body has called
'Nobody called'

In (51a), the semantic negation is introduced by *non*. The sentence without *non* simply means 'Gianni called'. In (51b), *nessuno* acts like an NQ, such as English *nobody*, and thus induces a semantic negation. However, if the two are combined in a sentence, only one semantic negation is yielded, whereas, from a compositional perspective, two semantic negations would be expected:

(52) Gianni *(*non*) ha telefonato a *nessuno*
Gianni NEG has called to NEG-body
'Gianni didn't call anybody'

The phenomenon where two (or more) negative elements that are able to express negation in isolation yield only one semantic negation when combined is called Negative Concord (NC) after Labov (1972), and has been discussed extensively in the past decades.

NC is exhibited in a large variety of languages. Within the Indo-European language family, almost every variety of the Romance and Slavic languages, and a number of Germanic languages (Afrikaans, West Flemish, Yiddish, and some Dutch and German dialects), as well as Albanian and Greek, exhibit NC.

NC comes about in different kinds. In some languages, for example Czech, an NM obligatorily accompanies all neg-words, regardless of their number and position. Those languages are called *Strict NC languages*, following terminology by Giannakidou (1998, 2000). In other languages, so-called *Non-strict NC languages*, such as Italian, NC can only be established between neg-words in postverbal position and one element in preverbal position, either a neg-word or an NM. Examples are below:

(53) a. Milan *(*ne-*)vidi *nikoho* (Czech)
Milan NEG.saw NEG-body
'Milan didn't see anybody'
b. Dnes *(*ne-*)volá *nikdo*
Today NEG.calls NEG-body
'Today nobody calls'
c. Dnes *nikdo*   *(*ne-*)volá
today NEG-body   NEG.calls
'Today nobody calls'

(54) a. Gianni *(*non*) ha telefonato a *nessuno* (Italian)
Gianni NEG has called to NEG-body
'Gianni didn't call anybody'

b. Ieri *(*non*) ha telefonato *nessuno*
   yesterday NEG has called NEG-body
   'Yesterday nobody called'
c. Ieri *nessuno* (*non*) ha telefonato (a *nessuno*)
   yesterday NEG-body NEG has called to NEG-body
   'Yesterday nobody called (anybody)'

The reader should note that this typology of NC languages is not exhaustive. In languages like Bavarian and West Flemish, NC is allowed to occur, but it is not obligatory (Den Besten 1989; Haegeman 1995). In French and Romanian, the combination of two neg-words gives rise to ambiguity between an NC reading and a reading with two semantic negations, standardly referred to as a Double Negation (DN) reading (cf. De Swart and Sag 2002; Corblin et al. 2004; De Swart 2010; Fălăuş 2009). And in other languages, multiple neg-words may not give rise to NC, but multiple NMs can, e.g. certain varieties of Afrikaans (cf. Biberauer and Zeijlstra 2012a, b).

The central question in the study of NC concerns the apparent violation of semantic compositionality in examples like (52). How is it possible that two elements that induce semantic negation when used by themselves yield only one negation when combined? In the literature, two approaches have been dominant: (i) the NQ approach, where every neg-word is taken to be semantically negative and where the missing negation in (52) results from some semantic absorption mechanism dubbed quantifier resumption; and (ii) the approach that takes neg-words to be semantically non-negative NPI-like indefinites, and the semantic negation in (51b) to be only covertly present—two positions we will discuss at length in Chapter 3.

But this is not the only question that pops up. A second question, given a neg-word's ability to yield a semantic negation in isolation, is why should it depend on another negative element in the first place? Why are the Italian and Czech examples in (55) (without the NMs) ungrammatical?

(55) a. *Gianni ha telefonato a *nessuno*   (Italian)
        Gianni has called to NEG-body
        'Gianni didn't call anybody'
     b. *Dnes *nikdo* volá   (Czech)
        today NEG-body calls
        'Today nobody calls'

We know from English that NQs can also give rise to sentential negation:

(56) a. Mary saw nothing
     b. Nobody left

Hence, expressing sentential negation is not restricted to NMs (and is even allowed in Non-strict NC languages like Italian, cf. (51b)).

The fact that the examples in (55) are ungrammatical shows that NC also involves negative dependencies, irrespective of how the phenomenon is explained. By definition, the neg-words in (51)–(55) are also NPIs if they cannot survive without negation.

Taking NC to be a special kind of NPI-hood appears to favour the approach that takes neg-words to be semantically non-negative. However, that must not necessarily be the case. It is very possible that neg-words are NQs that, for independent reasons, must co-occur in certain configurations with an NM. At the same time, it is not straightforwardly clear what such independent reasons may be. But an approach that takes neg-words to be NPIs faces serious questions as well. If neg-words are semantically non-negative, how can the readings of sentences such as (51b) (repeated here as (57)), where a single neg-word induces semantic negation, be derived?

(57) *Nessuno* ha telefonato (Italian)
 NEG-body has called
 'Nobody called'

In an influential proposal by Ladusaw (1992), neg-words are said to differ from plain NPIs in the sense that they are self-licensing, i.e., if nothing else licenses neg-words, NPIs license themselves. But then the question arises as to why certain NPIs are self-licensing and others not.

Hence, NC forms negative dependencies like (other) NPIs, but it also shows that the landscape of negative dependencies is more heterogeneous than is standardly assumed.

1.4.2 Positive Polarity-sensitivity

A final phenomenon that needs to be addressed concerns Positive Polarity Items (PPIs). While English *any*-terms require some DE licensing context, PPIs, by contrast, are known to be illicit in negative contexts.

At least four different types of PPIs have been discussed in the literature. The first type is represented by the English *some*-series and their counterparts in other languages (Jespersen 1917; Baker 1970; Progovac 1994; Van der Wouden 1994; Giannakidou 1998, 2011; Haspelmath 1997; Szabolcsi 2004; among many others). The second class consists of high-scale elements, such as *rather* (cf. Krifka 1995; Israel 1996, 2011). The third class of PPIs contains speaker-oriented adverbs, and has been thoroughly discussed by Nilsen (2003); Ernst (2009); and Giannakidou and Mari (2018). The final class of PPIs concerns deontic modals which obligatorily outscope negation, such as English *must* (cf. Israel 1996, 2011; Iatridou and Zeijlstra 2010, 2013; and Homer 2015). For an overview of all types of PPIs, the reader is referred to Van der Wouden (1994) and Israel (2011).

Each type is exemplified in (58). Note, though, that, contrary to most NPIs, PPIs in negative sentences do not always render a sentence ill-formed, but rather disambiguate it. Therefore, in (58a) and (58d), the sentences are not ruled out, but rather the readings with the PPI taking scope under the negation are excluded.

(58) a. John didn't see somebody
    *'John saw nobody'
    √'There is somebody John didn't see'
  b. I am (*not) rather ill
  c. They (*don't) possibly like spinach
  d. Mary mustn't leave
    *'Mary doesn't have to leave'
    √'It's obligatory that Mary doesn't leave'

What PPIs thus show is that they cannot scope below negation. In that sense, they appear to be the mirror image of NPIs, and various proposals have tried to account for the behaviour of PPIs in terms of anti-licensing (Ladusaw 1979; Progovac 1994; among others). On the other hand, it has recently been claimed by others, most notably by Van der Wouden (1994), Szabolcsi (2004), Ernst (2009), and Giannakidou (2011), that PPIs behave rather differently from NPIs and, therefore, should call for a different theoretical treatment.

Szabolcsi (2004), who pursues Postal's (2004) idea that NPIs underlyingly carry some negation or negative feature, proposes that PPIs like *some* actually have two underlying negative features. Since two negations cancel each other out, *some* can naturally survive in positive sentences/environments. In negative contexts, though, one negative feature is taken care of by the presence of an overt licenser, leaving the PPI behind with an unlicensed negation. Therefore, the PPI in a negative context makes the sentence bad.

A different line of reasoning is explored by Nilsen (2003). Following Krifka (1995), Nilsen argues that the pragmatic and semantic effects that Kadmon and Landman take to be responsible for NPI-hood naturally extend to PPI-hood. This idea is also manifest in Ernst (2009), which, whilst arguing against Nilsen's scale-based analysis of PPI-hood, endorses the idea that the PPI status of speaker-oriented adverbs ultimately reduces to speaker commitment and is therefore pragmatic/semantic in nature.

But again, nothing requires that all PPIs are treated alike. Just as we saw that it must be the case that different types of NPIs may have different sources for their NPI-hood, it is equally likely that different types of PPIs also have different sources for their PPI-hood. It is this line of reasoning that will be pursued throughout this book.

1.5 Conclusions

In this chapter, I have tried to sketch the major developments in the study of the syntax of negation and the study of negative polarity so far, and the ways in which these two phenomena can be taken to be connected.

While the first part of this chapter focuses on the notion of sentential negation and the way in which sentential negation can be expressed cross-linguistically, the second part discusses in more detail the types of negative dependencies that are empirically attested, and points out that the richness of the landscape of NPIs, NC (items), and PPIs indicates that negative dependencies should be taken to be a heterogeneous rather than a homogeneous phenomenon. This means that new research questions have to be formulated, and new hypotheses will have to be entertained.

Those research questions and hypotheses that guide such a pluriform approach to the study of negation and negative dependencies will be presented in detail in the next chapter.

2
Outline
The pluriform landscape of negative dependencies

2.1 The pluriform landscape of negative dependencies

In the previous chapter, negative dependencies were introduced against the background of the syntax and semantics of negative markers (NMs). Negative Polarity Items (NPIs) form classical examples of negative dependencies: an NPI cannot survive without the presence of an element that in some sense counts as negative. As we saw in Section 1.3, this has given rise to at least three questions: (i) why do NPIs have this particular requirement? (ii) What exactly counts as 'negative'? And (iii) what is the syntactic and semantic relation between an NPI and its licenser? But, as it turns out, it is not the case that these questions can be answered in the same way for each and every NPI. The landscape of NPIs is heterogeneous. In Section 1.3, I have already identified five major types of NPIs: superstrong NPIs, strong NPIs, strong/weak NPIs, weak NPIs, and superweak NPIs.

Superstrong NPIs are (mostly idiomatic) NPIs that may only appear in anti-morphic environments. Strong NPIs are restricted to Anti-Additive (AA) contexts. Strong/weak NPIs are NPIs that are fine in several (Strawson-)DE contexts, but, at the same time, are not licensed in every AA context. Weak NPIs are licensed in all (Strawson-)DE contexts. Superweak NPIs, finally, are distributionally restricted to non-veridical environments.

The sets of licensers of four out of five of these NPIs (superstrong, strong, weak, and superweak NPIs) have traditionally been taken to stand in a set–subset relation. These four sets of licensers together were said to form the Negative Hierarchy in Figure 2.1.

It should be noted, though, that this Negative Hierarchy is too much of an idealization of the way in which NPI-licensing contexts relate to each other. Since weak NPIs turn out be fine in contexts that, strictly speaking, do not count as DE (e.g., when weak NPIs appear in the prejacent of *only*, or in polar questions), the set of NPI-licensing contexts has been extended to Strawson-DE-ness (after von Fintel 1999). However, NPI-licensing contexts that are only Strawson-DE, and not DE in the regular sense, fall out of the hierarchy. For instance, *only* is veridical as it presupposes its prejacent; hence, it cannot be non-veridical. Moreover, the licensing contexts of so-called strong/weak NPIs do not fit in the Negative Hierarchy,

Negation and Negative Dependencies. Hedde Zeijlstra, Oxford University Press.
© Hedde Zeijlstra (2022). DOI: 10.1093/oso/9780198833239.003.0002

2.1 THE PLURIFORM LANDSCAPE OF NEGATIVE DEPENDENCIES

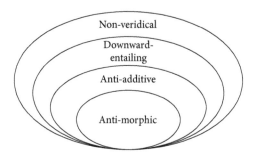

Fig. 2.1 The Negative Hierarchy (cf. Giannakidou and Zeijlstra 2017)

as these form a set that is a strict subset of the set of both AA and non-AA, DE contexts.

The fact that different types of NPIs are subject to different licensing conditions that do not always stand in a strict entailment relation has strong repercussions for the way in which NPIs are to be analysed. Traditionally, modulo a few exceptions (e.g. Giannakidou 2011, 2018), analyses on NPI-hood take variation among NPIs with respect to their licensing requirements to be an ancillary phenomenon. This has both been the case for approaches to NPI-hood that take NPIs to establish a syntactic dependency with their licensers (Klima 1964; Progovac 1994; Laka 1990; Postal 2004; Den Dikken 2006; Herburger and Mauck 2007; Collins and Postal 2014), as well as pragma-semantic approaches, such as Kadmon and Landman (1993); Krifka (1995); and Chierchia (2006, 2013), who have argued that a lack of informativity forms the basis of NPI-hood. Only Giannakidou (2011, 2018) argues that her approach to NPI-hood (which takes NPIs to have an inability to give rise to existential import, cf. Giannakidou 1998, 2000) may only apply to a particular subset of NPIs.

The fact that the landscape of NPIs is so much more heterogeneous than often assumed suggests that NPIs should not be analysed in a uniform way. After all, nothing requires that every instance of NPI-hood must stem from the same source. Differences in NPI strength may very well reduce to the existence of multiple sources of NPI-hood.

Moreover, negative dependencies are not restricted to NPIs. A variety of other phenomena yield negative dependencies, or can at least be analysed as such, as well. In addition, Positive Polarity Items (PPIs) form negative dependencies in the sense that their distribution bans them from environments that, again, are in some sense negative. Let us look at those other (potential) negative dependencies is slightly more detail.

I start with Negative Concord (NC). NC, as discussed in Subsection 1.4.1, concerns the phenomenon where two elements that, by themselves, in certain constructions, can render a sentence negative, but together yield only one semantic negation, illustrated below for Italian, taken from Zeijlstra (2004).

(1) a. *Nessuno* ha telefonato (Italian)
    NEG-person has called
    'Nobody called'

 b. *Ha telefonato *nessuno*
    has called NEG-person
    Int.: 'Nobody called'

 c. *Non* ha telefonato *nessuno*
    NEG has called NEG-person
    'Nobody called'

NC has been widely investigated, by Ladusaw (1992); Haegeman (1995); Haegeman and Zanuttini (1996); Zanuttini (1997); Giannakidou (2000); Herburger (2001); De Swart and Sag (2002); Weiss (2002); Zeijlstra (2004, 2008a, b); De Swart (2010); Haegeman and Lohndal (2010); and Blanchett (2015); among many others. The central question in the study of NC has always been whether NC Items, or neg-words as I refer to them in this book, are semantically negative or not.

For some of these authors (e.g. Haegeman 1995; Haegeman and Zanuttini 1996; De Swart and Sag 2002), NC involves a process of semantic absorption: two inherently negative (monadic) quantifiers (NQs) merge together into one bigger (polyadic) NQ. For others, neg-words are a special kind of NPI that, in the absence of an overt licenser, may trigger the presence of a covert negative licenser (cf. Ladusaw 1992; Giannakidou 2000; Zeijlstra 2004, 2008a, b).

However, equally (or, perhaps, even more) important is the question of why such neg-words (in Italian, at least in postverbal position) constitute a negative dependency: why must they be accompanied by a preverbal negative element like the NM *non*? Irrespective of how one analyses NC, the fact that certain elements require, at least in certain configurations, the presence of another NM means that such NC items also encode negative dependencies, rendering the landscape of negative dependencies even richer than it already is. At the same time, the substantial differences between neg-words and (other) kinds of NPIs must also be accounted for, as well as cross-linguistic differences with respect to NC systems. This, again, necessitates a heterogeneous approach to negative dependencies. Assuming that the source for the negative dependency of neg-words is different from that of other NPIs naturally opens up the way for understanding differences between neg-words and (plain) NPIs. Assuming that they share the same source, of course, does not do so.

This may also hold for other phenomena. It has been observed that certain readings of certain constructions only emerge in DE contexts. Take the German sentence (2) from Schwarz and Bhatt (2006):

(2) Susanne kann nicht eine Fremdsprache (German)
    Susanne knows NEG a foreign.language

This sentence means that either there is a foreign language that Susanne does not know or that Susanne does not know (even) one foreign language. It crucially lacks the reading 'Susanne knows no foreign language'. Interestingly, this reading becomes available again once the sentence is embedded in a DE context:

(3) Wir haben keinen angenommen, der nicht eine Fremdsprache kann
     we have hired NEG-person who NEG a foreign.language knows
     'We hired nobody who knows no foreign language'

Without entering into too much detail at this stage, the question arises whether these kinds of suppressed NPI readings should be analysed fully on a par with canonical weak NPIs, such as *any* or *ever*. Schwarz and Bhatt (2006) argue that the NM *nicht* in (3), which they take to be responsible for the wide-scope reading of negation over the (unfocused) indefinite, is an NPI, homophonous to the regular NM *nicht*. That would then explain why this reading is absent in (2).

But such an analysis is not without problems, and the question arises whether the source of the absence of this reading outside DE contexts should indeed lie in the existence of homophonous NMs that are also NPIs. Already the fact that, in this case, it is a particular construction that receives more readings in DE contexts rather than a particular element that may only appear in such constructions, suggests it is a different phenomenon from the kind of NPI-hood that has been introduced before. But if that is indeed the case, then the landscape of negative dependencies must be broadened even further.

Another phenomenon that, in this sense, deserves particular attention concerns the existence of so-called split-scope readings. As observed by Jacobs (1989), the most salient reading of German (4) is that where negation outscopes the modal, but where the indefinite takes scope under it, even though the negation and the indefinite form one single word *kein* ('no').

(4) Du   must keine Krawatte anziehen   (German[1])
     you must NEG   tie   wear
     'You don't have to wear a tie'

This suggests that *keine* ('no') is not a plain negative quantifier in itself, but rather may consist of two elements—a negation and an indefinite—that are only jointly realized as a single NI.

Split-scope readings have received a fair amount of attention in the literature, primarily focusing on the question of whether sentences like (4) consist of a separate negation and existential quantifier (Jacobs 1989; Rullmann 1995; Penka 2011; Zeijlstra 2011) or whether the split-scope reading is an entailment of a non-split-scope reading (Geurts 1996; De Swart 2000; Abels and Marti 2010). Penka (2007, 2011) has analysed these NIs as neg-words along the lines

---

[1] Example from Penka 2011.

of Zeijlstra (2004, 2008a, b). For her, NIs outside NC languages are also semantically non-negative elements that must agree with a covert negative operator, just as Zeijlstra (2004, 2008a, b) argues is the case for neg-words. The difference for her, though, is that these languages do not allow multiple agreement; every neg-word must agree with a unique negative operator. If that is correct, split-scope readings may reflect another type of negative dependency. If not, a treatment of NIs in different terms from that of plain NQs over individuals is still required.

A phenomenon that is closely related to the notion of negative dependencies concerns Neg-Raising. A sentence like *Mary doesn't believe that John likes her* is generally understood to mean 'Mary believes that John doesn't like her'; in other words, matrix negation seems to take narrow scope in the embedded clause under predicates like *believe, think,* or *hope*. For some scholars, Neg-Raising results from raising negation from the embedded clause into the matrix clause and having the negation interpreted in its base position, a stance going back to Fillmore (1963) and recently revived by Collins and Postal (2014). Others take Neg-Raising to result from a particular inference triggered by the negated main clause predicate (for instance, Bartsch 1973; Gajewski 2005, 2007; Romoli 2013; Zeijlstra 2017b; among many others). However, as it will turn out, whether negation can reconstruct or not has serious repercussions for various analyses of negative dependencies. For instance, Zeijlstra's (2011) analysis of split-scope phenomena is fully incompatible with the syntactic view on Neg-Raising. This also means that any theory of negative dependencies will have to account for the phenomenon of Neg-Raising.

Finally, PPIs form a type of negative dependencies, too. While English NPIs require some kind of negative licensing context, PPIs, by contrast, are banned from contexts that, in some sense, count as negative. English *somebody*, for instance, may appear in negative sentences, but only with a reading where *somebody* takes scope over the negation (5a). Other PPIs, such as *rather*, are just unacceptable in negative clauses (5b):

(5) a. Mary didn't see somebody
 √'There is somebody Mary didn't see'
 *'Mary saw nobody'
 b. I am (*not) rather ill

But these are not the only known PPIs. For instance, there are also PPIs that are speaker-oriented adverbs (cf. (6)–(7)), certain necessity modals (8), or even elements encoding illocutionary force. The clause-types in (9) remain the same under negation: (9a) is still a declarative, (9b) an interrogative, and (9c) an imperative. It is impossible to negate an element with the illocutionary force of a speech act.

(6) a. Fortunately, she didn't leave
    b. *She didn't fortunately leave

(7) a. Possibly, she didn't leave
    b. *She didn't possibly leave

(8) Mary mustn't leave
    *'Mary doesn't have to leave'
    √'It's obligatory that Mary doesn't leave'

(9) a. I didn't leave
    b. Didn't she leave?
    c. Don't leave!

So, all examples in (5)–(9) involve PPIs. But it is far from clear that, for all of these examples, the source of their PPI-hood is identical. As Israel (1996, 2011) shows, approaches that may account for the NPI-hood of lowest scalar end points may readily account for the PPI-hood of highest scalar end points, such as *rather* (see also Zeijlstra 2017a). But, strikingly, many PPIs do not denote highest scalar end points. Existential PPIs such as *somebody*, speaker-oriented adverbs like *unfortunately* or *possibly*, and features encoding illocutionary force require additional explanations for their PPI-hood. And it is by and large not straightforward that these explanations are similar. Again, just as the landscape of NPIs is much more diverse than sometimes assumed, the same holds for the landscape of PPIs. Since the landscape of NPIs already requires a heterogeneous explanation, it would be hard to understand why the landscape of PPIs should not.

The central research question that I address in this book is thus how the variety of negative dependencies that have currently been attested can be explained, and what the repercussions of this explanation are for the syntax and semantics of negative elements, negative dependencies, and related phenomena. Note that all these phenomena in the domain of negation and negative dependencies have been relatively well investigated, but hardly ever under one overarching perspective. Such an overarching perspective is especially called for, since particular approaches to one domain in the study of negation and negative dependencies can be incompatible with particular approaches in other domains. For instance, Penka's (2011) account for split-scope construction is an extension of Zeijlstra's (2004, 2008a, b) approach to NC and, therefore, incompatible with absorption approaches to NC. Moreover, various negative dependencies are related to other syntactic and semantic properties in intrinsic ways. For instance, Zeijlstra (2004, 2008a, b) has observed that the syntactic status of NMs is in some way related to whether a particular language exhibits NC or not. All of this calls for a unified theory of negation and negative dependencies.

In this book, I provide such a theory, one that integrates and explains all the phenomena I have set out (variation with respect to NMs, NC, split-scope, Neg-Raising, negative polarity, positive polarity) from a single overarching perspective, based sometimes on existing, sometimes on novel data from language variation, language acquisition, and language change.

The central hypothesis is that, to the extent applicable to negation, all possible ways to encode grammatical dependencies (at the lexical, syntactic, semantic, and pragmatic levels) should also be attestable in the domain of negative dependencies, unless these are ruled out independently (e.g. on functional, formal, or learnability grounds). This predicts a particular, heterogeneous landscape of negative elements and elements dependent on negation, which prediction indeed appears to be empirically confirmed. This constitutes a theory of negation and negative dependencies that accounts for all these dependencies in a unified way.

2.2 Outline

This book consists of four parts. The first part introduces the major phenomena that are under discussion and presents the central hypothesis and outline (Chapters 1 and 2).

The second part (Chapters 3–8) involves the syntax and semantics of NC and NQs. It presents the view that NC is an instance of syntactic agreement between neg-words and negative operators, much like subject–verb agreement. This sets NC items apart from both truly negative elements and other types of NPIs. This part will also discuss the behaviour of such truly negative elements, exploring the hypothesis that an NQ is the morphophonological realization of a merger of a semantic negation and an (existential) quantifier or indefinite. It also addresses related topics such as Neg-Raising and the absence of other kinds of single NQs, such as negated universal quantifiers.

After a short intermezzo, the third part (Chapters 10–15) concerns polarity sensitivity. It first argues that differences in NPI strength reduce to different sources for NPI-hood. Just as syntactic agreement establishes a particular negative dependency (realized as NC), other known grammatical dependencies, such as lexical, semantic, and pragmatic dependencies, may also apply in the domain of negation; and I show in this part how all other kinds of NPIs reflect these other dependencies. Next, I address the question of how these findings apply to the domain of PPIs, showing that the landscape of PPIs is as rich as, if not more pluriform than that of NPIs.

The final part (Chapters 16 and 17) spells out the major conclusions of this book and opens up further prospects of research in the domain of negation, negative dependencies, and in syntactic and semantic theory in general.

2.3 Relation to earlier work

As I have mentioned, this monograph is based on my own research on negation and negative dependencies over the past 20 years. Several of the ideas presented in this book are novel, but others have been published or presented in earlier works, though many of them, I have revised again. Below, I list which works have formed the basis for the current manuscript, though all of the works it is based on have been revised, most of them fairly substantially.

In Part I, Chapter 1 is based on Penka and Zeijlstra (2010); Dekker and Zeijlstra (2012); Giannakidou and Zeijlstra (2017); and Zeijlstra (2007, 2013b, 2015a, 2016a).

In Part II, the general account of NC presented in Chapter 3 is based on Zeijlstra (2004, 2008a, b). The analysis of Afrikaans in Chapter 4 is rooted in Biberauer and Zeijlstra (2011, 2012a, b), and the analysis of French has been presented in an earlier version (Zeijlstra 2010a). The Flexible Formal Feature Hypothesis (FFFH) (Chapter 5) was first published in Zeijlstra (2008b), and has been further elaborated in Zeijlstra (2014). The diachronic analyses in Chapter 6 stem from Zeijlstra (2016a, b), and the proposal on the *NALL*-problem has been presented in Zeijlstra (2012c). Chapter 7 is based on Zeijlstra (2011, 2020a), and Chapter 8 is a modest revision of Zeijlstra (2018b).

In Part III, Chapter 10 follows from work presented in Zeijlstra (2017b) and Iatridou and Zeijlstra (2017, 2021). The account of universal NPIs in Chapter 11 is based on Lin, Weerman, and Zeijlstra (2014, 2015, 2021 and partially on Iatridou and Zeijlstra (2013). Chapter 12 results from Zeijlstra (2012b). The account of universal PPIs (Chapter 13) has been published in Zeijlstra (2017a), and the analyses in the first parts of Chapter 14 are based on Zeijlstra (2017a) and Iatridou and Zeijlstra (2021. Chapter 15 is a revised version of Zeijlstra (2006, 2013a).

In Part IV, in Chapter 16, references are made to Iatridou and Zeijlstra (2013) and Lin et al. (2021) . Chapter 17 builds up on Kauf and Zeijlstra (2012, 2021); Bjorkman and Zeijlstra (2019); Koeneman and Zeijlstra (2014); and Zeijlstra (2008c, 2012a, 2020b, 2022).

PART II
NEGATIVE CONCORD AND NEGATIVE QUANTIFIERS

3
Negative Concord is syntactic agreement

3.1 Introduction: Negative Concord and neg-words

From a compositional perspective, one would expect that every negative element introduces a semantic negation. This is indeed the case in a language like Dutch. Dutch *niet* ('not') and *niemand* ('nobody') can both render a sentence negative (as shown in (1a–b)). When combined in a single clause, two semantic negations are yielded (1c). The reading that (1c) yields is called a *Double Negation* (DN) reading. Since, in Dutch, every combination of two negations yields a DN reading, Dutch is called a DN language.[1]

(1)   a. Suzanne belt *niet*   (Dutch)
　　　　Suzanne calls NEG
　　　　'Suzanne doesn't call'
　　b. *Niemand* belt
　　　　NEG-body calls
　　　　'Nobody calls'
　　c. Suzanne belt *niet niemand*
　　　　Suzanne calls NEG NEG-body
　　　　DN: 'Suzanne doesn't call nobody' = 'Suzanne calls somebody'

However, in many other languages, things work differently. Take Italian, for instance. As is shown in (2), even though both *non* ('not') and *nessuno* ('nobody') yield a semantic negation in (2a) and (2b), respectively, jointly, they do not yield two semantic negations, but only one (2c):

---

[1] It is not completely true that, in Dutch, combinations of two negative elements never give rise to non-DN readings. In particular contexts, two adjacent NQs, or a NQ with a right-adjacent NM, may yield an (emphasized) single-negation reading. Examples are (i) and (ii).

(i)   Ik heb nergens geen student gezien   (Dutch)
　　　　I have nowhere no student seen
　　　　'I haven't seen any student anywhere'
(ii)   Ik ben daar nooit niet geweest
　　　　I am there never not been
　　　　'I have never ever been there'

Such constructions are heavily restricted, and are not considered as instances of Standard Dutch. In Chapter 6, I will discuss such constructions in more detail, and show that these combinations of two negative elements with one negative meaning are lexically stored as such (see also Zeijlstra 2010b).

Negation and Negative Dependencies. Hedde Zeijlstra, Oxford University Press.
© Hedde Zeijlstra (2022). DOI: 10.1093/oso/9780198833239.003.0003

(2) a. Gianni *non* ha telefonato (Italian)
Gianni NEG has called
'Gianni didn't call'

b. *Nesssuno* ha telefonato
NEG-body has called
'Nobody called'

c. *Non* ha telefonato *nessuno*
NEG has called NEG-body
'Nobody called'

This phenomenon, where multiple negative elements jointly yield only one semantic negation, is known as *Negative Concord* (NC). Italian is thus an NC language. Negative Indefinites (NIs), such as *nessuno*, that can yield a semantic negation in isolation, but also participate in NC relations, are called *neg-words* (or *n-words*, after Laka's 1990 terminology).

Italian is not the only language that displays this phenomenon. In fact, many other languages are NC languages. Below, examples are shown from Catalan, Hungarian, Czech, Polish, Greek, and Japanese (taken from Giannakidou and Zeijlstra 2017), though this list of NC languages is far from exhaustive.

(3) a. *(*No*) he dit *res* (Catalan)
NEG have.1SG said neg-thing
'I haven't said anything'

b. Balász *(*nem*) látottt *semmit* (Hungarian)
Balász NEG saw NEG-thing
'Balász didn't see anything'

c. Milan *(*ne-*)vola *nikdo* (Czech)
Milan NEG calls NEG-person
'Milan doesn't call anybody'

d. Janek *(*nie*) pomaga *nikomu* (Polish)
Janek NEG help NEG-person
'Janek doesn't help anybody'

e. *(*Dhen*) ipa TIPOTA² (Greek)
NEG said.1SG NEG-thing
'I didn't say anything'

f. John-wa *nanimo* tabe-*(*nak*)-atta (Japanese)
John.TOP NEG-thing eat.NEG.PAST
'John didn't eat anything'

---

² In Greek all neg-words are emphasized.

3.1 INTRODUCTION: NEGATIVE CONCORD AND NEG-WORDS

At first sight, the readings of examples like (2c) and the ones in (3) seem to violate the principle of compositionality (cf. Frege 1892; Partee 1975, 1984; Janssen 1997). Why is it that these readings do not contain two semantic negations?

However, this essentially semantic question is not the only one that needs to be addressed. Languages also differ cross-linguistically with respect to whether they exhibit NC or not, as already indicated by the difference between Dutch and Italian. This shows that the availability of NC readings is not a universal phenomenon. Moreover, NC is also subject to further cross-linguistic variation. Traditionally, NC is said to come about in two kinds: *Strict NC* and *Non-strict NC* languages (after Giannakidou 2000, 2006b). In Strict NC languages, neg-words always need to be accompanied by an NM, irrespective of their clausal position. This is shown in (4) for Czech, where both preverbal and postverbal neg-words yield an NC relation with the NM *ne*, and which thus classifies as a Strict NC language.

(4) a. Dnes *nikdo* *(*ne-*)volá (Czech)
today NEG-body NEG-calls
'Today nobody calls'
b. Dnes *(*ne-*)vola *nikdo*
Today NEG-calls NEG-body
'Today nobody calls'

In Non-strict NC languages, every postverbal neg-word must be accompanied by a preverbal negative element (either an NM or another neg-word), but preverbal neg-words themselves may not be accompanied by another NM. This is shown in (5) for Italian, a Non-strict NC language.

(5) a. Ieri *nessuno* (*non) ha telefonato (a *nessuno*) (Italian[3])
Yesterday NEG-body NEG has called to NEG-body
'Yesterday nobody called'
b. Ieri *(*non*) ha telefonato *nessuno*
Yesterday NEG has called NEG-body
'Yesterday nobody called'

This is not, however, the only instance of variation that can be attested in the domain of NC. While Italian and Czech differ in one respect (whether preverbal neg-words can establish an NC relation with the additional NM), they behave similarly with respect to the obligatoriness of NC: when the NM can be there, it

---

[3] It has occasionally been claimed in the literature that examples such as (5a) give rise to DN readings when the NM is present. This is not fully correct. The DN reading only becomes available if the preverbal neg-word is heavily stressed and followed by an intonational break (#), as is shown in (i). Otherwise, speakers judge such constructions to be ungrammatical.

(i) NESSUNO (#) *non* ha telefonato a *nessuno* (Italian)
NEG-body (#) NEG has called to NEG-body
'Nobody did not call anybody'

must be there. The NMs in (4) and (5b) may simply not be removed. But not in every NC language is the presence of an NM always required. West Flemish, for instance, is a language where NC is optional (cf. Haegeman 1995; Haegeman and Zanuttini 1996). In (6), the NM *nie* can simply be left out, without this affecting the meaning or the grammaticality of the sentence.

(6) ... da Valère *niemand* (*nie*) ken (West Flemish)
 ... that Valère NEG-body NEG knows
 '... that Valère doesn't know anybody'

Moreover, as we will see later on, various other subtypes of NC can be attested as well. It is a core property of NC that it can manifest itself in different shapes, cross-linguistically. Therefore, two questions have to be addressed:

(i) How can the apparent violation of the compositionality problem be explained?
(ii) How can the range of variation that languages cross-linguistically exhibit with respect to the distribution and behaviour of NC be explained?

Most accounts of NC focus on (i), and either discuss only one subclass of NC languages, or ignore (ii) altogether. However, since, as we will see, several different approaches may be able to address (i), each with their own successes and shortcomings, (ii) might be a way to evaluate these approaches: to what extent are the existing approaches able to capture the cross-linguistic variation attested? Accounting for both (i) and (ii), rather than just (i), evidently leads to a much broader and better understanding of the nature of NC. Even if we know why *non* and *nessuno* in Italian yield a single negative reading together, we may still not understand why postverbal *nessuno* should always be accompanied by the NM. Why can it not render the sentence negative, as it does in subject position (5a), or as NQs in DN languages like Dutch do?

As for (i), generally, the major question for scholars investigating NC is whether neg-words are semantically negative or not. To see this, let us look again at the Italian examples in (2b–c), repeated in (7):

(7) a. *Nesssuno* ha telefonato (Italian)
 NEG-body has called
 'Nobody called'
 b. *Non* ha telefonato *nessuno*
 NEG has called NEG-body
 'Nobody called'

On the basis of (7a), one would expect that *nessuno* simply means something like 'nobody'; otherwise the negativity of the sentence could not be accounted for. Naturally, (7b) forms a problem for this assumption, as then the meaning of the sentence does not any longer follow compositionally. On the basis of (7b), one would rather assume that *nessuno* means something like 'anybody', which readily predicts the proper meaning of the sentence. However, under this assumption, the negative meaning of (7a) is completely unexpected.

These assumptions and related problems are representative for existing analyses of NC. Some scholars (e.g., Haegeman and Zanuttini 1991, 1996; Haegeman 1995; De Swart and Sag 2002; Collins and Postal 2014) take neg-words to be semantically NQs (like the ones in Dutch), and try to account for the compositionality violation in (7b) by means of some negative absorption mechanism (where all negations melt together into one big NQ). Other scholars (e.g. Ladusaw 1992; Giannakidou 2000) rather focus on (7b), and argue that this shows that neg-words are very similar to NPIs like English *anybody* or *anything*. For these scholars, (7a) is problematic, and they have to argue that, in this case, negation is covertly present. Not everybody took either one of these more rigid perspectives, though. Herburger (2001), following ideas from Longobardi (1991) and Van der Wouden and Zwarts (1995), has argued that neg-words are ambiguous between semantically negative elements and semantically non-negative elements.

In this chapter, I focus on question (i), and discuss the various possibilities that could account for NC; and I leave question (ii) to Chapters 4 and 5. In Section 3.2, I discuss the approach which takes every neg-word to be semantically negative, and which alludes to a general principle of negative absorption that may account for the existence of NC readings. In Section 3.3, I discuss the approach that takes the opposite perspective: such an approach takes neg-words to be semantically non-negative. Then, the major challenge is to understand why, in certain configurations, neg-words can still induce a semantic negation. In this section, I also discuss the approach that takes a hybrid perspective, where neg-words are considered to be ambiguous between semantically negative elements and semantically non-negative ones. It will be shown that each of these approaches faces some serious challenges. In Section 3.4, I will present my own analysis of NC, which is a particular implementation of the approach that takes neg-words to be semantically non-negative. This analysis takes NC to be an instance of syntactic agreement. Section 3.5 presents a summary and spells out the major conclusions, consequences, and open questions that this syntactic-agreement perspective triggers.

3.2 The negative-quantifier approach

3.2.1 Proposal

The idea that neg-words are NQs can be traced back to Zanuttini (1991), and has been further elaborated in Haegeman (1995) and Haegeman and Zanuttini (1996).

Subsequently, this proposal has been rephrased in a polyadic-quantification framework by De Swart and Sag (2002), and has been further implemented by Collins and Postal (2014). Since De Swart and Sag (2002) present the formally most elaborated proposal on NC using this approach, I will discuss and evaluate this proposal in the most detail. Towards the end of the section, I compare it to other proposals that also fall under the negative-quantifier approach.

Haegeman and Zanuttini (1991, 1996) argue that NC readings result from a factorization-and-absorption mechanism that is available in NC languages. Under this approach, neg-words are negative unary universal quantifiers that, once they are hosted in the same projection (yielding factorization), together form a single negative complex quantifier through negative absorption, as formalized in (8) (with round brackets denoting optionality).

(8) $[\forall x_\neg][\forall y_\neg]([\forall z_\neg]) = [\forall_{x, y(, z)}]_\neg$

Haegeman and Zanuttini motivate their proposal by pointing out that similar effects take place when multiple *Wh*-terms are combined, and that the syntactic treatment of *Wh* and that of negation are very similar. Haegeman (1995) lists a series of parallels between *Wh*-terms and negative elements, the most important one being the similarity between readings of multiple *Wh*-expressions and NC.

Expressions containing multiple *Wh*-terms can be interpreted as a pair-list question at LF. Higginbotham and May (1981) and May (1989) provide a formal description of *Wh*-elements in terms of polyadic quantification by arguing that *Wh*-terms are unary quantifiers that, in the same projection, may turn into one *n*-ary quantifier, binding *n* variables. Hence, two *Wh*-terms (each binding a separate variable) may together form one *Wh*-operator that binds two variables, a process shown in (9), provided they are in the same projection. The answers to such a question consist of one or more pairs of persons and things:

(9) a. Who read what? Mary read the NY Times; John read the Washington Post.
b. $Wh_x Wh_y[\mathbf{read}(x, y)] \rightarrow Wh_{x,y}[\mathbf{read}(x, y)]$

Following Haegeman and Zanuttini, factorization is the process that brings together two (or more) quantifiers of the same type (*Wh*-quantifiers, NQs, or other types of quantifiers), which then, in turn, undergo absorption. Haegeman and Zanuttini (1991, 1996) furthermore argue that factorization only takes place under Spec-head agreement within a particular functional projection. This means that factorization is syntactically driven. This syntactic motivation requires the presence of a syntactic feature [Wh] that drives movement to a CP. Rizzi (1991, 1997) formalized this syntactic requirement by arguing that all *Wh*-elements obey the Wh-*Criterion*.

(10) *Wh*-Criterion:
   a. A *Wh*-operator must be in Spec-head configuration with X°$_{[Wh]}$.
   b. An X°$_{[Wh]}$ must be in Spec-head configuration with a *Wh*-operator.

If negative factorization and absorption are similar to resumption of *Wh*-quantifiers, negative factorization and absorption can only take place under spec-head configuration as well. Hence, for Haegeman and Zanuttini, Rizzi's *Wh*-Criterion is to be extended with respect to negation. Therefore, they introduce the so-called *NEG-Criterion*, formalized as in (11).

(11) NEG-Criterion
   a. A NEG-operator must be in Spec-head configuration with X°$_{[NEG]}$.
   b. An X°$_{[NEG]}$ must be in Spec-head configuration with a NEG-operator.
   Whereby the following definitions hold:

   NEG-operator: a negative phrase in scope position;
   Scope position: a left-peripheral A'-position [Spec, XP] or [YP, XP].

This NEG-Criterion triggers the movement of every neg-word to a specifier or adjunct position of the functional projection NegP, from where they will undergo absorption.

Cross-linguistic variation then results from the timing of the application of the NEG-Criterion: the NEG-Criterion applies at surface structure in West Flemish, and at LF in Romance languages. Therefore, neg-words are moved to the left of the NM *nie* in West Flemish before spell-out, whereas, in languages like Italian, movement over *non* is postponed until LF (12).[4]

(12) a. S-Structure [$_{CP}$ dat [$_{NegP}$ niemand$_i$ *niet* [t_i belt]]]   (West Flemish)
               that NEG-body NEG calls
               'that nobody calls'

   b1. S-Structure [$_{NegP}$ e [$_{Neg°}$ *non* [ha telefonato *nessuno*]]]   (Italian)
   b2. LF   [$_{NegP}$ *nessuno*$_i$ [$_{Neg°}$ *non* [ha telefonato t_i]]]
                   NEG-body NEG has called
                   'Nobody has called'

Note that, for successful factorization, neg-words are forced to move to a position higher than the negative operator in Spec, NegP. Consequently, Haegeman and Zanuttini therefore assume that neg-words are universal quantifiers: if neg-words were negative existential quantifiers, they could not take scope over the negative

---

[4] Later, Haegeman (1995) replaces this assumption of cross-linguistic variation in the moment of application of the NEG-criterion with the assumption that all languages apply the NEG-Criterion at surface structure. This is due to her adoption of a representational framework (cf. Brody 1995) in which the notion of movement is replaced by the notion of *CHAIN*. The NEG-Criterion is applied to negative CHAINs that either are headed by an abstract operator with the phonological content in foot position (e.g. Italian), or have the entire neg-word in their head position (e.g., West Flemish).

operator ¬. However, as already discussed in Chapter 1 (and with more to come in Chapters 4, 7, 8, and 16), the idea that every neg-word is a universal NQ is highly problematic.

De Swart and Sag (2002), while adhering to the general idea developed by Haegeman and Zanuttini, criticize their factorization-and-absorption mechanism for its ad hoc character. As they argue, (8) still violates compositionality, since negative features are simply erased without further motivation. These considerations led De Swart and Sag (2002) to formulate an implementation of Haegeman and Zanuttini's original proposal in a polyadic quantification framework, thus preserving the negative status of neg-words.

De Swart and Sag adopt a framework in which occurrences of multiple NQs can be interpreted under two different modes of interpretation: functional application or polyadic quantification. In the former case, these quantifiers are interpreted as an iteration of monadic quantifiers, giving rise to a DN reading. In the latter case, two quantifiers [NO_E^A] and [NO_E^B] create a polyadic quantifier [$NO'_E^{A,B}$], where the sets A and B are provided by the denotation of the NPs. The interpretation of polyadic quantifiers follows from the definition of resumptive quantification, after Keenan and Westerståhl (1997), as shown in (13).

(13)   Resumptive quantification:[5]
$$Q'^{A_1, A_2, \ldots, A_k}_E (R) = Q^{A_1 \times A_2 \times \ldots \times A_k}_{E^k}(R)$$
whereby $A_1, A_2, \ldots, A_k \subseteq E$ and $A_1 \times A_2 \times \ldots \times A_k,\ R \subseteq E_K$

NC, for De Swart and Sag, is thus an instance of resumptive quantification that applies to multiple quantifiers of the 'same' kind. At the same time, their approach needs to specify what exactly counts as the same kind of quantifier. As NC does not apply to semi-negative expressions such as *hardly* or *seldom* (in NC languages, a sentence like *I rarely saw nobody* does not mean 'I rarely saw anybody'), De Swart and Sag formulate an additional requirement to NC that restricts this instance of resumptive quantification to AA expressions only. To do so, De Swart and Sag have to assume that, prior to undergoing resumptive quantification, negative elements need to share a semantic AA feature, thus replacing Haegeman and Zanuttini's syntactic agreement with an instance of semantic agreement.

Any combination of two or more NQs then yields both an NC and a DN reading. They illustrate this for French (14), which is indeed reported to be ambiguous. The composition of the DN reading is exemplified in (15), the NC reading in (16).

(14)   *Personne* aime *personne*   (French)
        NEG-body loves NEG-body
        DN: Nobody loves nobody
        NC: 'Nobody loves anybody'

---

[5] Example from De Swart and Sag 2002.

(15) $[\text{NO}_E^{\text{Human}}, \text{NO}_E^{\text{Human}}](\text{LOVE})$
NO(HUMAN, {x| NO (HUMAN, {y| x LOVE y})})
HUMAN ∩ {x| HUMAN ∩ {y| x LOVE Y} = ∅} = ∅
DN: ¬∃x¬∃y Love(x, y)

(16) $[\text{NO'}_E^{\text{Human, Human}}](\text{LOVE})$
$[\text{NO'}_{E2}^{\text{Human×Human}}](\text{LOVE})$
NC: ¬∃x∃y Love(x, y)

The main advantage of this approach is that the availability of NC readings does not have to be independently accounted for, but rather comes for free, once it is assumed that quantifier resumption applies to NQs. Moreover, since quantifier resumption (like Quantifier Raising, QR) must obey syntactic locality, it follows immediately why no NC readings are available between two neg-words in two different syntactic domains (though see Wurmbrand 2018 for a criticism of that). As shown in (17) for Italian, NC is indeed not available when an NM is in the main clause and a neg-word appears in an embedded indicative clause or in an adjunct island:

(17) a. *Gianni *non* ha detto che ha acquisito *niente* (Italian)
Gianni NEG has said that has bought NEG-thing
'John didn't say that he bought anything'
b. *Gianni *non* lavora per guadagnare *niente*
Gianni NEG works in.order.to earn NEG-thing
'Gianni doesn't work in order to earn anything'

Finally, it follows nicely for languages such as French that sentences containing multiple negative elements are felt to be ambiguous between a DN and an NC reading, although the NC reading is the one that is generally preferred.

3.2.2 Problems for the negative-quantifier approach

At the same time, the negative-quantifier approach faces serious problems. In brief, three major problems are: (i) that the cross-linguistic distribution of NC remains unexplained; (ii) that neg-words may also occur in certain non-AA contexts; and (iii) why, in most NC languages, neg-words need to be accompanied by NMs.

The prediction that every sentence containing two or more NQs is always ambiguous between an NC and a DN reading is too strong. Although French reflects this kind of ambiguity, similar constructions in most other languages are clearly unambiguous. Therefore, the question arises of why languages display cross-linguistic variation in this respect. For De Swart and Sag (2002: 390), this is 'really a question about the relation between language system and language use'.

For them, both interpretations are always available, but it is a matter of preference which reading surfaces in the end.

Support for this flexible distinction between DN and NC readings comes from the languages that De Swart and Sag primarily base their analysis on: French and English. As shown in (14), French expressions with two neg-words are indeed known to be ambiguous between DN and NC readings. A similar situation holds in English, where many (non-standard) varieties exhibit NC effects (mostly involving the weak NM *n't*), as shown in (18) (cf. Ladusaw 1992).

(18)   I did*n't* see *no one*   (Non-standard English)
       'I did not see anybody'

English and French are not representative of the NC-vs-DN distinction, however. Most other NC languages (Romance languages such as Romanian, Spanish, Italian, or Portuguese; Slavic languages, Albanian, Greek, Hebrew, and Hungarian) do not allow DN readings for standard NC constructions. Similarly, most DN languages cannot give rise to NC readings (Dutch, German, Scandinavian languages). The NC examples presented in the beginning of this chapter ((2)–(3)) only receive an NC reading; the DN examples (e.g. (1)) only receive a DN reading. Hence, the NC landscape consists of a large number of languages which only allow for one reading, and only a handful of languages where these sentences are indeed ambiguous. Obviously, any theory of NC should account for the fact that, in languages such as French and English, in most cases, both DN and NC readings are allowed, but also for the fact that, in most other NC languages, such ambiguities are absent.

In later work, De Swart (2006, 2010) acknowledges this point, and takes a different stand. Here, she argues that the cross-linguistic differences should indeed be captured by the grammar. For this, she develops an independent set of constraints in terms of a bidirectional Optimality Theory. Even though the semantics of clauses containing two NQs allows for both a DN and an NC interpretation, additional constraints may rule out one of the two. For instance, in a DN language, semantic transparency needs to be maximally realized, and, therefore, every negative form should have a reflex in the meaning and vice versa, whereas, in a (Strict) NC language, negation needs to be maximally marked, hence negative meaning should receive a maximal amount of negative markings. By introducing such additional constraints, the existence of various types of NC and DN languages can be grammatically accounted for. However, one may wonder whether the mechanism underlying the semantics of NC and the range of cross-linguistic variation that NC exhibits should be treated independently. Given scientific parsimony an explanation of NC should be preferred that correctly predicts not only the semantics of NC constructions, but also the types of NC that can be expected over two theories that apply independently.

Another problem for the negative-quantifier approach is the fact that, in many cases, mostly in Romance languages, neg-words can be used outside contexts that may license NPIs (such as *before*-clauses, predicates expressing doubt or prohibition, comparatives, and superlatives), which are not negative or AA. Still, in those contexts, these neg-words do not give rise to a negative meaning, but rather to an existential/indefinite interpretation. In this sense, neg-words do not seem to behave like NQs, but more like NPIs, as is shown in the Spanish examples from Herburger (2001) in (19), where the neg-words are translated by English *any*-terms.

(19) a. Antec de hacer *nada*, debes lavarle las manos (Spanish[6,7])
before of do NEG-thing, must.2SG wash.CL the hands
'Before doing anything, you should wash your hands'

b. Dudo que vayan a encontar *nada*
Doubt.1SG that will.3PL.SUBJ find NEG-thing
'I doubt they will find anything'

c. Prohibieron que saliera *nadie*
forbade.3PL that went_out.3SG.SUBJ NEG-body
'They forbade anybody to go out'

d. Es la última vez que te digo *nada*
is the ultimate time that you tell.1SG NEG-thing
'This is the last time I tell you anything'

e. Juan ha llegado más tarde que *nunca*
Juan has arrived more late than NEG-ever
'Juan has arrived later than ever'

These facts are completely unexpected under the negative-quantifier approach, as no polyadic quantifier relation can be established between these NPI licensers. These NPI licensers are not AA and, in some cases, not even quantificational. An obvious way to repair this approach is by arguing that, underlyingly, such expressions that license neg-words contain a decomposed negation. A predicate like *doubt* could be said to have a lexical semantics like NOT BE SURE, and it would be this negation that, then, licenses the neg-words. However, before even exploring this option, it first needs to be discussed what role NMs play in NC constructions in the first place.

A third problem for the negative-quantifier approach is that the necessity of NC never becomes clear. If neg-words are NQs, neg-words should be possible in postverbal position, just as is the case in English. Thus, the question immediately arises of why English (20) is accepted as grammatical, whereas Italian (21) is not.

---

[6] Herburger (2001: 297).
[7] Herburger (2001: 298).

(20) John has said *nothing*

(21) *Ieri ha detto *niente*   (Italian)
      Yesterday has said NEG-thing
      Int. 'Yesterday he didn't say anything'

If *niente* in (21) is a NQ, it is unclear why it is unable to yield the intended reading without any negative material present in preverbal position. The comparison between (20) and (21) triggers two questions. The first one, as already indicated, is why an NM should be obligatory in Italian if the NQ in Italian has the same semantics as in English; the second one is how the single negative reading comes about, given that the NM is not a NQ itself (it does not bind a variable).

As for the first question, De Swart and Sag, following Ladusaw (1992), argue that the NM or the preverbal neg-word in such cases functions as a scope marker. In order for sentential negation to be expressed, negation needs to outscope at least all the material inside the vP. If the neg-word is inside the vP, an additional NM may take over. At the same time, since the neg-word under the negative-quantifier approach should be able to undergo QR, as is the case in English, and thus outscope the rest of the vP, why could it not do so in Italian? Two different types of solutions have been provided in the literature.

According to the first solution, voiced in slightly different terms by De Swart (2010), this is a matter of (arbitrary) variation. In every type of language, a combination of an NM and a neg-word can, but does not have to, give rise to an NC reading. Additional syntactico-semantic rules then further specify the negative system. Alluding to a constraint called *Neg First* (after Horn 1989), a language might prefer to mark negation even at the beginning of the sentence (i.e., at least to the left of the vP), or to keep the number of negative forms in balance with the number of negative meanings. Italian would favour the first; English would favour the second.

Alternatively, one could argue that the presence or absence of the NM should give rise to different semantic effects. This is a position taken by Herburger (2001), who takes neg-words to be ambiguous between NQs and NPIs. She presents data like (22), where postverbal neg-words in an NC language do not have to be accompanied by an NM, and shows that, in these cases, the neg-words (i) bring in a semantic negation (supporting the idea that they are indeed NQs), and (ii) take scope differently from how a postverbal NQ would do in a DN language.

(22) a. El bebé pasa el tiempo mirando a *nadie*   (Spanish[8])
         the baby spends the time looking at NEG-thing
         'The baby spends the time looking at nothing'

---

[8] Example based on Herburger (2001: 303).

b. El bebé *no* pasa el tiempo mirando a *nadie*
the baby NEG spends the time looking at NEG-thing
'The baby doesn't spend the time looking at anything'

The reading in (22a) is one where the baby is staring in front of him- or herself. For Herburger, this is due to an independent constraint that bans QR of NQs across the existential quantifier binding the event variable in NC languages. If this constraint holds, then (22a) would indeed get a reading like (23):

(23) $\exists e.[\textbf{Look}(e)\ \&\ \textbf{Agent}(e, baby)\ \&\ \neg\exists y.[\textbf{Thing'}(y)\ \&\ \textbf{Theme}(e, y)]]$

(23) states that there is a looking event, but that there is no element that serves as this looking event's theme. The negation induced by *nadie* in (22a) scopes under the existential quantifier binding the looking-event variable. In line with the discussion in Chapter 1, sentential negation for her means that such existential event-binding quantifiers must take scope under negation; and she takes these event variables to be introduced by v. In (22b), where the entire vP is scope-marked for negation, there is a single wide-scope sentential negation, and the reading in (23) is absent. As, generally, readings of the kind in (23) are pragmatically highly infelicitous, constructions with sole vP-internal neg-words are extremely rare in NC languages. For instance, (21) would mean that there is a calling event, but at the same time nobody is being called, which yields a contradiction. While Herburger's analysis nicely derives the meaning differences between (22a) and (22b), it does so by stipulating that NQs in NC languages behave differently from NQs in DN languages, something that runs against the gist of the negative-quantifier approach.

But even if this problem is set aside, there is still the question of why, in (22b), the NQ and the NM establish an NC relation, even though the latter one is not a NQ and should therefore not be expected to undergo resumptive quantification. De Swart and Sag argue that NMs should be thought of as so-called zero-quantifiers, quantifiers that bind no variable. Being both quantificational and negative in nature, NMs can then participate in NC relations (as is the case in most languages). However, since NMs in NC constructions do not bring in any new semantic contribution (as they do not bind variables), languages may also choose to leave NMs out of NC. French would then be an example of a language that forbids one of its NMs, namely *pas*, to participate in NC relations (irrespective of its relative position to the neg-word, as shown in (24)), whereas other languages allow (e.g. West Flemish) or even require (e.g., Italian with postverbal neg-words; Czech with all neg-words) the NM to be present.

(24)   a.   *Personne* (*ne*) mange *pas*   (French)
            NEG-body NEG eats NEG
            *NC: 'Nobody eats'
            OKDN: 'Nobody doesn't eat'

b. Elle (*n'*)a vu *pas rien*
she NEG has seen NEG NEG-thing
*NC: 'She hasn't seen anything'
ᴼᴷDN: 'She hasn't seen nothing'

However, the French system, where the NM *pas* never participates in NC languages, is typologically very rare. Virtually every other NC language does allow NMs to participate in NC in at least certain configurations. As we will see in Chapters 4–6, *pas* should be treated as a kind of exceptional NM.

3.2.3 Concluding remarks

The negative-quantifier approach provides a strong mechanism to account for NC readings in a compositional fashion, but this mechanism, being universally available, does not explain why only some languages are NC languages, and why NC languages themselves may also vary in a number of dimensions, such as the optionality or obligatoriness of NC, or what kind of elements, including NMs, may or must participate in NC. The best way to think about the negative-quantifier approach is as a global approach that takes NC to be the result of universally available modes of interpretation rather than the result of any local specifications on lexical items. The so-called NPI approach aims at providing the latter.

3.3 The Negative Polarity Item approach

3.3.1 Proposal

In contrast to a global approach such as the one I have spelled out, a local approach to NC rather aims at accounting for the existence of NC patterns as a result of certain lexical specifications of neg-words and NMs. Focusing on constructions where a postverbal neg-word needs to be accompanied by an NM, one can assume that the neg-word must have a property that (i) requires it to be outscoped by a negation, and that, (ii) jointly with the negation, yields a single negative interpretation. In this sense, neg-words behave very similarly to NPIs, which are also required to appear in (semi-)negative contexts and do not bring in a separate negation of their own.

Given these strong similarities between NPIs and neg-words (or between negative polarity and NC), and in order to overcome the problems that the negative-quantifier approach has been facing, several scholars (e.g. Laka 1990; Ladusaw 1992; Suñer 1995; Giannakidou 1998, 2000, 2006b) have proposed that neg-words are in fact special kinds of NPIs. If the meaning of an element like Italian *nessuno*

3.3 THE NEGATIVE POLARITY ITEM APPROACH 59

is actually 'anybody' instead of 'nobody', the proper reading in (7b) follows immediately: the NM *non* introduces the negation in the semantics, while *nessuno* is semantically non-negative.

This approach tackles several problems that the negative-quantifier approach is facing. First, the difference between neg-words in NC languages and NQs in DN languages has been reduced to differences in their lexical properties: NIs in DN languages are semantically NQs (and always bring in a negation of their own) (though see Chapter 7 for some problems with this perspective); neg-words in NC languages are semantically non-negative NPIs. Moreover, the occurrence of neg-words in typical NPI-licensing contexts is also predicted, although it needs to be further specified why certain languages allow neg-words to be licensed by non-negative NPI licensers, whereas other languages do not. Finally, the obligatory co-occurrence of NMs and neg-words in most NC languages also follows immediately: just like plain NPIs, neg-words have to be licensed by a negation as well.

3.3.2 Challenges for the Negative Polarity Item approach

Despite its attractive properties, a series of arguments against the NPI approach have been put forward in the literature, mostly in defence of the negative-quantifier approach. These arguments all concern the fact that neg-words and NPIs do have different syntactic and semantic distributions.

For one, if neg-words are NPIs, how can the readings of sentences like (7a), repeated here as (25a), where a single neg-word induces semantic negation, be derived? A plain NPI, such as *anybody*, may not appear in an unlicensed subject position, let alone render a sentence negative by itself (25b).

(25) a. *Nessuno* ha telefonato (Italian)
NEG-body has called
'Nobody called'
b. *Anybody calls

It is a defining property of neg-words that, in certain configurations, they may induce a semantic negation by themselves. When this is not possible in preverbal position, as is the case with neg-words in Strict NC languages, this is still possible in fragment answers or certain coordinations, both in Strict and Non-strict NC languages, as illustrated for Greek (Strict NC) and Spanish (Non-strict NC) below:

(26) a. A Quién ha viste? {A *Nadie* / *A un alma} (Spanish[9])
To who has.2SG seen? NEG-body / a soul
'Who did you see? Nobody / A single soul' (Greek)

b. Ti idhes? {*TIPOTA* / *Tipota}
what saw.2SG? NEG-thing / anything
'What did you see? Nothing / anything'

(27) a. Me caso contigo o con {*nadie* / *un alma}   (Spanish)
me marry with-you or with NEG-body / anybody
'I marry you or nobody.'

b. Thelo na pandrefto ton Petro i {KANENAN / kanenan}
want SUBJ marry the Petro or NEG-body / anybody
(alo)   (Greek)
else
'I want to marry either Peter or nobody else'

In order to solve these problems, Herburger (2001) argues that neg-words are lexically ambiguous between NQs and NPIs. This means that every neg-word can in principle receive both the reading of an NPI and that of a NQ. Take for instance (28):

(28)   *Nessuno* ha detto *niente*   (Italian)
       NEG-body has said NEG-thing
       'Nobody said anything'

The first neg-word, *nessuno*, can only receive a negative-quantifier reading; the NPI reading is blocked since it does not appear in a downward-entailing (DE) context. The second neg-word should in principle be able to receive two interpretations: an NPI interpretation and a negative-quantifier interpretation. However, given Herburger's constraint that blocks vP-internal neg-words from covertly raising out of the vP, this second reading (there is nobody who participates in a calling event where nobody is called) is, again, pragmatically ill-formed (and trivially true).

Herburger's analysis suffers from both conceptual and empirical problems, though. First, lexical ambiguity is some kind of theoretical last-resort solution, as it is extremely hard to actually prove that there are two lexical entries for neg-words. Second, the mechanism that blocks postverbal movement of neg-words across the existential quantifier that binds the event variable is purely stipulated; it lacks any kind of independent motivation. This is especially problematic since it appears to only hold in NC languages. In DN languages, postverbal NQs are not constrained by this ban.

Moreover, the proposal does not extend to Strict NC languages. Take (4) again, repeated as (29) below.

---

[9] Example taken from Herburger (2001: 300).

(29) a. Dnes *nikdo* *(*ne-*)volá (Czech)
today NEG-body NEG-calls
'Today nobody calls'

b. Dnes *(*ne-*)vola *nikdo*
today NEG-calls NEG-body
'Today nobody calls'

Following Herburger, *nikdo* ('neg-body') must receive a negative-quantifier interpretation as it is not c-commanded by any DE operator. The NM *ne*, in Herburger's terms, is the negation itself (otherwise she could not explain why (29b) comes with an NC reading), and thus introduces a semantic negation, too. However, the entire sentence does not have a DN reading, but rather a plain NC reading, which is not predicted (unless one were to say that, in Strict NC languages, the NM itself is ambiguous between a semantic negation and a non-negative NPI, something Herburger alludes to as well).

Given the above-mentioned problems for a treatment of neg-words in terms of NQs (even if they are taken to be ambiguous with NPIs), it is legitimate to wonder to what extent neg-words actually do induce a semantic negation. Or, to put matters differently, how much evidence is there for the claim that neg-words are semantically negative, and how much evidence is there that shows that neg-words are semantically non-negative?

This question has already been addressed by Ladusaw (1992), and he concludes that there is ample evidence for the claim that neg-words are semantically non-negative: constructions with an NM and a neg-word, or with multiple neg-words, or with a neg-word in a DE context, clearly support this claim. On the other hand, there is actually not that much evidence that neg-words are semantically negative. As Ladusaw observes, at best there is evidence that every clause in which one or more neg-words surface must be interpreted negatively. For that reason, he concludes that the hypothesis that all neg-words are NPIs can be entertained as long as some mechanism is available that can license these NPIs in absence of an overt negation. In other words, neg-words that induce a semantic negation are nothing but NPIs, like the English *any*-terms, that are licensed by some covert negative operator.

Ladusaw's approach overcomes the problems that the previous approaches have been facing, but does do so at some price. It allows inclusion of abstract negative operators. However, inclusion of such abstract negative operators must be constrained to exactly those cases where neg-words appear overtly in the clause. To illustrate the problem: only in example (30a) may an abstract negative operator be assumed to be present; in (30b), an overt negation is already present, and (30c) is intended as a positive sentence and should never be able to receive a negative interpretation.

(30) a. *Nessuno* telefona (Italian)
   NEG-body calls
   'Nobody calls'

   b. *Non* telefona *nessuno*
   NEG calls   NEG-body
   'Nobody calls'

   c. Gianni telefona
   Gianni calls
   'Gianni calls'

Thus, the following two questions arise: (i) what is the exact mechanism that ensures that only neg-words in non-DE contexts may trigger the presence of an abstract negative operator, and (ii) why is it that neg-words have this self-licensing property, whereas all other known NPIs do not? Only if these questions can be satisfactorily answered can Ladusaw's hypothesis be successfully implied.

Ladusaw (1992) does not provide a full-fledged analysis of how this self-licensing mechanism can be implemented, although he does provide some suggestions. One suggestion, phrased in GPSG terms, would be to take NC to be an instance of syntactic agreement, an idea that actually predates the proposal presented in the next section. All neg-words are said to carry a negative feature ([NEG]). Combining multiple negative elements would then lead to a percolation of these negative features (cf. Gazdar, Klein, Pullum, and Sag 1985). An alternative solution, sketched in GB terms, is that the highest negative element in a functional projection NegP induces the semantic negation. But the compositionality problem remains unsolved under both types of analyses: if neg-words have a feature that can introduce a semantic negation, why does this featural equipment not prevent the introduction of multiple semantic negations in a multiple-negative construction?

What any analysis of NC then should do, when guided by the idea that neg-words are semantically non-negative, is to explain why neg-words are different from plain NPIs, which can never induce semantic negation in isolation and which can precede NMs (in Strict NC languages).

One such account, proposed by Giannakidou (2000), argues that, at least in Strict NC languages like Greek, the difference lies in the quantificational status of neg-words as opposed to that of 'plain' NPIs. Giannakidou (2000), following Szabolcsi (1981), takes these neg-words to be NPIs indeed, but holds that they differ from the English type of NPIs in the sense that the latter are indefinites, whereas the former are universal quantifiers that must outscope negation. Giannakidou supports this view by showing that Greek neg-words satisfy most diagnostics that apply to universal quantifiers. For instance, she demonstrates that Greek neg-words may be modified by *almost*, a property that holds for universals, but not for existentials (*I saw almost everything* vs **I saw almost something*):[10]

(31) En idha sxedhon KANENAN (Greek)
      NEG saw.1SG almost NEG-person / any person
      'I saw almost nobody'

If neg-words are licensed by negation in a reverse way, i.e., when all neg-words must outscope negation, it follows that, at LF, all neg-words must c-command negation. That preverbal neg-words already c-command negation at surface structure only supports this view and is no longer problematic.

Another potential problem for the NPI approach vanishes as well under this particular approach—and this concerns locality. As indicated in the previous section, NC is subject to syntactic locality. The relevant example that shows this is repeated below:

(32) a. *Gianni *non* ha detto che a acquisito *niente* (Italian)
         Gianni NEG has said that has bought NEG-thing
         'John didn't say that he bought anything'
      b. *Gianni *non* labora per guadagnare *niente* argente
         Gianni NEG works in.order.to earn NEG money
         'Gianni doesn't work in order to earn any money'

Neg-words cannot be licensed by an extra-clausal negation or by a negation outside an island if they are themselves inside an island.[11] As the translations show, NPIs like *any* can be licensed in such configurations. Hence, NPI-licensing does not appear to be subject to syntactic locality. QR, on the other hand, is subject to syntactic locality; and if neg-words have to undergo QR across negation (either overtly or covertly), locality of NC can be maintained.

This argument is valid, of course, but the potential challenge that the NPI approach faces when it comes to locality is weaker than has often been claimed, including by myself. It is indeed the case that the licensing of NPIs like *any* is not subject to syntactic locality, but that does not hold for every NPI. NPIs can be divided into strict NPIs and non-strict NPIs. Non-strict NPIs may be licensed by a negation or another DE operator outside the local domain they appear in; strict NPIs must be licensed locally. So, if neg-words are taken to be strict NPIs, locality is not a problem anyway. As Collins and Postal (2014) observe, strict NPIs are also strong NPIs (NPIs that can only be licensed in AA contexts; see also Chapters 8 and 10). Hence, the fact that neg-words are generally licensed by AA contexts would actually suggest that they should be licensed locally, if they are taken to

---

[10] But see Horn (2005) and Penka (2011) for a number of arguments against this diagnostic.
[11] It should be noted that this constraint can be overruled if the neg-word appears in a subjunctive clause, arguably because subjunctive clauses in general count as weaker syntactic domains than indicative clauses (see Zeijlstra 2004 for discussion and references).

be NPIs. However, that also means that examples like (19), which were initially taken as prime evidence in favour of the NPI approach, need to be re-explained, as, here, the licensers are DE, but not AA.

Since Giannakidou (2000) focuses only on Strict NC languages, the only cases in Greek (or any other Strict NC language) where a neg-word may occur without a corresponding NM are in fragment answers or in coordinations. I repeat the relevant examples below:

(33) a. Ti idhes? *Tipota*! (Greek)
what saw.2SG? NEG-thing
'What did you see? Nothing'

b. Thelo na pandrefto ton Petro i KANENAN (alo). (Greek)
want SUBJ marry the Petro or NEG-body else
'I want to marry either Peter or nobody else'

For Giannakidou, such cases involve ellipsis of the (semantically) NM. She argues that this negation, expressed by *dhen*, is deleted under ellipsis in (33). For her, (33a–b) come along with the underlying structures shown in (34) and (35), respectively, where strikethrough indicates deletion under ellipsis. Thus, the assumption that neg-words are semantically non-negative can be maintained.

(34) [[*TIPOTA* [dhen ida]] (Greek)
NEG-thing NEG saw.1SG
'Nothing'

(35) ... i [dhen thelo na pandrefto KANENAN (alo)] (Greek)
... or NEG want SUBJ marry NEG-body else
'... or I want to marry nobody else'

Watanabe (2004) argues that this analysis violates the condition that ellipsis may only take place under semantic identity (cf. Merchant's 2001 notion of e-GIVENness). As the question does not contain a negation, it may not license ellipsis of the NM *dhen*.

Giannakidou (2006b) argues in response that the NM in the deleted part of the answer is licensed under semantic isomorphism with the question. Following Karttunnen (1977), she takes the denotation of a question to be the set of all possible answers, including the negative one. This negative answer (or more precisely: the negation that this particular answer contains) would then license the deletion under ellipsis of *dhen*.

Apart from the theoretical question of exactly what mechanism is responsible for licensing elided material in answers to questions, this analysis makes incorrect empirical predictions. First, if questions may license elided negation, then it would be expected that any NPI, and not only neg-words, could be licensed in fragment questions. However, this is not the case. The English counterpart of (34) with *anybody* is ruled out, as is shown below.

(36) Who did you see? *Anybody ~~I didn't see~~!

Nevertheless, one could argue that (36) is ruled out because of the fact that English *anybody* is subject to a surface condition that requires it to always follow its licenser. But then it should be expected that NPIs that may or must independently precede negation should be felicitous as fragment answers. This prediction is not borne out either: Dutch *heel die vent* (lit.: whole that bloke) is an NPI meaning something like 'that bloke ... at all', and must precede negation (cf. Den Dikken 2006).

(37) Ik heb   heel   die   vent   *(niet) gezien   (Dutch)
     I   have whole   that   bloke   NEG   seen
     'I didn't see that bloke at all'

On the other hand, *heel die vent* cannot be used as a fragment answer, let alone receive a negative interpretation:

(38) Wie heb   je   gezien?   *Heel   die   vent.   (Dutch)
     who have you seen   whole that   bloke
     'Who did you see?'   'No/any bloke at all'

So, if elided *dhen* in the fragment answer in (34) could be licensed by the question, then an elided negation should also be able to license *heel die vent* in (38), contrary to fact.

The same applies to disjunction. Neg-words may appear in disjunctions receiving a negative reading, as shown in (27); but if disjunctions were able to license elided negation, other elements, especially NPIs, should be expected to be fine in such constructions as well. Again, this prediction is not borne out, as is shown below:

(39) *I want to marry you or anybody

For Watanabe, the acceptability of neg-words in fragment answers forms evidence that neg-words cannot be analysed as being semantically non-negative, as Giannakidou (2000) proposes. This conclusion, I will argue later on, is too strong. It may at best imply that the exact analysis by Giannakidou is problematic, but it does not prove that neg-words themselves are semantically negative.

3.3.3 Concluding remarks

The discussion so far has indicated that neg-words cannot be readily analysed as plain NQs or as plain NPIs. The reason is that treating neg-words as NQs leaves various language-specific properties of neg-words unexplained (such as their relation with NMs or potential non-AA licensers), and that analysing neg-words as being NPI-like also brings in particular problems, as neg-words, in at least one respect, crucially differ from other NPIs: if they are NPIs, they can self-license themselves, unlike all other kinds of NPIs. As we saw, alluding to lexical ambiguity of neg-words between NQs and NPIs also faces several problems.

At the same time, the NPI approach has two fundamental advantages. First, it is a local approach, and therefore able to integrate answers to the first central question (how to address the compositionality problems) with answers to the second central question (how to account for the attested variation among different NC systems or manifestations). Second, more bluntly, neg-words, in at least those languages where NC is obligatory, are NPIs. NPIs, by definition, are elements that need to be licensed by some kind of negation, and that is indeed the case with (vP-internal) neg-words. Even if they were NQs, they would still count as NPIs as they could not survive without an additional negation. Hence, any theory that takes neg-words to be NPI-like is, in this sense, on the right track. However, since certain NPIs (neg-words) are able to appear without an (overt) licenser in at least some contexts (at any rate, in fragment answers) and then induce a semantic negation, whereas others are not (plain NPIs), the notion of NPI-hood needs to be enriched in a way that covers both neg-words and plain NPIs. The following section will present an analysis of NC and neg-words that aims precisely at doing that.

3.4 Negative Concord is syntactic agreement

In this section, I present my own explanation of NC, which takes it to be an instance of syntactic agreement. The proposal falls indeed under the umbrella of NPI approaches, in that it takes neg-words to be semantically non-negative, and in that it takes neg-words to require the presence of a semantically negative operator. The crucial difference between this approach and other NPI approaches to NC is that it takes the relation between this negative operator and the neg-words to be an instance of syntactic agreement, whereas the dependency of a plain NPI to another (negative) operator lies elsewhere in the grammar, generally inside the semantic or pragmatic components. As a result of this, the negative operator in the case of NC may be covertly present, whereas negation cannot be covertly present when it comes to 'real' NPI licensing.

3.4.1 Proposal

Generally, agreement means that a semantic feature of one element is manifest on other elements as well (cf. Corbett 2006). In languages that exhibit subject–verb

3.4 NEGATIVE CONCORD IS SYNTACTIC AGREEMENT 67

agreement, semantic properties of the subject (like person or number) are reflected on the finite verb as well. In this section, I demonstrate that this idea naturally extends to negation: in NC languages, then, the presence of a negative operator is manifest on other elements as well.

Following standard minimalist ideas, I take agreement to be a relation between an element that carries a particular interpretable formal feature [iF] and one (or more) element(s) which carry the uninterpretable counterparts of the same formal feature (Chomsky 1995a, 2000, 2001; Pesetsky and Torrego 2004, 2007). Subject–verb agreement, for instance, is the manifestation of the relation between an interpretable φ-feature on the subject and a matching uninterpretable φ-feature on the finite verb, as is illustrated for second-person singular in (40) for German (though see Chapter 17 for more discussion).

(40) a. Du kommst (German)
you come.2SG
'You come'
b. [$_{TP}$ du$_{[i2SG]}$ komm-st$_{[u2SG]}$ [$_{VP}$ ...]]

Now, crucially, nothing forbids agreement (in terms of the syntactic operation Agree) to apply to other formal features. Even stronger, if agreement were restricted to, e.g., φ-features, this should be motivated independently. Hence, the account of agreement phenomena in terms of [iF]s and [uF]s should naturally extend to negation as well.

In that case, one could take negative agreement to be a relation between elements that carry an interpretable formal negative feature ([iNEG]) and elements that carry an uninterpretable one ([uNEG]). In the rest of this chapter, I defend the view that all instances of NC are instances of negative agreement, as formulated in (41), a view that finds predecessors in Brown (1999) and Weiss (2002).

(41) NC is an Agree relation between a single feature [iNEG] and one or more features [uNEG]

In order to explore (41) and its consequences, a few assumptions have to be spelled out. First, NC languages exhibit elements which are only formally negative, i.e., these elements carry [uNEG]. This entails that these elements have all the morphosyntactic properties that are characteristic of negation, but lack the semantics of negation. These elements are semantically non-negative. I argue, following Ladusaw (1992) and Zeijlstra (2004), that, at least in the NC languages discussed so far, neg-words are such elements: in those languages, neg-words are considered to be semantically non-negative existentials that are syntactically marked for negation, i.e., they carry a [uNEG]-feature. The semantic representation for neg-words is the one in (42).

(42) $[[\text{n-Q}]] = \lambda P. \exists [Q(x) \& P(x)]$ where $Q \in \{\textbf{Person'}, \textbf{Thing'}, \textbf{Place'}...\}$[12]

Second, I adopt Multiple Agree, along the lines of Ura (1996) and Hiraiwa (2001), who have argued on the basis of (among others) Japanese case-feature checking that single [iF]s may establish Agree relations with multiple [uF]s, provided that all Agree relations respect proper locality conditions. A slightly deviant version of Agree that I adopt in this chapter is that, contrary to standard probe-goal relations as they have been developed for case- and φ-feature checking (nowadays referred to as Downward Agree (DA)), feature checking operates in a top-down fashion, with the [iNEG]-feature being required to c-command the [uNEG]-features. This version of Agree, dubbed *Upward Agree* (UA), has predecessors in Adger (2003) and Neeleman and Van de Koot (2002), among many others, and has recently provoked a fair amount of discussion (cf. Wurmbrand 2012a, b; Zeijlstra 2012a; Preminger 2013; Polinsky and Preminger 2019; Bjorkman and Zeijlstra 2019; Preminger and Polinsky 2015; see also Chapter 17). In none of these papers, however, is the validity of UA for NC (or other phenomena that look like grammaticalized semantic dependencies) disputed; rather, the discussion is whether UA can extend to other types of agreement, such as φ-agreement. For that reason, I will not discuss the distinction between UA and DA here any further, and leave open the question whether UA and DA reflect two different syntactic operations or whether they can be unified in some way.

Third, I allow the possibility that, under certain circumstances, the element carrying [iNEG] (or any interpretable formal feature, for that matter) may be covert. Let me illustrate this again by means of subject–verb agreement. In many languages, it is the case that, if the uninterpretable person feature on the finite verb is overtly present, the pronominal subject carrying the interpretable person feature may be abstract, a phenomenon widely attested and well-known as *pro-drop* or *null subjects*. In Italian, as exemplified in (43), the *-o* affix on *canto* already suggests that this finite verb can only establish an Agree relation with an element carrying [iφ: 1SG]. Therefore, the subject does not have to be phonologically realized:

(43) a. Canto (Italian[13])
sing.1SG
'I sing'
b. [*pro*$_{[iφ: 1SG]}$ canto$_{[uφ: 1SG]}$]

Something similar applies to negation. If some overt element carrying [uNEG] already requires the presence of an element carrying [iNEG], this latter element itself does not necessarily have to be overtly realized. Of course, it remains a matter of language-specific properties whether this mechanism is actually applied (just as some rich-agreement languages, like German, do not exhibit pro-drop).

---

[12] Alternatively, one may think of neg-words in this respect as pure indefinites, introducing a free variable; but this discussion is tangential to the rest of the arguments presented in this book. For a detailed evaluation, the reader is referred to Penka (2007, 2011).

Naturally, when alluding to a covert negative operator, one must ensure that its appearance is reduced to those cases where it is required to be present, and nowhere else. The most straightforward way of doing so would be to say that only if, in a particular well-formed sentence, no overt element can be said to be responsible for the checking of a [uNEG]-feature, a covert element can be taken to be responsible for it. Such a formalization forbids adopting abstract material beyond any grammatical necessity. This way, it is prevented that sentences without any element carrying a feature [uNEG] may have a covert element carrying [iNEG]. The question emerges, however, of how such a constraint can be embedded in minimalist syntax. After all, nothing in principle would forbid merging an abstract negative operator in a non-negatively marked sentence (i.e., in a sentence without any element carrying a feature [uNEG]). However, it is well known that the acceptability of a sentence does not depend only on its syntactic derivability. Sentences are also subject to certain extra-grammatical factors, such as processability or parsability. Assuming that the human parser only includes covert operators if there is a clear signpost for them (such as an overt element carrying [uNEG]), this constraint follows directly from parsing conditions on covert material. Note that allusion to such parsing constraints is not unusual in syntax. Ackema and Neeleman (2002), Abels and Neeleman (2012), and Biberauer et al. (2014) allude to similar parsing constraints to limit rightward movement (though see Kayne 1994 and Nilsen 2003 for alternatives to and criticisms of this approach).

To summarize, the proposal amounts to saying that NC is nothing but a syntactic relation between a single negative operator, carrying [iNEG], which may be covert, and one or more elements carrying [uNEG]. In order to demonstrate how this mechanism functions in detail, in the next subsection, I apply it first to Non-strict NC, leaving the other types to Chapter 4.

3.4.2 Application

Thus far, nothing has been said about the interpretative status of the formal negative feature of NMs. Since every sentence that contains an NM is also semantically negative, it makes sense, as a first hypothesis, to assume that the NM is indeed the carrier of semantic negation. For Italian, the NM would then be the realization of the negative operator. Consequently, postverbal neg-words can have their features checked against the NM *non*. The syntactic representation of (44) is thus (45) (ignoring irrelevant functional projections). As *non* is the only semantic negation, the sentence receives an NC reading (44).

(44) *Non telefona a nessuno* (Italian)
 Gianni NEG calls to NEG-body
 'Gianni doesn't call anybody'

(45) [$_{NegP}$ non$_{[iNEG]}$ telefona [$_{vP}$ a nessuno$_{[uNEG]}$]]

(46)
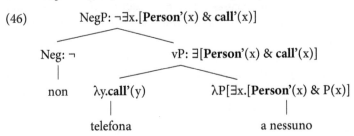

At the same time, under the requirement that if a neg-word c-commands, and therefore, precedes the NM, its [uNEG] feature cannot be checked against *non*'s [iNEG], sentences like (47) are correctly predicted to be ungrammatical with an NC reading.

(47) *Ieri *nessuno non* ha telefonato a *nessuno* (Italian)
 yesterday NEG-body NEG has called to NEG-body
 'Yesterday nobody called anybody'

If, however, in Italian, a neg-word precedes the verb in a sentence without an NM, then the syntax and semantics follow straightforwardly. In (48), which is grammatical, no overt element carries [iNEG], and *nessuno* carries [uNEG]. Hence, an abstract operator immediately c-commanding *nessuno* may be assumed to be present, as is demonstrated in (49).

(48) Ieri *nessuno* ha telefonato a *nessuno* (Italian)
 yesterday NEG-body has called to NEG-body
 'Yesterday nobody called anybody'

(49) [ieri Op$_{¬[iNEG]}$ *nessuno* ha telefonato a *nessuno*]

Note that this comes with the assumption that the external argument *nessuno* cannot have its feature checked under c-command in its base position. For the structures assumed here, external-argument subjects would, in terms of the VP-Internal-Subject-Hypothesis (VISH), be expected to originate within vP. If feature-checking involves Agree, however, it is not clear why checking prior to movement should be ruled out. One option is, of course, to reject VISH: if external-argument subjects originate vP-externally in their surface position above *non*, it is clear that the c-command condition on checking will not be met. But the evidence for VISH is quite overwhelming, so this solution can be rejected right away. However, a parsing solution along the lines just sketched can explain the ungrammaticality of (47). Since parsing applies in a direct left-to-right fashion,

---

[13] Cf. Alexiadou and Anagnostopoulou (1998) for a different view of the feature value of verbal-agreement affixes; see Chapter 17 for more discussion.

the moment the parsers encounters *nessuno*, which carries a feature [uNEG], it must include a negative operator right away. That means that even if *nessuno*'s [uNEG]-feature could have been checked off earlier, the parser would still include a negative operator on top of *nessuno* in (47).

Evidence for the inclusion of this abstract operator even follows from sentences (acceptable to most, though not all, speakers of Italian, albeit only with stress on the first neg-word, followed by an intonational break), where preverbal neg-words co-occur with an NM. Those constructions exhibit a DN reading, indicating that the sentence must contain an additional negative operator next to the NM.

(50) ?Ieri NESSUNO (#) *non* ha telefonato a *nessuno* (Italian)
yesterday NEG-body NEG has called to NEG-body
'Yesterday nobody didn't call anybody'

The syntactic approach is thus able to provide a compositional analysis of NC. It also circumvents several of the problems that other approaches suffer from. For instance, unlike the negative-quantifier approach, the syntactic agreement can easily distinguish between neg-words and NQs in DN languages. While the former are semantically non-negative indefinites, the latter are semantically negative and therefore always induce a semantic negation of their own. Also, unlike the negative-quantifier approach, it can easily account for the presence of the NM, at least in Non-strict NC languages. If sentential negation is the result of the existential quantifier binding the event variable, and this event variable is introduced by v, it should be marked that the negative operator, irrespective of whether it is overtly or covertly present, is higher than v. This is immediately guaranteed if the NM *non*, the overt negative operator, is present in some NegP that dominates vP. It is also immediately guaranteed if a neg-word is in a vP-external position, as, then, the covert negative operator must c-command this neg-word and, therefore, in turn, also v.

Now, let us see what happens if a neg-word appears in postverbal position, without any negative material being present outside vP. The prediction of the syntactic-agreement approach is still that there is a covert negative operator present (as is always the case when a neg-word is not checked by an overt higher element carrying [iNEG]). However, nothing ensures that this abstract negative operator is in vP-external position. In fact, given the line of reasoning that includes this negative operator only in those positions where the parser allows that, the negative operator should be in the lowest possible structural position from where it can c-command the (highest) neg-word. If that neg-word is inside vP, so should the abstract negative operator. This means that (51) is, strictly speaking, grammatical, as, in its syntactic representation, no [uNEG]- (or other) feature remains unchecked (52):

(51) #Ieri ha detto *niente* (Italian)
Yesterday has said NEG-thing
Int. 'Yesterday she didn't say anything'

(52) [TP ieri ha [vP detto *Op*¬[iNEG] *niente*[uNEG]]]

At the same time, the reading of (51)/(52) is internally contradictory. This follows directly from (53). (53) asserts that there is a saying event, but that nothing is said in that event. But when nothing is said, there cannot be any saying event in the first place. It is this contradiction that rules out (51).

(53) ∃e.[**Say**(e) & **Agent**(e, she) & ¬∃y.[**Thing'**(y) & **Theme**(e, y)]]

Only in those situations where a contradiction due to the appearance of a covert negative operator in vP-internal position would not arise, can neg-words remain unaccompanied by an NM in postverbal position. Indeed, all examples presented by Herburger are cases where this contradiction indeed does not arise, for example, in the example repeated from (22)/(23) here as (54)/(55):

(54) El bebé pasa el tiempo mirando a *nadie* (Spanish)
the baby spends the time looking at NEG-thing
'The baby spends the time looking at nothing'

(55) ∃e.[**Look**(e) & **Agent**(e, baby) & ¬∃y.[**Thing'**(y) & **Theme**(e, y)]]

This means that two of the major challenges for the negative-quantifier approach do not arise for the syntactic-agreement approach. Also, the two major challenges for the NPI approach do not extend to the syntactic-agreement approach. The first challenge was that a mechanism is needed that ensures that neg-words, but not plain NPIs, can be self-licensing in Ladusaw's terms. By assuming that the source for the negative-sensitivity of neg-words lies in syntax and that for other NPIs outside syntax, and by assuming that only syntactic dependencies can be satisfied by covert elements, it follows immediately that only neg-words can be licensed by a covert negative operator whose presence is manifested by the overt appearance of a neg-word. Naturally, if other NPIs are not negative-sensitive for syntactic reasons, the question arises why a syntax-external mechanism makes them negative-sensitive. This question will be addressed at length in Chapters 9–12 of this book, where I will carefully show that, indeed, any type of NPI other than neg-words comes with a property that forces it to appear under a negative or other NPI-licensing operator for reasons other than syntactic ones.

The other major challenge for the NPI approach concerns the appearance of neg-words in fragment answers and coordinations. Here, I restrict myself to Nonstrict NC languages, but, as we will see in the following chapter, the explanation also extends to the other type of NC languages. Take again the relevant examples repeated below:

3.4 NEGATIVE CONCORD IS SYNTACTIC AGREEMENT 73

(56) a. A Quién ha viste? {A *nadie* / **un alma*}   (Spanish[14])
who has seen? NEG-body / A soul
'Who did you see? Nobody / A single soul'

b. Me caso contigo o con {*nadie* / **un alma*}
me marry with-you or with NEG-body / anybody
'I marry you or nobody'

Given that the elided parts of the fragment answer may not contain any negation if the question itself contains no negation, the semantic negation of the answer may not come from this elided part. However, nothing forbids the inclusion of a covert operator in a case where a (preverbal) neg-word lacks an overt semantic negation. In fact, since the neg-word carries a feature [uNEG], such an operator is actually required to be present. The same holds for ellipsis in coordinations, where the elided part of the second conjunct must be semantically equivalent to the relevant part of the first conjunct. That means that the syntactic structures of (56) are as follows:

(57) a. [$Op_{\neg[\text{iNEG}]}$ *nadie*$_{[\text{uNEG}]}$ ho viste]
b. [Me caso contigo o $Op_{\neg[\text{iNEG}]}$ con *nadie* me caso]

As (57) shows, every negative feature is checked, semantic negations are present, and no negation has been elided. Since other NPIs cannot trigger the presence of a covert negation, the syntactic-agreement approach correctly predicts that neg-words, unlike other NPIs, can appear in fragment answers and coordinations.

3.4.3 Challenges for the syntactic-agreement approach

As has been discussed, another property of NC is that it is bound by syntactic locality conditions. Obviously, if syntactic agreement underlies NC, it is trivially bound to syntactic locality as syntactic agreement always is; so, the syntactic-agreement approach does not face any difficulties in this respect. However, as discussed in previous sections, neither the NQ approach nor the NPI approach (despite previous claims to the contrary) make any incorrect predictions in this sense either; so, this does not work to the advantage of the syntactic-agreement approach. At the same time, the syntactic-agreement approach faces two challenges of its own. The first concerns the variation attested among NC languages; the second, the fact that neg-words, at least in certain languages, can be licensed by typical NPI-licensing contexts that are not semantically negative in any straightforward sense.

Let us discuss each challenge in turn. The analysis developed for Non-strict NC cannot apply straightforwardly to Strict NC languages. The reason is twofold.

---

[14] Example taken from Herburger (2001: 300).

First, the explanation that rules out (58b) should also rule out (58a) if Strict and Non-strict NC were to be analysed in the same way. But (58a) is, of course, ruled in, as it is a defining characteristic of Strict NC.

(58) a. Dnes *nikdo* *(*ne-*)volá (Czech)
today NEG-body NEG-calls
'Today nobody calls'

b. *Ieri *nessuno non* ha telefonato (a *nessuno*) (Italian)
yesterday NEG-body NEG has called to NEG-body
'Yesterday nobody called'

Second, the explanation for fragment answers and coordination cannot hold for Strict NC languages either. The reason is that, while the examples in (57) are grammatically fine, the ones in (59) are not grammatical without the NMs. Greek being a Strict NC language, the elided parts should still carry an NM.

(59) a. [[*TIPOTA* [* ~~(dhen)~~ ~~ida~~]] (Greek)
NEG-thing NEG saw.1SG
'Nothing'

b. ... i [* ~~(dhen)~~ ~~thelo na~~ ~~pandrefto~~ *KANENAN* (alo)] (Greek)
... or NEG want SUBJ marry NEG-body else
'... or I want to marry nobody else'

At the same time, nothing within the syntactic-agreement approach forces the Strict and Non-strict NC languages to be analysed on a par. According to the syntactic-agreement approach, NC is a feature-checking relation between one element carrying a feature [iNEG] and one or more elements carrying [uNEG]. In Italian, neg-words carry [uNEG] and the NM [iNEG]; but other feature assignments are also possible. In the next chapter, I will show that, indeed, all logical possibilities of [iNEG] and [uNEG] assignment can be attested, and that this constitutes the landscape of NC varieties. In short, I will argue that, in Strict NC languages, both neg-words and the NM carry [uNEG], and show that, then, the attested challenges I have described disappear. In that chapter, I will also provide explanations for other types of NC languages, such as languages with optional NC (like West Flemish) and languages where NMs do not participate in NC, such as French. Since the syntactic-agreement approach is ultimately a local (in fact, even a lexical) approach to NC, it principally opens up space for variation along the lines I have suggested.

This leaves us with the final major challenge for the syntactic-agreement approach: the existence of examples like (19), repeated below as (60), where neg-words are licensed by typical NPI licensers that lack the semantics of a real negation.

3.4 NEGATIVE CONCORD IS SYNTACTIC AGREEMENT 75

(60) a. Antec de hacer *nada*, debes lavarle las manos (Spanish)
   before of do NEG-thing, must.2SG wash.CL the hands
   'Before doing anything, you should wash your hands'
 b. Dudo que vayan a encontar *nada*
   doubt.1SG that will.3PL.SUBJ find NEG-thing
   'I doubt they will find anything'
 c. Prohibieron que saliera *nadie*
   forbade.3PL that went_out.3SG.SUBJ NEG-body
   'They forbade anybody to go out'
 d. Es la última vez que te digo *nada*
   is the ultimate time that you tell.1SG NEG-thing
   'This is the last time I tell you anything'
 e. Juan ha llegado más tarde que *nunca*
   Juan has arrived more late than NEG-ever
   'Juan has arrived later than ever'

Such examples have typically been taken to form evidence for the NPI approach. For the syntactic-agreement approach, one would be forced to analyse these examples with a feature [iNEG] assigned to these NPI-licensers, illustrated for (60a–b) in (61).

(61) a. Antec[iNEG] de hacer *nada*, debes lavarle las manos (Spanish)
 b. Dudo[iNEG] que vayan a encontar *nada*

Intuitively, this is not very satisfying, as expressions like *before* or *doubt* are not semantically or syntactically negative. Of course, their meaning has some negative flavour (*before* has a similar meaning to *not after*; *doubt* means something like *not be sure*, cf. Herburger and Mauck 2007, among others). But even if such elements should indeed be lexically decomposable into a negation, that still does not mean that these items themselves should carry a feature [iNEG]; at best, the negations in their lexical decomposition should. Moreover, many other expressions with a negative flavour can be decomposed into a negation (and, presumably, many expressions without a negative flavour as well). *Bad* means something like *not good*. But *bad* cannot license any neg-words, as shown below for its equivalent *mal* in Spanish:

(62) Está mal hacer *nada* (Spanish)
   is bad do NEG-thing
   #'It is bad to do anything'

However, it should be noted that this problem appears only under the perhaps intuitive but also naïve assumption that it is the [iNEG] feature itself that is interpreted as a semantic negation. But is that really the case? Generally, it is assumed (after Chomsky 1995a) that features that can check off [uF]s are semantically interpretable themselves. But there are other ways to think of feature checkers. In the case of Italian *non*, one could also say that it is a semantic negation and that, by virtue of its being semantically negative, in addition, it has a formal feature, call it [iNEG], that is able to check off [uNEG] features. If that is the case, no different predictions would be made for the examples discussed so far, except for cases like (19)/(60). Saying that Spanish *antec* or *dudo* in (19)/(60) carries [iNEG], along the lines of (61), does not entail that they are both semantically negative as well. At the same time, if one disentangles carrying a feature [iNEG] from being semantically negative, one needs a proper theory which explains when [iNEG] is assigned to some particular element and which constrains the distribution of [iNEG] to only those elements that are known to license neg-words. It is exactly such a theory that I will develop and apply in Chapter 5.

3.5 Conclusions

In this chapter, I have argued that the best way to approach NC is by assuming that it is an instance of syntactic agreement where one element carrying [iNEG] checks off one or more elements carrying [uNEG]. In a Non-strict NC language like Italian, I take the NM *non* to be a semantic negation, carrying an interpretable formal feature [iNEG], and neg-words like *nessuno* ('neg-body') to carry an uninterpretable formal feature [uNEG]. In the absence of an overt element carrying [iNEG], a covert negative operator can be postulated to be present and to be responsible for introducing a semantic negation as well as for checking off the [uNEGs] on the neg-words.

This system, where a covert negative operator can be presumed to be present when, otherwise, any present neg-words would continue to have unchecked [uNEG]-features, can be seen as an implementation of Ladusaw's notion of self-licensing. In this sense, the analysis of NC differs from analyses of other types of NPIs, in the sense that these other types of NPIs do not involve syntactic agreement with a negation. Note that, since neg-words require a negation, or, to be more precise, an element carrying [iNEG], to be present, neg-words are NPIs, albeit NPIs of a different kind from the more standard examples. The analysis of NC formulated in this chapter is therefore a particular instance of the NPI approach to NC.

The question remains of how different types of NC can be reduced to different types of negative features present on negative elements and any other grammatical differences between the various languages, and the exact relation between carrying some [iF] or [uF] feature and the corresponding semantics. These questions will be dealt with in the next two chapters.

4
Types of Negative Concord systems

4.1 Variation on the domain of Negative Concord

In the previous chapter, I have argued that the best way to approach Negative Concord (NC) is by assuming that NC is an instance of syntactic agreement where one element carrying [iNEG] checks off one or more elements carrying [uNEG]. I have illustrated this for the Non-strict NC language Italian, where I take the NM *non* to be a semantic negation, carrying an interpretable formal feature [iNEG], and neg-words like *nessuno* ('neg-body') to carry an uninterpretable formal feature [uNEG], shown again in (1)–(2).

(1) Gianni *non* telefona *nessuno* (Italian)
 Gianni NEG calls to NEG-body
 'Gianni doesn't call anybody'

(2) [NegP *non*[iNEG] telefona [vP a *nessuno*[uNEG]]]

In absence of an overt element carrying [iNEG], a covert negative operator can be postulated to be present and be responsible for the introduction of a semantic negation as well as for checking off the [uNEG]s on the neg-words ((3)–(4)).

(3) Ieri *nessuno* ha telefonato a *nessuno* (Italian)
 yesterday NEG-body has called to NEG-body
 'Yesterday nobody called anybody'

(4) [ieri Op¬[iNEG] *nessuno*[uNEG] ha telefonato a *nessuno*[uNEG]]

What remains an open question is how different types of NC can be reduced to different types of negative features present on negative elements, or to any other grammatical differences between the various languages. In order to address these questions, we should first look at what types of NC languages have currently been attested. Once these systems have been identified, we can investigate how such systems may follow from the syntactic-agreement approach to NC. Naturally, when such an approach is able to account for different types of NC languages, it should also be assessed what other types of NC languages are predicted to be grammatically possible, and whether such types can be attested as well, and, if not, why so. In this chapter, I will discuss how the approach accounts for other known and unknown types of NC languages, and correctly predicts the full landscape of NC.

Negation and Negative Dependencies. Hedde Zeijlstra, Oxford University Press.
© Hedde Zeijlstra (2022). DOI: 10.1093/oso/9780198833239.003.0004

The range of variation among NC languages can best be described along the following three dimensions: Strict vs Non-strict NC languages, obligatory vs optional NC, and partial vs full NC languages. The first dimension has been discussed at length in the previous chapter; the second dimension has been illustrated for West Flemish, where, unlike most other NC languages, NC is always optional; the third dimension has briefly been introduced when discussing French NC (in Subsection 3.2.2), where the NM *pas* never participates in NC constructions. A fourth possible dimension would be the semantic status of neg-words: are neg-words existentials that scope under negation, or universals that take scope over negation (see the discussion on Greek NC in Subsection 3.3.2)?

In the following sections, I will discuss how the NC proposal in terms of [iNEG]/[uNEG] features can capture the attested variation. In Section 4.2, I first argue that the Strict vs Non-strict NC distinction is readily accounted for by assuming that in Strict NC languages, unlike Non-strict NC languages, the NM carries [uNEG]. Second, I discuss NC-optionality and argue that this NC-optionality results from the fact that, in certain languages, indefinites, including neg-words, raise to a vP-external position. I also address the consequences of this assumption for cases of NC languages where neg-words and NMs both obligatorily appear in a higher position. In Section 4.3, I show that the current analysis predicts another type of NC system to exist—namely a system where the NM carries [uNEG], but where every neg-word carries [iNEG] (i.e., the mirror image of Non-strict NC languages), and that such systems can indeed be attested. A particular variety of Afrikaans as well as several older varieties of German(ic languages) are good examples. Section 4.4 discusses partial NC systems, such as French, where only a subset of the negative elements can be assigned [iNEG]/[uNEG]-features; and I show that more languages exhibit these properties, including languages that do not seem to exhibit NC in the first place, such as (Standard) English or Hindi/Punjabi. Section 4.5 provides an overview of the range of variation that is predicted to arise under the current NC proposal, and introduces further potential dimensions of variation, including the question whether every neg-word is existential or not (focusing on a proposal by Shimoyama 2011, who claims that Korean and Japanese exhibit universal neg-words; see also Szabolcsi 1984 for Hungarian, and Giannakidou 2000 for Greek).

4.2 Strict vs Non-strict Negative Concord languages

4.2.1 Strict vs Non-strict Negative Concord

The major difference between Strict and Non-strict NC languages is that, in the former, preverbal, i.e., vP-external, neg-words still need to be accompanied by the

NM, whereas, in the latter, preverbal, vP-external neg-words may not. The relevant examples from Czech and Italian are repeated below.

(5) a. Dnes *nikdo* *(*ne-*)volá   (Czech, Strict NC)
today NEG-body NEG-calls
'Today nobody calls'

b. Dnes *(*ne-*)vola *nikdo*
today NEG-calls NEG-body
'Today nobody calls'

(6) a. Ieri *nesssuno* (**non*) ha telefonato   (Italian, Non-strict NC)
yesterday NEG-body has called
'Nobody called yesterday'

b. Ieri *(*non*) ha telefonato *nessuno*
yesterday NEG has called NEG-body
'Nobody called'

As both Strict and Non-strict NC languages allow multiple neg-words to yield a single semantic negation, as shown in (7), it seems straightforward to assign neg-words in both types of NC languages a feature [uNEG].

(7) a. Dnes *nikdo* ne-volá *nikomu*   (Czech, Strict NC)
today NEG-body neg-calls NEG-body
'Today nobody calls anybody'

b. Ieri *nesssuno* ha telefonato *nessuno*
yesterday NEG-body has called NEG-body
'Yesterday nobody called anybody'

Hence, the source of the difference between the two must lie outside the featural status of neg-words. One option for identifying that source would be to look at the featural status of NMs. Since, in Czech, the lower NM may agree with the negation that outscopes a higher neg-word, it would be hard to assign [iNEG]-status to Czech *ne*.[1] If, in Czech, the internal order between neg-words and the NM does not make any difference, it seems a straightforward step to assign [uNEG]-status to both of them. I therefore hypothesize that, in Strict NC languages, the NM also carries [uNEG], and all overt negative elements (carrying [uNEG]) establish an Agree relation with a single abstract negative operator Op¬ that carries a feature [iNEG]. In Non-strict NC languages, the NM carries [iNEG] itself. As the idea that

---

[1] See Fălăuş and Nicolae (2016) for an attempt to assign [iNEG] to NMs in Strict NC languages, though.

the NM, present in every negative sentence except for fragment answers and coordinations (as discussed in the previous chapter), is semantically non-negative may seem counter-intuitive, let us first put forward a number of arguments in favour of the idea that the NM in Strict NC languages, as opposed to the NM in Non-strict NC languages, lacks negative semantic content.

One argument is that it can be shown that negation behaves differently in Strict and Non-strict NC languages with respect to the scope of quantifying DPs. This is shown in (8). Although Czech *moc* ('much') dominates the NM, it is outscoped by negation. This reading is not obtained in a similar construction in Italian, where *molto (pizza)* ('much (pizza)') is not in the scope of negation. This is an indication that Italian *non*, in contrast to Czech *ne*, is semantically negative, as the latter, but not the former, does not coincide with its locus of (alleged) interpretation.

(8) a. Moc *ne*jedl (Czech)
    much NEG.eat.3SG.PRF
    ¬ > much: 'She hasn't eaten much'
    *much > ¬: 'There is much that she didn't eat'

   b. Molto (pizza) *non* ha mangiato (Italian)
    much pizza NEG has eaten
    *¬ > much: 'She hasn't eaten much (pizza)'
    much > ¬: 'There is much (pizza) that she didn't eat'

A second argument is that, in some Strict NC languages, the NM may be left out if it is preceded by a neg-word—something to be expected on functional grounds if the NM carries [uNEG] (if a neg-word appears in a higher position and, therefore, precedes it, the NM is no longer needed as a scope marker). This is, for instance, the case in Greek (a Strict NC language) with certain neg-words, such as *oute kan* ('even'). If *oute kan* precedes the NM *dhen*, the latter may be left out. If it follows *dhen*, *dhen* may not be removed (as Giannakidou's 2007 examples show in (9)). This forms an argument that Greek *dhen* is in fact not semantically negative itself: if it were, leaving it out should yield a semantic effect. As Greek is a Strict NC language, this strengthens the assumption that, in Strict NC languages, the NM carries [uNEG].

(9) a. O Jannis *(*dhen*) dhiavase *oute kan* tis Sindaktikes Dhomes (Greek[2])
    the Jannis NEG reads even the Syntactic Structures
    'Jannis doesn't read even *Syntactic Structures*'

---

[2] Examples taken from Giannakidou (2007).

b. *Oute kan* ti Maria (*dhen*) proskalese o pritanis
 even the Maria NEG invite the dean
 'Not even Maria did the dean invite'

Naturally, the question arises as to why *dhen* in these constructions may be left out, but not in other constructions. Barouni (2018) argues that this has to do with the fact that neg-words like *oute kan* ('(not) even') in Greek have a morphological negative reflex which emphasized neg-words lack (such neg-words are the emphasized forms of the regular weak NPIs). Her claim is that, only in cases where neg-words are not morphologically marked for negation, negation may be left out. Even though this argument seems intuitively plausible for Greek, it is not conclusive, though, as it is not clear why, in most other Strict NC languages, like Czech, where both neg-words and NMs are morphologically marked for negation, the NM may still not be dropped if it follows a neg-word.

A potentially stronger argument in favour of a treatment of NMs in Non-strict NC languages is that no known Non-strict NC language exhibits so-called *True Negative Imperatives* (TNIs), an issue I will address at length in Chapter 15. What is meant by TNIs is exemplified in (10) for Czech. In Czech, the NM always precedes the finite verb. This does not hold only for indicative verbs, but also for imperative verbs. As (10) shows, sentences with imperative verbs are negated in just the same way as indicative sentences are (with a preverbal NM *ne*). Therefore, Czech is said to allow TNIs: the sentence with the imperative verb can be negated in the same way indicative sentences are negated.

(10) a. Pracuj! (Czech)
    work.2SG.IMP
    'Work!'

 b. *Ne*pracuj! (TNI)
    NEG.work.2SG.IMP
    'Don't work!'

Things are different, however, in a language like Spanish, as illustrated in (11). In Spanish, the NM *no* always occurs in preverbal position (11a). However, if the verb has an imperative form as in (11b), it may not be combined with this NM (11c). Spanish does not allow TNIs. In order to express the illocutionary force of an imperative, the imperative verb must be replaced by a subjunctive (11d).[3] Such constructions are called *Surrogate Negative Imperatives* (SNIs).[4]

---

[3] Negative sentences with the illocutionary force of an imperative are often referred to as *prohibitives*.
[4] See Van der Auwera (2005) (and references therein) for many more examples of languages that ban TNIs, and on the way those languages express SNIs.

(11) a. Tu *no* lees (Spanish)
NEG read.2SG
'You don't read'

b. ¡Lee!
read.2SG.IMP
'Read!'

c. *¡*No* lee! (*TNI)
NEG read.2SG.IMP
'Don't read'

d. ¡*No* leas! (SNI)
NEG read.2SG.SUBJ
'Don't read!'

Han (2001) convincingly argues that the ban on TNIs does not follow from any syntactic requirements that have been violated, but from a semantic violation: the imperative operator, i.e., the operator that encodes the illocutionary force of an imperative, may not be in the scope of negation. The imperative operator is realized by moving V_{imp}, carrying a feature that encodes the illocutionary properties of an (imperative) speech act ([IMP]), to C°. Han takes negation in Romance languages to head a projection somewhere high in the IP domain. Hence, V_{imp} head-adjoins first to negation; then, as a unit, the NM and V_{imp} move further to C° (or Force°, in Rizzi's 1997 terms). As a result, [IMP] remains in the c-command domain of negation, which violates the constraint that negation may only apply to the propositional content of the clause (cf. Frege 1892; Lee 1988): a negative imperative can only mean that it is imperative not to do something, not that it is not imperative to do something. The structure in (12) is thus ill-formed.

(12) * CP (Spanish)

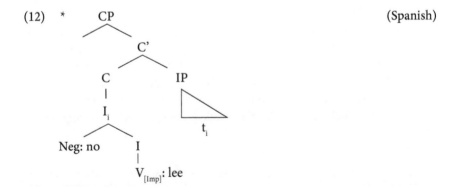

This means that it is predicted that, in all Non-strict NC languages, TNIs are banned. This prediction is indeed borne out (cf. Zeijlstra 2006, 2013a; and Chapter 15). Postponing a detailed analysis to Chapter 15, for now I take it to be the case that, if a language allows a NM in C°, this NM is not semantically negative.[5]

On the basis of these three arguments I conclude that NMs in Strict NC languages carry [uNEG], and that those in Non-strict NC languages carry [iNEG]. Now, let us see how the [iNEG]-[uNEG] proposal applies to the relevant Czech constructions.

In Czech, the NM *ne* is associated with Neg° and carries [uNEG]. The same feature is carried by both preverbal and postverbal neg-words. That means that, in every negative clause, semantic negation must always be introduced by an abstract negative operator. This is shown in (13)–(16) for the four relevant types of negative sentences.

(13) a. Milan *nevolá* (Czech)
    Milan NEG.calls
    'Nobody is calling'

   b. [$_{TP}$ Milan [$_{NegP}$ $Op_{\neg[iNEG]}$ $ne_{[uNEG]}$ [$_{VP}$ volá]]]

(14) a. *Nevolá nikdo*
    NEG.calls NEG-body
    'Nobody is calling'

   b. [$_{NegP}$ $Op_{\neg[iNEG]}$ $ne_{[uNEG]}$ [$_{VP}$ volá $nikdo_{[uNEG]}$]]

(15) a. *Nikdo nevolá*
    NEG-body NEG.calls
    'Nobody is calling'

   b. [$Op_{\neg[iNEG]}$ [$_{TP}$ $nikdo_{[uNEG]}$ [$_{NegP}$ $ne_{[uNEG]}$ [$_{VP}$ volá]]]]

(16) a. *Nikdo nevidi nikoho*
    Nikdo NEG.sees NEG-body
    'Nobody sees anybody'

   b. [$Op_{\neg[iNEG]}$ [$_{TP}$ $nikdo_{[uNEG]}$ [$_{NegP}$ $ne_{[uNEG]}$ [$_{vP}$ $vidi_{[uNEG]i}$ nikoho]]]]

As the reader can see, in each example, there is only one semantic negation present; the reading is thus fully compositional. I illustrate this for the first

---

[5] Note that such a generalization is always unidirectional. It does not guarantee that all Strict NC languages allow TNIs as TNIs can be banned on different grounds as well (see Zeijlstra 2013; and Chapter 15).

NC example (14) in (17), but the derivations work similarly for the other examples.

(17)

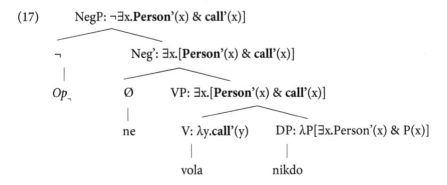

A few words should be said about the syntax. I assume that the position of NegP in the structure is in between TP and vP/VP, although not much hinges on that. However, that means that the abstract negative operator is sometimes inside NegP (as, for instance, in (13) and (14)) and sometimes outside NegP, for instance when the subject raises to Spec, TP. I see no objection to this. The abstract negative operator is an adjunct that is able to check *ne*'s and the neg-words' [uNEG]-features, and it can do so from any position in the tree where it c-commands them—arguably from the closest position where it can do so, given the parsing considerations discussed earlier. If one were to assume that the position of NegP is above TP, one would need to account for the fact that the NM always appears below the preverbal subject, and that the subject, therefore, needs to move to an even higher position than Spec, TP. I do not see any advantage to this, as it does not simplify the syntax in any sense (though the analysis presented here would be fully compatible with such a view).

The proposed analysis thus captures the fact that, in Strict NC languages, unlike Non-strict NC languages, neg-words can precede the NM. At the same time, the analysis presented for Non-strict NC gives rise to two new questions. First, the treatment of fragment answers needs to be modified, as the treatment of fragment answers in Non-strict NC languages involved no NM in the ellipsis site, given their semantic negativity. Second, the question arises of why the NM is obligatory in Strict NC languages.

As for the first question, one will have to assume that, just as was the case in Non-strict NC languages, fragment answers are the result of deletion under ellipsis of the remaining clause after the neg-word has been F-fronted (cf. Merchant 2001, 2004). I repeat below the relevant examples from Spanish and Greek that were used in the previous chapter.

4.2 STRICT VS NON-STRICT NEGATIVE CONCORD LANGUAGES 85

(18) a. A Quién ha viste? {A *Nadie* / *A un alma}   (Spanish[6])
 At whom has.2SG.PRF seen? At NEG-body / At a soul
 'Who did you see? Nobody / A single soul'

 b. Me caso contigo o con {*nadie* / *un alma}
 me marry with-you or with NEG-body/anybody
 'I marry you or nobody.'

(19) a. Ti idhes? *Tipota*!   (Greek)
 what saw.2SG? NEG-thing
 'What did you see? Nothing'

 b. Thelo na pandrefto ton Petro i KANENAN (alo) (Greek[7])
 want SUBJ marry the Petro or NEG-body else
 'I want to marry either Peter or nobody else'

In Spanish, the crucial part of the analysis is that, since the neg-word appears in a preverbal position, no NM is required in the ellipsis site. Therefore, the problem pointed out by Watanabe (2004)—that under an approach that takes neg-words to be semantically non-negative the ellipsis site should contain a semantic negation and therefore violate Merchant's semantic identity condition on ellipsis—no longer applies. The semantic negation is not deleted under ellipsis, but is realized by a non-deleted null operator in clause-initial position.

(20) a. [$Op_{\neg[\text{iNEG}]}$ A *Nadie*$_{[\text{uNEG}]}$ ho viste]
 b. [me caso contigo o $Op_{\neg[\text{iNEG}]}$ con *nadie* me caso]

In Greek, this position can only be partially maintained. Grammatically, the NM must be present in the ellipsis. But, at the same time, it is semantically vacuous, as, in Greek, being a Strict NC language, semantic negation is always introduced by the abstract negative operator. But if the NM is semantically vacuous, it does not alter the semantics of the ellipsis site, and Merchant's identity condition is not violated either. Hence, the existence of fragment answers in Strict NC languages does not pose any problem for the analysis pursued.

(21) a. [$Op_{\neg[\text{iNEG}]}$ [*TIPOTA*$_{[\text{uNEG}]}$ [~~dhen~~$_{[\text{uNEG}]}$ ~~ida~~]]]   (Greek)
 NEG-thing NEG saw.1SG
 'Nothing!'

 b. ... i [$Op_{\neg[\text{iNEG}]}$ ~~dhen~~$_{[\text{uNEG}]}$ ~~thelo na pandrefto~~ *KANENAN*$_{[\text{uNEG}]}$ (alo)]
 ... or NEG want SUBJ marry NEG-body else
 '... or I want to marry nobody else'

[6] Example taken from Herburger (2001: 300).
[7] Example taken from Giannakidou (2000).

4.2.2 Obligatoriness and optionality of Negative Concord

A potential problem for an analysis that takes NMs to be semantically vacuous might be that it is not clear why the NM should always be present. In the case of (13) or (14), the role of the NM is clear: in (13), it is the only instance of overt negation, and therefore marks the presence of a semantic negation in a vP-external position; in (14), where a neg-word appears in postverbal position, the role of the NM is again to ensure that the abstract negative operator takes scope outside vP, similar to the explanation of the presence of the NM with postverbal neg-words in Italian provided in Chapter 3.

However, it is unclear why the NM should be present in (15)–(16), as, here, the preverbal neg-word already marks the presence of the abstract negative operator. Hence, a functional-semantic account, as has been provided for the distribution of the NM in Strict NC languages, is not sufficient. That suggests that the presence of the NM in Strict NC languages is captured by more formal considerations. If the NM is an agreement marker in the strictest sense of the word, then it can be said to follow those properties that are generally assigned to agreement markers. Take again null-subject languages. In a null-subject language like Italian, it is not the case that the agreement marker all of a sudden drops when the subject is overtly realized.

(22) a. Canto (Italian)
    sing.1SG
    'I sing'
  b. Io canto/*cant
    I sing.1SG/sing
    'I sing'

(23) a. Parla
    talk.3SG
    'She/he talks'
  b. Catarina parla/*parl
    Catarina talk.3SG/talk
    'Catarina talks'
  c. Parla/*parl Caterina
    talk.3SG/talk Caterina
    'Catarina talks'

On a functional account, it would be expected that an agreement marker can be dropped if the subject is present. But agreement markers cannot be dropped, suggesting that they are indeed subject to some more formal, morphosyntactic constraint that states that agreement markers must always be realized when possible. As, in Strict NC languages, the NM, by virtue of its carrying [uNEG] and by virtue of its weak morphophonological properties, counts as an agreement marker, it is then predicted not to be droppable. In Non-strict NC languages, the NM is a semantic negation and thus does not count as an agreement marker—and therefore can be dropped when necessary (and, given its semantics, will have to be dropped then).

If this line of reasoning is correct, it is predicted that NC is, in principle, optional if the highest overt NC participant is outside vP, unless other grammatical requirements demand a lower negative element to be present as well. A general constraint on the obligatoriness of agreement markers, which accounts for the obligatory presence of the NM in Strict NC languages, irrespective of the NM, is an example of such a requirement. This predicts that, in languages where, for one reason or the other, the agreement marker does not have to appear obligatorily for formal reasons, and where, semantically, its inclusion is not forbidden, optional NC patterns may arise. Let me illustrate this prediction with two examples: West Flemish and Catalan.

In West Flemish, as is well known, indefinites obligatorily scramble outside vP to a position somewhere in the middle field (cf. Haegeman 1995; among others). Since, in West Flemish, the real NM *nie* is a phrasal element (cf. Haegeman 1995; see also Chapter 1) and phrasal elements lack the necessary morphophonological properties to constitute an agreement marker (cf. Tvica 2017 and references therein), West Flemish NC should always be optional. This is indeed the case, as has already been illustrated in Chapter 3, repeated below:[8]

(24)   ... da Valère *niemand* (*nie*) ken   (West Flemish)
        ... that Valère NEG-body NEG knows
        '... that Valère doesn't know anybody'

Even though NC in West Flemish is more complex than (24) suggests, no instances of NC have been found where NC has been obligatory. Whenever a NM does not head an NC chain, it can be freely removed; and any neg-word that is not the highest element in an NC chain does not have to be negatively marked, as has been extensively shown in Haegeman (1995).

---

[8] I ignore the contribution of the preverbal marker *en/ne* (see also Chapter 1), often taken to be a NM as well (cf. Haegeman 1995; Haegeman and Zanuttini 1991, 1996). The reason is that this marker *en/ne* is not able to render a sentence negative by itself and, therefore, given the definitions in Chapter 3 (see also Chapter 1), does not count as an NC participant (see also Section 4.4). For a description and analysis of *en/ne* as a focus marker, see Breitbarth and Haegeman (2014).

88   TYPES OF NEGATIVE CONCORD SYSTEMS

A second type of language where NC is predicted to be optional consists of Strict NC languages where, nevertheless, the preverbal NM is not subject to the constraint that requires (semantically uninterpretable) agreement markers to be always present. Examples of such languages are rare, as, generally, preverbal negative elements act as agreement markers, but they can be found among varieties of Catalan (see Chapter 5 for an explanation as to why such languages are less likely to appear). Espinal (2008) presents the following examples from the Central Catalan variety:

(25) a. *No* ha vist a ningú. (Central Catalan)
  NEG has seen to anybody
  '(S)he has seen no one'

  b. *Ningú (no)* ha vist res
  NEG-body NEG has seen anything
  'Nobody has seen anything'

As can be seen, Catalan *no* can be optionally left out in the presence of a preverbal neg-word without any further pragmatic or semantic effects. This shows that non-droppability of NMs is not an inherent property of languages that allow neg-words to precede NMs. Naturally, the question of why Catalan is more liberal than other languages in allowing semantically redundant NMs to be absent is left open. While I assume that this may have to do with other developments of negation in Catalan, most notably the fact that Catalan has already reached the second phase of Jespersen's Cycle (see Chapters 1 and 6), I have no proper explanation to offer at this stage and, therefore, leave this question for future research.[9]

4.3 In search of a missing language: A closer look at Afrikaans

What we have seen in the previous section is that the difference between DN and Non-strict NC languages in the context of our proposed system depends on the semantic value of neg-words, whereas the difference between Strict and Non-strict NC languages is dependent on the semantic value of the NM. However, a typological gap of the sort illustrated in (26) now arises:

---

[9] In a particular line of research, Deprez et al. (2015), Espinal et al. (2016), Espinal and Tubau (2016), and Etxeberria et al. (2018) try to account for the optionality of the NM by taking it to be an expletive negation rather a real NM. However, as they analyse expletive negation in terms of a [uNEG]-feature, it is not clear how their analysis in terms of expletive negation would be any different from an account in terms of Strict NC.

(26) Typology of NC and DN languages

	Neg-words semantically negative	Neg-words semantically non-negative
NMs semantically negative	DN-languages: *Dutch, German, Swedish*	Non-strict NC languages: *Spanish, Italian, Portuguese*
NMs semantically non-negative	?	Strict NC languages: *Czech, Serbo-Croatian, Greek*

As (26) shows, the feature-based analysis of the negation systems discussed so far (i.e., DN, and Strict and Non-strict NC systems) raises the question of whether a fourth type, where neg-words carry [iNEG] and NMs carry [uNEG], might exist. As Biberauer and Zeijlstra (2012a) have shown, one particular variety of Afrikaans counts as such a language, and other examples may be attested among Old and Middle High German and Old Saxonian.

In Afrikaans negation every negative sentence, regardless of whether it contains a neg-word or a NM, ends with the NM *nie* (cf. Waher 1978; den Besten 1986; Robbers 1992; Oosthuizen 1998; Biberauer 2008, 2009; Biberauer and Zeijlstra 2012a for discussion). This is illustrated below:

(27) Hy is *nie* moeg *nie* (Afrikaans[10])
he is NEG tired NEG
'He is not tired'

(28) Hy is *nooit* moeg *nie*
he is never tired NEG
'He is never tired'

Afrikaans negative sentences consist either of a neg-word and a NM or of a combination of two NMs. The only exception to this generalization arises when two NMs appear adjacent to each other; then only one *nie* is realized (see Biberauer 2008 for arguments that this scenario involves a real instance of haplology):

(29) Hy kom *nie* (*nie*)
he come NEG NEG
'He isn't coming'

It turns out that there are at least two distinct varieties of this language, which differ in respect of the way in which they express negation. Biberauer and Zeijlstra (2012a) refer to these varieties as *Variety A* and *Variety B*. Both varieties are spoken

---

[10] Unless indicated otherwise, all examples in this subsection come from Biberauer and Zeijlstra (2012a).

in South Africa, although Variety A, which corresponds to a more conservative variety, is losing ground to Variety B (see Biberauer and Zeijlstra 2011 for further discussion). Varieties A and B differ in two major respects. First, in Variety A two neg-words always yield a DN reading, see (30):

(30) *Niemand* het *niks* gekoop *nie* (Afrikaans: Variety A)
NEG-body has NEG-thing bought NEG
DN: 'No one bought nothing', i.e., 'Everyone bought something'

In Variety B, by contrast, multiple neg-words can yield both DN and NC readings (depending on the intonational contour of the clause, cf. Biberauer 2009; Huddleston 2010), as shown in (31):

(31) *Niemand* het *niks* gekoop *nie* (Afrikaans: Variety B)
NEG-body has NEG- thing bought NEG
NC: 'No one bought anything'
DN: 'No one bought nothing', i.e., 'Everyone bought something'

Second, in Variety A, a NM *nie* may only follow a neg-word if the neg-word is sentence-final, as in (32), or if it constitutes a fragmentary answer, as in (33); it cannot do so sentence-internally, as shown in (34):

(32) Hier slaap *niemand* *nie* (Afrikaans: Variety A)
here sleeps NEG-body NEG
'Nobody sleeps here'

(33) Wie het my boek gesien? *Niemand* (*nie*)
who has my book seen? NEG-body NEG
'Who saw my book? No one'

(34) a. *Niemand* (**nie*) het die werk voltooi *nie*
NEG-body NEG has the work finished NEG
'Nobody has finished the work'
b. Ek het vir *niemand* (**nie*) 'n boek gekoop *nie*
I have for NEG-one NEG a book bought NEG
'I didn't buy a book for anyone'

In Variety B sentences (32) and (33) are also fine; however, it also allows *nie* to occur in the final position of phrases containing a neg-word. This generally triggers an emphatic effect. The examples in (34) are therefore all well-formed. For this reason, Biberauer and Zeijlstra (2012a) argue that Variety A represents an instance of the type of negation system that is missing in (26). For them, in Variety A all neg-words carry [iNEG], while the NM *nie* carries [uNEG]; Variety B they take to be a Strict NC language in which both neg-words and the NM carry [uNEG].

If neg-words bear [iNEG] in Variety A, the expectation is that every combination of two neg-words will yield a DN reading. As demonstrated in (35), this is indeed the case.

(35) *Niemand*[iNEG] het *niks*[iNEG] gekoop *nie*[uNEG]   (Afrikaans: Variety A)
NEG-body   has   NEG-thing   bought   NEG
DN: 'No one bought nothing', i.e., 'Everyone bought something'

If neg-words carry [iNEG], a neg-word co-occurring with *nie* in sentence-final position, or in a fragment answer, is predicted to yield an NC reading only, resulting from the Agree relation between the neg-word's [iNEG]-feature and the [uNEG]-feature on *nie*. This is indeed borne out:

(36) Hier slaap *niemand*[iNEG] *nie*[uNEG]   (Afrikaans: Variety A)
here sleeps NEG-body   NEG
'Nobody sleeps here'

(37) Wie het my boek gesien? *Niemand*[iNEG] (*nie*[uNEG])
who has my book seen?   NEG-body   NEG
'Who saw my book? No-one'

Just as in every other Strict NC language, an abstract negative operator checks the [uNEG]-features on the NMs in structures lacking an overt negative item carrying [iNEG]. This is shown in (38) and explains why two NMs still yield one semantic negation:

(38) a. Hy is *nie* moeg *nie*   (Afrikaans)
       he is NEG tired NEG
       'He is not tired'

   b. [Hy is Op_[iNEG] *nie*[uNEG] moeg *nie*[uNEG]

However, one problem arises. If neg-words carry [iNEG] and NMs [uNEG], one would expect a construction of one neg-word followed by two NMs to yield an NC reading. However, this is not the case:

(39) *Niemand*[iNEG] het *nie*[uNEG] die werk voltooi *nie*[uNEG] (Afrikaans)
NEG-body   has   NEG   the work completed NEG
*NC: 'Nobody completed the work'
DN: 'Nobody didn't complete the work'

Of course, one could argue that the two NMs are lexically distinct and carry different negative features, the higher one [iNEG] and the lower one [uNEG]. This would in principle explain the facts. However, such an analysis cannot hold.

First, as Biberauer (2008) has shown, in constructions with one sentence-final negation, this negation is the result of haplology of the two NMs *nie*; such haplology effects would be hard to account for if the two NMs were different, homophonous morphemes. Moreover, homophony, also for language learners, is a last-resort option. Since all constructions except for constructions like (35) do not provide a cue for the language learner that the two instances of *nie* are homophonous, the child should only learn that on the basis of DN examples like (35). However, since DN constructions very rarely appear in natural language (cf. Horn 1989), and are especially rare in child-directed speech, children acquiring Variety A are not likely to be in a position to acquire the knowledge that the two are homophonous (see Chapter 5 for more discussion).

Biberauer and Zeijlstra, however, provide another possible explanation for the DN reading of (35). An important property of constructions like (35) is their heavy restriction. They can only be uttered felicitously in contexts where a speaker rejects a negative proposition previously asserted in the conversation. As with denial structures more generally (cf. Horn 1985, 1989; Gyuris 2009), these structures require (at least) one negated element to be focused. Thus, in the examples in (40), either the neg-word, or the NM, or both must receive stress for the utterance to be felicitous:

(40) a. Speaker 1: Net HANS het *nie* die werk voltooi *nie*, né?
                                                                                                 (Afrikaans: Variety A)
                only Hans has NEG the work completed NEG right
                'It was just Hans who didn't finish the work, right?'

       Speaker 2: Nee, *NIEMAND* het *nie* die werk voltooi *nie*
                        no   NEG-body has NEG the work completed NEG
                'No, NO ONE didn't finish the work'

b. Nee, *niemand* het *NIE* die werk voltooi   *nie*
   no NEG-body has NEG the work completed NEG
   'No, nobody has NOT finished the work / No, nobody DIDN'T finish the work'

c. Nee,   *NIEMAND*   het *NIE*   die werk voltooi   *nie*
   no   NEG-body   has NEG   the work completed   NEG
   'NOBODY has NOT finished the work'

d. *Nee,   *niemand*   het *nie*   die werk voltooi   *nie*
   no   NEG-body   has NEG   the work completed   NEG

What happens here is that the second speaker rejects a claim made by the first speaker; Speaker 2 takes herself to be more certain about the state of affairs in question than Speaker 1. This phenomenon, where a speaker conveys strong certainty of this type, is known as *Verum Focus* (Höhle 1992; Romero and Han 2004; Gyuris 2009) and is often attested in cases where a previous utterance is denied. This is illustrated below:

(41) a. Speaker 1: Mary is nice, isn't she?
       Speaker 2: No, Mary is NOT/ISN'T nice

   b. Speaker 1: You don't like spinach, do you?
       Speaker 2: No, I DO like spinach

Romero and Han (2004) propose that there are two instances of Verum Focus: *Positive Verum Focus* and *Negative Verum Focus*. Positive Verum Focus may be signalled by emphatic *do*-support in languages like English (41b), while Negative Verum Focus (referred to as *Falsum Focus* in Gyuris 2009), requires a stressed negative element (cf.(41a)).

When a negative element receives Verum Focus, this generally breaks up Agree relations (see Haegeman and Zanuttini 1996; Corblin et al. 2004; Biberauer and Zeijlstra 2012a). For instance, Biberauer and Zeijlstra (2012a) presents the following example from Serbo-Croatian, a Strict NC language where a focused neg-word triggers a DN reading:

(42) Speaker 1: Ko *nije* video *nikog*? (Serbo-Croatian)
 who NEG.have seen NEG-body
 'Who saw no one?'

 Speaker 2: NIKO (*nije* video *nikog*)
 NEG-body NEG.has seen NEG-body
 'NOBODY didn't see anybody'

Arguably, this results from the fact that the structure hosting the focus features (in Biberauer and Zeijlstra's terms) 'seals off' the phrase it is associated with and thereby effectively creates a syntactic island. The island effect arguably results from an intervention effect created by the focus operator (cf. Biberauer and Roberts 2011 for a speculation along these lines). This is fully in line with the idea that focused expressions are interpreted as structured meanings in terms of foreground–background semantics, and that focused phrases should be interpreted as an atomic unit at LF (cf. von Stechow and Zimmermann 1984; von Stechow 1990; Rooth 1992; Krifka 2001a). Consequently, the neg-word, carrying [iNEG], and the NM with [uNEG] can no longer establish an Agree relation yielding an NC reading.

Hence, it is clear that constructions like (35) should indeed yield a DN reading when used as denials. But why is it not possible to use such a construction as a plain sentence. Why is the NC reading of (43) absent?

(Afrikaans: Variety A)
(43) *Niemand*$_{[iNEG]}$ het *nie*$_{[uNEG]}$ die werk voltooi *nie*$_{[uNEG]}$
 NEG-body has NEG the work completed NEG
 *NC: 'Nobody completed the work'

One option might be to say that there is a blocking effect at stake: an NC reading is already guaranteed in the absence of the medial *nie*. Given the availability of such alternative utterances under standard (Neo-)Gricean pragmatics, (43) might be predicted not to express exactly the same meaning; the addition of any further NMs to have to be functionally motivated (see also Chapter 7). However, one might argue that then (43) could still receive an emphatically NC structure (i.e., 'NOBODY completed the work'). Moreover, we know from other NC languages, such as West Flemish or Catalan, that additional NMs may be included even if their presence is not necessary.

However, it should be noted that in Variety B, where sentence-medial *nie* is permitted, it only appears in the same phrase as the focused neg-word. *[Niemand nie] het die werk voltooi nie* is the alternative to the Variety A case in (34). Both in Variety A and in Variety B, a regular sentence-mediate NM is not allowed to occur in NC constructions, even though Variety B is a Strict NC language. Why that is the case, and whether this is due to pragmatic competition, are both still unclear. Hence, a complete answer to the above-raised question is thus still open, but the solution to this should lie in the fact that in both varieties, a sentence-mediate NM cannot be added in NC constructions, even though in Variety B, the fact that NMs (and neg-words) carry [uNEG] is not disputed.

Afrikaans A is not the only known variety that exhibits such an NC system. Breitbarth (2013, 2014, 2017) has also shown for Old Saxonian (OS) that this language appears to have had a similar NC system. Since this language is no longer spoken, it can only be investigated by means of corpus studies, which means that the evidence is rather indirect; but it is shown that, in such languages, both combinations of neg-words and NMs, as well as clauses with sole NMs, may appear, whereas combinations of multiple NMs hardly occur at all:

> NC only seems to take the shape of negative doubling—the cooccurrence of the marker of sentential negation with a negative indefinite—in OS; where more than one indefinite occurs in the scope of negation, at most one of them is morphologically negative.
>
> (Breitbarth 2017: 24)

Similar observations have been made for Old and Middle High German (Jäger 2008 and references therein). In a corpus with 171 clauses that express sentential negation and contain at least one neg-sword, 79 exhibit an NC pattern, but only one of those contains more than one neg-word (and appears to be a literal translation from Latin).[11] Jäger (2008) shows that, in Middle High German, combinations of multiple neg-words also hardly ever appear (though NC was generally much less available in Middle High German than it was in Old High German).

While these patterns would be hard to understand if neg-words carried a feature [uNEG], they follow immediately if neg-words carry [iNEG], especially given

---

[11] Jäger takes this example (and a few more attested examples in other texts) to indicate that the combination of multiple neg-words yielding NC is indeed possible (known as Negative Spread after Den Besten 1986, 1989), and tries to reduce the causes of their rarity to independent factors. However, if this line of reasoning is correct, it can no longer be explained why, in other NC languages, Negative Spread is pervasively present.

that, in languages where neg-words do carry [uNEG], instances of multiple neg-words yielding an NC reading are fairly standard. If, in these languages, neg-words indeed carry [iNEG] and NMs carry [uNEG], NMs are able to render sentences negative on their own, but are unable to add an additional negation in a clause that is already negative.

At the same time, various questions are left open. For one, why is it the case that the type of NC where neg-words carry [iNEG] and NMs carry [uNEG] is so rare? As such rarity can only be explained in terms of learnability (apparently, it is much harder to acquire that a NM carries [uNEG] with neg-words carrying [iNEG]), first the conditions under which such an NC system can be acquired need to be spelled out, which is the topic of the next chapter.

4.4 Partial and/or invisible Negative Concord

So far, the variation attested varies in two dimensions. One dimension involves the features that are attributed to neg-words and/or NMs, yielding the three types of NC systems discussed in Section 4.2. The second dimension involves the position of neg-words in the clause and whether such systems allow optional NC or not. However, in all these cases, all neg-words are taken either to carry [iNEG] or to carry [uNEG]. What we have not attested so far is variation where, say, one neg-word carries [iNEG] and another one [uNEG], or where only some negative elements carry a feature [iNEG]/[uNEG] and others not at all. Examples of the former type are tremendously rare and can only be attested when languages change from NC to DN systems or the other way around. Examples of languages where not every element participates are less exceptional, and I will discuss two examples in this section: French and English.

4.4.1 Negative Concord in French: Partial Negative Concord

French is a language that exhibits two particular characteristics with respect to the expression of (sentential) negation. First, it is an NC language: a clause-internal combination of elements that can independently induce a semantic negation together yields only one semantic negation, as illustrated in (44).[12]

(44) a. *Personne (ne) mange* (French)
 NEG-body NEG eats
 'Nobody eats'

---

[12] Under special intonation, multiple negative constructions also allow DN readings. (44c) can thus also have the reading 'nobody eats nothing' (cf. Corblin et al. 2004), as focus can generally disrupt NC (see the discussion in Section 4.3). However, crucial here is that (44c) allows for an NC interpretation.

b. Jean *(ne)* mange *rien*
   Jean NEG eats NEG-thing
   'Jean doesn't eat anything'

c. *Personne (ne)* mange *rien*
   NEG-body NEG eats NEG-thing
   'Nobody doesn't eat anything'

Apart from that, French also displays Embracing Negation, the phenomenon, discussed in Chapter 1, where a language has not one, but two NMs (in the case of Standard French: the preverbal NM *ne* and the postverbal NM *pas* that normally 'embrace' the finite verb, see (45)). *Ne* is mostly a feature of formal French; in colloquial registers, it is almost always dropped.

(45) Marie *(ne)* mange *pas*
     Marie NEG eats NEG
     'Marie doesn't eat'

Interestingly, French *ne* and *pas* differ quite drastically from each other in the sense that, while *ne* may participate in NC constructions and may be combined with *pas*, thereby yielding a single semantic negation, no combination of *pas* and a neg-word (such as *personne* or *rien*) may ever give rise to an NC reading. Inclusion of *pas* in a sentence containing one or more neg-words always yields an additional semantic negation:

(46) *Personne (ne)* mange *pas (rien)*
     NEG-body NEG eats NEG NEG-thing
     'Nobody doesn't eat (anything)'

This leads to the following questions: what are the properties of French neg-words, *ne* and *pas*, such that *ne* can combine with both neg-words and *pas*, while still yielding a single semantic negation? And why may *pas* and neg-words not be combined in such a way?

I will argue that part of the problem is that *ne* should not be analysed as an NC element or as an NM, but rather as a plain NPI. I will show that French *pas*, despite being semantically negative, cannot carry a formal negative feature [iNEG]. Under these two assumptions, the French pattern is fully captured.

Before setting up the argument, I would like to evaluate some earlier accounts of these French facts. As already discussed in Chapter 3, De Swart and Sag (2002) provides an account for the inability of French *pas* to participate in NC relations. De Swart and Sag argue that NMs should be thought of as zero-quantifiers, i.e., quantifiers that bind no variable. Being quantificational and negative in nature, NMs can then participate in NC relations (as is the case in most languages). However, since NMs in NC constructions do not bring in any new semantic contribution (as they do not bind variables), languages may also choose to leave NMs out of

4.4 PARTIAL AND/OR INVISIBLE NEGATIVE CONCORD   97

NC. French would then be an example of a language that forbids one of its NMs, namely *pas*, to participate in NC relations.

This analysis of French *pas* faces a number of problems. Apart from the general problems that it inherits from De Swart and Sag's treatment of NC in terms of quantifier resumption (see Subsection 3.2.2), the analysis seems to be too general, as it suggests that a salient subset of NC languages allows NMs to be banned from NC constructions. However, to the best of my knowledge, only French exhibits this particular kind of behaviour. No other NC languages, even languages close to French, share this property. So, it appears to be just a characteristic of French that *pas* cannot participate in NC constructions. But it is unclear, under De Swart and Sag's proposal, how this is motivated and, more importantly, how this property of French *pas* is lexically encoded. What is it that French *pas* has that all other NMs in NC languages lack (or the other way round)?

Penka (2007) addresses these questions and argues that it is not so much a special property of French *pas* that it cannot establish NC relations with a neg-word, but rather a special property of French neg-words themselves. Penka adopts the analysis of NC pursued in this book and takes NC to be an instance of syntactic agreement, but argues that such an analysis cannot extend to French: regardless of the feature status of *pas* ([iNEG] or [uNEG]), *pas* should be able to participate in at least some NC relations, contrary to fact.

In order to solve this problem, Penka proposes that neg-words in French do not carry a feature [uNEG], but rather a feature [uNEGØ] that states that neg-words can be checked only by an abstract negative operator (which, in French, she takes to carry the corresponding feature [iNEGØ]). French *ne*, in her system, carries a general feature [uNEG] that does not specify the phonological status of its checker. *Pas*, finally, is an overt negator, thus carrying [iNEG]. Now the patterns simply follow: neg-words and *ne* can be checked by a single abstract operator, yielding an NC reading (47a); *ne* can have its [uNEG] feature checked against *pas*' [iNEG]-feature (47b); and, finally, a combination of (one or more) neg-words with *pas* yields a DN reading, as *pas* cannot check the neg-words' [uNEGØ]-features (47c), and thus an additional abstract negative operator is required:

(47) a. $Op_{\neg[iNEGØ]}$ $Personne_{[uNEGØ]}$ ($ne_{[uNEG]}$) mange $rien_{[uNEGØ]}$
 b. Marie $ne_{[uNEG]}$ mange $pas_{[iNEG]}$
 c. $Op_{\neg[iNEGØ]}$ $Personne_{[uNEGØ]}$ ($ne_{[uNEG]}$) mange $pas_{[iNEG]}$ $rien_{[uNEGØ]}$

Although Penka's proposal seems to be an improvement on the original [iNEG]/[uNEG] system, as it can handle the French patterns illustrated above, it is problematic for two reasons. First, independent motivation is lacking for the existence of [iNEGØ]- and [uNEGØ]-features, especially since no other NC languages seems to exhibit such features, and also since syntactic features should generally be blind regarding the phonological status of the elements carrying them. But even more problematic is that Penka's analysis also makes a wrong prediction—namely that, if *ne* can be licensed by Op¬, it should be able to negate a sentence by itself, contrary to fact (see (48)).[13] Given these problems of earlier analyses, the explanation for French *pas*'s behaviour should lie elsewhere.

(48) *Marie *ne* mange (French)

The observation about (48) is important, as it shows that *ne* cannot be an NC item. Since NC is the phenomenon where elements that may induce a semantic negation on their own together only yield one semantic negation, *ne*, by definition, cannot appear in NC constructions (see also Breitbarth 2009 for a similar observation). If NC is taken to be an instance of syntactic agreement, instantiated by an underlying feature system, it follows as well that *ne* cannot have any formal negative feature at its disposal.

The question then arises of what properties *ne* exactly exhibits. Two properties immediately come to mind. First, *ne* is semantically non-negative, as it is unable to induce a semantic negation by itself, but may appear in sentences that are negative. Second, *ne* may also appear in all kinds of other (Strawson-)DE contexts, such as restrictive focus (49a), comparatives (49b), complement clauses of expressions of fear (49c), avoidance (49d), denial or doubt (49e), conditionals (49f), and temporal *before*-clauses (49g), as shown below (all examples have been taken from Rooryck 2017: 3–4).

(49) a. Jean (*ne*) voit que Marie (French)
       Jean NEG sees but Marie
       'Jean only sees Marie'

   b. Jean est plus malin que Pierre (*ne*) l'est
      Jean is smarter than Pierre NEG it is
      'Jean is smarter than Pierre is'

   c. Il a barricadé la porte de peur/crainte qu'on (*n'*) entre chez lui
      he has blocked the door of fear that one enters NEG enter with him
      'He blocked the door for fear that people might come in'

   d. Jean a évité que Lucienne (*ne*) tombe
      Jean has avoided that Lucienne NEG fall.SUBJ
      'Jean prevented Lucienne from falling'

   e. Nie-/doute-t-il que je (*ne*) dise la vérité?
      denies/doubts he that I NEG tell.SUBJ the truth?
      'Does he doubt/deny that I am telling the truth?'

---

[13] There are a few known cases where *ne* actually may negate a sentence by itself, such as *je ne sais* ('I don't know'), but these expressions form a closed class and are generally analysed as idiosyncratic properties of French, presumably remainders of a previous stage of the language (see also Chapters 6 and 8).

4.4 PARTIAL AND/OR INVISIBLE NEGATIVE CONCORD

f. Je viendrai à moins que Jean (*ne*) soit là
I will-come to less that Jean NEG is.SUBJ there
'I will come unless Jean is there'

g. Il est parti avant que nous (*n'*) ayons mangé
he is left before that we NEG too have eaten
'He left before we ate'

The contexts where *ne* may appear without being supported by a neg-word or by *pas*, and without giving rise to a semantic negation, are all contexts that are known to license NPIs. Thus, *ne* is best analysed as an NPI. Even though it may not appear in every known NPI licensing context (*ne*, for instance, is not accepted in *if*-clauses or restrictors of universal quantifiers), this does not run against the analysis. Not every NPI must be licensed in every NPI-licensing context (as discussed in Chapter 1, and as will be intensively discussed in Chapters 9–12). Note that this implies that constructions containing *ne* and *pas* also do not count as NC constructions; such constructions only show that *pas* is able to license NPI *ne*—not surprising, given that *pas* is a semantic negation.

Focusing on French neg-words, as these can independently induce a semantic negation, but together only yield one semantic negation, these neg-words should be taken to be equipped with a [uNEG] that may be licensed by an abstract negation. Application of this mechanism to French neg-words is illustrated for the sentences in (50). Note that *ne* is not equipped with such a feature, as it is an NPI, not an NC element.

(50) a. $Op_{\neg[iNEG]}$ *Personne*$_{[uNEG]}$ (*ne*) mange (French)
NEG-body NEG eats
'Nobody eats'

b. $Op_{\neg[iNEG]}$ Jean (*ne*) mange *rien*$_{[uNEG]}$
Jean NEG eats NEG-thing
'Jean doesn't eat anything'

c. $Op_{\neg[iNEG]}$ *Personne*$_{[uNEG]}$ (*ne*) mange *rien*$_{[uNEG]}$
NEG-body NEG eats NEG-thing
'Nobody doesn't eat anything'

But now the question arises again why, instead of the abstract operator $Op_\neg$, *pas* cannot be the checker of a neg-word's [uNEG]-feature. Why, for instance, is (51) impossible with an NC reading?

(51) *Jean (*ne*) mange *pas*$_{[iNEG]}$ *rien*$_{[uNEG]}$ (French)
Jean NEG eats NEG NEG-thing
'Jean doesn't eat anything'

Even though *pas* is a clear semantic negation (otherwise it could not license *ne*), *pas*' semantic status does not entail that *pas* must carry a formal negative feature as well (regardless of whether such a formal feature would be semantically interpretable or not). In fact, as *pas* appears to be unable to license any other negative element (except for *ne*), *pas* can actually not be said to carry an interpretable formal feature [iNEG]. *Pas* is only semantically, and not formally negative.

Consequently, whenever a neg-word and *pas* co-occur in one and the same clause, it must be the abstract negative operator Op¬ that checks off the neg-word's [uNEG]-feature, and the sentence thus contains two semantic negations: one introduced by Op¬ and one by *pas*. When one neg-word precedes and one neg-word follows *pas*, there is still one abstract negative operator that checks off both neg-words' [uNEG]-features, whereas *pas* introduces a semantic negation of its own. The fact that *pas* does not act as an intervener in the agreement relation between Op¬ and the two neg-words follows straightforwardly: since *pas* is morphosyntactically not marked for negation, any morphosyntactic process must be blind to *pas*' negative semantics. Examples are given below:

(52) a. Op¬[iNEG] Jean (*ne*) mange *pas rien*[uNEG]
       Jean NEG eats NEG NEG-thing
       'Jean doesn't eat nothing'

      b. Op¬[iNEG] *Personne*[uNEG] (*ne*) mange *pas rien*[uNEG]
         NEG-body NEG eats NEG NEG-thing
         'Nobody doesn't eat anything'

French *pas* is thus semantically negative, but not formally equipped with any negative feature: morphosyntactically, *pas* is not negative. French neg-words, on the other hand, form the mirror image of *pas*: they are semantically non-negative, but only formally equipped with a negative feature; they carry a [uNEG], which needs to be checked off by an element that carries an interpretable formal feature [iF]. This makes French a so-called *partial NC* language.

Naturally, one could argue that the idea that certain NMs in NC languages do not carry a feature [iNEG] needs independent motivation, as, otherwise, it may be as much ad hoc as the other accounts discussed. However, closer scrutiny shows that French is not the only partial NC language. As I will show below, English also counts as one.

4.4.2 Negative Concord in English: Invisible Negative Concord

English at first sight appears to be a DN language. Combinations of NIs and NMs (both *not* and *n't*) do not exhibit NC effects. All examples in (53) receive a DN reading:

(53) a. Mary did*n't* see *nobody*
b. Mary did *not* see *nobody*
c. *Nobody* did*n't* see Mary
d. *Nobody* did *not* see Mary
e. Mary *never* saw *nobody*
f. *Nobody never* saw Mary
g. *Nobody* saw *nothing*

Consequently, one would have to assume that all English negative elements are semantically negative. However, it is not really clear whether this is the case. Especially the examples involving *n't* (in (53a, c)) are also fairly easily interpreted with an NC reading. In fact, as Anderwald (2002) has shown, British non-standard varieties are almost invariably NC varieties, at least with respect to *n't*. This is different for other DN languages. As shown in Zeijlstra (2004) and Barbiers et al. (2008), many non-standard varieties in Dutch still exhibit DN.[14] Hence, something special is at hand in English, which calls for an explanation.

English negation is also deviant from negation in a number of other respects. First, the NM *n't* is a syntactic head (see Chapter 1), whereas the NMs in other DN languages are phrasal elements (*niet* in Dutch, *nicht* in German, *inte* in Swedish). Not only should this mean that, in English, unlike in Dutch/German/Swedish, the NM should head a negative projection NegP of its own; it also means that NMs may move up along with the verbal head whenever the latter raises to a higher projection. That is generally the case in English with auxiliaries, questions, and imperatives. Let us discuss each in turn.

Whenever the non-phrasal NM *n't* appears in a sentence, it must always attach to a non-lexical verb (that can raise up to TP). This is either a copula *be*, an auxiliary *be/have*, a modal, or the auxiliary *do* (in *do*-support constructions). While for the auxiliaries *have* and *do*, it would be hard to prove that they start out below vP, this can be more easily proven to be the case for copula *be* and modal auxiliaries. Take the following examples:

(54) a. Mary is *not* ill
b. Mary has *not* been ill

(55) a. Peter ca*n't* leave
b. Peter may *not* leave
c. Peter need*n't* leave

---

[14] This goes against Weiss (2002), who argues that every language is underlyingly NC, and that DN is just a prescriptive property of certain languages, based on the seeming 'illogicality' of two negations not cancelling each other out. A major problem for Weiss' analysis is that it cannot explain why certain languages gave up on NC, but others did not.

Assuming that *is* and *been* in (54) start out in the same position (as, in both cases, they select the predicate *ill*), *is* in (54a) must start out below the negation, head-adjoin to it in Neg°, and jointly with the latter move to T. Similarly, since the modal verbs in (55) all take scope below negation (in the case of (55b), under neutral intonation), they should be expected to start out below NegP and raise, via the negative head, into TP as well (see Iatridou and Zeijlstra 2013; Homer 2015; and see also the discussion in Chapter 13). The structure of such constructions is as in (56):

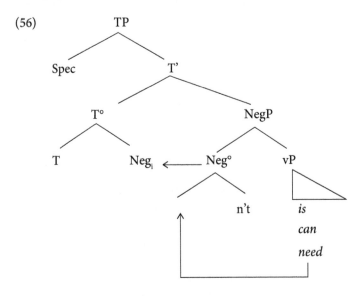

(56)

This has consequences for the way negation takes scope. If, indeed, negation takes scope from its surface position (and the NM would not reconstruct), the NM in (56) takes scope from a different position from where negation usually takes scope from—namely from a position where it c-commands vP. Crucially, in (56), *n't* does not c-command the vP in its surface position in T.

Naturally, this can be remedied by arguing that every instance of head movement leads to obligatory reconstruction. Then, negation heads NegP again, and all verbs would still take scope under it from their base position. Alternatively, one can argue that, even though *n't* doesn't c-command vP at surface structure, *isn't*, *can't*, and *needn't*, still being negative elements, do take scope over vP and therefore still yield semantic negation.

Evidence for the fact that head movement obligatorily reconstructs comes from negative constructions containing modals. Take the following sentences:

(57) a. Mary can *not* leave ¬ > ◊
 b. Mary may *not* leave ¬ > ◊
 c. Mary must *not* leave □ > ¬

In (57a–b), the modals *can* and *may* take scope below negation (under neutral intonation); in (57c), *must* takes scope above negation. In Iatridou and Zeijlstra (2013) and also Chapter 13, it is argued that these readings follow from a general mechanism that takes head movement to always reconstruct (see also Chomsky 1995a; Boeckx and Stjepanović 2001; Harley 2004), unless reconstruction yields ungrammaticality. For examples like (57c), they argue at length that *must* is a Positive Polarity Item (PPI), which is banned from appearing in a position where it takes direct scope under negation, and that, therefore, reconstructing *must* would render the sentence ungrammatical. I will discuss the PPI properties of modals and other elements at length in Chapter 13, but I would like to point out that evidence for the claim that, in (57c), *must* is exempt from reconstruction, comes from examples like (58), where *must* takes scope below negation. It is well-known (after Baker 1970; Ladusaw 1979; and Szabolcsi 2004) that PPIs can take scope under two (semi-)negative contexts. Hence, in (58), reconstruction of *must* should not be forbidden, and *must* is thus predicted to take scope below negation, which is indeed the case.

(58) Few students must*n't* leave   few > ¬ > □

At the same time, moving a NM may have a semantic effect indeed. Take, for instance, polar questions:[15]

(59) a. Have*n't* you filled in your tax forms?
     b. Have you *not* filled in your tax forms?

Two things are at stake here: first, the relative position of the NM is different in (59a–b); second, the two sentences are semantically slightly different. As Romero and Han (2004) have pointed out, sentences like (59a) come along with a bias that the hearer has filled in their tax forms, whereas sentences like (59b) lack such a bias. For Romero and Han (2004), this is due to the relative scope of negation with respect to VERUM focus. For them, in (59a), negation in higher position applies to VERUM focus, so that the meaning of the polar questions is {¬VERUM(p), ¬¬VERUM(p)} (where p = 'you have filled in you tax forms'), which is formally equivalent to {¬VERUM(p), VERUM(P)}.

If *haven't* should obligatorily reconstruct, these facts remain unexplained. However, if we assume that *haven't* takes scope in situ, another problem arises: while negation takes scope over VERUM focus, *have* itself does not. Only negation scopes over VERUM; the perfect tense takes scope below. But if *have* must reconstruct, so must *haven't*.

Hence, we reach a paradox. Obligatory reconstruction of the NM cannot explain the bias in polar questions with the negative head marker *n't*; but allowing

---

[15] See also Lechner (2004) for more discussion of semantic effects of head movement.

heads not to reconstruct in such and other constructions makes wrong predictions too.

At the same time, there is a way out, namely by assuming that *n't*, unlike *not*, contains a feature [uNEG] to be checked off by the abstract negative operator Op$_\neg$. If *n't* carries a feature [uNEG], to be checked by an abstract negative operator Op$_\neg$ that carries [iNEG] and c-commands it, it is ensured that the surface position of *n't* coincides with the surface position of negation, which is indeed the required result.

Additional evidence for *n't* being semantically vacuous comes, again, from negative imperatives. In English, negative imperatives raise to a position into the CP (evidenced by the fact that the imperative auxiliary *do* precedes the subject):

(60) a. Do (you) sit down
b. Do*n't* (you) sit down

Given the earlier discussion that states that only NMs that carry [uNEG] may appear in a position in C°, it follows again that *n't* should be semantically non-negative.[16]

If *n't* is not a semantic negation but an element that carries [uNEG] and triggers the presence of an abstract negative operator, the question arises what properties other negative elements such as the phrasal NM *not*, or NIs like *nobody* or *never* have.

As for *not*, the most likely answer is that it carries a feature [iNEG]. The reasons for that are twofold: first, it always introduces a semantic negation of its own; second, as with *n't*, it triggers certain morphosyntactic operations that are sensitive to negation. Hence, negation must be part of the formal, and not only the semantic properties of *not*.

The first claim is best illustrated by examples like (61):

(61) Mary did*n't not* leave

(62) a. [Mary Op$_{\neg[\text{iNEG}]}$ did*n't*$_{[\text{uNEG}]}$ *not*$_{[\text{uNEG}]}$ leave]
b. [Mary Op$_{\neg[\text{iNEG}]}$ did*n't*$_{[\text{uNEG}]}$ *not*$_{[\text{iNEG}]}$ leave]

If *not* in (61) carried [uNEG], (61) would be predicted to yield an NC reading, as both negative elements could have their [uNEG] features checked off by the same abstract negative operator (see (62a)), contrary to fact. By contrast, if *not* in (61) carries [iNEG], it is correctly predicted that a DN reading is yielded (62b). Note that the same question arises as in the discussion (in Section 3.3) of the analysis of Non-strict NC readings: why can't the higher element carrying [uNEG] have its feature checked against the element carrying [iNEG] in a derivational stage where it appeared below it? If *n't* heads the NegP of which *not* is the specifier, why couldn't

---

[16] See Chapter 15 for a discussion on how the covert negative operator takes exact scope in TNIs in Strict NC languages.

not have checked *n't*'s [uNEG]-feature? The same answer as before applies here as well: since Op₋ must be parsed into the structure, it is done in a position where the highest overt [uNEG]-element has not been locally c-commanded by an overt element carrying [iNEG].

This argument shows that *not* must be semantically negative. However, that leaves open the question of whether it carries [iNEG] or no formal negative feature at all (as French *pas* does). The reason to assume that both *not* and *n't* carry a formal negative feature is that both trigger *do*-support:

(63) a. *Mary *not* left
　　 b. Mary did *not* leave

(64) a. *Mary left*n't*
　　 b. Mary did*n't* leave

According to Bobaljik (1995), who implements Chomsky's (1957) conjecture that negation blocks affix lowering, the reason why the a-examples in (63)–(64) are out is that (PF-)merger of the verb with its tense/agreement morphology is blocked by intervening heads. If that is the case, both (63a) and (64a) should contain a negative head. In (64a), that head position is occupied by *n't*; in (63a), *not* must appear in the specifier of a NegP whose head is empty. But this means that *not* must have a feature in common with the negative head. Assuming that the feature that the negative head contains is a [NEG]-feature, *not* must also be formally marked for negation.

However, things are different for NIs. An NI like *never* or *nobody* never triggers *do*-support. Such NIs also never participate in NC constructions. Hence, there is no evidence that such elements contain any formal negative features at all. In fact, if they did, examples like (65) should trigger NC readings, contrary to fact, irrespective of whether or not they carried [iNEG] and checked off *n't*'s [uNEG]-feature directly, or if they carried [uNEG] and were both checked by the higher abstract negative operator.

(65) a. She *never* did*n't* leave
　　 b. *Nobody* did*n't* leave

Hence, I take English to be a language like French, where only some semantically negative elements carry a feature [iNEG], and other semantically negative elements do not carry any formal negative feature at all. This way, English also provides additional evidence for the claim that the French NC system is a partial NC system. It is no longer an ad hoc solution that applies only to French.

At the same time, English is different from French in the sense that English is an invisible NC language. That French exhibits instances of NC is crystal clear. But, in English, the number of overt negative elements always corresponds with the number of semantic negations. The English NC system is thus an NC system

106   TYPES OF NEGATIVE CONCORD SYSTEMS

in disguise. Therefore, one may still wonder whether the original case for partial NC is strong enough. If the additional empirical evidence for French comes with a new type of NC system, namely invisible NC, the question arises whether the existence of invisible NC systems can receive additional empirical support. Below, I argue that English, however, is not the only example of an invisible NC language.

4.4.3 Other invisible Negative Concord languages: Hindi and Punjabi

Not every language in the world has elements that look like NIs or neg-words. Hindi and Punjabi, for instance, are languages that lack any negatively marked quantificational element. The only negative items in Hindi/Punjabi are NMs themselves, such as *nahii/nayii* in (66)/(67).[17]

(66) Raam *nahii* gayaa   (Hindi)
      Ram.NOM NEG go.PRF.M.SG
      'Ram didn't go'

(67) raam *nayii* gayaa   (Punjabi)
      Ram.NOM NEG go.PRF.M.SG
      'Ram didn't go'

In order to convey an expression for which, in other languages, neg-words are used, Hindi and Punjabi exploit indefinite NPIs (where NPIs are formed by incorporating an *even*-particle in the indefinite; see Lahiri 1998). For instance, Hindi *koyii* is a plain indefinite, meaning 'somebody / a person'; *koyii bhii* ('somebody / a person even') is an NPI, meaning 'anybody'.

(68) a. raam-ne   kisii-ko   bhii   *nahii* dekhaa   (Hindi)
          Ram-ERG   somebody-ACC   even   NEG   see.PRF.M.SG
          'Ram didn't see anyone'

      b. raam-ne   kisii-nuu   vii   *nayii* vekhyaa   (Punjabi)
          Ram-ERG   somebody-ACC   even   NEG   see.PRF.M.SG
          'Ram didn't see anyone'

(69) a. koyii   bhii   *nahii*   gayaa   (Hindi)
          somebody   even   NEG   go.PRF.M.SG
          'No one went'

      b. koyii   vii   *nayii*   gayaa   (Punjabi)
          somebody   even   NEG   go.PRF.M.SG
          'No one went'

---

[17] These are not the only NMs. There are also NMs with restricted usages to subjunctives and/or imperatives, such as *na* or *mat* in Hindi. This distinction does not play a role for the rest of the discussion; so, I will focus only on *nahii/nayii*.

These NPIs are not neg-words, as they cannot appear as fragment answers, even though Hindi/Punjabi do allow fragment-answer DPs:

(70) Q: tum-ne kisko dekhaa? (Hindi)
you-ERG who.ACC see.PRF.M.SG
'Who did you see?'

A: sab-ko / *kisi-ko
all-ACC / *somebody-ACC
Int.: 'Everybody' / 'Nobody'

(71) Q: tuu kinnuu vekhyaa? (Punjabi)
you-ERG who.ACC see.PRF.M.SG
'Who did you see?'

A: sabb-nuu / *kisi-nuu
all-ACC / *somebody-ACC
Int.: 'Everybody' / 'Nobody'

Hindi and Punjabi differ from most other languages that exhibit similar NPIs, in that these NPIs do not always appear to be c-commanded by negation. However, as with any other NPI, such NPIs should be outscoped by negation at LF. Something strange is at hand here. If the subject NPIs in (69) were able to scope below negation, either negation should be in a higher position, or these NPIs should be able to reconstruct below negation. However, evidence for either is absent.[18]

Negation is not very likely to appear in a higher position than TP. In examples (72)–(73), the universal quantifier *sab(b)* generally takes scope below negation, but with extra stress on *sab(b)* it can also take higher scope. This suggests that negation is in between the surface and base position of the subject (Spec, TP and Spec, vP, respectively). That the NM occupies the head position of a NegP that is below TP has been independently motivated by Mahajan (1990); Dwivedi (1991); Kumar (2006).

(72) sab skuul *nahii* jaate haiN (Hindi)
everyone/all school NEG go.HAB.M.PL be.PRES.3.PL
'Everyone doesn't go to school' $\neg > \forall; {}^?\forall > \neg$

(73) sabb skuul *nayii* jaande ne (Punjabi)
everyone/all school NEG go.HAB.M.PL be.PRES.3.PL
'Everyone doesn't go to school' $\neg > \forall; {}^?\forall > \neg$

Hence, negation cannot be in a position higher than TP. At the same time, subjects can reconstruct below negation. But this does not involve all subjects. That

---

[18] A third option would be that negation covertly raises to a higher position, but there is no evidence for covert movement of NMs in general; see Chapters 7–8 for more discussion.

universal quantifiers can reconstruct below negation does not entail that existential NPI subjects can as well. In fact, looking at other instances of reconstruction, if a quantifier can reconstruct, it is generally the universal quantifier and not the existential one, as is shown for English below:

(74) a. Every boy did*n't* leave $\quad\forall > \neg; \neg > \forall$
b. A boy did*n't* leave $\quad\exists > \neg; *\neg > \exists$

While, in (74a), the universal quantifier can reconstruct (yielding the most salient reading), the existential one cannot. For Mayr and Spector (2012), this follows from a general constraint that forbids reconstruction to yield stronger readings. Hence, it is really questionable that, in (69), the NPIs reconstruct below negation.

But if, in (69), the NPIs cannot reconstruct below negation and negation is not above the NPIs, how can these NPIs still take scope below negation? One possibility that remains open is that the NMs are not semantically negative elements, but rather carry a feature [uNEG] to be checked by an abstract negative operator $Op_\neg$ carrying [iNEG]. If this operator is included immediately above the highest overt marker of negation (which, in Hindi/Punjabi, would be either a NM or an NPI), it would follow immediately that negation takes scope from the surface position of the NM, unless the NM is c-commanded by a higher NPI; then, $Op_\neg$ immediately c-commands this NPI. That is exactly the pattern attested in Hindi/Punjabi. For this reason, I assume that, in Hindi/Punjabi, semantic negation is always expressed by the abstract negative operator and that NMs carry a feature [uNEG]. The sentences in (66)/(69a), for example, would then have the following structure:

(75) a. [Raam [$Op_{\neg[iNEG]}$ *nahii*$_{[uNEG]}$ gayaa]] (Hindi)
b. [$Op_{\neg[iNEG]}$ koyii (bhii) [*nahii*$_{[uNEG]}$ gayaa]]

This makes Hindi/Punjabi just as much an instance of invisible NC language as English—with the only difference that English also has NIs (even though these lack a formal negative feature), whereas Hindi and Punjabi lack those. In both languages, agreement between [iNEG]- and [uNEG]-features takes place, even though the number of overt negation corresponds with the number of semantic negations. Hence, the claim that English is an invisible NC language does receive additional empirical support.

Naturally, the question arises why, in English, the covert negative operator may not outscope NPI-subjects. Why cannot the English covert negative operator outscope NPI-subjects too? Arguably, there are two potential reasons for this. First, the languages that lack neg-words are predominantly head-final languages, where parsing of covert operators works differently in the first place. Therefore, a covert operator in Hindi/Punjabi can still be 'parsed in' before the NPI subject, whereas, in English, it cannot. Alternatively, in languages like Hindi/Punjabi, this is the only way to convey that an existential subject is negated, whereas English also has NIs. The existence of the latter can then be said to block *any*-terms or other NPIs to be c-commanded by a covert negative operator when appearing in clausal subject position.

4.5 Conclusions

In this chapter, I have shown that the proposal for NC presented in the previous chapter predicts the currently attested landscape of NC. Differences between NC systems all reduce to the question of which negative elements carry a feature [iNEG] and which ones a feature [uNEG]. In Strict NC languages, all overt negative elements carry [uNEG], and the only negative element carrying [iNEG] is the abstract negative operator Op¬. In Non-strict NC languages, neg-words carry [uNEG], and the NM and the abstract negative operator Op¬ carry [iNEG]. The mirror image of Non-strict NC systems, such as Variety A of Afrikaans, is a system where all neg-words and the abstract negative operator Op¬ carry [iNEG], and the NM [uNEG].

I have also shown that not every negative element has to participate in NC. For instance, partial NC languages like French and English are examples of languages where only some negative elements carry a feature [iNEG] or [uNEG]. The result of this may be that, in some languages, the number of overt negative elements equals the number of semantic negation, so that the NC system in these languages is actually invisible, as I have shown is the case in English and Hindi/Punjabi.

Naturally, additional differences between languages apart from their NC system may also result in differences within the negation. This happens, for instance, in West Flemish and Catalan (at least in its Central Variety). Even though both West Flemish and Central Catalan are Strict NC languages, as all of their overt instances of negation carry [uNEG], they allow neg-words to not always be obligatorily accompanied by the NM for independent reasons. For instance, in West Flemish, this is due to the fact that all indefinites, including neg-words, undergo obligatory scrambling outside vP.

At the same time, the approach still raises a number of (follow-up) questions. The most important one is: what determines which element carries what kind of negative feature (if any negative feature at all)? This question already came up towards the end of Chapter 3, when it was claimed that the licensing of neg-words outside negative contexts requires other non-negative elements to carry [iNEG] features as well. In this chapter, it has become even more important to understand why, in some languages, all and, in other languages, only some negative elements carry [iNEG] or [uNEG]. Moreover, it should be made clear why, in some languages, neg-words or NMs carry [iNEG] and, in others, [uNEG]. These questions will all be addressed in the next two chapters. I will show that a particular, independently motivated learning algorithm determines the possible feature assignments of [i/uNEG]-features (and other features), and that the reason why a particular language displays a particular negative feature configuration lies in its diachronic development of negation.

Before closing off this chapter, I would like to address one other dimension of variation that has hitherto been left undiscussed. According to Shimoyama (2011), neg-words (or other kinds of NPIs) could either be perceived as existentials that take obligatory scope under negation, or universals that obligatorily outscope negation (see also Szabolcsi 1981; Giannakidou 2000). Under my proposal, it seems that all neg-words should take scope below negation. This means that the examples that Shimoyama takes to reflect universal neg-words should actually be existential neg-words.

Shimoyama's proposal has often been criticized for a lack of understanding of what properties could make a particular item obligatorily outscope negation. However, as I will argue in Chapter 16, it turns out that a particular class of PPIs, equipped with a [uNEG]-feature and certain other properties, can actually display this behaviour. However, in order to evaluate whether, under this particular conception, there is a need to reconsider the claim that all neg-words are existentials, we must first introduce this and other notions of PPI-hood. Therefore, I will come back to this discussion later.

5
The flexibility of negative features

5.1 The nature of negative features

The previous two chapters presented a theory of NC that took every instance of NC to be an instance of syntactic agreement between a semantically negative element carrying a feature [iNEG] and one or more semantically non-negative elements carrying a feature [uNEG]. It turns out that, when we assume that NC is an instance of syntactic agreement, various core facts about NC readily follow. First, it provides a compositional explanation for why every NC item can induce a semantic negation of its own, but, at the same time, does not introduce a second negation when it appears in an already negative context. Second, it explains why NC is subject to the same locality constraint as syntactic agreement. And, third, it explains why NC can be subject to cross-linguistic variation—not every language is an NC language, and, moreover, among NC languages, different types of NC can be attested.

At the same time, various questions are left open. The first one concerns DN languages—languages that do not exhibit NC. Naturally, in such languages, every morphosyntactically negative element should also be semantically negative. Then it follows immediately that every negatively marked element introduces a negation of its own. But the question has been left open whether, in such languages, every negative element carries a feature [iNEG] or whether such languages lack any kind of formal negative features. This question lies at the heart of the syntax–semantics interface, as it addresses the question to what extent semantic properties should always be reflected in the morphosyntax. Does every semantically negative element have to carry a semantic feature [iNEG]? Note that, in the discussion on French NC, I already provided a tentative negative answer to this question by arguing that French *pas*, despite being semantically negative, does not carry a feature [iNEG]. What then determines whether a semantically negative element carries [iNEG] or not?

I also argued that the mirror question of the one raised above, namely whether every element carrying [iNEG] is also semantically negative, does not necessarily have to be answered positively. Already in Chapter 3, we saw that, in particular NC languages such as Spanish, certain non-negative (but still (Strawson-)DE) elements could license neg-words. Two examples from Chapter 3 are repeated below:

Negation and Negative Dependencies. Hedde Zeijlstra, Oxford University Press.
© Hedde Zeijlstra (2022). DOI: 10.1093/oso/9780198833239.003.0005

(1) a. Antec de hacer *nada*, debes lavarle las manos   (Spanish)
       before of do NEG-thing, must.2SG wash.CL the hands
       'Before doing anything, you should wash your hands'

   b. Dudo que vayan a encontar *nada*
      doubt.1SG that will.3PL.SUBJ find NEG-thing
      'I doubt they will find anything'

Before and *doubt* are indeed not semantically negative predicates; but they are nevertheless able to check off the [uNEG] feature on *nada* (neg-thing). Hence, if the proposal that NC reduces to syntactic agreement is correct, at least in Spanish, such predicates should be said to carry a feature [iNEG]. But they are not inherently negative.

If, indeed, certain semantically negative elements do not carry [iNEG], and certain semantically non-negative elements may carry [iNEG], the question immediately arises what determines which element gets assigned a negative feature, and, if so, what kind of negative feature. Ultimately, this is a learnability question, as it amounts to asking how the language learner will know whether a particular lexical item carries some particular formal feature. Therefore, a learnability algorithm is required to account for the acquisition of formal (negative) features. In this chapter, I will provide such an algorithm, and I will show that it makes several empirical and theoretical predictions that appear to be borne out.

In Section 5.2, I will spell out this learnability algorithm for formal (negative) features. In this section, I first introduce the theoretical background that is necessary to understand the relation between syntactic and semantic features, then present the algorithm itself, and afterwards I discuss its theoretical consequences. In Section 5.3, I show how the feature configurations underlying the NC systems discussed in Chapter 4 emerge. Further empirical and theoretical consequences of the proposal for language variation, acquisition, and change will be discussed in Section 5.4, including a predicted and confirmed uni-directional generalization between the syntactic status of an NM and the existence of NC in a language. Section 5.5 concludes.

5.2 The Flexible Formal Feature Hypothesis

Ever since the introduction of formal features in syntactic theory, questions have arisen as to: (i) what constitutes the set of formal features in a particular grammar, i.e., is this pool of formal features in a particular grammar given by UG, or does it emerge in the process of language acquisition? And (ii) what are the syntactic and semantic properties of such formal features? Let us start this section by having a closer look at these two questions.

5.2.1 A universal set of formal features?

As for the first question: over the past two decades, several proposals have been formulated that aim at accounting for the presence of the set of formal features in natural language grammars. Initially, it was argued that UG provides this set of formal features, and that every language has the same set of formal features at its disposal—a view much in line with the so-called cartographic approach, which, in its most radical version, assigns a universal syntactic structure to all natural languages with variation lying in the way that (parts of) this structure are phonologically realised (cf. Pollock 1989; Beghelli and Stowell 1997; Rizzi 1997, 2004; Cinque 1999, 2002, 2006; Starke 2001, 2004; Caha 2009; Miyagawa 2010; Baunaz et al. 2018).

More recently, an alternative view arose which states that the set of formal features is as minimal as possible in every language. Under this view, sometimes referred to as *building block grammars* or *WYSIWYG (What You See Is What You Get)* approaches, formal features and, consequently, functional projections should only be assumed to be present if there is overt evidence for it (cf. Iatridou 1990; Grimshaw 1997; Bobaljik and Thráinsson 1998; Koeneman 2000; Nilsen 2003; Zeijlstra 2008b; Biberauer and Roberts 2015).

The main difference between these building block grammar / WYSIWYG approaches and the cartographic approach (in its most radical sense) is that the visible presence of a particular formal feature in a particular language (for instance, if it overtly heads a functional projection) does not, under the former approach, imply its presence in all languages, whereas this is the basic line of reasoning under the latter approach (cf. Chomsky 2001; Cinque 1999; Kayne 2000; Starke 2004; Miyagawa 2010). This reduces the question as to what constitutes the set of formal features to a question about the nature of UG. Is UG a rich body of knowledge that contains the set of all formal features that a language may be sensitive to, or is UG, as has been proposed in more recent minimalist views (cf. Chomsky 2005), much poorer in nature, and are the relevant formal features to be acquired in the course of first-language acquisition? Even though the latter view should be taken to be the default hypothesis (given that one should only postulate things in UG that otherwise cannot be accounted for), its correctness can only be evaluated against a concrete proposal of how these formal features can be acquired in the first place. Formulating such a proposal and evaluating its consequences, especially with respect to negation and NC, is one of the goals of this chapter.

In order to do so, in this chapter, I further elaborate my proposal from Zeijlstra (2008b, 2014), where it is argued that syntactic doubling is the only available cue to determine the presence of formal features. However, I also argue that the implementation of this proposal, if correct, drastically changes the way that the nature of formal features should be considered.

For Chomsky (1995a), the set of formal features, i.e., the set of features that may participate in syntactic operations, is a set that intersects with the set of semantic features (the architecture of grammatical features is depicted in (2)). Consequently, formal features come about in two kinds: interpretable and uninterpretable formal features. Interpretable formal features ([iF]s) are features that are part of the intersection of the sets of formal and semantics features; therefore, both participate in syntactic operations and receive an interpretation at LF. Uninterpretable features ([uF]s), by contrast, are features that are only formal, and not semantic in nature, and therefore cannot receive an interpretation at LF.

(2)   Phonological features   Formal features   Semantic features

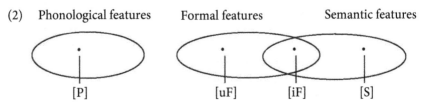

Chomsky (1995a, 2001) furthermore argues that every feature that reaches the interfaces must be interpretable (following his Principle of Full Interpretation):

(3) Full Interpretation (FI): Every element of an output representation should provide a meaningful input to the relevant other parts of the cognitive system.

To satisfy FI, all [uF]s must be deleted in the course of the derivation, as those, by definition, do not provide any meaningful input. For Chomsky (1995, 2000), Agree is the only available operation that is capable of deleting [uF]s: if a matching [iF] and [uF] stand in a particular (c-command) configuration, the [uF] can be checked off against the [iF] and, as a consequence, be deleted. Once every [uF] has been deleted, the derivation can be fully interpreted at the interfaces; after the deletion of those features that are only formal in nature, all features left over are either phonological or semantic features, which are interpretable at the relevant interfaces.

In later work, Chomsky (2001) argued that this view should be modified, as it would otherwise face a *look ahead problem*, originally pointed out by Epstein et al. (1998) and Epstein and Seely (2002). Since it can only be determined at the

5.2 THE FLEXIBLE FORMAL FEATURE HYPOTHESIS

level of LF whether a particular feature is interpretable, the (un)interpretability of a feature is not visible in the course of the derivation (which precedes transfer at LF). Hence, deletion of [uF]s as such cannot be a trigger for syntactic operations. For this reason, Chomsky argues that deletion of [uF]s cannot be the trigger of syntactic operations, but that, rather, feature valuation is. Every feature that has not been valued in the lexicon needs to be valued in the course of the derivation; valuation then takes place under Agree. For this, Chomsky postulates that all formal features that are interpretable are also lexically valued, and formal features that are uninterpretable are also lexically unvalued. Again, only the former type of features (lexically valued and interpretable features) are members of the set of semantic features. Furthermore, Chomsky argues that, during syntax, all lexically unvalued features that are valued during the derivation get deleted prior to LF. As a result, all and only those formal features that are interpretable survive at LF.

Chomsky's (2001) proposal in a way enriches the feature taxonomy by including a second parameter—feature (un)valuedness—but given that, for him, interpretability and valuedness always go hand in hand, the number of different types of formal features remains identical. There are two types of features: lexically valued and interpretable features, and lexically unvalued and uninterpretable ones (see (4), where '__' means *unvalued* and 'val' means *valued*).

(4)   Phonological features   Formal features   Semantic features

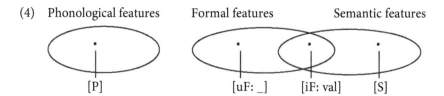

[P]   [uF: _]   [iF: val]   [S]

Note, however, that it is a pure stipulation that (un)valuedness and (un)interpretability should always coincide. If that stipulation is given up, as has been proposed by Pesetsky and Torrego (2007), who argue that valuedness and interpretability are disentangled notions, formal features come about in four kinds: (i) interpretable and unvalued features; (ii) interpretable and valued features; (iii) uninterpretable and unvalued features; and (iv) uninterpretable and valued features. Both types of [iF]s form a subset of the set of semantic features, and both types of [uF]s do not. Pesetsky and Torrego's (2007) taxonomy thus looks as follows:

(5) Phonological features   Formal features   Semantic features

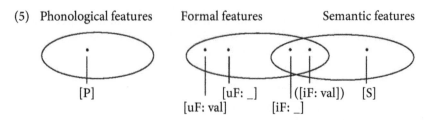

Hence, different views on the nature of formal features are available, with both (un)interpretability and lexical (un)valuedness playing a role. However, as to the best of my knowledge has never been noted thus far that, if feature (un)interpretability were not an LF phenomenon, but instead a purely formal property (as I will argue later on), this 'look ahead' problem immediately disappears. In this chapter, I argue for this alternative stand, at least when it comes to features like negation and other features involving grammatical reflexes of semantic operations. This does not mean that I propose to dismiss (un)valued features as a second parameter. As argued elsewhere (e.g. in Bjorkman and Zeijlstra 2019, following Pesetsky and Torrego 2007 and Arregui and Nevins 2012), valuation and checking are operationally, and even derivationally, distinct, and can account for the distribution of φ-values on φ-probes (see also Chapter 17).

The question that arises, then, is how the language learner can acquire which element carries [iF] and which one carries [uF], and how the alleged connection between [iF]-features (the 'checkers') and the corresponding semantics of F is captured by the proposed learnability algorithm.

In short, I argue that the acquisition of formal features is governed, after Zeijlstra (2008b, 2014), by so-called 'doubling cases', i.e., cases where the locus of interpretation of a particular semantic property (i.e., a semantic operator or feature) does not correspond 1:1 with its morphosyntactic manifestation(s). Hence, formal features, [iF] and [uF], can only be acquired against the background of form–meaning mismatches. We will later on see that as a result, most, but crucially not all, elements carrying [iF] will therefore also carry the semantics of F. The correspondence between semantic content and the ability to check off a particular formal feature is a property of language acquisition, not of grammar itself.

5.2.2 The algorithm

The only way to evaluate the claim that the set of formal features in a particular grammar is not part of UG, but rather emerges in the process of language acquisition (and therefore on the basis of language input only), is by evaluating a

5.2 THE FLEXIBLE FORMAL FEATURE HYPOTHESIS 117

particular procedure that may account for this emergence. In this subsection, I propose such a procedure. In short, I argue that formal features can only be acquired if a particular semantic feature is morphosyntactically doubled; this will form a cue for language learners to assume that this semantic feature is formalized, i.e., that it should be taken to involve a formal feature as well. Here, I start with outlining the general format of this learning algorithm.

Following/modifying earlier work (Zeijlstra 2008b, 2014), I argue that formal features should only be postulated by the language learner if the language input provides overt evidence for them. In terms of learnability, this entails that the null hypothesis must be that formal features are absent and that morphemes map phonological content directly to semantic content. Hence, the starting assumption should be that any element that appears responsible for the induction of a particular semantic context should also be taken to be the carrier of this semantic content:

(6) Assume a 1:1 correspondence between morphemes and semantic content.[1]

Assuming (6), it follows that, only if a 1:1 relation between some morpheme and its semantic contribution proves to be absent, other properties than semantic and phonological properties must be assigned. So, if a particular element, for instance a verbal agreement marker, manifests the presence of some semantic context (e.g. the semantic φ-features of the subject), then it must be taken to carry a corresponding uninterpretable formal φ-feature. If a language lacks any kind of φ-morphology, it therefore lacks formal φ-features as well; only if φ-agreement is present does this provide evidence for the language learner to assume that the verb contains some uninterpretable person, number, and/or gender features. So, only semantically redundant elements must be assigned [uF]:

(7) If some morphosyntactic element α manifests the presence of some semantic context F, but cannot be assumed to be the carrier of F itself, then assign a formal feature [uF] to α

Informally, (7) means that carrying [uF] may only take place if the element carrying [uF] is able to mark the presence of some semantic property F without actively carrying the semantics of F itself. Now, since a learnability requirement for the acquisition of [uF]s is that they appear in a particular semantic context, in principle, no [uF] feature can be present without a corresponding semantic operator F. But if it is a purely formal requirement that the element carrying this corresponding semantic property F must be present if an element carrying [uF] is present, this element should not only carry the semantics of F, but also a formal property that

---

[1] See also Clark (1987), whose Principle of Contrast states that every two different forms must also have a different meaning, which has its origin in von Humboldt (1836) (cf. Dressler 1987).

states that an element [uF] cannot survive in the sentence without it; this formal property is, by definition, a feature [iF]:

(8) Assign [iF] to all morphosyntactic elements that introduce the semantic context that is manifested by [uF]. If no overt morphosyntactic element is responsible, assume some covert element to be present that carries the semantics of F and that, therefore, should be assigned [iF]

So far, this is not new. As pointed out in Zeijlstra (2008b): if, under Chomsky's (1995a, 2001) analysis of formal features (2), formal features must be acquired during the process of language acquisition, [uF]s must form the cue, since [iF]s are still part of the set of semantic features and, therefore, semantically indistinguishable from them. The only distinguishing property of [iF]s in comparison to purely semantic features, under this approach, is their ability to check their uninterpretable counterparts. Also, the assumption that, if no overt morphosyntactic element is responsible, some covert element carrying [iF] must be assumed to be present, is trivially true. If the grammaticality of a sentence does not follow from its overt elements, it must follow from a covert element.

Now, (9) must be true as well. As we will see later on, this is an important and necessary step, although it may appear to be redundant now, given (8).

(9) Assign [iF] to all those elements that are responsible for the rest of the grammatical occurrences of [uF]

To summarize, a feature [uF] is learnable. If some element does not carry the semantics of F, but at the same time may only appear in a semantic context F, this element carries [uF]. If some [uF] appears in a grammatical sentence, some element must carry [iF]. Hence, [iF] features are learnable as well.

5.2.3 Consequences

A question that arises now concerns the interpretational status of [iF]s such as [iNEG]. Does an [iF] like [iNEG] have semantic content itself or not? Under the outlined proposal, two logical possibilities arise:

(10) [iNEG] (and, therefore, all [iF]s) are interpreted as carriers of the semantics of negation (or F)

(11) The element carrying [iNEG] (or [iF]) must be taken to carry a semantic negation (or the semantics of F) as part of its lexical semantics; this means that it is not the feature [iNEG](/[iF]) itself that is being interpreted at LF.

Solution (10) represents the current view on formal features and, at first sight, appears to be the preferred option. First, it immediately reduces the ability of [iF]s to check and delete [uF]s that match their semantic properties. Moreover, the fact

5.2 THE FLEXIBLE FORMAL FEATURE HYPOTHESIS 119

that only [uF]s have to be deleted (and, thus, to undergo Agree), whereas [iF]s do not, also immediately follows: all other elements are semantically interpretable and do not violate FI. However, the option in (10) comes at a particular price, as it faces several severe and some hitherto unobserved theoretical and empirical problems. I discuss these problems next, and argue that these problems do not surface under assumption (11).

First, as already mentioned in Subsection 5.2.2, the assumption that [uF]s must be checked and deleted, because otherwise they would make the derivation crash at LF (owing to FI), introduces a major look-ahead problem. For Chomsky (1995), [uF]s must be deleted at the level of LF, and feature checking is a necessary condition for feature deletion. However, at the stage in the derivation at which feature checking takes place, it is not yet known that the feature, if remained unchecked, would cause the derivation to crash at a later stage, as has been pointed out by Epstein et al. (1998), Epstein and Seely (2002), and others. However, this look-ahead problem arises only under this particular view on feature interpretability in (10). The view on feature interpretability in (11) does not face this problem, as, here, the difference between [iF]s and [uF]s is only formal in nature and thus visible in the course of the derivation; the only property of [iF] is that it is able to check the configurational needs of [uF].

Second, although it is an advantage that feature checking can be motivated in terms of FI, it can only do so by virtue of the stipulation that feature checking leads to LF deletion of [uF]s. However, it is unclear why feature checking should lead to deletion. Nothing principled motivates it; so, the conjecture that checked [uF]s are deleted is at best a stipulated one. In fact, one may even wonder why the appearance of [uF]s at LF should make the derivation crash. Take, for instance, the structure in (12):

(12)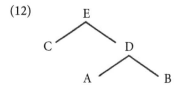

Now suppose that A is semantically empty, i.e., it contains only formal features at LF. In that case, the denotation of D is identical to the denotation of B. If no other grammatical condition is violated, and D can be a semantic complement of C (or vice versa), nothing renders (12) illegible at LF. Hence, the presence of [uF]s does not a priori violate FI.

In fact, not ignoring the vacuous meaning contribution of a [uF] even yields a logical contradiction. Given the definition by Svenonius (2006) in (13), a semantic feature is a feature that can constitute a distinction between two different semantic representations.

(13) A feature F is an X feature iff F can constitute a distinction between two different X representations

Now, if, all other things being equal, the presence or absence of a [uF] can make a sentence crash or converge, it is the [uF] that is solely responsible for that, and, by consequence, it should be taken to be a semantic feature. But if it were a semantic feature, FI should not mind its presence.

Under the view in (11), such problems do not necessarily arise. There is no need any more to allude to a principle such as FI, which gives rise to this logical contradiction. The triggering of syntactic operations simply takes place as a result of the need for certain learnable formal properties of lexical elements. As long as the outcome of the derivation is legible to the interfaces, no further constraints on the derivation have to be imposed.

However, apart from these theoretical considerations, the advantages of the view in (11) also pertain to the two questions raised in the introduction of this chapter: does every element with the semantics of F carry a feature [iNEG]? And does every element carrying a feature [iNEG] have the semantics of F? As we saw before, the approach to NC pursued in this chapter requires both questions to be answered by 'no'. However, only the view in (11) is compatible with that.

Hence, I take the connection between features that may check off other features and LF-interpretability not to be direct but rather indirect, and a result of language acquisition rather than a property of the formal system. Interpretable features are not semantic features themselves, as they lack LF-interpretability. Rather, the carrier of an [iF] (and not the [iF] itself) generally, but crucially not always, also carries the semantics of F as well. The feature taxonomy that I propose, then, is a simpler and more symmetric one, where the set of formal features is autonomous and consists of two types of formal features: [iF]s and [uF]s, where [uF] encodes a need to stand in a proper Agree configuration with [iF], and where [iF] encodes the ability to satisfy [uF]'s configurational needs. The taxonomy is depicted in (14). Note that, in this sense, '[iF]-feature' and '[uF]-feature' are actually misnomers (that, for conventional reasons, I will continue using). Better terms would be 'independent feature' and 'dependent feature' (see Chapter 17).

(14) Phonological features   Formal features   Semantic features

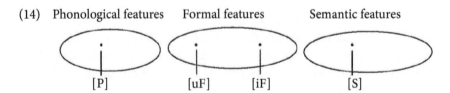

Now, let us therefore look at how, against the background of the developed learnability algorithm, the various types of NC languages and their particular properties come about.

5.3 Acquiring types of Negative Concord systems

Now, let us apply this proposal to the acquisition of formal negative features. As discussed earlier, in DN languages, every morphosyntactically negative element must also be semantically negative; but in NC languages, this is not the case. According to the algorithm in Subsection 5.2.2, this entails that NC languages should have formal negative features at their disposal, but that DN languages do not. Let us therefore go through the various types of languages in detail.

5.3.1 Double Negation: Dutch

In a DN language like Dutch, every morphosyntactically negative element corresponds to a semantic negation. These negative elements are either the NM *niet* or NQs, as illustrated in (15). Note that the locus of negation at LF in (15b) does not coincide with its relative position at surface structure; but since the NQ here undergoes QR to a higher position, this mismatch is independently accounted for.

(15)   a. *Niemand* komt $\neg\exists x.[\textbf{person'}(x) \,\&\, \textbf{come'}(x)]$ (Dutch)
         NEG-body comes
         'Nobody is coming'
   b. Jan doet *niets* $\neg\exists x.[\textbf{thing'}(x) \,\&\, \textbf{do'}(j, x)]$
         Jan does NEG-thing
         'Jan does nothing'
   c. Jan loopt *niet* $\neg\textbf{walk'}(j)$
         Jan walks NEG
         'Jan isn't walking'

Since there is no element that marks the presence of negation but is not semantically negative itself, condition (6) is always fulfilled with respect to negation; consequently, there is no need to assign any [uNEG]-feature, along the lines of (7). Since there are no [uNEG]-features to be assigned in Dutch, there is no reason to assign [iNEG]-features either (cf. (8)–(9)). The child cannot even acquire that there are formal negative features. The only types of negative elements in Dutch are the NM and the NIs, and these contain a semantic negation and no formal negative feature. The inventory of negative elements in Dutch is thus as follows:

(16)   Dutch negative elements:
      niet $\neg$
      negative indefinites $\neg\exists$

5.3.2 Non-strict Negative Concord: Italian

Things are different, however, in NC languages. Let us start by discussing the Non-strict NC language Italian. Both neg-words and the NM may render a sentence negative:

(17) a. Gianni *non* ha telefonato　　　¬**call'**(g)]　　　　　　　(Italian)
　　　　　Gianni NEG has called
　　　　　'Gianni didn't call'
　　　b. *Nessuno* ha telefonato　　　　¬∃x.[**person'**(x) & **call'**(x)]
　　　　　NEG-body has called
　　　　　'Nobody called'

At the same time, a combination of the NM and the neg-word gives rise to a single semantic negation. As, in Italian, postverbal neg-words obligatorily need to be accompanied by the NM *non* or a preverbal neg-word, a large proportion of negative sentences in the L1 input consists of sentences such as (18).

(18) Gianni *non* ha visto　　*nessuno*　　¬∃x.[**person'**(x) & **see'**(g, x)] (Italian)
　　　Gianni NEG has seen　　NEG-body
　　　'Gianni has seen nobody'

Since (18) contains more than one negative element, but only one negation in its semantics, only one of the negative elements can be semantically negative, and the other one must be semantically non-negative (otherwise, semantic compositionality would be violated). The reasons why it is the neg-word and not the NM that must be semantically non-negative are twofold. First, the scope of negation coincides with the surface position of *non*, not with that of the neg-word. Second, two neg-words in a single clause yield an NC-reading, as shown in (19), and this is also evidence for the child that the neg-words cannot be semantically negative.

(19) *Nessuno*　　ha　　　　telefonato　　a *nessuno*
　　　NEG-body　have.3SG　called　　　　to NEG-body
　　　¬∃x∃y[**person'**(x) & **person'**(y)
　　　& **call'**(x, y)]　　　　　　　　　　　　　　　　　　　　　　(Italian)
　　　'No one has called anyone'

Following (7), a neg-word must therefore carry an uninterpretable formal negative feature [uNEG].

Since *non* can still be assumed to be responsible for semantic negation, it must be assigned [iNEG] along the lines of (8).

The fact that *non* is the carrier of [iNEG] and neg-words carry [uNEG] triggers questions for sentences such as (19), which, as said, provide evidence against *nessuno*'s semantic negativity. Here, *non* is absent (and may not even be included). Hence, all overt negative elements carry [uNEG]. The solution to this problem lies

5.3 ACQUIRING TYPES OF NEGATIVE CONCORD SYSTEMS

in (8), according to which, then, some abstract negative operator must be assumed to be present, which carries [iNEG]. Otherwise, no element could be responsible for the checking of the neg-words' [uNEG]-features:

(20) Op¬   nessuno ha telefonato a *nessuno*
      [iNEG][uNEG]   [uNEG]

The inventory of Italian negative elements is thus as follows: the NM carries [iNEG] and contains a semantic negation, and so does the covert negative operator Op¬. The neg-words in Italian, however, are semantically non-negative and only carry an uninterpretable formal negative feature [uNEG].

(21) Italian negative elements:
      non   [iNEG]   ¬
      neg-words   [uNEG]   ∃
      Op¬   [iNEG]   ¬

The learning algorithm in (6)–(9) thus enables the language learner to acquire the negative inventory in (21).

5.3.3 Strict Negative Concord: Czech

In a Strict NC language like Czech, the application of the learnability algorithm leads to slightly different results. First, since Czech is an NC language, negation must be formalized, and neg-words must be attributed a feature [uNEG]. However, the (default) assumption that the NM carries [iNEG] cannot be maintained. To see this, take (22).

(22) Nikdo ne-volá   (Czech)
      NEG-body NEG.calls
      'Nobody calls'

If *ne* carried a feature [iNEG], the negative subject would appear outside its scope, which is in contrast with the fact that *nikdo* marks the presence of a negative context in which it appears.

(23) Op¬   Nikdo   ne-volá   ¬∃x.[**person'**(x) & **call'**(x)]
      [iNEG]   [uNEG]   [uNEG]

As a final consequence, single occurrences of *ne* cannot be taken to be realizations of the negative operator, but must be seen as semantically vacuous markers of such an operator. In (24), the NM indicates the presence of Op¬, which, in turn, is responsible for the negative semantics of the sentence.

(24) Milan   Op¬   ne-volá   ¬**call'(m)**
              [iNEG]   [uNEG]

Czech, thus, has a different inventory of negative elements from that of Italian. In Italian, the NM is semantically negative and carries [iNEG]. In Czech, on the other hand, it is semantically non-negative and carries [uNEG]. The only semantically negative element carrying [iNEG] in Czech is Op₋:

(25) Czech negative elements:
      ne   [uNEG]
      NEG-words [uNEG]   ∃
      Op₋   [iNEG]   ¬

The acquisitional procedure outlined in Section 5.2 thus predicts that Czech and Italian are languages that have a formal negative feature at their disposal, whereas Dutch does not. At the same time, this learning algorithm creates a space of possible variation with respect to what kind of formal and negative semantic features can be assigned to the various negative elements, as already shown for the differences between Czech and Italian. But more types of NC languages have been attested in Chapter 4; we will see how, according to the learnability algorithm, these types of NC systems emerge.

5.3.4 Negative Concord in Afrikaans Variety A

While the Strict NC system of Variety B of Afrikaans can be acquired along the lines of Czech, things are different in Variety A of Afrikaans. In this variety, both neg-words and NMs can render a sentence negative, with the additional peculiarity that Afrikaans exploits two identical NMs *nie*—one in a position in the middle field, and one in sentence-final position. Only if the two end up string-adjacent, just one is realized:

(26) a. Hy is *nooit* moeg *nie*   (Afrikaans A)
        he is never tired NEG
        'He is never tired'
    b. Hy is *nie* moeg *nie*
        he is NEG tired NEG
        'He is not tired'
    c. Hy kom *nie* (*nie*)
        he come NEG
        'He isn't coming'

The fact that the NM can appear twice in the sentence without yielding two semantic negations, even though, on its own, it can yield one semantic negation, forms evidence for the child that *nie* cannot be semantically negative itself, and that it must therefore carry [uNEG]. On the other hand, the initial hypothesis that neg-words induce a semantic negation never gets falsified. Consequently, the child must assume that neg-words in Afrikaans A are semantically negative. Since a combination of a neg-word and an NM (as in (26a)) contains only one semantic negation, it must be the neg-word that is responsible for the checking of the [uNEG]-feature of *nie*. Finally, in the absence of any overt element carrying [iNEG], [uNEG]-features on *nie* are to be checked by a covert negative operator carrying [iNEG]. The inventory of negative elements in Afrikaans Variety A is thus as follows:

(27) Afrikaans Variety A negative elements:
    nie   [uNEG]
    NEG-words [iNEG] ¬∃
    Op$_\neg$ [iNEG] ¬

5.3.5 Optional Negative Concord: Catalan and West Flemish

Optionality of NC does not play a big role in learnability of negative features, as the presence of NC forms a cue for a particular featural status of negative elements even in cases where these instances of NC are not obligatory. Catalan children (of the central variety) are confronted with input data like (28):

(28) a. *No funktiona*   (Central Catalan)
       NEG works
       'It doesn't work'
   b. *No ha vist a ningú*
       NEG has seen to NEG-body
       '(S)he has seen no one'
   c. *Ningú ha vist res*
       NEG-body NEG has seen NEG-thing
       'Nobody has seen anything'
   d. *Ningú no ha vist res*
       NEG-body NEG has seen NEG-thing
       'Nobody has seen anything'

Catalan differs from other NC languages in that a preverbal neg-word may, but does not have to, be accompanied by an NM.

Given data like (28b), the child must assume that neg-words carry [uNEG]. The question arises what the featural status of *no* is. However, whereas the data in (28a) and (28c) would be fully compatible with both an analysis of *no* carrying [iNEG] and an analysis of *no* carrying [uNEG], data like (28d) only call for a [uNEG] analysis. Consequently, an optional NC language like Catalan is not to be analysed any differently from how other Strict NC languages are. In fact, Catalan only differs from other types of NC in that the NM does not have to be present in constructions where it is functionally redundant. Consequently, the Catalan negative inventory is as in (29), at least for the Central Variety.

(29) Catalan (Central Variety) negative elements:
    no   [uNEG]
    NEG-words [uNEG]   ∃
    Op₋   [iNEG]   ¬

The same analysis applies mutatis mutandis to West Flemish. The examples taken from Haegeman and Lohndal (2010) show that, in West Flemish, the NM *nie* can optionally establish an NC relation with a higher neg-word as well as with both neg-words, and that *nie* is also independently able to induce semantic negation (30). Combinations of multiple neg-words also yield NC (31).

(30) a. ... da Valère *niemand* gezien oat   (West Flemish)
      ... that Valère NEG-body seen had
      '... that Valère had not seen anybody'
   b. ... da Valère dienen boek *nie* kent
      that Valère that book NEG knows
      '... that Valère doesn't know that book'
   c ... da Valère *niemand* (*nie*) ken
      ... that Valère NEG-body NEG knows
      '... that Valère doesn't know anybody'

(31) K een *nooit niets* gezien   (West Flemish)
    I have never NEG-thing seen
    'I have never seen anything'

These properties entail already that the feature inventory of West Flemish must be the same as that of other NC languages. Both the NM and neg-words can establish NC relations with higher neg-words, and must therefore be taken to carry [uNEG]. The only source for semantic negation must then be the abstract negative operator:

(32) West Flemish negative elements:
    nie   [uNEG]
    NEG-words [uNEG]   ∃
    Op₋   [iNEG]   ¬

However, two caveats are to be made here. First, the NC system in West Flemish appears to be richer than other systems, given the fact that there seems to be an optional second preverbal NM present in the language. This optional NM *en*, or *ne*, has to left-attach to the finite verb and may appear in every negative sentence:

(33) a. K'(*en*)-een *niet* gewerkt (West Flemish)
I (NEG)-have NEG worked
'I haven't worked'
b. K'(*en*)-een *niets* gezien
I (NEG)-have NEG-thing seen
'I haven't seen anything'

However, this NM is not able to render a sentence negative on its own. The following examples are ungrammatical:

(34) a. *K'*en*-een gewerkt (West Flemish)
I NEG-have worked
'I haven't worked'
b. *K'*en*-een iets gezien
I NEG-have anything seen
'I haven't seen anything'

This means that, under the current learning algorithm, this marker *en/ne* does not count as an NM in the first place, and cannot be assigned a feature [iNEG]/[uNEG] (nor a semantic negation). Naturally, the question that arises is what the exact meaning contribution (if any) of *en/ne* is. One option would be to treat it analogously to French *ne* (see Subsection 4.4.1). Breitbarth and Haegeman (2014) takes a different stand and considers *en/ne* to be a discourse marker that instructs discourse participants on how to integrate the utterance containing it into the discourse context. For Breitbarth and Haegeman, *en* expresses that there is a contrast between the negative proposition in the utterance and an assumption or expectation of the contrary state of affairs entertained by one or more discourse participants. Either way, however, this marker *en/ne* cannot be taken to be an NM in the strict sense and thus not be said to carry a feature [iNEG]/[uNEG], either.

Another property of the West Flemish NC system is that not every combination of negative elements can give rise to an NC interpretation. For instance, if, instead of a neg-word, a negated adverb like *nie dikkerst* ('not often') precedes the NM, only a DN reading may emerge:

(35) ... da Valère doa *niet* dikkerst *niet* gewerkt eet (West Flemish)
... that Valère there NEG often NEG worked has
'... that Valère has neg often neg worked there'

Also, the reverse combination of the NM, as in (36), can only yield a DN reading:

(36) ... da Valère *nie niemand* ken (West Flemish)
... that Valère NEG NEG-body knows
'... that Valère doesn't know nobody'

Haegeman and Lohndal argue that examples like (35) suggest that more features than just [iNEG] and [uNEG] may be involved, and develop a richer agreement system to account for these cases. Their account, however, does not apply to the example in (36). As their account also argues that both the NM and the neg-word carry [uNEG], their account does not make any different predictions with respect to negation, and I therefore do not further discuss it here. Neither their account nor my account can readily explain the DN pattern in (36), though I note that, to a large extent, it is similar to the Afrikaans (Variety A) examples involving two *nies* and a neg-word, which also yield a DN reading. Arguably, the sketched solution to that problem in Section 4.3 can also apply to these West Flemish cases (though see Stelling 2019 for a different solution in terms of expletive negation; see also Chapter 16).

5.3.6 Partial Negative Concord: French

Given the proposal, there is nothing that forces every negative item to be assigned a feature [iNEG]. Only those negative elements that can license the presence of a semantically non-negative interpreted neg-word are assigned [iNEG]. As a consequence, it is actually predicted that a language learner cannot acquire the French negation system with French *pas* being assigned a formal negative feature. To see this, let us look at the relevant data again.

(37) a. *Personne (ne) mange.* (French)
 NEG-body NEG eats
 'Nobody eats'
 b. *Jean (ne) mange rien*
 Jean NEG eats NEG-thing
 'Jean doesn't eat anything'
 c. *Personne (ne) mange rien*
 NEG-body NEG eats NEG-thing
 'Nobody doesn't eat anything'

(38) *Marie (ne) mange pas*
 Marie NEG eats NEG
 'Marie doesn't eat'

(39) *Personne (ne) mange pas (rien)*
 NEG-body NEG eats NEG NEG-thing
 'Nobody doesn't eat (anything)'

Since *ne* never renders a sentence negative, and, moreover, may also appear in various kinds of other NPI-licensing contexts, such as restrictive focus, comparatives, complement clauses of expressions of fear, avoidance, denial or doubt, conditionals, and temporal *before*-clauses, *ne* can never be acquired with a feature [uNEG] or [iNEG]. For that to happen, French *ne* should be able to at least render some sentences negative by itself, contrary to fact. *Ne* is actually an NPI (cf. Zeijlstra 2010a), which may freely occur in a wide subset of DE contexts. Furthermore, assuming, along the lines of Kadmon and Landman (1993), Krifka (1995), and Chierchia (2006, 2013), that the licensing requirement by NPIs lies in their pragma-semantic properties (though see Chapters 9–11 for more refined discussion), the fact that *pas* is semantically negative already accounts for *ne*'s possible co-occurrence with *pas*. At the same time, *pas* is never able to establish an NC relation with a neg-word.

These facts are mysterious under analyses where [uNEG] needs to be checked by any semantically negative element. However, once the demand that *pas*, being a semantic negation, must carry a feature [iNEG] is dropped, the facts follow immediately. *Pas* is semantically negative but lacks a feature [iNEG], and therefore cannot establish Agree relations with neg-words. Given the learnability algorithm, this follows directly: if there is no instance of *pas* responsible for the checking of a feature [uNEG], it cannot be assigned a feature [iNEG]. This gives rise to the following inventory of French negative elements: the only element carrying [iNEG] is the abstract negative operator Op$_\neg$; neg-words carry [uNEG] and therefore must be checked by this abstract negator. *Ne*, finally, is an NPI and may appear under the scope of Op$_\neg$, *pas* and other DE contexts.

(40) French negative elements:
  pas   ¬
  ne   NPI
  NEG-words   [uNEG]   ∃
  Op$_\neg$ [iNEG]   ¬

This connection between so-called [uF]s and their corresponding semantics seems weaker than previously assumed—something unexpected under (10), but predicted under (11), which can therefore be taken as evidence in favour of this position.

5.3.7 Invisible Negative Concord: English and Hindi/Punjabi

Finally, the question arises of how the invisible NC patterns in English and Hindi/Punjabi may be acquired. At first sight, these examples seem to be more problematic for the learnability algorithm, as the number of negative forms and negative meanings in a sentence are the same. Hence, the initial assumption in (6), repeated below as (41), is not immediately falsified by the input data.

(41) Assume a 1:1 correspondence between morphemes and semantic content

At the same time, as we already saw in Subsection 4.4.2, English *n't* shows characteristic that do not match being a semantic negation. For one, the surface position of *n't* does not always coincide with the locus of semantic interpretation. This means that (6)/(41) has to be given up. As *n't* is nevertheless able to induce a semantic negation in isolation, the algorithm determines that it must carry a feature [uNEG]. This also entails that, when *n't* renders a sentence negative by itself, the semantic negation comes from an abstract negative operator carrying [iNEG].

The question remains open, then, how English *not* should be analysed. Given the fact that English *not*, unlike negative adverbs like *never*, is involved in *do*-support, it is taken to be a specifier of a dedicated NegP, and it is likely to assume that it carries [iNEG] and is not just a semantic negation. This begs the question of how children acquire the information that *not* carries [iNEG] in the absence of any NC relations between *n't* and *not*. A cue for that is the fact that English exhibits *do*-support in negative sentences, as in (42).

(42) Mary does *not* walk

The fact that *not* triggers *do*-support, but other negative phrases do not do so, shows that *not* must share a (negative) feature with *n't*. Since the position of *not* in the sentence coincides with the locus of semantic negation, this forms evidence for the child that *not* carries [iNEG] and can't carry [uNEG].

As for the syntactic/semantic status of NIs, given that verbs may raise across them (see (43)), the child is able to work out that these NIs do not occupy the specifier position of a NegP (contrary to Haegeman 1995 and many others).

(43) a. Mary has₁ never t₁ left
      b. Is₁ *nobody* t₁ willing to believe this?

Also, since every NI induces a semantic negation of its own, the first step of the learning algorithm triggers the hypothesis that such NIs are purely semantic negations and do not carry any feature [iNEG]/[uNEG]. As NIs do not participate in any NC configuration and never check off the [uNEG] feature of any negative head, this initial hypothesis will not be falsified.

This leads to the following feature inventory of English negative elements:

(44) English negative elements:
      n't   [uNEG]
      Op¬   [iNEG]   ¬
      not   [iNEG]   ¬
      negative indefinites   ¬∃

The learnability of other examples of invisible NC languages is more straightforward. In Hindi and Punjabi, languages that crucially lack neg-words, the

NM may appear in a position where it appears below an NPI, even though this NPI itself is under the scope of negation, as shown below (repeated from Subsection 4.4.3):

(45) a. koyii   bhii   nahii gayaa   (Hindi)
        somebody even   NEG   go.PRF.M.SG
        'No one went'
     b. koyii   vii   nayii gayaa   (Punjabi)
        somebody even   NEG   go.PRF.M.SG
        'No one went'

As indicated in Subsection 4.4.3, such NPIs cannot reconstruct to a position below negation; hence, the conclusion is inevitable to the child that the NM itself is not the semantic negation, but rather marks the presence of a higher covert negative operator. Consequently, the child reaches the following conclusion about the feature inventory of Hindi/Punjabi negative elements:

(46) Hindi/Punjabi negative elements:
     nahii/nayii [uNEG]
     Op₋   [iNEG]   ¬

5.3.8 Non-negative licensers of neg-words

The learning algorithm thus correctly predicts what feature inventories emerge in what kind of NC language, including partial or invisible NC languages. In addition, this feature learnability algorithm provides the solution to the missing puzzle that the NC analysis has been facing so far: how can (Strawson-)DE, but non-negative (i.e., non-AA) elements license neg-words, and why is this only the case in a number of NC languages?

As I have outlined, under the proposed learnability algorithm, the mapping between a semantic and a corresponding [iF] is not always 1:1. As long as it can be acquired that a particular element carries a feature [iNEG], there is no requirement that it must be semantically negative—just as semantic negativity does not require that a particular element carries a feature [iNEG], as we saw is the case for French. This then solves one of the open problems for the analysis of NC, namely those cases where semantically non-negative (albeit DE) elements can license (semantically non-negative) neg-words in the sense that they appear to be able to check off the neg-words' [uNEG]-features.

Take again the relevant Spanish examples from Herburger (2001):

(47) a. Pedro compró el terreno sin contarselo a *nadie* (Spanish)
Pedro bought the land without telling to NEG-body
'Peter bought the land without telling anybody'
b. Antec de hacer *nada*, debes lavarle las manos.
before of do NEG-thing, must.2SG wash.CL the hands
'Before doing anything, you should wash your hands'

Given the learning algorithm, and especially the rule in (9) that states that [iF] must be assigned to all those elements that are responsible for the rest of the grammatical occurrences of [uF], it follows that *sin* ('without') and *antec* ('before') in Spanish must be assigned a feature [iNEG]. Otherwise, the grammaticality of the examples in (47) cannot be accounted for by the language learner. For an element to be assigned [iNEG] it is no longer necessary that it is semantically negative. In fact, one cannot even allude to an abstract negative operator being present, since the semantic negation that it would bring in is absent from the meaning of the sentence it appears in.

If, however, semantic negation is not a prerequisite for such licensers of neg-words to carry [iNEG], this may lead to an overgeneralization. In principle, now, every expression could be assigned a feature [iNEG] (as long as this feature can be acquired to be present), but the facts suggest that only (Strawson-)DE elements carry them. Hence, the question arises of what is responsible for the restriction of such non-negative licensers to (Strawson-)DE elements?

This can be readily explained in diachronic terms. Neg-words historically emerge from NPIs (see Roberts and Roussou 2003; Jäger 2010), as do many NMs (see Chapter 6 for more discussion and examples). So, what used to be an instance of NPI licensing must have been reanalysed as an instance of syntactic Agree. An original NPI got licensed in the standard NPI licensing contexts. After these NPIs have been reanalysed into neg-words, the child, confronted with what is still a robust enough quantity of such licensed neg-words, cannot do anything else but assign to the original NPI licenser a feature [iNEG], according to step (9) in the learning algorithm. The diachronic pattern is then as in (48). The fact that semantically non-negative licensers of neg-words are DE is then the mere result of the diachronic development of neg-words out of NPIs. Since the presence of a feature [iNEG] on semantically non-negative licensers of neg-words must be diachronically motivated and since NPIs are the predecessors of neg-words, the fact that only DE elements may carry [iNEG] now immediately follows, without having to postulate that this is a formal requirement on NC systems.

(48) DE context   NPI   →
      DE context$_{[iNEG]}$ NEG-word$_{[uNEG]}$

The fact that such semantically non-negative NPI licensers are only attested in some NC languages now has to do with the fact that a robust input is needed for the child to be able to assign these licensers a feature [uNEG]. If the relevant input decreases in terms of frequency, there is no longer a cue present, and the relevant elements can no longer be acquired as carrying a feature [iNEG]. This may explain the difference, for instance, between Russian and Czech *bez* ('without'). Under the assumption that Czech *bez* still carries [iNEG] (at least for those speakers who accept (49a)), but that Russian *bez* does not do so (49b), it follows that expressions like *bez* can, but do not have to, participate in NC relations:

(49) a. %Bez_[iNEG] *nikoho*_[uNEG]   (Czech)
without NEG-body
'without anybody'
b. *Bez *nikogo*_[uNEG]   (Russian)
without NEG-body
'without anybody'

This view thus correctly answers the questions I have raised. By contrast, under any of the alternative views of NC where all non-negative licensers of neg-words should contain some underlying negation, these facts cannot be derived. Under such a view, any non-negative licenser should still have some negation as part of its lexical decomposition. As all these licensers are in some sense still felt to be somewhat negative (they are all DE), such an assumption might not be too unnatural. However, such accounts would face serious problems.

First, as noted, languages vary both cross-linguistically and intra-linguistically to quite a large extent with respect to whether these contexts may license neg-words, as I have shown for Russian and Czech *bez* ('without'). While, in Russian, *bez* is systematically excluded from participating in NC constructions, this is possible for most speakers of Czech. Consequently, languages should then cross-linguistically and language-internally differ with respect to whether some DE contexts are lexically decomposed into some negative element and others not. However, as there is no independent motivation for this assumption, this would be an instance of circular reasoning (though see Chapters 6–7 and 11 for more discussion on lexical decomposition of negative elements). Second, even if expressions like Spanish *antec* ('before') or Czech *bez* ('without') contained an abstract negative operator in their lexical decomposition, the [iNEG] feature on this operator could never stand in a c-command relation with any of the neg-words it licenses, unless specific ad hoc assumptions were to be made. Hence, the facts show that one cannot straightforwardly assume that every element that may license an element carrying [uNEG] contains a decomposable semantic negation.

5.4 Consequences in the domain of language variation, acquisition, and change

The proposal outlined in the previous sections makes several empirical predictions in the domains of language variation, language acquisition, and language change. I will discuss these predictions for each empirical domain separately in the three following subsections.

5.4.1 Types of Negative Concord systems: Language variation

Although the range of variation that can be attested among types of NC systems is fairly rich—and richer than has generally been assumed in the literature—it is not the case that every imaginary NC system is a possible one. The learnability algorithm also directly or indirectly rules out various negation systems.

One of the strongest predictions in this sense is that languages without NC may not exhibit an overt NM that occupies a head position in the clausal spine. The acquisitional procedure outlined in Section 5.2 predicts that NC languages are languages that have a formal negative feature at their disposal, whereas DN languages do not. Only if there is some instance of NC present in the language, can [uF]s and [iF]s be acquired. A consequence of that is that, if non-NC languages do not have a formal negative feature at their disposal, they cannot project such a feature either (following Giorgi and Pianesi 1997), as illustrated in (50).

(50)   a. NC: [u/iNEG]/[X]   b. No NC: [X]

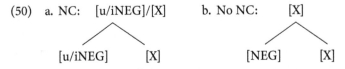

As a result, negative heads (X°) are predicted to be unavailable in languages without NC. This prediction is borne out (on the basis of the extensive cross-linguistic and language-internal survey in Zeijlstra 2004; see also Zeijlstra 2008a, b). There appears to be no language without NC which exhibits an NM that is a syntactic head. Traditional counterexamples to this prediction, English or languages like Hindi/Punjabi, which have an NM that heads a projection in the clausal spine but which nevertheless do not yield classical NC patterns, underlyingly turn out to be (invisible) NC languages.

Apart from this main constraint on types of NC languages, it is not the case that anything goes when it comes to NC languages. For instance, what has not been attested so far either, are partial NC systems where the boundary between formal and semantically negative elements lies within the series of neg-words. There are no languages, to the best of my knowledge, where an indefinite like *nobody* would always behave like an NQ, but where an indefinite like *never* would exhibit prototypical neg-word behaviour. This is, however, not ruled out by the proposed algorithm. At the same time, as we will see in Chapter 6, even though such languages would be formally possible, they may be independently ruled out (or be extremely rare) for diachronic reasons; it would be extremely hard, if not outright impossible, for such languages to emerge out of other, more standard, NC or DN systems.

5.4.2 Types of Negative Concord systems: Language acquisition

The learning algorithm for (negative) features also makes particular predictions with respect to the acquisition of negation and NC. In short, it predicts that children take as their starting assumption that every negative form corresponds to a negative meaning. Only if the language input violates this original hypothesis can the child postulate the presence of formal [iNEG]s and [uNEG]s.

This prediction has two related consequences. First, DN languages are the default when it comes to the acquisition of negation; and, second, NC is a derived system. As for the first consequence, this explains the learnability of DN languages. DN constructions are relatively rare and are generally used only to negate previously uttered negative claims (cf. Horn 1989; Zeijlstra 2014). Given their poor frequency, DN constructions can hardly be taken as sufficient cues for the acquisition of DN. However, if DN is nothing but the absence of NC, i.e., renders a plain 1:1 relation between negative form and negative meaning, it is readily learnable as such. In fact, it is even predicted that children should go through a DN stage before they acquire NC.

This latter prediction seems to be borne out. As shown initially in Klima and Bellugi (1966), and Bellugi (1967), and later on confirmed in de Villiers and de Villiers (1985), Déprez and Pierce (1993), Drozd (1995), and, more recently, in Thornton and Tesan (2013) and Thornton et al. (2016), children go through various stages when acquiring the way negation is expressed in their target language. Crucial is that these stages do not necessarily reflect high-frequency instances of ways of expressing negation in the adult grammar. This is especially telling in the case of English, where children first go through a stage where negation is expressed by a sentence-initial NM, as the following examples, taken from Thornton and Tesan (2013), who quote Bellugi (1967), show.

(51) a. No sit there
 b. Not a teddy bear
 c. Not the sun shining

After this first stage, they reach a second stage where they always use the negation as a sentence-internal adverbial. Examples, again taken from Thornton and Tesan

(2013), are in (52), where the position of the negation is similar to that of other adverbs:

(52) a. He no bite you
      b. I no want envelope

In this stage, children also start using what look like negative auxiliaries (53), but, as Bellugi argues, those should still be interpreted as adverbials and not as real auxiliaries. One of the reasons for this is that the children's early such elements are restricted to *don't* and *can't*, also in third-person contexts. Another reason why such elements are more likely to be adverbial units is that the adult-like auxiliary system is 'largely absent' at this second stage (Bellugi 1967: 64); NMs, therefore, cannot have been integrated in the tense-agreement system.

(53) a. I can't catch you
      b. I don't sit on Cromer coffee
      c. It don't fit in here

Only in the third stage will children use negative auxiliary verbs (*don't, doesn't, can't*, etc.).

The question that immediately arises is why children do not take over the most frequently used form to negate a sentence in the adult language, but rather go through a stage that significantly deviates from that. According to Thornton and Tesan (2013), and followed up on in Thornton et al. (2016), the idea is that the children indeed follow a trajectory along the lines of the proposed learning algorithm (after Zeijlstra 2008b, 2014) and use a single form for semantic negation.

Still, that does not fully explain why children would not use the negative head *n't* when expressing negation. However, according to the learnability algorithm, a negative head (i.e., the negative feature that can syntactically project) can only be acquired if the language input contains NC. Thornton and Tesan (2013) and Thornton et al. (2016) hypothesize that children recognize that English has a negative head (i.e., *n't*), and, therefore, must also assign NC interpretations to sentences with two negations, despite the absence of evidence for this interpretation in the adult input. The existence of *n't* must involve [uNEG]s, and, therefore, the child must take the inventory of English negative elements to contain formal negative features [iNEG]/[uNEG]. Naturally, the question arises why children would not only assign [uNEG] to *n't* and no [iNEG]-feature to any other overt negative element (apart from *not*).[2] However, if children, at the stage where they acquire that auxiliaries like *don't, doesn't,* and *can't* consist of a separate negative head, infer

---

[2] In addition, one may allude to Roberts' (2007) principle of Input Generalization, which takes children to maximally exploit a formal feature once acquired. According to Input Generalization, the child may then assign [iNEG] features to neg-words and later on remove them again if there is evidence for that.

that the language must exhibit NC constructions, even if the direct evidence at first sight is lacking, this forms strong support for the proposed learning algorithm.

Thornton and Tesan (2013) present a longitudinal study where they show that this indeed the case. Data come from Adam and Sarah, in (54) and (55), respectively, who indeed use NC constructions after having acquired that *n't* is a syntactic head.

(54) a. She is not having no picnic (3;11) file 40
b. I just don't want nothing in there (4;0) file 42
c. I don't want to share none of my books (4;6) file 49
d. I'm not scared of nothing (4;7) file 51

(55) a. I didn't do nothing (3;5) file 63
b. I didn't call him nothing (3;8) file 72
c. Because nobody didn't broke it (4;5) file 107
d. I don't think I can do this no more (4;8) file 121

Strikingly, these children do not use NC constructions in earlier stages. This cannot be due to the semantic complexity of such expressions, given that they could already produce counterparts involving an NPI like *any*, as the following examples from Bellugi, presented again in Thornton and Tesan (2013), show:

(56) a. Boomer's not hungry any more. (2;0.3)
b. Don't touch anything! (2;0.7)
c. I not a dog any more (2;0.15)
d. I'm not scared any more (2;0.18)
e. There's no any more [= no cookies left] (2;0.24)
f. Girl's not sad any more (2;0.25)

Hence, it appears that English children went from a DN stage, via a full NC stage, to the target stage—a development strongly in line with the proposed learning algorithm. In Thornton et al. (2016), this hypothesis has further been investigated in a comprehension study with 20 three- to five-year-old children and a control group of 15 adults. Again, the adult participants mostly assigned a DN interpretation to the relevant sentences containing multiple negative expressions, whereas the child participants assigned an NC interpretation, thus confirming the earlier conclusions based on the longitudinal studies.

Note that the proposed algorithm makes more predictions than discussed here. One question that arises, for instance, is whether, in other NC languages, children also pass through a DN stage, or whether children acquiring strict NC languages must go through a Non-strict NC stage, as they would first have to hypothesize that the NM is [iNEG]. Such questions thus call for future research along the lines I have presented (see Chapter 16).

5.4.3 Consequences for language change

A third empirical domain where the consequences of the learnability algorithm become manifest is language change. As outlined in the previous subsection, children must pass through a DN phase before they can acquire NC (systems). If NC systems are derived and more marked in terms of both acquisition and featural complexity (the former naturally relating to the latter), the question arises as to why languages would exhibit NC in the first place, and, moreover, why NC languages across the world show the attested range of variation.

The most natural explanation for this is language change. If independently triggered changes somewhere in the negation system may alter the language input for new generations, that would force them to analyse the negation system of their target language differently from the one belonging to the previous stage. As it is a very well-known fact that markers of negation undergo a substantial amount of change, it makes sense to investigate how changes in the domain of NMs may trigger changes from DN to NC and vice versa, as well as other changes, such as the emergence of partial or invisible NC or other unusual NC systems, such as the system attested in Afrikaans A. The same holds for the change from Strict to Non-strict NC languages. If such changes can indeed trigger the emergence of the various NC systems attested, the cross-linguistically attested landscape of types of NC (and DN) can be naturally explained. In the next chapter, diachronic patterns attested in the domain of negation and NC, for that reason, will be discussed in detail.

5.5 Conclusions

In this chapter, I have focused on the relation between carrying an interpretable formal negative feature [iNEG] and being semantically negative, and I have argued, both theoretically and empirically, that, even though the two often go hand in hand, they should be formally disentangled. There are cases where a particular element may carry [iNEG] despite being semantically non-negative, as is the case with licensers of neg-words that are not negative (such as adverbs meaning 'before', or predicates conveying doubt in NC languages like Spanish). There are also examples of semantically negative elements that lack formal negative features, such as the French NM *pas* or English NIs, such as *nobody* or *never*.

If the relation between an [iNEG] and being semantically negative is not 1:1, this calls for a learnability algorithm that determines which element should be assigned a formal negative feature (if any). In this chapter, I have presented such a mechanism, and I have also outlined the conditions under which existing types of NC systems can be acquired. Furthermore, I have spelled out the empirical consequences of this learnability algorithm for the domains of language variation, acquisition, and change. For one, it is predicted that only in NC languages can formal negative features be acquired, which, in turn, can project; consequently, every language that exhibits an NM that is a syntactic head in the clausal spine must also be an NC language, a prediction that appears to be borne out. Also, it has been pointed out that every language learner must start with the hypothesis that the target language is a DN language, unless there is evidence to the contrary—again, a prediction that appears to be correct (though see Nicolae and Yatsushiro 2020 for different results; see also Chapter 16). Finally, and relatedly, I have argued that the emergence of NC and/or particular kinds of NC systems must always be the consequence of additional syntactic changes in the domain of negation. As we will discuss more thoroughly in the next chapter, changes with respect to the presence and type of NC are indeed generally due to independent syntactic developments of NMs in the language, often along the lines of Jespersen's Cycle.

6
Diachronic developments in the domain of negation and Negative Concord

6.1 The nature of negative features

If NC systems are more marked in terms of both acquisitional and featural complexity (the former naturally relating to the latter), the question arises of why languages would exhibit NC in the first place, and, moreover, why NC languages across the world show the attested range of variation. Why would not every language adhere to Humboldt's principle, which, in this case, would mean a 1:1 correspondence between negative form and negative meaning? Why would languages exploit formal negative features [i/uNEG] in the first place, given that their existence is not something given by UG?

As argued for in the previous chapter, the most natural explanation for this is language change. If independently triggered changes somewhere in the negation system may alter the language input for new generations, that would force these new generations to analyse the negation system of their target language differently from the previous one. As it is a very well-known fact that markers of negation undergo a substantial amount of change, it makes sense to investigate how changes in the domain of NMs can trigger changes from DN to NC and vice versa, as well as other changes, such as the emergence of partial or invisible NC or other unusual NC systems, like the one attested in Afrikaans A, or the change from Strict to Non-strict NC languages. If such changes can indeed trigger the emergence of the various NC systems attested, the cross-linguistically attested landscape of types of NC (and DN) receives a natural explanation.

In the subsequent sections, we will discuss such patterns of language change at length. First, in Section 6.2, I will discuss the general pattern that is known as *Jespersen's Cycle*. In Section 6.3, I will discuss patterns where NC emerges or where one type of NC changes into another type of NC—changes involving the emergence of formal negative features [i/uNEG]. In Section 6.4, I will focus on the mirror image, namely the disappearance of NC or the disappearance of [i/uNEG] features. In Section 6.5, I will briefly address the question why, in the course of time, only negated existentials have emerged (first as neg-words, then as NIs), but apparently no negated universals—a problem known as the *NALL*-problem: Why is there no language in the world with a single lexical item meaning 'not all'? Section 6.6 concludes.

6.2 Jespersen's Cycle

As outlined in Section 6.1 and in the previous chapter, changes in the domain of NMs may have strong effects on the emergence of particular types of NC and DN. Let us therefore look at what kinds of changes in the domain of NMs can be attested in the first place.

Already in 1917, the Danish grammarian and philosopher Otto Jespersen observed a general tendency in the expression of negation in various languages:

> The history of negative expressions in various languages makes us witness the following curious fluctuation; the original negative adverb is first weakened, then found insufficient and therefore strengthened, generally through some additional word, and in its turn may be felt as the negative proper and may then in course of time be subject to the same development as the original word.
>
> (Jespersen 1917: 4).

Jespersen supports this claim with a number of examples from different languages in which such a development can indeed be found. This change did not only happen in English or the Germanic languages (such as Dutch or German) where the development was very similar, but also in other languages where historical data have remained (e.g., the Slavic languages, the Romance languages, Greek, and several varieties of Arabic). Take, for instance, the way that the expression 'I don't say' changed from Old Latin to Colloquial French or French-based creoles.

(1)   a. ˚Ne dico   Proto-Latin[1]
      b. ˚Ne dico oinom/oenum   Proto-Latin
      c. Non dico   Classical Latin
      d. Jeo ne di   Old French
      e. Je ne dis (pas)   Middle French
      f. Je ne dis pas   Modern French
      g. Je (ne) dis pas   Colloquial French
      h. Je dis pas   Quebecois
      i. Je pa di   Haitian French Creole

Without providing full examples (these can be found in Zeijlstra 2004, 2016a, among others, and references therein), what we see is that, in Latin, the weaker form *ne* was strengthened by an additional minimizer ˚*oinom/oenum* ('one (thing)'), which merged into Classical Latin *non*. In Old French, it got weakened to *ne* and emphasized by a second element *pas*, which originally meant 'step' and nowadays, in spoken colloquial French, fully replaces the original NM *ne*. In some

---

[1] The asterisk (˚) here indicates that the examples are reconstructed. I put this asterisk in superscript to distinguish it from the plain asterisk (*) that marks ungrammaticality.

French-based creole languages such as Haitian French Creole, *pas* has phonologically weakened yet again, displaying the same behaviour as Old Latin and Old French *ne*. Other examples, also from languages outside the Indo-European language family, and additional discussion can be found in, for instance, Chatzopoulou 2012; Devos et al. 2010, 2013; Van der Auwera 2010, 2011; Van Gelderen 2008, 2009, 2011; Eckardt 2006, 2012; and Willis et al. 2013.

Now, two types of questions arise. First, why is it that such changes happen? What causes the original NM to weaken, such that it seems to require the additional support of a second NM? And why does this new NM take over the role of the original one? Second, what is the source of these NMs? In English, the NM stemmed from *nawiht*, an NQ meaning 'nothing'. But in French, *pas* originally meant 'step', a meaning that at first seems quite remote from the meaning of 'not'. Let's look at both questions in more detail.

Jespersen attributes the negative cycle to the tension between the phonological weakness of the old NM and the need to strongly mark the sentence as being negative. If an NM such as English or French *ne* becomes phonologically too weak to fully function as the negator of the sentence, a second, supporting NM jumps in.

Jespersen's hypothesis has raised some criticism, both empirically and theoretically. Empirically, second NMs can also emerge in languages in which the original NM does not count as phonologically weak, as was the case in Greek (cf. Kiparsky and Condoravdi 2006). More importantly, phonological weakening in general does not drive morphosyntactic change, but rather results from it. Even phonologically weak elements can be very robust markers of a particular semantics (e.g., past-tense morphology is quite often phonologically rather weak, but, nevertheless, does not fail in fulfilling its function). Partly for these reasons, Kiparsky and Condoravdi (2006) argue that something else must be at hand. These scholars argue that every language must be able to express both plain negation and emphatic negation. To get a feeling for the distinction, look at the minimal pair in (2).

(2) a. I didn't read
    b. I didn't read anything

Truth-conditionally, the two sentences in (2) are identical: If somebody did not read anything, that person did not read; and if somebody did not read, she did not read anything. Yet, (2b) feels more emphatic than (2a), because (2b) puts a strong focus on the absence of anything that could have been read by the speaker. English is a language that expresses plain negation by means of an NM (often *n't*, sometimes *not*) and has a number of additional means at its disposal to further emphasize negation (such as indefinites of the *any*-series, cf. Haspelmath 1997). In general, languages can add two types of elements to emphasize what would otherwise be a plain negation: *minimizers* and *generalizers*. Minimizers are elements that denote (extremely) small amounts of something. *A sip* in *I didn't drink a sip* is a good example of a minimizer that gives rise to an emphatic effect in negative contexts. The reading that emerges is that the speaker did not even drink the smallest amount possible. Generalizers are elements that, in contrast, extend the domain of quantification. *Anything* in (2b) is a good example: It says that, of an extended set of things that could have been read, the speaker did not read even one. But why would the requirement that negation can be expressed both emphatically and non-emphatically trigger syntactic change? Why could the two strategies in a particular language not remain constant over time?

Following work by Dahl (2001), Kiparsky and Condoravdi (2006) allude to a general semantic weakening mechanism, saying that what is marked emphatically loses its emphatic power in the course of time. If a particular emphasizing strategy is used more and more often, it tends to inflate and become less emphatic. As a result, it will be used even more frequently, given that the originally emphasized expression can also be used to describe situations that require less of a negative emphasis. If this trend continues, at some point, the original strategy for emphasizing negation ends up being the plain way of expressing negation, and becomes obligatory. The old NM then loses its function of expressing plain negation and, being superfluous, will disappear. The new marker (and, originally emphasizer) of negation, then, has taken over the role of the plain negator, and new supportive elements to express emphatic negation may emerge, thus continuing the cycle.

A particular prediction of Kiparsky and Condoravdi's proposal is that NMs may have different diachronic sources: They could have developed out of minimizers or out of generalizers (generally, quantifiers). This prediction seems to be borne out. In the languages discussed thus far, we can already identify these two possible origins, and other languages confirm this picture.

French *pas*, as mentioned earlier, developed from the meaning 'step'. Although this meaning is quite remote from the semantics of negation, it is clear how it can be used as a minimizer. Verbs expressing movement can be readily emphasized by including an element denoting a very small amount of moved distance, such as a step. The question that arises, though, is why exactly this minimizer was developed into the novel NM instead of any other minimizer. Eckardt (2006) has investigated the development of *pas* and similar French minimizers, and shown that, in the early stages, a whole series of supporting minimizers in French were exploited: *pas* ('step'), *point* ('point'), *mie* ('crumb'), *goutte* ('drop'), and many more. All of these, to a greater or lesser extent, were grammaticalized into more general minimizers (losing their original lexical meaning), and it was in a way a historical accident that, in the end, *pas* became the standard minimizer that took over the role of negation (in various southern varieties of French, *point* is still used). However, it was certainly not an accident that a minimizer ended up as a second NM.

Other languages employ generalizers rather than minimizers to emphasize negation. Kiparsky and Condoravdi present data not only from Greek, where various generalizers reinforced plain negation, but also from English, where *nawiht* (> *naught* > *not*) is an example of a quantifier that was initially used to emphasize an additional NM before it became a marker of negation itself. Interestingly though, the morphology of *nawiht* is already marked for negation, suggesting that it is better translated as 'nothing' than as 'a thing'. However, since English (like all other Germanic languages at this stage) was an NC language, the combination *ne* and *nawiht* jointly had a meaning contribution that contained one semantic negation; *nawiht* alone contributed an additional indefinite meaning contribution like 'anything', not an extra negation. Thus, *nawiht* counts as a generalizer as well.

With this in mind, let us look at how the various changes in the system of NMs triggered the emergence of DN and NC systems in the various languages discussed.

6.3 The emergence of Negative Concord

Perhaps the most striking question in the domain of negation and NC is how it is possible that an NC system emerges in a language. Why would it be that languages deviate from a 1:1 mapping between negative form and meaning, and instead exhibit a many:1 mapping? One hypothesis that immediately comes to mind is that, because of Jespersen's Cycle, a second NM emerges independently, which, when it forms a joint negation with the original NM, renders the language an NC language. Then, the strict 1:1 mapping between negative form and meaning is disrupted. In order to test this hypothesis, one should look at a language where, along the lines of Jespersen's Cycle, this 1:1 relation between negative form and negative meaning became obsolete. Unfortunately, there are not that many languages that have shown such a change in their history. For instance, English and Greek, were already NC languages in the earlier phases of Jespersen's Cycle. What happened in those languages was that the original NM (*ne* in English; *ou* in Greek) got reinforced by an already existing neg-word (*nawith* 'neg-thing' in English; *oudhen* 'neg-thing' in Greek). In such languages, one cannot investigate the emergence of NC, as the languages were already NC languages before entering the second phase of Jespersen's Cycle.

Other languages, however, provide a better window into the emergence of NC and the various subtypes thereof. First, by considering the case of French in Subsection 6.3.1, we will see how NC systems could have emerged in general. Then, in Subsection 6.3.2, we will look at the emergence of Non-strict NC out of Strict NC (illustrated for Romance languages), the emergence of the mirror system in Afrikaans A (Subsection 6.3.3), and the emergence of the partial NC systems of French (Subsection 6.3.4) and English (Subsection 6.3.5). The next section will then spell out how NC systems may disappear in a language.

6.3.1 The emergence of French Negative Concord

Luckily for our purposes, certain languages also had positive expressions becoming negative reinforcers. Those are languages where, instead of negatively marked generalizers, a positive minimizer or generalizer took up the role of additional NM. A good example of such a language, as mentioned in the previous section, is French, though similar patterns have also been observed for various (northern) varieties of Italian (cf., among others, Zanuttini 1997; Poletto 2008).

As shown by Eckardt (2006), and also discussed in detail in Roberts and Roussou (2003), French *ne* (and, before that, *non*) started out as a single NM that, according to Kiparsky and Condoravdi, was not able to yield emphatic negation any more, and therefore required additional material to express increased negative force. Owing to the unavailability of existing neg-words, in this language, positive generalizers, such as *personne* ('person') or *rien* ('thing'), or positive minimizers, such as *pas* 'step', *point* ('point'), *mie* ('crumb'), were added to the negation to strengthen it.

While, originally, in Old French (appr. AD 900–1300), those expressions could only be literally interpreted, as shown in (3) below for *pas* ('step') and *rien* ('thing'), taken from Eckardt (2003), later on, they could also yield a more general interpretation. For instance, in (4), *pas* no longer means 'step', nor does *mie* mean 'crumb'.

(3)   a. *Ne* vus leist pas aler avant   (Old French[2,3])
         NEG you is-allowed step to-go forward
         'You may not go forward a step'

      b. D'avanture *ne* sai je rien ...
         of adventure NEG know I thing
         'Of adventure, I don't know anything ...'

(4)   a. N' i ot rei, prince ne baron, Qui *pas* m' i pöust contrester
                                              (Middle French[4,5])
         NEG there has king prince nor baron who 'pas' me there could contradict
         'There is no king, prince or baron who could even/at all contradict me there'

      b. Quel part qu'il alt, *ne* poet *mie* cäir
         which part that-he goes NEG can 'mie' fall
         'Wherever he goes, he cannot fall a bit'

---

[2] [Benedeit SBrendan 1793], TL 6, 411, 26.
[3] [Ch. lyon 368], TL 8, 1279, 38.
[4] [Troie 16865], TL 7, 410, 31.
[5] [Ch. Rol. 2034], TL 6, 15, 23.

As Eckardt shows, the minimizers that originally meant 'step', 'thing', 'crumb', etc. were used to strengthen the negation. However, in line with Kiparsky and Condoravdi, such strengtheners became obligatory over time, lost their literal reading, and got semantically bleached into expressions meaning 'even', 'at all', or 'a bit'. As is well-known from the literature on NPI-hood, and as will be discussed in great detail in Chapters 9–10, minimizers or other indefinite expressions that are obligatorily focused behave as NPIs. Hence, the new strengtheners were all NPIs with a bleached interpretation. The originally positive expressions *personne* and *rien* were reanalysed as 'anybody' and 'anything' accordingly.

At this stage, virtually every occurrence of *ne* should be accompanied by such NPIs, that were either indefinites or pure strengtheners. Such NPIs could, in the earlier stages of the change, appear in all kinds of DE contexts, and thus count as weak NPIs (see (5)), but were later on restricted to purely negative contexts—presumably an effect of the relatively high frequency of negation as their licenser (cf. Roberts and Roussou 2003; Eckardt 2006; though see also Chapter 10)—and became strong NPIs.

(5) a. Je doute que personne y réussisse. (Middle French[6,7,8])
    I doubt that anyone there succeed
    'I doubt that anyone might succeed at it'
  b. Suis je pas bele dame e gente, Digne de servir un preudome?
    am I 'pas' beautiful lady and gentle worthy to serve a gentleman
    'Am I not a beautiful lady and gentle, worthy to serve a gentleman?'

Now, the following cocktail emerged. French *ne* could not be used without an additional strengthener, even though the strengthening effect has become obsolete itself, and these (now semantically vacuous) reinforcers of negation only appeared in sentences that were fully negative themselves—therefore, they all contained *ne*. In addition, the competition between the various possible strengtheners disappeared, basically leaving *pas* (and sometimes *point*) and the future neg-words as the only available candidates to be an additional negation.

Therefore, at this stage, language learners had to analyse *pas* as an obligatory part of the negation. It only appeared in negative sentences and served no other function than co-expressing negation. Thus, language learners, following the learnability algorithm presented earlier, would assign formal features [uNEG] to both *pas* and *ne* (as neither of the two could be taken to be the main negator). In the same vein, with *ne* no longer being able to act as a main negation itself, elements like *personne* and *rien* were taken by language learners to be part of the negation system and got assigned [uNEG] as well—also because multiple occurrences of such elements would not add more semantic negations. When interpreting a sentence like *Je ne dis rien* (I neg say thing 'I don't say anything'),

[6] Maurice Grevisse, *Le bon usage*, § 981.
[7] *Roman de la Rose*, CFMA, 5768, SATF 5798.
[8] The negation in the translation is included to reflect the strengthened rhetoric effect of *pas*. *Pas*, at this stage, could not be used as a single negation in itself.

a language-learning child could no longer assume that *ne* was the only source for the negation. The behaviour of *ne* in the language input was no longer compatible with that of a plain NM. Consequently, the child should take *rien* (and *personne*, etc.) to contain formal negative features as well.

Crucially, now arriving in the Middle French era, the language was a Strict NC language where *ne*, *pas*, and the neg-words could freely be included in a single clause and thus yield an NC reading, as the following example from Molière (taken from Zeijlstra 2010a) shows:

(6) On ne veut pas rien faire ici qui vous déplaise ... (17th-c. Fr.)
    we NEG want NEG NEG-thing do that you displeases ...
    'We don't want to do anything that displeases you ...'

The emergence of Strict NC in Old / Middle French can thus be understood as the result of the need for a NM to be strengthened. This strengthening initially led to an emphatic negation reading, but the joint meaning contribution of the NM and the original strengthener shortly afterwards became the plain negation, the original strengthener being a second NM. Because of this, the language turned into an NC language, given that, now, two negative forms corresponded to one negative meaning. Strengtheners that contained an indefinite (such as elements meaning 'person' or 'thing') also became part of the negative inventory for the same reasons, and got reanalysed as neg-words (after already having undergone a change from positive indefinites, via weak NPIs, into strong NPIs). The French developments thus clearly show how the cause underlying Jespersen's Cycle triggered the emergence of NC as an epiphenomenon.

Naturally, however, this cannot be the full picture. As outlined earlier, French further developed from a Strict NC language into a partial NC language, and other languages ended up having other NC systems as well, such as Non-strict NC, the Afrikaans-A type of NC, or invisible NC. So far, we have dealt only with the emergence of Strict NC. I will next spell out how such other NC systems emerged, including French partial NC. After that, I will also discuss the mirror image of the emergence of NC and demonstrate how Jespersen's Cycle also triggered the disappearance of NC in other languages.

6.3.2 From Strict to Non-strict Negative Concord

A particular question arises with respect to the development of Non-strict NC languages. Even though they are fully learnable, one may wonder why languages would opt for the NM being semantically negative but not so for neg-words. Again, the cause of Non-strict NC is historical. At least for the Romance Non-strict NC languages, it turns out that, at earlier stages, they were Strict NC languages, as illustrated for Old Spanish in (7) and for Old Italian in (8).[9]

---

[9] For an overview of the development of Spanish negation, see Herburger (2001) and references therein. See Martins (2000) on negation in Old Romance in general.

(7) Qye a myo Cid Ruy Diaz, que *nadi* no diessen posada
    that to my Lord Ruy Diaz, that NEG-body NEG gave lodging
    (11th-c.Spanish[10])
    'that nobody gave lodging to my lord Ruy Diaz'

(8) Mai *nessuno* oma *non* si piò guarare (Old Italian[11])
    NEG-ever NEG-even-one man NEG himself can protect
    'Nobody can ever protect himself'

Given the fact that the language input during L1 acquisition contained expressions of the forms in (7)–(8), the NM was assigned a formal feature [uNEG]. However, at some point, speakers began to omit the NM *no* in such constructions (cf. Zanuttini 1997; Martins 2000). This change is not surprising, since the NM in these constructions did not contribute in any way to the semantics of the sentence, not even as a scope marker; it is semantically fully redundant. An NM preceding a neg-word can still function as a scope marker for negation (and therefore yield sentential negation), but the fact that there is an abstract negative operator located in a higher position than the preceding neg-word in examples like (7) and (8) already follows from the presence of these preverbal neg-words themselves. Note that this redundancy of the NM preceded by the neg-word has raised questions already in Subsections 4.2.2 and 5.3.5, where we discussed contemporary varieties of Catalan that display the same effect. In (Central Variety) Catalan the NM can also be optionally left out, as the example in (9) shows.

(9) *Ningú (no)* ha vist res (Central Variety Catalan)
    nobody NEG has seen NEG-thing
    'Nobody has seen anything'

Now, if the L1 input included few examples like (10) and an increasing relative frequency of examples like (11), at a certain point, the absence of cases of *no(n)* following *nessuno/nadie* should become so high that they can no longer form a cue for the NM to carry [uNEG]. As a result, following the learnability algorithm, *no(n)* must be reanalysed as [iNEG], leading to the standard Non-strict NC patterns. Hence, the reinterpretation of *no(n)* leading to the change from Strict to Non-strict NC thus correctly follows from the proposed learning algorithm.

(10) Op¬ nessuno/nadie no(n) V
     [iNEG][uNEG]   [uNEG]

---

[10] Example taken from Herburger (2001).
[11] Examples taken from Martins (2000: 194).

(11) Op¬ nessuno/nadie V
      [iNEG][uNEG]

6.3.3 The emergence of the Negative Concord system of Afrikaans A

As outlined in Section 4.3, Afrikaans A exhibits a fairly irregular NC pattern, where the NM *nie* carries [uNEG] and neg-words [iNEG]. From a synchronic perspective, it is hard to understand why Afrikaans would display such an NC pattern; but diachronically, the special circumstances under which Afrikaans, or, more specifically, its somewhat unusual negation system, emerged naturally account for that.

Standard Afrikaans / Variety A is a relatively new language, having only been codified in 1925. Many of its properties stem from its Germanic ancestry, most notably from varieties of Dutch (cf. Ponelis 1993 and Roberge 1994 for overview and discussion). However, its negation system is very different from Dutch (See den Besten 1986 and Roberge 2000). As Biberauer and Zeijlstra (2012b) argue, this is due to the fact that certain Standard Afrikaans properties have been selected for ideological reasons, most notably to establish the language as a different language from Dutch (see Deumert 2004 for more discussion).

One such departure form Dutch concerned negation. As discussed in detail in Chapter 4, every sentence containing a NI or an NM *nie* must feature the sentence-final NM *nie* (with the additional constraint that a sentence may not end with two adjacent NMs, in which case one of the two *nies* is unpronounced; cf. Biberauer 2008):

(12)   a. Ek het *nooit* die argument verstaan   *nie*   (Afrikaans A)
          I   have never the argument understood NEG
          'I have never understood the argument'
       b. Ek het *nie* die argument verstaan   *nie*
          I   have NEG the argument understood NEG
          'I did not understand the argument'
       c. Ek loop *nie*
          I   walk NEG
          'I don't walk'

Now, given the fact that the child cannot recognize that there are two NMs *nie*, the only option it has is to analyse Afrikaans *nie* as an element carrying [uNEG]: it is able to render a sentence negative in isolation (12c); but together with another marker *nie*, no DN reading is yielded (12b). For this reason, in sentences like

150   DIACHRONIC DEVELOPMENTS

(12b–c), the presence of a covert negative operator carrying [iNEG] must be postulated.

At the same time, there is no reason for the Afrikaans A language learner to assume that NIs are semantically non-negative: every NI brings in a semantic negation and is only repeated by an NM carrying [uNEG]. As there is no other negation present in the sentence (and compatible with the meaning of the sentence), the child must further postulate that NIs must carry [iNEG]. This, then, leads to the introduction of the Afrikaans A NC system.

Again, the introduction of a particular NC system directly follows from the emergence of a second NM, albeit that the reasons for this extra NM may appear slightly less natural than in other cases.

6.3.4 The emergence of French partial Negative Concord

As described above, French *pas* developed from a noun meaning 'step' via a minimizer ('a bit') into a full NM (cf. Déprez 1997; Rowlett 1998; Roberts and Roussou 2003; Eckardt 2006), along the lines of Jespersen's Cycle. While Old French had only the NM *ne* at its disposal, during the period of Middle French *ne* was more often combined with the additional minimizer *pas* (as well as various competitors, such as *point* 'point', *grain* 'piece of grain', etc.), until the embracing negation *ne ... pas* became the standard way of expressing sentential negation. As I have described (see also Roberts and Roussou 2003; Kiparsky and Condoravdi 2006; Eckardt 2006, for an overview and analyses), in Middle French, it was felt that *ne* was no longer able to express sentential negation by itself and should always be accompanied by an indefinite or minimizer.

However, in cases where there was already an indefinite reinforcer present, there was no need for *pas* to strengthen *ne*. And this was exactly the case with neg-words. Thus, combinations of *ne* and neg-words did not need an additional reinforcer, *pas*, and, therefore, combinations of *ne* with a neg-word and combinations of *ne* with *pas* have both been frequently attested, but combinations of *ne* with both a neg-word and *pas* much less so.

Note that this does not entail that it must have been forbidden by then to reinforce combinations of a neg-word and *ne* by an additional minimizer, *pas*. Early Middle French was a Strict NC language. Indeed, such combinations have been attested, such as the famous follow-up of the example in (13a) (repeated from (6)) shows:

(13) a. On ne veut pas rien faire ici qui vous déplaise ...   (17th-c. Fr.)
          One NEG want NEG NEG-thing do that you displeases ...
          'We don't want to do anything that displeases you ...'

b. ... de pas mis avec rien tu fais la récidive,
    et c'est, comme on t'a dit, trop d'une negative
... with pas put with rien you do the reoffending,
    and it.is as one you.has said too.many of.one negative
'... with "pas" put together with "rien", you repeat yourself,
    and it is, as they say, a negation too many'

However, as the follow-up in (13b) suggests, such combinations of *ne* + neg-words, reinforced by *pas*, were very rare. Most cases of negation involved either the combination of *ne* and *pas*, or *ne* and a neg-word. The reason for this rarity of combinations of *ne*, *pas*, and a neg-word is functional in nature. The need to reinforce *ne* was absent in cases where *ne* already had been reinforced by an additional indefinite, and could only lead to a very strong emphasis.

However, as from the Middle French period onwards, every instance of negation involved either *ne* and *pas*, or *ne* and a neg-word, *ne* by itself was no longer able to render a sentence negative and started to be optionally dropped. Consequently, under the learnability algorithm presented in this chapter, *ne* was no longer able to act as a cue for language learners to assign it a feature [i/uNEG], and had to be reinterpreted as an NPI. Hence, neg-words and *pas* were the only elements that could induce a semantic negation. Since neg-words could co-occur in the same clause and establish an NC relation, the loss of *ne* did not trigger a difference in their featural status. French neg-words remained carriers of [uNEG]. However, *pas*, which hardly ever co-occurred with any other neg-word in a clause, was always the sole source of negation, and could consequently no longer be assigned a formal negative feature. Language learners would start to take it to be the semantic negation and had no information present in their language input to reject that initial hypothesis. This way, the French partial NC system was born. The same development that led to *pas* becoming a NC-item also caused its absence from NC in later stages.

6.3.5 The emergence of English invisible Negative Concord

Finally, the question arises as to how the invisible NC systems like the one attested in contemporary English emerged. While, in English, Jespersen's Cycle took place in a fairly standard way—not in any substantial way different from other Germanic languages such as Dutch and German—more recent changes, starting in the 15th century, departed from the development of negation in these Germanic languages. To provide a brief history of the changes: in Old English, it was possible to include a particle *no* at the beginning of the sentence to render it negative. Examples of such sentences starting with *no*, like (14), can be found in the epic *Beowulf*, which is said to reflect the oldest versions of English, probably stemming from the 7th or 8th century.

(14)   *No ic me an herewæsmun hnagran talige, guþgeweorca, þonne Grendel hine*   (Old English; 7th–8th c.[12])
NEG I me in less battle-power count, fighting-acts, than Grendel him
'I don't count myself less than Grendel in battle power, fighting acts'

This way of expressing negation is already rather rare in this text (and might be used here to indicate contrastive focus on *ic* 'I'). A more common strategy in *Beowulf* and other Old English texts is to express negation by attaching (or prefixing) a weaker NM *ne* to the finite verb, as in (15). This NM *ne* started out as an NM for auxiliary verbs only, before its usage became more widespread.

(15)   *Nolde eorla hleo ænige þinga pone þwealcuman cwicne forlætan*
(Old English; 7th–8th c.[13])
NEG-wanted nobles protector some thing the.murderer alive free
'The protector of the nobles didn't want at all to free the murderer alive'

It looks as if Old English underwent a change in expressing negation where the phonological strong form *no* made room for weaker *ne*. Following Jespersen's observation and Kiparsky and Condoravdi (2006), one would expect to find occurrences of a second, supporting negative element to express emphatic negation. Indeed, these examples show up in 11th- and 12th-century English in many different forms: *na*, *nauht*, or *noht*. These elements have often been analysed as contracted forms of Old English *nawiht* ('no thing'), although the weaker form *na* can also be analysed as a weaker form of *no*.

(16)   *Ne het he us na leornian heofonas te make*   (Late Old English; 11th c.[14])
NEG called he us NEG learn heavens to make
'He didn't order us to make heavens'

(17)   *þis ne habbe ic nauht of earned*   (Early Middle English; 12th c.[15])
this NEG have I NEG deserved
'I haven't deserved this'

In these 11th- and 12th-century English sentences, the co-occurrence of the two NMs is the rule, but occasionally the older NM *ne* is already dropped. Consequently, *naught* could take over the role of carrier of negation and, in the end,

---

[12] *Beowulf*: 677.
[13] *Beowulf*: 791.
[14] Ælfric Lives of Saints. XVI.127.
[15] Vices and Virtues 7.9.

become the main NM, resulting in the final loss of *ne*. By the 14th century, English presented hardly any examples of this preverbal NM *ne*; only *not* (in any of its forms) was responsible for the expression of negation.

(18)   He yaf *nat* of that text a pulled hen   (Middle English; 14th c.[16])
       he gave NEG of that text a plucked hen.
       'He didn't care a thing about that text'

In this way, Jespersen's Cycle in English did not much deviate from what was attested in other languages, and ended in a way that is still the standard way of expressing negation in most Germanic languages. Sentential negation can be expressed by means of a single negative adverb *not*, that does not have to stand next to the finite or auxiliary verb, as is the case with Dutch *niet* or German *nicht*. This pattern can still be found in current English sentences such as (19).

(19)   a. She is hopefully not ill
       b. She has not written to Bill

However, the cycle continued, and, in the 15th century, *do*-support entered English and negative expressions with a *do*-auxiliary became standard. In these sentences, the NM attaches again to the auxiliary verb.

(20)   a. Dyd *not* I send unto yow one Mowntayne ...
                                    (Early Modern English; 12th c.[17])
       'Didn't I send you a Mowntayne ...'
       b. Have *not* I chosen you twelve

Later on, in these cases, *not* got reduced to the phonological weaker *n't*, as is available in Standard English, often followed by an *any*-indefinite. Two strategies for negation are thus available: either using *n't* or using *not*. While *n't* started out as a contracted form of *not*, nowadays, it behaves as a negative affix (see Zwicky and Pullum 1983).

(21)   a. I did*n't* move to England
          I did *not* move to England
       b. I did*n't* do anything
          I did *not* do anything

When available, the reduced form *n't* is nowadays the standard way of expressing negation in colloquial English, and has become the obligatory method in most American English varieties. The increasing preference of *n't* over *not* in colloquial use is illustrated by the use of *not*-contractions by American presidents from Kennedy to Clinton. While Kennedy and Nixon still used the uncontracted form

[16] Chaucer, Canterbury Tales, General Prologue, 177–8.
[17] Mowntayne. 210.

not in the majority of cases (during public debates), Bush Sr. and Clinton used this form in only in 14–17% of all cases (Yaeger-Dror and Hall-Lew 2002).

As discussed at length in Section 4.4.2, the fact that the NM could move along with the auxiliary all the way up to C is an indication that the syntactic position of this NM no longer coincides with its locus of semantic negation. Under the presented learnability algorithm, this entails that *n't* can no longer be taken to be a purely semantic negation and must be reassigned a feature [uNEG]. For the reasons spelled out in Section 4.4.2, this reanalysis could only affect those NMs that appear in a position inside NegP, namely *n't* and *not*, which are now taken to carry [uNEG] and [iNEG], respectively. Since there was no cue present for the language learner to have NIs like *nobody* or *never* become part of the NC system, such NIs did not reanalyse and remained purely semantically NIs, lacking any kind of formal negative feature. Since *n't* is the only negative element carrying [uNEG], and since *n't* cannot be overtly c-commanded by *not* in the same local domain, every instance of *n't* needs to be checked by the covert operator $Op_¬$, and hence the system of invisible NC has emerged in English.

6.4 The disappearance of Negative Concord and the emergence of double negatives

6.4.1 En/ne-deletion in Dutch

So far, we have looked at the emergence of NC systems and have seen that, for all systems, including the rarer ones, there are clear diachronic motivations for how they came into being. Now, let us look at the mirror image of the emergence of NC: the disappearance of NC and the emergence of DN. Again, it turns out that diachronic developments with respect to Jespersen's Cycle underlie such a change.

A good example language for investigating the disappearance of NC is Dutch. While Modern Dutch is clearly a DN language, Middle Dutch was an NC language, as the examples in (22), taken from Hoeksema (1997), show.

(22) a. Ic   en   sag   niemen   (Middle Dutch[18,19,20,21])
       I   NEG   saw   NEG-body
       'I didn't see anybody'

   b. Die   niemen   en   spaers
       that NEG-body   NEG   saves
       'That saves nobody'

---

[18] Taken from Hoeksema (1997).
[19] Vanden levene ons heren 2018.
[20] Brabantsche yeesten 7957–9.
[21] Middelnederlandsche gedichten en fragmenten: 189.

c. Den onderseten *niet en* was // gheoorlooft *niets* *niet* met
the shepherds NEG was // allowed NEG-thing NEG with
allen // aen enen andren paus te vallen
all PRT an other pope to attack
'The shepherds were not at all allowed to attack another pope together'
d. Welc es .i groet berch, ende een hoech,
which is a big mountain and a high,
daer *noyt* *niemen* over *ne* vloech?
there NEG-ever NEG-body about NEG flew
'Which is a big and high mountain, that nobody ever flew above?'

In terms of Jespersen's Cycle, Middle Dutch has two NMs: a negative head *en/ne* and a phrasal NM *niet*, as shown in (23):

(23) a. En laettine mi spreke niet (13th-c. Dutch,[22,23,24])
NEG let.he me speak NEG
'If he doesn't let me speak'
b. Sine ware niet genedert heden
she.NEG were NEG humiliated currently
'She wasn't humiliated at that time'
c. Dat si niet en sach dat si sochte.
that she NEG saw that she looked-for
'That she didn't see what she looked for'

Even though *ne/en* started out as the sole NM in Old Dutch (cf. Zeijlstra 2004), which was also an NC variety, in Middle Dutch, the NM *en/ne* must occur in all sentences containing sentential negation, but may not occur by itself and, thus, should be licensed by another negative element (except in a limited number of special contexts; cf. Postma 2002). In negative sentences without indefinite arguments (i.e., without neg-words), the additional NM *niet* licenses the presence of *en/ne*. In contexts with a neg-word, the neg-word may license *en/ne* as well, and *niet* can be left out. Adding *niet* or additional neg-words to a combination of *en/ne* and a neg-word may yield NC readings as well, as has been shown in (22).

Given the fact that Old Dutch and the earlier phases of Middle Dutch were Strict NC languages, this NM *en/ne* should be said to carry [uNEG]. However, it has been known since Jespersen's seminal work that preverbal NMs such as Middle Dutch *en/ne* lost force and gradually started to disappear—just as in French and the other Germanic languages discussed. Its usage became optional, as is shown below in (24), which consists of two examples from the same text: one where *en* is lacking, one where *en* is still present.

---

[22] Lanceloet: 20166.
[23] Lanceloet: 20316.
[24] Lanceloet: 20042.

Table 6.1 *En*-deletion in Holland Dutch per context (in %) (Burridge 1993)

	V1	V2	V-final
1300	43	28	8
1400	75	25	36
1500	77	48	28
1600	100	30	8
1650	100	100	98

(24) a. Maer *niemant* gaf gehoor (Dutch; 1638[25,26])
 but NEG-body gave obeying
 'But nobody obeyed'

 b. Dat *niemant* zich het woên der vyanden *en* kreunde
 that NEG-body REFL the raging of.the enemies NEG moaned
 'That nobody cared about the raging of the enemies'

In the middle of the 17th century, for instance, the usage of *en/ne* was almost entirely gone. This development of *en*-deletion in Holland Dutch is shown in Table 6.1 (for different verbal positions).

Clearly, when the NM *en/ne* was no longer actively part of the Dutch negative system, it could not be acquired as such. That means that negative doubling, i.e., the co-occurrence of an NM and a neg-word, could no longer function as a cue for the acquisition of [uNEG] and [iNEG] features. Consequently, if the language input existed of examples like (22a–b), but with the preverbal NM being absent, such examples would count again as examples with a 1:1 relation between negative form and negative meaning. Children learning this new variation could not reach a target language with NC any more. At first sight, this clearly shows how Jespersen's Cycle triggers the disappearance of NC as well. It is certainly not a coincidence that all Germanic languages that nowadays are DN languages (Dutch, German, Swedish, Norwegian) all lost their NC property after reaching the stage in Jespersen's Cycle where the preverbal NM became obsolete.

At the same time, not every Germanic language where the preverbal NM got dropped became DN languages. For instance, Bavarian or Yiddish are still NC languages, despite the fact that the preverbal NM dropped.

(25) a. Gestan han'e *neamd ned* gseng (Bavarian)
 yesterday have.I NEG-body NEG seen
 'Yesterday I didn't see anybody'

---

[25] Gysbrecht V: 1368.
[26] Gysbrecht V: 1410.

6.4 THE DISAPPEARANCE OF NEGATIVE CONCORD 157

    b. ... daß'ma *koana ned* furtgehd
       ... that.me NEG-body NEG leaves
       '... that nobody is leaving'

(26) a. Ikh hob *nit* gezen *keyn* moyz   (Yiddish)
       I NEG seen NEG mice
       'I haven't seen any mice'
    b. *Keiner* efnt *nit* mayn tir
       NEG-body opens NEG my door
       'Nobody opens my door'

This shows that the drop of the preverbal NM is rather a necessary, but not a sufficient, condition for the loss of NC and the emergence of DN. I argue that this has to do with the fact that not every instance of NC in the language input consisted of the preverbal NM plus one other negative element. Focusing on the Dutch developments, examples like (22c–d) remained examples of NC after the drop of the preverbal NM *en/ne*. Hence, why would those examples not count as instances of NC for the Dutch language learner, especially when such examples may have formed evidence for NC in languages like Bavarian or Yiddish?

In Middle Dutch, though, these instances were fairly infrequent. In a corpus study, Deurloo (2009) presents results from the period of 1500–1640, where she attests 285 sentences (of a total of 8,621 negative sentences in her corpus of that period) which consist of either two or more neg-words, or one or more neg-words and the NM *niet*. She attributes this very low frequency (roughly 3.3%) to the fact that the inclusion of an additional negative element does not alter the semantics and is therefore redundant. Thus, in Middle Dutch, most instances of NC were cases of negative doubling with the preverbal NM *en/ne*. Cases of negative spread or negative doubling with the (optional) NM *niet* were much less frequently attested, as they could only be used to mark emphasis (see Burridge 1993; Jäger 2008).

If the cue to set the parameter to NC is robust enough, the language will be taken to be an NC language. For the NC/DN distinction, such a cue is formed by sentences with more than one morphosyntactic instance of negation that is interpreted with only a single semantic negation. As the majority of such cues consisted of examples with *en/ne* in combination with either *niet* or a single neg-word, *en*-deletion resulted in the disappearance of a cue that is robust enough to set the language as an NC language. This led to the following situation: the majority of NC expressions disappeared from Dutch and the language could no longer be acquired as an NC language. But there are still these far less frequent former negative-spread expressions consisting of multiple neg-words or neg-word(s) in combination with *niet*. Even if language learners cannot take examples with two neg-words or a neg-word plus the NM *niet* to instantiate NC, they are still confronted with such examples and, therefore, must deal with them in some way. Since the language learner could not interpret these instances as instances of NC, as a last resort, these must be analysed as complex lexical items.

6.4.2 Emphatic Multiple Negative Expressions in Dutch and German

Evidence for the existence of such complex lexical items comes from so-called *Emphatic Multiple Negative Expressions* (EMNEs) in DN languages like Dutch and German. Such examples, illustrated below, are fixed constructions that are (substandardly) acceptable with an emphasized negative reading:

(27) a. Zij heeft *nergens* *geen* zin in (Dutch)
    she has NEG-where NEG desire in
    'She doesn't feel like anything at all'
  b. Hij gaat *nooit* *niet* naar school
    he goes NEG-ever NEG to school
    'He never ever goes to school'
  c. Zij hebben *nooit* *geen* geld
    they have NEG-ever NEG money
    'They never have any money'

(28) Sie hat *nie* *keine* Lust (German)
    she has NEG-ever NEG desire
    'She never feels like anything'

Despite their superficial similarities, EMNEs cannot be taken to be instances of NC, but should rather be analysed in terms of fixed lexical expression, given four below-listed differences between EMNEs and regular NC constructions:

(29) Differences between EMNEs and NC constructions:
  a. EMNEs always have an emphatic reading; NC constructions usually do not;
  b. The formation of EMNEs is not productive; speakers generally differ with respect to which EMNE they accept and which they do not accept;
  c. EMNEs are subject to strict adjacency conditions, contrary to NC constructions;
  d. Only the first element of the EMNE may carry stress, whereas, in NC constructions, all elements may do so.

Let us discuss each of these in turn. One of the striking differences between plain NC constructions and EMNEs is the fact that EMNEs always give rise to emphatic negative readings. NC expressions, on the other hand, yield plain negative readings. Even stronger, in pure NC languages, such as Italian, the usage of NC constructions is dispreferred if an emphatic reading is intended; in such a case, an NPI usually replaces the neg-word. This is shown in (30) and (31) for Dutch and Italian. The reading of the Dutch example in (30a) is identical to the reading of Italian (31a), and the same holds for the readings in the (b) examples. Such facts only follow if the emphasis is cooked into the (lexical) meaning of the fixed expression.

(30) a. Hij heeft *niemand niet* gezien (Dutch)
 he has NEG-body NEG seen
 'He didn't see ANYbody'
 b. Hij heeft *niemand* gezien
 He has NEG-body seen
 'He didn't see anybody'

(31) a. *Non* ha visto alcunché (Italian)
 NEG has seen anybody
 'He didn't see ANYbody'
 b. *Non* ha visto *nessuno*
 NEG has seen NEG-body
 'He didn't see anybody'

The second difference between EMNEs and NC is that, while several EMNEs are accepted by most speakers of Dutch (such as *nooit niet* or *niks geen*), many other EMNEs are only accepted by some speakers of Dutch. Only a minority of informants accepts, for instance, the examples in (32).

(32) a. %Ik heb *niemand niets* gegeven (Dutch)
 I have NEG-body NEG-thing given
 'I didn't give anything to anybody at all'
 b. %Ik heb *nergens niet* gezocht
 I have NEG-where NEG looked.for
 'I didn't look (for it) anywhere'

The fact that the examples in (32) are acceptable to only some speakers of Dutch would be puzzling if EMNEs were taken to be instances of NC, since NC constructions are hardly ever subject to such language-internal variation. However, since EMNEs, being lexical items, have to be acquired on an item-by-item basis, variation of this kind is not surprising at all.

The third difference between EMNEs and NC constructions is that the two negative elements of an EMNE have to be strictly adjacent, as already observed by de Vries (1910), whereas two elements that have established an NC relation still allow other material to intervene. In Italian, as shown in (33), the two NC elements are separated by the verbs *ha* and *telefonato*. In (34), however, it is shown for Dutch that, whenever other lexical material intervenes between the two negative elements, only a DN reading can be obtained.

(33) Ieri   non   ha   telefonato   nessuno   (Italian)
     yesterday NEG   has   called   NEG-body
     'Nobody called yesterday'

(34) a. Gisteren   heeft   niemand   niet gebeld   (Dutch)
        yesterday has   NEG-body   NEG called
        'Nobody at all called yesterday'
     b. Niemand   heeft   gisteren   niet gebeld.
        NEG-body   has   yesterday NEG called
        *'Nobody at all called yesterday'
        √'Nobody didn't call yesterday'

Since complex lexical items are stored as a unit in the lexicon, their adjacency can hardly be said to be surprising.[27]

The fourth difference between EMNEs and plain NC constructions is that, for EMNEs, the stress must fall on the first element. If the second element carries stress, again, only the DN reading is yielded, as shown in (35). Stress patterns do not, however, change the semantics in NC languages in this respect.

(35) a. Hij   heeft   NIKS   niet gezegd   (Dutch)
        he   has   NEG-thing   NEG said
        'He didn't say anything (at all)'
     b. Hij   heeft   niks   NIET gezegd
        he   has   NEG-thing   NEG   said
        *'He didn't say anything (at all)'
        √ 'There is nothing he didn't say'

(36) a. Gianni NON   ha   detto   niente   (Italian)
        Gianni neg   has   said   NEG-thing
        'Gianni did NOT say anything.'

---

[27] It is not the case that no EMNE may intervene. Certain examples have been attested that contain a preposition as well:

(i) Hij   heeft   nooit   van   geen   gesprek   geweten   (Dutch)
    he   has   never   of   NEG   conversation   known
    'He never knew about any conversation (at all)'

However, such examples do not run against the provided analysis. Remainders of Dutch NC need not have to consist of neg-words and negative marker *niet* only. If an object had been introduced by a preposition, which is likely to happen in a language like Dutch, as is the case in (ii), this would lead to a situation where the two negative elements with the intervening preposition were reanalysed as complex lexical items.

(ii) Na   dien   tyd   wist   Reintje nooit   van   geen   betalen   (Dutch; 1728;
     after that   time   knew   Reintje never   of   NEG   pay   Apollo's Marsdrager 321)
     'After that Reintje couldn't pay anything'

This explains why some current EMNEs may still carry an intervening preposition, such as *nooit van geen*. The two negations in (i) cannot be the result of NC; therefore, they can only be analysed as complex lexical items, similar to plain EMNEs.

b. Gianni *non* ha detto *NIENTE*
   Gianni NEG has said NEG-thing
   'Gianni didn't say ANYthing'

Again, the fact that the stress patters are fixed and cannot be altered (while maintaining the single negative reading) again shows that such elements cannot readily be interpreted as NC constructions.

The fact that EMNEs arose out of remnants of the former NC stage of the language immediately explains these differences. In addition, this analysis also explains why not every EMNE construction is possible. For example, (37) is never attested as an EMNE, and informants only assign a DN reading to them.

(37) Ik heb *niet niemand* gezien. (Dutch)
    I have NEG NEG-body seen
    *'I didn't see anybody'

The unavailability of those examples can hardly, if at all, be explained in lexical terms only. If these constructions are never part of the lexicon, this is obviously in need of explanation. However, if, for independent reasons, constructions such as the one in (37) were not grammatical in Middle Dutch, as is reflected by their current West Flemish ungrammaticality (see Section 4.2.2), it also follows that those examples could never have been lexicalized in the first place. Here, this is due to the fact that neg-words in Middle Dutch always have to scramble out of the vP in order to participate in an NC relation with the NM.

Hence, the death of Dutch NC, so to speak, led to the birth of EMNEs. And in other languages that have undergone a similar development with respect to their NMs, similar effects arose as well. The languages closest to Dutch in this respect are Frisian and German. Indeed, both languages exhibit EMNEs, too. Research executed for the *Syntactic atlas of the Dutch dialects* (Barbiers et al. 2008) shows that various Frisian dialects exhibit EMNEs—such as Anjum Frysian, where the following expressions are taken from.

(38) a. Der wol *net* ien *net* dansje (Anjum Frysian[28])
       there wants NEG one NEG dance
       'Nobody wants to dance'
    b. Zitte hjir nergens *gjin* muizen?
       sit here NEG-where NEG mice
       'Are there any mice here?'

German, which underwent a similar development (cf. Jäger 2008), also exhibits EMNEs, as shown in (28). German EMNEs are, however, less frequent and belong to (even) less formal registers than Dutch EMNEs. But this is by no

---

[28] Examples from Zeijlstra (2004: 115).

162   DIACHRONIC DEVELOPMENTS

means surprising, since German is known to be much more sensitive to normative pressure on language use than Dutch (see Weiss 2002; Weerman 2006).

However, as the examples in Bavarian and Yiddish show, in some other languages, the residue of NC expressions after the drop of the preverbal NM must have been substantially larger, or at least large enough to pass the robustness threshold for the acquisition of NC, again along the lines of the learnability algorithm proposed in this chapter. One of the reasons is that, if using more than two negative elements in a sentence may trigger an empathic effect, this effect, along the lines of Kiparsky and Condoravdi (2006), gets lost over time, and it would be less marked to use such an expression. If that is the case, this could explain why such examples would be used more frequently, thus providing more evidence in the language input for NC. Indeed, the examples from Bavarian and Yiddish in (24)–(25) are generally not felt to be emphatic.

6.5 Possible and impossible changes: The *NALL*-problem

So far in this chapter, I have argued that external diachronic developments, most notably changes in the expression of negation along the lines of Jespersen's Cycle, have had as a side effect that the situation in which negative elements were acquired altered and that, therefore, negative elements could be assigned [iNEG]/[uNEG] features, or could be reanalysed without them. This explains the variety attested within the landscape of NC systems. At the same time, these changes are not the only (possible) changes in the domain of negation. In this section, I will discuss the emergence of neg-words out of indefinites within NC systems, as well as another kind of change that actually never happened: the lexicalization of negated or negatively marked universal quantifiers.

6.5.1   Emerging negative indefinites

What we have not yet discussed is the emergence of NIs or neg-words out of indefinites with or without attached NMs. In French, one can see a clear reanalysis pathway from plain indefinites into NPIs into neg-words. Similar reanalyses from indefinites/NPIs into neg-words took place in Greek (cf. Giannakidou 1998; Kiparsky and Condoravdi 2006), Scandinavian Germanic languages (Jäger 2008), or Hebrew (Haspelmath 1997). In other languages, neg-words also contain a clear morphologically negative reflex, as is the case in the English *no*-series or the Old High German and Slavic *ni*-series. In these languages, neg-words cannot be said to have undergone such a reanalysis. Such morphological forms suggest historic changes where these neg-words are the result of lexical merger of an NM and an indefinite. For instance, the Old High German *ni*-series consists of the original NM *ni-* plus an indefinite, although, already in the earliest documents, these NIs were fully lexicalized and not synchronically formed with the NM. Similar patterns have been observed for Slavonic, Celtic, and Baltic languages, and Sanskrit (see Jäger 2010 for more discussion and overview). It should be emphasized, though, that, often, these changes are not supported by actual diachronic evidence—as they had already taken place before their first occurrences in the written documents—but rather evidenced by reconstruction based on their etymology.

From the NC perspective, it is far from surprising that such neg-words may emerge. If the NM carries a feature [uNEG], it is not necessarily the case that it is syntactically restricted to attach to finite verbs only, and not to other quantificational or other scope-taking elements. With a freer distribution, NMs can be expected to attach to other elements as well, and it is therefore not that surprising that a number of them have lexicalized into morphologically complex combinations of NMs and indefinites/NPIs. In fact, as we will see in the next chapter, there are good arguments to even nowadays think of NQs like English *no* or their Dutch/German counterparts *geen/kein* as morphosyntactically complex expressions.

6.5.2 The *NALL*-problem

At the same time, a question emerges with respect to the formation of NQs and the like. If NQs like *nobody* or *never* are diachronically (or even synchronically) the result of an NM incorporating an existential/indefinite element, why have similar patterns not been attested for NMs incorporating in other quantificational elements, such as universal quantifiers? In other words, why do we not find expressions like *nall*, with the intended meaning 'not all'?

The observation that no language in the world has a single lexical item with the meaning 'not all' or 'not every' is well established and goes back to the works of Thomas Aquinas. Horn (1972, 1989, 2007) extends the observation to a ban on lexicalization of the so-called O-corner in the Square of Opposition (see also Levinson 2000).

The Square of Opposition is a diagram depicting the four major types of propositions under Aristotelian logic: universal affirmatives (A), universal negatives (E), existential affirmatives (I), and existential negatives (O), each of them exemplified below (the abbreviations stem from Latin *affIrmo* ('I assert') and *nEgO* ('I deny')):

(39) a. Universal affirmative (A): every car is red
b. Universal negative (E): no car is red
c. Existential affirmative (I): some car is red
d. Existential negative (O): some car is not red
= not every car is red

Boethius (lived 480–524) formalized this insight in his Square of Opposition. He gave labels to each of the four basic sentence types—A and I on the affirmative side of the square, and E and O on the negative side—and included the entailment relations.

(40)   Square of Opposition

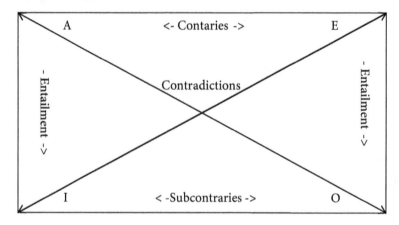

Horn's and others' observations boil down to an alleged ban on lexicalizing the O-corner of the Square of Opposition. English quantifiers like *every*, *some*, and *no* can be seen as lexicalizations of the A-, I-, and E-corner, respectively. But English lacks a single quantifier meaning 'not all' (the unattested word *nall*, hence the name of the problem). Similarly, while English has *both*, *either*, and *neither*, there is no *noth*, a word that would mean 'not both'. Propositional connectives can also appear in the Square of Opposition, as they are subject to the same entailment relations. And again, *and* (A) (inclusive), *or* (I), and *nor* (E) exist, but *nand* (with the intended meaning 'not and') does not.

This is not a particular quirk of English. Languages in general have no problem in lexicalizing the A-, I-, and E-corners, albeit that the E-corner is not always lexicalized; for instance, not every language exhibits NQs, NIs, or neg-words (see Section 4.4.3). However, across languages, the O-corner is systematically excluded from lexicalization (see Jaspers 2005 and references therein for more overview and discussion).

The question of why it is impossible to lexicalize the O-corner of the Square of Opposition has received several answers, but has never been fully and satisfactorily solved. With the exception of Hoeksema (1999b), most existing solutions to the *nall*-problem alluded to particular synchronic, grammatical, or logical mechanisms to rule out O-lexicalization.

One grammatical principle that can be alluded to in order to exclude O-lexicalization is blocking: the existence of the lexicalization of the I-corner blocks lexicalization of the O-corner, as argued for by Horn (1972, 1989, 2007). His argument is that, while I- and O-type sentences are semantically different, their pragmatic contributions are similar. To see this, let us take into consideration the joint meaning contribution of the assertions and the scalar implicatures of the following two examples:

(41) Assertion   Some car is red
      Implicature   Not every car is red
      Joint meaning contribution: Some, but not every, car is red

(42) Assertion   Not every car is red
      Implicature   Some car is red
      Joint meaning contribution: Some, but not every, car is red

Since the joint meaning contributions made by the corresponding I- and O-type sentences are the same, natural language need only exploit one. Since negative expressions are always marked in comparison to their positive counterparts, for Horn, the possible existence of I-type terms blocks the existence of O-type terms. If a language is to lexicalize one of the I/O-corners, it should be the I-corner.

As Hoeksema (1999b) points out, though, pragmatic equivalence is much weaker than semantic equivalence. One can easily utter the assertion in (41) about a particular subset of cars without knowing anything about the colours of the other cars. But then the pragmatic equivalence of (41) and (42) is already disrupted. Moreover, if conveying I-type sentences blocks conveying O-type sentences, the question emerges why utterances containing expressions like 'not... every' or 'not ... all' are still fine. In fact, their appearance is abundant.

Hence, Horn's theory is, in one way, too weak (pragmatic equivalence is too weak to account for such blocking), and, in another, too strong (it predicts the exclusion of usage of O-type sentences, not of O-lexicalization only).

For these and other reasons, other scholars have looked for other kinds of arguments to account for the ban on O-lexicalization. Most notably, Jespersen (1924) and Seuren (2006), following up on work by De Morgan (1858), argued that the Square of Opposition should actually be replaced by a triangle where either the O-corner would be dropped altogether or where it would conflate with the I-corner. Jespersen proposes a tripartition of logical operators (including only *every*, *some*, and *no*), which, therefore, require only three corners. Naturally, if there is no O-corner left, there is no O-problem to begin with. Alternatively, other ways of designing the square (cf. Löbner 1987, 1990) and other geometric representations (such as hexagons) have been proposed as well (see Van der Auwera 1996; Jaspers 2005; Horn 2007; see also Béziau and Basti 2017 for overview and discussion on geometrical alternatives to the Square of Opposition). Under such richer geometrical representations, there are still O-corners, but these are no longer the only ones that are excluded from lexicalization.

At the same time, as Jaspers (2005) mentions, even if there is no O-corner left any longer, the question still remains open why logically accessible meanings, such as 'not all', 'not both', or 'not and' still cannot be lexicalized. Again, this point becomes especially relevant in the light of Hoeksema's earlier observation that the complex construction '*not ... every*' is highly pervasive.

6.5.3 A diachronic solution

Attempts to provide a synchronic explanation for the *NALL*-problem have thus far not been very successful. For this reason, one may instead opt for a diachronic approach. Maybe it is not the case that there is a grammatical or logical reason why elements living in the O-corner cannot be lexicalized, but rather that the conditions under which such a lexicalization could take place are never met. In this section, I argue that this perspective is indeed on the right track.

As a starting point, consider that every negative expression is marked in comparison to its positive counterpart, as has clearly been demonstrated by Horn (1989). Negative quantifiers, therefore, should be the result of some process that made their positive counterparts negative. We have seen two examples of that: lexical merger of an NM and an indefinite/NPI (as sketched in Section 6.5.1), and reanalysis of an indefinite/NPI (as discussed in detail for French in Section 6.3.1).

Now let us look at the scenarios under which these processes can take place. First, note that, under the reanalysis process, an element that is initially intended to strengthen the negation (cf. Kiparsky and Condoravdi 2006) is first reanalysed in such a way that it becomes a semantically bleached NPI. This NPI, always co-occurring with negation, is then felt to be a negative element (i.e., an NM or a neg-word), leaving the original NM a superfluous element. Examples for French were *pas* and *personne*, which originally meant 'step' and 'person'. Later on, these got grammaticalized as minimizing NPIs (meaning something like 'a single bit' and 'anybody', respectively), and finally became an NM and a neg-word, respectively.

For a universal quantifier to undergo the same process, it should first appear in a stage where (i) it is used to strengthen a negation, and (ii) it only or mostly appears in negative sentences. However, as pointed out by Hoeksema (1999b), in order to strengthen a negation, a universal quantifier should outscope negation rather than scope under it. Universals scoping under negation rather yield weakened readings. But if this universal may not appear under the scope of negation, it can never be said to be an NPI, an element which, by definition, may only appear under the scope of negation. In fact, an element that may not appear under the scope of negation is, by definition, a PPI. But PPIs are not restricted to negative clauses where they would outscope negation. Hence, the two conditions (i)–(ii), which would require universals to enter the first stage of reanalysis into negated universal quantifiers, are in conflict, and reanalysis of this type is thus correctly predicted not to take place.

The only candidate left for lexicalizing negated universal quantifiers (and other inhabitants of the O-corner) over time would then be lexical merger. Hoeksema excludes this option by arguing that it would be very hard for the NM expressing sentential negation to immediately precede the universal quantifier, a necessary condition for a negative element to undergo lexical merger with a universal. Neither in SVO nor in SOV languages would such an NM easily appear in a string-adjacent position next to the universal. However, it is very well possible that a negative prefix that can be attached to verbs may be attached to quantifying elements as well. That something of the kind must have happened can be straightforwardly assumed, as string-adjacency between an NM and an indefinite is also a necessary condition for lexical merger of NIs, a process that has occurred frequently over time. Consequently, Hoeksema's diachronic approach might not fare better in explaining the universal absence of lexicalized negated universal quantifiers.

But there may be another option, if it is also very well possible that a negative prefix that can be attached to verbs may also be attached to quantifying elements. As seen in Chapter 5, languages where such affixal NMs, being syntactically non-phrasal, are available in must-be NC-languages, given the workings of the learning algorithm (a negative head can be acquired only in NC languages). In such languages, an NM must attach to the finite verb in most, if not all, negative sentences, as well. But if that is the case, attaching an NM to a quantificational or other scope-taking element can take place only in scenarios where (i) the relevant sentence is already marked for negation, and (ii) the negation attached to the quantificational or other scope-taking element does not induce a second semantic negation; what attaching an NM to such a quantificational or other scope-taking element does can only be scope-marking it for negation.

There is a major functional difference, however, between scope-marking an existential or low-scale element for negation and scope-marking a universal or high-scale element for negation in sentences that are already negative. This holds equally well for quantifiers and connectives. Let me first illustrate that for connectives, and, after that, for quantifiers. Take (43). (43) is ambiguous between (44a) and (44b).

(43) I didn't see John or Mary

(44) a. [I didn't see [John or Mary]]   ¬ > or
      b. I didn't see John or I didn't see Mary   or > ¬

In (44a), the entire disjunction takes scope below negation; in (44b), negation is part of both disjuncts, the second disjunct being subject to ellipsis. Now, if *or* in (43) is scope-marked for negation, only the reading in (44a) survives. Example

(45) (with 'neg' standing for an affixal negative scope-marker) can thus only mean that I saw neither John nor Mary.

(45) I didn't see John NEG-or Mary

Since (44a) entails (44b), scope-marking *or* strengthens the sentence. Generally, strengthening is functionally motivated (as leaving out a strengthener under standard (neo-)Gricean pragmatics generally leads to a weaker reading).

Now, let us see what happens when a conjunction is scope-marked for negation:

(46) I didn't see John and Mary

(47) a. [I didn't see [John and Mary]] ¬ > and
b. I didn't see John and ~~I didn't see~~ Mary and > ¬

(48) I didn't see John NEG-and Mary

Again, scope-marking the connective for negation would block the structure and reading of (47b). As the entailment relations in (47) are reversed ((47b) entails (47a)), however, scope-marking *and* for negation, as in (48), would only weaken the utterance. Without the scope marker, both the weaker and the stronger readings are available. Scope-marking for negation lets only the weak reading prevail. Scope-marking the negation does not bring in any new meaning effect, and is thus functionally ill-motivated.

The same applies for quantificational elements. Assuming that quantifiers can in principle take scope above or below negation, scope-marking a quantificational element for negation must, again, have a pragmatic effect. Here, a complicating factor, is, however, that scopal orderings between negation and quantificational elements are sometimes fixed and sometimes not. Take the following examples (where I deliberately did not pick *somebody* or *anybody*, as these elements are polarity-sensitive):

(49) a. Everybody didn't leave $\forall > \neg; \neg > \forall$
b. A person didn't leave $\exists > \neg; *\neg > \exists$

(50) a. I didn't see everybody $\neg > \forall; *\forall > \neg$
b. I didn't see a person $\neg > \exists; \exists > \neg$

Universal quantifiers cannot raise across negation, but can reconstruct below negation. Existentials show the reverse pattern: they can raise across negation, but cannot reconstruct below it. This, arguably, is the result of the fact that LF-operations cannot yield non-weaker readings (cf. Mayr and Spector 2012). Now let us see what negative scope-marking on a preverbal quantifier would bring:

(51) a. NEG-everybody didn't leave $\neg > \forall$
b. NEG-a person didn't leave $\neg > \exists$

Scope-marking the universal in (49) yields a weaker reading (51a); scope-marking the existential in (49) yields a stronger reading (51a). In fact, it yields a reading that would otherwise be absent. This shows, again, that scope-marking an existential quantifier for negation is functionally well-motivated, but that scope-marking a universal quantifier for negation is not. A similar pattern appears when the postverbal quantifiers in (50) are scope-marked for negation:

(52) a. I didn't see NEG-everybody   ¬>∀
     b. I didn't see NEG-a person   ¬>∃

Scope-marking the universal is superfluous, as it was already restricted to a narrow-scope reading of the quantifier with respect to negation. Scope-marking the existential is, again, an instance of pragmatic strengthening, as it renders the weaker wide-scope reading of the existential over negation absent, and is, therefore, again functionally well-motivated. Note that this already shows for the ambiguous cases that scope-marking a universal quantifier for negation is pragmatically ill-motivated, and that scope-marking an existential quantifier for negation is pragmatically well-motivated. Hence, even if languages were more liberal with respect to ambiguity between a quantifier and negation, that would never lead to a situation where, all of a sudden, scope-marking a universal quantifier would turn out to be pragmatically motivated.

Under this account, attaching a negative affix to a universal quantifier or conjunction is never functionally apt; but attaching a negative affix to an existential quantifier or disjunction is. Therefore, it is unexpected that, in such languages, many instances of negatively marked universal quantifiers or conjunctions surface. But if such elements are absent or occur very infrequently at best, they cannot form the input for lexical merger either.

Naturally, one could object to this analysis, that, even in NC languages, it is not unnatural to combine universal quantifiers with negation. But it should be noted that, in those cases, a negated universal often comes with an existential inference. This has some consequences for the proposed analysis. A crucial ingredient of it is that there is an entailment relation between (53a) and (53b): (53a) entails (53b).

(53) a. Everybody didn't go to the party
     b. Not everybody went to the party

However, if (53b) has an explicit existential inference, generally triggered by some focus on the universal quantifier, the entailment relation is disrupted: (53a) does not entail (54).

(54) Not EVERYbody went to the party, but some went

Hence, negating a universal quantifier can only be functionally motivated if it is not entailed by the non-scope-marked version of the sentence in the scenarios

I have sketched. However, as (54) shows, in order to trigger a proper functional effect by scope-marking the universal quantifier (or any other inhabitant of the O-corner), this quantifier must be focused. At the same time, lexical merger of two elements requires that these elements can be reanalysed as a single prosodic word. This means that such adjacent elements cannot stand in an internal-focus relation, since morphological words lack internal-focus structure in general (cf. Williams 1981). Hence, we arrive at the following situation, where a functionally well-motived negated universal quantifier cannot form the input for lexical merger, and where a possible candidate for lexical merger is functionally ill-motived.

(55) [NEG + ∀/and]   Functionally ill-motivated   Possible input for
                                                                   lexical merger
      [NEG + [FOC ∀/and]]   Functionally well-motivated   Impossible input for
                                                                   lexical merger

The two scenarios in (55) thus jointly explain the *NALL*-problem, and also explain why universal quantifiers can still be abundantly negated in natural language.

6.6 Conclusions

In this chapter, I have explained how variation among NC systems may have emerged diachronically, most notably as a side effect of Jespersen's Cycle (Section 6.2). We saw in Subsection 6.3.1 that, when additional NMs become part of the negative system, this can lead to the emergence of NC. All of a sudden, the 1:1 mapping between negative form and negative meaning is disrupted. In the same way, if NMs disappear, become optional, or have their syntactic properties changed, NC systems may disappear or change in type. This has happened in the case of emergence of Non-strict NC languages (Subsection 6.3.2), the NC system of Afrikaans A (Subsection 6.3.3), the partial NC systems of French and English (Subsections 6.3.4–5), and the emergence of DN, as illustrated for Dutch in Section 6.4. Where the learnability algorithm constitutes the space of variation with respect to the existence and types of NC, actual diachronic developments determine which types of NC languages may actually emerge when.

In addition, in Section 6.5, I also have shown how the emergence of NIs / neg-words as well as the exclusion of their universal counterparts can be accounted for, thus, among others, providing a solution for the so-called *NALL*-problem. Again, we see that, where grammar allows for a range of variation in the domain of negation, diachronic effects further limit it.

7
Negative indefinites and split-scope readings

7.1 The problem

Negative Indefinites, such as English *nobody*, *nothing*, or *no boy*, are generally considered to be generalized quantifiers that are semantically negative:

(1) [[nobody]] = λP.¬∃x[**body'**(x) & P(x)]   or equivalently
    [[nobody]] = λP.∀x[**body'**(x) → ¬P(x)]

This, among other things, explains why they can appear in object position and induce sentential negation from there by means of QR, as well as why two NIs give rise to a DN reading. However, the view that NIs in languages such as Dutch, German, and English should be regarded as NQs has been challenged by examples such as (2), which seem problematic for analyses of NIs in terms of NQs.

(2) Du   musst keine Krawatte anziehen   (German[1])
    You must   no   tie   wear
    a. 'It is not required that you wear a tie'   ¬ > must > ∃
    b. 'There is no tie that you are required to wear'   ¬ > ∃ > must
    c. #'It is required that you don't wear a tie'   must > ¬ > ∃

In (2), the most salient reading is the so-called split-scope reading in (2)a, where the negation outscopes the modal auxiliary, which, in turn, outscopes the indefinite. Note that readings where the entire NI has wide or narrow scope with respect to the modal verb are also available (2b–c), albeit that the wide-scope reading of *must* is only available with extra focus on the modal (see Chapter 13).

Split-scope readings form a serious problem for a treatment of NIs in terms of NQs, as the negation associated to the NI and the indefinite part are allowed to take scope from different clausal positions. In a recent and influential work, Penka (2011) has argued for a universal treatment of NIs: all NIs are semantically non-negative indefinites, carrying a syntactic feature [uNEG], following Ladusaw (1992) and Zeijlstra (2004, 2008a, b), as well as the theory spelled out in the previous chapters. The only difference then, for Penka, between neg-words and NIs in DN languages is that the former may be licensed under multiple agreement

---

[1] Unless mentioned otherwise, the German data are all taken from Zeijlstra (2011).

(i.e., one—possibly covert—semantic negation may license multiple neg-words), whereas the latter may only be licensed under single agreement (every NI must be licensed by a unique licenser). This position is hardly compatible with the learnability algorithm spelled out in Chapter 5, which takes NIs to be fully semantically negative and would not allow the language learner to postulate any formal negative features on them in the first place.

Penka's analysis runs against previous analyses that have been proposed in the literature. The first approach takes split-scope effects to result from lexical decomposition by means of some process of amalgamation (Jacobs 1980) or incorporation (Rullmann 1995). The second approach takes NIs to be plain NQs and derives split-scope readings as an entailment of quantification over kinds (Geurts 1996) or properties (De Swart 2000).

In this chapter, however, I argue that both Geurts' and De Swart's approach, which takes NIs to be NQs, and Penka's approach, which takes neg-words to be semantically non-negative in all languages, face serious problems. I also point out several problems for the amalgamation/incorporation approaches, but I argue that these problems can easily be overcome once it is assumed that NIs in DN languages are the single spell-out of a syntactic treelet consisting of two sisters: a negation and an indefinite. Under this analysis, the meaning of an NI is in most cases equivalent to the meaning of a NQ, but this approach accounts for split-scope interpretations as well—namely as a result of partial reconstruction after of NIs QR. The chapter thus concludes that split-scope readings can only be accounted for in terms of decomposition of NIs, and not in terms of plain NQs or neg-words.

The chapter is set up as follows: after introducing the relevant data in Section 7.2, I present my analysis of NIs and apply it to the problematic cases in Section 7.3. This analysis is then, in Section 7.4, compared to previous accounts. In this section, I demonstrate that analyses that take NIs to be NQs face serious problems, as do analyses that take NIs in Dutch and German to be neg-words. Section 7.5, finally, concludes.

7.2 The phenomenon

In this section, I discuss the phenomenon, occurring in West Germanic languages, that challenges the view that NIs in these languages are NQs. This phenomenon was first noted in Bech (1955/1957) and later discussed in, among others, Jacobs (1980) for German, and Rullmann (1995) for Dutch. It is generally referred to as scope-splitting, since, semantically, the negation and the indefinite meaning component of NIs take scope independently. This can be seen in environments where the negation takes wide scope over some other scope-taking element, while the indefinite meaning component has narrow scope with respect to it. A split-scope reading is generally available for NIs embedded under modal or object-intensional verbs and with NIs in idiomatic expressions.

7.2.1 Modal verbs

Consider the following German example in which an NI is embedded under a modal verb:

(3) Du musst keine Krawatte anziehen (German)
You must no tie wear
    a. 'It is not required that you wear a tie'   ¬ > must > ∃
    b. 'There is no tie that you are required to wear'   ¬ > ∃ > must
    c. #'It is required that you don't wear a tie'   must > ¬ > ∃

The most salient reading of this sentence is paraphrased in (3a). As can be read off from this paraphrase, negation has wide scope over the modal, whereas the indefinite has narrow scope. This reading, however, cannot be derived under the assumption that the NI *keine Krawatte* is a plain NQ. The only readings that the negative-quantifier analysis derives are the ones paraphrased in (3b) and the marginally available one in (3c). In (3c), the NI is interpreted with surface scope, and both the negation and the indefinite have narrow scope with respect to the modal. This reading, equivalent to 'it is required that you don't wear a tie', is hard to get, and available only with lots of help from the context, because there is a strong tendency in German that negation outscopes modals (see De Haan 1997, and Chapter 13). The only way the modal can end up in the scope of the negation under a negative-quantifier analysis is by means of LF-movement of the NQ across the modal, resulting in reading (3b), in which both the negation and the indefinite outscope the modal. But this wide-scope reading has very weak truth conditions: (3b) is true if and only if there is no specific tie that you are required to wear. This does not exclude that the occasion under discussion might require that you wear some tie or other. This is contrary to intuitions, according to which the sentence in (3) denies that wearing ties is obligatory. The same line of argumentation carries over to the following Dutch example (from Rullmann 1995: 194), again with the reading where the modal takes wide scope being marginally available:

(4) Ze mogen geen verpleegkundige ontslaan (Dutch)
They may no nurse fire
    a. 'They are not allowed to fire any nurse'   ¬ > may > ∃
    b. 'There is no nurse who they are allowed to fire'   ¬ > ∃ > may
    c. ?'They are allowed not to fire a nurse'   may > ¬ > ∃

As Penka (2007, 2011) has shown, the case for the split-scope reading can be made even stronger. In the context of German expletive *es* ('there'), an indefinite embedded under a modal can take only narrow scope:

(5) Es   muss ein   Arzt   anwesend sein   (German)
    There must a   physician present   be
   a. ?'It is required that there be a physician present'   must > ∃
   b. *'There is a physician who is required to be present' ∃ > must

Similarly, an NI embedded under a modal in a *there*-insertion context cannot take scope above the modal. But in the salient reading, the negation nevertheless outscopes the modal.

(6) Es   muss kein Arzt   anwesend sein   (German)
    There must no   physician present   be
   a. 'It is not required that there be a physician present'   ¬ > must > ∃
   b. *'There is no physician who is required to be present'   ¬ > ∃ > must
   c. ?'It is required that there be no physician present'   must > ¬ > ∃

And, even stronger, if (6) contains a modal verb that is an NPI, which therefore requires narrow scope with respect to negation, the split-scope reading is the only available one, as shown below:

(7) Es   braucht kein Arzt   anwesend zu sein.   (German)
    There needs   no   physician present   to be
   a. 'It is not required that there be a physician present'   ¬ > need > ∃
   b. *'There is no physician who is required to be present'   ¬ > ∃ > need
   c. *'It is required that there be no physician present'   need > ¬ > ∃

These considerations show that the salient reading cannot be somehow derived from the wide- or narrow-scope reading of a NQ, thereby confirming that scope-splitting of NIs is real.

Most of the literature on split-scope readings focuses on Dutch and German, but split-scope readings are not restricted to these languages. English NIs exhibit split-scope readings under modals as well, although things look slightly different there, since English modals have different and, generally speaking, more fixed interpretational scopal restrictions with respect to negation (see Chapter 13). As described by Iatridou and Sichel (2011), English *must*, for instance, must always outscope negation; thus, under *must*, no split-scope readings arise:

(8) You must do no homework
   a. 'It is required that you do no homework'   must > ¬ > ∃
   b. *'It is not required that you do homework'   ¬ > must > ∃
   c. *'There is no homework that you are required to do' ¬ > ∃ > must

Have to, however, normally scopes under negation. And indeed, when *have to* is combined with an NI, split-scope effects show up, although variation with respect to that emerges among different speakers. Not every speaker of English accepts split-scope readings. But for those who do, sentence (9) is clearly ambiguous between a split-scope and a non-split-scope reading (data from Iatridou and Sichel 2011); only the reading where the modal outscopes negation is ruled out:

(9) You have to do no homework
   a. *'It is required that you do no homework'   must > ¬ > ∃²
   b. 'It is not required that you do homework'   ¬ > must > ∃
   c. 'There is no homework that you are required to do'   ¬ > ∃ > must

English thus, in principle, also allows split-scope readings, in a similar way to Dutch and German: The only reason why not all English modal auxiliaries may give rise to those readings is that they can be blocked due to independent properties of modal auxiliaries, or other factors that may play a role. One reason why not every speaker of English accepts split-scope readings is that, in English, split-scope readings can also be conveyed unambiguously by using NPI-indefinites of the *any*-series: (10) has the same reading as (9b).

(10) You don't have to do any homework

7.2.2 Object-intensional verbs

Scope-splitting also occurs when an NI is the object of a transitive intensional verb like *seek*, *need*, or *owe*, as demonstrated in the following examples from German, Dutch, and English, respectively.

(11) Perikles schuldet Socrates kein Pferd   (German)
     Perikles owes Socrates no horse
   a. 'Perikles is not obliged to give Socrates a horse'   ¬ > owe > ∃
   b. 'There is no horse that Perikles is obliged to give to Socrates'   ¬ > ∃ > owe
   c. *'Perikles is obliged not to give Socrates a horse'   owe > ¬ > ∃

(12) Hans zoekt geen eenhoorn   (Dutch)
     Hans seeks no unicorn
   a. 'Hans is not trying to find a unicorn'   ¬ > seek > ∃
   b. 'There is no unicorn Hans is trying to find'   ¬ > ∃ > seek
   c. *'Hans is trying not to find a unicorn'   seek > ¬ > ∃

(13) Mary needs no secretary
   a. 'It is not the case that Mary needs a secretary'   ¬ > need > ∃
   b. 'There is no secretary that Mary needs'   ¬ > ∃ > need
   c. *'What Mary needs is no secretary'   need > ¬ > ∃

---

[2] In certain contexts and for certain speakers, this reading can still be obtained (cf. Iatridou and Sichel 2011).

As before, the split-scope reading (a) is the salient one. Under intensional verbs, the narrow-scope reading (c) is never available at all. Note that, while the wide-scope reading (b) is possible, it has, again, very weak truth conditions. (12b), for instance, is true if unicorns do not exist in the evaluation world, independently of Hans' activities.

7.2.3 Idiomatic expressions

Finally, German, Dutch, and English idioms involving an indefinite are generally negated by replacing the indefinite with an NI. The negation then applies to the entire idiom as such (see (14)–(15)).

(14) a. Hans hat mir einen Bären aufgebunden (German)
 Hans has me a bear up-tied
 'Hans has fooled me'
 b. Hans hat mir keinen Bären aufgebunden
 Hans has me no bear up-tied
 'Hans hasn't fooled me'

(15) a. Hij heeft een scheve schaats gereden (Dutch)
 He has a diagonal skate ridden
 'He made a mistake'
 b. Hij heeft geen scheve schaats gereden
 He has no diagonal skate ridden
 'He didn't make any mistake'

(16) a. Mary has got a bone to pick with you
 'Mary has something to fight with you about'
 b. Mary has got no bone to pick with you
 'Mary doesn't have anything to fight with you about'

Occurrences of NIs in idioms themselves are already problematic if NIs are taken to be plain NQs. But what is important for the present discussion is the fact that NIs in idioms also invoke split readings when they are embedded under modal verbs. Furthermore, within idioms, the negative component of NIs may outscope the operator that has scope over its indefinite part.

(17) Mir kannst du keinen Bären aufbinden (German)
 Me can you no bear up-tie
 'You can't fool me'

(18) Hij mag geen scheve schaats meer rijden (Dutch)
 He may no diagonal skate more ride
 'He is not allowed to make any more mistakes'

(19) Mary can't have a bone to pick with you
 'It is not possible that Mary has something to fight with you about'

7.2.4 Concluding remarks

The data presented above indicate that, whenever an NI can take wide or narrow scope with respect to some particular operator, a third reading is available where the negation takes wide scope and the indefinite takes low scope, and that such split-scope readings are also available if, for instance, the narrow- or wide-scope reading is ruled out on independent grounds (as is the case with, for instance, object-intensional verbs selecting NIs). These data are problematic for the assumption that NIs are NQs—i.e., the assumption adopted so far to account for the behaviour of NIs in DN languages—since, without adopting additional machinery, a treatment of NIs as NQs cannot account for this third type of reading.

In this chapter, I offer an alternative explanation of NIs, arguing that they constitute a piece of syntactic structure, consisting of both a negation and an indefinite which together spell out as a single morphological word.

7.3 Proposal

The fact that the negative and the indefinite part of an NI in the languages I have discussed may take scope from different positions is in need of explanation. In this section, I formulate a proposal that accounts for this. In short, I propose that, in these languages, NIs constitute pieces of syntactic structure consisting of a negation and a non-negative indefinite in a sisterhood relation, which can be further merged in the derivation.

In Subsection 7.3.1, I elaborate this proposal in more detail, and, in the subsequent subsections, I demonstrate how all the different readings available for the NIs discussed in Section 7.2 can be derived: modal verbs (Subsection 7.3.2), intensional verbs (Subsection 7.3.3), and idiomatic expressions (Subsection 7.3.4). Subsection 7.3.5 contains some concluding remarks.

7.3.1 NIs as pieces of syntactic structure

It is often assumed that NIs lack internal syntactic structure and that an NI is an atomic lexical item. The semantics of an NI, then, is that of a NQ, and its semantic force is induced from one point in the syntactic structure. A simplified illustration is given in (20).

(20) No car is red

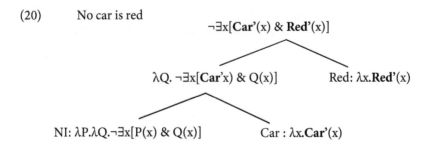

However, the structure in (20) is not the only way to generate the meaning of a construction containing an NI. Even though, from a morphosyntactic perspective, (20) consists of three lexical elements (not taking the copula into account), semantically, it exhibits at least four distinct objects: the predicates *car* and *red*, the indefinite, and the negation. From this semantic point of view, it is far from unnatural to assume that all these objects can express their semantic force from a different point in the syntactic structure, as shown in (21). Since (21) yields exactly the same reading as (20), it follows that NIs do not have to be negative quantifiers: they can also be semantically non-negative, as long as there is some grammatical mechanism which forces a negation to enter the derivation along with the indefinite and which has to end up in an appropriate position.

(21) No car is red

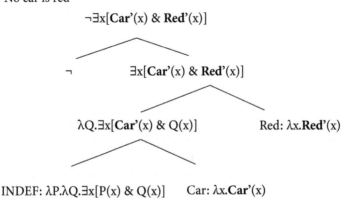

The main difference between (20) and (21) is that the indefinite and the negation occupy different positions in the structure. Consequently, the structure in (21), in contrast to the structure in (20), does not prevent other material from intervening between the position of the negative operator and the indefinite. Once intervening material between the negation and the indefinite is allowed, the existence of split-scope readings follows as an immediate result. The question of how the structure in (21) is derived is what everything boils down to, and is therefore the topic of this section.

The fact that it is possible that the two parts of the NI form one unit at PF while simultaneously occupying two different structural positions at the level of LF introduces two questions. First, how does it follow from the structure in (21) that the two different nodes—the negation and the indefinite—are realized as a single morphophonological object? Second, what is the relation between the negation and the indefinite such that, on the one hand, they are linked together (an NI is always a combination of one negation with one indefinite), but on the other hand, they may appear in different positions in the structure?

In order to address these questions, I propose that an NI is the phonological realization of a piece of syntactic structure. Rather than merging with an atomic object, the derivation is expanded with another piece of syntactic structure, spelled out as *kein*, *geen*, or *no* for German, Dutch, and English, respectively (a standard case of morphological fusion resulting in suppletive forms)—much in the same vein as has been proposed for pronouns (cf. Weerman and Evers-Vermeul 2002; Neeleman and Szendrői 2007; Gruber 2013; and references therein) and for Wh-terms (Barbiers et al. 2010). Now, the two problems vanish: first, the fact that the complex structure corresponds to one morphophonological object, despite being syntactically complex, follows straightforwardly. Second, the fact that the relation between the negative operator and the indefinite is 1:1 follows as well: no other object than a syntactic structure consisting of those two nodes could be spelled out as *kein/geen/no*.

An example of such a spell-out rule is given in (22) for German *kein* 'no'.

(22)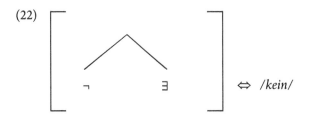

The figure in (22) shows that what is spelled out as *kein* is a syntactically and semantically complex piece of structure that contains both a negation and an indefinite component which stand in a sisterhood relation.

But it does not follow yet, how a spell-out rule such as (22) could allow for material intervening between the negation and the indefinite while still being spelled out as one morphological word.

However, since NIs, under this proposal, are not syntactically atomic, they are not subject to the principle of lexical integrity, which states that the internal structure of words is not accessible to syntax (Di Sciullo and Williams 1987; Ackema and Neeleman 2004). NIs are not created within the lexicon (as a result of some lexicon-internal morphological process), but they are the result of a syntactic process in accordance with a postsyntactic PF rule. Consequently, NIs differ from morphologically negative words (arguably being the output of the morphological component) such as *unwise* or *non-smoker*, that will never give rise to split-scope effects.

The NI forms a syntactic constituent that can be subject to syntactic operations such as movement or QR. As I will illustrate in detail in the next subsection, this means that the entire NI, being quantificational in nature, can undergo QR (raising across another scope-taking element), followed by partial reconstruction of the indefinite part of the NI at the level of LF. As a result, then, at PF, the entire copy is spelled out, whereas, at LF, the negation and the indefinite structure allow intervening, scope-taking material.

The syntactically complex status of NIs now enables us to derive a structure like the one in (21), and thus to derive split-scope readings. I first demonstrate how the different readings of sentences consisting of a modal verb and an NI follow. Then, I show in a similar fashion how the different readings come about in sentences with an object-intensional verb and in idiomatic expressions.

7.3.2 Deriving the split-scope readings: Modal verbs

Let us reconsider the data like (3) (presented here as subordinate clauses, to avoid V2 effects). The LFs of the three readings are given in (23a–c), with the first one being the split-scope reading, the most salient one.

(23) ... dass du keine Krawatte anziehen musst
... that you no tie wear must

    a. '... that it is not obligatory that you wear a tie'   ¬ > must > ∃
        [Neg [$_{IP}$ you [$_I$ must [$_{VP}$ a tie wear]]]]

    b. '... that there is no tie that you must wear'   ¬ > ∃ > must
        [Neg [a tie [$_{IP}$ you [$_I$ must [$_{VP}$ wear]]]]]

    c. '... that it is obligatory that you don't wear a tie'   must > ¬ > ∃
        [you [$_I$ must [$_{VP}$ Neg a tie [$_V$ wear]]]]

Let us first consider the base-generated structure, where the NI *keine Krawatte* ('no tie') is merged with the verb, which, in turn, merges with the modal verb *musst* 'must'. Finally, the subject merges, and the IP is created.[3]

---

[3] The exact position where the subject is base-generated (Spec, vP or Spec, IP) is irrelevant for the present discussion.

7.3 PROPOSAL   181

(24) Base structure of (23):

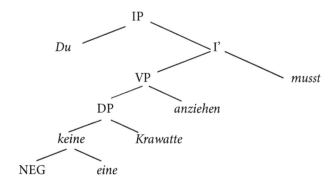

This base structure already yields the narrow-scope reading (23c), where both the negation and the indefinite are in the scope of the modal verb. Now, the object is allowed to move under QR to a higher position to get wide scope. Adopting the Copy and Deletion Theory of Movement (Chomsky 1995a), that creates a copy of the object raising under QR, while the original element is subject to deletion or trace conversion (Fox 2000). This is illustrated in (25).

(25) Application of QR:

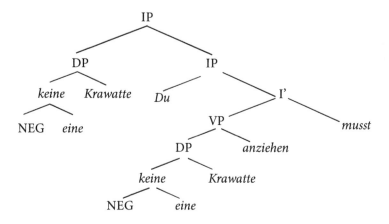

The structure in (25) contains two identical copies of the syntactic object [NEG eine Krawatte], with the lower copy being interpreted phonologically, and the higher copy being interpreted semantically. The interpretation of the higher copy of this object yields the reading in which both the negation and the indefinite outscope the modal verb (23b). The LF of this structure is given in (26).

(26) [IP [DP NEG eine Krawatte]ᵢ Du [I' [VP [DP ~~NEG eine Krawatte~~]ᵢ anziehen] musst]]

However, as I have argued, the NI is not a syntactic atom, but rather constitutes a piece of syntactic structure. Given that the negation and the indefinite are sisters within that structure (and thus within each copy of that piece of structure), nothing requires that both be interpreted at LF in one and the same copy. Hence, it is possible that the semantic component interprets the negation within *keine Krawatte* in the higher copy and the indefinite in the lower copy. This yields the LF in (27), where the highest copy is partially reconstructed at LF.[4]

(27) [$_{IP}$ [$_{DP}$ NEG ~~eine Krawatte~~]$_i$ Du [$_{I'}$ [$_{VP}$ [$_{DP}$ ~~NEG~~ eine Krawatte]$_i$ anziehen] musst]]

The reading that (27) yields is exactly the one where the negation outscopes the modal verb, whereas the modal verb, in turn, outscopes the indefinite: the split-scope reading. The assumption that NIs are syntactically complex lexical items is in accordance with the Copy Theory of Movement, and thus correctly predicts that a sentence like (23) gives rise to (at least) three readings, including the split-scope reading.

A potential problem for this analysis is that it seems to overgeneralize. In principle, nothing would prevent the semantic component from interpreting the indefinite in the higher copy and the negative operator in the lower one, yielding a reading that is not possible for NIs. This reading cannot be yielded, however, on independent grounds: Negation never reconstructs at the level of LF (cf. Horn 1989; Zanuttini 1997; Penka and von Stechow 2001; Zeijlstra 2004, 2017b; see also Chapter 8), a principle that is in line with the more general ban on adverbial reconstruction at LF.

Thus, movement of the entire NI, followed by partial reconstruction of the negative operator, is blocked, as this violates the ban on LF reconstruction of negation. In (28), the negative operator receives too low an interpretation. This implies that the negation may not be interpreted below if the indefinite is interpreted in the higher copy. The interpretation in (29), where the indefinite outscopes the negation, is therefore ruled out.

(28) *[$_{IP}$ [$_{DP}$ ~~NEG~~ eine Krawatte]$_i$ Du [$_{I'}$ [$_{VP}$ [$_{DP}$ NEG ~~eine Krawatte~~]$_i$ anziehen] musst]]

However, the question remains open as to why the reverse reading could not emerge as a result of movement of the indefinite part out of the NI, if the NI does not raise to the highest position itself, as is sketched in (29).

(29) *[$_{IP}$ [$_{DP}$ eine Krawatte]$_i$ Du [$_{I'}$ [$_{VP}$ [$_{DP}$ NEG ~~eine Krawatte~~$_i$] anziehen] musst]]

---

[4] See Fox 2000; Fanselow and Cavar 2001, 2002 for more thorough discussion on the exact constraints on partial reconstruction; the view presented here for partial deletion basically mirrors Fanselow and Cavar's 2002 analysis of partial deletion at PF.

The structure in (29), however, can never be derived either. Under this proposal, the internal structure of an NI such as *keine Krawatte* can only consist of merger of *keine* (in itself a merger of the negation with the indefinite) with the NP *Krawatte*:

(30)   [[NEG eine] [Krawatte]]

The only syntactic constituents containing the indefinite in a construction such as (29) that could undergo movement are thus either the entire structure in (30), which gives rise to either wide-scope or split-scope readings, or *Krawatte* by itself. The latter type of movement cannot give rise to a semantic effect, as the NP needs to remain in the scope of the indefinite in order to avoid semantic anomalies. Note, however, that some languages, e.g. German, are sometimes analysed as allowing movement of the NP outside the NI—but if such raising is allowed, the interpretation of the NP remains in situ.[5] Hence, it is impossible for the indefinite to scope over the negation.

(31)   Bücher   hat   er   keine   geschrieben   (German)
       Books   has   he   no   written
       'He hasn't written any books'

7.3.3 Deriving the split-scope readings: Object-intensional verbs

The analysis also applies to split-scope readings in the case of object-intensional verbs, such as German *schulden* 'to owe'. The only difference between these cases, illustrated in (32), and the cases with modal verbs is that the narrow-scope reading is not available either.

(32)   ... dass   Perikles   Sokrates   kein   Pferd   schuldet
       ... that   Perikles   Sokrates   no   horse   owes
   a. '... that Perikles is not obliged to give Socrates a horse'   ¬ > owe > ∃
   b. '... that there is no horse that Perikles is obliged to give   ¬ > ∃ > owe
       to S'
   c. *'... that Perikles is obliged not to give Socrates a horse'   owe > ¬ > ∃

In a similar fashion to (25), the object moves to a Spec, IP position, and the structure in (33) is derived.

---

[5] See Fanselow and Cavar (2002) for a discussion of these facts and how they are related to other partial deletion phenomena. Note that I do not suggest that cases such as (32) must involve raising of *Bücher* ('books'). I only intend to show that, if these constructions are analysed as such, they do not form any counterexamples to what is claimed here.

(33)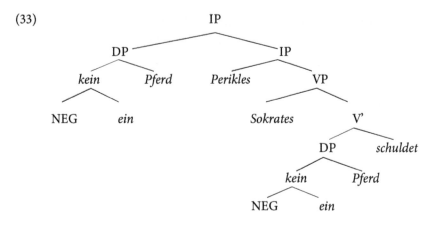

Now, the entire copy can be interpreted in the higher position, which yields the wide-scope reading (34).

(34) [IP [DP NEG a horse] Pericles [VP Socrates [DP NEG a horse] owes]]

But, similarly to the case of modal verbs, the negation may be interpreted high and the indefinite below. This yields the split-scope reading (35).

(35) [IP [DP NEG a horse] Pericles [VP Socrates [DP NEG a horse] owes]]

The reading where the negation is interpreted low and the indefinite is interpreted high is independently ruled out, owing to the movement constraints discussed in the previous subsection.

The question remains open why the narrow-scope reading is not possible where both the negation and the indefinite are interpreted below. Zimmermann (1993) argues that object-intensional verbs take properties but not quantifiers as their arguments (an analysis that is at odds with the analysis presented here), as can be seen from the fact that determiners that are invariably interpreted as quantifiers, such as *every*, cannot have a narrow-scope reading, as illustrated in (36).

(36) Hans seeks every unicorn   (wide scope only)

It is unclear, however, whether this constraint results from the semantics of transitive intensional verbs, or from the pragmatics that make such utterances salient. Several examples containing NIs have been reported to be compatible with a narrow-scope reading like (37).

(37) For once, I need no children in the house[6]

Hence, Zimmermann's account is probably too restrictive for these cases, and it seems that pragmatic constraints are involved (as well). Therefore, I take it that

---

[6] The example is attributed to von Fintel (exact reference unknown). See also Iatridou and Sichel (2011).

the ill-formedness of (38) follows from the pragmatics that goes with transitive intensional verbs: (38) is not syntactically ill-formed, but pragma-semantically infelicitous.

(38) #[IP [DP ~~NEG a horse~~] Perikles [VP Socrates [DP NEG a horse] owes]]

The exact nature of this ban, however, is beyond the scope of this chapter. Crucial for now is that the QR-based analysis predicts that NIs selected by object-intensional verbs give rise to split-scope readings, a prediction that is indeed borne out.

7.3.4 Deriving the split-scope readings: Idiomatic expressions

Finally, the analysis I have presented also accounts for the split-scope readings of sentences that combine an idiomatic expression with a modal verb. Let us (again) look at the German example in (39).

(39)   ... dass du mir keinen Bären aufbinden kannst   (German)
       ... that you me no bear up-tie can
       Literal: 'that it is not possible that you tie me up a bear'
       Idiomatic: 'that you can't fool me'

Note that the exact idiomatic expression does not require the NI. The true idiomatic expression is rather *einen Bären aufbinden* (a bear up-tie 'to fool').[7] This is shown again in (40):

(40)   Du willst mir einen Bären aufbinden   (German)
       you want me a bear up-tie
       'You want to fool me'

In (39) again, the entire idiomatic expression (including the negation) is first merged within VP; and later on, the NI moves out of VP under QR to an IP-adjunct position.

---

[7] In some cases, *kein* cannot be directly interchanged with *ein*. This is, for instance, the case in (i):

(i)   Damit kommst du auf {keinen/* einen} grünen Zweig   (German)
      with.that come you at no/ a green twig
      'You won't be successful with that'

This is, however, due not to the fact that the negation is part of the idiom, but to the fact that the idiom is an NPI. As shown below, the idiom containing a non-negative indefinite is well-formed when it is combined with, for example, a negative subject.

(ii) Niemand ist auf einen grünen Zweig gekommen   (German)
      nobody is at a green twig come
      'Nobody has been successful'

(41)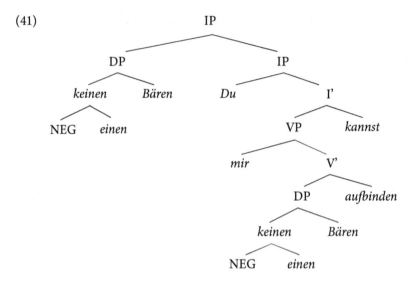

Now, the lower negation and the higher indefinite may delete under the Copy and Deletion Theory of Movement, yielding the structure (42), which correctly expresses the intended truth conditions.

(42) [IP [DP NEG ~~a bear~~] you [I' can [VP me [DP ~~NEG~~ a bear] tie up]]]

Of course, the other possible readings are still available, both literal and idiomatic, as is shown in (43) for the narrow-scope reading (literal and idiomatic) and (44) for the wide-scope reading (only literal).

(43) [IP you [I' can [VP me [DP NEG a bear] tie up]]]

(44) [IP [DP NEG a bear] you [I' can [VP me [DP ~~NEG a bear~~] tie up]]]

A crucial step in this line of argumentation is that the idiom (*einen Bären aufbinden*) needs to be interpreted as a unit. That is, the idiomatic reading is only available if the indefinite is interpreted inside the VP. Therefore, (44), which represents the wide-scope reading of (39), only receives the non-literal reading. It should be noted that, under this analysis, the syntactic process of QR feeds the non-literal interpretation of the idiomatic expression, even when the non-literal reading itself does not involve quantification.

7.3.5 Concluding remarks

The analysis I have presented explains how split-scope readings arise and how they are constrained. It does so by assuming that NIs such as German *kein* realize syntactic structures (as is thought to be the case with pronouns and *Wh*-terms). As a result of QR and the syntactic principle that demands that copies need to be deleted as well, split-scope readings are expected to arise as well. Note that the entire analysis does not allude to any principle that is not independently motivated.

Apart from the emergence of split-scope readings, the proposal solves another problem concerning the interaction between NIs and ellipsis. German and Dutch NIs that are deleted under ellipsis sometimes seem to have lost their negation, as illustrated in (45) and (46) for German and for Dutch.

(45) ... dass er im Garten keinen Mensch antraf und
 ... that he in.the garden no person met and
 im Haus auch nicht (German)
 in.the house also NEG
 '... that he didn't see anybody in the garden nor in the house'

(46) ... dat hij geen mens in de tuin aantrof en
 ... that he no person in the garden saw and
 ook niet in het huis (Dutch)
 also NEG in the house
 '... that he didn't see anybody in the garden nor in the house'

Given that deletion under ellipsis may only take place under semantic identity (cf. Merchant 2001), it is strange that the deleted VP in the second clause does not contain a negation. After all, the expected underlying representation of (45) would be (47), which would be expected to contain a negation of its own, as shown below (where double strikethrough indicates deletion under ellipsis):

(47) ... dass er im Garten [$_{VP}$ keinen Mensch antraf] und im Haus auch nicht [~~keinen Mensch antraf~~]

But following the analysis pursued in this section, it is, in fact, expected that the negation does not have to be part of the deleted VP: The fact that QR may apply followed by partial reconstruction makes it possible that only the indefinite is interpreted in situ in the first conjunct, and not the negative operator. Consequently, the deleted VP does not have to carry a semantic negation either:

(48) ... dass er im Garten [NEG ~~einen Mensch~~] [$_{VP}$ [~~NEG~~ einen Mensch] antraf] und im Haus auch nicht [$_{VP}$ ~~einen Mensch antraf~~]

Note that, so far, this only partially answers the question why the deleted VPs in (45) and (46) must be interpreted non-negatively: the account only makes it possible, not obligatory. The obligatory non-negative interpretation, however, is required owing to the contribution of *auch nicht* in German and *ook niet* in Dutch. German *auch nicht* and Dutch *ook niet* can only be felicitously included in the second conjunct of a sentence if the first conjunct is negative and if it is *auch nicht / ook niet* (not anything else) that renders the second conjunct negative, as shown below:

(49) a. Er hat *(nicht) gegessen und auch nicht getrunken (German)
       he has   NEG   eaten   and also NEG   drunk
       'He didn't eat and neither did he drink'
       *'He didn't eat and neither did he not drink'
    b. Hij heeft *(niet) gegeten en   ook niet gedronken   (Dutch)
       he has   NEG   eaten   and also NEG drunk
       'He didn't eat and neither did he drink'
       *'He didn't eat and neither did he not drink'

The data in (49) show that the negation may not be part of the deleted part of the second conjunct as a result of the semantic/pragmatic behaviour of *auch nicht / ook niet*. Similarly, the deleted VPs in (45) and (46) may not contain a negation either, which can only be the case if the VPs in the first conjuncts do not do so.[8]

Note that this analysis predicts that, in those cases, the first conjunct may only receive a split-scope reading, as, only under the split-scope reading, the VPs of both the first and the second conjunct only contain the indefinites, a prediction that is indeed borne out:

(50) Du   musst am   Vormittag keine Krawatte anziehen
     you must in.the evening   no   tie   wear
     und am   Nachmittag auch nicht   (German)
     and in.the morning   also NEG

  a. 'It is not required that you wear a tie'   ¬ > must > ∃
  b. *'There is no tie that you are required to wear' ¬ > ∃ > must
  c. *'It is required that you don't wear a tie'   must > ¬ > ∃

(51) Ze   mogen in het   ziekenhuis geen verpleegkundige ontslaan
     they may   in the   hospital   no   nurse   fire
     en   in de   kliniek ook niet   (Dutch)
     and   in the   clinic also NEG

  a. 'They are not allowed to fire any nurse'   ¬ > may > ∃
  b. *'There is no nurse who they are allowed to fire'   ¬ > ∃ > may
  c. *'They are allowed not to fire a nurse'   may > ¬ > ∃

7.4 Comparison with other accounts

The facts I have presented strongly indicate that NIs should be considered as being distinct from NQs, and the proposed analysis correctly predicts how and when split-scope readings may arise. In this section, I evaluate other analyses that have

---

[8] For more discussion on the absence of negation in VP-ellipsis licensed by the VP-antecedent's containing an NI, see also Temmermans (2012), and Temmermans and Van Craenenbroeck (2017) and references therein.

attempted to cope with the problems introduced in Section 7.2. First, I discuss a previous analysis by Jacobs (1980) and Rullmann (1995), who posit that NIs result from amalgamation or incorporation processes. After that, I evaluate three accounts —Geurts (1996), De Swart (2000), and Abels and Marti (2010)—which have maintained that NIs are NQs despite the facts that seem to argue against this analysis, resulting from independent semantic principles. Finally, I discuss the work by Penka (2007, 2011), who takes the opposite view and argues that split scope should be treated analogously to NC. For her, NIs in Dutch and German are semantically non-negative and are equipped with a formal feature [uNEG] that requires them to be bound by an abstract negative operator carrying [iNEG]. The difference between NC and DN languages, for her, does not depend on the presence or absence of formal negative features [uNEG]/[iNEG], but on whether an abstract covert negation carrying [iNEG] may check exactly one or multiple features [uNEG]—a conclusion that is incompatible with the conclusions reached in Chapter 5.

In this section, I show that, despite surface similarities with the presented analysis, these accounts all face problems which do not arise under the presented analysis.

7.4.1 Amalgamation and incorporation (Jacobs/Rullmann)

One of the first analyses of this phenomenon was Jacobs (1980) (relatively close in spirit to the analysis I propose), which states that, in German, the NM *nicht* amalgamates with an indefinite, e.g. *jemand* ('somebody') or *etwas* ('something'). That is to say that the NM *nicht* and the adjacent indefinite *ein* fuse into the single word *kein*. The major difference between this analysis and the one I have presented is that, for Jacobs, amalgamation applies to adjacent negations and indefinites, and not only to negations and indefinites that are syntactic sisters.

A similar approach is the proposal put forward by Rullmann (1995), based on Klima's (1964) rules of incorporation. If, superficially, the negation and the indefinite are adjacent, the negation incorporates in the indefinite, yielding an NI. For Dutch *niet* and *geen*, this would be:

(52) niet D_{indef} ⇒ geen

Both analyses have been criticized by Penka (2011), who argues that such an amalgamation process is problematic in grammatical frameworks that assume different levels for semantic and phonological representations. Since such an amalgamation rule cannot take place at the level of LF (otherwise, the split-scope reading could never be derived), it must be purely phonological and take place at PF. But this requires a phonological rule that, for example, renders *nicht* and *etwas* into *nichts*. Such phonological rules are not known in other phonological processes.

One could assume (as I do as well), though, that amalgamation does not apply to the NM or indefinites such as *jemand* or *etwas*, but rather to abstract material: an abstract negative operator and/or an abstract determiner. For Penka, this only makes things worse: Abstract material, i.e., material that lacks phonological content in the first place, is invisible at PF by default; hence no amalgamation rule can apply.

All these criticisms rely, however, on what kind of rules are allowed at the phonology–morphology–syntax interfaces. Under a purely lexicalist point of view (where every lexical item comes in with all its phonological features present), Penka's arguments may hold. But over the past decade, work on Distributed Morphology (Halle and Marantz 1993, and subsequent works) have provided frameworks in which morphophonological realization takes place after spell-out— i.e., abstract syntactic structures are the input for morphophonological processes. Under such a view of the syntax–morphology interface, Penka's arguments against amalgamation or incorporation lose their validity.

However, an analysis only in terms of postsyntactic morphophonological realization is a necessary, but not a sufficient analysis of the facts. Both Jacobs' and Rullmann's proposals, rephrased in terms of postsyntactic spell-out, crucially rely on phonological string-adjacency of the negation and the indefinite; the gist of the analysis is that what appears as adjacency at surface structure does not have to be structurally adjacent at the level of LF:

(53) [NEG [[eine Krawatte anziehen] musst]]

In (53), NEG and *eine Krawatte* may somehow be spelled out as *keine Krawatte*, even though the indefinite scopes under the modal, whereas the modal scopes above. However, there are two problems with such an analysis.

First, such a mechanism would not directly apply if the language in question were VO instead of OV, as, then, such a configuration would no longer be possible. However, as demonstrated in Section 7.2, English, being an SVO language, allows, at least for some speakers, split-scope readings as well, even though the (vP-external) position where negation is interpreted at LF is never string-adjacent to the (vP-internal) position where the indefinite appears at PF.

(54) You have to do no homework

Under the analysis pursued here, *kein/geen/no* are to be considered not as the phonological realization of two string-adjacent elements at the level of PF, but as the realization of a piece of syntactic structure that consists of a top node dominating two syntactic sisters: the negation and the indefinite, which may jointly undergo QR. Then, these problems do not hold any more.

The second problem for the adjacency analysis is that that it is not the case that negation and an indefinite may not appear string-adjacent to each other.

7.4 COMPARISON WITH OTHER ACCOUNTS 191

The following examples are fine, albeit with some focus on the indefinite (see Chapter 12 for more discussion).

(55) Fritz kann nicht eine Fremdsprache (German)
Fritz knows not a foreign.language
Int.: 'Fritz doesn't know a foreign language'

Of course, one can argue that this focus is introduced by a covert focus element intervening between the negation and the indefinite, and thus disrupting the strict adjacency between the negation and the indefinite. However, for reasons that will become clear in Chapter 12, the focus on the indefinite disappears once they are both embedded in a DE environment. The examples in (56) have the same reading. Hence, intervention by focus could not explain why, in (56a), the negation should not incorporate in the indefinite. However, one can still maintain that, in (56a), the negation is a syntactic sister not of *eine Fremdsprache*, but rather of the entire vP *eine Fremdsprache kann*—a position I will defend in Chapter 12. In that case, the analysis presented in the earlier subsection predicts that the negation and the indefinite are spelled out independently.

(56) a. Wir haben keinen angenommen der nicht eine
we have nobody hired who not a
Fremdsprache kann (German)
foreign.language knows
'We hired nobody who doesn't know a foreign language'

b. Wir haben keinen angenommen der keine
we have nobody hired who no
Fremdsprache kann
foreign.language knows
'We hired nobody who doesn't know a foreign language'

So, the major difference between the analysis presented in this chapter and Jacobs' and Rullmann's analyses is that, in the former, negation is always part of the NI (until the level of LF, when partial deletion may apply), whereas, in the latter, NIs result from coincidental string-adjacency of the negation and the indefinite.

7.4.2 Quantification over abstract individuals (Geurts)

Geurts (1996) tries to overcome the problems of taking NIs to be NQs by arguing that split readings of NIs arise when the article *kein* does not quantify over simple individuals as usual, but rather quantifies over kinds in the sense of Carlson (1977). He derives the split reading of (57), as sketched in (58).

(57) Ich suche keine Putzfrau (German)
    I seek no cleaning-lady
    'I'm not looking for a cleaning lady'

(58) a. [no cleaning lady] λx. I seek x
     b. ¬∃x ∃ {CLEANING LADY}: I seek x

First, the NQ *keine Putzfrau* moves across the verb at LF (58a). Geurts then assumes that *kein*, in this configuration, quantifies over the singleton set consisting only of the kind term CLEANING LADY. This yields (58b), which asserts that the speaker is not a cleaning-lady seeker. This is equivalent to the reading in which the indefinite quantifier ranges over concrete individuals and the negation has wide scope: the split-scope reading.

But Geurts' proposal has a number of problems, both conceptually and empirically (see De Swart 2000 for a more thorough discussion of these problems). First, it cannot simply appeal to the notion of abstract individual or natural kind as used in Carlson (1977). To account for split readings, in some cases, very specific and strange kinds would have to be assumed. For instance, to get the paraphrased reading of (59), Geurts would have to appeal to the kind STUDENT WHO ATTENDED ARNIM'S LECTURE YESTERDAY.

(59) Ich suche keinen Student, der gestern in Arnims Vorlesung
    I seek no student who yesterday in Arnim's lecture
    war (German)
    was
    'I'm not looking for a student who attended Arnim's lecture yesterday'

Another problem for this analysis is the fact that *kein* can combine with numerals while scope-splitting is still possible. It remains unclear how Geurts' account could deal with a sentence such as (60), under the paraphrased reading, as *two cars* does not refer to a particular kind in terms of Carlson (1977).

(60) Wir müssen keine zwei Autos haben (German)
    we must no two cars have
    'We don't need to have two cars'

Even more problematic is the fact that NIs can occur in idiomatic expressions and give rise to split-scope readings, as shown in (61)–(62). Occurrences of NIs in idioms themselves are a problem for the negative-quantifier analysis. But what is important for the present discussion is the fact that NIs in idioms also yield split readings when they are embedded under modal verbs:

(61) Mir kannst du keinen Bären aufbinden (German)
    me can you no bear up-tie
    'You can't fool me'

(62) Hij mag geen scheve   schaats meer rijden   (Dutch)
     he   may   no   diagonal skate   more ride
     'He is not allowed to make any more mistakes'

In the cases of (61) and (62), the split reading cannot be derived by assuming quantification over abstract individuals, since this would only yield the literal interpretation. To get the idiomatic meaning of the expression *(k)einen Bären aufbinden* in (61), the indefinite must be interpreted together with the rest of the idiom in the scope of the modal while the negation still takes wide scope.

7.4.3 Higher-order quantification (De Swart)

The account of De Swart (2000) is similar to that of Geurts (1996) in so far as both assume that some special kind of quantification is responsible for scope-splitting of NIs, thus maintaining the quantificational status of NIs. But rather than assuming quantification over abstract individuals, which causes several of the problems already mentioned, De Swart (2000) employs higher-order quantification. She argues that scope-splitting occurs when *kein* quantifies over properties, and proposes that there is an additional lexical entry for *kein*, according to which *kein* is a NQ over properties:

(63) $[[\text{kein Buch}]] = \lambda w.\lambda P_{<<s,<e,t>>,t>}.\neg \exists P_{<s,<e,t>>} (P=\lambda w'.\lambda y.(\textbf{Book'}_{w'}(y)) \,\&\, P(P))$

Using this translation for *kein* then derives the split-scope reading for the sentence in (64), as sketched in (65):

(64) Hanna sucht kein Buch   (German)
      Hanna seeks no   book

(65) no book (seek) (hanna)
      $\neg \exists P(P= \lambda w'.\lambda y.(\textbf{Book'}_{w'}(y)) \,\&\, \textbf{Seek'}(\textbf{h}, P))$
      $= \neg \textbf{Seek'}(\textbf{h}, \lambda w'.\lambda y.(\textbf{Book'}_{w'}(y))$
      'Hanna is not a book seeker'
      = 'Hanna doesn't seek a book'

But, as Penka (2007) has pointed out, there are reasons to believe that higher-order quantification is not what is responsible for scope-splitting. First, such an analysis cannot derive intermediate-scope readings of the indefinite for sentences with two scope-bearing elements besides negation and the indefinite, i.e., readings where the negation takes widest scope and the indefinite takes scope in between the two operators. This is the case because the higher-order interpretation of *kein* invariably gives the indefinite narrowest scope. De Swart claims that this is actually a virtue of her analysis, and argues that intermediate-scope readings are not available for NIs, an argument she puts forward against Kratzer (1995). But this claim seems to be empirically too strong. For example, (66) does indeed have the paraphrased reading, in which negation takes widest scope and the indefinite scopes in between *kann* 'can' and *wollen* 'want'. This is confirmed by the fact that the speaker can elaborate on (66) with 'as she doesn't know one'. If the indefinite necessarily had narrow scope with respect to 'want', this continuation would not be felicitous, because Julia might still have the idea that Norwegians make good husbands and want to marry some Norwegian or other even without knowing any Norwegian.

(66) Julia kann keinen Norweger heiraten wollen (German)
Julia can no Norwegian marry want
'It's not possible that there is a Norwegian that J. wants to marry'
¬ > can > ∃ > want

Moreover, the fact that NIs in idioms can have a split reading is also a problem for De Swart's account. The NI somehow has to isolate itself from the idiom to be able to apply to the remaining property. But if the NI is part of the idiom itself (e.g. in (61) and (62)), the idiom cannot be interpreted *en bloc* any more—a crucial property for the interpretation of idioms. This predicts that split-scope readings of idiomatic expressions receive a literal reading, contrary to fact. Hence, (61) and (62) are also problematic for this analysis.

Note that this problem does not appear under the analysis I proposed, as the indefinite part of the idiom will be interpreted in the lower copy of the NI, whereas negation will be interpreted in the higher copy. The actual idiom that needs to be interpreted as a unit thus still contains the indefinite, but not necessarily the negation.

7.4.4 Negative Indefinites and choice-functions (Abels and Marti)

All analyses of split-scope I have discussed are designed to account for split-scope readings yielded by NIs. However, it has been observed that split-scope readings may also be triggered by other quantifiers that are not upward monotonic. Take the following examples from Hackl (2000) and Rullmann (1995), quoted in Abels and Marti (2010):

(67) At MIT one must publish fewer than three books in order to get tenure
'At MIT one must publish at least n books in order to get tenure, and n is less than three'[9]

---

[9] Example from Hackl 2000.

(68) How many books does Chris want to buy?
'What is the number n such that Chris wants it to be the case that there are n books that he buys?'[10]

That split-scope readings may emerge in comparatives and comparative quantifiers is well known since Hackl (2000), De Swart (2000), and Heim (2001). The question that arises is whether these two types of split-scope effects reflect different grammatical phenomena, or whether they can be said to follow from a single, unified analysis.

One reason for a non-unified approach to split scope, put forward by Jacobs (1980) and Penka (2011), is that NIs can also give rise to split-scope readings across universal quantifiers with a particular hat contour (cf. Büring 1995). For many speakers of German (69), with a special intonational hat contour, receives a reading where not every doctor has a car.

(69) /JEDER Arzt hat KEIN\ Auto   (German)
      every doctor has no car
      'Not every doctor has a car'

Crucially, however, such split-scope readings do not emerge with other non-upward monotonic quantifiers:

(70) ??/JEDER Arzt hat weniger als DREI\ Autos   (German)
      every doctor has fewer than three cars
      'Every doctor has at least n cars, and n is less than three'

(71) */JEDER Arzt hat GENAU\ drei Autos
      every doctor has less three cars
      'Every doctor has at least three cars'

Since examples like (69) are not available for every speaker of German, but split-scope readings with NIs are, Abels and Marti take split-scope involving the hat contour to be an independent phenomenon from other types of split-scope, thus paving the way for a unified approach for split-scope involving negative and other non-monotone increasing quantifiers, such as comparative quantifiers and numerals. For them, a NQ like German *kein* is a NQ over choice functions, which scopes from its raised position. The noun phrase is interpreted below where the trace of the quantifier leaves a choice function variable that takes the denotation of the noun as its argument. Since Abels and Marti take common noun denotations to be indexed by a world variable, which can be bound by a higher intensional operator, the impression of a split-scope reading is the result. The split-scope reading of (72a) results from the LF in (72b) (where '@' stands for the actual world).

---

[10] Taken from Rullman (1995).

(72) a. Du   musst   keine   Krawatte   anziehen   (German)
       you   must   no   tie   wear
       'It is not required that you wear a tie'   ¬ > must > ∃
    b. ¬∃f CF(f) & ∀w'R@, you wear f(tie$_w$') in w'

However, even though a unified approach to split scope is conceptually attractive, it is not clear whether the two types of split-scope readings they distinguish are truly independent. Speakers who accept split-scope readings with the hat contour also accept split-scope readings across intensional operators, though not necessarily the other way around—something that is not immediately clear if the two phenomena are truly independent. But if the phenomena are not independent, the analysis in terms of choice-functions does not carry over to those instances of split scope like (69). In fact, as we will see in Chapter 13, the absence of split-scope readings involving universal quantifiers for speakers who do accept other kinds of split-scope readings can indeed be explained independently. This suggests that the two types of split-scope readings involving NIs should have the same source and not be taken separately.

Following Hackl (2000) and Heim (2006), I take monotone decreasing expressions, such as *few* or *little*, or comparatives, to invoke split-scope readings owing to the fact that these expressions are not plain generalized quantifiers but rather that they underlyingly consist of two quantifiers: one quantifier over individuals and one quantifier over degrees. Split-scope readings then follow, since the degree quantifier can move to a position scoping either under or over the modal. This latter type of movement of the degree operator to a position higher than the modal then yields the split-scope reading (see Penka 2007, 2011 for a more detailed discussion of these facts).

7.4.5 Negative Indefinites are neg-words (Penka)

A recent analysis that forms the opposite of Geurt's, De Swart's, and Abels and Marti's analyses, is the one by Penka (2007, 2011), who takes NIs to be semantically non-negative. Penka (2011), following Penka (2007) and Penka and von Stechow (2001), draws a parallel between split scope and NC.

Penka adopts the analysis of NC (after Zeijlstra 2004, 2008a, b), as formulated in Chapters 3–4, and takes neg-words to be semantically non-negative, carrying an uninterpretable negative feature ([uNEG]) that needs to be checked against a negative operator, which may be phonologically abstract. In addition, Penka argues that, in Dutch and German, the same process is going on, the only difference being that multiple agreement with respect to negation is not allowed in these languages. Hence, every NI is a semantically non-negative indefinite carrying a [uNEG]-feature and needs to have its feature checked against an abstract negative operator $Op_{¬[iNEG]}$. In the case that two NIs show up in the sentence,

7.4 COMPARISON WITH OTHER ACCOUNTS

each NI must be licensed by a separate $Op_{\neg[iNEG]}$. Thus, Penka derives split-scope readings by having the abstract negative operator outscope the intervening scope-taking operator, which, in turn, outscopes the indefinite DP, as illustrated in (73).

(73) ... dass Du keine Krawatte anziehen musst (German)
... that you no tie wear must
[dass Du [$Op_{NEG[iNEG]}$ [[keine$_{[uNEG]}$ Krawatte anziehen] musst]]]
'It is not required that you wear a tie' ¬ > must > ∃

However, at least two problems arise for this analysis. First, it is not clear what determines the licensing conditions of the abstract negative operator. Penka (2007, 2011) states that adjacency at surface structure is the proper licensing domain for NIs; otherwise, the three readings in (74) could not have been derived.

(74) [dass Du [$Op_{NEG[iNEG]}$ [[keine$_{[uNEG]}$ Krawatte anziehen] ¬ > must > ∃
musst]]]
[dass Du [[$Op_{NEG[iNEG]}$ keine$_{[uNEG]}$Krawatte] [anziehen ¬ > ∃ > must
musst]]]
[dass Du [[$Op_{NEG[iNEG]}$ [keine$_{[uNEG]}$ Krawatte anziehen]] must > ¬ > ∃
musst]]

But if this were correct, it would no longer be possible to account for the split-scope readings in English VO constructions, as, there, the position left-adjacent to the NI is not a position where negation takes scope.

Second, Penka (2007, 2011) takes every language to exhibit formal negative features, and reduces the difference between NC and Double Negation languages (i.e., languages that always exhibit a 1:1 correspondence between morphosyntactic and semantic negation) to a single parameter, namely whether negative agreement may be subject to multiple agreement or not. In Chapter 5, on the other hand, it was stated that only real NC languages have a formal negative feature, and that, in Double Negation languages, the negative feature does not have any formal status: It is a purely semantic feature; the acquisition of formal negative features in a Double Negation language is impossible. Moreover, this analysis makes a strong empirical prediction, namely that, if non-NC languages do not have a formal negative feature at their disposal, they cannot project such a feature either, as illustrated in (75).

(75) a. NC: [u/iNEG]/[X]   b. No NC: [X]

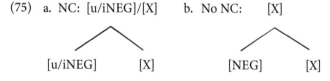

[u/iNEG]   [X]   [NEG]   [X]

As shown in Chapter 5, as a result, negative heads (X°) are predicted to not be available in non-NC languages, a prediction that has proven to be borne out: There is no language without NC which exhibits an NM that is a syntactic head (see Chapter 5). This prediction remains unexplained, though, under Penka's analysis, where every language has a formal negative feature.

Now, this is not a principled argument against Penka, as she may argue that this unidirectional relation is motivated by something else; but if two different analyses of split scope have more or less the same explanatory power, and one is compatible with the only explanation thus far for some other phenomenon, whereas the other is not, this speaks in favour of the former analysis. To conclude, Penka's analysis, which tries to unify NC and split-scope readings, faces problems that the QR-based analysis for split scope does not suffer from. As it stands, despite surface similarities, split-scope effects and NC differ much more in nature, and the theory of NC presented in this book cannot be naturally extended to split-scope constructions without modifying it to such an extent that it seriously loses its explanatory force with respect to NC.

7.5 Conclusions

In this chapter, I have argued that NIs in languages like Dutch, German, and English are not NQs (in the Montegovian sense), but pieces of syntactic structure that consist of a negation and an indefinite, which are postsyntactically spelled out as a single morphological word. Split-scope effects are derived as a result of the Copy Theory of Movement. I have proposed that, in split-scope constructions, after QR, the negative operator is interpreted in a higher copy and the indefinite in a lower copy of the NI. Furthermore, I have demonstrated that alternative analyses that take NIs in Dutch and German to be NQs or neg-words, or to be resulting from amalgamation or incorporation processes, face problems that the analysis presented in this chapter does not encounter. A crucial ingredient of the analysis, necessary to rule out partial reconstruction of the negation below the indefinite in split-scope constructions, is that negation, once raised, does not reconstruct. While that constraint seems empirically well-founded, it is at odds with certain approaches to NEG-raising, the phenomenon where matrix negation is felt to be interpreted in the embedded clause, as in (76).

(76) I don't think she left
 'I think she didn't leave'

In the next chapter, we will look at this phenomenon in detail, and show that NEG-raising does not involve syntactic reconstruction.

8
Neg-raising

8.1 Introduction

Neg-raising concerns the phenomenon, illustrated in (1), by which certain negated predicates (e.g. *think, believe, expect*) can give rise to readings where negation seems to take scope from an embedded clause: for instance, (1a) may have a reading (1a′) (alongside the literal interpretation where, indeed, I do not entertain the thought that you are right), and the same holds for the b- and c-pairs.

(1) a. I don't think you're right
 a′. I think you're not right
 b. She doesn't believe John is ill
 b′. She believes John isn't ill
 c. They don't expect to win the race
 c′. They expect not to win the race

By contrast, most other predicates do not give rise to such inferences. Negated predicates like *predict* or *claim* lack readings where negation seems to take lower scope, as shown in (2). (2a) does not imply (2a′), and (2b) does not imply (2b′):

(2) a. I don't predict you're right
 a′. I predict you're not right
 b. She doesn't claim John is ill
 b′. She claims John isn't ill

Predicates that can give rise to such readings are referred to as *Neg-raising predicates*. Predicates that do not yield such readings are dubbed *non-Neg-raising predicates*. Readings invoked by Neg-raising predicates, where negation seems to take scope from the embedded clause, are called *Neg-raising readings*.

The standard analysis, which treats Neg-raising in pragma-semantic terms, goes back to Bartsch (1973) and has further been elaborated in Horn (1978, 1989), Horn and Bayer (1984), Horn (1989), Gajewski (2005, 2007), and Homer (2015), among many others. Under this approach, Neg-raising predicates are assumed to come along with an excluded middle or homogeneity presupposition. For instance, the predicate *think p* presupposes that either p is thought, or not-p.

Applying this to (1), (1a) presupposes that the speaker either thinks you are right or thinks that you're not right. Together with this presupposition, (1a) entails (1a'):[1]

(3) Assertion: I don't think you're right (1a)
    Presupposition: I think you're right or I think that you're not right
    I think that you're not right (1a')

Recently, this standard approach has been challenged by Collins and Postal (2014, henceforth CP14), who argue that Neg-raising involves syntactic movement of the negation from a lower clause into a higher clause (a proposal tracing back to Fillmore 1963, and also adopted in Horn 1971, 1972). Ignoring *do*-support effects, the syntactic structure of (1a) would then be as in (4), and the reading (1a') would follow from interpreting the negation in its base position (<NEG> indicating a lower copy/trace of NEG).

(4) I NEG think you're <NEG> right

Collins and Postal (2014 adopt a principle that states that only base occurrences of NEG are interpreted. Under this approach, the lowest copy of NEG must be semantically interpreted, whereas the highest copy of NEG is phonologically realized (in this case as *n't*).[2]

The syntactic approach to Neg-raising has often been rejected, as it seems to make incorrect predictions about Neg-raising constructions involving NIs (see e.g. Horn 1989; Gajewski 2007; Homer 2015 for discussion). To see this, take the following example from Horn (1989):

(5) Nobody supposes that nuclear war is winnable

If *nobody* is the realization of a negated indefinite (NEG ∃-body), the underlying structure of (5) under the syntactic approach should then be like (6). The predicted Neg-raising reading would then be that somebody supposes nuclear war is not winnable (with the raised negation taking scope from its base position).

(6) NEG ∃-body supposes that nuclear war is <NEG> winnable

However, this is not the Neg-raising reading that (5) has. The Neg-raising reading is rather 'everybody supposes that nuclear war is not winnable'. Under the conceived wisdom that NIs are negated existentials (and not universals scoping over

---

[1] Gajweski (2007) takes these excluded middle presuppositions to be soft presuppositions (in the sense of Abusch 2002, 2010), as they behave differently from so-called hard presuppositions. These excluded middle presuppositions can easily be suspended, e.g. in the case of (1a), in contexts where the speaker has made it clear that they have no thoughts about the issue, whereas hard presuppositions cannot be that easily suspended. For this and other reasons, Romoli (2013) takes the excluded middle inference to be a scalar alternative and takes Neg-raising readings to result from scalar implicatures.

[2] Naturally, this yields the question of what would trigger this movement. Collins and Postal (2014) are not explicit about this issue, but rather state that the syntactic and semantic properties of these constructions force an analysis in terms of movement.

negation, see Chapter 7), this Neg-raising reading cannot be yielded by raising the negation and incorporating it in the quantifier.[3]

Note that this is not a problem for the standard, pragma-semantic approach to Neg-raising; the excluded middle presupposition plus the assertion jointly entail the attested Neg-raising reading. If *suppose* in (6) presupposes that it is supposed that nuclear war is either winnable or not, then, if nobody supposes that nuclear war is winnable, everybody supposes that nuclear war is not winnable. This is indeed the attested Neg-raising reading.

Collins and Postal (2014) acknowledge this fact, but argue that this reading can, nevertheless, be accounted for under the syntactic approach to Neg-raising once it is assumed that constructions like (5) contain two, covert negations, next to the NI subject, as in (7).

(7) Nobody NEG$_1$ supposes that nuclear war is NEG$_2$ winnable

For CP14, (7) is the logical form of (5), and it has indeed the attested Neg-raising reading. Truth-conditionally, (7) ('nobody doesn't suppose that nuclear war is not winnable') is equivalent to 'everybody supposes that nuclear war is not winnable'. However, the negations NEG$_1$ and NEG$_2$ are not pronounced. In order to account for the phonological deletion of these two negations, CP14 postulate a mechanism by which (under particular circumstances) an even number of negations can be phonologically deleted under a clause-mate DE operator.[4]

Concretely, CP14 assume that, in (7), the lower negation (NEG$_2$) raises into the matrix clause. Again, using <...> serves to indicate lower copies of moved elements, as indicated in (8).

(8) Nobody NEG$_1$ NEG$_2$ supposes that nuclear war is <NEG$_2$> winnable

---

[3] Note that this objection would disappear if NIs were taken to be universal quantifiers that outscope negation (as has been argued for Greek neg-words by Giannakidou 2000 and for Japanese neg-words by Shimoyama 2001, 2006). For non-Negative Concord languages, like English, there is strong evidence that NIs are indeed existentials/indefinites under the scope of negation (cf. Penka 2011; Zeijlstra 2011; Iatridou and Sichel 2011 for an overview and discussion), though, and in the current debate, nobody has pursued an alternative analysis in terms of universal quantifiers. See Chapter 16 for more discussion.

[4] Collins and Postal (2014) employ various Neg-deletion rules (cf. CP14: ch. 8 for an overview). The Neg-deletion rule applying here states that an NPI-licenser can license the deletion of a clause-mate negation, provided that the total number of deleted negations is even and provided they stand in a c-command chain. CP14 do not postulate this rule just for these Neg-raising constructions, but they also apply it to account for weak NPI-hood in general. For CP14, a sentence like (i) also contains two covert negations, and has the underlying structure (ii) (see also Chapters 9, 11 for more discussion):

(i) At most three students ate any apples
(ii) At most three students ate ~~NEG NEG~~ some apples

After having raised NEG$_2$ into the matrix clause, NEG$_1$ can license the phonological deletion of (now clause-mate) NEG$_2$, after which *nobody* licenses the phonological deletion of NEG$_1$. Using ~~strikethrough~~ as an indication of phonological deletion, (8) then becomes (9), which is phonologically realized as (5).

(9) Nobody ~~NEG$_1$NEG$_2$~~ supposes that nuclear war is <NEG$_2$> winnable

Semantically, every NEG is interpreted in its lowest position (irrespective of whether it is realized or not), which gives rise to the attested Neg-raising reading: 'nobody does not suppose that nuclear war is not winnable', which is truth-conditionally equivalent to 'everybody supposes that nuclear war is not winnable'.

Naturally, the innovative—and perhaps somewhat unintuitive—step here is the presence of two negations that are phonologically zero. However, for CP14, this step can already be motivated on the basis of the following line of reasoning. First, there is syntactic evidence that the negation, at least in certain cases, discussed in detail in the next sections, *must* have started out below in the embedded clause. Consequently, the standard, pragma-semantic approach, which computes the Neg-raising reading on the basis of the negation taking scope from its surface position, then *cannot* be on the right track for them. Second, CP14 claim that there is independent evidence for such unpronounced negations. Together, this for them provides the necessary ingredients for an analysis as in (7)–(9).

In Section 8.2, I will present what I take to be the three most important arguments from CP14 in favour of the syntactic approach, including the proposed mechanism of Neg-deletion, and against the standard, pragma-semantic approach. Then, in Section 8.3, I will present three problems for this syntactic approach. In Section 8.4, I show that, upon closer inspection, the arguments presented in Section 8.2 in favour of the syntactic approach actually involve facts that are sometimes equally well, and sometimes even better, explained by the standard, pragma-semantic approach. In short, I conclude that the arguments provided by CP14 show that, maybe, in some, but certainly not in all cases of Neg-raising, negation must have started out of the embedded clause. However, nothing requires that negation must be interpreted in a lower position. In fact, there are good reasons to assume that negation never takes scope from a position lower than its surface position. As I conclude in Section 8.5, these facts reinstall the standard, pragma-semantic approach to Neg-raising.

8.2 Arguments in favour of the syntactic approach

The three most important arguments by CP14 in favour of their syntactic approach to Neg-raising centre around the licensing of embedded strict NPIs by negated Neg-raising predicates, the possibility of negated Neg-raising predicates to embed so-called *Horn-clauses*, and the syntactic behaviour of negative parentheticals. For

CP14, all these arguments indicate that the negation present in a higher clause with a Neg-raising predicate must have started out in a lower clause. These arguments will be discussed consecutively in Subsections 8.2.1, 8.2.2, and 8.2.3, respectively. Subsection 8.2.4 contains some concluding remarks.

8.2.1 Neg-raising and strict Negative Polarity Items

Strict NPIs, such as *breathe a word* or punctual *until* (see also Chapter 10, 14), differ from other, non-strict NPIs (such as *any* or *ever*) in the sense that the licensing of the former (10)–(11), but not the latter (12)–(13), is subject to syntactic locality constraints, such as clause-boundedness. Strict NPIs cannot be licensed by a clause-external licenser; non-strict NPIs can, as the following examples from CP14 demonstrate.

(10) a. Carolyn will *(not) breathe a word about it
 b. *Stanley doesn't predict that Carolyn will breathe a word about it

(11) a. Calvin {didn't move/*moved} in until June
 b. *Calvin didn't claim that Mona moved in until June

(12) a. Carolyn {won't/*will} say anything about it
 b. Stanley *(doesn't) predict that Carolyn will say anything about it

(13) a. Mona {didn't ever move in/*ever moved in}
 b. Calvin {didn't claim/*claimed} that Mona ever moved in

Strikingly, as CP14 show, a negated Neg-raising predicate may license embedded strict NPIs, though, as shown in (14).

(14) a. Stanley doesn't believe that Carolyn will breathe a word about it
 b. Calvin didn't think that Mona moved in until June

For CP14, this suggests that the negation must have started out clause-internally in order to locally license the NPI before it raises into the matrix clause. Further evidence, for CP14, for such a raising analysis comes from the fact that, once the embedded clause containing the strict NPI forms a syntactic island, i.e., a syntactic domain which is closed for external syntactic operations such as extraction, licensing of strict NPIs by negated Neg-raising predicates is no longer possible either.

For instance, embedded clauses with a clause-internal topic (15a) or an internal topic-cleft (15b) do not allow any *Wh*-element to further raise out of them, as shown below (again, based on CP14's examples), whereas, in the corresponding examples without clause-internal topics or where an internal topic clefts, *Wh*-extraction is fine (as shown in (15a′, b′)).

(15) a. *When does Mona believe that Irene, Jim should call?
    a'. When does Mona believe that Jim should call Irene?
    b. *What do you expect that it's Tony who says?
    b'. What do you expect that Tony says?

All embedded clauses containing the strict NPI in (16)–(18) are syntactic islands, i.e., constituents from which no element can be extracted. As is illustrated for such clause-internal topics in (16) and for clause-internal clefts in (17) (examples after CP14), strict NPIs in the embedded clause can no longer be licensed by the negated Neg-raising predicate in the higher clause. The same is illustrated for topic islands in (18), which also form syntactic islands (where the attested ungrammaticality follows from an alleged absent c-command relation between the higher copy of the negation and the surface position of its lower, unpronounced copy).

(16) a. *Stanley doesn't believe that about that, Carolyn will breathe a word
    b. *Calvin didn't expect that Mona, Jim should call until tomorrow

(17) a. *Stanley doesn't believe that it is Carolyn who will breathe a word about it
    b. *Calvin didn't expect that it was Mona who moved in until June

(18) a. *That Carolyn will breathe a word about it, Stanley doesn't believe
    b. *That Mona moved in until June, Calvin didn't expect

Now, for CP14, it follows that, contexts from which extraction is forbidden are also contexts in which negated Neg-raising predicates cannot license strict NPIs: Neg-raising involves movement of the negation from a lower clause into a higher clause. Once this movement is forbidden, syntactic Neg-raising can no longer take place.

However, this argument is not watertight. What the island effects show is that, if the strict NPI is in a different syntactic domain from that of its licensers, this NPI can no longer be licensed by it. While, in (14), the NPI and the negation must be in the same syntactic domain—otherwise NEG-movement should be impossible—in (16)–(18), they are not, as here NEG-movement is indeed impossible. But if strict NPI-licensing is subject to syntactic locality, there is nothing that a priori shows that the negation should have moved out of the lower clause in (14). One can equally well maintain that the negation licenses the NPI from its surface position in (14), given that it is in the same syntactic domain as the NPI, while the fact that (16)–(18) are out is then because the NPI and the negation are in different syntactic domains. What the facts show is only that negation can license strict NPIs in exactly those domains from which movement is also possible—a conclusion that is not surprising, as syntactic locality is not restricted to extraction, but to all kinds of syntactic operations, including agree(ment) (see also Chapter 10). The difference between Neg-raising and non-Neg-raising predicates is then a difference in locality (see Chapter 13). The complement of a Neg-raising predicate belongs to the same syntactic domain as the Neg-raising predicate, whereas the complement of a non-Neg-raising predicate belongs to a different domain. This conclusion is a necessary assumption for CP14 as well, since otherwise it cannot be explained in their approach why only Neg-raising predicates allow an embedded negation to raise into the higher clause and other predicates do not, and it suffices to account for the differences in terms of strict NPI-licensing by the negated Neg-raising and negated non-Neg-raising predicates discussed in this section.[5,6]

8.2.2 Neg-raising and Horn-clauses

Stronger evidence in favour of a syntactic approach to Neg-raising comes from so-called *Horn-clauses*. Horn-clauses, named after the person who first observed these constructions, are clauses where a clause-externally negated (strict) NPI in the specifier position of its CP triggers Negative Inversion.

Normally, Negative Inversion is possible only if the element present in Spec, CP is a negation or a (semi-)negative element, such as *few* or *only*.[7]

(19) a. No student has she liked
 b. Never has she liked me
 c. Not every student has she liked
 d. Few students has she liked
 e. Only Bill has she liked

Strikingly, under negated Neg-raising predicates, a clause that contains a (strict) NPI in its edge can also trigger/license Negative Inversion (20), but not under non-Neg-raising predicates (21).

(20) a. I don't think that ever before have the media played such a major role in a kidnapping
 b. I don't suppose that under any circumstances would she help me

(21) a. *I don't claim that ever before have the media played such a major role in a kidnapping
 b. *I don't predict that under any circumstances would she help me

---

[5] One could argue that this would predict that *Wh*-terms cannot be extracted from the complements of non-Neg-raising predicates, contrary to fact. *When does Mona say/claim that Jim should call Irene?* is perfectly grammatical. However, there is a rich body of (uncontroversial) evidence in syntactic theory that, in these cases, the *Wh*-term does not move directly from its base position to its final position, but first lands in an intermediate position, which is at the edge of its original syntactic domain, but already visible for the next syntactic domain (cf. Chomsky 1973, 2001).

[6] For more discussion on strict NPIs, Neg-raising and island effects, see also Romoli (2013).

[7] For an overview and discussion about when exactly negation licenses Negative Inversion, see Jackendoff (1972), May (1985), Haegeman (2000), Büring (2004), CP14.

For CP14, the availability of Horn-clauses under negated Neg-raising predicates shows that the negation must have started out in the Horn-clause itself. CP14 argue that those sentences have underlying structures with the negation starting out in the embedded clause, where the negation licenses the strict NPI and the subject–auxiliary inversion, before it raises into the matrix clause (where it gets phonologically realized as *n't*), as shown in the derivation in (22). Note that, if the negation had not raised into the main clause, it would have been incorporated into the NPI (with the realization *never before*).

(22) a. I think that the media have [NEG ever before] played such a major role
b. I think that [NEG ever before] have the media <have> played <[NEG ever before]> such a major role
c. I NEG think that [<NEG> ever before] have the media <have> played <[NEG ever before]> such a major role

For CP14, the licensing of strict NPIs and Horn-clauses forms strong evidence for a syntactic approach to Neg-raising. And, indeed, the existence of such examples has not been explained by any other account to Neg-raising. Moreover, as CP14 show, Horn-clauses give rise to the same island effects that apply to strict NPI licensing under negated Neg-raising predicates. Focusing on tropicalized islands, the data in (23) demonstrate that, if the embedded CP (with Negative Inversion) forms an island, the negation cannot license it either.

(23) a. *That ever before have the media played such a major role in a kidnapping, I don't expect
b. *That under any circumstances would she help me, I don't suppose

Collins and Postal (2014) show that not only NMs can license lower Horn-clauses; NIs also can also do so.

(24) a. Nobody thinks that ever before have the media played such a major role in a kidnapping
b. No person supposes that under any circumstances would she help me

This point is important, as it shows that Horn-clauses cannot only be licensed by those instances of Neg-raising that are not problematic for the syntactic approach, but also by those that need special treatment in terms of multiple phonologically deleted negations (see Section 8.1).

While one can argue that strict NPIs can be licensed by clause-external negations, under the assumption that the clause containing the strict NPI does not constitute a syntactic domain, no one has claimed before (at least to the best of my knowledge) that Negative Inversion can be licensed on a distance. That does not entail, though, that it is impossible to argue that Horn-clauses do not involve movement of negation.

8.2 ARGUMENTS IN FAVOUR OF THE SYNTACTIC APPROACH   207

To see this, take into consideration what the ingredients of Negative Inversion are. These are (i) the presence of subject–auxiliary inversion in the lower clause (i.e., T-to-C movement in syntactic terms), and (ii) the presence of a negation in the specifier position of this C-head. For CP14, in Horn-clauses, this negation has been raised into the higher clause. Now, no movement has to be postulated if one were to rephrase the ingredients for Negative Inversion as follows: (i) the presence of subject–auxiliary inversion in the lower clause (i.e., T-to-C movement in syntactic terms), and (ii) the presence of a *signpost of a negation* in the specifier position of this C-head, where a signpost of a negation is either a negative element or an element that is fully dependent on the presence of a (local) negation (aka an NPI). Now, this rephrasing covers both regular cases of Negative Inversion (where there should be a negation present in the specifier of the CP, since that it is the highest position of the syntactic domain that the C-head is part of) and Horn-clauses (where there is an NPI in the specifier position of the CP and a negation in the higher clause containing a Neg-raising predicate). Since Neg-raising predicates (and, as we will see in Subsection 8.3.1, a few others) are the only predicates that form a single syntactic domain with their complements (see the previous subsection), only negated Neg-raising predicates (and other predicates that form a syntactic domain with their complement clauses) can license Horn-clauses.

Naturally, the question arises whether such a step can be independently motivated. If there were no independent motivation to favour this rephrasing over the original formulation of Negative Inversion, the reasoning would be ad hoc and would not yield any further understanding. However, there are actually reasons to assume that Horn-clauses resemble, or even reduce to, another phenomenon, known as parasitic licensing, where additional NPIs can intermediate in a long-distance NPI-licensing relation that would otherwise apply locally only (cf. Klima 1964; Den Dikken 2006; Hoeksema 2007). Take the following Dutch examples from Hoeksema (2007).

(25) a. Ik hoop dat je niet meer van mening verandert
    I hope that you not any more of opinion change
    'I hope you will not change your opinion any more'
  b. *Ik hoop niet dat je meer van mening verandert
    I hope not that you any more of opinion change
    Intended: 'I hope you won't change your opinion any more'

The examples in (25) show that *meer* is a strict NPI. However, if the embedded clause also contains another (non-strict) NPI, such as *ooit* ('ever'), the sentence is fine again. NPI *ooit* can license strict NPI *meer*, as long as *ooit* is properly licensed itself.

(26) Ik hoop niet dat je ooit meer van mening verandert
   I hope not that you ever any more of opinion change
   'I hope that you will never change your opinion any more'

Much in the same vein, one can argue that T-to-C movement (unless triggered independently) is a strict NPI, albeit a strict NPI that needs to be licensed very locally (i.e., in the specifier of this C-head). However, if a properly licensed NPI appears in this position, this NPI could still mediate in the licensing of the strict NPI in the C-head. And if this NPI in the specifier position needs to stand in a local relation with its licenser itself (cf. CP14), it follows that Horn-clauses can be analysed as a special case of parasitic NPI-licensing.

There are good reasons to assume that Horn-clauses are actually instances of parasitic licensing. One of the reasons is that, even though many elements in Spec, CP could have contained a raised negation, Horn-clauses are restricted to NPIs appearing in that position. While CP14 need a special stipulation to rule out examples like (27) (for which they provide a condition that Horn-clauses must be restricted to existentials appearing in Spec, CP), under the idea that Horn-clauses instantiate an instance of parasitic licensing, the unwellformedness of such examples follows directly.

(27) a. I do NEG think that <NEG> always have the media played such a major role in a kidnapping
b. I do NEG suppose that under <NEG> many circumstances would she help me

Does that mean that Horn-clauses no longer provide evidence for movement of negation out of the embedded clause? Not necessarily. Ultimately, this depends on what exactly is taken to be the underlying mechanism behind parasitic licensing. If parasitic licensing involves movement of negation from the position of the intermediate NPI into the higher clause (cf. Den Dikken 2002; Hoeksema 2007), Horn-clauses still provide evidence for movement or incorporation of a lower negation. If parasitic licensing does not involve movement, one can argue that Horn-clauses do not involve movement either (provided that Horn-clauses indeed reflect parasitic licensing). Currently, parasitic NPI-licensing is not well enough understood to settle the debate, and I concur with CP14 that Horn-clauses may provide evidence that, in cases where Horn-clauses appear under negated Neg-raising predicates, this negation must have started out in the lower clause, as long as it has not been established that parasitic licensing does not involve negative movement.

8.2.3 Neg-raising and negative parentheticals

The third piece of evidence provided by CP14 for the syntactic approach to Neg-raising concerns negative parentheticals, such as parenthetically used *I don't fear* or *I don't think*. Negative parentheticals are generally forbidden, as shown by Ross (1973), and illustrated in (28):

8.2 ARGUMENTS IN FAVOUR OF THE SYNTACTIC APPROACH

(28) a. Max is a Martian, I fear
 b. Max is not a Martian, I fear
 c. *Max is a Martian, I don't fear
 d. *Max is not a Martian, I don't fear

However, as Ross (1973) observed, Neg-raising predicates can be used in negative parentheticals, provided that the main clause is negative as well.

(29) Max is not a Martian, I don't {think/believe/expect/*claim/*assert}

Note that negative parentheticals are also possible when the predicate is a Neg-raising predicate and the subject of the parenthetical is an NI—again, provided that the main clause is negative as well:

(30) Cathy will not, nobody {thinks/believes/expects/*claims /*asserts}, divorce Fred

Collins and Postal (2014), focusing on a wide array of instances of negative parentheticals, show that parentheticals are subject to two conditions: (i) a requirement that the elided complement of the parenthetical is semantically equivalent to the main clause; and (ii) a requirement that the parenthetical is not a DE context (and thus not semantically negative) itself. It is condition (ii) that generally rules out negative parentheticals. Now, if negative parentheticals involve syntactic movement of the negation out of their elided complement clause, as may be the case with Neg-raising predicates, both of these conditions are met in examples (29)–(30).

To see this, take (29) with its underlying structure (31). Here, the lower copy of the negation is interpreted, and the parenthetical is thus semantically non-negative; it contains only a negative form, not a negative meaning, for CP14. Therefore, both the identity condition, (i), and the condition that the parenthetical is semantically not DE (and thus not negative), (ii), are met.

(31) Max is not a Martian, I NEG think [Max is <NEG> a Martian]

The same applies to (30), which, as with every Neg-raising construction involving an NI, CP14 take to contain two phonologically deleted negations. As shown in (32), the negative parenthetical in (30), in full analogy to (5)/(7), then contains two negative elements (nobody and NEG$_1$), which jointly render the parenthetical positive (*nobody does not think that ...* is equivalent to *everybody thinks that ...*), and a raised negation (NEG$_2$) that is interpreted in the elided clause, satisfying the identity condition.

(32) Cathy will not, nobody NEG$_1$ NEG$_2$ thinks [Cathy will <NEG$_2$> divorce Fred], divorce Fred

Collins and Postal (2014) argue that the fact that negative parentheticals need a negation to be interpreted in the elided clause and not in the parenthetical itself forms another argument in favour of the syntactic approach to Neg-raising. For them, there is no way that these facts can be accounted for under the standard, pragma-semantic approach to Neg-raising, with the negation taking scope in situ.

However, whether the pragma-semantic approach cannot account for the existence of negative parentheticals primarily depends on the question of at what grammatical level these conditions hold, taking for granted that CP14's conditions (i)–(ii) are indeed correct.

For CP14, syntactic base positions are also the positions where negations are interpreted; so, there is no distinction to be made between these conditions applying at a syntactic level and their applying at a semantic/pragmatic level. However, using the perspective that negation is not interpreted lower than its surface position, there is a distinction to be made. At first sight, it does not look as if the pragma-semantic approach can get the facts right. Negation is interpreted in its surface position, and that would violate both conditions on negative parentheticals. The assertion of the negative parentheticals in (33) is DE, and the elided complement contains no negation:

(33) a. [I don't think [Max is a Martian]]
b. [Nobody thinks [Cathy will divorce Fred]]

However, once the presuppositional meaning contributions are taken into account, things shift. If the presuppositional content (which projects the excluded middle projection) is taken into consideration as well, and conditions (i)–(ii) are checked only after the enriched meaning contribution of the sentences is computed, the sentences in (33) yield the same meaning as the ones in (34), which then again meet both conditions (i) and (ii).

(34) a. I think [Max is not a Martian]
b. Everybody thinks [Cathy won't divorce Fred]

If the conditions on negative parentheticals have to be respected at a post-grammatical level, the pragma-semantic approach can deal with them just as well as CP14's syntactic approach. Hence it is indeed a question at which level negative parentheticals must fulfil the two conditions.

There is, I think, good evidence that these conditions indeed have to be licensed at a post-grammatical, pragmatic level. As CP14 show, it is not only Neg-raising predicates that can appear in negative parentheticals. Also, certain inherently negative verbs do. Collins and Postal (2014) provide the following examples:

(35) a. Cathy was not, I don't deny, divorced from Fred
b. Cathy was not, I don't doubt, divorced from Fred

Collins and Postal (2014) argue that these examples fit in, as the joint meaning contribution of 'not deny' or 'not doubt' is no longer DE, given the fact that *deny* and *doubt* are, in a way, negative verbs, too (since *deny* has a similar meaning to *not confirm*, and *doubt* means something like *not be certain*), and known, for instance, to license weak NPIs.

However, at a purely semantic level, the assertions of negated *doubt* and *deny* still count as negative. This is evidenced by the fact that such negated predicates can license both *either*-continuations (and not *too*-continuations) and strict NPIs like *in years*:

(36) a. Mary doesn't doubt it, and Bill doesn't doubt it either/*too
     b. Mary doesn't deny it, and Bill doesn't deny it either/*too

(37) a. Mary has*(n't) doubted it in years
     b. Mary has*(n't) denied it in years

But that means that, at a purely semantic level, *not deny* and *not doubt* still count as negative. If the conditions for negative parentheticals should hold at this level (or earlier), the examples in (35) are predicted to be ungrammatical. However, since negated predicated *not deny* and *not doubt* pragmatically imply *confirm* or *be certain*, they no longer count as DE if the two conditions that capture the acceptability of negative parentheticals apply post-grammatically. Then, again, it is correctly predicted that the examples in (35) are fine. But if that is the case, the pragma-semantic proposal makes at least the same predictions with respect to the distribution of negative parentheticals as CP14, if not better ones, given the facts in (35)–(37). The distribution of negative parentheticals does thus not form an argument in favour of the syntactic approach to Neg-raising.

8.2.4 Summing up

Collins and Postal (2014) provide three arguments in favour of the syntactic approach to Neg-raising, their central conclusion being that only under a syntactic approach to Neg-raising can the facts discussed in this section be explained. The emphasis here should be on *only*, as these arguments would no longer hold in favour of the syntactic approach if they were also compatible with the standard, pragma-semantic approach.

So far, the evidence provided by CP14 appears rather mixed in strength. The facts concerning strict NPIs and negative parentheticals do not form any major problem for the standard, pragma-semantic approach, as the latter is fully compatible with such facts. However, the facts concerning Horn-clauses have not yet received an explanation in alternative terms. Hence, unless Horn-clauses, despite CP14's claims, appear to be compatible with the standard, pragma-semantic approach to Neg-raising, they indeed call for a syntactic approach to Neg-raising. However, as we will see later on, under the standard, pragma-semantic approach to Neg-raising, these facts can be explained as well (irrespective of whether they involve negative movement or cross-clausal long-distance parasitic licensing).

8.3 Problems for CP14

Collins and Postal (2014)'s proposal is an important and original contribution to the understanding of the phenomenon of Neg-raising, but it also faces several challenges. First, as pointed out by Horn (2014), it is not the case that only Neg-raising predicates can license Horn-clauses; other negated predicates can do so as well, even though they do not trigger Neg-raising readings. In a reply, Collins and Postal (2018a), henceforth CP18, argue that these cases can be accounted for in a different way—but, as I will show next, in Subsection 8.3.1, this alternative account suffers from the same problem as the original account. Second, it turns out that the proposed independent motivation for phonologically deleted negation, apart from covert negative operators triggered by neg-words, is flawed (Subsection 8.3.2). Third, not every instance of Neg-raising can follow from the suggested movement mechanism, which has the effect that the proposed analysis of Neg-raising in syntactic terms should coincide with the standard, pragma-semantic approach rather than replace it (Subsection 8.3.3). Subsection 8.3.4 sums up.

8.3.1 Horn-clauses and Cloud-of-Unknowing predicates

Horn (2014) observes that not every negated predicate that licenses Horn-clauses also triggers Neg-raising readings. He presents examples of non-Neg-raising predicates, such as non-factive *know* and other predicates expressing particular subject or speaker knowledge—dubbed *Cloud-of-Unknowing predicates*—that, when negated, can also license Horn-clauses. Horn's example is presented below in (38a); (38b) is another example.

(38) a. I *(don't) know that ever before had all three boys napped simultaneously
 b. She's *(not) convinced that ever before had all three boys napped simultaneously

However, the examples in (38) clearly lack a Neg-raising reading. They are not semantically or pragmatically equivalent to their counterparts in (39).

(39) a. I know that never before had all three boys napped simultaneously
 b. She's convinced that never before had all three boys napped simultaneously

This shows that the negation that is phonologically realized in the main clauses in (38) cannot be the same negation that could license *ever before*. That means that the underlying structure of (38a) cannot be similar to the one in (22c), repeated as (40) below.

(40) I NEG think that [<NEG> ever before] have the media <have> played <[NEG ever before]> such a major role

To solve these problems, CP18 reply to Horn (2014) by arguing that examples such as (38) again contain two phonologically unrealized negations, i.e., (38a) would underlyingly be like (41). For CP18, syntax dictates that there must be (minimally) one negation present in the embedded clause; otherwise, Negative Inversion could not be accounted for. Since the presence of this negation does not give rise to a semantic effect, CP18 argue that the embedded clause must contain a second negation (taking immediate scope above it), which then semantically cancels out the other negation. In order to account for the fact that both negations are not phonologically realized, CP18 propose that negated Cloud-of-Unknowing predicates form again a context under which (clause-mate) phonological deletion of two negations may take place.

(41) [I do NEG$_1$ know ~~NEG$_2$~~ [<NEG$_2$> that ~~NEG$_3$~~ ever before had all three boys napped simultaneously]]

Let us go step by step through the derivation of (41). In (41), NEG$_2$ starts out in the embedded clause and licenses phonological deletion of NEG$_3$ (which is responsible for the subject–auxiliary inversion). NEG$_2$ then raises into the matrix clause to be phonologically deleted under [NEG$_1$ *know*], just as was the case in the constructions involving NIs. Since NEG$_2$ raises from the embedded clause into the main clause, all deleted negations and their licensers of the deletion are clause-mates.

An important ingredient of this analysis is the raising of one of the negations (NEG$_2$) from the embedded clause into the main clause. Empirical evidence for the fact that, under such an approach, raising must have taken place, again, comes from island effects. Horn-clauses cannot constitute syntactic islands when licensed by a Cloud-of-Unknowing predicate.

(42) a. *That ever before had all three boys napped simultaneously, I don't know
    b. *That ever before had all three boys napped simultaneously, she's not convinced of

Collins and Postal (2018a) are correct that, in their system, (41) is an alternative solution. However, what is problematic is that, if raising a negation (NEG$_2$) out of a Horn-clause into a matrix clause is possible, nothing rules out (43) as an additional underlying structure. If negations may raise out of embedded clauses into their respective matrix clauses, both (41) and (43) should be grammatical. If such movements were forbidden, both (41) and (43) would be ruled out.

(43) [I do NEG₁ know [that <NEG₁> ever before had all three boys napped simultaneously]]

But since (41b) is the structure that gives rise to the Neg-raising reading, it is predicted that the sentences in (38) should exhibit the corresponding Neg-raising readings in (39) as well, contrary to fact.

Collins and Postal (2018a) argue that one can rule this out by stipulating as a condition that, if a negation raises into a clause containing a negated Cloud-of-Unknowing predicate, this predicate must be under the scope of a distinct negation (CP18: ex. 70). But note that such a condition is not independently motivated: its primary motivation is that negated Cloud-of-Unknowing predicates do not yield Neg-raising readings. The question thus remains open as to why this condition is necessary and why it would not be possible to have a negation raised into such a main clause.

Apart from this, it makes empirically incorrect predictions. Take (44a).

(44) a. Nobody doesn't know [that ever before had all three boys napped simultaneously]
 b. Nobody knows that never before had all three boys napped simultaneously

This sentence contains one element (*nobody*) that must have been base-generated in the matrix clause. Hence, the condition is independently met. Then, according to CP18, an embedded negation may raise into the matrix clause, and the sentence is predicted to have the reading in (44b), contrary to fact.

Naturally, one can reformulate the condition in such a way that this particular problem disappears. However, the problem at stake is bigger: the explanans here is actually the explanandum. Positing a condition like CP18's (70) is, at best, descriptively adequate, but does not explain why Cloud-of-Unknowing predicates could not give rise to Neg-raising readings. Hence, the solution CP18 provide in order to account for the syntactic/semantic behaviour of Horn-clauses under negated Cloud-of-Unknowing predicates still suffers from the same problem (a predicted, but unattested Neg-raising reading) as their original proposal. Unless such readings are ruled out by ill-motivated brute force, both the Collins and Postal (2018a) and the CP18 proposals overgeneralize.

8.3.2 Phonologically deleted negations

To defend their proposal that (optionally present) semantic negations can be phonologically deleted in certain contexts, CP14 present several other cases of alleged phonological deletion of semantic negations, so that the proposal can be independently motivated. The most important examples are negated modals in French and optionally negative minimizers in German.[8]

As for the first, French has an expletive marker *ne* that, in principle, requires co-occurrence of an additional negation (usually *pas* or a NI), as discussed at length in Chapters 4 and 5.[9]

(45) Marie ne mange *(pas/rien) (French)
 Marie NEG eats not/nothing
 'Marie doesn't eat/Marie doesn't eat anything'

However, when combined with a few particular modals, such as *pouvoir* 'must', *savoir* 'know', or the verb *cesser* ('stop'), *ne* suffices to express negation. Collins and Postal (2014) present examples like (46).

(46) a. Je ne peux (pas) (French)
  I NEG can not
  'I can't'
 b. Il ne cessait (pas) de crier
  he NEG stopped not of cry
  'He didn't stop crying'
 c. Tu ne sais (pas)
  you NEG know not
  'You don't know'

Collins and Postal (2014) take this to be evidence for the deletion of a semantic negation. They formulate a rule stating that NEG can be deleted in the contexts of verbs such as *pouvoir, cesser, savoir* (and *oser* ('dare')). For them, examples like (46) contain a semantic negation that has been deleted.

However, as such examples are restricted to only a handful of modals, they can alternatively be analysed as remnants of previous stages of the languages that have fossilized into idiomatic expressions. As has been known at least since Jespersen (1917), Old French lacked the NM *pas* and used only the preverbal NM *ne* to express negation (see Chapter 5). Hence, it could very well be the case that expressions like (46) merely reflect Old French negation and should be thought of as idiomatic expressions (see Haegeman 1995; Zeijlstra 2004 for an overview and discussion of such facts). The existence of such an alternative analysis means that these examples do not form any hard evidence for the presence of phonologically

---

[8] A third case study concerns *too+infinitive* cases (e.g. *Bill is too lazy to work*), which I do not discuss in detail in this chapter. I refer to Romoli (2013) for a discussion that aims at discarding *too+infinitive* constituting evidence for phonologically deleted negations.
[9] For more discussion on the fact that French *ne* is an expletive negation, see Godard (2004); Zeijlstra (2010a); and references therein.

deleted negations. At the same time, it must be acknowledged that this alternative analysis also lacks proper evidence.

This is, however, different for the second kind of example that CP14 provide. Here, it can actually be shown that they contain no phonologically deleted negation. The examples concern particular German pejorative NPIs. As Sailer (2006) observes, for many (though not all) German speakers, certain sentences containing a minimizer (and similar pairs of sentences with other pejorative minimizers) with a negation have the same meaning as they would have without a negation. The construction is quite restricted and only works with a few verbs that express concern, interest, etc. An example is given in (47).

(47) a. Das interessiert mich einen Dreck (German)
 that interests me a dirt
 'I'm not interested at all'
 b. Das interessiert mich keinen Dreck
 that interests me no dirt
 'I'm not interested at all'

For CP14, the fact that the sentences with and without negation have the same meaning is evidence that (47a), which lacks an overt negation, must contain a covert negation. Hence, they argue that there is another rule that allows phonological Neg-deletion in these German constructions.

However, the semantic similarity of the two readings need not follow from the postulation of a covert negation in (47a). Here, an alternative analysis is possible too. One could argue that the two sentences have different readings whose usage conditions are more or less identical. If the reading of (47a) is that the degree of interest of the speaker is extremely low—even lower than some contextual threshold that indicates a minimal degree of interest, or simply as low as the degree of the speaker's interest in dirt—(47a) expresses that the speaker's interest lies below this threshold. That means that (47a) expresses that the speaker has no contextually salient degree of interest.

If that is the case, (47a), as well as other cases where an expression containing an extremely low degree can be uttered in exactly the same situations as those in which the speaker expresses no degree of interest at all by uttering (47b). Hence, the similarity of the readings in the minimal pair in (47) can be explained without postulating any covert negation.

Since such constructions require that the used minimizer denotes a degree even lower than the contextual threshold that indicates a minimal degree of concern, knowledge, etc., such minimizers are generally pejorative expressions (as is the case here). This analysis would also extend to Postal's treatment of *squat* (cf. Postal 2004), where the same pattern emerges: Both *I know squat about negation* and *I don't know squat about negation* have the same meaning or usage conditions. Expressions containing minimizers that do not denote degrees even lower than such contextual thresholds lack this effect. *I didn't mean a word of it* still has a different reading from *I meant a word of it*, since the latter (to the extent to which such an expression is grammatical) still conveys that there is some contextually salient degree to which 'I meant what I said'. Arguably, this also explains why such expressions are restricted to predicates expressing interest or knowledge (and why they generally involve pejorative minimizers).

Interestingly, the two analyses make different predictions. For the alternative analysis, (47a) is a positive sentence and (47b) a negative sentence. Under CP14's proposal, both are negative sentences.

As discussed in Chapter 7, sentential negation can be diagnosed in German by *auch (nicht)* ('also (not)') continuations. In German, positive clauses can be continued by *auch*, but they cannot be continued by *auch nicht*. Negative clauses, on the other hand, trigger *auch nicht*-continuations and only marginally allow *auch*-continuations:

(48) a. Hans geht und Marie auch (*nicht)   (German)
          Hans goes and Marie also not
          'Hans goes and Marie does too'
    b. Hans geht nicht und Marie auch ??(nicht)
          Hans goes not and Marie also not
          'Hans doesn't go and Marie doesn't either'

Exactly the same pattern can be observed for (47), as shown in (49). Hence, the test shows that (47b) carries a semantic negation, but (47a) does not, disproving CP14's covert-negation analysis.

(49) a. Das interessiert mich einen Dreck, und ihn auch (*nicht)   (German)
          that interests me a dirt, and him also not
          'I'm not interested at all, and neither is he'
    b. Das interessiert mich keinen Dreck, und ihn auch ??(nicht)
          that interests me no dirt, and him also not
          'I'm not interested at all, and neither is he'

This test shows that, in the German cases, independent evidence can be provided for the absence of covert negations in examples such as (47a).[10] As such examples (along with the indeterminate cases concerning French negated modals) form the major empirical evidence for the type of phonological Neg-deletion that CP14 employ, this renders the allusion to covert negations in the examples

---

[10] Again, similar diagnostics apply to *squat*: *I know squat about negation, and Mary knows squat about negation, too.* vs. *I don't know squat about negation, and Mary doesn't know squat about negation, either.* Thanks to Larry Horn for pointing this out to me.

involving Neg-raising and Cloud-of-Unknowing predicates void of independent motivation.[11]

This, I think, is a welcome step, as the allusion to pairs of phonologically deleted negations seems the most counter-intuitive assumption CP14 make. For one, processing of double negation is notoriously hard and generally restricted to special denial contexts (cf. Horn 1989). An example like (50a) is not easy at all to parse, and speakers have to take quite a bit of trouble to grasp its meaning. The question then immediately arises of why speakers would no longer have trouble if the additional negations in such sentences were not phonologically realized (and for this there is only indirect evidence). Even more puzzling is the assumption that language users would also have to resolve the fact that one of these covert negations underwent raising. In those cases where there is a clear signpost of negation present in the embedded clause (such as a strict NPI or a Horn-clause), there may be evidence in support of parsing a lower, raised, covert negation, but in examples like (50b), even such a signpost is lacking. Hence, it remains unclear why language users would have no problems in understanding a sentence like (7) (repeated as (50b)) with its Neg-raising reading under CP14's approach.[12]

(50) a. Nobody doesn't suppose that nuclear war is not winnable
b. Nobody NEG$_1$ supposes that nuclear war is NEG$_2$ winnable

I therefore conclude that the absence of evidence of phonologically deleted negations à la CP14 so far suggests that an approach to Neg-raising that entails phonologically deleted negations is on the wrong track. However, one might legitimately wonder whether these criticisms of the postulation of covert negations are not at odds with the fact that the latter are adopted in my analysis of NC. It should nevertheless be noted that the arguments I have presented do not entail that phonologically covert negations cannot exist at all. In Chapters 3–5, I argued that, in Negative Concord (NC) languages, neg-words enter a syntactic Agree relation with a possibly covert negation. In such configurations, covert negations are, however, syntactically licensed by an agreeing overt negative element, and there is, thus, clear morphological evidence, encoded in terms of [iNEG]- and [uNEG]-features, for the presence of a silent negation. In fact, covert operators can be acquired only if elements that may induce semantic negation in isolation do not do

---

[11] In more recent work, Collins and Postal (2017) address the fact that, in every Neg-raising construction, the matrix clause behaves negatively, given standard Klima-tests for sentential negation. For this reason, they entertain the hypothesis that every Neg-raising construction contains three negations, one overt negation base-generated in the matrix clause and two covert negations, one starting out in the matrix clause and one starting out in the embedded clause, which, in turn, raises into the main clause, giving rise to phonological deletion of the two, licensed by the third negation. In that sense, every Neg-raising construction has a similar structure as attributed by CP14 to Neg-raising constructions involving NIs. Given the discussion in this and previous sections, this makes the problems observed for CP14 only bigger.
[12] Note that this cannot easily be remedied by assuming that the parser may always postulate that negations may have raised, as in the large majority of negative sentences this is not the case.

so when combined with other elements that can induce semantic negation. Those cases are very different from the French and German examples presented here, where the appearance of a covert negation is dependent on the choice of verb. Moreover, covert negative operators must always remain unrealized, unlike the cases in (46)–(47), where Neg-deletion applies optionally. The existence of covert negative operators, therefore, does not extend to the kind of examples presented and discussed in CP14.

8.3.3 Islands and Neg-raising

A third problem for CP14 concerns island effects. Collins and Postal (2014) take Neg-raising to involve syntactic movement out of a lower clause into a higher clause. Evidence for that view comes from cases where a Horn-clause or a strict NPI is licensed by a clause-external, negated Neg-raising predicate. As shown before, if such strict NPIs or Horn-clauses are in a syntactic island (or form an island themselves), this movement is blocked, and such licensing is no longer possible, as is exemplified for strict NPIs in (51) and for Horn-clauses in (52):

(51) *That Carolyn will breathe a word about it, Stanley doesn't expect

(52) *That ever before had all three boys napped simultaneously, I don't believe

But if that is correct, and Neg-raising is indeed the result of syntactic movement, Neg-raising readings should not be allowed when the clause in which the negation appears to be interpreted is a syntactic island. However, this prediction is not borne out. Examples (51) and (52) can easily give rise to a Neg-raising reading if the strict NPI is absent or if subject–auxiliary inversion does not take place, as illustrated in (53) and (54). See also Romoli (2013), who presents more evidence for this claim.

(53) That Carolyn will breathe, Stanley doesn't expect
      'Stanley expects that Carolyn won't breathe'

(54) That all three boys napped simultaneously, I don't believe
      'I believe that all three boys didn't nap simultaneously'

But where does the Neg-raising reading come from? Clearly, it cannot be the case that the negation emerged in the embedded clause—otherwise the raising of a negation in (51) and (52) should not be problematic either. The only way to account for Neg-raising readings in (53) and (54) is by alluding to some pragma-semantic mechanism along the lines of Bartsch (1973) and her successors.

This has important consequences. It shows that under CP14's approach, the pragma-semantic approach must be valid throughout, as acknowledged in Collins and Postal (2018b). That means that a sentence like (1a), repeated in (55), is actually ambiguous between two types of Neg-raising readings. After all, there is no reason why the pragma-semantic approach would apply in (53)/(54), but not in (1a)/(55). The example in (1a)/(55) has thus two readings if CP14's approach is correct (next to the literal, non-Neg-raising reading): one where the Neg-raising reading comes from the low interpretation of the raised negation, and one as a result of the inference that comes from the excluded middle presupposition.

(55) I don't think you're right
    a. I NEG think you're <NEG> right   (syntactic NEG-raising)
    b. I NEG think you're right   (pragma-semantic NEG-raising)

However, the syntactic approach is then no longer an alternative analysis to the standard, pragma-semantic approach, but rather an account that is at best co-existent with it. Note that this seriously undermines the strength of CP14's proposal, as it is no longer clear why (55) should also have a parse with a negation starting out below. Why would syntactic Neg-raising not only apply when there is some trace of the negation visible in the embedded clause (such as subject–auxiliary inversion)?

8.3.4 Summing up

What we observed in this section is that CP14/18a's approach both overgeneralizes and undergeneralizes. It predicts Neg-raising readings where they are not attested, and it predicts the absence of Neg-raising readings where they are found. Moreover, one of the most important assumptions that this syntactic approach to Neg-raising builds on, Neg-deletion of the type illustrated in examples (46)–(47), cannot be motivated independently, despite claims to the opposite. A minimal requirement for this approach to be compatible with the observed facts is stating that the syntactic and the pragma-semantic approaches are both correct and that there are two different sources for Neg-raising readings (cf. Collins and Postal 2018b).

From a perspective of scientific parsimony, this is unattractive. It is also unattractive that particular stipulations have to be made for the alleged phonological deletion of negations and the absence of Neg-raising readings with negated Cloud-of-Unknowing predicates.

However, at the same time, as we saw in Section 8.2, it appears that the licensing of Horn-clauses under negated Neg-raising predicates seems to favour the syntactic approach, and has not been explained under the standard, pragma-semantic approach to Neg-raising. But only if this standard, pragma-semantic approach to Neg-raising is able to account for these facts as well can the syntactic approach be rejected and the phenomenon of Neg-raising exclusively be the result of inferences resulting from excluded middle presuppositions.

8.4 Reinstalling the standard, pragma-semantic approach

So, where do we stand? Collins and Postal (2014)'s approach faces at least three serious problems: it predicts Neg-raising readings to be possible in cases where they are not attested; it predicts Neg-raising readings to be impossible in cases where they are actually found; and, moreover, the treatment of Neg-raising readings invoked by NIs can only be maintained by making very specific assumptions, which, on closer inspection, turn out to not be independently motivated. However, CP14 can straightforwardly account for the fact that strict NPIs and Horn-clauses can be licensed by higher negated Neg-raising predicates. Hence, in order to reinstall the standard, pragma-semantic approach, it must be shown that this approach can also capture the observed facts concerning Horn-clauses. This may not be a straightforward task, as the standard, pragma-semantic approach to Neg-raising does not take the negation to start out in the lower clause in order to have it reconstructed at a later stage. However, as I will show now, it is still possible to unify the facts presented by CP14 with this standard, pragma-semantic approach to Neg-raising.

The central claim of the pragma-semantic approach is that, in Neg-raising readings, the negation is interpreted in its surface position. Collins and Postal (2014)'s central claim is that the negation starts out in a lower clause and is interpreted there. It is important to observe that CP14's central claim (negation starts out in a lower clause and is semantically interpreted there) is actually a twofold claim: one claim that the negation starts out below, and the other claim that negation must also be interpreted in this lower position. However, CP14 only provide evidence for the first claim. To the extent that the evidence is valid, Horn-clauses licensed by negated Neg-raising predicates show that the negation may in some cases indeed start out in the lower clause. However, nothing forces it to also be interpreted in this lower clause.

Hence, it is still possible to reconcile CP14's observations with the pragma-semantic approach to Neg-raising, even if Horn-clauses involve negative movement, as it is a logical possibility that, in particular cases, negation starts out below, raises into the higher clause, and is interpreted (only) there, with the excluded middle or homogeneity presupposition of the Neg-raising predicate triggering an additional inference that, together with the assertion, yields the Neg-raising reading. Under such an account, it is possible to derive the Neg-raising readings of sentences that contain lower strict NPIs or Horn-clauses. The examples in (56) would then have syntactic structures as in (57), with <NEG> again indicating the base position of NEG. Subject–auxiliary inversion is licensed by the lower negation before it raises into the higher position, where it will be semantically interpreted.

(56) a. Stanley doesn't believe that Carolyn will breathe a word about it
b. I don't think that ever before have the media played such a major role in a kidnapping

(57) a. Stanley does NEG believe that Carolyn will <NEG> breathe a word about it
b. I do NEG think that <NEG> ever before have the media <have> played <NEG ever before> such a major role in a kidnapping

Such an analysis already makes all the relevant correct predictions. First, it can account for the relevant aspects concerning the distribution of strict NPIs, including their island sensitivity: if the embedded clause is an island, the negation can never move into the matrix clause. Furthermore, the existence of Neg-raising readings involving island clauses (Section 8.3.3) naturally follows. In (53), repeated as (58), there is no movement going on, but the assertion and the presupposition together still trigger the Neg-raising reading. Because Neg-raising does not involve any kind of syntactic reconstruction, movement of negation is not a prerequisite for Neg-raising readings.

(58) That Carolyn will breathe, Stanley doesn't expect
'Stanley expects that Carolyn won't breathe'

In fact, following standard minimalist ideas on syntactic movement (cf. Chomsky 1995a), movement takes place only when it is necessary. That is indeed the case in the examples in (56), but in other examples—for instance (1a) repeated as (59)—no negative movement has been going on. The surface position of negation is also its base position here.

(59) I don't think you're right

Adopting this version of the pragma-semantic approach to Neg-raising also avoids alluding to deleted double negations. In examples such as (60), the universal Neg-raising follows immediately. Negation is simply interpreted in its surface position (which is also its base position), and the excluded middle or homogeneity presupposition does the rest of the job. Note also that, if in (61a), where the negation must have started out below to license Negative Inversion, it can still raise into the position where it is interpreted together with the existential realized as *nobody* (61b), presuming that NIs are the phonological realization of an adjacent negation and indefinite (cf. Penka 2011; Zeijlstra 2011; see also Chapters 7 and 12). Consequently, no phonologically deleted double negations are needed.

(60) Nobody supposes that nuclear war is winnable

(61) a. Nobody thinks that ever before have the media played such a major role in a kidnapping
b. NEG ∃-body Nobody thinks that <NEG> ever before have the media played such a major role in a kidnapping

Finally, the facts concerning Cloud-of-Unknowing predicates follow. What Neg-raising predicates—at least the ones discussed thus far—and Cloud-of-Unknowing predicates share is that they do not impose strict locality conditions on their embedded clauses; other predicates, such as *say* or *claim*, do. Therefore, Neg-raising predicates and Cloud-of-Unknowing predicates can license embedded strict NPIs and Horn-clauses. As the other predicates impose stronger locality conditions, negation cannot move out of them, and, therefore, they also cannot license embedded strict NPIs and Horn-clauses. However, Cloud-of-Unknowing and Neg-raising predicates differ with respect to the excluded middle- or homogeneity presupposition: Neg-raising predicates have it; Cloud-of-Unknowing predicates do not. Hence, the latter class of predicates does not trigger Neg-raising readings.

One may wonder, then, why Neg-raising predicates have two distinguishing properties: weak locality conditions imposed on their complement clauses, and the excluded middle- or homogeneity presupposition responsible for the Neg-raising readings. Ideally, what renders some predicate a Neg-raising predicate should ideally follow from one distinguishing property only. There is no reason why predicates with an excluded middle- or homogeneity presupposition should also impose weak locality conditions on their complement clauses to yield a Neg-raising reading, unless it can be proven that these two properties are independent.

But this independency can indeed be proven. Interestingly, there are predicates that only have this excluded middle- or homogeneity presupposition, and lack the weaker locality restrictions. *To be of the opinion* is a good example (Chris Collins, pers. comm.). Example (62a) clearly has the reading (62b). However, it cannot license strict NPIs or Horn-clauses.

(62) a. I am not of the opinion you're right
b. I am of the opinion you're not right

(63) a. *I am not of the opinion that Carolyn will breathe a word about it
b. *I am not of the opinion that ever before have the media played such a major role in a kidnapping

Hence, predicates' imposition or not of weak and strong locality conditions on their complement clauses, and predicates coming with an excluded middle- or homogeneity presupposition, are independent properties. This predicts that there are indeed 2*2=4 possible predicates with respect to the presence or absence of an excluded middle- or homogeneity presupposition, and with respect to the weaker or stronger locality conditions, as is demonstrated in the following table.

(64) Four types of predicates

	Imposes weak locality constraints on its complement	Imposes strong locality constraints on its complement
Excluded middle- or homogeneity presupposition present	*think, believe, expect*	*to be of the opinion, to be true, to be the case*
Excluded middle- or homogeneity presupposition absent	*know, to be convinced* (Cloud-of-Unknowing predicates)	*say, claim, predict*

It may be striking, though, that the large majority of predicates that come with the excluded middle- or homogeneity presupposition also impose weak locality constraints on their complements. However, this may very well be because most predicates in this class are also non-factive, and it has been claimed in syntactic theory that non-factive predicates often impose weaker constraints on extraction from complement clauses than factive predicates do (cf. Giorgi 2004 and others). Both Neg-raising and Cloud-of-Unknowing predicates are indeed always non-factive.[13]

The crucial property that distinguishes predicates that allow licensing of strict NPIs and embedded (Horn-)clauses from predicates that do not lies in the weaker locality conditions they impose on their complement clauses. The fact that clauses containing such predicates form a single syntactic domain with their complement clause can account for both the presence of extraction facts and the presence of domain-internal long-distance licensing. Both phenomena are known to be subject to the same kind of syntactic locality conditions. Hence, in Horn-clauses licensed by negated Neg-raising predicates, negation may start out in the embedded clause, depending on how parasitic licensing works exactly.

8.5 Conclusions

As shown in the previous sections, the proposed alternative in this chapter reinstalls the standard, pragma-semantic approach to Neg-raising. While the syntactic approach suffers from various problems, none of the arguments presented in favour of it form an argument against the standard, pragma-semantic approach,

---

[13] The reverse does not always hold, though: not every non-factive is a Neg-raiser. To date, it is not fully clear what constitutes the set of Neg-raisers (arguably an argument in favour of the syntactic approach), though see Zuber (1984) for an attempt to define this class.

8.5 CONCLUSIONS 225

as it is equally apt to account for the relevant distribution of strict NPIs and Horn-clauses (irrespective of whether the proposed evidence by CP14/18a involves movement of a negation or not), as well as the behaviour of negative parentheticals. There are thus no non-theory-internal reasons to maintain CP14's syntactic approach to Neg-raising to explain why negation sometimes seems to take scope from a position inside an embedded clause. The wide range of novel and striking facts presented in CP14 is fully compatible with the standard, pragma-semantic approach to Neg-raising.

9
Intermezzo
The landscape of polarity-sensitive elements
Convergence vs divergence

9.1 Neg-words and/or (other) Negative Polarity Items

One of the central questions addressed in the previous part was whether neg-words were NQs or NPIs. It has become clear that neg-words are indeed not NQs; they are semantically non-negative.

However, it is not that straightforward to assess whether they are NPIs or not. *Strictu sensu*, they are. They are semantically non-negative elements that need to be licensed by an element carrying an interpretable negative formal feature [iNEG], which is generally carried only by NMs or covert negative operators, albeit it that, in some languages, other elements may also carry such a feature [iNEG]. At the same time, neg-words crucially differ from all other known NPIs, in the sense that they are self-licensing in the terms of Ladusaw (1992). More formally, they are able to license the presence of a covert operator that, in turn, can license them. That suggests that neg-words are also crucially different from what is generally assumed to be an NPI.

For this reason, scholars have sometimes argued that there is a general set of elements called *Negative-Sensitive Items* (NSIs; cf. Miyagawa et al. 2017) that comprises both neg-words and 'plain' NPIs. Even though this terminology can be very useful, there is something unsettling about separating neg-words from 'plain' NPIs—not only because one would need a definition of NPI-hood that does not capture neg-words (providing such a definition in itself is not impossible), but, more importantly, because it suggests that NPIs form a single category. However, there is nothing that unifies all NPIs to the exclusion of neg-words in a principled way. What we see is that there are all kinds of elements that, for one reason or another, are distributionally restricted in such a way that they are all fine under the (direct) scope of negation. But that makes NPI-hood a non-homogenous notion. The question of whether neg-words are NPIs or not, then, essentially becomes a non-question. Even though neg-words are semantically non-negative and distributionally restricted, there is no point in wondering whether they belong to the class of elements to which *any*, *ever*, *need*, *in years*, or (punctual) *until* belong. These elements do not belong to a single class, either. It may actually very well be the case that certain NPIs share more properties with other non-NPIs, PPIs, or neg-words than with other NPIs.

What this calls for is an approach to negative dependencies, including all known cases of neg-words, NPI-hood, and PPI-hood, that is not based on the assumption that all NPIs (or PPIs) share a common core, irrespective of whether neg-words would belong to that core. In Section 9.2, I sketch the outline of such an approach, which I dub a *convergent* approach, to negative dependencies, and which, in the remaining Chapters, 10–15, will be applied to a series of different NPIs and PPIs. After that, in Section 9.3, I briefly introduce the different kinds of NPIs and PPIs that we will come across in the coming chapters.

9.2 Convergence vs divergence

Most approaches to NPI-hood—and also to PPI-hood, even though PPI-hood is a less well-investigated research area than NPI-hood—are so-called *divergent* approaches. They assume some common core for NPI-hood and then take the existing variation to be ancillary. This is depicted in (1).

(1)

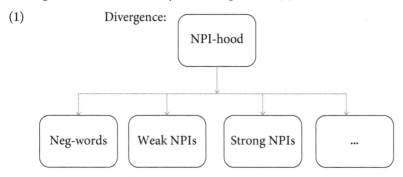

A good example of such a divergent approach is Chierchia (2013), who takes NPI-hood to be the result of the introduction of domain alternatives that need to agree with a covert exhaustifier. This, for him, is behind all the NPIs he discusses, and also applies to neg-words. To account for the differences between such elements, he assumes that, for neg-words, these NPIs have an additional uninterpretable negative feature [uNEG] (following Zeijlstra 2004, 2008a, b), and, for strong NPIs, that these must be exhaustified with respect to their entire meaning contribution (including presuppositions and implicatures), and not with respect to their assertive content only, as is the case for weak NPIs. This opens up questions as to why neg-words should have this NPI-behaviour in addition to their

[uNEG] feature, or whether the mechanism that triggers the exhaustifier to be present is the same across all these types of NPIs. The latter would be unexpected, as neg-words pattern with strong NPIs in their sensitivity to syntactic locality conditions with respect to their licensers. Only weak NPIs can be licensed across syntactic domains, such as islands. Moreover, Chierchia (2013) does not address other types of NPIs, such as so-called strong/weak NPIs (like universal modals such as English *need*), or superweak NPIs that appear to be fine in all kinds of non-DE, non-veridical contexts. The NPI-hood of such elements would actually be very hard to account for under his system.

Giannakidou (2018) questions the above-mentioned exhaustification approach and argues that it suffers from both theoretical and empirical problems. An assessment of the theoretical problems will take place later—it turns out that most criticisms can be either tackled or circumvented by slightly modifying the approach. Empirically, she argues that various Greek, Korean, and Mandarin Chinese NPIs are licensed outside the set of DE contexts. Instead, she argues that these are best analysed in terms of deficient referentiality. These empirical problems, however, only affect the exhaustification approach if every NPI is taken to be subject to it. If the landscape of NPIs is more diverse, as Giannakidou strongly argues for herself, nothing excludes different types of NPIs from coexisting. In that light, the criticism of the exhaustification approach she presents in Giannakidou (2018) seems somewhat at odds with the overall conclusion she reaches with respect to the diversity of NPI-hood.

Again, this shows that a proper approach to NPI-hood must take into consideration that NPI-hood is not a grammatical category in its own right, but rather the result of various elements converging towards one joint property. In the remaining chapters, I argue that this convergence approach, as depicted in (2), provides a natural way to understand the heterogeneous nature of NPIs and PPIs.

(2) Convergence:

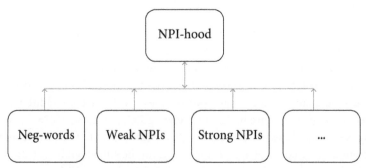

9.3 Outline

An advantage of the convergent approach is that various proposed theories of NPI-hood no longer necessarily contradict each other. In fact, the remaining chapters will show that various proposed analyses turn out to be correct in their own right, albeit it with a more limited domain of application, and sometimes also with due modification.

For instance, in Chapter 10, I will essentially follow Chierchia's approach to weak and strong NPIs, but argue that there can only be a syntactic feature-checking relation between a strong NPI and its exhaustifier. Weak NPIs are exhaustified for purely pragmatic reasons. This approach to weak NPIs, therefore, resembles Krifka's (1995) approach, on which Chierchia's alternative was originally considered an improvement. Also, going back to the early nineties, Kadmon and Landman (1993) have observed that various NPIs display domain-widening effects, and suggest that domain-widening is what underlies NPI-hood. This hypothesis appeared too strong, but that does not mean that no NPI can be an NPI because of its domain-widening properties. I will demonstrate, basing myself on Iatridou and Zeijlstra (2017, 2021), that the English NPI *in years* is actually such a domain-widening NPI.

Of course, that does not mean that all NPIs are captured in these terms. It turns out that at least three more types of NPIs can be identified. There are superstrong NPIs, only licensed in anti-morphic contexts, which, as I will argue in Chapter 11, must be considered idiomatic in nature. In addition, there is a class of strong/weak NPIs that indeed have a distribution that lies in between that of strong and weak NPIs, for which neither a scalarity nor a referential-deficiency approach proves to be tenable. In fact, I argue that it is not even a semantic but rather a lexico-syntactic property that makes them NPIs, much along the lines of what Collins and Postal (2014) refer to as unary NPIs. As for the referential-deficiency approach, I follow Giannakidou (2000 et seq.), but I differ from her by arguing that this approach applies to superweak NPIs only.

Finally, the above-mentioned types of NPIs do not even fully exhaustify the set of NPI-like elements. In Chapter 12, I will discuss constructions that may only give rise to a particular reading when these constructions are embedded in DE contexts. While it has sometimes been argued that such constructions contain a hard-to-notice NPI, I conjecture that the presence or absence of such readings is purely pragmatically captured.

The convergent approach does not only hold for NPIs. It also holds for PPIs. The landscape of PPIs is as much a heterogeneous landscape as that of NPIs. In fact, the two landscapes do not fully overlap, either. There are PPIs that can be considered the mirror image of NPIs, but there are also NPIs (like strong/weak NPIs) that lack any PPI-counterpart, and, as we shall see, there are PPIs that lack an NPI-counterpart. Examples of PPIs that mirror certain NPIs are universal quantifier

PPIs: strong universal PPIs are PPIs for the same reason as weak existential NPIs are weak NPIs; and weak universal PPIs are PPIs for the same reason as strong existential NPIs are strong NPIs. These PPIs will be discussed in Chapter 13.

At the same time, these are not the only PPIs that mirror NPIs attested. Various existential NPIs can also be seen as the mirror image of superweak NPIs, albeit that they have the distribution of a weak PPI, something that will be explained in Chapter 14. The same chapter also discusses elements like English *until* that are polarity-sensitive, but where the kind of polarity-sensitivity is dependent on the grammatical context. When combined with a perfective, *until* is NPI-like; when combined with an imperfective, it is PPI-like.

And finally, as Chapter 15 will reveal, there are PPIs that lack any NPI-counterpart. Elements that carry features with the illocutionary force of a speech act are such PPIs. These may not be outscoped by negation (though they can be outscoped by other elements), but there are no examples of illocutions that must be embedded under a negation.

PART III
POLARITY-SENSITIVITY

10
Strong vs weak Negative Polarity Items

10.1 Introduction: Strong and weak Negative Polarity Items

As shown in the previous chapter, NPIs come about in various kinds. One of the most prototypical kinds of NPIs are weak NPIs, such as *any* or *ever*. Weak NPIs are only licensed in (Strawson) DE contexts, as shown in (1)–(2), where DE is defined as in (3):

(1) a. We *(didn't) read *any* books
 b. Nobody ready *any* books
 c. Every student who knows *anything* about linguistics will join the event
 d. Do you want *any* cookies?
 e. At most three students did *any* homework
 f. John hardly likes *any* cookies

(2) a. We *(didn't) *ever* read a book
 b. Nobody *ever* read these books
 c. Every student who has *ever* been there before will join the event
 d. Did you *ever* want to succeed?
 e. At most three students *ever* did their homework
 f. John hardly *ever* liked cookies

(3) δ is downward entailing iff $\forall X \forall Y (X \subseteq Y) \rightarrow ([[\delta]](Y) \subseteq [[\delta]](X))$[1,2]

At the same time, as already discussed in Chapters 1, 2, and 9, not every NPI fits in the class of weak NPIs. Strong NPIs like *in years* and punctual *until* are ruled out in DE contexts that are not AA, such as *few* or *at most N*.

(4) a. He hasn't had a seizure *in years*
 b. *He has had a seizure *in years*
 c. Nobody has had a seizure *in years*
 d. *Few patients have had a seizure *in years*
 e. *At most 10 patients have had a seizure *in years*

---

[1] Definition adopted from Van der Wouden (1994).
[2] For a discussion and overview of whether polar questions are DE, see Mayr (2013); Nicolae (2015).

(5) a. She didn't leave *until* 5pm / my departure / I left
    b. *She left *until* 5pm / my departure / I left
    c. Nobody *until* 5pm / my departure / I left
    d. *Few people left *until* 5pm / my departure / I left
    e. *At most 10 people left *until* 5pm / my departure / I left

Naturally, the question arises why weak NPIs are restricted to (Strawson) DE contexts and strong NPIs restricted to AA contexts? What sets the two apart?

In this chapter, I first introduce the basic tenets of a current strong proposal on the nature of NPI-hood (Chierchia 2006, 2013), taking NPI to be subject to obligatory exhaustification, and I discuss how the distinction between strong and weak NPIs can be captured under this approach, following Gajewski (2011) and by providing novel evidence in favour of it. Then, in Section 10.3, I show that the way in which the strong–weak NPI-distinction is currently captured under Chierchia's approach still faces certain problems. In Section 10.4, I provide a solution for this problem by alluding to two different mechanisms—one syntactic, one pragmatic—that trigger obligatory exhaustification, and I show that, when these two mechanisms are adopted, the strong–weak distinction follows naturally. Section 10.5 discusses the role of domain-widening in strong and weak NPI-licensing. Section 10.6 concludes.

10.2 Exhaustification approaches to NPI-hood and the strong–weak distinction

In order to address the above-mentioned questions, I will first (in Subsection 10.2.1) discuss the approach to weak-NPI-hood that is currently most successful in describing the contextual restrictions of weak NPIs, the so-called exhaustification approach by Chierchia (2013), with predecessors in Kadmon and Landman (1993); Krifka (1995); Lahiri (1998); and Chierchia (2006). After that, in Subsection 10.2.2, I will discuss how, within this approach, the distinction between weak and strong NPIs is generally derived, following work by Gajewski (2007, 2011) and Chierchia (2013). I conclude this section by spelling out several problems for the exhaustification approach and the way it disentangles weak from strong NPIs.

10.2.1 Exhaustification approaches to NPI-hood

According to a recent line of thinking (Krifka 1995; Lahiri 1998; Chierchia 2006, 2013; and others), NPIs that are only fine in DE contexts are ruled out outside such contexts because then their semantics would give rise to a contradiction. That means that the sentences in (6), even though they are judged unacceptable, are,

10.2 EXHAUSTIFICATION APPROACHES TO NPI-HOOD 235

strictly speaking, not syntactically ill-formed, but rather violate their usage conditions (Kadmon and Landman 1993) or yield a semantic anomaly (Krifka 1995; Lahiri 1998; Chierchia 2006, 2013).

(6) a. *Mary has ever been there
    b. *I read any book

Following Chierchia's (2006, 2013) implementation of this idea, NPIs are equipped with an uninterpretable feature [uσ,D] which obligatorily introduces all its domain and scalar alternatives and which must be checked by a covert c-commanding exhaustifier that carries an interpretable feature [iσ,D]. Chierchia then argues that the combination of these two requirements triggers a semantic contradiction for every NPI outside a DE context. To illustrate this, let us focus on (6b). For Chierchia, the uninterpretable feature [uσ,D] of *any book* needs to be checked ((7a) is ungrammatical). Once it gets checked by the covert exhaustifier (the only element able to check this feature), it yields a logical contradiction (7b).

(7) a. [I read [any book] $_{[uσ,D]}$]
    b. [EXH$_{[iσ,D]}$ [I read [any book] $_{[uσ,D]}$]]

The question is, of course, why (7b) yields a contradiction. Following Chierchia, the uninterpretable feature [uσ.D] introduces all scalar and domain alternatives. The scalar alternatives are all elements on the scale <*some/any*, ..., *all*>. The domain alternatives are all subdomains of the domain of quantification of the *any*-term. If, in (7b), the domain of quantification is the set of books {a, b, c}, the domain alternatives are all subdomains of {a, b, c}, such as {a, c}, {b, c}, or the singleton set {a}. The idea behind the introduction of domain alternatives has originally been guided by the intuition that NPIs are felt to be domain-wideners. In terms of Kadmon and Landman (1993), domain-wideners are elements that extend their domain of quantification beyond their contextual restrictions, including elements that are usually felt to be outside the domain of quantification. The claim that all NPIs are domain-wideners has proven to be false (cf. Krifka 1995; Chierchia 2013; see Section 10.5) and has, therefore, in this approach, been replaced by the claim that all NPIs obligatorily introduce not only scalar but also domain alternatives.

The second factor behind the unacceptability of (7b) comes from the introduction of the exhaustifier. An exhaustifier that is applied to some proposition states that all non-weaker alternatives of that proposition are false. Chierchia (2013) introduces two exhaustification operators, **O** and **E**. **O** is the covert counterpart of *only*; **E** is the overt counterpart of *even*.[3] **E** is an exhaustifier that applies to

---

[3] Note, though, that **O** and **E** do not have to be semantically identical to *only* and *even*, respectively. For instance, under Horn's (1969) presuppositional view, *only p* presupposes its prejacent *p* and asserts its exhaustification, whereas, for Chierchia, in **O** and **E**, both meaning components are part of the assertion.

emphatic minimizing NPIs only (such as *lift a finger*). Since *any* or *ever* do not count as emphatic NPIs, we focus here on **O** and adopt that EXH has the following semantics of **O**:

(8) $[[EXH]] = [[O]] = \lambda p.p \wedge \forall q \in Alt(p)[p \not\subseteq q \rightarrow \neg q]$

Now, suppose again that the domain quantification is the set of books {a, b, c}. Then [[I read any book]] denotes $\exists x.[x \in \{a, b, c\} \& read(I, x)]$. Now, the domain alternatives of $\exists x.[x \in \{a, b, c\} \& read(I, x)]$ are:

(9) a. $\exists x.[x \in \{a, b, c\} \& read(I, x)]$
b. $\exists x.[x \in \{a, b\} \& read(I, x)]$
c. $\exists x.[x \in \{a, c\} \& read(I, x)]$
d. $\exists x.[x \in \{b, c\} \& read(I, x)]$
e. $\exists x.[x \in \{a\} \& read(I, x)]$
f. $\exists x.[x \in \{b\} \& read(I, x)]$
g. $\exists x.[x \in \{c\} \& read(I, x)]$

Apart from (9a), all domain alternatives in (9) are stronger than $\exists x.[x \in \{a, b, c\} \& read(I, x)]$. That means that, if EXH applies to $\exists x.[x \in \{a, b, c\} \& read(I, x)]$, all these stronger domain alternatives must be false.

(10) $[[EXH(I\ read\ any\ books)]] =$
$[\lambda p.p \wedge \forall q \in Alt(p)[p \not\subseteq q \rightarrow \neg q]](\exists x.[x \in \{a, b, c\} \& read(I, x)]) =$
$\exists x.[x \in \{a, b, c\} \& read(I, x)] \&$
  $\neg \exists x.[x \in \{a, b\} \& read(I, x)] \&$
  $\neg \exists x.[x \in \{a, c\} \& read(I, x)] \&$
  $\neg \exists x.[x \in \{b, c\} \& read(I, x)] \&$
  $\neg \exists x.[x \in \{a\} \& read(I, x)] \&$
  $\neg \exists x.[x \in \{b\} \& read(I, x)] \&$
  $\neg \exists x.[x \in \{c\} \& read(I, x)]$

But the conjunction of all negated stronger domain alternatives entails that there is no element, member of the set {a, b, c}, that has been read by me. This already follows from the three negated domain alternatives where the domain of quantification is a singleton set: $\neg \exists x.[x \in \{a\} \& read(I, x)] \& \neg \exists x.[x \in \{b\} \& read(I, x)] \& \neg \exists x.[x \in \{b\} \& read(I, x)] \leftrightarrow \neg \exists x.[x \in \{a, b, c\} \& read(I, x)]$. But then [[EXH(I read any books)]] must have the denotation in (11), which forms a logical contradiction.

(11) $\exists x.[x \in \{a, b, c\} \& read(I, x)] \& \neg \exists x.[x \in \{a, b, c\} \& read(I, x)]$

Chierchia, following Gajewski (2002), takes sentences that are logically contradictory to be judged as unacceptable. If logically contradictory statements indeed trigger unacceptability judgements, the unacceptability of (7b) directly follows.

10.2 EXHAUSTIFICATION APPROACHES TO NPI-HOOD

Note that, for Chierchia, following Gajewski (2002), only logically contradictory expressions are ungrammatical; not just any contradictory expression. An expression is logically contradictory if and only if, under all significant rewritings of its non-logical parts, the contradiction remains, as is the case for unlicensed NPIs of the relevant kind. This is not the case for non-logical contradictions, such as *It rains and it doesn't rain*, since one could rephrase the second *rain* with *snow* and the contradiction disappears.

Now, if the NPI is embedded in a DE context, things change. To see this, take (12).

(12) I didn't read any book

Again, exhaustification of (12) will result in all stronger domain alternatives of (12) being false. But now, no domain alternative of (12), listed in (13), is actually stronger than (12), as, in DE contexts, entailment relations are reversed. Apart from (13a), all of them are weaker, owing to the fact that the negation, being DE, reverses the direction of the inference.

(13) a. $\neg\exists x.[x\in\{a, b, c\} \ \& \ \text{read}(I, x)]$
 b. $\neg\exists x.[x\in\{a, b\} \ \& \ \text{read}(I, x)]$
 c. $\neg\exists x.[x\in\{a, c\} \ \& \ \text{read}(I, x)]$
 d. $\neg\exists x.[x\in\{b, c\} \ \& \ \text{read}(I, x)]$
 e. $\neg\exists x.[x\in\{a\} \ \& \ \text{read}(I, x)]$
 f. $\neg\exists x.[x\in\{b\} \ \& \ \text{read}(I, x)]$
 g. $\neg\exists x.[x\in\{c\} \ \& \ \text{read}(I, x)]$

Consequently, exhaustification in (12) applies vacuously: [[EXH(I didn't read any book)]] = [[I didn't read any book]] and the sentence just has the reading $\neg\exists x.[x\in\{a, b,c\} \ \& \ \text{read}(I, x)]$ and is thus acceptable.

10.2.2 The strong–weak distinction among Negative Polarity Items

The next question that emerges is how to account for the distinction between weak NPIs (which are fine in all DE contexts) and strong NPIs (which are only fine in AA contexts). Here I follow Gajewski (2011) who, basing himself on Krifka (1995), takes the strong–weak distinction to lie in the distinction between whether the exhaustifier is looking only at the semantics of the NPI licenser, or looking also at its pragmatics (both the presupposition and the implicatures) (see also Chierchia 2013: weak NPIs want EXH to look at the semantics of the licenser only; strong NPIs want EXH to also look at the licenser's enriched meaning contribution.

Let's illustrate this with *few N* and *at most N*. Is the semantics of *few* 'not many of' or 'not many of, but some'? 'If *few* meant 'not many of, but some', nothing would follow about (14b) on the basis of the context in (14a) (examples taken from Iatridou and Zeijlstra 2021):

(14) a. If all students pass the state exam, the school will receive a $10K bonus
If half the students pass the state exam, the school will receive a $5K bonus
If few students pass the state exam, the school will face budget cuts
b. This year, no students pass the state exam, so the department will face budget cuts

Yet, intuitively, (14b) follows, which means that 'but some' should be a (cancellable) inference. But this means that the semantics of *few* is just 'not many of', not 'not many of, but some'. Crucially, since the semantics of *few* is just 'not many of', *few* is also DE, which explains why it can license NPIs (as in (15)).

(15) a. Few MIT students have ever been to Antarctica
b. Few Göttingen students have eaten anything with saffron in it

If the semantics of *few* had been 'not many of, but some', it would not have been able to license NPIs. The reason for this is that it would not have been DE. If not many, but still some students wear a shirt, it is not entailed that not many, but still some students wear a red shirt. Naturally, one might ask why elements like *few* trigger existential inferences (*not many, but some*). The reason is that there are competing scalar alternatives that make no existential inference. *No students passed the exam* is stronger than *Few students passed the exam*, so, if the speaker utters the latter, the hearer may infer that the speaker does not hold the former to be true. The difference between AA and other DE elements is that only AA elements do not trigger existential implicatures. It is this distinction that the strong–weak NPI dichotomy embarks on.

A potential NPI-licenser can thus have pragmatic inferences that eradicate its DE-ness, but if EXH looks only at its semantics and not at its pragmatic inferences, the environment can remain DE and it can shield an NPI from yielding a contradiction and, thereby, unacceptability. Negative Polarity Items that are only evaluated by EXH with respect to the DE-ness of the assertion are weak NPIs, like *any* and *ever*. Such NPIs are thus also fine even when there are existential inferences, which would render the overall meaning contribution non-DE, as long as these inferences are not part of the assertion.

On the other hand, there are also NPIs that do not survive in environments with pragmatic existential inferences. Those, for Gajewski (2011), are strong NPIs. For strong NPIs, there should be no existential inferences whatsoever, not even in non-asserted content, not even in the enriched meaning. As Gajewski (2011) shows, DE elements that can give rise to an implicature that would ruin their DE-ness are DE elements that are not the strongest scalar endpoints. Hence, the only DE elements that do not give rise to such non-DE implicatures are scalar endpoints like *not*, *nobody*, *never*, *no X*, etc. Such DE elements are, again, AA.[4]

In summary, NPIs in AA contexts do not trigger a contradiction even if the exhaustifier looks at the enriched meaning contribution of its complement. This, then, captures, for Gajewski (2011) and also for Chierchia (2013), the difference between strong and weak NPIs. What is crucial is that strong NPIs require a DE context whose non-truth-conditional meaning contribution does not contribute a non-DE-inference either. That is, strong NPIs also require the non-truth-conditional meaning component to be free of existential inferences.

10.2.3 Preliminary evidence for this treatment of the strong–weak distinction

Naturally, the question arises what determines whether a particular NPI is strong or weak. Why is it that *in years* and *until* are strong NPIs? Existing accounts so far have not addressed the question of why particular elements can only be strong or weak NPIs. Whether a particular NPI is weak or strong still appears arbitrary. As Gajewski (2011) puts it:

> [I]mplicatures and presuppositions introduced by an NPI licenser interfere with the licensing of strong NPIs, but not with the licensing of weak NPIs. At this point, I do not have an explanation of why this is so. Ultimately, the answer should be sought in the semantics of the NPIs themselves.
>
> Gajewski (2011: 19)

Assuming that arbitrariness is what is behind the strong–weak distinction seems unnatural. For the cases of *in years* and *until*, which are both strong, Iatridou and Zeijlstra (2017, 2021) instead argue that the fact that the time spans they introduce are presupposed and not asserted forces them to behave like strong NPIs. This, then, may actually open up the window towards a better understanding of which NPIs are strong and which ones are weak.

Let us therefore look at the semantic/pragmatic behaviour of strong NPIs like *in years* and punctual *until* in more detail. Iatridou, Anagnostopoulou, and Izvorski (2001) describe a perfect like (16) as in (17)–(19) (see also Von Fintel and Iatridou 2019):

(16)   I have visited Cape Cod three times since 1990

---

[4] Gajewski (2011) points out that *few*, on its proportional reading, may be considered a scalar end point and, therefore, not give rise to an existential inference (see the previous footnote). In those cases, it is correctly predicted that *few* can license strong NPIs.

240   STRONG VS WEAK NEGATIVE POLARITY ITEMS

(17) a. There is a time span (the Perfect Time Span/PTS);
b. The Right Boundary (RB) of the PTS is manipulated by Tense, and since (16) is a Present Perfect, RB is the time of utterance (t^u);
c. The Left Boundary (LB) of the PTS is the argument of *since*: (some time in) 1990;
d. In the PTS, there are 3 non-overlapping subintervals at which that the speaker visits Cape Cod.

(18) $\exists t: RB(t^u, t)$ and $LB(1990, t)$ & $\exists t', t'', t''' \subseteq t$: I visit Cape Cod at t', t'', t'''

(19)

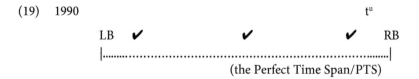

(the Perfect Time Span/PTS)

The LB of the PTS can be set by an adverbial ('PTS-adverbs'), as in (16)–(19), or contextually:

(20) I have visited Cape Cod three times (= since the beginning of my life, or since I entered the US)

Strikingly, the existence of the PTS of temporal adverbs similar to *in years*, such as *in the last 5 years*, is presuppositional in nature and not part of the assertion. The classical tests for presuppositions (projection above negation, questions, and *if*-clauses) clearly show this.

(21) I have been there in the last 5 years
Given a PTS [-5y, t^u], it is the case that within [-5y, t^u] I have been there

(22) I haven't been there in the last 5 years
Given a PTS [-5y, t^u], it is the case that within [-5y, t^u] I haven't been there

(23) Have you been there in the last 5 years
Given a PTS [-5y, t^u], I wonder whether within [-5y, t^u] you have been there

(24) If you have been there in the last 5 years, …
Given a PTS [-5y, t^u], if it is the case that you have been there within [-5y, t^u] …

Here, the diagnostics have only been applied to *in the last 5 years*, the closest non-NPI cousin to *in years*. *In years* itself cannot be licensed in positive sentences, questions, or clauses. But if *in the last 5 years* and *in years* behave in the same way, then it follows that the source of the introduction of domain alternatives does not come from the assertion, but rather lies in the presupposition. Moreover, for *in years*, it can be shown that the PTS also projects above negation. *I haven't been there in years* means that, given a particular PTS, it is not the case that I have been there within that PTS. Also note that in negative questions and conditionals the PTS of *in years* projects over questions and conditionals, indicating as well that this PTS is presupposed.

The same also holds for *until*. The same diagnostics show that the time span introduced by *until* (henceforth UTS) is also presupposed and not asserted (note that since punctual *until* is an NPI, the other cases involve durative *until*; see Chapter 14 for more discussion):

(25) I lived there until 2010
 Given a UTS [t, 2010], it is the case that within [t, 2010] I lived there.

(26) I didn't leave until 2010
 Given a UTS [t, 2010], it is the case that within [t, 2010] I didn't leave.

(27) Did you live there until 2010?
 Given a UTS [t, 2010], I wonder whether within [t, 2010] you lived there.

(28) If you lived there until 2010, ...
 Given a UTS [t, 2010], if it is the case that you have been there within [t, 2010], ...

If the domain alternatives of an NPI make reference to elements that follow from its presuppositional meaning contribution, the exhaustifier should have access to the enriched meaning contribution of the context of this NPI. In the case of *in years*, the domain alternatives are all alternatives that make reference to a PTS/UTS that is different from the one originally presupposed. The exhaustifier should then not only look at the licensing context of *in years* in the assertion if the alternative propositions are alternatives with respect to the presupposition *in years*.

This reflects a suggestion, voiced in Homer (2008, 2009), that strong NPIs are sensitive to all non-truth-conditional meaning because they are more 'pragmatic' in nature somehow (cf. Gajewski 2011). For this reason, the exhaustifier should look at the enriched meaning contribution of the context in which *in years* appears. Since it is the obligatory presence of an exhaustifier that looks at the enriched meaning contribution of an NPI's licensing context that renders NPIs strong NPIs, it follows that both *in years* and *until* must be strong NPIs. Naturally, this does not apply only to *in*-adverbials like *in years* or to punctual *until*. The prediction that emerges is that other NPIs that presuppose or implicate (as opposed to assert) the existence of a particular domain of quantification that obligatorily introduces domain alternatives should also be strong NPIs. So far, *in years* and *until* confirm this prediction. Whether there are any counterexamples should be subject to further research.

10.3 Problems for the exhaustification approach and the strong–weak Negative Polarity Item distinction

We have seen that the exhaustification approach can very well deal with the fact that weak NPIs are subject to DE contexts. Also, this approach opens up a way to differentiate between strong and weak NPIs, by requiring that the EXH that scopes over weak NPIs only evaluates the assertive meaning contribution of its complement, whereas the EXH that scopes over strong NPIs takes the entire, enriched meaning contribution of its complement into consideration.

At the same time, this approach faces several problems. One of them concerns the alleged arbitrariness of strong and weak NPIs; but, as shown in Subsection 10.2.3, this problem might be overcome by taking into account whether the source for the introduction of domain alternatives of an NPI lies inside or outside the assertion. In the latter case, the NPI should be a strong NPI, and in the former case, a weak NPI. But there are two more problems. One concerns the way in which it is encoded on an NPI whether the exhaustifier whose presence it manifests must evaluate only the assertive content of its complement, or rather its enriched meaning contribution. And second, there is a problem that concerns the difference in locality conditions involved in weak and strong NPI-licensing.

10.3.1 Encoding weak and strong NPI-hood

One problem that has emerged so far concerns the encoding of weak and strong NPI-hood. What determines whether an NPI triggers the presence of an exhaustifier that will or will not look into the enriched meaning contribution of its complement? We saw earlier that, if the domain alternatives of an NPI are introduced by its presupposition, its NPI-hood should be the result of an exhaustifier evaluating the enriched meaning contribution; but this NPI-hood is not guaranteed to follow just from the fact that its presupposition introduces domain alternatives. It could very well be that, despite introducing such alternatives, an exhaustifier would still only look at the assertive part of its complement and apply vacuously. In that case, no strong NPI-effect is expected to emerge in the first place.

Hence, it needs to be encoded on an NPI, in one way or another, that the context that an NPI appears in is subject to enriched exhaustification. For the sake of exposition, let us introduce the following types of exhaustifiers:

(29) EXH: an exhaustifier that looks only at the assertive part of its complement, and that is thus responsible for weak NPI licensing;
EXH+: an exhaustifier that looks at both the assertive part of its complement and the non-assertive part, and that is thus responsible for strong NPI licensing.

10.3 PROBLEMS FOR THE EXHAUSTIFICATION APPROACH

Using these terms, the question at stake is: how is it encoded on a weak NPI that it triggers the presence of EXH, and how is it encoded on a strong NPI that it triggers the presence of EXH+?

One solution, captured fully in Chierchia's terms, is by distinguishing different types of features involved in the Agree relation between the exhaustifier and the NPI. One could postulate that EXH carries a formal feature [iEXH], and EXH+ carries a formal feature [iEXH+]. Then, as a next step, one could postulate as well that weak NPIs carry a feature [uEXH], and strong NPIs a feature [uEXH+]. The exact same Agree mechanism that, for Chierchia, is behind NPI-licensing and is also taken to be behind NC in this monograph would then be responsible for the weak vs strong NPI distinction. Despite this analogy, such a solution faces two major problems.

First, it would again render the distinction between weak and strong NPIs completely ad hoc. The solution, in a sense, then appears as a description of the same problem in more formal terms, rather than a principled explanation. But more importantly, it ignores a general problem that Chierchia's theory faces when it comes to feature-checking. How is it possible that feature-checking of weak NPIs may violate syntactic locality? In (30a), *any* appears in an embedded finite clause, and, in (31a), in an adjunct island. The same applies to *ever* in (31a)–(32a). Since embedded clauses are syntactically opaque (modulo the phase edge), as are adjunct islands (though see Truswell 2007, 2011 for more discussion), the Agree relations between [iEXH] and [uEXH] in the b-examples should not be allowed, and the sentences should be predicted to be ungrammatical, contrary to fact.

(30) a. I didn't say that I bought any cookies
b. [EXH$_{[iEXH]}$ I didn't say [that I bought [any$_{[uEXH]}$ cookies]]]

(31) a. I don't work in order to make any money
b. [EXH$_{[iEXH]}$ I don't work [in order to make any$_{[uEXH]}$ money]]

(32) a. I didn't say that I ever saw him
b. [EXH$_{[iEXH]}$ I didn't say [that I ever$_{[uEXH]}$ saw him]]

(33) a. I don't travel in order to ever see him
b. [EXH$_{[iEXH]}$ I don't travel [in order to ever$_{[uEXH]}$ see him]]

10.3.2 Syntactic locality and the exhaustification approach

In order to properly understand how the strong–weak distinction should be captured in Chierchia's system, this system should first be amended to accommodate the locality problem I have raised. One possibility, suggested by Chierchia as well, is to follow Bošković (2007) in assuming that only movement is subject to syntactic locality, but Agree proper is not. Then, the grammaticality of (30)–(33) should no longer be problematic. However, this assumption would be illicit, for the following three reasons.

First, it is known since Polinsky and Potsdam (2001) that φ-agreement is sensitive to syntactic locality. It is only possible to establish an Agree relation with a φ-probe in a higher clause and a φ-goal in a lower clause if that goal appears in its CP phase edge. This can be illustrated, for instance, by the following minimal pair from Tsez, taken from Polinsky and Potsdam (2001):

(34) a. Enir [užā magalu b-āc'rułi] b-iyxo (Tsez)
mother [boy bread.ABS(III) III-ate] III-know
'The mother knows that (as for the bread) the boy ate it'
b. Enir [užā magalu b-āc'rułi] r-iyxo
mother [boy bread.ABS(III) III-ate] IV-know
'The mother knows that the boy ate the bread'

In (34), an embedded absolutive object can only control noun-class agreement on the finite verb if it receives a topical interpretation. In (34a), the embedded topic controls the agreement on the verb; in (34b), it does not and default agreement (noun class IV agreement in Tsez) pops up. The standard analysis for this is that the Agree relation must be mediated by the embedded Topic/C-head in the embedded left periphery, either by covertly raising the object (Potsdam and Polinsky 2001) or by valuation of the Top°/C°-head by the object and having the valued Top°/C°-head control agreement on the matrix verb (Bjorkman and Zeijlstra 2019). Either way, if φ-agreement can only be controlled by lower goals in the left periphery, this shows that agreement, like movement, is subject to syntactic locality.

Second, as has been discussed in detail in Chapters 3 and 4, NC is subject to syntactic locality as well. Example (35) (repeated from Section 3.3.2) shows that an element carrying [iNEG] cannot check a feature [uNEG] in an embedded (indicative) clause.

(35) a. *Gianni *non* ha detto che ha acquistato *niente* (Italian)
Gianni NEG has said that has bought NEG-thing
'John didn't say that he bought anything'
b. *Gianni *non* labora per guadagnare *niente*
Gianni NEG works in.order.to earn NEG-thing
'Gianni doesn't work in order to earn anything'

This shows that the syntactic locality of Agree is not restricted to φ-agreement. It applies to all instances of Agree, including the ones that Chierchia's proposal builds on.

Finally, and perhaps more importantly, giving up syntactic locality in the domain of NPI-licensing would obscure the fact that, while some NPIs can indeed be licensed across syntactic domains or islands, other NPIs actually cannot. Take the following examples:

(36) a. *I don't travel in order to have seen him in years
     b. *I don't say that I have seen him in years

(37) a. *I don't stay here in order to move in until June
     b. *Nobody claims she has moved in until June

The examples in (36)–(37) show that certain NPIs, such as *in years* and punctual *until*, are actually sensitive to syntactic locality. That *in years* and punctual *until* are such NPIs is not coincidental. As Collins and Postal (2014) observed, strong NPIs are also strict NPIs, i.e., NPIs that must be licensed within a local syntactic domain such as a finite clause or an island, and vice versa. This shows that syntactic locality plays a role for at least some kinds of NPIs. The most intuitive step would then be to restrict the underlying Agree-based approach for NPI licensing to strict NPIs only. That means that strong NPIs are equipped with an uninterpretable feature that can only be checked by a covert exhaustifier.

Collins and Postal's observation that all strict NPIs are also strong NPIs, and vice versa, now enables us to restrict the exhaustifier that can check off such features to EXH+. Then, the underlying structures of (38a) and (39a) are as in (38b) and (39b).

(38) a. I haven't seen him in years
     b. [EXH+$_{[iEXH+]}$ I haven't seen him in years$_{[uEXH+]}$]

(39) a. *I don't stay here in order to move in until June
     b. [EXH+$_{[iEXH+]}$ I didn't move in [until June]$_{[uEXH+]}$]

Naturally, the question arises of how the licensing of weak NPIs takes place if no instance of syntactic agreement is involved. More concretely, what triggers the presence of the regular exhaustifier EXH if its presence is not manifested by Agree? For this, I propose to make a distinction between so-called syntactic vs pragmatic exhaustification.

10.4 Syntactic vs pragmatic exhaustification

I assume that there are, in principle, two ways in general to trigger the presence of an exhaustifier: one way is by syntactic agreement (as has been shown in this chapter at various places); another one would be the result of a pragmatic mechanism that states that, if some (domain) alternatives have been introduced in the sentence and no operator applies to these alternatives, as a last resort, the entire clause is exhaustified. This, then, leads to the following picture:

(40) a. Syntactic exhaustification: - is triggered by agreement;
- is subject to syntactic locality constraints;
- may apply at any position in the clause, provided its complement is of the right semantic type;
- involves the 'enriched' exhaustifier EXH+.

b. Pragmatic exhaustification: - takes place as a last-resort operation;
- is not subject to syntactic locality constraints;
- may apply at the CP level only (given that it is a last-resort operation applying at clausal level).
- involves the regular exhaustifier EXH.

Implicitly or explicitly, such mechanisms have been suggested in the literature before. Krifka (1995) has argued that the ungrammaticality of NPIs comes from the fact that enriching them in the (Neo-)Gricean way would trigger implicatures that contradict the assertion. Since such contradictions would not emerge in DE contexts, NPIs can be felicitously uttered in such contexts only. At the same time, Krifka's approach has been criticized because implicatures can, in general, be cancelled, thus giving rise to the question why such contradictory implicatures would not be cancelled then. However, the question is open whether the cancellability of inferences that are related to (domain) alternatives is due to such inferences being inherently cancellable, or to such alternatives only being optionally introduced. If the latter is correct, inferences would not be cancellable if they involve obligatorily introduced alternatives, as would be the case for weak NPIs like *any* or *ever*.

Following this line of reasoning, one can adopt from Krifka and Chierchia the idea that NPIs obligatorily introduce both domain and scalar alternatives, and subsequently argue that these alternatives must be applied to by some focus-sensitive operator. The next step would then be that, in the absence of an overt operator, exhaustification steps in as a last-resort operator. Both steps have been proven to be correct for scalar alternatives. First of all, (41a–b) will be taken by hearers to make a different meaning contribution, suggesting that the focus on *two* cannot simply be ignored.

(41) a. Two students passed the exam
b. TWO students passed the exam

And focused *TWO students* can be applied to by a focus-sensitive operator:

(42) a. Even TWO students passed the exam
b. Only TWO students passed the exam

10.4 SYNTACTIC VS PRAGMATIC EXHAUSTIFICATION 247

Crucially, (41b), when uttered out of the blue, means the same as (42b). In a context where a minimal requirement for a course to be subject to extension is that at least two students pass the exam, the continuation in (43a) is fine, but the one in (43b) is not. This shows that, for scalar alternatives, if no overt focus-sensitive operator is present, as a last resort, the utterance is interpreted with an exhaustified interpretation.

(43) a. Q: How many students passed the exam?
   A: Two students passed the exam. In fact, even five did.
   b. Q: How many students passed the exam?
   A: TWO students passed the exam. #In fact, even five did.

The same, then, applies to introduced domain alternatives. Introduced domain alternatives must be exhaustified as a last resort if no other operation applies to them. The difference between scalar and domain alternatives, however, is that, while various focus-sensitive operators apply to scalar alternatives, this is not the case with domain alternatives. Consequently, domain alternatives introduced by indefinite elements will be exhaustified by default; and given the contradiction that arises in upward entailing or non-monotonic contexts, their restriction to DE contexts straightforwardly follows.

Now the Strict vs. Non-Strict distinction among NPIs can be naturally captured: both types of NPIs obligatorily introduce all scalar and domain alternatives, but Strict NPIs must syntactically agree with the exhaustifier; Non-Strict NPIs are subject to pragmatic exhaustification. But if Strict NPIs are exhaustified by a different exhaustifier from the one for Non-Strict NPIs, nothing forbids that these two exhaustifiers may have different semantic properties. This opens up ways to understand the strong–weak distinction and its correlation with the Strict–Non-Strict distinction. Since weak NPIs are subject to pragmatic exhaustification, it is plausible to assume that the pragmatic exhaustifier has the same properties that we assigned thus far to EXH. In this sense, EXH functions like a classical (Neo-)Gricean operation. However, if syntactic exhaustification always considers the implicatures of the licenser as well, it rather makes sense to assume that this is a different type of exhaustifier, call it EXH+, which also considers the implicatures generated in its entire complement.

The proposal just introduced captures the connection between the strong–weak distinction and syntactic locality that is attested. The type of exhaustifier that is responsible for the licensing of strong NPIs (by applying to the overall meaning contribution of the utterance that the NPI appears in), EXH+, stands in a syntactic Agree relation with the NPI; the type of exhaustifier that is responsible for the licensing of weak NPIs (by applying only to the assertion of the utterance that the NPI appears in) only appears as a last-resort operation to apply to otherwise unaffected domain alternatives.

This account provides a solution for the two problems addressed before. First, it predicts that all weak NPIs, unlike strong NPIs, can be licensed by a licenser outside their syntactic domain. Since exhaustification may apply at every clausal level, a weak NPI may even be fine under a clause-external negation, since then exhaustification applies at the highest clausal level. Second, it is now possible to syntactically encode the difference between weak and strong NPIs —by postulating that all NPIs obligatorily introduce domain alternatives (which is what renders them NPIs), but that only strong NPIs carry an uninterpretable feature [uEXH+] that triggers the presence of EXH+ that they agree with; weak NPIs are simply subject to the pragmatic exhaustification requirement (given that they obligatorily introduce domain alternatives). Note that an additional advantage is that what underlies NPI-hood under the exhaustification approach boils down to only one requirement (obligatory introduction of domain alternatives) and not two (obligatory introduction of domain alternatives and the presence of a [uσ,D]-feature on the NPI), as was the case in Chierchia's original proposal.

At the same time, it is important to understand the differences between EXH and EXH+. In Chierchia (2013), the major distinction between the exhaustifier that is involved in strong-NPI licensing and the exhaustifier that is involved in weak-NPI licensing is that the former applies to both scalar and domain alternatives, whereas the latter applies to domain alternatives only. In that sense, EXH+ is a 'smart' exhaustifier that computes and exhaustifies all alternatives present. In a sentence like (44), it must exhaustify an enriched version of the prejacent, as, otherwise, the NPI would still be evaluated within a DE context.

(44) Few students have been there in years

Chierchia encodes that by assigning to what I call EXH+ both an [iσ] and an [iD] feature ([iσ, D]), whereas the exhaustifier that is responsible for weak NPIs is actually one that only exhaustifies over domain alternatives (and is subject to a later round of scalar exhaustification).

In principle, I fully adopt this view, but as feature-checking is restricted to strong NPIs, I only take EXH+ to behave on a par with all other focus-sensitive operators that apply to focus alternatives. These are operators applying to both types of available alternatives. In this sense, EXH+ is different from EXH. While EXH+ is a clear operator, application of EXH is rather an instance of (Neo-)Gricean reasoning, where, against a body of alternatives, the assertion gets pragmatically strengthened. In this sense, it is not an operator but an operation. Note that this reflects the presence of triggers of both local and global inferences in the realm of NPI-hood.

10.5 Negative Polarity Items and domain-wideners: A re-appreciation

Chierchia's and also Krifka's approaches in terms of domain and scalar alternatives are based on Kadmon and Landman (1993), who are the first to provide a pragma-semantic approach to NPI-licensing. For Kadmon and Landman (1993), NPIs are not in need of exhaustification, but are rather domain-wideners that extend the contextually restricted domain of quantification. This domain-widening property is, for them, (partly) responsible for NPIs being NPIs. Kadmon and Landman (1993: 360) present the following example to show how *any* behaves as a domain-widener.

(45) YOU: Will there be French fries tonight?
ME: No, I don't have potatoes.
YOU: Maybe you have just a couple of potatoes that I could take and fry in my room?
ME: Sorry, I don't have ANY potatoes.

For Kadmon and Landman (1993), domain-wideners like *any* are subject to a strengthening requirement that forces the utterance containing the domain-widener to be stronger than its non-domain-widening alternatives: The utterance which contains *any potatoes* must be stronger than the utterance which contains just *potatoes*. Since extending the domain of quantification of an existential quantifier in a positive context makes the utterance less informative (*I saw a car* is less informative than *I saw a BMW*), this strengthening requirement can be met only if the existential is embedded in an environment that reverses inferences, i.e., in DE contexts. This, for Kadmon and Landman, is what makes domain-wideners NPIs. Note that this strengthening requirement, however, for Kadmon and Landman is not specified as being a lexical requirement.

As I have shown, more recent approaches to NPI-hood adopt the basic insight of Kadmon and Landman (1993), in which there is a relationship between NPIs and domain-widening; but they argue contra Kadmon and Landman that the property of domain-widening itself does not underlie NPI-hood. Rather, NPI-hood may underlie domain-widening. The reasons why Chierchia rejects domain-widening as the primitive source of NPI-hood are twofold. First, it is argued that the original account by Kadmon and Landman is non-compositional: their strengthening requirement, i.e., the requirement that an utterance containing an NPI can only be used if the utterance with the NPI is stronger than the one with its non-NPI counterpart, as has been said, is not part of the lexical meaning of an NPI, nor does it follow from it. Second, not every NPI is always used as a domain-widener. Chierchia points out that, out of the blue, a sentence like (46b) can be uttered without any domain-widening effect. Only in contrast with an alternative like (46a) does the domain-widening effect arise.

(46) a. I don't have eggs
b. I don't have any eggs

So, while, for Kadmon and Landman, all NPIs are domain-wideners, for Chierchia, an NPI does not necessarily have a domain-widening effect.

Chierchia (2013) argues that the main characteristic of NPIs is the fact that NPIs introduce subdomain alternatives and that the sentences they occur in are obligatorily exhaustified. Domain-widening comes about when an item which introduces subdomain alternatives is contrastively focused under negation. Once contrastively focused, NPIs are domain-wideners in the sense of Kadmon and Landman. Or, as Chierchia (2013: 36) puts it in discussing *any*: when contrastively focused, *any* acts as a 'domain-widener', but when it is not contrastively focused (in DE contexts), it is interchangeable with a plain indefinite.

However, there may be reasons to flag up the relation between NPIs and domain-wideners. First, while NPIs like *any* and *ever* can be used as non-domain-wideners, a substantial set of NPIs cannot. This could suggest that whereas some NPIs are NPIs that only introduce domain alternatives and only become domain-wideners under contrastive focus, other NPIs might even be lexically specified for being domain-wideners.

This is, for instance, the case for minimizing NPIs like *a red cent* or *a single zip*, which clearly extend their domain of quantification beyond contextual restrictions.

(47) a. I don't own a red cent
b. I didn't drink a single sip

The examples in (47) imply that the speaker really does not have any money at all, or that the speaker really stayed fully sober. Not that they 'just' are not in possession of money or happened not to have a drink.

Another set of NPIs that always act like domain-wideners is formed by *in*+Bare-Plural-Temporal-Noun combinations, such as *in days, in months, in ages, in weeks*, or *in hours*, which were discussed in Subsection 10.2.3. The reason why these NPIs are domain-wideners is twofold. First, they differ with respect to other temporal *in*-adverbials, such as *in the last 5 years*, in the sense that they have a non-cancellable actuality inference (AI), something Iatridou and Zeijlstra (2017, 2021) refer to as *Constant's observation*. This can be witnessed in the following minimal pairs.

(48) a. She hasn't had a seizure in the last five years. I don't know about earlier.
b. She hasn't had a seizure in the last five years. In fact, she has never had one.

(49) a. She hasn't had a seizure in years. [#]I don't know about earlier.
b. He hasn't had a seizure in years. [#]In fact, he has never had one.

10.5 NPIS AND DOMAIN-WIDENERS: A RE-APPRECIATION 251

Both *in the last 5 years* and *in years* imply that the relevant event took place before, but this implication is only cancellable in (48), not in (49).

Another difference between these two *in*-adverbials is that *in years* and its kin come with what Iatridou and Zeijlstra call a 'beyond expectation inference', as shown in the following examples:

(50) I know Mary does not like to visit our common aunt Trudy. So when I visited aunt Trudy myself, I expected to hear that Mary had not been there in the past few weeks. But, it was
   a. ... worse than I thought. She had not been there in the past two months.
   b. ... better than I thought. She had (just) not been there in the past two days.

(51) I know Mary does not like to visit our common aunt Trudy. So when I visited aunt Trudy myself, I expected to hear that Mary had not been there in the past few weeks. But, it was
   a. ... worse than I thought. She had not been there in months.
   b. ... #better than I thought. She had (just) not been there in days.

Once it is assumed that *in years* is a domain-widener that stretches its domain of quantification beyond *any* contextual restrictions, these two non-cancellable inferences naturally follow. Since the domain of quantification in the case of *in years* is the PTS, contextual restrictions that may normally apply to PTSs no longer do so. The PTS, for instance, cannot be restricted to a contextual time span, such as a lifetime. Against this background, *in years* has two jobs to do: Being a PTS-adverb, it has to set the LB of this PTS, and, being a domain-widener, it has to widen (i.e., extend) the PTS as much as possible. *In-* (or *for-*)adverbials can only do so by having the PTS stretching backwards from the RB, which, for perfect adverbials, is always set by tense. Putting these properties together, the result is that *in years* stretches backwards as far as possible from the RB.

Now, the only point in time which *in years* cannot skip over on its stretch-backwards-from-RB path is the point in time where an event of the relevant sort took place. Stretching the PTS any further back would make the sentence false, as the assertion is that no event of the relevant sort occurred in the PTS. In the example at hand, *in years* can stretch the PTS back until the first seizure that it meets, which is effectively the most recent seizure (the example is schematized with the RB at the time of utterance (t^u)):

(52) Seizure 1....................Seizure 2................................. RB: t^u
   ←---------------------------------

The occurrence of an event of the relevant sort is thus the only way to enable the resolution of conflicting requirements on *in years* to set the LB and to set it as far as possible backwards from RB. This explains why, with *in years*, there unavoidably is an event of the relevant sort, why that event unavoidably occurs at the LB, and why the time of the event is unavoidably earlier than any other contextually salient alternatives, as the event being earlier translates into the PTS being bigger. In other words, the domain of quantification is extended. None of these facts are unavoidable with other PTS-adverbials. This, then, derives Constant's observation, i.e., the non-cancellability of the AI with *in years*, and the beyond expectation inference (BEI).

Hence, elements that introduce domain alternatives can become polarity-sensitive. A subset thereof always gives rise to domain-widening effects. This is, however, not something that follows from Chierchia's proposition directly. Let us see why.

First, for Chierchia, elements like *in years* outside DE contexts should yield a contradiction. That is indeed the case if *in years* obligatorily introduces subdomain alternatives. Take the assertion and domain alternatives in (53), where Run(e) is the run time of an event e.

(53)   Given a PTS τ, such that RB(UT, τ) and LB (τ - weeks, τ)
Assertion: $\exists e.[\text{meet}(e, \text{Joe}, \text{Mary}) \land \text{Run}(e) \subseteq \tau]$
Domain alternatives: $\langle \exists e.[\text{meet}(e, \text{Joe}, \text{Mary}) \land \text{Run}(e) \subseteq \tau'] \mid \tau' \subseteq \tau \rangle$.

Now, if an event takes place in a subdomain of the PTS τ' smaller than τ, it also takes place in τ, whereas the reverse does not hold. That means that all alternatives in (53) entail the assertion. Exhaustification results in all alternatives that are stronger than the assertion being made false, which means that, apart from the assertion, all alternatives of the kind in (53) must be false. Then we reach a logical contradiction again. If in no subdomain of the PTS did a meeting event take place, it cannot have taken place in the PTS either. This contradiction does not arise when the sentence is embedded in a DE context. Since the assertion in (54a) entails all domain alternatives in (54b), exhaustification takes place vacuously, as there is no non-weaker alternative that is to be negated any more.

(54)   Given a PTS τ, such that RB(UT, τ) and LB (τ - weeks, τ)
Assertion: $\neg\exists e.[\text{meet}(e, \text{Joe}, \text{Mary}) \land \text{Run}(e) \subseteq \tau]$
Domain alternatives: $\langle \neg\exists e.[\text{meet}(e, \text{Joe}, \text{Mary}) \land \text{Run}(e) \subseteq \tau'] \mid \tau' \subseteq \tau \rangle$.

Hence, this representation of *in years*, couched within Iatridou et al. (2001) and von Fintel and Iatridou (2019), follows Chierchia's general approach to NPI-hood in that *in years* introduces smaller subdomains of the PTS as domain-alternatives. This does not make it a domain-widener itself, though. Only if *in years* is furthermore always contrastively focused, an assumption that Chierchia also makes, is it also a domain-widener, and everything works out.

For *in years* this may indeed be the case. One option is that it is lexically encoded (i.e., *in years* would be inherently accented or stressed) or that it follows from the prosodic configuration that *in years* appears in. As noted in Iatridou and Zeijlstra (following Edward Fleming, pers. comm.), it does not seem possible to check this phonetically because, given that *in years* has to be in the scope of negation, and therefore appears at the right edge of the clause, the stress contour that it receives would be the same regardless of the presence or absence of contrastive focus. If it is indeed correct that *in years* always carries some stress, this is consistent with the position that is inherited from Chierchia, namely that it is always contrastively focused.

This may, however, not be the case for every NPI that behaves like a domain-widener. Apart from the minimizing examples mentioned before, we will see in Chapter 14 that there may be other NPIs (such as punctual *until*) that are very similar domain-wideners to *in years*, but lack any hearable inherent stress. Hence, the question that emerges is whether domain-widening should not be taken as a more inherent property of certain NPIs and be only a contextual property (under contrastive focus) for others. In that case, the domain-widening effects of *in years*, NPI minimizers, and punctual *until* are lexically encoded, whereas for other NPIs domain-widening may result from contrastive stress.

10.6 Conclusions

In this chapter, I have discussed a well-known distinction between NPIs, namely that between weak NPIs and strong NPIs. I argued that only a modified version of the approaches made by Chierchia and Gajewski to account for this distinction gets the facts right. Exhaustification of strong NPIs takes place in the syntax; exhaustification of weak NPIs in pragmatics. Apart from the fact that this explains the differences between strong and weak NPI licensing in terms of syntactic locality, it also leads us to a better understanding of these NPIs in the first place. What makes an NPI an element that must appear in a DE context is simply the obligatory introduction of domain alternatives and does not necessitate the existence of particular syntactic features—the latter only play a role in the licensing of strong NPIs.

This, of course, does not entail that weak and strong NPIs are the only types of NPI possible. In fact, in the previous section, I raised the question whether NPIs that are always domain-wideners should be treated as a special class or not, a question that will return in Chapter 14. But as we saw in the previous chapter, there are other types of NPIs, apart from weak and strong NPIs. These are the so-called superstrong, strong/weak, and superweak NPIs, which will be discussed in the next chapter.

11
Other types of NPIs

11.1 Introduction: Superstrong, strong/weak, and superweak Negative Polarity Items

In Chapter 9, we saw that the landscape of NPIs is pluriform: various NPIs of different strengths can be attested. In the previous chapter, I discussed two well-known types of NPIs—weak NPIs and strong NPIs—and I argued that these differ with respect to the way in which they trigger the presence of the exhaustifier that underlies their NPI-hood.

In this chapter, I introduce three further types of NPIs: superstrong, strong/weak, and superweak NPIs. The first type is an NPI whose distribution is much more restricted than that of strong NPIs. This is illustrated for two Dutch idiomatic NPIs. Dutch *voor de poes* ('for the cat') can have a reading 'soft' and *mals* (tender) can mean 'mild', but only when taking scope under some, but crucially not all, AA elements. The idiomatic interpretation of *voor de poes* only emerges under *niet* ('not') (1), and *mals* only under *niet* and *nooit* ('never') (2).

(1)   a.   Zij is niet voor de poes   (Dutch)
             she is not for the cat
             'She is tough'

         b.   Niemand is voor de poes
             nobody is for the cat
             *'Everybody is tough'

         c.   Geen mens is voor de poes
             no person is for the cat
             *'Everybody is tough'

         d.   Zij is nooit voor de poes
             she is never for the cat
             *'She is always tough'

(2)   a.   De kritiek was niet mals   (Dutch)
             the criticism was not tender
             'The criticism was harsh'

         b.   De kritiek was nooit mals
             the criticism was never tender
             'The criticism was always harsh'

c. Geen kritiek was mals
   no criticism was tender
   *'All criticism was harsh'

d. Niets was mals
   nothing was tender
   *'Everything was harsh'

The fact that these NPIs are idiomatic expressions already suggests that they are lexically stored with their negations as such, which means that the source of their NPI-hood can just be said to be lexically encoded.

However, the other two types of NPIs cannot be said to be idiomatic. The first type concerns modals such as English *need*, which are fine in some, but not all, DE contexts, and another one is exemplified by the Chinese indefinite *shenme*, which appears in all non-veridical contexts, but not outside those. NPIs of the former type are referred to as strong/weak NPIs, of the latter type as superweak NPIs. In this chapter, I argue that these two types of NPIs have a different source for their NPI-hood than strong or weak NPIs. Whereas I apply a Chierchia-style approach to both strong and weak NPIs in Chapter 10, in this chapter I argue that strong/weak NPIs are very similar to what Collins and Postal (2014) refer to as unary NPIs, and that superweak NPIs are NPIs because of referential deficiency along the lines of Lin (1996, 1998) and Giannakidou (2011, 2018). In addition, in this chapter, I present acquisitional data from Lin et al. (2015, 2018, 2021) that further support this conclusion, and, therefore, also the conclusion that superstrong, strong, strong/weak, weak, and superweak NPIs are all NPIs for different reasons.

Section 11.2 discusses strong/weak NPIs. Section 11.3 discusses superweak NPIs. In Section 11.4, I compare the acquisitional data presented in Sections 11.2–3 for Dutch *hoeven* ('need') and Chinese *shenme* with the way in which English *any* is acquired. Section 11.5 concludes.

11.2 Strong/weak Negative Polarity Items

11.2.1 Distribution

This section focuses on a particular type of NPI whose strength is somewhere between those of strong NPIs and weak NPIs, and which I will refer to as strong/weak NPIs (following Lin et al. 2015). Examples of such NPIs are modals like English *need* (the *need* that does not select *to*-infinitivals) and its Dutch and German counterparts *hoeven* and *brauchen* (the latter only when it selects clausal arguments). These modals are strong necessity modals and restricted to some, but crucially not all, AA or DE contexts (Zwarts 1981, 1986, 1995; Van der Wouden 1994).

Concretely, these modals are unable to appear outside DE contexts (3). They can appear, though, in the scope of the NM *not/niet/nicht* 'not' (4), with NIs such as *nobody/niemand/keiner* ('nobody'), both in subject and object position (5), and (modulo *need*) in the scope of *without/zonder/ohne* 'without', which are all AA contexts.[1]

(3) a. *John need cook
Int.: 'John has to cook'

    b. *Jan hoeft te koken   (Dutch)
       Jan need to cook
       Int.: 'Jan has to cook'

    c. *Hans braucht zu kochen   (German)
       Hans need to cook
       Int.: 'Hans has to cook'

(4) a. John need not cook

    b. Jan hoeft niet te koken   (Dutch)
       Jan need not to cook
       'Jan does not have to cook'

    c. Hans braucht nicht zu kochen   (German)
       Hans need not to cook
       'Hans does not have to cook'

(5) a. No student need cook

    b. Geen student hoeft te koken   (Dutch)
       no student need to cook
       'No student has to cook'

    c. Kein student braucht zu kochen   (German)
       no student need to cook
       'No student has to cook'

(6) a. You need do nothing

---

[1] Dutch and German are SOV languages with Verb Second. This means that *hoeven* and *brauchen* are base-generated in the sentence-final position, where they takes scope under a negative operator, even though these modal verbs precedes the negative operator at surface structure owing to the verb movement. See Iatridou and Zeijlstra (2013) and Chapter 13 for more discussion and arguments on why modal verbs such as Dutch *hoeven* always reconstruct.

11.2 STRONG/WEAK NEGATIVE POLARITY ITEMS

    b. Je hoeft niets te doen (Dutch)
       you need nothing to do
       'You don't need to do anything'

    c. Du brauchst nichts zu tun (German)
       you need nothing to do
       'You don't need to do anything'

(7) a. Jan was klaar zonder te hoeven haasten (Dutch)
       Jan was finished without to need hurry
       'Jan finished without having to hurry'

    b. Hans stellte einen neuen Rekord auf, ohne dass er
       Hans set.PST a new record up, without that he
       sich zu beeilen brauchte (German)
       REFL to.hurry.INF need.PST
       'Hans set a new record without (even) having to hurry'

However, not all AA contexts license *need/hoeven/brauchen*. The restriction of a universal quantifier (8) or the antecedent of a conditional, for instance, do not license these modal verbs (9).

(8) a. *Everybody who need cook, has to start now

    b. *Iedereen die hoeft te koken moet nu beginnen (Dutch)
       everyone that need to cook must now start
       Int.: 'Everyone that has to cook must start now'

    c. *Jeder, der zu kochen braucht, muss jetzt
       everyone that to cook need, must now
       anfangen. (German)
       start
       Int.: 'Everyone that has to cook must start now'

(9) a. *If Mary need cook, she has to start now

    b. *Als Marie hoeft te koken moet zij nu beginnen (Dutch)
       if Marie need to cook must she now start
       Int.: 'If Mary has to cook then she must start now'

    b. *Wenn Marie zu kochen braucht, muss sie jetzt
       if Marie to cook need must she now
       anfangen (German)
       start
       Int.: 'If Mary has to cook then she must start now'

Examples of non-AA, DE contexts which license *need/hoeven/brauchen* are semi-negative adverbs like *seldom/zelden/selten* ('seldom') (10), second arguments of negated universal quantifiers (11), and exclusives like *only/alleen/nur* ('only') (which is Strawson-DE, cf. von Fintel 1999) (12).

(10) a. John need seldom cook

    b. Jan hoeft zelden te koken (Dutch)
       Jan need seldom to cook
       'Jan seldom has to cook'

    c. Hans braucht selten zu kochen (German)
       Hans need seldom to cook
       'Jan seldom has to cook'

(11) a. Not everybody need cook at the weekend

    b. Niet iedereen hoeft in het weekend te koken (Dutch)
       not everybody need in the weekend to cook
       'Not everybody has to cook at weekends'

    c. Niet jeder braucht am Wochenende zu kochen
       not everybody need in.the weekend to cook
       'Not everybody has to cook at weekends'

(12) a. Only John need cook

    b. Alleen Jan hoeft te koken (Dutch)
       only Jan need to cook
       'Only Jan has to cook'

    c. Nur Hans braucht zu kochen (German)
       only Hans need to cook
       'Only Hans has to cook'

Polar or *Wh*-questions do not license *need/hoeven/brauchen*, as shown in (13)–(14):

(13) a. *Need John cook?

    b. *Hoeft Jan te koken? (Dutch)
       need Jan to cook
       Int.: 'Does Jan have to cook?'

    c. *Braucht Hans zu kochen? (German)
       need Hans to cook
       Int.: 'Does Hans have to cook?'

(14) a. *What need John cook?
　　 b. *Wat hoeft Jan te koken?　　　　　　　　　　　(Dutch)
　　　　 what need Jan to cook
　　　　 Int.: 'What does Jan have to cook?'
　　 c. *Was braucht Hans zu kochen?　　　　　　　　(German)
　　　　 what need   Hans to cook
　　　　 Int.: 'What does Hans have to cook?'

The question arises why modals like *need/hoeven/brauchen* are restricted to these kinds of contexts. But this is not the only question that emerges. A second question concerns the reason why these modals have such restrictions; what makes them strong/weak NPIs. And, finally, this type of NPI does not occur very often. Most NPIs attested are either strong or weak NPIs (cf. Van der Wouden 1994), not strong/weak NPIs. Negative Polarity Items of this type rarely occur, and, to the best of my knowledge, only among necessity modals. Hence, the question also emerges as to why this type of NPI is much less common than other types of NPIs.

11.2.2 Strong/weak Negative Polarity Items and split-scope constructions

In order to account for the special NPI-status of *need/hoeven/brauchen*, I start by focusing on the two types of licensers that such NPIs require. The first type is exemplified by (4) and (11), where the NM *not/niet/nicht* is overtly included in the licenser. The second type of example, however, also turns out to include an NM, albeit covertly. Closer inspection of the remaining examples reveals that all licensers of *need/hoeven/brauchen* of this second type are also able to give rise to split-scope readings. This can already be straightforwardly illustrated for *no/geen/kein* in the examples in (5), which can clearly be paraphrased in split-scope terms: it is not the case that there is a necessity for any student to cook.

　　As outlined in Chapter 7, every NI is able to give rise to split-scope readings, albeit that English speakers do not always accept them that easily, presumably because of competition with *any*-phrases that yield similar readings. But these are not the only elements that may give rise to split-scope readings. Expressions such as *seldom*, *few*, and *only* can also give rise to split-scope readings (cf. Hackl 2000; Heim 2006; von Fintel and Iatridou 2007; see also Chapter 7). Von Fintel and Iatridou (2007), for instance, point out that (15) has a reading where negation outscopes *may* (on its deontic interpretation), but where the modal outscopes an exceptive quantifier:

(15) He may only have one cookie   ¬ > may > ∃$_{exc}$

In fact, they argue that *only* is lexically decomposed into a negation and an exceptive existential quantifier, and with respect to generating split-scope readings behaves similarly to other NIs. That *only* is indeed decomposable into negation and an exceptive existential quantifier, for them, also follows from the fact that, in many other languages, exceptive constructions transparently consist of negation and exceptives, as illustrated in (16) for Greek *dhen ... para mono* (not ... except):

(16) Dhen idha para mono ton Yani   (Greek)
     NEG saw.1SG para mono the Yani
     'I didn't see anyone except Yani'

So, it appears that licensers of *need/hoeven/brauchen* consist either of an overt NM, or of expressions that may give rise to split-scope readings, where a negation is scopally separated from an existential quantifier.

As we already saw, in order to solve this problem, two different types of approach have been proposed. Within the so-called *decomposition approach*, it is argued that split-scope effects result from (lexical) decomposition of the NI into a separate negation and an existential. Scholars differ with respect to whether this decomposition is to be accounted for in terms of amalgamation (Jacobs 1980), incorporation (Rullmann 1995), syntactic agreement (Penka 2011), or a postsyntactic spell-out rule (Zeijlstra 2011; Chapter 7).

Others have argued that NIs are negative quantifiers (NQs), but that these quantifiers do not only quantify over individuals, but also over kinds (Geurts 1996), properties (De Swart 2000), and choice-functions (Abels and Marti 2010). Quantification over non-individuals then entails the split-scope readings. Proposals along these lines are referred to as the *negative quantifier approach*.

Both approaches make different predictions for the syntax underlying split-scope constructions. Crucially, for the NQ approach, the split-scope reading is reflected only in the semantics. However, under the decomposition approach, split-scope readings also have a syntactic reflex, as the negation and the existential occupy different terminal nodes in the tree.

Under the decomposition approach to split-scope, the licensing conditions of NPIs like *need/hoeven/brauchen* can straightforwardly be captured: these NPIs are licensed by a phrase that contains, as its highest scopal element, a negation, either overtly realized or incorporated in its sister (following the version of the decomposition approach defended in Zeijlstra 2011 and Chapter 7). The question that naturally arises now is why this is the case.

11.2.3 The source of *need/hoeven/brauchen*'s NPI-hood

Clearly, the source of the NPI-hood of elements like *need/hoeven/brauchen* cannot be similar to that of weak or strong NPIs, given that these are not existentials but universal quantifiers (assuming that modals are quantifiers over possible worlds; cf. Kratzer 1981, 1991; pace Lassiter 2011). As will be shown in Chapter 13, to the extent that scalarity approaches to polarity-sensitivity can apply, these can only account for PPIs, and not for NPIs. Hence, alternative sources for the NPI-hood of *need/hoeven/brauchen* need to be sought.

One clear alternative suggests itself. The history of accounting for NPI-hood has always been divided between syntactic and semantic approaches. The approaches discussed in the previous chapter are all semantic in nature, not least because they focus on DE-ness, the reversal of entailment relations. As is well-known, DE-ness has a profound effect on semantics, but hardly on morphosyntax. At the same time, there is also a strong tradition aiming for syntactic explanations to NPI-hood.

The alternative tradition that takes NPIs to come along with a syntactic requirement that they be licensed by a (semi-)negative operator goes back to Klima (1964), and has also been presented by Progovac (1992, 1993, 1994), who takes NPI-licensing to be some special instance of syntactic binding, and by Laka (1990), who relates NPIs to the obligatory presence of an affective phrase (ΣP), and has most recently been revived by Collins and Postal (2014), who follow Postal (2004), by reintroducing Klima's theory and claiming that NPIs underlyingly carry a negation. Under this approach, what underlies an NPI like English *any* is the following lexico-syntactic representation.[2]

(17) any: [$_D$ NEG [SOME]]

For Postal, the complex [$_D$ NEG [SOME]] gets morphophonologically realized as in (18):

(18)   a. *no one* if the negation stays in place: *I saw no one*
      b. *anyone*
         i. if the negation raises out: *I didn't see anyone*
         ii. if the negation is deleted by another negative operator:
            in *no one saw anyone*, the negation on the subject absorbs the negation in the object.

The condition in (18b-ii) applies to cases of NC, where Postal ultimately assumes a polyadic quantification approach (where two or more monadic NQs can form one polyadic quantifier; see Chapter 3), and will not be further discussed here. The

---

[2] Den Dikken (2006) adopts the essence of Postal's analysis, but recasts it within terms proposed by Chomsky (1995a, etc.): Some NPIs carry a [uNEG] that must be checked against a negative head in the clause. Independently, and for different reasons, Neeleman and Van de Koot (2002) and Herburger and Mauck (2007) reached this conclusion as well.

crucial condition is (18b-i). Under this approach, *any* can only surface in structures where it is c-commanded by a negation.

The main difficulty that such purely syntactic approaches face is to understand why most types of NPIs frequently have very particular semantics, namely denoting the endpoint of a scale, e.g. *lift a finger, have a red cent*. If being an NPI is merely a matter of having certain syntactic features, then we would expect a more random distribution of NPIs, and not the observed higher concentration within the class of scalar items.

Herburger and Mauck (2007) are aware of this problem, and try to countenance it by arguing that the scalar-end-point property is a necessary, but not a sufficient condition for NPI-licensing. Their approach is more nuanced than others' within the syntactic approach: It is indeed a pragmatic and/or semantic issue whether some element may be a candidate for becoming an NPI, but it is only the presence of some uninterpretable negative feature [uNEG] that turns an element into an NPI. Nevertheless, as discussed in the previous chapter, the pragma-semantic approach to NPI-hood can already explain why low-scalar elements can be NPIs—hence, adding an additional syntactic component seems theoretically superfluous.

Apart from that, two additional problems are still open. The first one concerns the licensing of NPIs by DE determiners. For Postal, this means that an NPI-licensing expression, such as *few*, must contain an underlying (incorporated) negation. Under the feature-checking analysis, *few* must contain some negative feature that checks the negative feature of the NPI. However, it is unclear what determines the distribution of negative features to non-negative elements. Not every semi-negative element can license NPIs (e.g. *it is bad that ... cannot*, but *it is regrettable that ... can*).

A second problem, especially for feature-checking approaches, is that the locality restrictions on weak-NPI-licensing are weaker than those for regular movement. Weak NPIs, such as *any*, can be licensed across the boundaries of a clause, even across an island, in fact, which is not possible for syntactic movement (without intermediate landing sides) (19), as discussed in detail in the previous chapter.

(19) a. I didn't say that Mary bought any biscuits
b. I don't work in order to make any money

Collins and Postal (2014) address these problems by arguing that there are two types of NPIs, so-called unary and binary NPIs. Unary NPIs consist of one negation, which moves to a higher position; and binary NPIs contain two negations that, when licensed by a DE operator, remain unpronounced (see Chapter 8 for how the same mechanism applies in Neg-raising constructions). A weak NPI like *any* then comes in two guises, one as a unary NPI and one as a binary NPI. A strong NPI like *in years* is only a unary NPI. This, then, explains why strong NPIs

11.2 STRONG/WEAK NEGATIVE POLARITY ITEMS

can only be licensed by AA elements, which clearly contain a negative core, and why they must be licensed locally (as movement is subject to syntactic locality).

As discussed in Chapter 8, assuming that constructions with NPIs appearing in non-AA, DE contexts contain two unpronounced negations appears highly problematic for a variety of reasons. One of them is that double negation is notoriously hard to process, but understanding a sentence with a licensed weak NPI is not. Also, it does not follow from anything why licensing unpronounced double negations must take place under non-AA, DE contexts only. For these reasons, as well as the reasons spelled out in Chapter 8, I hold Collins and Postal's account of binary NPIs untenable.

However, that does not mean that the account for NPI-hood in terms of unary NPIs is on the wrong track as well. In fact, I argue that this is what underlies modal NPIs like *need/hoeven/brauchen*. The representation of NPI modals would be as follows, where the negation has to be spelled out in a higher position than the modal's base position:

(20) need/hoeven/brauchen: [$_V$ NEG [□]]

Strong/weak NPIs are actually better NPI candidates for Collins and Postal's (2014) proposal of unary NPIs than weak or strong NPIs, as these modals are restricted to those contexts that seem to spell out a separate negation, not to DE contexts. It straightforwardly rules out restrictive clauses of universal quantifiers, *if*-clauses, and polar and *Wh*-clauses as licensers of *need/hoeven/brauchen*, as these cannot be readily considered as consisting of covert negations (though see Herburger and Mauck 2007; Ludlow 2002 for an approach along these lines); there is simply no morphosyntactic evidence for that assumption.[3]

However, one criticism that this approach was confronted with is that it renders NPI-hood vulnerable to arbitrariness. It becomes unclear why certain elements are NPIs or not. Why is it that so few strong/weak NPIs are attested, and why is it that they are only attested (so far) among universal modals? Is there anything in the syntax or semantics of these elements that makes them prone to becoming NPIs, and why is it that other elements are not likely to become unary NPIs? For this, I argue, we need to focus on the learnability of NPIs in the first place. How is it that children acquire that certain elements are restricted to a particular distribution with respect to negative contexts?

11.2.4 Acquiring *hoeven*

In order to acquire an NPI, children must acquire the underlying property that is responsible for its NPI-hood. In the case of *need/hoeven/brauchen*, the child

---

[3] Note that, if such elements were to contain covert negations, given that, for instance, a universal quantifier ∀ is formally equivalent to ¬∃¬, this would massively overgeneralize. In the end, then, every predicate may contain one or two covert negation, and NPIs would be licensed in every grammatical context.

should acquire that it is lexically connected to a negation that must be spelled out or incorporated higher in the clause. But how does the child acquire such knowledge?

Since the ungrammaticality of an NPI in non-licensing contexts does not logically follow from the absence of such constructions in the input, the existence of NPIs raises an important learnability problem. How can children detect an NPI's restricted distribution in the absence of substantial or reliable negative feedback? How do children acquire, in the absence of negative evidence, exactly which types of contexts can and cannot license an NPI?

As argued for in Lin et al. (2014, 2015, 2018, 2021), the learnability problem of NPIs due to the absence of negative evidence can only be solved once a learning model is adopted that relies on positive evidence only, given that children generally do not acquire linguistic knowledge on the basis of negative evidence (see Brown and Hanlon 1970; Braine 1971; Pinker 1984, 1995, 2013; Gropen et al. 1991; Marcus et al. 1992; Marcus 1993; Cowie 1997; Boyd and Goldberg 2011; Goldberg 2011).

One possible learning strategy in this respect is conservative widening (Manzini and Wexler 1987; see Koster and Van der Wal 1996; Van der Wal 1996; Tieu 2011, 2013; Snyder 2008 for earlier applications to the acquisition of NPI-hood). Conservative widening is a general learning mechanism in language acquisition that can best be described in terms of the Subset Principle (Manzini and Wexler 1987): 'Briefly, the subset principle demands that a learning procedure should guess the narrowest possible language, consistent with positive evidence seen so far. By hypothesizing as narrow a target language as possible, the acquisition procedure is protected from disastrous overgeneralization' (Berwick and Weinberg 1986: 233, quoted in Lin et al. 2015). If children, for some reason, acquire that NPIs can only appear in anti-morphic context, they could reach a target stage, based on positive evidence only, that NPIs can also be licensed in other AA or DE contexts. This way, a conservative-widening learning mechanism can prevent children from making overgeneralization errors, which can then no longer be unlearned.

But how are children supposed to make the first step in analysing an NPI? Lin et al. take the children's establishment of their initial analysis to be input-based only, in a similar way to that proposed for category learning via a distributional approach (Cartwright and Brent 1997; Mintz et al. 2002; Mintz 2002; Redington et al. 1998). They adopt Mintz (2002, 2003) and Mintz et al. (2002) in that a distribution-based learning mechanism plays a crucial role in early language acquisition. Children's first attempts to analyse a target NPI can only be guided by investigating positive evidence available at the beginning of acquisition in terms of distributional properties.

Such a hypothesis, then, must take the acquisition of NPIs to exhibit several developmental stages. Children start with the strictest analysis possible of their target language, based on distributional properties of the limited input data available in the acquisitional onset. Even though such an analysis may not be identical to that of an adult speaker, it is at least compatible with all the input data a child has perceived and analysed so far. Later on, such an analysis can be easily falsified by more input data processed in a succeeding stage. This can eventually lead language learners to weaken down the initial analysis to construct a reanalysis explaining the input data perceived and processed in both stages. Such an iterative process then continues until, at a certain stage of language acquisition, children establish an analysis that explains all input data throughout the whole process of language development. This conservatively widening pathway in acquisition is subject to the Subset Principle: the set of the output of an analysis at a certain stage is always a subset of the set of the output generated by its reanalysis at the subsequent stage.

Lin et al. (2015), on the basis of a Childes corpus study (MacWhinney 2000), show that, for Dutch *hoeven*, this is indeed correct. They present the following results, that show that children start out using *hoeven* only in sentences that contain the NM *niet*. Only later on do they start using *hoeven* also in certain other AA or DE contexts (Table 11.1).

Table 11.1 Usage of NPI *hoeven* (need) by children

Licensing condition	Stage I (age: 1–3)	Stage II (age: 3–4)	Stage III (age: 4–5)
Sentential negation (*niet* 'not')	101 (99.02%)	67 (98.53%)	42 (85.71%)
Negative indefinites (*green* 'no(ne)', *niks* 'nothing', etc.)	1 (0.98%)	0	5 (10.2%)
Weaker negation (*alleen* 'only', *weining* 'few', etc.)	0	1 (1.47%)	2 (4.08%)
TOTAL	102	68	49

Lin et al. show that the distribution of *hoeven* across different types of negative contexts in Stage I does not significantly differ from its distribution in Stage II. They do find a significant difference between children younger than four years old and their older counterparts in Stage III. The contributor to this significant effect is the emergence of NIs and exceptives as a new type of licensers for *hoeven* in Stage III. This means that children in Stage III employ significantly more types of negative contexts to license the target NPI than children below the age of four. The distribution of *hoeven* is indeed more restricted in early than in late child Dutch (Figure 11.1).

The acquisition of *hoeven* thus exhibits two distinctive developmental periods, with the age of four as a watershed. In the first stage, *hoeven* is always attested as taking scope under the NM *niet*; in late child Dutch, it then appears in negative contexts introduced by an NI as well. That *hoeven* starts out co-occurring with the NM *niet* only is not surprising: it is the most frequent licenser of *hoeven* attested in child-directed speech (80.81% of all occurrences). Also, the percentage

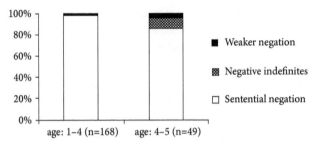

Fig. 11.1 Distribution of NPI *hoeven* (need) in child Dutch, taken from Lin et al. (2015)

of co-occurrence of *hoeven* and *niet* with a distance between zero (i.e., adjacent co-occurrence) and three syllables reached 97.32%. The distribution of *hoeven* is restricted to negative contexts introduced by *niet* in the child's initial analysis, and is expanded later on.

Following Lin et al.'s findings, which have been confirmed experimentally in Lin et al. (2018), *hoeven* starts out as a lexical chunk [HOEVEN NIET]. However, 20% of the input data cannot be captured by this initial analysis. These concern cases of *hoeven* appearing in the scope of NIs (such as *geen* ('no') or *niks* ('nothing')), negated universal quantifiers (like *niet iedereen* 'not everybody') and exceptives like *alleen* 'only'. Such input data force the children to reanalyse *hoeven*. Given the fact that all these other licensers contain a decomposable negation, in late child Dutch, *hoeven* must then be lexically associated with an abstract negation that is present in all licensers. Referring to this abstract negation as NEG, the adult analysis is represented as [HOEVEN NEG].

Naturally, the question may arise, though, whether Dutch children at that stage already have acquired split-scope readings, which form the necessary evidence that NIs and the like are indeed available. Lin et al. argue that this is indeed the case, and they provide the following naturally produced examples which suggest that children are able to understand that NIs are to be decomposed.

(21) a. Je mag geen deurtje lenen   (2:11;09)   (Dutch[4])
        you may no door borrow
        'You are not allowed to borrow a door' NEG>may > ∃
     b. Ik kan niks horen   (3:06;21)
        I can nothing hear[5]
        'I am not able to hear a thing'   NEG>can> ∃-thing

With this in mind, it is safe to conclude that children indeed follow an acquisitional pathway that starts out with an analysis of *hoeven* as a lexical chunk [HOEVEN NIET] and ends up with a complex lexical element [HOEVEN NEG].

---

[4] Example from Wijnen and Bol (1993: jos21109.cha: line 356).
[5] Example from Wijnen (1988: 30621.cha: line 1133).

This means that the acquisition of unary NPIs à la Collins and Postal (2014) is indeed possible—but under special circumstances only. The NPI should co-occur most frequently with the NM, and also appear almost adjacent to it. This is indeed the case with verbal auxiliaries, but is likely not the case for other potential NPIs. Hence, even though there are no grammatical restrictions on the possible kinds of strong/weak NPIs, learnability requirements put severe constraints on them.

Naturally, this is not the entire story. If strong/weak NPIs must be acquired along these lines, it must also be the case that other kinds of NPIs, such as strong or weak NPIs, are acquired differently. In Section 11.4, I will show that this is indeed the case. However, before doing so, I first discuss another type of NPI, namely superweak NPIs.

11.3 Superweak Negative Polarity Items

11.3.1 Non-veridicality

As discussed in Chapter 9, Giannakidou (2000), basing herself on Zwarts (1986, 1995), argues that NPIs are not necessarily sensitive to AA or DE contexts, but also (or rather) to non-veridicality. (Non-)veridicality is defined in terms of truth:

(22) (Non)veridicality for propositional operators:
A propositional operator F is veridical, iff F(p) entails p; otherwise F is non veridical

Informally, a veridical context is a context in which the truth of a proposition can be entailed. Complement clauses of factive verbs, for instance, are veridical, since the truth of the proposition (23b) is entailed by (23a).

(23) a. I know you are 25 years old
b. You are 25 years old

On the other hand, a non-veridical context is a context in which the truth of a proposition cannot be entailed. Contexts that are non-veridical are polar questions, imperatives, complement clauses of intensional verbs, etc. Polar questions are non-veridical as sentences like (24a) do not entail the truth of (24c). In the same vein, complement clauses of intensional verbs are non-veridical as well: (24b) does not entail the truth of (24c), either.

(24) a. Are you 25 years old?
b. I guess you are 25 years old
c. You are 25 years old

Non-veridical contexts form a weaker type of negative context than DE contexts. As proven in Zwarts (1995), DE contexts and non-veridical contexts stand in a subset relationship with each other. All DE contexts are non-veridical, but not the other way around.

Giannakidou argues that non-veridicality is, in general, what is responsible for NPI-hood. For her, DE-ness is not always a necessary condition for it. For instance, the Greek indefinite *tipota* ('anything') can be licensed under modals meaning 'may' or 'want', or in subjunctive clauses (Giannakidou 1998, 1999, 2000). Similar observations have been made for Chinese (Lin 1996), Salish (Mathewson 1998), Navajo (Fernald and Perkins 2007), and Romanian (Fălăuş 2009). Also, for the English NPI *any*, she has argued that it has a much broader distribution than DE contexts:

(25) a. *John saw anybody
 b. Did John see anybody?
 c. John didn't see anybody
 d. Few students saw anybody
 e. John can see anybody (from where he is)
 f. Any minor must be accompanied by an adult
 g. Pick any card
 h. Ariadne will talk to anybody
 i. Any cat hunts mice

Indeed, (25e–i) are not DE. However, it is not clear that the instances of *any* in these examples are indeed NPIs. Instead, they are generally assumed to be Free Choice Items (FCIs). Of course, the fact that members of the English *any*-series can be used both as NPIs and as FCIs can be no coincidence. In many languages, indefinites display both NPI and FC effects, such as Serbo-Croatian *ko bilo* ('anybody'), Malagasy *na inona na inona* ('or what or what', 'anything', cf. Paul 2005), English *any* being the most stereotypical example. English *any* may surface, as exemplified in (25), in (a limited number of) positive contexts, as long as it acts as an FCI. For this reason, NPIs and FCIs are often analysed on a par, the immediate question being whether English *any*, as well as other elements that may manifest both FC and NPI behaviour, is lexically ambiguous between an NPI and FCI or has a single lexical representation. However, there are also NPIs, such as English *ever*, that lack an FC effect, or FCIs that lack an NPI effect, for instance Spanish *cualquiera* ('whoever'). This suggests that, even though FCIs and NPIs can form a unified class, they should, at the same time, still constitute two independent subclasses, even within a language where NPIs and FCIs are syncretic. Before evaluating Giannakidou's proposal of NPI licensing in terms of non-veridicality, it thus first needs to be assessed to what extent FCI-usages of NPIs like *any* should be taken into consideration when accounting for their NPI status.

11.3.2 Negative Polarity Items and Free Choice Items

As Alonso-Ovalle and Menendez-Benito (in press) point out in their overview of FCIs and other indefinites, the major difference between FCIs and NPIs is that

11.3 SUPERWEAK NEGATIVE POLARITY ITEMS

NPIs generally have an indefinite interpretation, but FCIs seem to behave more like universals rather than indefinites. This is shown in (26), taken from van Rooij (2008), where both examples convey that all students in Mary's class are working on NPIs, not just some—albeit that the example containing *any*, but not the one with *every*, comes along with a sort of 'and that's not an accident' implicature.

(26) a. Any student in Mary's class is working on NPIs
   b. Every student in Mary's class is working on NPIs

The question of why FCIs receive an apparent universal force is related to the question of whether FCIs and NPIs should indeed receive a unified analysis. A number of researchers have aimed to unify the two uses of *any* by proposing that this item is an indefinite, one of the reasons being that, morphologically, such FCIs resemble NPIs and not universal quantifiers.

According to these approaches, the universal force attested for the FCI usage comes about via the kind of pragmatic strengthening effect that is generally also said to underlie NPI-hood (cf. Aloni 2007; Kadmon and Landman 1993; Chierchia 2006, 2013). For Kadmon and Landman (1993), pragmatic strengthening (domain-widening, in their terms) is a property of both FCIs and NPIs. Just as *I don't have any potatoes* has a stronger reading than *I don't have potatoes* (see Chapter 10), Kadmon and Landman argue that (26a) is stronger than *A student in Mary's class is working on NPIs*. As, for them, the same effect that drives NPIs to be subject to certain licensing constraints is responsible for the FC effects, Kadmon and Landman take FCI *any* and NPI *any* to be a single lexical item. On similar grounds, Aloni (2007), Aloni and Van Rooij (2007), Chierchia (2006, 2013), Dayal (2013), and Van Rooij (2008) also opt for a unified analysis of FC and NPI *any*. All of these are thus cases where morphological considerations underlie semantic analyses. The FCI effects then follow from pragmatic effects involving the element's scalar alternatives. For instance, for Chierchia, the FC effect of (27) results from two rounds of exhaustification: first, domain alternatives are exhaustified, and, in turn, the assertion plus the exhaustified domain alternatives and scalar alternatives are exhaustified again, illustrated below for a scenario when there are two biscuits, a and b:

(27) You may eat any biscuit
   a. Assertion: $\Diamond[a \vee b]$
   b. Scalar alternative: $\Diamond[a \wedge b]$
   c. D-alternatives: $\Diamond a; \Diamond b$
   d. Exhaustified D-alternatives: $O(\Diamond a) = \Diamond a \wedge \neg \Diamond b; O(\Diamond b) = \Diamond b \wedge \neg \Diamond a$
   e. Free Choice effect:
   OExh-ALT $(\Diamond[a \vee b]) = \Diamond[a \vee b] \wedge \neg[\Diamond a \wedge \neg \Diamond b] \wedge \neg[\Diamond b \wedge \neg \Diamond a]$
   $\wedge \neg \Diamond[a \wedge b] = [\Diamond a \rightarrow \Diamond b] \wedge [\Diamond b \rightarrow \Diamond a] \wedge \neg \Diamond[a \wedge b] = \Diamond a \wedge \Diamond b \wedge \neg \Diamond[a \wedge b]$

In earlier work, Dayal (1998, 2004, 2009) has proposed breaking with the idea that FCI *any* is an indefinite, and analysing it instead as a universal quantifier. FCI *any* and NPI *any*, in her view, are homophonous. Also, Menéndez-Benito (2005, 2010) and Saebo (2001) have proposed taking NPIs and FCIs to be different types of elements. Apart from the fact that the attested homophony between FCIs and NPIs would remain unexplained, a problem with analyses that are based on a treatment of FCIs like *any* as a universal quantifier, indicated by Giannakidou (2001), is that the universal reading of FC *any* is not always available. Example (28) does not mean 'pick every card'.

(28) Pick any card

Thus, for Dayal and others who maintain the idea that FCIs are underlyingly universals, it is necessary to derive the indefinite reading of FC *any* from an underlying universal semantic representation, and the reader is referred to Dayal (1998, 2004, 2009) for the specifics of her proposal.

Hence, even though it is not clear whether NPIs and FCIs indeed have a joint semantic core (as the widely attested morphological overlap between NPI and FCI indefinites would suggest), most existing analyses at least seem to point in that direction. However, if the FC effects follow from the same semantic core as the NPI, the examples in (25) no longer necessarily form an argument for the view that NPIs like *any* need to be licensed in non-veridical contexts, instead of DE contexts. This in itself is a welcome result, as such NPIs cannot be licensed in every non-veridical context. The following examples, for instance, are all degraded.

(29) a. *Mary probably read any book
b. *She intends to read any book

Moreover, even though FCIs often appear in non-veridical contexts, it is not the case that they can appear in non-veridical contexts only. Cases of subtrigging, illustrated in (30), show that FCIs are also fine outside non-veridical contexts. The same holds for Strawson-DE contexts that are clearly veridical, but still license weak NPIs (31).

(30) a. She read any book you can imagine
b. Any student who knows Mary attends her lecture

(31) a. Only Mary bought any biscuits
b. I regret having bought any biscuits

Hence, I take the fact that various NPIs can also have a second life as FCIs not to be an argument to extend the domain of weak NPI-licensing from DE-ness (and Strawson DE-ness) to non-veridicality.

11.3.3 Chinese *shenme*: A superweak Negative Polarity Item

What I have just set out shows that weak NPIs like *any* should not be considered as elements that are licensed by non-veridical contexts. They are not superweak NPIs. However, that does not entail that superweak NPIs cannot exist in their own right. It may very well be the case that certain elements appear in all non-veridical environments and only in such contexts, with the same kind of semantic contribution.

One example, presented in Lin et al. (2014), Lin (2017), and Lin et al. (2021), concerns Mandarin Chinese *shenme*. *Shenme* can be categorized as an existential indefinite or as an interrogative pronoun, depending on its syntactic and semantic contexts. Its interpretation depends on the environment it appears in. It can have an interrogative interpretation like English *what*; it can also have an indefinite interpretation like English *a*, *any*, or *some*. *Shenme* even seems to get an FC-like reading when it appears in the scope of the universal quantifier *dou*.

In questions, *shenme* may act as a *Wh*-term, very similarly to English *what*. The examples in (32), a matrix and an embedded question containing *shenme*, illustrate this (see for instance Huang 1982; Cheng 1991, 1994; Lin 1996).

(32) a. Yuehan mai le *shenme* shu (ne)? (Mandarin Chinese)
John buy PRF shenme book Q
'What kind of book(s) has John bought?'

b. Wo xiang zhidao Yuehan mai le *shenme* shu
I want know John buy PRF shenme book
'I wonder what kind of (books) John has bought'

In addition to (embedded) *Wh*-questions, *shenme* can also be attested in a variety of non-veridical contexts. Examples of such contexts that license *shenme* are in the scope of an NM (33a–b), an NI (33c–d), the antecedent clause of a conditional (34a), the restriction of a universal quantifier like *meige* (34b), questions—both polar and *Wh*-questions—(35), and epistemic modal contexts (36) (Huang 1982; Cheng 1991, 1994; Lin 1996, 1998; Lin et al. 2014; and others). In these examples, *shenme* functions like the English indefinites *a*, *any*, or *some*.

(33) a. Yuehan mei mai *shenme* shu (Mandarin Chinese)
John not buy shenme book
'John did not buy (a) book'

b. Bie rang ta mai *shenme* Shu
not let him buy shenme book
'Don't let him buy (any/a) book(s)'

c. Zuotian meiren mai *shenme* shu
yesterday nobody buy shenme book
'Nobody bought (a) book(s) yesterday'

d. Ta   congwei mai   guo   *shenme*   Shu
    s/he   never   buy   PRF   shenme   book
    'S/he never bought (any/a) book(s) before'

(34) a. Ruguo Yuehan gei   ni   mai   guo   *shenme* liwu, (Mn. Ch.)
        if   John   for   you   buy   PRF   shenme   present
        ni   yiding   yao   haohao   xiexie   ta
        you   certainly   should well   thank   him
        'If John has ever bought a present for you, you should thank him a lot'

   b. Meige   yao   gei   nvpengyou   mai   *shenme*   liwu   de
       every   want   for   girlfriend buy   shenme   gift   REL
       nansheng   dou   hui   dedao   ta   de   yige   wen
       boy   all   will   get   s/he   GEN   one   kiss
       'Every boy that wants to buy a gift for his girlfriend will get a kiss from her'

(35) a. Yuehan   mai   *shenme*   shu   le   ma?   (Mandarin Chinese)
        John   buy   shenme   book   PER   Q
        'Has John bought (any) book?'

   b. Yuehan   yao   kan   duoshao   shu   cai   neng
       John   need   read   how many   book   then   able
       fabiao   *shenme*   wenzhang   ne?
       publish   shenme   paper   Q
       'How many books does John need to read before he can publish a paper?'

(36) a. Yuehan   keneng   mai   le   *shenme*   shu   (Mandarin Chinese)
        John   maybe   buy   PER   shenme   books
        'Maybe John has bought a/some book(s)'

   b. Yuehan   kending   mai   le   *shenme*   shu
       John   must   buy   PER   shenme   book
       'John must have bought a/some book(s)'

   c. Mali   zuotian   haoxiang   mai-le   *shenme*   shu
       Mary   yesterday   probably   buy- PRF   shenme   book
       'Mary has probably bought a book yesterday'

Next to its interrogative *what*-reading and existential *a/any/some*-reading, *shenme* can also obtain an FC-like interpretation when it appears in the scope of the universal quantifier *dou* 'all' (see, for instance, Cheng 1995; Lin 1998). In this context, *shenme* seems to have the same universal reading as *every* in English, as shown in the two examples in (17).[6]

---

[6] As is already established in the Chinese literature, *dou* is a universal quantifier that quantifies over a phrase or a clause that precedes it (Cheng 1995; Lee 1986; Lin 1998; Pan 2006). This means that the

(37) a. Yuehan *shenme* shu   dou xihuan kan   (Mandarin Chinese)
       John   shenme   book   all like   read
       'John likes to read every book'
   b. *Shenme* ren   dou keyi xue   zuofan
      Shenme   person all can   learn cook
      'Every person can learn cooking'

However, this does not entail that *shenme* must be taken, here, to be an FCI. The reasons for that are twofold. First, without the presence of *dou*, it is impossible for *shenme* to trigger an FC effect (38a–b). Second, bare NPs and DPs, when quantified over by *dou*, also trigger a universal effect (38c–d). This shows that the universal effect arguably comes from *dou*, and not from *shenme* itself.

(38) a. *Yuehan *shenme* shu   xihuan kan   (Mandarin Chinese)
        John   shenme   book   like   read
        Int.: 'John likes to read every book'
   b. *Yuehan xihuan kan   *shenme* shu
      John   like   read shenme   book
      Int.: 'John likes to read every book'
   c. Yuehan shu   dou xihuan kan
      John   book   all like   read
      'John likes to read every book'
   d. Yuehan zhexie shu   dou xihuan Kan
      John   these   book all like   read
      'John likes to read each of these books'

Therefore, it looks like *shenme*'s appearance in the scope of *dou* is not an FCI usage but rather that of an NPI in the restrictive clause of a universal quantifier.

Note, finally, that outside non-veridical contexts *shenme* is ungrammatical (Cheng 1994; Li 1992; Lin 1996; Xie 2007; see also recent work by Chierchia and Liao 2015), as shown in (39).

(39) *Yuehan zuotian   mai le   *shenme* shu   (Mandarin Chinese)
      John   yesterday buy PRF a   book
      Int.: 'John has bought (a) book(s) yesterday'

Naturally, the question arises as to whether the *shenme* that is used as an interrogative pronoun is the same as the indefinite one. It could be the case that the only difference between the two usages comes from the structural position of *shenme* in the clause and the relevant features on the interrogative heads. Alternatively, it can be the case that there are two different *shenme*s in the lexicon. However, irrespective of this question, since *shenme* may also appear as

---

restriction of this universal precedes rather than follows it, differently from other universal quantifiers in Mandarin, such as *meige* 'every' (as claimed in Lin et al. 2021).

274   OTHER TYPES OF NPIS

an indefinite in both polar and *Wh*-questions, it remains the case that *shenme* is indeed a superweak NPI. This also means that superweak NPIs exist in their own right.

11.3.4 The Non-Entailment-of-Existence Condition and non-veridicality

Naturally, the question arises why *shenme*'s distribution is much broader than that of *any* or *ever* (in their NPI usages). Here, I follow Lin (1996, 1998), who argues that the source of this kind of NPI-hood lies in a lexically encoded *Non-Entailment-of-Existence Condition*. In this framework, certain elements may not appear in contexts that would entail the existence of a referent satisfying their description, where such contexts are formed by the proposition whose widest scope operator is a scope operator that the NPI is in the scope of. The example in (36c), repeated in (40) without the modal, is bad as the sentence would entail that there is a book bought yesterday by Mary; if the modal is present, or a negation as in (33a), the sentence is fine; the existence of a book bought yesterday by Mary is no longer entailed.

(40) a. Mali zuotian *(haoxiang) mai-le senme shu   (Mandarin Chinese)
          Mary yesterday probably bought-PRF what/any book
          'Mary has (probably) bought a book yesterday'
      b. Mali zuotian mei mai senme shu
          Mary neg bought what/any book
          'Mary didn't buy any book yesterday'

Strikingly, this restricts the environments in which *shenme* can occur to the set of non-veridical contexts.

However, the question still arises why *shenme* may not appear in contexts that would entail the existence of a referent satisfying their description. But this may directly result from Giannakidou (2011, 2018) where it is argued that expressions that are restricted to non-veridical contexts exhibit lexical referential deficiency: these elements lack the ability to refer to an existing discourse referent. This way, every (existential) quantifier that is referentially deficient ends up as a superweak NPI.

In this account, I deviate from Chierchia and Liao (2015) who argue that *shenme* is similar to *any*: it comes with the feature complex [uσ,D], which introduces both scalar and domain alternatives, and is subject to a covert exhaustifier, just like other weak or strong NPIs in Chierchia's system. This would then account for its appearance as an existential indefinite or pronoun in various DE contexts, as sketched along the same lines for *any* in his earlier work. As for *shenme*'s function as an interrogative pronoun, which English *any* lacks, Chierchia and Liao propose that *shenme*, in addition, carries an unconstrained *Wh*-feature, which can be valued either positively, and is then responsible for *shenme*'s interpretation and distribution as a *Wh*-term, or negatively, when it does not behave like a *Wh*-term. This unconstrained *Wh*-feature, represented as [U-WH] in their system, thus explains the possible but not mandatory appearance of *shenme* as a *Wh*-term (see further Chierchia and Liao 2015: exx. 55 and 59). A problem for this analysis is, though, that it does not address the question of how other occurrences of *shenme* in non-DE, non-veridical contexts can be accounted for.

11.3.5 Acquiring *shenme*

If *shenme* is indeed an NPI whose restricted distribution lies in its referential deficiency, the question also arises how this property can be acquired, and how this acquisitional pathway precludes NPIs of other strengths from this referential deficiency. Following Lin et al. (2021), the fact that NPI *shenme* is homophonous or even polysemous to interrogative *shenme* forms a cue for understanding this.

Lin et al. (2021) show that, at an early stage, Mandarin children virtually only use *shenme* in *Wh*-questions with an interrogative *what*-meaning (at 96.5%), whereas older children also use *shenme* in different non-DE, non-veridical contexts (at 13.2%), such as those introduced by an epistemic modal adverb (see also Lin et al. 2014). The results are given in Figure 11.2.

Following the non-referentiality approach, the attested acquisition pathway of *shenme* can be explained as follows: below the age of four, children consider *shenme* just as a *Wh*-term. This initial analysis is triggered by massive frequency of *shenme* as a *Wh*-term in the language input (97.7%) and explains why *shenme* is only attested as a *Wh*-term in early child Mandarin. After the age of four, children reanalyse *shenme* as a non-referential indefinite (either alongside *Wh-shenme* or

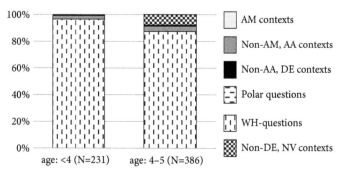

Fig. 11.2 Distribution of *shenme* in early and late child Mandarin (Lin et al. 2021)

not). This reanalysis is triggered by input evidence containing *shenme* appearing in those contexts that do not require the existence of a relevant discourse referent, such as polar questions or epistemic modal contexts.

As for this transition from a *Wh*-term to a referential deficient item, one might further adopt Giannakidou's approach by assuming that *shenme* contains a dependent variable (see also Giannakidou and Lin 2016). According to Giannakidou (2011, 2018), not only non-referential indefinites but also *Wh*-terms contain a dependent variable. The analysis of *shenme* as having a dependent variable is then automatically made when children make their first step in acquisition to take *shenme* as a *Wh*-term. The reanalysis process of *shenme* as exhibiting referential deficiency is therefore a modifying process based on language input within the same category of expressions that contain a dependent variable. The fact that *shenme* is first acquired as a *Wh*-term and then reanalysed as a referentially deficient NPI may thus explain why *shenme* has become a superweak NPI.

11.4 Acquiring weak Negative Polarity Items

So far, five types of NPIs have been disentangled and discussed, and different sources for NPI-hood have been assigned to superstrong, strong, strong/weak, weak, and superweak NPIs. Superstrong NPIs are idiomatic and stored as such with their licensers. Both strong and weak NPIs introduce domain alternatives that, when exhaustified outside DE contexts, yield a contradiction; in the case of strong NPIs, exhaustification is triggered syntactically and applies to every level of meaning contribution; in the case of weak NPIs, exhaustification is triggered pragmatically and applies to the assertion only. Strong/weak NPIs are lexically connected with a negation that needs to be spelled out higher in the structure, either as an NM or incorporated in another expression. Superweak NPIs are referentially deficient and therefore only fine in non-veridical contexts; they may not entail the existence of a referent satisfying their description.

We also saw that strong/weak and superstrong NPIs are acquired in different ways. Different acquisitional pathways may lead to NPIs of different strengths. In that sense, it would be worthwhile to investigate how strong or weak NPIs are acquired. It would be strange if their acquisitional pathways were identical to those of *hoeven* or *shenme*.

As shown by Tieu and Lidz (2016) and Lin et al. (2021), English children below the age of four systematically use *any* in the scope of *not* (at 76.3%); they also show evidence for polar questions in *any*-licensing (at 19.8%). Older children, on the other hand, are capable of using *any* in more types of semantic contexts, such as in FC-inducing contexts with an FC interpretation (6.7%), and various DE contexts,

11.4 ACQUIRING WEAK NEGATIVE POLARITY ITEMS   277

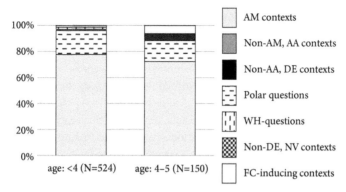

Fig. 11.3 Distribution of *any* in early and late child English (Lin et al. 2021)

which are introduced neither by *not* nor by polar questions (4.7%), for instance, conditional clauses. The results from Lin et al. are given in Figure 11.3.

As presented in Figure 11.3, English children exploit two kinds of licensing environments for *any* at the early stage: in the scope of the sentential negation *not* at 78.6%, and in polar questions at 18.7% (see also Tieu 2013 for similar results). At the subsequent stage, children start to use *any* in a variety of other DE contexts (and FC-inducing environments as well). In the language input, we find that *any* appears in the scope of *not* at 57.7%, and in polar questions at 32.3%. Lin et al. assume, given the frequency effect attested for *hoeven* and *shenme* before, that *any*'s overwhelming appearance in these two contexts triggers the children's initial analysis of the indefinite.

In order to explore the children's initial analysis of *any*, however, a better understanding is needed of the semantics of polar questions in early child grammar; in particular, what exactly polar questions containing *any* represent. Lin at al. analyse polar questions containing *any* uttered by English two- and three-year-olds (i.e., children at the early stage), and the contexts in which such polar questions are attested. Altogether, 96 polar questions with *any* were found in early child language, of which at least 72.9% seem to convey a negative bias: 15.6% exhibit a negative answer indicated by the child her-/himself, and 57.3% are responded to by parents or investigators with either a negative answer (27.1% direct; 17.7% indirect) or a positive answer with counter-evidence (12.5%)—two kinds of felicitous responses associated with negatively biased polar questions (Krifka 1995; Van Rooij 2003).

At the same time, polar questions without *any* do not tend to convey such a bias in early child language. An investigation of 103 polar questions without *any*, randomly selected in early child English, shows that in only 25.2% of the cases can such questions be analysed as expressing a negative bias.

A comparison of the response patterns observed with polar questions with and without *any* leads to the conclusion that polar questions containing *any* express a negative bias in early child language. This gives rise to the assumption that the early child grammar (not the adult grammar) associates polar questions containing *any* only with some kind of negative meaning. Following the semantics of polar questions proposed in Hamblin (1973) and the analysis of polar questions with a negative bias proposed in Asher and Reese (2005), one may assume that the meaning of a negatively biased polar question with *any*, uttered by English two- and three-year-olds, containing two parts is the set $\{\neg(...any...), \neg\neg(...any...)\}$.[7] Under this assumption, we see that *any* stays in the scope of a logic negation in each part of a negatively biased polar question, just as when it appears in the scope of *not*. Based on what has been assumed so far, it is thus hypothesized that *any* must be analysed as bearing an immediate scope relation with a semantic negation in early child language.

The question then arises as to how children, on the basis of input data with *any* appearing in other (DE) contexts, reach the conclusion that it introduces domain alternatives. I do not have a clear answer here, but it may very well be the case that, if *any* always appears under the immediate scope of negation, it always gives rise to a strengthening effect. Any sentence with *any* under the immediate scope of negation is stronger than its relevant (domain and scalar) alternatives. On a speculative note, children may be able to understand *any* to trigger a strengthening effect and use that to jump to the conclusion that *any* introduces domain alternatives that are to be exhaustified.

Crucially, though, the acquisitional pathway of *any* is substantially different from that of *hoeven* or *shenme*, suggesting that NPIs of different strengths are indeed NPIs for a different reason, reflected by the way they are acquired.

11.5 Conclusions

In this chapter, three other types of NPIs than strong and weak ones have been discussed. I have argued that superstrong NPIs are idiomatic and stored as such with their licensers. Strong/weak NPIs are lexically connected with a negation that needs to be spelled out higher in the structure, either as an NM or incorporated in another expression, along the lines of Collins and Postal's (2014) analysis of unary NPIs. Superweak NPIs, I have argued, following Lin et al. (2014, 2021), are

---

[7] Other approaches to negatively biased polar questions are Guerzoni (2003) and Van Rooij (2003). From a syntactic perspective, Guerzoni argues that polar questions with a negative bias are negative assertions, i.e., $\neg p$, rather than questions. Van Rooij, however, analyses negatively biased polar questions as true questions denoting $\{p, \neg p\}$, but differing from their neutral counterparts in that they necessarily carry a strong negative presupposition or implicature. It is not the goal here to participate in the debate on the semantics and/or pragmatics of polar questions with a negative bias. See Asher and Reese (2005) and the references therein for a related discussion (cf. Lin et al. 2021).

referentially deficient and therefore only fine in non-veridical contexts; they may not entail the existence of a referent satisfying their description (cf. Lin 1996, 1998; Giannakidou 2011, 2018). In addition, I have shown that acquisitional data appear to confirm these analyses, and also that (strong and) weak NPIs like *any* indeed form a different type of NPI from superstrong, strong/weak, and superweak NPIs.

This suggests that NPIs of different strengths are NPIs for different reasons. But does the reverse also hold? Are all NPIs of the same strength also NPIs for the same reason? It may very well be the case that there are different types of NPIs that are equally strong. In the next chapter, I will argue that that is indeed the case, and present another kind of weak NPI whose distribution cannot be accounted for along the lines of Chierchia (2006, 2013).

12
Not a light negation

12.1 Introduction

In languages like Dutch and German, certain constructions of negation yield readings that may only emerge in DE contexts, rendering such readings NPI-like. German examples of such cases, taken from Schwarz and Bhatt (2006), are presented in the next examples. The sentences in (1), which contain an indefinite DP, a definite DP, or a disjunction of two DPs, cannot be regularly negated by having the NM *nicht* immediately precede them, as is shown in (2). To the extent that they are grammatical, they cannot give rise to a reading where Fritz knows no foreign language or where he didn't answer question 3, or question 3 or 4. By contrast, the examples in (3) show how such readings can be realized. In (3a), for this reading, an NI (*keine* 'no') is used; in (3bc-i), *nicht* appears in a position following a definite DP or a disjunctive expression. Alternatively, a disjunctive construction *weder ... noch* ('neither ... nor') can be used (cf. (3c-ii)).

(1) a. Fritz kann eine Fremdsprache (German)
    Fritz knows a foreign.language
    'Fritz knows a foreign language'

   b. Fritz hat Frage 3 beantwortet
      Fritz has question 3 answered
      'Fritz answered question 3'

   c. Fritz hat Frage 3 oder 4 beantwortet
      Fritz has question 3 or 4 answered
      'Fritz answered question 3 or 4'

(2) a. *Fritz kann nicht eine Fremdsprache (German)
       Fritz knows not a foreign.language
       Int.: 'Fritz doesn't know a foreign language'

   b. *Fritz hat nicht Frage 3 beantwortet
      Fritz has not question 3 answered
      Int.: 'Fritz didn't answer question 3'

   c. *Fritz hat nicht Frage 3 oder 4 beantwortet
      Fritz has not question 3 or 4 answered
      Int.: 'Fritz didn't answer question 3 or 4'

Negation and Negative Dependencies. Hedde Zeijlstra, Oxford University Press.
© Hedde Zeijlstra (2022). DOI: 10.1093/oso/9780198833239.003.0012

(3) a. Fritz kann keine Fremdsprache (German)
    Fritz knows no foreign.language
    'Fritz doesn't know a foreign language'

  b. Fritz hat Frage 3 nicht beantwortet
     Fritz has question 3 not answered
     'Fritz didn't answer question 3'

  c. i. Fritz hat Frage 3 oder 4 nicht beantwortet
        Fritz has question 3 or 4 not answered
        'Fritz didn't answer question 3 or 4'

    ii. Fritz hat weder Frage 3 noch 4 beantwortet
        Fritz has neither question 3 nor 4 answered
        'Fritz answered neither question 3, nor 4'

The same applies to Dutch, where the intended readings in (5) cannot be yielded and have to be conveyed by the corresponding sentences in (6):

(4) a. Frits kent een vreemde taal (Dutch)
       Frits knows a foreign language
       'Frits knows a foreign language'

  b. Frits heeft vraag 3 beantwoord
     Frits has question 3 answered
     'Frits answered question 3'

  c. Frits heeft vraag 3 of 4 beantwoord
     Frits has question 3 or 4 answered
     'Frits answered question 3 or 4'

(5) a. *Frits kent niet een vreemde taal (Dutch)
       Frits knows not a foreign language
       Int.: 'Frits doesn't know a foreign language'

  b. *Frits heeft niet vraag 3 beantwoord
     Frits has not question 3 answered
     Int.: 'Frits didn't answer question 3'

  c. *Frits heeft niet vraag 3 of 4 beantwoord
     Frits has not question 3 or 4 answered
     Int.: 'Frits didn't answer question 3 or 4'

(6) a. Frits kent geen vreemde taal (Dutch)
       Frits knows no foreign language
       'Frits doesn't know a foreign language'

  b. Frits heeft vraag 3 niet beantwoord
     Frits has question 3 not answered
     'Frits didn't answer question 3'

c. i. Frits heeft vraag   3 of 4 niet beantwoord.
        Frits has   question 3 or 4 not answered
        'Frits didn't answer question 3 or 4'

   ii. Frits heeft (noch) vraag   3 noch 4 beantwoord
       Fritz has   neither question 3 nor 4 answered
       'Fritz answered neither question 3, nor 4'

However, the examples in (2)/(5) with their intended readings all of a sudden become fine once they are embedded in contexts that license weak NPIs: DE contexts, such as NIs (e.g. (7)/(10)), polar questions (as in (8)/(11)), and (counterfactual) conditionals (as in (9)/(12)).[1]

(7) a. Wir haben keinen angenommen der nicht eine
       we   have nobody hired   who not   a
       Fremdsprache   kann   (German)
       foreign.language knows
       'We hired nobody who doesn't know a foreign language'

   b. Wir haben keinen angenommen der nicht Frage   3
      we   have nobody hired   who not   question 3
      answered has
      beantwortet hat
      'We hired nobody who didn't answer question 3'

   c. Wir haben keinen angenommen der nicht Frage   3
      we   have nobody hired   who not   question 3
      oder 4 beantwortet hat
      or   4 answered   has
      'We hired nobody who didn't answer question 3 or 4'

(8) a. Kann   Fritz nicht eine Fremdsprache?   (German)
       knows Fritz not   a   foreign.language
       'Doesn't Fritz know a foreign language?'

   b. Hat Fritz nicht Frage   3 beantwortet?
      has Fritz not   question 3 answered
      'Didn't Fritz answer question 3?'

   c. Hat Fritz nicht Frage   3 oder 4 beantwortet?
      has Fritz not   question 3 or   4 answered
      'Didn't Fritz answer question 3 or 4?'

---

[1] See Mayr (2013) and Nicolae (2015) for arguments that polar questions are DE.

12.1 INTRODUCTION 283

(9) a. Wenn Fritz nicht eine Fremdsprache könnte, wäre er
   if Fritz not a foreign.language knew, were he
   durchgefallen (German)
   failed
   'If Fritz hadn't known a foreign language, he would have failed'

   b. Wenn Fritz nicht Frage 3 beantwortet hätte, wäre er
   if Fritz not question 3 answered had, were he
   durchgefallen
   failed
   'If Fritz hadn't answered question 3, he would have failed'

   c. Wenn Fritz nicht Frage 3 oder 4 beantwortet hätte,
   if Fritz not question 3 or 4 answered had,
   wäre er durchgefallen
   were he failed
   'If Fritz hadn't answered question 3 or 4, he would have failed'

(10) a. We hebben niemand aangenomen die niet een
   we have nobody hired who not a
   vreemde taal kent (Dutch)
   foreign.language knows
   'We hired nobody who doesn't know a foreign language'

   b. We hebben niemand aangenomen die niet vraag 3
   we have nobody hired who not question 3
   heeft beantwoord
   has answered
   'We hired nobody who didn't answer question 3'

   c. We hebben niemand aangenomen die niet vraag 3
   we have nobody hired who not question 3
   of 4 heeft beantwoord
   or 4 has answered
   'We hired nobody who didn't answer question 3 or 4'

(11) a. Kent Frits niet een vreemde taal? (Dutch)
   knows Frits not a foreign.language
   'Doesn't Frits know a foreign language?'

   b. Heeft Frits niet vraag 3 beantwoord?
   has Frits not question 3 answered
   'Didn't Frits answer question 3?'

   c. Heeft Frits niet vraag 3 of 4 beantwoord?
   has Frits not question 3 or 4 answered
   'Didn't Frits answer question 3 or 4?'

(12) a. Als   Frits   niet   een   vreemde taal sprak,   zou   hij
       if   Frits   not   a   foreign.language   knew,   would he
       gezakt zijn   (Dutch)
       failed be
       'If Fritz hadn't known a foreign language, he would have failed'

   b. Als   Frits   niet   vraag   3   beantwoord   had,   zou   hij
      if   Frits   not   question 3   answered   had,   would   he
      gezakt zijn
      failed be
      'If Fritz hadn't answered question 3, he would have failed'

   c. Wenn   Fritz   nicht   vraag   3   of   4   beantwoord   had,
      if   Frits   not   question 3   or   4   answered   had,
      zou   hij   failed   be
      would   he   gezakt   zijn
      'If Fritz hadn't answered question 3 or 4, he would have failed'

As we saw, the sentences in (2)/(5) are indeed unacceptable with the intended or unmarked readings.[2] However, that does not mean that they are ungrammatical. These sentences can still be used grammatically, but only with other readings. For instance, (2a)/(5a) is ungrammatical with the intended reading in which a negation outscopes the indefinite without any additional focus effects. However, (2a)/(5a) can be uttered felicitously when it either gives rise to a reading where the indefinite takes wide scope with respect to negation, or when the indefinite itself is focused; in that case, it may even receive two readings. These cases, where marked readings arise, are shown below:

(13) Fritz   kann   nicht   eine   Fremdsprache   die   man   in
      Fritz   knows   not   a   foreign.language   that   one   in
      Frankreich   spricht   (German)
      France   speaks
      ∃ > ¬: 'Fritz doesn't know a foreign language spoken in France'

(14) a. Fritz   kann   nicht   EINE   Fremdsprache;   er   kennt
        Fritz   knows   not   A/ONE   foreign.language;   he   knows
        DREI   (German)
        THREE
        'Fritz doesn't know one foreign language, but three'

---

[2] It may sound odd to refer to the reading that is absent outside DE contexts as the 'unmarked reading'; however, this is indeed the most salient reading once there is embedding in an NPI context. For this reason, and other reasons that will become clear in the remainder of this chapter, I stick to the term 'unmarked reading' here.

12.1 INTRODUCTION

    b. Fritz kann nicht (einmal) EINE Fremdsprache
       Fritz knows not (even) A/ONE foreign.language
       'Fritz doesn't even know one foreign language'

(15) Frits kent niet een vreemde taal die men in Frankrijk
     Frits knows not a foreign.language that one in France
     spreekt   (Dutch)
     speaks
     ∃ > ¬: 'Frits doesn't know a foreign language spoken in France'

(16) a. Frits kent niet EEN vreemde taal; hij kent er
       Fritz knows not A/ONE foreign.language; he knows there
       DRIE   (Dutch)
       THREE
       'Fritz doesn't know one foreign language, but three'

    b. Frits kent (zelfs) niet EEN vreemde taal
       Fritz knows (even) not A/ONE foreign.language
       'Fritz doesn't even know one foreign language'

In the case of a negated definite, the only reading that is available is one in which the focus is on the definite description:

(17) Fritz hat nicht Frage DREI beantwortet, sondern Frage
     Fritz has not question THREE answered, rather question
     VIER   (German)
     FOUR
     'Fritz didn't answer question three, but rather question four'

(18) Frits heeft niet vraag DRIE beantwoord, maar vraag
     Frits has not question THREE answered, but question
     VIER   (Dutch)
     FOUR
     'Frits didn't answer question three, but question four'

Also, in the case of negated disjunctions, the sentence can be repaired once (some parts of) the disjunction receives focus as well.

The two questions that now arise are the following: (i) Why is it that certain constructions involving negation are always available with a marked reading, but are in DE contexts also available with an unmarked reading; and (ii) why is it that the unmarked reading does not arise outside these weak NPI licensing contexts?

In the remainder of this chapter, I address both questions. First, in Section 12.2, I discuss an earlier account of this phenomenon, proposed by Schwarz (2004) and by Schwarz and Bhatt (2006). I argue that this account, which takes the negative constructions in examples like (2)/(5) to be a special type of NPI containing so-called *light negation*, is incorrect. In Section 12.3, I propose an alternative account that takes the blocking of the marked readings to be the result of an implicature that arises by virtue of the fact that the unmarked readings could also have been yielded by alternative and, in some way, simpler sentences. The fact that such implicatures generally dissolve in (weak) NPI licensing contexts accounts for the availability of these unmarked readings in NPI licensing contexts. Section 12.4 concludes.

12.2 Light negation (Schwarz and Bhatt)

Schwarz (2004) and Schwarz and Bhatt (2006) argue that German has two lexically ambiguous, homophonous NMs: a plain NM *nicht*, which generally renders sentences negative, and a second NM *nicht*, dubbed *light negation* (after Ladusaw 1979), which is a (weak) NPI. For them, examples like (2), with the intended unmarked reading, contain this light negation, whose occurrence, being an NPI, is naturally restricted to DE contexts. The same would hold for Dutch (5).

The idea that NMs are ambiguous between a plain and a light variant stems from Ladusaw (1979), who argues that it is this light NM that is involved in constructions like (19) (with *something* taking scope below negation):

(19) a. *I am happy that you didn't see something
     b. I am surprised that you didn't see something

As is well known, *something* is a Positive Polarity Item (PPI) and therefore banned from negative contexts, as illustrated in (19a). However, once the negated PPI is included in an NPI licensing context, as is the case in (19b), it is fine again. Krifka (1992) and Szabolcsi (2004) argue that this is due to some mechanism that changes negated PPIs into NPIs. If *not something* is indeed taken to be an NPI, the pattern in (19) directly follows. For Krifka and Szabolcsi, negated PPIs can thus be rescued. Also Homer (2020) provides an account of why negated PPIs may occur in NPI licensing contexts (see Chapter 13 for more discussion).

Ladusaw (1979), on the other hand, has a different view on PPI-hood. For him, a PPI can never be rescued: once a PPI is anti-licensed, it can no longer give rise to a well-formed sentence. This entails, however, that *something* in (19b) can never be said to have been rescued, and, therefore, not have been anti-licensed in the first place. In order to account for the grammaticality of (19b), Ladusaw proposes that the negation here is not a regular NM but rather this alternative light negation, which he takes to be an NPI that never anti-licenses PPIs. Since this light negation is an NPI, the negation in (19a) must be the regular NM, as such a light negation would be banned from non-NPI licensing contexts.

For Schwarz and Bhatt, the data presented in Section 12.1 confirm Ladusaw's proposal. They see these data as additional evidence for the presence of a light negation marker alongside a regular one.

However, Schwarz and Bhatt's analysis faces a number of serious problems. First, their approach cannot account for the fact that the regular NM *nicht* may not be included in examples such as the ones in (2)/(5). Also, it remains unclear why such constructions still yield a marked reading only, as the data in (13)–(18) show. One could potentially argue that inclusion of the regular negation is fine in examples such as (2)/(5), but that this regular NM can only give rise to the marked reading. However, it is unclear, under this proposal, why the regular NM would be subject to such a restriction and why the light negation marker would not, especially given the fact that, semantically, both denote a semantic negation.

Another problem for this analysis is the fact that there does not seem to be any additional evidence for the existence of a second NM *nicht*. As long as no independent evidence for the existence of a second homophonous NM is presented, any analysis of the facts presented in Section 12.1 that does not have to allude to such a lexical ambiguity is superior.

Finally, as Schwarz and Bhatt point out themselves, the distribution of negative constructions that appear to be subject to NPI licensing constraints does not completely coincide with the distribution of other well-known NPIs. In one particular type of context, namely non-counterfactual conditionals, such constructions are still bad, even though plain NPIs are generally licensed in such contexts. To illustrate this, Schwarz and Bhatt (2006) claim that, in a discourse like (20), the expressions in (9) cannot be used as a continuation of the answer (although speakers that I consulted sometimes find these judgements hard to confirm).

(20) A: Was   glaubst   Du   warum   Fritz   durchgefallen   ist? (German)
         what   believe   you   why   Fritz   failed   is
         'Why do you believe Fritz failed?'

      B: Ich   bin   mir   nicht   sicher,   aber ...
         I   am   me   not   sure,   but
         'I'm not sure, but ...'

By contrast, in the consequents of counterfactual conditionals, such negative NPI-like constructions are fine again, even though consequents of counterfactual conditionals do not license NPIs.

(21) a. Wenn   Fritz   dumm   wäre,   könnte   er   nicht   eine
         if   Fritz   stupid   were,   could   he   not   a
         Fremdsprache   (German)
         foreign.language
         'If Fritz were stupid, he wouldn't know a foreign language'

b. Wenn Fritz dumm wäre, hätte er nicht Frage 3 beantwortet
if Fritz stupid were, had he not question 3 answered
'If Fritz were stupid, he wouldn't have answered question 3'

c. Wenn Fritz dumm wäre, hätte er nicht Frage 3 oder
if Fritz stupid were, had he not question 3 or
4 beantwortet
4 answered
'If Fritz were stupid, he wouldn't have answered question 3 or 4'

As Schwarz (2004) and Schwarz and Bhatt (2006) point out, in those contexts where the distributions of plain NPIs and constructions like (2)/(5) do not overlap, the distribution of negated PPIs patterns with the distribution of negated indefinites, definites, and disjunctions.[3] They argue that *some* can only receive a reading where it scopes below negation in counterfactual conditionals like (22a), and not in non-counterfactual conditionals such as (22b) (cf. Baker 1970; Karttunen 1971; Schwarz 2004), though, again, the judgements are subtle and not shared by all my informants.

(22) a. If John didn't know some foreign language, he would have failed
b. If John doesn't know some foreign language, he may fail

Schwarz and Bhatt take this to be further evidence against the Krifka/Szabolcsi/Homer-type of analysis of PPI-rescuing and in favour of an analysis in terms of light negation. Nevertheless, it remains unclear, under their proposal, why the distribution of light negation deviates from that of plain NPIs, given that they take this light negation to be an NPI. Apparently, for them, appearing in a DE licensing context is a necessary but not a sufficient condition for being licensed in these cases.

12.3 Proposal

In order to overcome the problems outlined in Section 12.2, I propose a different analysis, which, crucially, does not rely on the presence of a second, homophonous NM. Instead, I argue that all the facts I have described can be naturally explained by assuming that *nicht/niet* is always a regular NM and that all unavailable readings are the result of the application of standardly adopted pragmatic principles.

The reasoning goes as follows: Suppose that the examples in (2)/(5) may semantically give rise to both the unmarked readings and the marked readings (as in

---

[3] On a terminological note: I distinguish the term 'negated indefinites' from 'negative indefinites' (NIs). The first refers to plain indefinites that are negated by an additional NM (e.g. *nicht ein* ('not a')); the second one to single morphological words such as *kein* ('no').

(13)–(18)). Nevertheless, another, minimally differing, expression may also give rise to the unmarked readings that are intended in (2)/(5), such as the examples in (3)/(6), but only to those. Then, the set of all readings that the examples in (2)/(5) may give rise to forms a superset of the readings that can be expressed by the examples in (3)/(6). Uttering a sentence like the ones in (2)/(5) may consequently give rise to an implicature that states that, by uttering such a sentence, the speaker does not want to convey the readings of the expressions in (3)/(6), for, if she had wanted to convey those, she would have used a more specified expression like one in (3)/(6) instead. Since the unmarked readings of the examples in (2)/(5) are the same as those of (3)/(6), sentences as in (2)/(5) can only be used to give rise to marked readings, as shown in (13)–(18). However, as is known since Gazdar (1979) and much subsequent work (Chierchia 2004, Sauerland 2004a, b; Gajewski and Sharvit 2008, 2012; Fox and Spector 2018 and many others), implicatures are suppressed in DE licensing contexts. This means that, in those contexts, the implicature that blocks the unmarked readings of (2)/(5) no longer arises and that, consequently, in NPI licensing contexts, expressions such as the ones in (2)/(5) can be used to convey their unmarked readings as well.

Of course, such an account raises a number of questions. First, the question arises of what selects the alternative readings of the expressions in (2)/(5). And if these are indeed the examples in (3)/(6), why is it that exactly those examples count as alternatives of the ones in (2)/(5)? In order to address these questions, let us first have a look at the three types of examples in (2)/(6) and their alleged alternatives in (3)/(6). For the sake of exposition, these examples are repeated in (23)–(25), henceforth focusing on the German examples only.

(23) a. *Fritz kann nicht eine Fremdsprache (German)
     Fritz knows not a foreign.language
     Int.: 'Fritz doesn't know a foreign language'

   b. Fritz kann keine Fremdsprache
      Fritz knows no foreign.language
      'Fritz doesn't know a foreign language'

(24) a. *Fritz hat nicht Frage 3 beantwortet (German)
     Fritz has not question 3 answered
     Int.: 'Fritz didn't answer question 3'

   b. Fritz hat Frage 3 nicht beantwortet
      Fritz has question 3 not answered
      'Fritz didn't answer question 3'

(25) a. *Fritz hat nicht Frage 3 oder 4 beantwortet (German)
     Fritz has not question 3 or 4 answered
     Int.: 'Fritz didn't answer question 3 or 4'

b. i. Fritz hat Frage 3 oder 4 nicht beantwortet
Fritz has question 3 or 4 not answered
'Fritz didn't answer question 3 or 4'

ii. Fritz hat weder Frage 3 noch 4 nicht beantwortet
Fritz has neither question 3 nor 4 not answered
'Fritz didn't answer question 3 or 4'

What is striking is that the alleged alternatives (now in the b-examples of (23)–(25)) do not form a homogeneous class. For expressions containing a negated indefinite, the alternative contains a morphological variant (*keine* instead of *nicht eine*); for negated definites, by contrast, the alternative is a syntactic variant (*Frage 3 nicht* instead of *nicht Frage 3*); for negated disjunctions, there are even two different alternatives, a syntactic one (cf. (25b-i)) and a morphological one (cf. (25b-ii). At the same time, as I argue in the remainder of this chapter, following the ideas spelled out in Chapter 7, the morphological alternatives can be taken to also be syntactically different. Therefore, the alternative expressions listed in (23)–(25), in the end, all count as syntactic alternatives.

I first discuss how this account works for negated indefinites (Subsection 12.3.1), and then I show how the account extends to negated definites (12.3.2) and disjunctions (12.3.3).

12.3.1 Negated indefinites

Let us first focus on the syntactic structures of the two examples in (23). At first sight, the example in (23a) may be structurally ambiguous, i.e., it seems compatible with three syntactic structures: one in which the *v*P contains the indefinite, and *nicht* takes the *v*P as its complement (i.e., (26a)), and one in which the negated indefinite forms a constituent that is part of the *v*P that may overtly or covertly raise outside *v*P (as in (26b-c)):

(26) a. [Fritz kann$_i$ [nicht [$_{vP}$ [$_{DP}$ eine Fremdsprache] t$_i$]]]
b. [Fritz kann$_i$ [$_{vP}$ [$_{DP}$ [nicht eine] Fremdsprache] t$_i$]]
c. [Fritz kann$_i$ [$_{DP}$ [nicht eine] Fremdsprache]$_j$ [$_{vP}$ t$_j$ t$_i$]]

At the same time, it is less clear what the underlying structure of the example in (23b) is. This is due to the fact that it is problematic to think of *keine* as a plain negative existential quantifier, since *keine* is able to give rise to so-called *split-scope effects*. As discussed extensively in Chapter 7, split-scope effects (the original observation due to Jacobs 1980) involve instances of *keine* or other NIs where some scope-taking element intervenes between the scope of the negation and the scope of the indefinite. The example that was used in Chapter 7 is (27):

(27) Du musst keine Krawatte anziehen (German)
you must no tie wear
i. 'It is not required that you wear a tie' ¬ > must > ∃
ii. 'There is no tie that you are required to wear' ¬ > ∃ > must
iii. ^{?'}It is required that you don't wear a tie' must > ¬ > ∃

The most salient reading of (27) is the first reading, where negation outscopes the modal, but where the modal, in turn, outscopes the indefinite. However, this reading does not directly follow if *keine* is taken to be a plain negative existential quantifier.

As we already saw in Chapter 7, in order to solve this problem, two different types of approaches have been proposed. Within the so-called *decompositional approach*, split-scope effects are taken to result from lexical decomposition of the NI into a separate negation and an existential. Scholars differ on whether this decomposition is the result of amalgamation (Jacobs 1980), incorporation (Rullmann 1995), syntactic agreement (Penka 2011), or a postsyntactic spell-out rule (Zeijlstra 2011; Chapter 7).

Others have argued that NIs are NQs, but that these quantifiers do not quantify only over individuals but also over kinds (Geurts 1996), properties (De Swart 2000), or choice-functions (Abels and Marti 2010). Quantification over non-individuals, then, entails the split-scope readings. Proposals along these lines are referred to as the *negative quantifier approach*.

Both approaches make different predictions for the underlying syntax of the examples in (23). Under the NQ approach, *keine* is a determiner and the syntactic structure of (23b) should be similar to that of (28):

(28) [Fritz kann [$_{vP}$ [$_{DP}$ keine Fremdsprache] t$_i$]]

Note that under this approach, the ambiguity of (27) is not syntactic. All readings are derived from (28). Both (27-i) and (27-ii) are the result of QR, and the oddity of (27-iii) results from the fact that German *musst* ('must') does not outscope negation (see Chapter 13). This also means that the sentence in (23a) is compatible with all three structures in (26), but the one in (23b) only with (26b) (and (26c) after QR).

Under most of the decomposition analyses, however, the structures underlying the different readings in (27) are syntactically different. Under this approach, an NI like *keine* consists of a negation and an indefinite part that, for most accounts, are subject to a string-adjacency requirement. In other words, the negation and the indefinite may form a constituent, but do not have to, as long as the negation and the indefinite are adjacent at PF. Most accounts make no clear predictions as to when an adjacent negation and indefinite must be jointly spelled out as an NI. This means that, under this approach, both (23a) and (23b) would be compatible with the three structures in (29), where the adjacent negation and indefinite are separate syntactic morphemes. In (23a), the two would be spelled out as individual words; in (23b), they would be jointly realised as *keine* under PF-adjacency.

(29) a. [Fritz kann$_i$ [¬ [$_{vP}$ [$_{DP}$ ∃ Fremdsprache] t$_i$]]]
　　 b. [Fritz kann$_i$ [$_{vP}$ [$_{DP}$ [¬ ∃] Fremdsprache] t$_i$]]
　　 c. [Fritz kann$_i$ [$_{DP}$ [¬ ∃] Fremdsprache] [$_{vP}$ t$_i$]]

However, the decomposition analysis presented in Chapter 7 (based on Zeijlstra 2011) makes a different prediction. Under this analysis, NIs such as *keine* are taken to be the output of a spell-out rule that states that, only if the negation and the existential stand in a syntactic sisterhood relation, they can and must be spelled out as a single NI. If the negation and the indefinite do not stand in a sisterhood relation, they must be realized separately. The spell-out rule for German *kein* is thus as in (30):

(30)　[¬ ∃] ⇔ /kein/

Consequently, the structure in (29a) can only be the structure underlying (23a), and the structures in (29b, c) only the structures underlying (23b). (23a) and (23b) are thus syntactically different. (23a) is syntactically unambiguous; (23b) is syntactically ambiguous between a wide-scope reading and a narrow-scope reading of the NI with respect to the modal. However, since a narrow-scope reading with negation taking scope under an existential modal is generally degraded (for reasons to be discussed in Chapter 13), from now on, I will take it to carry the wide-scope reading only.

The advantage of this view is that, unlike other accounts, the underlying syntactic structures of (23a–b) are now fully distinct. (23a) aligns with (30a), and (23b) with (29b) (and (29c)). This contrasts both with the NQ approach, where (23a) is compatible with all three structures in (28), and with the decomposition approach, where (23b) is compatible with all three structures in (28).

With this in mind, the semantic differences between (23a) and (23b) follow as well. (23b) can only give rise to a reading where negation must scope over the indefinite. A wide-scope reading of the indefinite over the negation is impossible. For that to happen, *eine* plus *Fremdsprache* should jointly move across the negation at LF, but such movement is illicit, since *eine* and *Fremdsprache* do not form a constituent. Also, (23b) does not allow the existential to be focused with the focus being associated to the negation, since the existential is part of a single word, and word-internal focus is not possible either, as has been known since Williams (1981). However, as the reader can verify, all these readings are possible for (23a), since, here, *eine* and *Fremdsprache* do form a single constituent, and negation can freely focus-associate to *eine*.

Adopting the analysis presented earlier for NIs and split scope, it is thus predicted that a sentence like (23a) can give rise to a set of readings that forms a superset of the set of readings that can be yielded by (23b). Both can give rise to the three readings where negation takes scope over the existential, but, in addition, (23a) can also give rise to a reading where the indefinite takes scope over negation, or where the indefinite is focused under negation. The next step, then, is to account for the fact that sentences like (23a) are only fine with the unfocused reading where negation outscopes the indefinite in DE contexts, and not in any other environments. Why is it that, outside DE contexts, the unmarked reading is blocked? The most straightforward way of answering this question is to relate this to pragmatic competition. By uttering (23a) instead of (23b), the speaker conveys that she does not take (23b) to hold.

In principle, there are two possible ways of accounting for this. One way is to allude to Horn's (1984) division of linguistic labour, which states that a marked form always corresponds to a marked reading. The question thus arises, of course, as to why (23a) would be a more marked expression than (23b). The most plausible answer for this is morphological blocking: since it is possible to jointly spell out a negation and an indefinite using a simpler morphological element, there must be a reason not to do so. This automatically renders utterances containing morphologically more complex forms marked with respect to those containing simpler ones. Horn's division of linguistic labour could potentially also be handled in terms of the Gricean Maxim of Manner, which states that a speaker should not be unnecessarily unclear (as pointed out to me by Paul Portner (pers. comm.)). If the speaker had wanted to unambiguously express an unfocused wide-scope reading of the indefinite, she would have employed the simplest way of doing so, using the NI *keine*. Hence, when a different, vaguer expression like *nicht eine* is used, the reading that *keine* gives rise to must be inferred not to hold.

An alternative option would be to say that (23b) always entails (23a), but not necessarily the other way round, as the readings of (23a) together form a strict superset of the set of readings of (23b). Then one might argue that, since (23b) is stronger than (23a), the interplay of the Gricean Maxims of Quantity and Quality triggers an implicature that states that, by uttering (23a), the speaker does not want to commit herself to the truth of (23b).

Although I do not want to a priori exclude the latter possibility, I do want to point out several problems that this latter approach faces. First, it would require that the computation of alternatives takes place prior to LF, since the unidirectional entailment relation between (23a) and (23b) holds only if all the possible readings are taken into account, and not the reading that is generated at LF. However, standardly, the selection of alternatives is computed at the level of LF.

Secondly, under this approach, the relative ordering of the negation and the indefinite no longer plays a role, since any sentence without an NI that is more ambiguous than the one with the NI should be blocked. This, however, is not the case. Both language-internally and language-externally, once the adjacency relation between the negation and the indefinite is broken, the indefinites can be negated without any readings being blocked. For German, this is shown for cases where a preposition intervenes, as in (31).

(31) Hans denkt nicht an eine Fremdsprache (German)
Hans thinks not to a foreign.language
'Hans doesn't think about a foreign language'

But also languages where the negation and the indefinite are normally not string-adjacent have no problem with expressing the unmarked reading by having an NM take scope over an indefinite, even if the language has a special NI at its disposal. English is a good example of such a language, where both (32a) and (32b) are fine:

(32) a. John didn't read a book
b. John read no book

Under the Horn/Manner type of account, these examples are, however, not problematic. Since no sentence is available in which the negation and the indefinite could have been merged together as a single NI without changing the rest of the word order, there is no way in which examples (31) and (32a) are marked; consequently, no unmarked alternative could give rise to a blocking effect.

To summarize, a negation and an indefinite are realized as a single NI if and only if they stand in a syntactic sisterhood relation; a sentence with a negated indefinite must thus be assigned a different syntactic structure from one with an NI. Since an NI is unmarked with respect to a negated indefinite, uttering a sentence with a negated indefinite instead of an NI in the same position comes with an implicature that states that the speaker is not committed to the truth of a sentence where the negated indefinite would have been replaced by an NI.

The final step in our reasoning is then to show that this implicature does not arise once the negated indefinite is embedded in an NPI-licensing context. But that should not come as a surprise once it is assumed that local implicatures are cancelled, or at least suppressed, under DE operators (cf. Gazdar 1979; Chierchia 2004, Sauerland 2004a, b; Gajewski and Sharvit 2008, 2012; Fox and Spector 2018, and many others). If this implicature is absent, the sentence with the negated indefinite should no longer be ill-formed under its unmarked reading. This, then, accounts for the exact distribution of negated indefinites in- and outside DE contexts without alluding to an additional homophonous NM.

Moreover, this analysis makes one additional prediction that Schwarz (2004) and Schwarz and Bhatt (2006) do not make. Since the analysis proposed in this chapter takes the blocking of the unmarked reading of a sentence containing a negated indefinite to be an implicature which, in principle, should be cancellable, it is predicted that the blocking of the unmarked reading can be cancelled as well. This is indeed the case, as the data in (33) show:

(33) a. Kann   Fritz   nicht   eine   Fremdsprache?   (German)
       knows   Fritz   not   a   foreign.language
       'Doesn't Fritz know a foreign language?'

   b. Nein, Fritz kann   nicht eine Fremdsprache; er   kann
      no,   Fritz knows not   a   foreign.language; he knows
      keine Fremdsprache
      no   foreign.language
      'No, he doesn't speak a foreign language; he knows no foreign language'

So, this alternative analysis correctly predicts the behaviour and distribution of negated indefinites in languages like Dutch and German. However, the question is still open of how this analysis extends to the cases of negated definites and disjunctions. This will be discussed in the next two subsections.

12.3.2 Negated definites

In Subsection 12.3.1, the unavailability of the unmarked readings of negated indefinites in DE contexts was said to be due to the fact that it can be inferred that, since the speaker did not select a less marked form (an NI instead of a negated indefinite), the speaker is not committed to the truth of that alternative expression. In this subsection, the question of the extent to which this line of reasoning applies to negated definites is addressed.

Let us start the discussion on negated definites by repeating the examples in (24) in (34). These examples contain a negated definite lacking an unmarked reading, and a minimally different alternative that can grammatically convey this unmarked reading.

(34) a. *Fritz hat   nicht   Frage   3   beantwortet   (German)
        Fritz has   not   question 3   answered
        Int.: 'Fritz didn't answer question 3'

   b. Fritz hat   Frage   3   nicht   beantwortet
      Fritz has   question 3   not   answered
      'Fritz didn't answer question 3'

The examples in (34) differ from the minimal pairs in the discussion of negated indefinites in the sense that the alternative in (34b) involves a word-order difference, whereas the alternatives for the negated indefinites were morphologically different (although this morphological difference corresponded to a syntactic difference as well).

At the same time, the examples in (34) also differ in their semantics. As is known since Jackendoff (1972), for negation to associate to its focus, it must linearly precede it (see also Jaeger and Wagner 2003). Consequently, while, in (34b), *nicht* cannot be focus-associated to *Frage 3*, in (34a), *nicht* can. In fact, as discussed earlier, even in contexts that do not license weak NPIs, a sentence like (34a) is fine with focus on *Frage 3*, as (35) shows:

(35) Fritz hat nicht Frage DREI beantwortet (sondern
Fritz has not question THREE answered (rather
Frage VIER) (German)
question FOUR)
'Fritz didn't answer question THREE (but question FOUR)'

So, what appears to be the case is that, even though, semantically, (34a) is ambiguous between a focused and a non-focused reading of the definite, in DE contexts, only the focused reading is available. Therefore, the question arises as to whether it can be inferred that, by uttering a sentence like (34a) instead of (34b), the speaker is not committed to the reading that (34b) yields, and that, for that reason, (34a) can only yield a reading with focus on the definite. Then, the entire distribution of sentences containing negated definites follows—again, if it is assumed that inferences following from conversational implicatures do not emerge in DE contexts.

That the absence of the non-focused reading is indeed an implicature can, again, be proved by the fact that this inference is cancellable, as the following example shows:

(36) a. Hat Fritz nicht Frage 3 beantwortet? (German)
has Fritz not question 3 answered
'Didn't Fritz answer question 3?'

b. Nein Fritz hat nicht Frage 3 beantwortet; er hat keine
No Fritz has not question 3 answered; he has no
Frage beantwortet
question answered
'Fritz didn't answer question 3; he didn't answer any question'

The problem that arises now is that, on the one hand, it appears that (34b) is a proper alternative of (34a), such that, by uttering (34b), it can be inferred that the speaker is not committed to the truth of (34a); on the other hand, it is not clear what kind of an alternative (34b) is. Note that it does not suffice to say that (34b) is more informative than (34a), since this would entail that, for any syntactic construction A, any other syntactic construction B that yields a subset of the readings that A yields counts as an alternative; and as we discussed in Subsection 12.3.1, that would massively overgeneralize. The implicature cannot follow from the interplay between the Gricean Maxims of Quality and Quantity.

However, this implicature can be derived from either Horn's division of linguistic labour or the Gricean Maxim of Manner, which states that a speaker should not be unnecessarily unclear. Now, if the speaker had wanted to unambiguously express an unfocused reading involving the definite, she would have employed the simplest way of doing so, with the NM in its canonical position at the *v*P boundary, below any definite expressions, which, in German, always scramble out of *v*P. With the negation in a position where it could be used to focus-associate with the definite DP—which is, actually, the most salient way to have negation being focus-associated with the DP—uttering (34a) without intending a focused reading of the definite DP would make the utterance unnecessarily vague.

Thus, as a result of Horn's division of linguistic labour or Grice's Maxim of Manner, it may be inferred that, by uttering (34a), the speaker only intends to express a focused reading of the definite, and all other readings can be inferred to be unavailable. Again, once an expression like (34a) is embedded in a DE licensing context, this implicature is suppressed and the sentence can have the unfocused reading as well.

12.3.3 Negated disjunctions

Now the question arises why negated disjunctions are only fine in DE contexts, since the minimally differing alternatives can be either morphological in nature or syntactic, as the data in (25), repeated below as (37), reveal.

(37) a. *Fritz hat nicht Frage 3 oder 4 beantwortet (German)
       Fritz has not   question 3 or   4 answered
       Int.: 'Fritz didn't answer question 3 or 4'

   b. i. Fritz hat Frage 3 oder 4 nicht beantwortet
         Fritz has question 3 or 4 not   answered
         'Fritz didn't answer question 3 or 4'

      ii. Fritz hat weder Frage 3 noch 4 beantwortet
          Fritz has neither question 3 nor 4 answered
          'Fritz didn't answer either question 3 or 4'

However, the two readings in (37b) are not identical. While (37b-ii) exclusively states that both question 3 and question 4 have not been answered by Fritz, the reading of (37b-i) is weaker and states that at least one of the two questions has not been answered. In fact, the stronger reading is a possible reading for (37b-i) as well, but this reading is harder to obtain, presumably again as a result of morphological blocking by (37b-ii) (see Gajić 2020 for more discussion).

Sentence (37a) is only fine when it receives a focused interpretation of the entire disjunction or parts of it, and the exact reading thus depends on what exactly has been focused. Unless the focus is on *oder* ('or'), the focused readings that (37a) yield do not require that both questions have been answered. Consequently, it is hard to assume that the availability of (37b-ii) is behind the fact that the unmarked reading of (37a) does not come up outside DE contexts. Rather, it seems that (37b-i) is responsible for this.

If that is indeed correct, then it automatically follows that whatever is behind the exclusion of the unmarked readings of negated definites is also behind the exclusion of the unmarked readings of negated disjunctions. Since I tentatively assume that this is the result of the application of Horn's division of linguistic labour, arguably voiced in terms of Grice's Maxim of Manner, this then naturally extends to negated disjunctions.

12.4 Conclusions

The results thus far show that the unavailability of the unmarked readings of negated indefinites, definites, and disjunctions follows from the fact that these readings are blocked by an implicature that states that those readings cannot have been intended by the speaker, as the speaker, in that case, would have selected a simpler alternative expression. As such an implicature is suppressed in DE contexts for NPIs, the distribution of the facts presented in Section 12.1 can be explained.

This shows that the phenomenon, taken by Schwarz and Bhatt to represent a special kind of NM, can actually be straightforwardly explained without postulating the existence of this second homophonous NM. It has also been shown that this phenomenon is the result of an implicature triggered by virtue of competing alternative sentences. This shows that not everything that looks like a weak NPI, such as the readings that appear only under DE contexts, must be a weak NPI in the sense of Chapter 10.

At the same time, several questions remain open. First, it is not really clear which mechanism exactly underlies the selection of competing alternatives for sentences containing a negated indefinite, definite, or disjunction. What is clear is that an implicature is triggered, but not how exactly this implicature is triggered. While morphological blocking seems to underlie the triggering of the alternative propositions in the case of negated indefinites (the alternative proposition containing a morphologically simpler NI instead of a negated indefinite, which gives rise to a smaller set of possible readings), in the case of negated definites and disjunctions, the fact that only those constructions give rise to a focused reading of the definite or disjunction appears to invoke an implicature that the speaker cannot have intended an unfocused reading. This also shows that what has been presented as a single phenomenon in the introduction of this chapter constitutes a single phenomenon only to some extent. Negated indefinites, negated definites, and negated disjunctions can all only give rise to their unmarked readings in NPI-licensing contexts because of a particular implicature that arises—but they do so for different reasons.

12.4 CONCLUSIONS 299

Second, this chapter shares with Schwarz (2004) and Schwarz and Bhatt (2006) the conclusion that the distribution of negated indefinites, definites, and disjunctions must be limited to NPI-licensing contexts, but Bhatt and Schwarz present some data that show that this distribution is not completely identical. Typical NPI-licensing contexts, such as non-counterfactual conditionals, do not license negated indefinites, definites, or disjunctions, whereas, at the same time, unexpectedly, consequents of counterfactual conditionals do. As both types of contexts also allow rescuing of negated PPIs, they take this to be further evidence for the existence of light negation, though without showing why what appears to be PPI-rescuing is subject to these specific constraints.

The case of consequents of counterfactual conditionals, however, also follows straightforwardly from the analysis presented in this chapter. Let us look at the data again:

(38) a. Wenn Fritz dumm wäre, könnte er nicht eine
if Fritz stupid were, could he not a
Fremdsprache (German)
foreign.language
'If Fritz were stupid, he wouldn't know a foreign language'

b. Wenn Fritz dumm wäre, hätte er nicht Frage 3
if Fritz stupid were, had he not question 3
beantwortet
answered
'If Fritz were stupid, he wouldn't have answered question 3'

c. Wenn Fritz dumm wäre, hätte er nicht Frage 3 oder
if Fritz stupid were, had he not question 3 or
4 beantwortet
4 answered
'If Fritz were stupid, he wouldn't have answered question 3 or 4'

Counterfactual conditionals always give rise to an inference that the antecedent does not hold in the actual world, i.e., in uttering the examples in (38), it is understood that Fritz actually is not stupid. Scholars have different opinions on whether this inference arises as a result of an implicature, presupposition, or is rather entailed by the antecedent; but regardless of the exact nature of this inference, it follows that the sentence seems to make an additional claim about the actual world (see Iatridou 2000; Ippolito 2002; Karawani 2014 for different proposals and overview discussions). (38a) clearly suggests that Fritz does speak at least one foreign language. But for this effect to arise, a proposition that takes Fritz to speak at least one foreign language must be part of the alternatives of the consequents, and thus *eine Fremdsprache* must be focused. This focus effect, as discussed earlier, cannot arise when the negated indefinite is replaced by a NI. Therefore, the inclusion of the negated indefinites in (38a) and, for the same reasons, for the negated definite and disjunction (38b–c) is well-motivated.

The question as to why such negated indefinites, definites, and disjunction may not appear in a non-counterfactual conditional is not accounted for yet. The examples already presented in (9), one of them repeated in (39), may only give rise to a counterfactual interpretation of the antecedent.

(39) Wenn Fritz nicht eine Fremdsprache könnte, wäre er
 if Fritz not a foreign.language knew, were he
 durchgefallen (German)
 failed
 'If Fritz hadn't known a foreign language, he would have failed'

There are two ways of interpreting these facts, though. One way is to argue that non-counterfactual conditionals do not allow negated indefinites, negated definites, and negated disjunctions to yield their unmarked readings. The second way of approaching it is saying that conditionals, to the extent that they license NPIs (cf. Heim 1984), also allow negated indefinites, definites, and disjunctions, but still impose additional restrictions on their interpretation. Under this latter view, such constructions are fine, even with their unmarked reasons, but, still, in NPI licensing contexts, subtle pragmatic competition may take place between a sentence with a conditional containing a negated indefinite and one with an NI. In other words, under that view, the primary implicature that rejects the unmarked readings for negated indefinites is suppressed, but as secondary or local implicature it may still play a role (albeit a much weaker one, as is generally the case with secondary implicatures; cf. Panizza et al. 2009 for discussion). That would then open up a way to account for the data in (9)/(39). Such effects (which are also visible in other examples that Schwarz and Bhatt provide), could potentially underlie the counterfactuality inferences in (39) as well (see also Chapter 16).

13
Universal Quantifier PPIs

13.1 Introduction

13.1.1 Exhaustification approaches to Negative Polarity Items

According to the line of thinking spelled out by Krifka (1995), Lahiri (1998), Chierchia (2006, 2013), among others, NPIs that are only fine in DE contexts are ruled out outside DE contexts, since, then, their semantics would give rise to a contradiction. This means that the sentences in (1), even though they are judged unacceptable, are, strictly speaking, not syntactically ill-formed, but rather violate their usage conditions (Kadmon and Landman 1993) or even yield a semantic anomaly (Krifka 1995; Lahiri 1998; Chierchia 2006, 2013).

(1)   a.   *Mary has ever been there
       b.   *I read any book

Following Chierchia's (2006, 2013) implementation of this idea, discussed at length in Chapter 10, NPIs are equipped with an uninterpretable feature [uσ,D], which obligatorily introduces all its domain and scalar alternatives and which must be checked by a covert c-commanding exhaustifier that carries an interpretable feature [iσ,D]. Chierchia then argues that the combination of these two requirements triggers a semantic contradiction for every NPI outside a DE context. To briefly illustrate this again, let us focus on (1b). For Chierchia, the uninterpretable [uσ,D] of *any book* needs to be checked ((2a) is ungrammatical). Once it gets checked by the covert exhaustifier (the only element able to check this feature), it yields a logical contradiction (2b).

(2)   a.   [I read [any book]$_{[u\sigma,D]}$]
       b.   [EXH$_{[i\sigma,D]}$ [I read [any book]$_{[u\sigma,D]}$]]

Suppose that the domain quantification is the set of books {a, b, c}. Then, [[I read any book]] denotes $\exists x.[x \in \{a, b, c\} \& read(I, x)]$. Now, the domain alternatives of $\exists x.[x \in \{a, b, c\} \& read(I, x)]$ are:

(3) a. ∃x.[x∈{a, b, c} & read(I, x)]
    b. ∃x.[x∈{a, b} & read(I, x)]
    c. ∃x.[x∈{a, c} & read(I, x)]
    d. ∃x.[x∈{b, c} & read(I, x)]
    e. ∃x.[x∈{a} & read(I, x)]
    f. ∃x.[x∈{b} & read(I, x)]
    g. ∃x.[x∈{c} & read(I, x)]

Apart from (3a), all domain alternatives in (3) are stronger than ∃x.[x∈{a, b, c} & read(I, x)]. This means that, if EXH applies to ∃x.[x∈{a, b, c} & read(I, x)], all these stronger domain alternatives must be false.

(4) [[EXH(I read any books)]] =
    [λp.p & ∀q∈Alt(p)[p ⊈ q → ¬q]](∃x.[x∈{a, b, c} & read(I, x)]) =
    ∃x.[x∈{a, b, c} & read(I, x)] &
    ¬∃x.[x∈{a, b} & read(I, x)] &
    ¬∃x.[x∈{a, c} & read(I, x)] &
    ¬∃x.[x∈{b, c} & read(I, x)] &
    ¬∃x.[x∈{a} & read(I, x)] &
    ¬∃x.[x∈{b} & read(I, x)] &
    ¬∃x.[x∈{c} & read(I, x)]

But the conjunction of all negated stronger domain alternatives entails that there is no element, member of the set of books {a, b, c}, that has been read by me. This already follows from the three negated domain alternatives where the domain of quantification is a singleton set: ¬∃x.[x∈{a} & read(I, x)] & ¬∃x.[x∈{b} & read(I, x)] & ¬∃x.[x∈{c} & read(I, x)] ↔ ¬∃x.[x∈{a, b, c} & read(I, x)]. But then [[EXH(I read any books)]] must have the denotation in (5), which forms a logical contradiction.

(5) ∃x.[x∈{a, b, c} & read(I, x)] & ¬∃x.[x∈{a, b, c} & read(I, x)]

For Chierchia, following Gajewski (2002), sentences that are logically contradictory are judged as unacceptable.[1] If logically contradictory statements indeed trigger unacceptability judgements, the unacceptability of (2b) directly follows.

---

[1] Note that, for Chierchia, following Gajewski (2002), only logically contradictory expressions are ungrammatical—not just any contradictory expression. An expression is logically contradictory if and only if, under all significant rewritings of its non-logical parts, the contradiction remains, as is the case for unlicensed NPIs of the relevant kind. This is not the case for non-logical contradictions such as *It rains and it doesn't rain*, since one could rephrase the second *rain* with *snow* and the contradiction disappears. See Chapter 10 for more discussion.

13.1 INTRODUCTION

However, if the NPI is embedded in a DE context, things change. To see this, take (6).

(6) I didn't read any book

Again, exhaustification of (6) will result in all stronger domain alternatives of (6) being false. But now, no domain alternative of (6) is actually stronger than (6), owing to the fact that the negation reverses the direction of the inferences. Consequently, exhaustification of (6) applies vacuously: [[EXH(I didn't read any book)]] = [[I didn't read any book]], and the sentence just has the reading ¬∃x.[x∈{a, b, c} & read(I, x)] and is thus acceptable.

13.1.2 Question: Universal Positive Polarity Items

According to Chierchia's proposal, the combinatorial properties of [uσ,D], the introduction of domain alternatives, and the exhaustification requirement ensure that any existential quantifier or other element denoting low-scale end points that is equipped with such a feature [uσ,D] is an NPI. At the same time, even though this has not been explicitly claimed within this framework, Chierchia's proposal also predicts that any universal quantifier that carries such a feature should be a PPI. To see this, take the non-existing word *pevery* (with the intended meaning 'every') to contain such a feature. Then, the underlying syntax of (7a), with this feature [uσ,D] being checked by EXH, would be (7b).

(7) a. I read pevery book
    b. [EXH$_{[i\sigma,D]}$ [I read [pevery book]$_{[u\sigma,D]}$]]

The exhaustifier in (7b) applies vacuously. The reason is that none of the domain alternatives of *I read pevery book* are stronger than *I read pevery book* itself: Of all the propositions in (8), (8a) is the strongest.

(8) a. ∀x.[x∈{a, b, c} → read(I, x)]
    b. ∀x.[x∈{a, b} → read(I, x)]
    c. ∀x.[x∈{a, c} → read(I, x)]
    d. ∀x.[x∈{b, c} → read(I, x)]
    e. ∀x.[x∈{a} → read(I, x)]
    f. ∀x.[x∈{b} → read(I, x)]
    g. ∀x.[x∈{c} → read(I, x)]

However, things are different with the negated counterpart of (7):

(9) a. I didn't read pevery book
    b. [EXH$_{[i\sigma,D]}$ [I didn't read [pevery book] $_{[u\sigma,D]}$]]

The semantics of (9b) yields a logical contradiction, for the very same reason as (2b) does: All domain alternatives of $\neg \forall x.[x \in \{a, b, c\} \rightarrow \text{read}(I, x)]$, listed in (10), entail $\neg \forall x.[x \in \{a, b, c\} \rightarrow \text{read}(I, x)]$.

(10) a. $\neg \forall x.[x \in \{a, b, c\} \rightarrow \text{read}(I, x)]$
    b. $\neg \forall x.[x \in \{a, b\} \rightarrow \text{read}(I, x)]$
    c. $\neg \forall x.[x \in \{a, c\} \rightarrow \text{read}(I, x)]$
    d. $\neg \forall x.[x \in \{b, c\} \rightarrow \text{read}(I, x)]$
    e. $\neg \forall x.[x \in \{a\} \rightarrow \text{read}(I, x)]$
    f. $\neg \forall x.[x \in \{b\} \rightarrow \text{read}(I, x)]$
    g. $\neg \forall x.[x \in \{c\} \rightarrow \text{read}(I, x)]$

Then, the meaning of (9b) is contradictory again, and should render the sentence unacceptable:

(11) [[EXH(Ididn't read pevery book)]] =
    $[\lambda p.p \land \forall q \in \text{Alt}(p)[p \not\subseteq q \rightarrow \neg q]](\neg \forall x.[x \in \{a, b, c\} \rightarrow \text{read}(I, x)]) =$
    $\neg \forall x.[x \in \{a, b, c\} \rightarrow \text{read}(I, x)]$ &
    $\forall x.[x \in \{a, b\} \rightarrow \text{read}(I, x)]$ &
    $\forall x.[x \in \{a, c\} \rightarrow \text{read}(I, x)]$ &
    $\forall x.[x \in \{b, c\} \rightarrow \text{read}(I, x)]$ &
    $\forall x.[x \in \{a\} \rightarrow \text{read}(I, x)]$ &
    $\forall x.[x \in \{b\} \rightarrow \text{read}(I, x)]$ &
    $\forall x.[x \in \{c\} \rightarrow \text{read}(I, x)]$

The universal counterpart of NPI *any*, given Chierchia's approach, is thus predicted to be a PPI. But languages do not seem to employ universal quantifiers such as *all*, *everybody*, or *everything* that are PPIs. Such quantifiers can all take scope below negation, even when they appear above negation in their surface position. Within the domain of quantifiers over individuals, most PPIs have been taken to be existential quantifiers (e.g. English *some*), not universal quantifiers. This gives rise to the question of why universal quantifiers like *all*, *everybody*, or *everything* that show PPI behaviour have not been attested thus far.

Some answers may suggest themselves. For instance, it may be the case that, for some reason, polarity effects may only appear among existential quantifiers. In this way, the *pevery* problem—the fact that no language seems to exhibit a PPI with a logically accessible meaning like *pevery*—would be similar to the absence of the so-called *nall*-quantifier: no language in the world has a single lexical item meaning 'not all' (see Chapter 6). But this cannot be correct.

First, the existing analyses for the explanation of the *nall*-problem all focus on the fact that universal quantifiers cannot be negatively marked. But the universal counterpart is a PPI, which, at best, is being positively marked. Second, if the account in Chapter 6 is correct in the sense that the solution to the *nall*-problem lies in diachronics, it is far from straightforward that universal quantifier PPIs should be ruled out this way. Third, and perhaps most importantly, it turns out that, in another domain of quantification, namely quantification over possible worlds, universal quantifier PPIs are indeed attested. For example, English *must* is a PPI (cf. Iatridou and Zeijlstra 2010, 2013; Homer 2015). This shows that it is not inherently impossible for a universal quantifier to be a PPI. Hence, the apparent absence of universal quantifiers over individuals that are PPIs needs an independent explanation.

13.1.3 Outline

In Section 13.2, it is demonstrated that, at least certain universal modals are indeed PPIs, following primarily Iatridou and Zeijlstra (2013), by providing four diagnostics for PPI-hood and applying them to modals like *must* and *should*. In Section 13.3, I argue that these modal PPIs are PPIs for the very same reason why, under Chierchia's approach, NPIs are NPIs. I show that the exact implementation of this approach predicts that such universal quantifier PPIs may actually surface under negation, as the exhaustifier whose presence they trigger may scopally intervene between the negation (or any other anti-licenser) and the PPI itself. I argue that, consequently, universal quantifier PPIs are fine under negation as long as they appear under negation at surface structure, but may not reconstruct under negation when they appear above negation at surface structure. In Section 13.4, I present several cases of such universal quantifier PPIs, showing that universal quantifiers, albeit in disguise, can indeed be attested, both in the domain of quantifiers over possible worlds and in the domain of quantifiers over individuals. Section 13.5 spells out predictions that this account makes and to what extent it applies to other kinds of PPIs (in terms of strength and in terms of type of domain of quantification); these predictions and applications will then be addressed in the next chapter.

13.2 Modal Positive Polarity Items

13.2.1 Modal auxiliaries and their scope with respect to negation

As has been pointed out by Israel (1996); Iatridou and Zeijlstra (2010, 2013); and Homer (2015), universal modals that take wide scope with respect to sentential negation, like English *must*, *should*, or *ought to*, should be analysed as PPIs.

(12) a. She must not leave $\square > \neg$
b. She should not leave $\square > \neg$
c. She ought not to leave $\square > \neg$

The reason why these modals are analysed as PPIs is that only these modal auxiliaries outscope negation. Other modal auxiliaries, existential modals, and other universal modals alike, in principle, take scope under negation:

(13) a. She doesn't have to leave $\neg > \square$
b. She doesn't need to leave $\neg > \square$

(14) a. She cannot leave $\neg > \lozenge$
b. She may not leave $\neg > \lozenge$

In fact, in the domain of deontic modals, all existential modals scope under sentential negation. Iatridou and Zeijlstra (2010, 2013) argue that modal auxiliaries are base-generated in a position below negation, where they should also be interpreted, regardless of whether they raise to a higher position at surface structure or not.[2] This, then, explains that the modals in (13) and (14) take scope below negation. Only if an interpretation under the scope of negation would lead to ungrammaticality, it is argued in Iatridou and Zeijlstra (2010, 2014), may the modal be interpreted in its surface position or even raise to a higher position above negation. Assuming that modals that outscope negation are PPIs thus ensures that these, but no other, modals take scope above negation if they appear in a negative clause.

However, it is not a priori clear that the scopal construals in (12)–(14) follow from the polarity-(in-)sensitivity of the modal auxiliaries involved. How can it be established that those modals that outscope negation are PPIs? Just saying that these are PPIs because they cannot take scope under negation is not sufficient. Are there additional arguments that those modals that outscope negation are indeed PPIs?

---

[2] The assumption that modal auxiliaries are base-generated below I⁰ goes against received wisdom for English. It is assumed since Chomsky (1957) that English modal verbs appearing in I⁰ are base-generated in I⁰. The argument for generation in I⁰ stems from the fact that these modals always *appear* in I⁰. Such modals are taken to differ in two ways from regular verbs: they only come in tensed forms *and* they are generated in I⁰. However, only the first of these characterizations is needed, as it automatically derives the second one. We know that these deontic modal auxiliaries are moving verbs since they can make it up to C⁰:

(i) Can/may/must he leave?

If these modals are movers, and if they are always tensed, then it follows that, if they are generated below I⁰, they will always move to at least I⁰, since tensed verbs that are able to move always move to I° or higher. So, the view that modals that show up in I° originate in a position lower than I° is thus as consistent with the facts as the generation-in-I⁰ view is. Moreover, it is superior to the latter, as it requires only one assumption (modals are always tensed) instead of two assumptions (modals are always tensed and are always base-generated in I°).

Empirical evidence for the PPI status of universal modals that outscope negation comes from two facts. First, other polarity-sensitive verbs/auxiliaries have been attested in the domain of modals as well. English *need* (the *need* that does not select *to*-infinitivals) as well as its German and Dutch translations (*brauchen* and *hoeven*, respectively) are all NPIs, as the following examples show (see the discussion in Chapter 11):

(15) a. John need*(n't) leave
 b. Hans braucht *(nicht) zu gehen (German)
    Hans needs not to go
    'Hans doesn't have to go'
 c. Jan hoeft *(niet) te vertrekken (Dutch)
    Jan needs not to leave
    'Jan doesn't have to leave'

Given that PPIs generally surface in domains where NPIs appear (cf. Van der Wouden 1994), it is likely to expect that modal PPIs can be attested as well.

Second, it turns out that modals that outscope negation share several relevant distributional properties (when it comes to negation) with better known PPIs, such as English *some*. If the distributional properties of those modals that take scope over negation are similar to those of other PPIs (or if any differences between them receive independent explanation), it can safely be concluded that the scopal properties of such modals follow from their PPI-hood.

The behavioural characteristics of PPIs distribute along four dimensions. Szabolcsi (2004) and references cited there show that, although PPIs are generally banned from negative contexts, there are actually three types of negative contexts in which all known PPIs, such as English PPI *some*, may surface under the scope of negation. Taking these behavioural properties as diagnostics for PPI-hood, it will be shown for three different languages (English, Dutch, and Greek), which vary syntactically in the way they express negation and/or modality, that, according to these diagnostics, modals outscoping negation are also PPIs, using the data from Iatridou and Zeijlstra (2013). The fourth dimension is based on the observation that, just like NPIs, PPIs may vary with respect to the exact logical properties of their licensing contexts: as discussed in Chapter 9, some PPIs are banned in all DE contexts (so-called strong PPIs), whereas other PPIs are banned in AA or anti-morphic contexts only (weak PPIs and weak superweak PPIs, respectively). The same kind of variation is also attested among English, Dutch, and Greek PPI modals. Now, PPIs that count as weak PPIs are fine under negation once that negation itself is embedded in a DE context. Strong

PPIs, by contrast, cannot appear in such contexts. Again, it will be shown that this contrast also applies to PPI modals. Given that the distributional patterns discussed here are the same for better-known PPIs and for modals that take scope over negation, it can indeed be concluded that those modals are PPIs as well.

13.2.2 Metalinguistic/contrastive negation

As shown by Szabolcsi (2004) (and references therein), PPIs may appear under the scope of metalinguistic negation and/or contrastive negation, as is shown for English *something* below ((17) based on an example by Roger Schwarzchild (pers. comm. to Anna Szabolcsi), quoted in Iatridou and Zeijlstra 2013).

(16) You didn't do SOMETHING wrong, you did everything wrong!

(17) If you push the red button, you will see something, but if you press the blue button, you WON'T see something

It is thus predicted that, if modals such as Dutch *moeten*, Greek *prepi*, or English *must* are PPIs, they should also be fine under the scope of metalinguistic negation and/or contrastive negation. For Greek *prepi* and Dutch *moeten*, this straightforwardly appears to be the case, as is shown in (18) and (19).

(18) Se   afto to scholio prepi na dhiavazis poli.   Se   ekino to
 in   this the school   must read   much. in   that the
 scholio dhen prepi na dhiavazis poli   (Greek)
 school NEG must read   much
 'If you go to this school you will have to study a lot. If you go to that school, you needn't study a lot'

(19) Op deze school moet je hard werken; maar op die school moet je niet
 hard werken   (Dutch)
 at this school must you hard work; but at that school must you NEG
 hard work
 'At this school you must work hard; but at that school you needn't work hard'

Similarly, as observed in Iatridou and Sichel (2011), contrastive focus on the modal itself in Greek and in Dutch permits modals that normally scope over negation to scope under it:

(20) A: o Kostas prepi na grapsi 2 arthra fetos (Greek)
the Kostas must write 2 article this year
'Kostas must write 2 articles this year'

B: dhen PREPI na grapsi 2 ala kala tha itan ¬ > □
neg MUST write 2 but good FUT be-PST
'He doesn't have to, but it would be good'

(21) A: Theresa moet op negatie werken (Dutch)
Theresa must on negation work
'Theresa must work on negation'

B: Ze MOET niet op negatie werken, ¬ > □
she must NEG on negation work
ze wordt hooguit aangemoedigd
she is at best encouraged
'She doesn't have to work on negation; she is at best encouraged'

On the other hand, English *must* cannot be contrastively focused when it appears in a sentence with an NM:

(22) A: He must read 5 books
B: #He MUST not read 5 books, but he is encouraged to do so

However, this is due to an independent property of English contrastive focus. Following Jackendoff's (1972) discussion on licensing of focus, if negation licenses focus, it must c-command the focus already at surface structure. This explains why (22B) is ruled out. However, it is possible to find cases in English where *must* is c-commanded by negation, and then we can duplicate this phenomenon. Iatridou and Sichel (2011) point out that negative subjects scope in exactly the same way with respect to modals as plain NMs do, while, at the same time, preceding the modal at surface structure. Therefore, the negation in a negative subject is expected to license the modal's focus. Consequently, a modal like *must* should be allowed to take scope under contrastive negation induced by a negative subject. This is indeed the case, as is shown in (23), with stress on the modal enabling the metalinguistic reading of the example. Thus, English *must* can appear under the scope of metalinguistic and/or contrastive negation as well, thus meeting the first diagnostic of PPI-hood, too.

(23) A: One student must read 5 articles on the topic
B: No student MUST read 5 articles on the topic, but one student is encouraged to do so

13.2.3 Intervention effects

A sentence with a PPI in the immediate scope of an anti-licensing operator is bad. However, when the PPI is not in the immediate scope of the anti-licenser, other intervening elements may shield the PPI from the anti-licenser, resulting in a fine sentence again (cf. Kroch 1979; Szabolcsi 2004 and references therein). This is illustrated in the following examples taken from Szabolcsi (2004).

(24) a. John didn't offend someone because he was malicious (but because he was stupid)   √ not > because ... > some
     b. Not every student said something   √ not > every > some
     c. John didn't say something at every party   √ not > every > some
     d. John doesn't always call someone   √ not > always > some
     e. John didn't show every boy something   √ not > every > some

Again, it is predicted that, if a modal that outscopes negation is a PPI, it can appear under the scope of negation (or any other anti-licensing operator) as long as some other scope-taking element intervenes between that operator and that modal.

This is indeed the case. As is shown in the following examples, the intervention tests straightforwardly apply to Greek *prepi* and Dutch *moeten*, and, as is indicated by the translations, to English *must* as well. The readings that (25)–(26) give rise to have the scopal relations: negation > because > must; the readings of (27) and (28) are: negation > always > must.

(25)   Dhen prepi na ton pandrefti epidhi ine oreos ala epidhi ine eksipnos   (Greek)
     NEG must him marry because is handsome but because is smart
     'She must not marry him because he is handsome but because he is smart'

(26)   Ze moet niet met hem trouwen omdat hij er goed uit ziet,   (Dutch)
     she must NEG with him marry because he there good out looks
     maar omdat hij een goede taalkundige is
     but because he a good linguist is
     'She must not marry him because he looks good but because he is a good linguist'

(27)   A: Panda esi prepi na vgazis ta skupidia?   (Greek)
         always you must take-out the garbage
         'Must you always take out the rubbish?'

       B: Dhen prepi na ta vgazo panda. Polles fores ta vgazi o yios mu
         NEG must always take out the rubbish. Many times it take-out the son my
         'I mustn't always take the rubbish out. Many times my son does that'

(28) A: Moet je altijd het vuilnis buiten zetten? (Dutch)
must you always the rubbish outside put
'Must you always put the rubbish outside?'
B: Nee, ik moet niet altijd het vuilnis buitenzetten; vaak doet Jan het
no I must NEG always the rubbish outside-put; often does Jan it
'No, I mustn't always take the rubbish out; Jan often does that'

So, English *must*, Greek *prepi*, and Dutch *moeten* also obey this second criterion of PPI-hood.

13.2.4 Clause-external negation

A third property of PPIs is that they are fine in the scope of negation or any other context that is known to ban PPIs if the latter is extra-clausal (Szabolcsi 2004: 24–7), as illustrated in (29):

(29) a. I don't think that John called someone   not > [$_{CP/IP}$ some
     b. No one thinks/says that John called someone   no one > [$_{CP/IP}$ some
     c. I regret that John called someone   regret > [$_{CP/IP}$ some
     d. Every boy who called someone got help   every [$_{CP/IP}$ some

As expected, clause-external negation is also able to scope above Greek *prepi*, English *must*, and Dutch *moeten*, showing one more environment where these behave like better-known PPIs.

(30) Dhen nomizo oti prepi na figi (Greek)
NEG think that must leave
'I don't think that s/he must leave'

(31) Ik denk niet dat ze moet vertrekken (Dutch)
I think NEG that she must leave
'I don't think that she must leave'

13.2.5 Variation among Positive Polarity Items

A well-known observation about PPIs is that they may differ with respect to the logical properties of their licensing contexts. Just like NPIs, certain PPIs are sensitive to AA environments and others to DE ones. Negative Polarity Items that are fine in all DE contexts are weak NPIs; NPIs that are fine in AA contexts only are strong NPIs. Similarly, PPIs that are anti-licensed in all DE contexts are strong PPIs; those that are banned from AA contexts only are weak PPIs. The stronger a polarity-sensitive element is, the more it is restricted in its distribution.

Example of weak PPIs are Dutch *een beetje* ('a bit') or English *some*, which both are anti-licensed by AA context only (examples after Van der Wouden 1994):

(32) a. *De monnik is niet *een beetje* gelukkig (Dutch)
 the monk isn't a bit happy
 Int.: 'The monk isn't a little happy'
 b. *Niemand is *een beetje* gelukkig
 nobody is a bit happy
 Int.: 'Nobody isn't a little happy'
 c. Weinig monniken zijn *een beetje* gelukkig
 few monks are a bit happy
 'Few monks aren't a little happy'

(33) a. I didn't see some girl some>not; *not>some
 b. Nobody saw some girl some>nobody; *nobody>some
 c. Few students saw some girl some>few; few>some

An example of a strong PPI (of which we will come across a few more) is Dutch *allerminst* ('not in the least'):

(34) a. *De monnik is niet allerminst gelukkig (Dutch)
 the monk is not not.in.the.least happy
 Int.: 'The monk isn't not in the least happy'
 b. *Niemand is allerminst gelukkig
 nobody is not.in.the.least happy
 Int.: 'Nobody is not in the least happy'
 c. *Weinig monniken zijn allerminst gelukkig
 few monks are not.in.the.least happy
 Int.: 'Few monks are not in the least happy'

If such variation is attested among 'plain' PPIs, it might be expected that such variation is also attested in the domain of modals outscoping negation if these are taken to be PPIs. Again, this is indeed the case. *Should*, for instance, is a PPI which cannot appear in the direct scope of any DE context. *Must*, by contrast, is a weaker type of PPI, since it may appear in those contexts that are (Strawson) DE, but not AA, such as *few*, *at most*, and *only*:

(35) a. Few students should leave should > few; *few > should
 b. Few students must leave must > few; few > must

(36) a. At most five students should leave should > at most five
 *at most five > should
 b. At most five students must leave must > at most five
 at most five > Must

(37) a. Only John should leave   should > only; *only > should
     b. Only John must leave   must > only; only > must

However, in order to ensure that the differences between *must* and *should* are a consequence of their differences in PPI-strength, and not due to something else, it must be shown that *should* patterns with *must* with respect to the three diagnostics of PPI-hood discussed in Sections 13.2.2–4. *Should* indeed exhibits similar behaviour in those respects, as is shown for metalinguistic/contrastive negation (38), intervening scope-takers (39), and clause-external negation (40).

(38) No student SHOULD read Shakespeare; they are just encouraged to

(39) a. A student's mistakes shouldn't necessarily be hurled on the shoulders
     of his teachers   ¬ > necessarily > should
     b. She should marry him not because he looks smart but because
     he is a good linguist   ¬ > because > should

(40) The doctor doesn't say that Peter should stop smoking   ¬ > should

So, English exhibits variation between strong and weak modal PPIs. This kind of variation can also be attested in Greek and Dutch. It should be noted, though, that the Greek and Dutch modals that are comparable with *should* are composites of the regular universal modal (*prepi/moeten*) and counterfactual morphology (in Greek, future plus past imperfective; in Dutch, a past future auxiliary; cf. Iatridou 2000; Von Fintel and Iatridou 2007). As is shown in the following examples, the Greek and Dutch modals expressing *should* cannot take scope below (Strawson) DE, but non-AA operators, such as 'few' and 'only', whereas the regular universal modals *prepi* and *moeten* can.

(41) a. Ligi fitites tha eprepe na figun   should > few; *few > should
     few students FUT must SUBJ leave
     'Few students should leave'   (Greek)
     b. Mono o Iannis tha eprepe na figi   should > only; *only > should
     only Iannis FUT must SUBJ leave
     'Only Iannis should leave'

(42) a. Weinig studenten zouden moeten vertrekken
     should > few; *few > should
     few students would must leave   (Dutch)
     'Few students should leave'
     b. Alleen Jan zou moeten vertrekken   should > only; *only > should
     only Jan would must leave
     'Only John should leave'

Now, a striking fact about PPIs is that, while they cannot be in the immediate scope of a clause-mate negation/AA operator, this configuration becomes licit for weak PPIs when this negation/AA operator is in the scope of an NPI licensing environment. This has been first observed by Baker (1970) and is also discussed at length in Szabolcsi (2004), for whom they are crucial to her explanation of PPI-hood (Szabolcsi 2004: 35–41; see also Homer 2015). For this reason, these facts are referred to as the *Baker-Szabolcsi facts*. By contrast, strong PPIs cannot be rescued in this way. The relevant configurations of the Baker-Szabolcsi facts are represented and illustrated below for the English weak PPI *some* and the Dutch strong PPI *allerminst* ('not in the least'):

(43) a. *Neg > PPI
 b. √ NPI licenser > Neg > PPI

(44) a. I am surprised that John didn't call someone √ surprise > not > some
 b. I regret that John didn't call someone √ regret > not > some
 c. If we don't call someone, we are doomed √ if [not > some]
 d. Every boy who didn't call someone ... √ every [not > some]
 e. Only John didn't call someone √ only > not > some
 f. Few boys didn't call someone √ few > not > some

(45) a. *Ik ben verbaasd dat je niet {allerminst/inderdaad/verre van} tevreden bent (Dutch)
 I am surprised that you are not not.in.the.least / indeed / far from happy
 b. *Het spijt me dat Jan niet {allerminst / inderdaad / verre van} tevreden is
 I regret that you are not not.in.the.least / indeed / far from happy
 c. *Als we niet {allerminst / inderdaad / verre van} tevreden zijn, gaat het mis
 if we are not not.in.the.least / indeed / far from happy, goes it wrong
 d. *Iedereen die niet {allerminst / inderdaad / verre van} tevreden is, –
 everybody, who is not not.in.the.least / indeed / far from happy, ...
 e. *Alleen Jan is niet {allerminst / inderdaad / verre van} tevreden
 only John is not not.in.the.least / indeed / far from happy
 f. *Weinig mensen zijn niet {allerminst / inderdaad / verre van} tevreden
 few people are not not.in.the.least / indeed / far from happy

If modals outscoping negation are indeed PPIs, it is expected that weak PPIs, like English *must*, can occur under the scope of negation embedded in DE contexts, but that strong PPIs, such as English *should*, cannot. This is indeed the case, as is shown for English in (46)–(51).

(46) a. If he must not work tonight he is allowed to go out with his boyfriend
√ ¬ > must
b. If he should not work tonight he is allowed to go out with his boyfriend
* ¬ > should

(47) a. Every boy who must not work tonight is allowed to go out with his boyfriend
√ ¬ > must
b. Every boy who should not work tonight is allowed to go out with his boyfriend
* ¬ > should

(48) a. Only John must not work tonight √ ¬ > must
b. Only John should not work tonight * ¬ > should

(49) a. Very few doctors must not work tonight. Most of them are on duty
√ ¬ > must
b. Very few doctors should not work tonight * ¬ > should

(50) a. I regret that John must not write a paper on that topic √ ¬ > must
b. I regret that John should not write a paper on that topic * ¬ > should

(51) a. I am surprised that he must not write a paper about the Romans
√ ¬ > must
b. I am surprised that he should not write a paper about the Romans
* ¬ > should

Finally, the Baker-Szabolcsi facts also extend to Greek and Dutch modals, as is shown below (restricting the examples for the first argument of universal quantifiers, and for *only*):

(52) a. Kathe pedhi pu dhen prepi na dhulepsi apopse bori na vgi me tin filenadha tu
every boy who NEG must work tonight can go out with the girlfriend his
(Greek)
'Every boy who doesn't have to work tonight is allowed to go out with his girlfriend'
every [¬ > must]

b. Kathe pedhi pu dhen tha eprepe na dhulepsi apopse bori na vgi me tin filenadha tu
every boy who NEG FUT must-PST work tonight can go out with the girlfriend his
'Every boy who should not work tonight is allowed to go out with his girlfriend'
*every [¬ > should]

(53) a. Monacha o Yanis dhen prepi na dhulepsi apopse (Greek)
only the John NEG must work tonight
'Only John doesn't have to work tonight' only [¬ > must]

b. Monacha o Yanis dhen tha eprepe na dhulepsi apopse
only the John NEG FUT must-PST work tonight
'Only John should not work tonight' *only [¬ > should]

(54) a. Iedereeen die vanavond niet moet werken, kan uitgaan (Dutch)
everybody who tonight NEG must work, can out.go
'Everybody who doesn't have to work tonight is allowed to go out'
every [¬ > must]

b. Iedereeen die vanavond niet zou moeten werken, kan uitgaan
everybody who tonight NEG would must work, can out.go
'Everybody who shouldn't have to work tonight is allowed to go out'
*every [¬ > should]

(55) a. Alleen Jan moet vanavond niet werken (Dutch)
only Jan must tonight NEG work
'Only John doesn't have to work tonight' only [¬ > must]

b. Alleen Jan zou vanavond niet moeten werken
only Jan would tonight NEG must work
'Only John shouldn't work tonight' *only [¬ > should]

Hence, a fourth parallel between modal and other PPIs has been identified: both modal and other PPIs exhibit the Baker-Szabolcsi facts if they are weak, but not if they are strong. On this basis, one can safely conclude that modal auxiliaries that outscope negation are indeed PPIs.

13.3 Why Positive Polarity Items?

13.3.1 Universal modal Positive Polarity Items as the mirror image of existential Negative Polarity Items

If modals like *must* and *should* and all other modal auxiliaries that outscope negation are PPIs, the question naturally arises of why they are PPIs in the first place. One answer, in the light of the discussion, suggests itself: they are universal quantifiers that have the same properties that Chierchia (2006, 2013) attributes to existential quantifiers that are NPIs. If *must* and *should* are introducers of domain alternatives that require the presence of a covert exhaustifier, it follows immediately that they may not take scope under negation: That would give rise to a semantic contradiction again.

To see this, take (56). Let us assume that the modal base of (57) consists of the worlds w_1, w_2, w_3. The semantics of *She must not leave* (without the exhaustifier) is then as in (57a). Since no domain alternative is stronger than (57a), exhaustification applies vacuously, and the meaning of (56b) is as in (57a).

13.3 WHY POSITIVE POLARITY ITEMS? 317

(56) a. She must not leave
 b. [EXH$_{[\sigma,D]}$ [she must$_{[u\sigma,D]}$ not leave]]

(57) a. $\forall w.[w \in \{w_1, w_2, w_3\} \to \neg leave_w(she)]$
 b. $\forall w.[w \in \{w_1, w_2\} \to \neg leave_w(she)]$
 c. $\forall w.[w \in \{w_1, w_3\} \to \neg leave_w(she)]$
 d. $\forall w.[w \in \{w_2, w_3\} \to \neg leave_w(she)]$
 e. $\forall w.[w \in \{w_1\} \to \neg leave_w(she)]$
 f. $\forall w.[w \in \{w_2\} \to \neg leave_w(she)]$
 g. $\forall w.[w \in \{w_3\} \to \neg leave_w(she)]$

Now suppose that *must* were to reconstruct under negation. The logical form of (58a) would then be as in (58b). But now, all relevant domain alternatives are stronger than the proposition [she *e* -n't must$_{[u\sigma,D]}$-leave], and, therefore, (58b) has the semantics shown in (59). But (59) is a contradiction, as it states that not in all worlds w_1, w_2, w_3 does she leave, and, at the same time, that she leaves in all worlds w_1, w_2, w_3. This proposal thus correctly predicts that *must* cannot reconstruct below negation.

(58) a. She mustn't leave
 b. [EXH$_{[\sigma]}$ [she *e* -n't must$_{[u\sigma]}$-leave]]

(59) $\neg\forall w.[w \in \{w_1, w_2, w_3\} \to leave_w(she)]$ &
 $\neg\neg\forall w.[w \in \{w_1, w_2\} \to leave_w(she)]$ &
 $\neg\neg\forall w.[w \in \{w_1, w_3\} \to leave_w(she)]$ &
 $\neg\neg\forall w.[w \in \{w_2, w_3\} \to leave_w(she)]$ &
 $\neg\neg\forall w.[w \in \{w_1\} \to leave_w(she)]$ &
 $\neg\neg\forall w.[w \in \{w_2\} \to leave_w(she)]$ &
 $\neg\neg\forall w.[w \in \{w_3\} \to leave_w(she)]$ =
 $\neg\forall w.[w \in \{w_1, w_2, w_3\} \to leave_w(she)]$ &
 $\forall w.[w \in \{w_1, w_2\} \to leave_w(she)]$ &
 $\forall w.[w \in \{w_1, w_3\} \to leave_w(she)]$ &
 $\forall w.[w \in \{w_2, w_3\} \to leave_w(she)]$ &
 $\forall w.[w \in \{w_1\} \to leave_w(she)]$ &
 $\forall w.[w \in \{w_2\} \to leave_w(she)]$ &
 $\forall w.[w \in \{w_3\} \to leave_w(she)]$

One caveat should be made, though. The toy model used in (57)–(59) contains only three possible worlds. In more realistic models, the number of worlds is, of course, much bigger (and can even be infinite). More importantly, the alternatives will not reduce down to singleton sets, as there is never enough information for a speaker/hearer to narrow down the domain of worlds into a singleton set. Note, though, that, for this approach to yield the contradiction, it is only necessary that the domain alternatives are partitioned and that the union of all domain alternatives is already the same set as the original domain of quantification. For instance, in (59), the contradiction would also be yielded without any singleton alternatives. In fact, if there is already a partition with two subdomains, with, for some proposition p, one subdomain consisting of all and only all p-worlds and the other subdomain consisting of all and only all not-p-worlds, the contradiction is yielded. Both subdomain alternatives would then be stronger, whereas the union of these subdomains of quantification is still identical to the original domain of quantification.

This approach derives the PPI-hood of these modal auxiliaries in a natural and straightforward way. However, this does not mean that it must be the correct way to analyse them. There could be alternative ways to account for the PPI-hood of the modals discussed. Such potential alternative explanations, therefore, first need to be evaluated and excluded before it can be concluded that these modals are indeed the mirror image of existential weak NPIs.

One potential alternative that comes to mind is that certain modals like *must* or *should* are in some sense performative and would therefore require a higher LF position than negation. However, such an analysis, especially for *must*, runs at odds with the fact that, in various cases, the modal PPI may indeed take scope below negation and is thus allowed in an LF-position below the position of negation, for instance when there is an intervener between the negation and *must/should*, or when *must* exhibits the Baker-Szabolcsi facts. Another alternative would be Giannakidou and Mari's (2018) approach to PPI-hood of epistemic modal adverbs, which takes a positive speaker's perspective to be the source of the PPI-hood of speaker-oriented modal adverbs such as *unfortunately* or *probably*. Giannakidou and Mari's approach particularly focuses on modal adverbs, but less so on modal auxiliaries. More importantly, their approach only applies to non-universal epistemic modal PPIs, whereas the reported modal PPIs here are all deontic modals (cf. Iatridou and Zeijlstra 2013; Homer 2015).[3]

Thirdly, however, the strongest piece of evidence comes from the observation that PPIs, under this approach, should be able to 'self-intervene'. The argument is quite complex, but has at its heart the possibility that the exhaustifier that the PPI induces may appear in a scopal position between the PPI and its anti-licenser, and, therefore, allow the PPI to take (indirect) scope under it. In the following subsection, this argument will be spelled out in detail.

---

[3] Even though Giannakidou and Mari (2018) is a substantially different approach to polarity-sensitivity than Chierchia (2013), they both reduce the unacceptability of utterances containing unlicensed polarity items to inherent contradictions. For Chierchia, an unlicensed NPI yields a contradictory assertion; for Giannakidou and Mari, the assertion of a clause containing an unlicensed (epistemic) PPI contradicts its presupposition.

13.3.2 Universal Positive Polarity Items as self-interveners

Under Chierchia's approach, every NPI that is exhaustified gives rise to a logical contradiction unless some DE operator intervenes between the exhaustifier and the NPI:

(60) EXH > DE > NPI

All scopal configurations of EXH, DE, and NPI other than (60) give rise to either a feature-checking violation (if, for instance, the uninterpretable feature [uσ,D] remains unchecked) or a logical contradiction. However, in the domain of PPIs, things are different. While (61) is a scopal configuration that yields ungrammaticality, other scopal configurations between EXH, a DE operator, and a PPI are fine. The only formal requirement for these scopal construals is that EXH outscopes the PPI (given the feature-checking mechanism by Chierchia).

(61) *EXH > DE > PPI

One such configuration that is fine is one where the DE operator appears under the scope of the PPI (as in (62)), which we saw was the scopal configuration that emerges when the modal does not reconstruct (in the case of *She must not leave*).

(62) EXH > PPI > DE

But another licit scopal configuration that has not been discussed so far is the one in (63).

(63) DE > EXH > PPI

Nothing in (63) violates any rule of grammar. The PPI's uninterpretable feature [uσ,D] has been checked by higher EXH; application of EXH over its (propositional) complement does not give rise to any contradiction (as no DE operator is embedded in the complement of EXH); and, finally, since exhaustification applies vacuously, nothing forbids the DE operator to take scope over its own complement that contains the vacuously exhaustified PPI. Since no further EXH is included, (63) can underlie acceptable sentences.

To see this, take (64a) again, repeated from (9), but now with the logical form in (63)/(64b):

(64) a. I didn't read pevery book
       b. [not [EXH$_{[\sigma,D]}$ [I read [pevery book]$_{[u\sigma,D]}$]]]

The exhaustifier in (64b) now applies vacuously. The reason is that *I read pevery book* is first exhaustified before negation applies. But then, exhaustification applies vacuously: of all the propositions in (65), (65a) is the strongest.

(65) a. $\forall x.[x\in\{a, b, c\} \rightarrow read(I, x)]$
    b. $\forall x.[x\in\{a, b\} \rightarrow read(I, x)]$
    c. $\forall x.[x\in\{a, c\} \rightarrow read(I, x)]$
    d. $\forall x.[x\in\{b, c\} \rightarrow read(I, x)]$
    e. $\forall x.[x\in\{a\} \rightarrow read(I, x)]$
    f. $\forall x.[x\in\{b\} \rightarrow read(I, x)]$
    g. $\forall x.[x\in\{c\} \rightarrow read(I, x)]$

Hence, the meaning of [EXH [I read [pevery book]]] is the same as the meaning of [I read [pevery book]] (both mean $\forall x.[x\in\{a, b, c\} \rightarrow read(I, x)]$), which can subsequently be negated without any problem (yielding $\neg\forall x.[x\in\{a, b, c\} \rightarrow read(I, x)]$). Thus, a universal quantifier PPI can actually take scope below negation, provided the logical form is one where negation does not take scope in between the (higher) EXH and the (lower) PPI.

The only difference between unacceptable (61) and acceptable (63) concerns the position of the covert exhaustifier. The question thus arises of what determines the position of a covert operator in a sentence. In this, we follow Zeijlstra (2008a, b, 2012a), and Chapters 3–5, where it is argued that, for the inclusion of abstract negative operators, the locus of the abstract operator must be in a position c-commanding the highest overt marker of it at surface structure. As discussed at length in previous chapters, neg-words in NC languages (where multiple negatively marked elements give rise to one semantic negation only) carry an uninterpretable feature [uNEG] that, much like NPIs/PPIs under the approach pursued here, must be c-commanded by a (possibly) covert operator that carries the matching interpretable feature [iNEG].

In full analogy to the inclusion of abstract negative operators, the following should hold:

(66) In any sentence with an NPI/PPI that needs to be checked by a covert exhaustifier, this exhaustifier must be present in a position where it c-commands the NPI/PPI at surface structure.

This brings us into a position to determine which scopal configurations are fine for exhaustified PPIs and which ones are not. The question at stake is when a scope configuration like (63), repeated in (67), is licit. After all, when (63)/(67) would reflect a possible LF, it shows that PPIs may indeed appear under the scope of their anti-licenser, provided that the exhaustifier they induce acts as an intervener. The answer to this question is now straightforward: if a PPI is in a position lower than its anti-licenser, EXH may c-command the PPI under the DE operator, provided that the complement of EXH is propositional. Then, the PPI can take scope under its anti-licenser:

(67) DE > EXH > PPI

If, however, the PPI c-commands its anti-licenser at surface structure, the exhaustifier must be in a position c-commanding both the PPI and the DE anti-licenser:

(68)　EXH > PPI > DE

Note that both (67) and (68) are acceptable scope construals. However, a consequence of this is that any sentence where the exhaustifier which checks off the uninterpretable feature [uσ,D] of a PPI that c-commands a DE operator at surface structure would forbid the PPI to reconstruct below the DE operator, even in cases where non-PPIs would be allowed to reconstruct. The reason is that, then, this PPI would end up in the illicit scope configuration (69), which yields a logical contradiction.

(69)　*EXH > DE > PPI

So, a particular prediction that I take the application of Chierchia's (2006, 2013) mechanism to make is that PPIs, at least those PPIs that are PPIs due to the presence of [uσ,D], are elements which (i) may appear and take scope under DE operators at surface structure; and (ii), when they appear above a DE operator at surface structure, may not reconstruct below it.

Now, strikingly, all modal PPIs in English appear above the NM:

(70)　a. She mustn't leave
　　　b. She oughtn't to leave
　　　c. She shouldn't leave
　　　d. She isn't to leave

Also, several other languages discussed in Iatridou and Zeijlstra (2013) place PPI modals in a position above the negation, such as (Northern/Western) Dutch *moeten* ('must') or German *sollen* ('should'):

(71)　Zij　moet　niet　vertrekken.　　　　　　　　　(Dutch)
　　　 she　must　not　 leave　　　　□ > ¬
　　　'She mustn't leave'

(72)　Sie soll nicht gehen.　　　　　　　　　　　　　(German)
　　　 she should not go　　　　　　□ > ¬
　　　'She shouldn't go'

The other languages involving modal PPIs discussed in Iatridou and Zeijlstra (2013) and above do not place the modals in a position below negation, but rather have them form one morphophonological unit, suggesting that these complex expressions occupy the same position in the syntactic structure. Examples here come from Greek and Spanish.

(73) Dhen-prepi na to kanume afto (Greek)
 NEG-must PRT it do this □ > ¬
 'We must not do this'

(74) Juan no-debe ir (Spanish)
 John NEG-must leave □ > ¬
 'John must not leave'

Both Greek *dhen* and Spanish *no* are clitic-like elements (hosted in Neg°) that head-adjoin to the modal head (cf. Zanuttini 1997, 2001; Giannakidou 1998; Zeijlstra 2004; Merchant 2006a, for a cross-linguistic survey of the morphosyntactic status of such NMs; see also Chapter 1). Arguably, no abstract operator can intervene in such complex words, and the PPI may only appear at LF in between the negation and the DE operator.

Hence, all modal PPIs attested so far either appear above negation or form a morphophonological complex with it. This is already strongly in line with the proposed analysis. But even more evidence can be provided. Dutch is a language that exhibits V-to-C movement in main clauses, but not in embedded clauses. Modal auxiliaries, being verbal in nature, thus appear above negation in main clauses, but below negation in subordinate clauses. Consequently, Dutch *moeten* ('must') in negative main clauses can only yield the scopal configuration EXH > MUST > DE and behaves PPI-like:

(75) Zij moet niet vertrekken (Dutch)
 she must not leave EXH > MUST > DE
 'She mustn't leave'

However, in embedded clauses, two scopal orderings should be fine: one where EXH intervenes between the negation and the modal, and one where EXH takes widest scope:

(76) ... dat zij niet moet vertrekken (Dutch)
 ... that she not must leave EXH > MUST > DE
 '... she mustn't leave' / '... she doesn't have to leave' DE > EXH > MUST

Example (76) is thus predicted to be ambiguous, unlike (75), a prediction that is indeed borne out:

(77) a. *Zij moet niet vertrekken, maar het mag wel (Dutch)
 she must not leave, but it may PRT
 'She mustn't leave, but it is allowed'
 b. Zij moet niet vertrekken, omdat het verboden is
 she must not leave, because it forbidden is
 'She mustn't leave, because it is forbidden'

(78) a. Ik   weet dat   zij   niet moet vertrekken, maar dat   het
        I   know that she   not   must leave,   but   that it
        wel mag   (Dutch)
        PRT may
       'I know that she doesn't have to leave, but that it is allowed'

    b. Ik   weet dat   zij   niet moet vertrekken, omdat het verboden is
       I   know that she   not   must leave,   because it forbidden is
       'I know that she mustn't leave, because it is forbidden'

The fact that the Dutch pattern shows exactly the predicted behaviour can be taken as a piece of evidence in favour of the proposal which takes PPI modals to be universal quantifiers that introduce domain alternatives and that require covert exhaustification. But this not the only piece of evidence. Take the following examples from English:

(79) a. Nobody must leave   must > nobody; nobody > must
     b. You must read nothing   must > nothing; *never > must
     c. You must never leave   must > nothing; *never > must

What these examples show is that, when *must* follows a negation, *must* can also take scope below it. However, if *must* precedes a negation, it may not. These facts are, again, straightforwardly predicted under the account just presented, but do not follow under any other account. The same facts can also be replicated in Dutch:

(80) a. Niemand moet vertrekken   must > nobody; nobody > must   (Dutch)
        nobody must leave

     b. Je moet niets lezen   must > never; *never > must
        you must read nothing

     c. Je moet nooit vertrekken must > nothing; *never > must
        you must never leave

Hence, the predictions that the approach pursued makes for modal PPIs are all met. But it gives rise to a new question as well: why have universal quantifier PPIs only been attested in the domain of modal auxiliaries and never in the domain of quantifiers over individuals?

13.4 Positive Polarity Items in the domain of universal quantifiers over individuals

Nothing in this proposal on the PPI status of modals hinges on the fact that they are quantifiers over possible worlds. After all, the approach to NPI-hood has even been developed for quantifiers over individuals. Hence, nothing in the approach should forbid the existence of universal quantifiers over individuals that are PPIs (for the same reason). However, no such PPI has been attested so far.

In this section, I argue that the reason why universal PPIs have been attested only among quantifiers over possible worlds and not among quantifiers over individuals, again, lies in the fact that universal quantifier PPIs may actually scope under negation, and, therefore, do not appear to be PPIs. To see this, take again the scopal ordering of a universal quantifier with a feature [uσ,D], negation, and the covert exhaustifier that gives rise to the logical contradiction—the ordering in (81):

(81) #EXH > NEG > ∀

If negation intervenes between the exhaustifier and the universal, a contradiction arises. But, as I have argued, nothing requires that a universal quantifier with a feature [uσ,D] (henceforth ∀$_{[uσ,D]}$) has its exhaustifier scope higher than the negation: the feature [uσ,D] requires only that the exhaustifier c-commands the ∀$_{[uσ,D]}$ and thus has scope over it, but it does not require that it has immediate scope. An alternative underlying syntactic configuration for such a universal quantifier carrying a feature [u$_{σ,D}$] is (82):

(82) NEG > EXH > ∀

But (82) does not give rise to a logical contradiction. As shown in (64)–(65), the proposition *I read every*$_{[uσ,D]}$ *book*, denoting ∀x.[x∈{a, b, c} → read(I, x)], would be exhaustified (a vacuous operation, since it is already stronger than any of its alternatives) before it gets negated. The denotation of (82) is then just (83), where the exhaustifier intervenes.

(83) ¬∀x.[x∈{a, b, c} → read(I, x)]

Universal PPIs (or, to be more precise: universal quantifiers that obligatorily introduce domain alternatives that must be exhaustified) are fine in negative / DE contexts as long as the exhaustifier takes scope in between the anti-licenser and the universal quantifier itself. Universal quantifier PPIs may appear under negation without being unacceptable, and, therefore, are unrecognizable as such.

How do we know, then, if PPIs that are universal quantifiers over individuals exist in the first place? As discussed before, we can only know this on the basis of examples where a universal quantifier negation appears above a morphologically independent NM at surface structure. In that case, the surface scope order would be EXH > ∀ > NEG. Under such a configuration, the universal quantifier that is equipped with a feature [uσ,D] cannot reconstruct below negation (as this would give rise to a logical contradiction), but a universal quantifier that is lacking [uσ,D] would be able to reconstruct below negation.

Interestingly, variation between those universal quantifiers that may and those that may not reconstruct under negation when appearing above it at surface structure has indeed been attested (and never been properly explained). In the remainder of this section, I argue that the only distinction between such quantifiers is the presence or the absence of a feature [uσ,D] on ∀. Following this line of reasoning, it can actually be established that English *everybody* is not a PPI, but that Dutch *iedereen* ('everybody') is a PPI (see Zeijlstra 2017a).

In English and most other languages (cf. Zeijlstra 2004 for an overview), for almost all speakers, a universal quantifier that precedes negation may reconstruct under negation. Sentence (84) is ambiguous between a wide-scope reading of the universal quantifier with respect to the negation ('nobody left') and a narrow-scope reading ('not everybody left'), the latter being the most salient reading. This shows that English *everybody* cannot carry a feature [uσ,D].

(84)   Everybody didn't leave   ∀>¬;¬>∀

However, for a small number of languages, this is not the case. For most speakers of Dutch (and several Northern German varieties), this reconstructed reading is not available (cf. Zeijlstra 2004; Abels and Marti 2010). The same holds for (Levantine/Jordanian) Arabic and Japanese.

(85)   Iedereen vertrok niet   (Dutch)
       everybody left not   ∀>¬;*¬>∀
       'Nobody left'

(86)   Kul t-tulaab   ma mashu   (Jordanian Arabic)
       all the-students not walked   ∀>¬;*¬>∀
       'No student walked'

(87)   Zen'in-ga sono testo-o uke-nakat-ta   (Japanese)
       all-NOM that test-ACC take-not-PAST ∀>¬;*¬>∀
       'Nobody took that test'

This observation has never received a satisfactory explanation, but directly follows once universal quantifiers in Dutch, Northern German, (Levantine/Jordanian) Arabic, and Japanese are taken to be PPIs. Focusing here on the Dutch example, if *iedereen* is a PPI, it must be c-commanded by EXH at surface structure, and reconstructing it below negation would result in the contradictory reading EXH>NEG>∀, thus providing a simple solution for this hitherto unsolved problem. Moreover, if *iedereen* is a PPI, the prediction that our analysis makes with respect to universal quantifiers, namely that universal quantifiers equipped with a feature [uσ,D] should also be attested (since nothing, in principle, rules them out), is also confirmed.

However, how can we independently investigate whether Dutch *iedereen* is indeed a PPI? As shown by Szabolcsi (2004) and discussed earlier, PPI-hood can be diagnosed in four different ways. First, PPIs should be fine under metalinguistic negation. This is indeed the case for Dutch *iedereen*, which may take scope under metalinguistic negation:

(88) Speaker A: Iedereen gaat de kamer uit (Dutch)
everybody goes the room out
'Everybody leaves the room'
Speaker B: Nee, onzin. Iedereen gaat niet de kamer uit;
no, nonsense. everybody goes not the room out;
alleen Jan en Piet
only Jan and Piet
'No, nonsense. Not everybody leaves the room, only John and Piet do'

Second, PPIs can scope under negation if a proper intervener scopes between the PPI and its anti-licenser. In a way, we already saw that this is the case for those PPIs that appear under the surface scope of negation (since EXH then acts as an intervener), but more examples of intervention effects can be attested. Example (89) can be true in a situation where it is not always the case that everybody leaves the room. Note that this reading is facilitated by adding extra stress on *altijd* ('always').

(89) Iedereen gaat niet altijd de kamer uit (Dutch)
everybody goes not always the room out
'It is not always the case that everybody leaves the room'

Thirdly, PPIs can take scope under clause-external negation. Again, this applies to *iedereen* as well:

(90) Ik zeg niet dat iedereen vertrekt; alleen Jan vertrekt (Dutch)
I say not that everybody leaves; only Jan leaves
'I'm not saying that everybody leaves; only John leaves'

Fourthly, and finally, (weak) PPIs can be rescued under two anti-licensers (with the highest one being a non-AA anti-licenser). Again, this is the case for Dutch *iedereen*. Take (91). The most salient reading of this sentence is the one where the speaker is surprised that some people left (i.e., that not everybody stayed). Again, this reading is only possible if *iedereen* is allowed to reconstruct under negation.

(91) Het verbaast me dat iedereen niet blijft (Dutch)
it surprises me that everybody not stays
'It surprises me that not everybody stays'

So, Dutch *iedereen*, when preceding negation, exhibits all the diagnostics of PPI-hood, thus allowing us to safely conclude that it is indeed a PPI in the classical sense (i.e., in the same way that *anybody* and *ever* are NPIs). The fact that it may appear under the scope of surface negation when negation precedes it, immediately follows as this PPI introduces an exhaustifier, which, in turn, may act as an intervener between the PPI and its anti-licenser.

13.5 Conclusions

To conclude, universal quantifier PPIs do exist, both in the domain of quantifiers over individuals and in the domain of quantifiers over possible worlds, as is predicted by Chierchia's (2006, 2013) approach to NPI-hood, which, in turn, is based on Kadmon and Landman (1993), Krifka (1995), and Lahiri (1998). Since the exhaustifier that is induced by these PPIs can act as an intervener between the PPI and its anti-licenser (at least for weak PPIs), universal quantifier PPIs may appear in disguise and take scope below their anti-licenser. Their PPI-like behaviour becomes visible only once they morphosyntactically precede their anti-licenser.

At the same time, many questions are open. These questions especially address the potential type of PPIs that this approach predicts to be possible and to be impossible. For instance:

What is the difference between *must* and *should*? One is a weak PPI and the other a strong one? But what underlies these differences? Is the mechanism behind strong and weak NPIs the same one that underlies strong and weak PPIs? This is predicted to be the case, but it needs to be evaluated.

Second, whether something is an NPI or a PPI depends on whether its domain alternatives are weaker or stronger in an upward-entailing context. This also predicts that elements whose domain of quantification can give rise to both types of domain alternatives should be ambiguous between NPIs and PPIs. The question thus arises whether such elements can indeed be attested.

Third, not every PPI is a universal quantifier. *Some*, maybe the best-known PPI, is existential, and the current approach can therefore not account for its PPI-hood. The same holds for certain existential modals: *May* is polarity-insensitive in its deontic usage, but PPI-like when it is used epistemically:

(92)   a.   You may leave
         b.   You may not leave   not > may

(93)   She may not be alive any more   may > not

A full theory of PPI-hood should also provide answers to these (and other) questions. In the next chapter, an attempt in that direction will be made.

14
The landscape of PPIs

14.1 Introduction

The previous chapter has shown that one particular approach to NPI-hood can be mirrored, thus explaining the existence and distributional properties of a class of universal PPIs. The source that underlies classical weak and strong NPIs has been said to also underlie these universal PPIs (the question of how exactly the strong–weak distinction applies being left open). At the same time, we saw that the landscape of NPIs is heterogeneous and that different types of NPIs exist, each of them having a different source for its NPI-hood. Hence, the question arises whether other types of NPIs also find their counterparts in the landscape of PPIs.

For some NPIs (in the broad sense, including neg-words that carry a feature [uNEG]), this is not readily the case. It would be hard to see how elements carrying a particular [uNEG]-feature would be restricted to positive contexts. As has already been discussed in Chapter 1, positivity is never grammatically reflected. Also, NPIs of the *hoeven* type, which require the presence of a higher negation that can be incorporated in another element, do not easily extend to PPIs (though see Szabolcsi 2004, who argues that such PPIs may contain two negations that are either both realized or both unrealized).

This leaves open the weak and strong NPIs discussed earlier whose NPI-hood follows under Chierchia's approach, and the superweak NPIs that result from being referentially deficient under the approaches by Lin (1996, 1998) and Giannakidou (1998 2000). In this chapter, we will see that all these NPIs indeed find their mirror images in the landscape of PPIs. First, in Section 14.2, we will see that the account for the strong–weak NPI distinction presented in Chapter 10 naturally extends to strong and weak PPIs, and even accounts for some hitherto unattested facts. Second, in Section 14.3, we will see that elements whose logical properties of their domain of quantification are not lexically fixed, but depend on their grammatical contexts can indeed be both NPIs and PPIs, as predicted in Section 13.5. And, finally, in Section 14.4, we will see that the mirror image of superweak NPIs, as discussed in Chapter 11, find their counterparts in weak existential PPIs. Section 14.5 concludes.

14.2 Strong vs weak Positive Polarity Items

As discussed in the previous chapter, different modal PPIs can be subject to different strength requirements. Focusing on English, at least the following two PPIs can be distinguished: strong PPIs (banned from all DE contexts) and weak PPIs (banned from AA contexts only). English *should* is a strong PPI. For instance, it cannot take scope below *few*, *at most N*, or *only*, whereas English *must*, which is a weak PPI, can:

(1) a. Few students should leave   should > few; *few > should
    b. Few students must leave   must > few; few > must

To capture the difference between these two scopal construals, take a scenario where we know of two (out of twenty) students, namely Mary and Suzanne, that they ought to leave. In such a scenario, *few>should* holds, a scenario under which the sentence *Few students should leave* cannot be felicitously uttered. In a scenario where, according to the fire regulations, there are two students too many in the room (and, therefore, two students have to leave, no matter who), the scopal reading is *should>few*, which is indeed an available reading for *Few students should leave*. Similar scenarios can be used to differentiate between the readings in other examples, such as (2) and (3).

(2) a. At most five students should leave   should > at most five;
                                              *at most five > should
    b. At most five students must leave   must > at most five;
                                              at most five > must
(3) a. Only John should leave   should > only; *only > should
    b. Only John must leave   must > only; only > must

As discussed in Chapter 10, the distinction between strong and weak PPIs is reminiscent of the distinction between strong and weak NPIs. For instance, English *in years* is a strong NPI, since it can be licensed by AA contexts only ((4)–(6)), whereas, by contrast, English *ever* is fine in all DE contexts ((7)–(10)):

(4) a. *I have seen him in years
    b. *Somebody has seen him in years

(5) a. I haven't seen him in years
    b. Nobody has seen him in years

(6) a. *Few people have seen him in years
    b. *At most five students have seen him in years
    c. *Only John has seen him in years

(7) a. *I ever saw him
    b. *Somebody ever saw him

(8) a. I didn't ever see him
    b. Nobody ever saw him

(9) a. Few people ever saw him
    b. At most five students ever saw him
    c. Only John ever saw him

Also discussed in Chapter 10 was the observation, due to Collins and Postal (2014), that strong NPIs are also strict NPIs, NPIs that must be licensed within a local syntactic domain such as a finite clause or an island. Licensing strong/strict NPIs across such locality boundaries, like adjunct islands, is not possible:

(10) a. *I don't travel in order to have seen him in years
     b. *I don't say that I have seen him in years

Again, weak NPI-licensing is not subject to such syntactic locality constraints and may apply across locality boundaries:

(11) a. I don't travel in order to ever see him
     b. I didn't say that I ever saw him

Following Gajewski (2011) and Chierchia (2013), the strong–weak distinction lies in the question whether the exhaustifier (EXH) only looks at the semantics of the NPI licenser, or also at its pragmatics (both its presupposition and its implicatures). Weak NPIs trigger EXH to look at the semantics of the licenser only; strong NPIs also trigger an EXH to look at the licenser's pragmatics.

I assume, as outlined in Chapter 10, that there are, in general, two ways to trigger the presence of an exhaustifier: one way is by syntactic agreement (as has been shown in this chapter at various places); another one would be the result of a pragmatic mechanism that states that, if some (domain) alternatives have been introduced in the sentence and they have not been applied to by any focus-sensitive operator that applies to alternatives, as a last resort, the entire clause is exhaustified. Implicitly or explicitly, such mechanisms have been suggested before in the literature (cf. Krifka 1995). This amounts to the following picture:

(12) a. Syntactic exhaustification:
    - is triggered by agreement;
    - is subject to syntactic locality constraints;
    - may apply at any position in the clause, provided its complement is of the right semantic type.
    b. Pragmatic exhaustification:
    - takes place as a last-resort operation;
    - is not subject to syntactic locality constraints;
    - may apply at the CP level only (given that it is a last-resort operation applying at propositional level).

14.2 STRONG VS WEAK POSITIVE POLARITY ITEMS 331

Now, the strict-vs-non-strict distinction among NPIs naturally follows. Both types of NPIs obligatorily introduce all scalar and domain alternatives, but strict NPIs must syntactically agree with the exhaustifier; non-strict NPIs are subject to pragmatic exhaustification. And, since strict NPIs are exhaustified by a different exhaustifier from that for non-strict NPIs, nothing forbids that these two exhaustifiers may have different semantic properties: the pragmatic exhaustifier has the same properties that were thus far assigned to EXH. In this sense, EXH functions like a classical (Neo-)Gricean operation. However, syntactic exhaustification involves a different type of exhaustifier, EXH+, which also considers the presuppositions and implicatures triggered in its complement.

This predicts that all weak NPIs, unlike strong NPIs, can be licensed by a licenser outside their syntactic domain. Also, it is predicted that all NPIs obligatorily introduce domain alternatives (which is what renders them NPIs), but only strong NPIs carry an uninterpretable feature [uEXH+] that triggers the presence of EXH+, which they agree with; weak NPIs are simply subject to the pragmatic exhaustification requirement. This has indeed the additional advantage that what underlies NPI-hood under the exhaustification approach boils down to only one requirement—obligatory introduction of domain alternatives—and not two (obligatory introduction of domain alternatives *and* the presence of a [uσ,D]-feature on the NPI).

This solution can naturally be extended to PPI-hood, where, as we will see, it makes even more fine-grained predictions. If the presence or absence of an uninterpretable feature [uEXH+] is what distinguishes weak from strong existential NPIs, this should also be behind the distinction between strong and weak universal PPIs—again, in the reverse configuration (as weak NPIs and strong PPIs have a distribution described in terms of DE, whereas strong NPIs and weak PPIs have a distribution described in terms of AA): Whatever makes a weak NPI a weak NPI, makes a strong PPI a strong PPI, and whatever makes a strong NPI a strong NPI, makes a weak PPI a weak PPI. Both weak and strong PPIs introduce domain alternatives, but only weak PPIs carry a feature [uEXH+] (and trigger EXH+ rather than EXH).

Now the presence of EXH+ no longer causes non-AA DE operators to give rise to a contradiction when they scope over universal PPIs. As we saw before, a plain DE operator like *few* is no longer DE when its implicatures are taken into consideration; and if DE-ness is what is behind the semantic contradiction that renders anti-licensed PPIs unacceptable, *few* under EXH+ can no longer give rise to this contradiction when it scopes over a PPI.

So, now we may assume that English *must* carries an uninterpretable feature [uEXH+], whereas English *should* does not do so and is subject to a pragmatic exhaustification constraint. This, however, has serious repercussions for the analysis presented so far. If only weak PPIs (the ones like *must* with an uninterpretable feature [uEXH+]) syntactically trigger the presence of EXH+, and strong PPIs like *should* do not, then the mechanism that is responsible for postulating the covert exhaustifier EXH+ in a position between the anti-licenser and the PPI is only available for weak PPIs like *must* and not for strong PPIs like *should*. Strong PPIs trigger the presence of EXH, which can only be present at clausal/CP level. Hence, we predict that only weak PPIs are fine under higher clause-mate anti-licensers and that strong PPIs are not. The relevant configurations are below:

(13)   NEG > EXH+ > PPI   Possible under syntactic exhaustification
Impossible under pragmatic exhaustification

(14)   EXH(+) > NEG > PPI   Possible under both syntactic exhaustification and pragmatic exhaustification

Now, for English, given the fixed position of modal auxiliaries in the clause, this may at first sight be hard to test; but as we saw, other languages exhibit constructions that can be used to evaluate these predictions. As stated before, Dutch exhibits V-to-C movement in main clauses only. We already established that, while Dutch *moeten* behaves like a typical PPI in main clauses, it can easily appear under the scope of negation in embedded clauses. Dutch *moeten* is also a weak PPI:

(15)   a.   Weinig   mensen   moeten   vertrekken   few > must;   (Dutch)
            few   people   must   leave   must > few
            'Few people must leave'
       b.   Hoogstens vijf mensen moeten vertrekken   at most 5 > must;
            at most five people must leave   must > at most 5
            'At most five people must leave'
       c.   Alleen Jan moet vertrekken   only > must;
            only John must leave   must > only
            'Only John must leave'

This is in line with our predictions, and has already been shown in the previous chapter. But Dutch also exhibits a universal modal PPI meaning 'should' (as discussed, of the form *would must*). This modal, however, is a strong PPI. The same applies to German *sollen* ('should').

(16)   a.   Weinig mensen zouden moeten vertrekken   *few> should;   (Dutch)
            few people would must leave   should >few
            'Few people should leave'
       b.   Hoogstens vijf mensen zouden moeten   *at most five>should;
            vertrekken
            at most five people would must leave   should>at most five
            'At most five people should leave'
       c.   Alleen Jan zou moeten vertrekken   *only>should;
            only Jan would must leave   should>only
            'Only Jan should leave'

(17) a. Wenige Leute sollen gehen   *few>should;   (German)
few people should go   should>few
'Few people should go'

b. Höchstens fünf Leute sollen gehen   *at most five>should;
at most five people should go   should>at most 5
'At most five people should go'

c. Nur Hans soll gehen   *only>should;
only Hans should go   should>only
'Only Hans should go'

Now, the prediction is that, in an embedded clause (both Dutch and German exhibit V-to-C movement in main clauses only), these stronger PPIs, being pragmatically exhaustified only, must still outscope negation, unlike the weak ones: The pragmatic exhaustifier EXH can only be introduced at clausal/CP level. And, indeed, they are:

(18) ... dat Jan niet zou moeten vertrekken *neg>should; (Dutch)
... that Jan neg would must leave   should>neg
'... that Jan shouldn't leave'

(19) ... dass Hans nicht gehen soll   *neg>should; (German)
... that Hans neg go should   should>neg
'... that Hans shouldn't go'

Hence, the evidence presented so far shows that, when applied to the domain of PPI modals, the amendment, suggested in Chapter 10, to Chierchia's theory, which was independently necessary given the different syntactic and semantic behaviour of weak and strong NPIs, again makes correct predictions for the treatment of universal PPIs. Finally, note that this predicts that Dutch *iedereen* must also be a weak PPI (and not a strong PPI), as, otherwise, it would also behave PPI-like when appearing in object position.

Also for English, it can be shown that the predictions hold. Recall the following examples from the previous chapters:

(20) a. Nobody must leave   must > nobody; nobody > must
b. You must read nothing   must > nothing; *nothing > must
c. You must never leave   must > nothing; *never > must

(21) a. Niemand moet vertrekken   must > nobody;   (Dutch)
Nobody must leave   nobody > must
b. Je moet niets lezen   must > nothing;
You must read nothing   *nothing> must
c. Je moet nooit vertrekken   must > nothing;
You must never leave   *never > must

In English and Dutch, weak modal PPIs only obligatorily outscope negation if they precede it at surface structure. However, in these languages, and also in German, the moment the (weak PPI) modal is replaced by a strong PPI modal, it always outscopes negation, irrespective of its surface position (though the Dutch examples might be a little less telling here, since the modal construction is spread over two verbs, one preceding, one following negation):

(22) a. Nobody should leave   should > nobody;
 *nobody > should
 b. You should read nothing   should > never;
 *never > should
 c. You should never leave   should > nothing;
 *never > should

(23) a. Niemand zou moeten vertrekken   should > nobody;   (Dutch)
 Nobody should leave   *nobody > should
 b. Je zou niets moeten lezen   should > never;
 You should read nothing   *never > should
 c. Je zou nooit moeten vertrekken   should > nothing;
 You should never leave   *never > should

(24) a. Keiner soll abfahren   should > nobody;   (German)
 Nobody should leave   *nobody > should
 b. Du sollst nichts lesen   should > never;
 You should read nothing   *never > should
 c. Du sollst nie abfahren   should > nothing;
 You should never leave   *never > should

Again, these facts show that strong PPIs, unlike weak PPIs, are insensitive to their clause-internal surface position with respect to negation, and always obligatorily take wide scope. This further corroborates the conclusions drawn in this section.

14.3 Hybrid Polarity Items

As discussed before, whether an element behaves like an existential NPI or a universal PPI depends on the logical strength of the propositional domain alternatives it introduces. The propositional domain alternatives of an NPI like *any* or *ever* are, unless they appear in a DE context, all non-weaker. The propositional domain alternatives of a PPI, such as *must* or Dutch *ieder* ('every'), are not stronger. The reason for the latter is that the first argument of a universal quantifier is DE itself. In order to yield the logical contradiction that gives rise to the unacceptability judgements of unlicensed PIs, propositional domain alternatives should be logically stronger and jointly contradict the assertion.

14.3 HYBRID POLARITY ITEMS

This makes it also possible that certain elements that obligatorily introduce domain alternatives can be both NPIs and PPIs, depending on the grammatical context they appear in. If a particular PI obligatorily combines with an operator that makes its domain alternatives either non-weaker or non-stronger, it is predicted that, depending on the operator it combines with, it is either an NPI or a PPI. In this section, I will show, largely following Iatridou and Zeijlstra (2021), that such hybrid PIs indeed exist.

14.3.1 Durative vs punctual *until*

The lexical item *until* is an adverbial that sets up a time span which Iatridou and Zeijlstra (2021) dub the *Until Time Span* (UTS). It has a Left Boundary (LB) that is contextually set, and a Right Boundary (RB) that is set by the argument of *until*. Strikingly, the literature makes reference to two different usages of until: so-called *durative until* (until-d) and *punctual until* (until-p) (cf. Karttunen 1974; Mittwoch 1977; Declerck 1995a; Giannakidou 2002; Condoravdi 2008). The two differ in various ways. For one, until-d is said to be polarity-insensitive, whereas until-p is an NPI. Second, until-d combines with imperfective predicates (basically, statives or progressives), whereas until-p combines with negated (telic) predicates. Examples of until-d, modifying positive predicates, can be found in (25) and (26).

(25) He was asleep / composing a sonnet until 5 pm / my departure

(26) He was asleep / composing a sonnet until I left

When a sentence with until-d and a durative predicate is negated, an ambiguity arises:

(27) He was not asleep / composing a sonnet until 5 pm / until I left

The sentence in (27) merely asserts that there was no sleeping or composing that reached the RB of the UTS. It is not specified whether there was no sleeping or composing at all, or whether there was some which terminated before the RB of the UTS. The transparent terms *throughout-not* and *not-throughout* are used to refer to the two cases respectively. From (27), it is unclear whether these two readings result from vagueness or (scopal) ambiguity. However, (28) seems to argue in favour of scopal ambiguity, since here only the *throughout-not* reading is available:

(28) Until 5 pm / Until I left, he was not asleep / composing a sonnet

The predicates used in connection with *until* so far are all imperfective (*composing a sonnet*) or stative (*asleep*). Strikingly, all imperfectives have the so-called subinterval property, which is essentially an instance of DE: a predicate P has the subinterval property iff, whenever it holds at an interval, it also holds at every one of its subintervals (cf. Dowty 1979). Predicates in perfective aspect behave quite differently in this respect. (Non-negative) perfectives generally lack the subinterval property. Using *for*-modification as a diagnostic, this becomes clear in the following examples:

(29) a. The plant was alive for five weeks
b. The plant was dying for five weeks

(30) *The plant died for five weeks

Karttunen (1974), among many others, observed that, when combining with a perfective predicate, *until*-modification is only possible if the predicate is negated, as shown below.

(31) a. *She left / reached the summit until 5 pm / I left
b. She didn't leave / reach the summit until 5 pm / I left

In this sense, *until* behaves like an NPI. This NPI-usage of *until* is referred to as until-p. In fact, until-p is a strong NPI, as demonstrated in (32)–(35).

(32) a. Nobody left until 5 pm
b. Nobody left until I left

(33) a. She never left until 5 pm
b. She never left until I left

(34) a. *Few people left until 5 pm
b. *Few people left until I left

(35) a. *Every student who left until 5 pm ...
b. *Every student who left until I left ...

The question now arises whether these two usages of *until* reflect lexical ambiguity or whether there is one underlying semantics for the two usages of *until*. At first sight, one would argue that there is only one *until*, the reason being that, unlike positive perfective predicates, negative perfects also have the subinterval property. Negation creates predicates with the subinterval property (cf. Mittwoch 1977; Krifka 1989; De Swart 1996; De Swart and Molendijk 1999; Verkuyl 1993; among others). Hence, negated perfectives thus behave on a par with imperfectives. The following examples are, therefore, fine:

(36) a. For five weeks, the plant didn't die. (Finally, it succumbed to the extreme draught.)
b. For five weeks, no plant died. (Finally, they succumbed to the extreme draught.)

Nevertheless, most scholars working on the semantics of *until* (inter alia, Karttunen 1974; Declerck 1995a; Giannakidou 2002; Condoravdi 2008) have argued that until-d and until-p are different lexical items. The reason is that until-p comes along with a non-cancellable Actuality Inference (AI), whereas until-d does not. The continuations in (37) are bad (for until-p), whereas the continuations in (38)–(39) (for until-d) are fine.

(37) She didn't leave until 5 pm / I left
 #... I don't know if she left later
 #... in fact, she didn't leave at all

(38) He was asleep / composing a sonnet until 5 pm
 ... and possibly well beyond that. I'm not sure
 ... and well beyond that

(39) He wasn't asleep / composing a sonnet until 5 pm
 ... and possibly well beyond that. I'm not sure
 ... and well beyond that

In addition, Iatridou and Zeijlstra (2021) have shown that until-p, unlike until-d, has a non-cancellable BEI. The RB of the UTS (time span introduced by *until*) of until-p (40) is always later than expected, whereas this is not the case for until-d ((41)–(42)):

(40) a. I expected her to arrive before 5 pm, but/and she didn't arrive until 7 pm
 b. # I expected her to arrive before 5 pm, but/and she didn't arrive until 3 pm

(41) a. I expected her to be sleeping until 5 pm, but she was sleeping until 7 pm
 b. I expected her to be sleeping until 5 pm, but she was sleeping until 3 pm

(42) a. I expected her to be sleeping until 5 pm, but she wasn't sleeping until 5 pm
 She slept until 7 pm
 b. I expected her to be sleeping until 5 pm, but she wasn't sleeping until 5 pm
 She slept until 3 pm

It is far from straightforward to see how these differences can follow from the same underlying semantics of *until*. At the same time, as Iatridou and Zeijlstra have argued, these differences do not follow under the lexical-ambiguity approach either. The reason is that what distinguishes until-d from until-p is that until-d modifies predicates for which the subinterval property holds. Those are imperfectives, but also, as shown before, negated perfectives. This means that the examples in (37) and (40) should actually be ambiguous between until-p and until-d. And while the parses with until-p should indeed disallow the continuations, the parses with until-p should be fine with it. Hence, more needs to be said.

14.3.2 Durative until *is* punctual until

Approaches that deal with the difference between until-d and until-p generally assign special properties to until-p, so as to explain the fact that it is an NPI and brings in special inferences, whereas until-d appears to be polarity-insensitive and does not bring in any special inferences. However, as we saw in the previous chapter, it is not only polarity-insensitive elements that can take scope under negation, but also universal PPIs. Universal PPIs, at least weak ones, are elements that cannot reconstruct below negation, but may appear below it. This opens up the way to hypothesize that both until-p and until-d are polarity-sensitive, one being an NPI and the other a PPI. But that also allows us to take one step further. Since the imperfective renders the predicates it modifies holding the subinterval property, but the perfective (unless negated) does not do so, one can even hypothesize that *until* itself is an element that obligatorily introduces elements that are in need of exhaustification (by means of feature-checking with the enriched exhaustifier), but that the perfective/imperfective distinction determines whether its propositional domain alternatives are non-weaker or non-stronger and, therefore, do or do not yield the contradiction.

To see how this works, let us first look at the meaning contribution that imperfectives and perfectives make. Following Klein (1994), Kratzer (1998), and many others, the contribution of the perfective and imperfective are the following relationships between Situation Time (ST) and Topic Time (TT):

(43) a. ST ⊆ TT (Perfective aspect)
b. TT ⊆ ST (Imperfective aspect)

Or, more formally (see von Fintel and Iatridou 2019):

(44) a. $[[\text{PRF } \phi]]^t = 1$ iff $\exists t' \subseteq t: [[\phi]]^{t'} = 1$
b. $[[\text{IMPF } \phi]]^t = 1$ iff $\exists t' \supseteq t: [[\phi]]^{t'} = 1$

Now, let us assume that the TT of predicates modified by *until* is the UTS (i.e., the time under consideration) and the ST the run time of the event discussed. Moreover, let us assume that *until* always obligatorily introduces domain alternatives that need to be exhaustified. Then, the distribution and attested readings of *until*, combined with positive and negative perfective and imperfective predicates, readily follows. To see this, let us assign the following (simplified) semantics of (46) to (45), with t^0 a contextually set LB, 7 pm the RB of the UTS τ, and Run(e) the run time of an event e; here, Run(e) is thus the ST, and the UTS τ is the TT.

14.3 HYBRID POLARITY ITEMS 339

(45) Sue didn't arrive until 7 pm

(46) Given a UTS τ, such that τ = [t⁰, 7]
Assertion: ¬∃e.[arrive(e, Sue) ∧ Run(e) ⊆ τ]

(46) presupposes that there is a UTS τ, and asserts that there is no arriving event with Sue as the agent in τ. It is clear that, if no such event took place in τ, no such event took place in any subinterval τ' of τ. Hence, all of the subdomain alternatives of τ in (47) are propositions that are entailed by (46).

(47) {¬∃e.[arrive(e, Sue) ∧ Run(e) ⊆ τ'] |τ' ⊆ τ}

This means that (46) has no stronger subdomain alternatives, and so exhaustification of (46) takes place vacuously, and no contradiction arises.

A contradiction would arise, though, if the negation was absent. To see this, take the (ungrammatical) positive counterpart of (46):

(48) *Sue arrived until 7 pm

Given the perfective in the matrix predicate, (48) should have the denotation in (49):

(49) Given a UTS τ, such that τ = [t⁰, 7]
Assertion: ∃e.[arrive(e, Sue) ∧ Run(e) ⊆ τ]

(49) asserts that there was an arriving event somewhere in between t⁰ and 7 pm. Now, let us see what happens when we try to exhaustify (49). The relevant domain alternatives of (49) are:

(50) {∃e.[arrive(e, Sue) ∧ Run(e) ⊆ τ'] |τ' ⊆ τ}

In this case, two concrete domain alternatives are:

(51) a. ∃e.[arrive(e, Sue) ∧ Run(e) ⊆ [t⁰, 6]]
b. ∃e.[arrive(e, Sue) ∧ Run(e) ⊆ [6, 7]]

Now if an event took place in between 6 pm and 7 pm, or in between t⁰ and 6 pm, it also took place in between t⁰ and 7: both alternatives in (51) entail the assertion in (49). This means that the alternatives in (50)/(51) are non-weaker than (49). This also means that they need to be falsified under exhaustification. Exhaustification then makes the following true:

(52) ¬∃e.[arrive(e, Sue) ∧ Run(e) ⊆ [t⁰, 7]]

But (52) is the negation of (49), and a contradiction arises. This, again, is the contradiction that makes the sentence in (48) ungrammatical. Therefore, until-p can only be used with negated predicates.

Now, let us see what happens with predicates in the imperfective. Both negative and positive predicates in the imperfective can combine with *until*. How does that follow under an approach where *until* always introduces domain alternatives that are to be exhaustified? It turns out that *until* here works exactly like a universal PPI. On this proposal, then, (53) has the meaning in (54):

(53) Miranda was reading *Anna Karenina* until yesterday

(54) Given a UTS τ, such that $\tau = [t^0, \text{yesterday}]$
Assertion: $\exists e.[\text{read}(e, \text{Miranda}, AK) \land \tau \subseteq \text{Run}(e)]$

The imperfective contributes that the TT (here, the UTS) is a subset of the ST (the event of reading *Anna Karenina*). In other words, the imperfective contributes the '$\tau \subseteq \text{Run}(e)$' part. Hence, the UTS is 'filled' with *Anna Karenina*-reading.

Given the fact that, now, the subinterval property holds of the predicate, it follows that all subdomain alternatives in (53) are actually entailed by the assertion. If Miranda has been reading *Anna Karenina* throughout the interval whose RB is yesterday, she has also been reading it in all of its subintervals. So there are no stronger domain alternatives of the assertion, and exhaustification takes place vacuously. In other words, one can actually maintain that for affirmative imperfectives, what looks like until-d is actually until-p.

Now let us look at negated until-d sentences to see whether, here, *until* can also be analysed under the unified approach. Take the following example:

(55) He wasn't reading *Anna Karenina* until yesterday

Such sentences are ambiguous between the *throughout-not* and *not-throughout* readings, which results from negation taking scope under or over until-d. Recall that, in both cases, the matrix predicate has the subinterval property because the imperfective yields the relationship in which the TT (here, the UTS $\tau = [t^0, \text{Yesterday}]$) is contained inside the ST.

The *throughout-not* reading involves low scope of negation (56):[1]

(56) Given a UTS τ, such that $\tau = [t^0, \text{Yesterday}]$
Assertion: $\exists e.[\neg\text{read}(e, \text{Miranda}, AK) \land \tau \subseteq \text{Run}(e)]$

Wide-scope negation, on the other hand, yields the *not-throughout* reading (57).

(57) Given a τ, such that $\tau = [t^0, \text{Yesterday}]$
Assertion: $\neg\exists e.[\text{read}(e, \text{Miranda}, AK) \land \tau \subseteq \text{Run}(e)]$

Now, with the semantics in (56), the acceptance of the *throughout-not* reading is predicted to be fine with *until* obligatorily introducing domain alternatives (58).

---

[1] Note that here a negated eventuality 'not-be-reading Anna Karenina' has been created. Following Iatridou and Zeijlstra (2021), here I only talk about negated events in this chapter, not negative events. If negative events were to be included in our discussion, then the negative event of 'not-reading-AK' holding at an interval would be obtained, which would be too weak a reading, as it would be true of an interval in which Miranda was not reading *Anna Karenina*. Alternatively, one could replace the event variable with a state variable s, and have Run(s) be the ST.

(58) Domain alternatives: $\{\exists e.[\neg \text{read}(e, \text{Miranda}, \text{AK}) \wedge \tau' \subseteq \text{Run}(e)] \mid \tau' \subseteq \tau\}$

If, throughout the entire interval, Miranda has not been reading AK, she has not been reading this book in any subinterval either; so, no domain alternative in (58) is stronger than the assertion. Exhaustification thus applies vacuously, and no contradiction arises.

But how about the *not-throughout* reading in (57)? Here, negation takes scope over the existential quantifier over the event variable. However, this predicts that, since the predicate has the subinterval property, exhaustifying (57) should yield ungrammaticality. It is indeed the case that all domain alternatives of (57), presented in (59), are non-weaker than (57).

(59) Domain alternatives: $\{\neg \exists e.[\text{read}(e, \text{Miranda}, \text{AK}) \wedge \tau' \subseteq \text{Run}(e)] \mid \tau' \subseteq \tau\}$

If Miranda has not been reading *Anna Karenina* throughout the day before yesterday—for instance, if, that day, the reading was interrupted for a while—it is entailed that she has not been reading *Anna Karenina* throughout in any larger interval either. Negating these stronger alternatives would entail that, in every smaller subinterval of interval $\tau = [t^0, \text{Yesterday}]$, Miranda has been reading *Anna Karenina* throughout, which contradicts the original assertion that Miranda reading *Anna Karenina* does not hold throughout in the entire UTS $\tau = [t^0, \text{Yesterday}]$.

But just as was shown for universal PPIs in the previous chapter, there is another possible parse for the *not-throughout* reading that does not give rise to this contradiction. Following the idea, already applied, that the *not-throughout* reading is the result of negation scoping over *until* instead of scoping below it (which yields the *throughout-not* reading), it is possible to first exhaustify the sentence without negation before applying negation itself.

The *not-throughout* reading is then derived as follows. First take the assertion (60), which would be the assertion of (57) without the negation:

(60) $\exists e.[\text{read}(e, \text{Miranda}, \text{AK}) \& \tau \subseteq \text{Run}(e)]$

As a next step, have the obligatorily introduced alternatives of (60) (presented in (61)) exhaustified.

(61) $\{\exists e.[\text{read}(e, \text{Miranda}, \text{AK}) \wedge \tau' \subseteq \text{Run}(e)] \mid \tau' \subseteq \tau\}$.

As seen before, this exhaustification takes place vacuously. No domain alternative in (61) is stronger than the assertion. Consequently, EXH((60)) is identical to (60). As a final step, negation applies to exhaustified (60), and the result is (57).

Hence, in total, there are three possible scope construals involving *until*, exhaustification, and negation. Since exhaustification must outscope *until*, these are: (i) NEG>EXH>UNTIL, (ii) EXH>NEG>UNTIL, and (iii) EXH> UNTIL>NEG. As I have shown, (i) is the only available scopal construal for *until* modifying a negative perfective predicate, and (ii) and (iii) the only available scopal construals for *until* modifying a negative imperfective predicate. In addition, positive imperfectives can also be modified by *until*. These results are listed in the table in (62).

(62) Possible scopal configurations of *until*:

	Perfective	Imperfective
EXH>UNTIL	⊥	OK (until-d in positive clauses)
EXH>NEG>UNTIL	until-p	⊥
EXH>UNTIL>NEG	⊥	OK (until-d with the *throughout-not* reading)
NEG>EXH>UNTIL	⊥	OK (until-d with the *not-throughout* reading)

These are indeed the facts we want to derive and that we can derive with our unified analysis for *until*.

14.3.3 Deriving the inferences

Hence, the distribution of *until* with negation can be explained under the assumption that *until* introduces domain alternatives that have to be exhaustified. When combined with the perfective, this renders *until* an NPI, and when combined with the imperfective, a PPI. But how can the fact that until-p, unlike until-d, gives rise to the non-cancellable AI and the BEI?

Following Chierchia (2013), NPIs act as domain-wideners only when used contrastively, an argument that was laid out already in Chapter 10. This opens up the following possibility: The fact that *until* sometimes comes with a non-cancellable AI and BEI and sometimes not, despite always introducing domain alternatives, is the result of the fact that sometimes it is contrastively focused, in which case it functions as a domain-widener and the inferences are there, and sometimes it is not contrastively focused, in which case the inferences are absent. As discussed in Chapter 10, domain-wideners stretch their domain of quantification beyond any contextual restrictions (with t^0 being fixed). In that case, the RB of the UTS can only be set by the moment the event takes place; that would be the maximal stretch of the UTS. If the usage of *until* that is known as until-p has indeed a domain-widening property, the non-cancellable AI and BEI follow straightforwardly, just as was the case before with the domain-widening NPI *in years*.

But why do (negated) perfective predicates require *until*-modification with contrastive focus, whereas imperfective predicates do not? First, note that the only configuration where negation has immediate scope over (unexhaustified) *until* is the one involving *until* in negated perfectives. In all the other cases, either negation is absent, or *until* scopes below negation, or *until* scopes only indirectly below negation, with the exhaustifier intervening.[2] This means that only in negated perfectives can *until* receive contrastive focus under negation. This way, it follows that only those instances of *until* that the literature calls until-p have the potential to be domain-wideners and yield the BEI and the non-cancellable AI. However, that does not explain yet why until-p must be a domain-widener. Then again, if it is assumed that *until* is always emphatically used, so that, when it appears under the direct scope of negation, it becomes contrastively focused under negation and therefore a domain-widener, everything follows.

Unfortunately, even though the assumption that *until* is always stressed yields the right result, this cannot be verified this phonetically (Edward Fleming, pers. comm., quoted in Iatridou and Zeijlstra 2021). Given that *until*-phrases have to be in the scope of negation and, therefore, appear at the right edge of the clause, the stress contour that they receive would be the same, regardless of the presence or absence of stress. If *until* is indeed always stressed, it does not only follow why only those instances of *until* that the literature calls until-p can yield the BEI and the non-cancellable AI, but also why they must do so. A unification approach to English *until* is possible, and the duality of its behaviour is due to the scopal ordering of the elements involved, as well as the resulting presence/absence of contrastive stress triggering domain-widening effects.

However, following the line of reasoning in Chapter 10, this could also be an argument that domain-widening, at least for some polarity-sensitive elements, should be a property that is already lexically encoded. This has been suggested for *until* by Yael Greenberg (pers. comm.), who argues that it could also be possible that *until* is lexically restricted to introducing all contextually salient domain alternatives as its domain alternatives. This would also derive the desired result, without making particular assumptions about inherent stress. To get back to the discussion about *in years* and its kin, in Chapter 10, the behaviour of *until* may actually suggest that certain polarity-sensitive elements are inherent domain-wideners where others are not (and may at best become domain-wideners under contrastive focus).

14.4 Existential Polarity Items

14.4.1 Existential Negative Polarity Items and Positive Polarity Items

The approach so far has been able to capture the behaviour of strong and weak PPIs that are universal quantifiers. At the same time, it is well-known that not every PPI

---

[2] Here following Rooth 1985, 1992; Chierchia 2013, and others, in that contrastive focus under negation is not possible when EXH intervenes between negation and the focused item, the reason being that contrastive focus requires negation to apply to focus alternatives; and, therefore, these alternatives cannot be applied to by the exhaustifier first.

is a universal quantifier. In fact, some of the best-known PPIs are actually existential quantifiers or indefinites. This is shown in (63) for *somewhat*, which simply cannot appear under negation, and for *some*, which can appear in negative causes, but only when it takes scope over negation (modulo the four types of exceptions discussed at length in the previous chapter).

(63) a. *Mary isn't somewhat ill
 b. Mary didn't see some girl (∃>¬;*¬>∃)

However, the PPI-hood of such existential PPIs does not follow from most theories of polarity-sensitivity. For instance, Chierchia's (2013) approach can only account for NPIs that denote lower scalar end points and PPIs that denote higher scalar end points. The existence of existential or low-scalar PPIs has not yet received a proper explanation (though see Israel 1996; Szabolcsi 2004 for particular attempts).

Naturally, that does not mean a priori that Chierchia's or other theories cannot be modified in such a way that existential PPIs, or universal NPIs, for that matter, can also be accounted for. An example of the latter would be to truncate scales such that the relevant element comes out as a scalar end point, as has, for instance, been argued by Chierchia to be the case for NPIs like *much*. *Much*, for him, simply forms the lowest scalar end point of a scale <much, most, all> (cf. Chierchia 2013). In a similar vein, truncating a scale on the other side could render other elements higher scalar end points. However, it is at least questionable whether such an extension could apply to elements like *somewhat* and *some*, which would then denote not only the lower but also the higher end point of a scale <some(what)>. It is far from clear that this way of introducing domain alternatives would result in positive polarity-sensitivity.

Alternatively, as has been proposed by Nicolae (2012), and also more recently by Staniszewski (2019), one could argue that existential elements that do not introduce subdomain alternatives, but rather introduce superdomain alternatives, under the same kind of reasoning, become PPIs. Then, *some(what)* could be said to introduce an existential quantifier that introduces superdomain alternatives. However, it is not the case that such elements become PPI-like when their superdomain alternatives are exhaustified. To see this, let us assume a domain of quantification {a}, with {a, b}, {a, c}, and {a, b, c} as its superdomain alternatives. Then *I saw something* would simply have a denotation like (64).

(64) ∃x.x∈{a} & see(I, x)

None of the superdomain alternatives of (64), listed in (65), are stronger than (64).

(65) a. ∃x.x∈{a} & see(I, x)
 b. ∃x.x∈{a, b} & see(I, x)
 c. ∃x.x∈{a, c} & see(I, x)
 d. ∃x.x∈{a, b, c} & see(I, x)

Hence, exhaustification takes place vacuously, at least under the exhaustifier that is the counterpart of *only*. But under negation, exhaustification does not yield a contradiction either. Take (66), (67):

(66) ∃x.x∈{a} & see(I, x)

(67) a. ∃x.x∈{a} & see(I, x)
      b. ∃x.x∈{a, b} & see(I, x)
      c. ∃x.x∈{a, c} & see(I, x)
      d. ∃x.x∈{a, b, c} & see(I, x)

Even if all (super)stronger alternatives of (66), namely the alternatives in (67b–d), are false, (66) is still not contradicted. As Nicolae (2012) points out, only under *even*-exhaustification would a contradiction arise. However, under Chierchia's system, NPIs that are exhaustified by a silent *even* are all NPIs that have some natural emphasis. This does not hold for plain NPIs such as *any* or *ever*, and there is no reason to assume it should hold for *some* or *somewhat* either. Hence, even a modified version of Chierchia's account can still not readily account for the nature of existential PPIs.

In Chapter 13, and in the previous chapter, I tried to distil an account of PPI-hood by mirroring existing accounts of NPI-hood. At the same time, as discussed already in Chapter 9, the landscape of NPIs is heterogeneous, given convergence. That is, different types of NPIs are NPIs for different reasons. In Chapter 11, we also identified a class of superweak NPIs, for which Chierchia's account cannot provide an explanation either (though see Chierchia and Liao 2015). An example of such an NPI, discussed in Chapter 11, is Chinese *shenme* ('what/any'), which is fine in non-veridical contexts (68):

(68) a. Mali zuotian *(haoxiang) mai-le senme shu   (Chinese)
         Mary yesterday probably bought-PRF what/any book
         'Mary has (probably) bought a book yesterday'
      b. Mali zuotian mei mai senme shu
         Mary NEG bought what/any book
         'Mary didn't buy any book yesterday'[3]

A likely explanation for the source of this kind of NPI-hood is Lin's (1996, 1998) lexically encoded *Non-Entailment-of-Existence Condition*. In this framework, certain elements may not appear in contexts that would entail the existence of a referent satisfying their description, where such contexts are formed by the proposition whose widest scope operator is a scope operator that the *Wh*-phrase is in the scope of. The sentence in (68a) without the modal is bad, as the sentence would entail that there is a book bought yesterday by Mary; if the modal is present, or a

---

[3] Example from Lin (2017).

negation, as in (68b), the sentence is fine; the existence of a book bought yesterday by Mary is no longer entailed.

For this reason, phrases like *shenme* may only appear in non-veridical contexts, as has been proven correct by Lin (2017) and shown in Chapter 11. Following Lin, Giannakidou (1998, 2011) argues that NPIs that are sensitive to non-veridicality (i.e., NPIs that, unlike *any* or *ever*, are licensed by all non-veridical operators, and not only by DE ones) are NPIs because they are referentially deficient, and thus cannot give rise to an existentiality entailment of the kind. In veridical contexts, such existential import is warranted.

This alternative approach readily offers an opening to capture the PPI-hood of existentials like *some* or *somewhat*. Let us assume that such existential PPIs are indeed the mirror image of these NPIs. Then they can be said to always give rise to possible existential import. They should then be subject to the reverse of Lin's *Non-Entailment-of-Existence Condition*, which I dub the *Non-Entailment-of-Non-Existence Condition*: Such elements may not appear in contexts that would entail the non-existence of referents satisfying their description, where, again, such contexts are formed by the proposition whose widest scope operator is a scope operator that they are in the scope of.

To see this, let us focus on plain existential PPIs. The reason that (69) does not allow a reading with a scopal construal *nobody>some* is that its assertion under this scopal construal would entail that there is no book read by anybody.

(69) Nobody read some book   (*nobody>∃; ^{OK}∃>nobody;)

This violates the Non-Entailment-of-Non-Existence Condition, which forbids excluding the existence of such books. When the scopal construal is reversed (*some>nobody*), it is asserted that there is a book ready by nobody, which no longer violates the Non-Entailment-of-Non-Existence Condition. The same line of reasoning holds for (63b) and for any other case where a negation or a NQ outscopes *some*. All these elements are not fine under AA or anti-veridical operators (the two are formally identical), as these operators entail this non-existence. This renders them PPIs.

By contrast, in (70), under both construals, there can be books read by few or at most three students: Either there are few / at most three students who read some book (surface scope), or some book is read by few / at most three people (inverse scope). In neither case is the non-existence of such books entailed.

(70) a. Few students read some book   (^{OK}few>∃; ^{OK}∃>few;)
      b. At most three students read some book (^{OK}ar most>∃; ^{OK}∃>at most;)

It is thus predicted that PPIs of this kind are fine in DE contexts that are not AA or anti-veridical, a prediction that, to the best of my knowledge, is borne out (see Chapter 9), thus providing evidence for the assumption that the Non-Entailment-of-Non-Existence Condition underlies existential PPI-hood.

14.4.2 Modal existential Positive Polarity Items

More fine-grained predictions for the idea that existential PPI-hood results from the Non-Entailment-of-Non-Existence Condition are made in the domain of modals. As discussed before, in the domain of deontic modals, all existential modals appear to be polarity-insensitive. However, as was shown already in Iatridou and Zeijlstra (2013), in the domain of epistemic modals, both NPIs and PPIs can be found. An example of an existential NPI is *can*, which, when used epistemically, can only appear in AA contexts:

(71) a. *She can have done it
  b. She can't have done it
  c. *Few / at most three students can have done it

Focusing on the topic of this chapter, certain existential epistemic modals are PPIs as well. *Might* is a good example, as it obligatorily scopes over negation, even though other existential epistemically used modals, such as *could*, do not (cf. Iatridou and Zeijlstra 2013), and generally take scope under negation:

(72) a. She might not have been there   (*¬>might; ^{OK}might >¬)
  b. She could not have been there   (^{OK}¬>could; $^?$could >¬)

May is a PPI when used epistemically, but polarity-neutral when used deontically (and then also generally takes scope under negation, at least under neutral intonation):

(73) a. She may not have been there   (*¬>may; ^{OK}may >¬)   *epistemic*
  b. She may not leave now   (^{OK}¬>may; $^?$may>¬)   *deontic*

Now, if the Non-Entailment-of-Non-Existence Condition is applied to these existential modal PPIs, the distinction between the epistemic PPI and the deontic polarity-neutral versions can be naturally explained. To see this, let us first look at the following examples from Kratzer (1991):

(74) a. Hydrangeas can grow here
  b. There might be hydrangeas growing here

In a context where the speaker talks about some land where it is clear that no hydrangeas grow, even though the physical circumstances (such as fertile soil, etc.) would make it possible, (74a) could be felicitously uttered, but (74b) could not. The difference between epistemic and deontic (or other) modal flavours, along the lines of Kratzer (1991), is that epistemic modals have an epistemic modal base, whereas the other ones have a circumstantial modal base. *Might*, being an epistemic modal, thus has a modal base that is restricted to those worlds that are compatible with the speaker's knowledge and beliefs.

Modals are, however, relative to not just one, but two conversational backgrounds. The second conversational background, based on the ordering source, consists of a set of ideals which impose an ordering on the worlds of the modal base. Modals end up quantifying over the best worlds of the modal base, given the ideals set by the ordering source (see Hacquard 2011, among others, for overview and discussion). The effect of these ordering sources is, however, different for epistemic modals than for others. For epistemic modals, the ordering source is assumed to be a stereotypical ordering source, which would force the modal to quantify only over the most normal worlds of the (epistemic) modal base. For circumstantial modals, the ordering sources can be different: deontic, bouletic, teleological, or even empty (in the case of circumstantial modals).

Applying this to the examples in (74), (74b) asserts that there is at least one (normal) world compatible with the speaker's knowledge and beliefs where hydrangeas grow in the land, even though the speaker clearly knows and believes that no hydrangea grows in this land–a clear contradiction. By contrast, in (74a), there can still be a world in the circumstantial modal base (consisting of the set of worlds that are compatible with the circumstances) where hydrangeas grow in the land, even though the speaker knows/believes that such a world has not been actualized.

Consequently, one can hypothesize that *may* and *might*, unlike other modals, may not appear in contexts where the existence of the worlds in their modal base that meet their description is denied, which is, in full essence, the same type of restriction that *some* or *somewhat* impose on their domain of quantification; they are subject to the Non-Entailment-of-Non-Existence Condition. This, then, explains *may*'s and *might*'s scopal behaviour with respect to negation. For deontic *may* (73b), with the construal ¬>*may*, the sentence asserts that there is no world in line with the speaker's demands where she leaves, but the Non-Entailment-of-Non-Existence Condition is nevertheless met: there can still be worlds part of the circumstantial modal base where she leaves. By contrast, (73a), with the construal ¬> *may*, would assert that there is no (normal) world according to the speaker's knowledge/belief where she has been there. But this would violate the Non-Entailment-of-Non-Existence Condition, which excludes non-existence of such worlds. The Non-Entailment-of-Non-Existence Condition thus contradicts the assertion. This anomaly disappears once the scopal relations are reversed: then, the sentence means that there is a world where she has not been, which is fully in line with the speaker's knowledge/belief state and the Non-Entailment-of-Non-Existence Condition.

Consequently, modals that are lexically marked for being subject to the Non-Entailment-of-Non-Existence Condition behave PPI-like when used epistemically, and polarity-neutrally when used with another modal flavour. Since the usage of *might* is (lexically) restricted to epistemic usages, it must always behave PPI-like (cf. Iatridou and Zeijlstra 2013); *may*, on the other hand, must behave

PPI-like only when used epistemically, and not when used deontically. Other existential modals, such as *could*, lack this lexically encoded Non-Entailment-of-Non-Existence Condition and can thus freely take scope below negation when a negation is present:

(75) a. She could not have been there (^{OK}¬>could; $^{?}$could >¬) *epistemic*
     b. She could not leave now (^{OK}¬>could; $^{?}$could >¬) *deontic*

Further evidence for this analysis comes from the strength of such existential modal PPIs. If, indeed, the Non-Entailment-of-Non-Existence Condition underlies their PPI-hood, they must be weak and not strong PPIs. This prediction is again borne out:

(76) a. Few students may not have been there (few>may; may>few) *epistemic*
     b. Few students might not have been there (few>may; may>few) *epistemic*

(77) a. At most three students may not have been there (few>may; may>few) *epistemic*
     b. At most three students might not have been there (few>may; may>few) *epistemic*

Hence, there is a class of PPIs that are polarity-sensitive because they are subject to the Non-Entailment-of-Non-Existence Condition. This class is constituted by both existential NPIs and existential PPIs, and gives rise to at least two predictions. First, existential PPIs of this kind are always weak PPIs; they are banned from AA contexts only, and not from other DE contexts. Second, when these existential PPIs are modals, they only behave PPI-like when used epistemically. To the best of my knowledge, these predictions have not been falsified.

14.5 Conclusions

What we have seen in this chapter is that both Chierchia's approach to NPI-hood and Lin's approach in terms of the Non-Entailment-of-Existence Condition can be naturally applied to account for PPI-hood as well. Chierchia's approach, with its predecessors in Kadmon and Landman (1993) and Krifka (1995), naturally accounts for both strong and weak universal PPIs, and also predicts hybrid PIs to be possible, as shown for *until*. The mirror image of Lin's Non-Entailment-of-Existence Condition, the Non-Entailment-of-Non-Existence Condition, predicts that there are weak existential PPIs, which can be attested among both quantifiers over individuals and quantifiers over possible worlds. Strong existential PPIs, to the best of my knowledge, have not been attested.

What this chapter has tried to show is that what underlies the landscape of NPIs also partially underlies the landscape of PPIs. Naturally, this does not mean that these are the only kinds of PPIs possible in this sense. Giannakidou and Mari (2018), following work by Ernst (2009) and Nilsen (2003), have proposed that certain modal adverbs, such as *probably*, are PPIs, because, otherwise, the assertions they appear in are conflict with their presuppositions. In principle, such an approach should also be applicable to NPI-hood.

However, a question that arises is whether PPIs that lack any kind of NPI counterpart may also be attested, just as other types of NPIs lack a PPI counterpart. This question will be addressed in the next chapter, where we will argue that features encoding illocutionary force are indeed such PPIs, following Han (2000, 2001). This will then account for the ban of certain negatively marked clause-types like the ban on TNIs, which has already been discussed in the context of NC and the difference between Strict and Non-strict NC languages.

15
Negation and clause types

15.1 Introduction: Two phenomena

As discussed in Chapter 1, negation is an operator that applies propositionally. One might therefore perhaps expect NMs to appear in sentence-initial position. However, NMs cross-linguistically rather tend to occur in the so-called middle field of the clause (cf. Payne 1985; Horn 1989; Chapter 1), somewhere between CP and vP/VP. In fact, in several cases, negation is even banned from sentence-initial position. In this chapter, I discuss two such cases: (i) the ban on TNIs that is attested in many languages, and (ii) the ban on single NMs in sentence-initial position in V-to-C languages. I argue that both phenomena can be explained in a unified way as a result of the interplay between the syntactic and semantic status of NMs and the fact that operators that encode the illocutionary force of a speech act take scope from C^0.

I first introduce these two phenomena. In Subsection 15.1.1, I discuss what is meant by the ban on TNIs, and in Subsection 15.1.2, I introduce some data concerning the ban on single NMs in sentence-initial position in V-to-C languages. After that, in Subsection 15.1.3, I present an outline of the structure of the remainder of the chapter and the explanation I provide.

15.1.1 The ban on True Negative Imperatives

The first phenomenon addressed in this chapter is that not every language accepts so-called TNIs (terminology after Zanuttini 1994), a phenomenon that was already briefly introduced in Chapter 4. What is meant by TNIs is exemplified in (1) and (2) for Dutch and Polish, respectively. In Dutch main clauses, the finite verb precedes the NM *niet* (1a). In imperative clauses, where the finite verb is in V1 position (1b), the negation also follows the finite imperative verb without yielding ungrammaticality (1c). Therefore, Dutch can be said to allow TNIs: the sentence with the imperative verb can be negated in the same way as indicative sentences are negated. The same holds for Polish. In Polish, the NM always precedes the finite verb. This does not hold only for indicative verbs, but also for imperative verbs. As (2) shows, sentences with indicative and imperative verbs are negated in the same way. Polish is thus a language that allows TNIs as well.[1]

(1) a. Jij   slaapt   niet   (Dutch)
       you   sleep   NEG
       'You don't sleep'

   b. Slaap!
      sleep.IMP
      'Sleep!'

   c. Slaap *niet*!   (TNI)
      sleep.IMP neg
      'Don't sleep!'

(2) a. (Ty)   *nie*   pracujesz   (Polish)
       you   NEG   work.2SG
       'You don't work'

   b. Pracuj!
      work.2SG.IMP
      'Work!'

   c. *Nie*   pracuj!   (TNI)
      NEG   work.2SG.IMP
      'Don't work!'

Things are different, though, in a language like Spanish, as shown in (3). In Spanish, the NM *no* always occurs in preverbal position (3a). However, if the verb has an imperative form, as in (3b), it may not be combined with the NM (3c). Spanish does not allow TNIs. In order to convey the meaning of a negative imperative (sometimes referred to as a prohibitive), the negated imperative verb must be replaced by a subjunctive (3d). Such constructions are called Surrogate Negative Imperatives (SNIs).[2]

(3) a. Tu   *no*   lees   (Spanish)
       you   NEG   read.2SG
       'You don't read'

   b. ¡Lee!
      read.2SG.IMP
      'Read!'

---

[1] It should be noted that TNIs in Slavic languages always take imperfective morphology, even if their positive counterparts take the perfective (cf. Despic 2020), an issue I will not further address in this chapter.

[2] See Van der Auwera (2005) and references therein for many more examples of languages that ban TNIs and the way those languages express SNIs.

c. *¡No   lee!   (*TNI)
   NEG   read.2SG.IMP
   'Don't read!'
d. ¡No   leas!   (SNI)
   NEG   read.2SG.SUBJ
   'Don't read!'

This immediately leads to two questions: How can this ban on TNIs in languages such as Spanish be explained, and how can the attested cross-linguistic variation be explained?

15.1.2 The ban on single negative markers in sentence-initial position in V2 languages

In V-to-C languages (such as Dutch, German, or Swedish), negative expressions, including those containing NMs, are in principle allowed to occur in sentence-initial position (i.e., in Spec, CP), as shown in (4) and (5), sometimes facilitated by a contrastive continuation.

(4) a. *Niemand*   komt   (Dutch)
       nobody   comes
       'Nobody comes'
    b. *Niet*   iedereen   komt
       NEG   everybody comes
       'Not everybody comes'
    c. *Nooit*   neem   ik   een   hond
       never   take   I   a   dog
       'I'll never get a dog'

(5) a. *Niet*   Marie   heb   ik   gebeld #(, maar   Jan)   (Dutch)
       NEG   Marie   have   I   called,   but   Jan
       'I didn't call Marie but Jan'
    b. *Niet*   kippen   hebben   vier   poten #(, maar   koeien)
       NEG   chickens have   four   legs,   but   cows
       'Chickens don't have four legs, cows do'

However, the occurrence of single *niet* 'NEG' in Dutch is banned in this position. Sentence (6) is completely ruled out:

(6) *Niet*   komt   Jan   (Dutch)
    NEG   comes Jan
    'John doesn't come'

All V-to-C languages, in principle, ban single NMs in Spec, CP, although, as I will discuss in Section 15.3, some particular contexts allow for exceptions. This means that, in those languages that exhibit V-to-C movement in main clauses, single NMs are not allowed to occupy this position, but complex constituents including negation are, as is illustrated for German and Swedish below.

(7) a. *Nicht hat er Hans gesehen (German)
NEG has he Hans seen
'He didn't see Hans'

b. Keiner hat das gemacht
nobody has that done
'Nobody did that'

c. Nicht Hans hat er gesehen, sondern Peter
NEG Hans has he seen, but Peter
'He didn't see Hans, but Peter'

(8) a. *Inte var det Selma (Swedish[3])
NEG was it Selma
'It wasn't Selma'

b. Inte all kom till festen
NEG all came to party.the
'Not everybody came to the party'

c. Inte Selma utan Sven var det
NEG Selma but Sven was it
'It wasn't Selma but Sven'

The fact that constructions like (4) and (5) are plainly grammatical, whereas constructions like (6) are not, indicates that the following generalizations are correct: an NM may only appear in Spec, CP if it combines with an additional XP; NQs, on the other hand, can always appear in Spec, CP, not surprisingly as they underlyingly also consist of negations that combine with an additional XP (see Chapter 7).

(9) *[$_{CP}$ NM [$_{C^0}$ V$_{fin}$]]

(10) [$_{CP}$ [NM XP] / [NQ] [$_{C^0}$ V$_{fin}$]]

---

[3] Example from Brandtler 2006.

This leads to the following question: why is (9) ruled out, whereas (10) is permitted?

15.1.3 Outline

The general aim of this chapter is to show that both phenomena can be explained as a result of the interaction between features that encode the illocutionary force of a speech act and features that are responsible for the expression of negation. In short, such features are PPIs, which, therefore, are not allowed under the scope of negation.

In Section 15.2, I discuss the ban on TNIs. After discussing some previous analyses, I argue, in the spirit of Han's (2001) account, that this ban follows from the fact that no semantically active NM may stand in such a syntactic relation that this NM semantically outscopes the feature in C^0 that encodes the illocutionary force of a speech act. This correctly predicts that all languages in which such a semantically NM is syntactically non-phrasal ban TNIs. In Section 15.3, I extend the analysis presented in Section 15.2 to the ban on single NMs in sentence-initial position in V-to-C languages. I argue that this ban also results from the fact that no negative material is allowed to outscope the illocutionary features in C^0 and that, therefore, negative constituents may only appear in Spec, CP if they can be reconstructed at LF. Section 15.4 concludes.

15.2 The ban on True Negative Imperatives

This section presents a full explanation of the ban on TNIs and is set up as follows. First, in Subsection 15.2.1, I discuss three previous accounts for the ban on TNIs: first Rivero's (1994) and Rivero and Terzi's (1995) account, second Zanuttini's (1997) account, and third Han's (2001) account. I argue that, while the first two accounts face serious difficulties, Han's account is essentially correct for the analysis of Romance languages, but fails to extend to, e.g., Slavic languages, where TNIs are accepted despite their NMs being syntactic heads. I demonstrate that this problem disappears once it is adopted that NMs are not always semantically negative, as argued for intensively in Chapter 5.

In Subsection 15.2.2, then, I argue that adopting Han's (2001) analysis in combination with a proper treatment of the semantics and syntax of NMs explains both the ban on TNIs and its cross-linguistic distribution. In Subsection 15.2.3, I show that, now, two typological generalizations are predicted: (i) every language with an overt NM X^0 that is semantically negative bans TNIs; and (ii) every language that bans TNIs exhibits an overt NM X^0. I demonstrate that both predictions appear to be borne out, at least for the languages investigated.

15.2.1 Previous analyses

Rivero (1994); Rivero and Terzi (1995)
Rivero (1994) and Rivero and Terzi (1995) assume that the clausal spine (of negative sentences) always has structural relations as in (11).

(11)   CP > NegP > IP > VP

They further propose that the difference between Slavic languages (which generally allow TNIs) and Romance languages (which generally disallow them) concerns the position where imperative force takes scope in the sentence. This is either IP (induced by movement of V_{imp} to I^0) or CP (induced by verbal movement to C^0). Now the difference between Slavic and Romance languages immediately becomes clear: If the Neg^0 position is filled by an overt element, i.e., by an NM, then verbal movement from I^0 to C^0 is no longer allowed, because of the Head Movement Constraint (HMC) (Travis 1984). Hence, Slavic languages, such as Polish, where the verb is assumed to raise to I^0, allow TNIs, whereas Romance languages, such as Italian, where the verb moves to C^0, do not (see (12)).

(12) a. [$_{CP}$ [$_{NegP}$ [$_{Neg}{}^0$ *Nie*] [$_{IP}$ [$_{I}{}^0$ pracuj$_{[IMP]i}$] [$_{VP}$ t$_i$]]]]   (Polish)
                     NEG   work.2SG.IMP
   'Don't work!'
   b. *[$_{CP}$ [$_{C}{}^0$ Parla$_{[IMP]i}$] [$_{NegP}$ [$_{Neg}{}^0$ *no*] [$_{IP}$ [$_{I}{}^0$ t$_i$] [$_{VP}$ t$_i$]]]]   (Italian[4])
                  talk.2SG.IMP   NEG
   'Don't talk!'

Rivero and Terzi defend their view that the position of the imperative verb is subject to parametric variation (either in I^0 or C^0) by presenting data from languages such as Serbian, in which imperatives generally precede their clitics. This indicates that the verb resides in C^0, unless the cliticized verb is preceded by some other element (e.g. a fronted object).[5]

(13) a. Čitaj   je!   (Serbian)
         read-2SG.IMP it
         'Read it!'

---

[4] At first sight, the ban on TNIs seems to apply only to the singular imperative forms in Italian. However, the Italian plural imperative form and the corresponding 2nd-person indicative are phonologically identical. I follow Zanuttini (1997), who takes plural imperatives to be banned as well and takes the (phonologically identical) indicative forms as the corresponding SNI. This adoption is in line with the observation that no other language banning TNIs makes a distinction between singular and plural imperatives.
[5] Examples taken from Rivero and Terzi (1995), also cited in Han (2001) and Zeijlstra (2013a).

b. Knjige imčitajte!
   books to-them.read-2PL.IMP
   'Read books to them!'

For Rivero and Terzi, these data show that the imperative verb only fronts to C° in order to avoid the ban, imposed by the phonological constraint known as the Tobler-Mussafia Law, on clause-initial clitics (13a). In cases where the Tobler-Mussafia Law cannot apply because some other element precedes these clitics anyway, the verb may remain in I⁰ (13b). The data in (13), though, do not show that the finite verb stays in I°: the data show only that the verb may keep its clitics in preverbal position if these clitics are preceded by a leftward object. An alternative analysis may very well be that, in both examples, the imperative verb is in C°, but that, in cases where the verb is also in clause-initial position, clitics are spelled out in a lower position (either because they are stranded or because some lower copy of the clitics is spelled out). Two arguments plead in favour of the latter.

First, since the Tobler-Mussafia Law is a phonological constraint, it would be a puzzle how I-to-C movement is triggered in examples such as (13a): at this stage of the derivation, it is not known that not moving the verb to C⁰ will make the derivation crash at a later stage. Second, apart from these southern Balkan languages, all other studied languages front their imperative verbs to C⁰, suggesting then that fronting imperative verbs to C⁰ rather applies universally. The only reason not to assume imperative-verb movement to C⁰ is that it opens up a way to account for the presence of negative imperatives and examples such as (13b). As I will show in the remainder of this chapter, though, negative imperatives in those languages do not form an argument against a universal C⁰ position for imperative verbs either.

Apart from this, Rivero's and Rivero and Terzi's analysis faces two serious problems. The first problem is that it is unclear why, in Romance languages, the NM is not allowed to cliticize onto V$_{imp}$, so that they move together to C⁰ as a unit, a point already addressed by Han (2001). Han follows Rizzi (1982) by arguing that, in constructions such as (14), which consist of a participle or an infinitive, the subject occupies a Spec, IP position and the auxiliary moves to C⁰. In case of negation, the NM *non* then joins the verb on its way to C⁰. Rizzi refers to these structures as Aux-to-Comp constructions.[6]

(14) a. [[$_C$⁰ avendo] Gianni fatto questo]   (Italian)
        having Gianni done this
        'Gianni having done this, ...'

    b. [[$_C$⁰ non avendo] Gianni fatto questo]
        NEG having Gianni done this
        'Gianni having not done this, ...'

---

[6] Examples taken from Rizzi (1982). These examples are also discussed in Han (2001) and Zeijlstra (2013a).

If, in the cases above, *non* is allowed to attach to the auxiliary verb, it is unclear why this movement would not be allowed in the case of V_{imp}.[7]

The second problem, also put forward by Han, is that, in the structure in (12a), the operator that encodes the illocutionary force of an imperative is c-commanded by the negation. It has already been noted by Frege (1892) and Lee (1988) that negation cannot operate on the illocutionary force of the sentence, but only on its propositional content. A negative assertion remains an assertion, a negative question remains a question, and a negative command has to remain a command. If negation is part of the proposition, and illocutions apply to propositions, negation can never take scope over any illocutionary operator. This renders illocutionary elements effectively PPIs.[8] Hence, in Rivero and Terzi's analyses for Slavic languages, either negation takes scope from too high a position, or the imperative operator takes scope from too low a position.

Zanuttini (1997)
Zanuttini (1997) discusses different types of NMs, basing herself on a number of Romance dialects (mostly from Northern Italy). She distinguishes, for instance, between NMs that can negate a clause by themselves and those that require an additional NM in order to express sentential negation. The differences are given in (15): Italian *non* can negate a clause by itself, French *ne* cannot, as discussed in Chapter 4 as well.

(15) a. Gianni non telefona (Italian)
     Gianni NEG calls
     'Gianni doesn't call'
  b. Jean ne téléphone *(pas) (French)
     Jean NEG calls NEG
     'Jean doesn't call'

Zanuttini argues that the difference between Italian *non* and French *ne* can be reduced to the properties of the functional projections they occupy: Italian *non* occupies a different functional projection in the clausal spine from the one that French *ne* does. As she observes that all Italian varieties she has studied have an NM of the *non*-type (i.e., an NM that can negate a clause by itself), which bans TNIs, she relates the ban on TNIs to particular properties of this functional head.

---

[7] Rivero and Terzi (1995) argue that, in these cases, the $V_{part/inf}$ does not raise to C^0, but to a position lower than Neg^0, and that the subject is in an even lower position. This analysis seems to be contradicted by the fact that *(non) avendo* may even precede speaker-oriented adverbs such as *evidentemente* 'evidently', which occupy a position higher than NegP, as pointed out by Cinque (1999) and repeated in Han (2001).

[8] Note that this does not mean that no other particles or focus-sensitive operators may apply to illocutionary elements. See, for instance, Krifka (2001b) and Iatridou and Tatevosov (2016) for a discussion on quantification into questions or on particles like *even* having entire questions as their focus, respectively.

Moreover, Zanuttini also observes that, in several of those varieties, these NMs are sensitive to mood. In those varieties, negative subjunctives quite often require different NMs from those indicatives require, an observation that goes back to Sadock and Zwicky (1985). In order to account for the ban on TNIs, Zanuttini elaborates on Sadock and Zwicky's observations. She assumes that for all languages/varieties where NMs can negate a clause by themselves, these come about in two kinds: NMs for indicatives and NMs for non-indicatives (i.e., subjunctives and, in principle, also imperatives). In those varieties where there seems to be only one NM (which can negate a clause by itself), she also presumes two lexically different NMs to be present, which happen to be homophonous.

Thus, she claims that, in Italian, the NM *non* is lexically ambiguous between *non*-1, which may occur in clauses with subjunctive or imperative mood, and *non*-2, which may only appear in indicative clauses. Furthermore, Zanuttini proposes that *non*-1 subcategorizes a MoodP, whereas *non*-2 does not:

(16) a. [$_{NegP}$ *non*-1 [$_{MoodP}$ … [$_{VP}$]]]   subjunctive/imperative clauses
 b. [$_{NegP}$ *non*-2 … [$_{VP}$]]   indicative clauses

Now, Zanuttini has to demonstrate why the construction in (16a) is doomed to be ungrammatical when the finite verb has imperative mood. In order to do so, she takes the fact that imperative verbs are often morphologically defective to indicate that they lack any [MOOD]-feature. Consequently, the [MOOD]-feature on Mood⁰ cannot be checked and the sentence becomes ungrammatical. In other clauses, e.g. indicatives, no MoodP is selected, and thus the sentence is grammatical, as shown in (17). In subjunctives, the verb is strong enough to check the [MOOD]-feature on Mood⁰.⁹

(17) a. *[$_{NegP}$ *Non*-1 [$_{MoodP}$ [$_{Mood'[Mood]}$ telefona$_{[IMP]i}$] a Gianni [$_{VP}$ t$_i$]]] (Italian)
  └─x─┘
   NEG   call.2SG.IMP to Gianni
   'Don't call Gianni!'

 b. [Io [$_{NegP}$ *non*-2 telefono$_i$ a Gianni [$_{VP}$ t$_i$]]]
   I   NEG   call.1SG to Gianni
   'I don't call Gianni'

This analysis suffers from three problems, however. First, the lexical distinction between *non*-1 and *non*-2 does not seem well-motivated. The piece of evidence that *non* is lexically ambiguous comes from the observation that, in languages that have two distinct NMs, these markers are often sensitive to mood distinctions in the verbal paradigm (cf. Sadock and Zwicky 1985), resulting in one NM that is used in indicatives and another that is used in subjunctives. However, no language-internal evidence is presented for the homophony of two different NMs *non*.

---

⁹ Since no MoodP is selected in affirmative clauses, positive imperatives are not problematic.

Moreover, it is unclear that the NM that must appear in imperatives is the same as the one that appears in subjunctives. Take, for instance, Greek, which is a language that exhibits such a mood distinction with respect to NMs. In Greek, the NM *dhen* is only used in indicative clauses, and the NM *mi* only in subjunctive clauses; TNIs are not only ruled out if *dhen* is the NM, but also if the negation is expressed by *mi*. The SNI can only be formed using the NM *mi* in combination with a subjunctive verb, as the following data from Rivero and Terzi (1995: 304) show:

(18) a. **Dhen* to diavase! (Greek)
     neg   it read.IMP
     'Don't read it!'
  b. **Mi* to grapse!
     neg it write.IMP
     'Don't write it!'
  c. *Mi* to grapsis![10]
     neg it write.SUBJ
     'Don't write it!'

Therefore, it cannot be stated a priori that a language like Greek exhibits one NM for imperatives/subjunctives, on the one hand, and one for indicatives, on the other; it rather has one NM for indicatives and one NM for subjunctives, and no NM for imperatives.[11] Consequently, the fact that several languages have different NMs for different moods does not hold as an argument for the alleged lexical ambiguity of, e.g., Italian *non*, along the lines of mood.

Second, it is doubtful whether imperative verbs actually lack mood features. Morphologically, Greek verbs, for instance, do exhibit mood inflection, but rather lack temporal features. Hence, Greek would then be expected to rule in TNIs, contrary to fact. The question thus arises whether the apparent morphological defectiveness of imperative verbs can be taken to indicate that imperative verbs lack [MOOD]-features in the first place.

Finally, Zanuttini's analysis is too strong. It predicts that all languages with an NM that can negate a clause by itself are languages that ban TNIs, but this prediction is not borne out. Many Slavic languages have a negative head marker (such as Polish *nie*) that negates a clause by itself, yet these languages allow TNIs. Note that, in most Slavic languages, the imperative seems to be morphologically defective as well. Zanuttini is aware of these facts and takes her analysis to apply to Romance languages only. Nevertheless, as acknowledged by Zanuttini, even within Romance, one may find varieties which allow TNIs. Old Italian (19) is an example from Zanuttini (1997):

---

[10] The position of the pronominal clitic *to* 'it' is related to the imperative/subjunctive distinction. Imperatives require the clitic to appear encliticized to the verb; subjunctives require left-adjunction.
[11] For more discussion on Greek negative imperatives and subjunctives, see Oikonomou (2016).

15.2 THE BAN ON TRUE NEGATIVE IMPERATIVES

(19) *Ni   ti   tormenta   di   questo!*   (Old Italian)
     NEG yourself torment.2SG.IMP of this
     'Don't torment yourself with this!'

Han (2001)

Han (2001), finally, argues that the ban on TNIs does not follow from syntactic requirements that have been violated, but from a semantic violation: the imperative operator (i.e., the operator that encodes the illocutionary force of an imperative, henceforth Op$_{IMP}$) may not appear in the scope of negation, as discussed before. Op$_{IMP}$ is realized by moving V$_{imp}$, carrying a feature [IMP] (or [DIR] for directive), onto C^0. Han takes negation in Romance languages to head a projection somewhere high in the IP domain. Hence, first, negation head-adjoins to V$_{imp}$, and then, as a unit, they jointly move further, to C^0. As a result, [IMP] remains in the c-command domain of negation, which violates the constraint that negation may only operate on the propositional content of the clause. The structure (20) is thus semantically anomalous.

(20)   *   (Spanish)

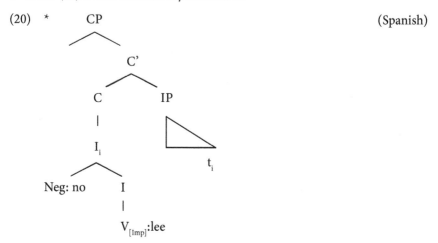

Under this analysis, it becomes immediately clear why TNIs are allowed in languages like Dutch. In those languages, NMs are phrasal, i.e., they do not occupy a head position in the clausal spine, and thus do not block movement of V$_{imp}$ to C^0, as illustrated in (21).

(21) [$_{CP}$ slaap$_{[Imp]i}$ [$_{vP}$ *niet* t$_i$]]   (Dutch)

For Slavic languages, Han assumes that V$_{imp}$ does not move to C^0. Consequently, this would mean that V$_{imp}$ remains under the scope of negation (as the NM occupies an intervening head position in those languages, V$_{imp}$ cannot move across it). Han argues that, in those cases, the feature [IMP] moves out of V$_{imp}$ and moves to C^0. Thus, Op$_{IMP}$ outscopes negation, as demonstrated in (22) for Polish.

(22)   [$_{CP}$ [IMP]$_i$ [$_{NegP}$ *nie* [$_{IP}$ pracuj$_i$]]]   (Polish)

Han's analysis suffers from two problems, though. First, there is no reason, as discussed before, to assume that Slavic imperatives do not raise to C. Second, the fact that Han allows feature-movement for the Slavic languages speaks against the analysis for Romance languages, since it remains unclear why such feature-movement would not be possible in Romance languages. If movement of the verb to C inevitably results in ungrammaticality, why could the verb not stay below C and have its [IMP] features still raise to C? If featural movement can apply in Slavic languages, nothing should ban it from applying in Romance languages as well.[12]

It must be noted, though, that this is only problematic for Han as she tacitly assumes that NMs always have the semantics of a negative operator. However, as I have argued in Chapter 4, this assumption is incorrect. Once it is adopted that NMs may be semantically non-negative themselves, this problem to Han's analysis disappears.

Concluding remarks
To conclude, the first two analyses that I have discussed so far face serious problems. The third analysis, on the other hand, faces problems that do not necessarily prove this analysis wrong, but may rather be the result of some incorrect assumptions on the semantics of NMs in general.

15.2.2 Explaining the ban on True Negative Imperatives

Given the discussion of the previous analyses of the ban on TNIs and the semantic and syntactic status of NMs in Chapter 4, the tool set is now complete that is needed to explain the peculiar behaviour of TNIs. Both the ban on TNIs and its cross-linguistic distribution can be explained on the basis of the following three well-motivated assumptions.

First, following Han (2001), imperative force is hosted on V$_{imp}$ in C^0, and, therefore, the operator inducing the illocutionary force of the imperative speech act must take scope from C^0, triggering movement of V$_{imp}$ to this position, a standard analysis in the syntax of imperatives. Second, operators that encode illocutionary force may not be operated on by a (semantic) negation. Third, according to the HMC (Travis 1984), an instance of relativized minimality (cf. Rizzi 1989), heads may not move across other (overt) heads.

From these assumptions, it follows that, if an NM that is semantically negative occupies an intervening head position, the verb is not allowed to move across this NM, and the semantic negative feature will therefore c-command the imperative feature on V$_{imp}$, ruling out TNIs.

---

[12] Though as the ill-formedness of TNIs is purely semantic, this argument may suffer from a look-ahead problem.

15.2 THE BAN ON TRUE NEGATIVE IMPERATIVES

As the availability of TNIs thus depends on two different properties of NMs, I analyse the ban on TNIs by discussing different classes of languages: Class I languages, languages that have an NM that both is semantically active (carrying [iNEG]) and occupies some Neg⁰ position; Class II languages, languages that also have a non-phrasal NM, but where this marker carries a feature [uNEG]; Class III languages, languages that have only phrasal NMs.

Class I languages

The first class of languages consists of languages that exhibit a non-phrasal NM which carries an [iNEG]-feature. To these languages, Han's analysis applies straightforwardly. V_{imp} must raise to C⁰, and as the NM Neg⁰ must be attached to V⁰, this NM c-commands [IMP]. Since [IMP] has the illocutionary force of a speech act, it follows that the imperative operator takes scope from V_{fin} in C⁰. Given the syntactic head status of the NM (and the fact that it has already targeted the highest head position available in the clausal spine), V_{imp} cannot escape from this unit. This is illustrated for Spanish in (23a).

If, however, the imperative verb is replaced by a subjunctive, nothing leads to ungrammaticality (see (23b)). This suggests that subjunctives themselves do not encode any illocutionary feature of their own, i.e., they do not carry a feature that encodes illocutionary force. Subjunctives do come along with particular illocutionary effects, yet this does not entail that these illocutionary effects must be due to their lexical semantics. Instead, I take subjunctives to be lexically-semantically underspecified for illocutionary force and their illocutionary effects (such as the prohibitive readings of SNIs) to be derived pragmatically (though see Schlenker 2005 for an alternative proposal). Speakers need to fill the functional gap and use the non-imperative construction with the subjunctive as a replacement. The SNI does not yield the reading of a prohibitive, but it just implicates one.[13]

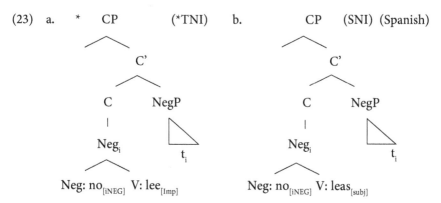

(23) a. *CP (*TNI)   b. CP (SNI) (Spanish)

---

[13] Han (2001) suggests that the fact that the subjunctive encodes an irrealis plays a role in the imperative interpretation, but this is contradicted by the fact that (for instance) an indicative can fulfil this function as well (Italian plural SNIs exhibit an indicative).

Class II languages

Languages that have non-phrasal NMs carrying [uNEG] behave differently with respect to the ban on TNIs. Czech, Polish, Bulgarian, and Bosnian/Serbian/Croatian, on the one hand, accept TNIs, whereas Romanian, Hungarian, and also Greek, on the other, disallow them. I begin with the first kind of languages.

In Czech, Polish, Bulgarian, Serbian, and Croatian, the NM is always in preverbal position. All these Slavic languages are Strict NC languages, and their (preverbal) NMs thus carry a feature [uNEG]. These NMs are semantically non-negative, and semantic negation is thus introduced by $Op_\neg$.

This $Op_\neg$ occupies a position below CP, arguably in Spec, NegP. The clausal structure, therefore, does not block TNIs.[14] In Polish, V_{imp} moves to Neg^0, attaches to *nie*, and, as a unit [$_{Neg}$ *nie*-V_{imp}], moves along to C^0. $Op_\neg$ is Spec, NegP, and [IMP] takes scope from C^0 and outscopes negation. Thus, in these languages, the scopal condition imperative > negation is met. This is illustrated for Polish in (24).

(24)
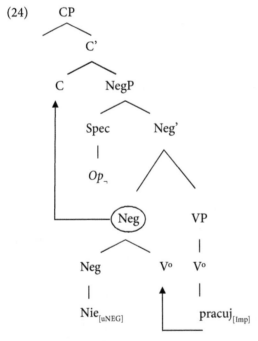

Still, not every language that exhibits a semantically non-negative head marker allows TNIs. Examples are Romanian, Hungarian, and Greek. These languages also exhibit X^0 NMs carrying [uNEG]-features, but, contrary to what would be

---

[14] One may wonder, given the parsing analysis presented in Chapters 4–5 for $Op_\neg$, why $Op_\neg$ must not be included in a higher position. However, if the parser knows that $Op_\neg$ cannot take scope from such a position, it can be included in the highest propositional layer of the clause. Only semantically non-anomalous parses can be generated.

15.2 THE BAN ON TRUE NEGATIVE IMPERATIVES

expected, they ban TNIs. Hence, additional explanations are required to account for the ban on TNIs in these languages. Of the three languages studied here, two languages have an additional NM for subjunctives. Hungarian *nem* is replaced by *ne* in subjunctives, and Greek *dhen* is replaced by *mi*.

Let us first focus on Hungarian. Hungarian imperative verbs are fine with this other NM *ne*, as is shown in (25).

(25) a. **Nem* olvass! (Hungarian)
NEG read.IMP
'Don't read!'
b. *Ne* olvass!
NEG read.IMP
'Don't read!'

Ne and *nem* are both allowed to participate in Strict NC constructions, and, therefore, both carry [uNEG]. They behave similarly to the Slavic NMs. The only difference is that *nem* and *ne* differ in their feature make-up with respect to mood. A suggestion would be that *nem* carries a feature [−IRR], which disallows it from participating in subjunctives and imperatives, and that *ne* would carry [+IRR]. (This is much in line with Zanuttini's 1997 analysis.) Crucially, though, the mood distinction of Hungarian NMs is not related to the ban on TNIs. Strictly speaking, Hungarian does allow TNIs, and imperatives and subjunctives cannot be combined with *nem* for independent reasons. Hungarian is, in this sense, similar to the Slavic languages, and the structure in (24), mutatis mutandis, applies to Hungarian as well.

Now, Romanian needs to be discussed. Romanian is a Strict NC language that lacks an additional NM for non-indicative mood. Even so, it still disallows TNIs (26):

(26) **Nu* lucreaza! (Romanian)
NEG work.IMP
'Don't work!'

Thus, TNIs in this language must be blocked for a different reason. The explanation of the ban on TNIs lies with a particular property of the Romanian NM that forbids further verbal movement after cliticization with the finite verb. This is independently motivated by the fact that Romanian verbs allow inversion with respect to their clitic cluster: In (27b), the verb moves to a higher position, leaving its clitic cluster in a stranded position.

(27) a. M-as mira se vina Ion (Romanian)
me-AUX.SUBJB be.surprised AUX.SUBJB come Ion
'I would be surprised if Ion came'

b. Mira   m-as   se   vina   Ion
   be.surprised me-AUX.SUBJB AUX.SUBJB come   Ion
   'I would be surprised if Ion came'

This movement is forbidden, however, in the case of cliticization with NMs. Both verbal movement out of the clitic cluster and clitic inversion below Neg⁰ are forbidden in Romanian, as has been demonstrated by Monachesi (2001) and Alboiu (2002), and as is illustrated in (28).[15]

(28) a. *Nu*   m-as   mira   se   vina   Ion   (Romanian)
         NEG   me-AUX.SUBJB be.surprised AUX.SUBJB come   Ion
         'I wouldn't be surprised if Ion came'
     b. *Mira   nu   m-as   se   vina   Ion
         be.surprised   NEG me-AUX.SUBJB AUX.SUBJB come   Ion
         'I wouldn't be surprised if Ion came'
     c. *Mira   m-as   *nu* se   vina   Ion
         be.surprised   me-AUX.SUBJB NEG AUX.SUBJB come   Ion
         'I wouldn't be surprised if Ion came'

The data in (27) and (28) show that Romanian *nu* blocks verbal movement to a higher position than Neg⁰, and thus acts differently from how other clitics in Romanian act. If verbal movement to a higher position is ruled out in Romanian negative clauses, a negated imperative verb may never raise to C⁰, and this immediately explains the ban on TNIs in this language. Hence, the ban on TNIs in Romanian does not follow from the general mechanism outlined in this chapter, but rather from independently motivated properties of Romanian cliticized verbs. This explanation of the Romanian ban on TNIs may also extend to other languages, such as Greek. It is arguably the case that the clitical behaviour of the Greek NM blocks TNIs in this language, too.

Hence, the languages that seem to be counterexamples to the analysis of the ban on TNIs presented here appear actually not to be that.

Class III languages

It also follows that, if an NM is phrasal, TNIs should, in principle, be accepted. Regardless of its position, the NM cannot block movement of V_{imp} to C⁰. Hence, the imperative can always take scope from C⁰, and all scopal requirements are met.

Let us show this for Dutch. As the position of the NM in Dutch is a vP-adjunct position, the structure of a TNI in Dutch would be like (29).

(29) [CP slaap[Imp]i [vP niet tᵢ]]   (Dutch)

The analysis of Class III languages extends to NC languages without a negative head marker, such as Bavarian, Quebecois, and Yiddish. Given the explanation

---

[15] Thanks to Adrian Brasoveanu (pers. comm.) for providing me these examples.

I've provided, it is not expected that TNIs are banned in these languages either. As shown in (30) for Yiddish, verbal movement to C^0 is not blocked, and, therefore, TNIs are allowed.

(30) Kuk nit! (Yiddish)
 look NEG
 'Don't look!'
 [$_{CP}$ kuk$_{[Imp]i}$ [$_{vP}$ nit [$_{VP}$ t$_i$]]]

15.2.3 Additional evidence

The analysis I have presented predicts that there is a unidirectional relation between the semantic value of NMs and the ban on TNIs, as well as a unidirectional relation between the ban on TNIs and the syntactic status (phrasal or non-phrasal) of the NM. This implies that the analysis can be evaluated crosslinguistically, to see whether these generalizations hold, both synchronically and diachronically. Moreover, this analysis now only applies to imperatives, whereas, in principle, it should rule out all kinds of illocutionary features being outscoped by negation.

Typological evidence
On the basis of the assumptions I've set out, the two following generalizations, **G1** and **G2**, must hold:

(31) **G1**: Every language with an overt NM occupying Neg^0 and carrying [iNEG] bans TNIs.
 G2: Every language that bans TNIs exhibits an overt NM occupying Neg^0.

G1 follows, for reasons I have explained: if an NM in Neg^0 carrying [iNEG] attaches to V$_{imp}$, it illegitimately c-commands the feature that encodes the illocutionary force. Since this NM occupies an intervening head position between C^0 and V^0, the verb can by no means move out of this c-command constellation. Therefore, TNIs are ruled out in languages with overt NMs in Neg^0 carrying [iNEG].

G2 also follows from the HMC. If a language does not exhibit an NM occupying Neg^0, this marker can never block verbal movement to C^0, and TNIs must be allowed.

These generalizations indicate that both the semantic value of the NM and its syntactic status play a role in determining whether and why a language bans TNIs. **G2** has already been observed by Zanuttini (1997); **G1** has first been presented in Zeijlstra (2013a).

A number of languages have been investigated for the syntactic status of their NMs and their semantic value. Moreover, it has been investigated whether these languages allow TNIs or not. The results are shown in (32) and indicate that the generalizations that follow from this analysis are indeed correct (at least for the studied languages), thus providing additional evidence for the proposed analysis.[16]

(32)　Language sample

Class:	Language:	Neg. marker in Neg⁰	Neg. marker: [iNEG]	TNIs allowed
I	Spanish	+	+	−
	Italian	+	+	−
	Portuguese	+	+	−
II	Czech	+	−	+
	Polish	+	−	+
	Bulgarian	+	−	+
	Serbian/Croatian	+	−	+
	Albanian	+	−	−
	Greek	+	−	−
	Hebrew	+	−	−
	Romanian	+	−	−
	Hungarian	+	−	−
III	Dutch	−	+	+
	Danish	−	+	+
	German	−	+	+
	Norwegian	−	+	+
	Swedish	−	+	+
	Bavarian	−	−	+
	Yiddish	−	−	+
	Quebecois	−	−	+

Diachronic evidence

The analysis is also confirmed by diachronic facts. In Non-strict NC languages with an NM X⁰ (carrying [iNEG]), TNIs must be banned. This holds, for instance,

---

[16] In order to make truly typological claims, the language sample should be made much broader and include languages from all kinds of language families. This is still a task for further research. For a typological overview of languages that (seem to) ban TNIs, the reader is referred to Van der Auwera (2005).

for Italian. However, it is known that Old Italian allowed TNIs (as pointed out by Zanuttini 1997 and shown in (33)).[17]

(33) a. *Ni   ti   tormenta   di questo!*   (Old Italian)
          NEG yourself torment.2SG.IMP   of this
          'Don't torment yourself with this!'

    b. **Non*   telefona   a   Gianni!*   (Cont. Italian)
          NEG   call.2SG.IMP to Gianni
          'Don't call Gianni!'

The analysis presented here predicts that it should be impossible for the NM in Old Italian to carry a feature [iNEG]. In other words, the analysis predicts that the NM in Old Italian must have carried [uNEG]. Consequently, Old Italian cannot have been a Non-strict NC language. This prediction is indeed borne out. Old Italian was, in fact, a Strict NC language, as confirmed by the data in (34), and discussed in Chapter 6.[18]

(34) a. *Mai   nessuno   oma non   si   piò   guarare* (Old Italian)
          n-ever n-even-one   man NEG   himself   can   protect
          'Nobody can ever protect himself'

    b. *Nessuno   (*non)   ha   detto   niente*   (Cont. Italian)
          n-body   neg   has   said   n-thing
          'Nobody said anything'

Apparently, Italian developed from a Strict NC language into a Non-strict NC language. Since, in Old Italian, TNIs were allowed, the change from Strict NC into Non-strict NC must have caused the ban on TNIs. Similar observations can be made for the development of Portuguese, which used to be a Strict NC language that allowed TNIs, but transformed into a Non-strict NC language that bans TNIs (see Martins 2000, Zeijlstra 2008a, b, and Chapter 6 for a more detailed analysis of the development of Romance languages with respect to NC).

The analysis I have presented predicts that the diachronic developments with respect to the acceptance of TNIs and the kind of NC that a language exhibits are related. That this prediction has been confirmed by the (Old) Italian data further supports the presented account for the ban on TNIs.

Finally, if the explanation I have presented is correct, it follows that not only should imperatives be banned, but all sentences in which a feature that encodes the illocutionary force of a speech act is outscoped by a semantic negation. In the next section, I demonstrate that this is exactly what blocks single NMs in Spec, CP. The fact that the ban on single NMs in Spec, CP follows from the analysis presented here is a final piece of evidence in its favour.

---

[17] Example taken from Zanuttini (1997).
[18] Examples taken from Martins (2000: 194).

15.3 The ban on single negative markers in sentence-initial position in V-to-C languages

In this section, I address the problem of the ban on single NMs in Spec, CP in V-to-C languages, formalized as in (35) (repeated from (9)).

(35) *$[_{CP}$ NM $[_{C}{}^{0}\, V_{fin}]]$

In the first subsection, I discuss why a previous analysis of this problem proposed by Barbiers (2002) is incorrect. After that, I argue that the same principles underlying the ban on TNIs are also responsible for the ban on topicalized NMs in V-to-C languages, alongside the well-established Merge-over-Move Constraint (Chomsky 1995a), thus providing additional evidence for the correctness of that explanation. In this section, I take Dutch as a standard example for V-to-C languages, but the analysis extends to other Germanic languages as well.[19]

15.3.1 Previous analysis: Barbiers (2002)

In order to account for the unacceptability of (35), Barbiers (2002) adopts Chomsky's (1995b) Bare Phrase Structure theory and proposes that the phrasal status of Dutch *niet* is actually flexible: It may appear in head position (a projection of a NegP) as well as in phrasal position. Apart from that, Barbiers takes *niet* to have some properties that are similar to those of expletives: (i) it carries a case feature ([uT(ense)], in Barbiers' analysis), and (ii) it cannot receive a theta-role.

These expletive-like properties of *niet* strongly limit its distribution. Either *niet* heads a projection of its own, or it appears in those phrasal positions that respect its syntactic conditions. As *niet* needs to have its case feature checked, it may not appear in adjunct positions and thus cannot appear in a verb's fixed argument position either, as it would receive a theta-role there. The only non-head position where *niet* would be allowed to appear is the position where a verb assigns case but no theta-role, i.e., the position where one usually attests expletive objects, e.g., the object position of verbs with an extraposed CP object. Such verbs, as illustrated for *zien* 'to see', allow objects to appear in two possible positions, depending on

---

[19] Dutch is standardly analysed as a V-to-C language after Den Besten (1983), as it exhibits Verb Second (V2). Nevertheless, some scholars have argued that not every instance of V2 should be analysed in terms of V-to-C movement. Zwart (1993) argues that non-inverted Dutch main clauses exhibit V-to-I movement, and Iatridou and Kroch (1992) have analysed cases of Icelandic and Yiddish (embedded) Verb Second as V-to-I movement, too. However, these arguments are not uncontroversial and have been countered elsewhere in the literature. I refer the reader to Weerman (1989), Vikner and Schwartz (1996), and Koeneman (2000), who all retain the original V-to-C hypothesis, for an evaluation of these arguments. In this chapter, I follow these authors in taking all instances of Germanic V2 to be V-to-C movement.

the syntactic category of the object (DP/CP). If the object is an extraposed CP, an expletive *het* 'it' may appear in the position where a DP object would appear:

(36) a. ... dat Jan die vrouw ziet (Dutch)
...that Jan that woman sees
'... that Jan sees that woman'
b. ... dat Jan (het) ziet dat die vrouw rondloopt
... that Jan (it) sees that that woman around.walks
'... that Jan sees that that woman walks around'

The verb thus has different positions for DP and CP complements, as shown in (37).

(37) [$_{VP}$ <DP> V <CP]

As DPs, contrary to CPs, require the verb to assign case to them, the DP position is a position that receives case. If, however, the verb selects for a CP complement, which receives the verb's theta-role, the DP position must still be available for elements that receive case, but do not receive a theta-role. Such examples are (object) expletives, and, according to Barbiers (2002), also Dutch *niet*.

This means that, except when it occupies an object position of a verb with an extraposed object, *niet* must be a syntactic head in other cases; and owing to its syntactic head status, *niet* may not move to a phrasal position, such as Spec, CP.

Barbiers consequently argues that, only in those cases where *niet* is able to occupy a specifier position, it may move out to Spec, CP, as, otherwise, we would be dealing with illicit head-to-spec movement. Barbiers motivates this analysis by presenting examples of exactly such constructions, where he shows that *niet* can indeed be fronted, such as (38), where *niet* is allowed in Spec, CP.

(38) Ik had wel gezien dat Jan aankwam, maar niet$_i$
I had PRT seen that Jan arrived, but NEG
had ik t$_i$ gezien dat Eddy vertrok
had I seen that Eddy left
'I did see that Jan arrived, but I didn't see that Eddy left' (Dutch)

However, Barbiers' analysis is problematic in several respects. First of all, it is unclear how verbal movement across the NM can be explained if *niet* constitutes a functional projection of its own: in Dutch main clauses, finite verbs are always able to move across *niet*, which would be unexpected if *niet* were a head (see also Chapter 1 and Chapter 5, which show that such negative adverbials are phrasal).

(39) Ik kom niet (Dutch)
I come NEG
'I don't come'
[$_{CP}$ Ik kom [$_{VP}$ [$_{Neg}$^{0} niet] [$_{VP}$ t$_i$]]]

Apart from that, Barbiers' analysis suffers from both overgeneration and undergeneration. For instance, it predicts that, in positions where expletive objects may occur, *niet* is always allowed to occupy the DP position (see (36)) and be fronted to Spec, CP if a complement CP has been selected. This prediction is false, as shown in (40).

(40) *Niet had ik gezien dat Eddy vertrok   (Dutch)
       neg   had I   seen   that Eddy left
      'I didn't see that Eddy left'

Apparently, the grammaticality of (38) does not depend on the base position of *niet*, as that is identical to the one in (40).

Furthermore, (38) is not the only type of construction where *niet* may topicalize. In (41), no CP complement has been selected by the verb, but *niet* is allowed to appear in Spec, CP as well.[20]

(41) Níet moeten in de lijst worden aangekruist de planten
      NEG   must   in the list   be   crossed   the plants
      die   je al   hébt
      that you already   have
      'You must not mark the plants on the list that you already have' (Dutch)

The arguments presented here indicate that Barbiers' analysis faces serious problems, both theoretically and empirically. In the next subsection, I argue that the alternative analysis, i.e., application of the explanation of the ban on TNIs, can account for (35) and also predicts the grammaticality of examples such as (38) and (41) by adopting Chomsky's (1995a) Merge-over-Move Constraint (see also Chomsky 2000).

15.3.2 Account

In this section, I demonstrate that the analysis of the ban on TNIs applies also to *niet*-topicalization. The central goal of this analysis is to account for the generalizations in (9) and (10), repeated as (42) and (43), and the apparent counterexamples presented here.

(42) *$[_{CP}$ NM $[_{C^0}$ V$_{fin}]]$

(43) $[_{CP}$ [NM XP] / [NQ] $[_{C^0}$ V$_{fin}]]$

First, again, operators that encode illocutionary force may not be outscoped / operated on by a semantic negation. Second, I adopt the analysis that V-to-C movement is triggered by the illocutionary force of the clause (see Wechsler 1991;

---

[20] Example taken from Haeseryn et al. (1997: 1280).

15.3 THE BAN ON SENTENCE-INITIAL SINGLE NMS

Lohnstein 2000; Gärtner 2000; and most notably Truckenbrodt 2006, among many others). As with the imperative cases, this amounts to saying that the features that encode operators with the illocutionary force of a speech act take scope from C^0. Consequently, these features may not be c-commanded by negation. Hence, in principle, no negative material is allowed to occur in Spec, CP.

However, such a constraint would be much too strong, as all sorts of negative material is allowed in Spec, CP, as shown in (44)–(45) (= (4)–(5)).

(44) a. *Niemand komt* (Dutch)
Nobody comes
'Nobody comes'

b. *Niet iedereen komt*
neg everybody comes
'Not everybody comes'

c. *Nooit neem ik een hond*
never take I a dog
'I'll never get a dog'

(45) a. *Niet Marie heb ik gebeld* ??(*maar Jan*) (Dutch)
NEG Marie have I called, but Jan
'I didn't call Marie (but Jan)'

b. *Niet kippen hebben vier poten,* *(*maar koeien*)
NEG chickens have four legs, but cows
'Chickens don't have four legs, cows do'

The fact that all these constructions are grammatical is due to the fact that Spec, CP is not the base position of these negative expressions. Each of these expressions is realized either as a temporal adverb (in the case of *nooit* 'never') or as an argument (all others). Therefore, they must have been base-generated in a lower position in the clause.[21] Given that movement to Spec, CP is an instance of A'-movement, all these expressions are to be reconstructed at LF, and do not violate the condition that operators with illocutionary force are outscoped by negation.

The question now arising is why *niet* itself is not able to be base-generated in the middle field, from where it would have been raised overtly to Spec, CP and be reconstructed at LF again. Such an instance of movement of the NM is, however, ruled out under minimalist reasoning. Based on the idea that movement/Remerge is a costly operation, which should thus be prevented when possible, Chomsky (1995a, 2000) has formulated the Merge-over-Move Constraint, from which it can be derived that, if some lexical item can be directly base-generated in some position, it cannot be said to have moved to that position. Hence, if *niet* is part of

---
[21] Note that the same holds for negative markers that head a NegP. These must be base-generated below CP as well.

the numeration and thus able to be base-generated in Spec, CP, it may not merge earlier and subsequently move to Spec, CP.

Since phrasal negation is a semantically flexible operation (in the sense that it can apply to different types of complements) and since it, being phrasal, does not select another functional projection, it is not necessarily fixed to some particular clausal position. Therefore, the NM *niet* can be base-generated in Spec, CP, and fronting *niet* from a lower position is thus forbidden. Consequently, base-generated *niet* cannot be lowered at LF and must therefore scope over the illocutionary feature in C⁰.[22]

Now (42) and (43) follow immediately. An expression of the form [*niet* XP] may move to Spec, CP and reconstruct to the base position of XP at LF, thus yielding no problem for pragmatics/semantics. Single *niet*, on the other hand, cannot lower at LF and renders the sentence unacceptable.

However, the counterexamples against the observation that *niet* cannot appear solely in Spec, CP are now in need of an explanation. Let me repeat them:

(46) Ik had wel gezien dat Jan aankwam, maar niet$_i$
     I   had PRT seen   that Jan arrived,   but   NEG
     had ik t$_i$ gezien dat Eddy vertrok   (Dutch)
     had I   seen   that Eddy left
     'I did see that Jan arrived, but I didn't see that Eddy left'

(47) Níet moeten in de   lijst worden aangekruist de   planten
     NEG   must   in the list   be   crossed   the plants
     die   je   al   hébt   (Dutch)
     that you   already   have
     'You must not mark the plants on the list that you already have'

In both cases, the element *niet* is disconnected from the elements over which it takes direct scope. In (46), the speaker says she saw John's arrival, but not Eddy's departure. In (47), the speaker asserts that only those plants that you already have marked do not need to be marked, but all others do. These readings strongly suggest that the kind of negation exhibited here is actually constituent negation, with *niet dat Eddy vertrok* and *niet de planten die je al hebt* being negative constituents. If that is indeed the case, what (46) and (47) reflect is partial topicalization. Being part of a larger constituent, *niet*, in these examples, is then indeed expected to reconstruct at LF.

These constructions are not the only cases of partial topicalization in Dutch. Other examples are given in (48):

---

[22] Note that sentence-initial *niet* is not syntactically ill-formed, and thus, strictly speaking, not ungrammatical, but that it yields a pragma-semantically infelicitous expression, just like banned TNIs under Han's (2001) analysis.

15.3 THE BAN ON SENTENCE-INITIAL SINGLE NMS

(48) a. *Boeken heb ik over Mulisch *niet* gelezen (Dutch)
books have I about Mulisch NEG read
'I didn't read books about Mulisch'

b. Boeken heb ik over die arrogante schrijver
books have I about that arrogant writer
uit Amsterdam *niet* gelezen, *(wel artikelen)
from Amsterdam NEG read, PRT chapters
'I didn't read books about that arrogant writer from Amsterdam, but chapters'

c. Boeken heb ik over Mulisch, die onder
books have I about Mulisch who amongst
andere *De ontdekking van de hemel* heeft
others The discovery of heaven has
geschreven, *niet* gelezen, *(wel artikelen)
written NEG read, PRT chapters
'I didn't read books about Mulisch, who, amongst other things, wrote *The Discovery of Heaven*, but chapters'

The example in (48a) is clearly out, but the b- and c-examples there are not. This illustrates that, in cases where the stranded XP is sufficiently heavy, it does not have to move along with the NM. As the stranded CP and NP in (46) and (47) are heavy enough, these examples indeed allow for partial topicalization.

The idea that (46) involves an instance of constituent negation, which undergoes partial topicalization, also explains the ungrammaticality of (40), repeated as (49).

(49) *Niet had ik gezien dat Eddy vertrok (Dutch)
NEG had I seen that Eddy left
'I didn't see that Eddy left'

Normally, constituent negation induces a contrastive effect. This can be illustrated for Dutch in the following way in (50), where both sentences exhibit constituent negation but where the example with the given contrast is much better than the sentence without such a contrast.

(50) a. ??Zij heeft *niet* Hans gezien (Dutch)
she has NEG Hans seen
'It wasn't Hans whom she saw'

b. Zij heeft *niet* Hans gezien maar Piet
she has NEG Hans seen but Piet
'It wasn't Hans but Piet whom she saw'

In (46) and (47), such contrastive effects are present as well (as in (48)), but not in (49). Hence, the markedness of (49) also follows from the analysis in terms of partial topicalization.

The idea that those cases that allow a single fronted *niet* are cases of partial topicalization and, therefore, cases of constituent, and not sentential, negation is also motivated by the following example from Swedish, which exhibits V-to-C movement too. Here, *inte* 'neg' can be fronted in cases such as (51).[23]

(51) A: Inte kom SVEN, utan BERTIL till festen
NEG came Sven but Bertil to party-the
igår (Swedish)
yesterday
'Not Sven, but Bertil came to the party yesterday'
B: Ja, det gjorde han, och Arne också/ *heller
yes that did he and Arne too/ either
'Yes, he did, and so did Arne'

Swedish exhibits the same type of *too/either*-pair (*också/heller*), which can be used as a diagnostic for the distinction between sentential and constituent negation, just like their English counterparts (cf. Klima 1964). *Också* 'too' can be used in cases of constituent negation, whereas *heller* 'either' is included in cases of sentential negation. The fact that the reply in (51) includes *också* indicates that *inte* has scope over *Sven* only, and not over the entire vP.[24]

Therefore, all counterexamples against the ban on single NMs in Spec, CP reduce to partial topicalization. This entails that, if partial topicalization does not apply, the single NM is banned from Spec, CP for the same reasons for which TNIs are banned. Hence, the two phenomena introduced in Section 15.1 have now received a unified explanation.

15.4 Conclusions

In this chapter, I have provided a unified explanation for two puzzling phenomena concerning the syntax and semantics of sentence-initial negation: the ban on TNIs that is attested in many languages, and the ban on sole NMs in sentence-initial position in V-to-C languages.

I have argued that both phenomena can be explained on the basis of the following three well-motivated assumptions: (i) features that encode the illocutionary force of a speech act are hosted on V_{fin} in C^0, and, therefore, speech-act operators take scope from C^0 (Han 2001); (ii) operators that encode illocutionary force

---

[23] Examples based on Brandtler (2006).
[24] Den Dikken (2016) argues that, in Dutch, partial fronting shows characteristics of sentential negation and that, therefore, the fronted *niet*-constituent, having stranded its complement, makes an intermediate landing site in the middle field, from where sentential negation is induced. Nothing in the analysis presented in this chapter is incompatible with that claim. In fact, languages may very well vary in this respect.

may not be operated on by a semantic negation (Frege 1892), i.e., they are PPIs; and (iii) the HMC (cf. Travis 1984), an instance of relativized minimality (cf. Rizzi 1989).

Furthermore, I have argued that the explanation provided in this chapter correctly predicts that all languages where an NM is both semantically negative and non-phrasal ban TNIs, and that it also correctly predicts that every language that bans TNIs exhibits an NM that occupies some head position Neg^0.

Moreover, I have shown that, on the basis of these assumptions, it also follows that no negative material may outscope any illocutionary features present in C^0, and that, for that reason, negative constituents may only appear in Spec, CP if they can be reconstructed at LF. This explains why sole NMs in V-to-C languages may not appear in Spec, CP, unless they involve instances of partial topicalization.

Finally, it shows that the landscape of PPIs is not a mirror image of (parts of) the landscape of NPIs, but that there are also elements that are PPI-like, such as the illocutionary features discussed in this chapter, that lack an NPI-like counterpart.

PART IV
CONCLUSIONS, OPEN QUESTIONS, AND AVENUES FOR FURTHER RESEARCH

16
Conclusions and open questions

16.1 Outline

In the previous two parts, I have spelled out an overarching theoretical perspective on the syntactic and semantic nature of negation and negative dependencies. In this chapter, I present the most important conclusions of this study and introduce several further research questions within the domains of negation and negative dependencies, some of them already part of ongoing work.

Section 16.2 spells out the conclusions of Part II of this study, focusing on NC, and NQs and their internal complexity. Section 16.3 summarizes the main conclusions of Part III, involving the landscape of Negative Polarity Items (NPIs) and Positive Polarity Items (PPIs).

In Section 16.4, I will outline which questions are still open and in need of further investigation, particularly focusing on other attested systems of NC, including the potential role that expletive negation plays in this regard, the acquisition of NC, and the predictions that the Flexible Formal Feature Hypothesis (FFFH) makes in this respect, and open questions in the domain of language change with respect to negation and negative dependencies. I also address a number of open questions concerning other types of attested NPIs, other types of attested PPIs, the learnability of NPI/PPI-hood in general, and the consequences of this study for the analysis of clause-types and their illocutionary effects.

Section 16.5 spells out some final remarks.

16.2 Conclusions concerning Negative Concord, and negative quantifiers and their internal complexity

In this section, I spell out the conclusions of the first main part of this study. Subsection 16.2.1 focuses on NC, Subsection 16.2.2 on NQs and their internal complexity.

16.2.1 Negative Concord

Back in Chapter 3, I argued that the best way to approach NC is by assuming that it is an instance of syntactic agreement where one element carrying [iNEG] checks off one or more elements carrying [uNEG]. In a Non-strict NC language like Italian, I take the NM to be a semantic negation, carrying an interpretable formal feature [iNEG], and neg-words like *nessuno* ('neg-body') to carry an uninterpretable formal feature [uNEG]. In the absence of an overt element carrying [iNEG], a covert negative operator can be postulated to be present and to be responsible for the introduction of a semantic negation and for checking off the [uNEG]s on the neg-words.

This system, where a covert negative operator can be presumed to be present when, otherwise, any present neg-words would remain having unchecked [uNEG]-features, can be seen as an implementation of Ladusaw's (1992) notion of self-licensing and also implements his idea that neg-words form a particular subset of polarity-sensitive elements that, unlike other NPIs, can be licensed by a covert licenser. In this way, the analysis of NC departs from analyses of other types of NPIs in the sense that the latter do not involve syntactic agreement between the NPI and the negation. Note that, since neg-words require a negation, or, to be more precise, an element carrying [iNEG], to be present, neg-words are ultimately NPIs, albeit NPIs of a different kind than the more standard examples. The analysis of NC formulated in this chapter is therefore a particular instance of the NPI approach to NC.

As shown in Chapter 4, my proposal for NC predicts the possibility of various other subtypes of NC as well. One dimension of variation follows from the question, which negative elements carry a feature [iNEG] and which ones a feature [uNEG]. In Strict NC languages, all overt negative elements carry [uNEG], and the only negative element carrying [iNEG] is the abstract negative operator Op¬. In Non-strict NC languages, neg-words carry [uNEG], and the NM and the abstract negative operator Op¬ carry [iNEG]. The mirror image of Non-strict NC systems, such as Variety A of Afrikaans, and, arguably, also Old High German and Middle Low German, is a system where all neg-words and the abstract negative operator Op¬ carry [iNEG], and the NM [uNEG].

A second dimension of variation is whether every negative element has to participate in NC, or only a subset thereof. NC languages like French and English are examples of languages where only some negative elements carry a feature [iNEG] or [uNEG]. The result of this may be that, in some languages, the number of overt negative elements equals the number of semantic negations, so that the NC system in these languages is actually invisible, as I have shown is the case in English and Hindi/Punjabi.

Naturally, additional differences between languages outside their NC system may also result in differences concerning NC. This happens, for instance, in West Flemish and Catalan (at least in its Central Variety). Even though both West Flemish and Central Catalan are Strict NC languages, in the sense that all of their overt instances of negation carry [uNEG] (though see Subsection 16.4.1), they allow neg-words to not always be accompanied by the NM for independent reasons.

16.2 CONCLUSIONS CONCERNING NEGATIVE CONCORD 383

For instance, in West Flemish, this is due to the fact that all indefinites, including neg-words, undergo obligatory scrambling out of vP, and can independently scope-mark sentential negation.

In Chapter 5, I have focused on a remaining problem that my proposal was still facing, namely the fact that, in some NC languages, certain non-negative, i.e., non-AA elements, such as predicates expressing doubt or fear, can also license neg-words. This, I argued, addresses what the exact relation is between carrying a formal negative feature [iNEG] and being semantically negative; and I concluded, on both theoretical and empirical grounds, that, even though the two often go hand in hand, formally, they should be disentangled. There are cases where a particular element may carry [iNEG] despite not being semantically negative, as is indeed the case with the above-mentioned non-negative licensers of neg-words. There are also examples of semantically negative elements that lack formal negative features, such as the French NM *pas* or English NIs such as *nobody* or *never*.

If the relation between a formal interpretable negative feature and being semantically negative is not 1:1, a learnability algorithm is called for that determines which element should be assigned a formal negative feature (if any). In Chapter 5, I have presented such a mechanism, the FFFH, and I have also outlined the conditions under which existing types of NC systems can be acquired. Unsurprisingly, this learnability algorithm comes with particular empirical consequences for the domains of language variation, acquisition, and change.

For one, this proposal predicts that only in NC languages can formal negative features be acquired that may project; consequently, every language that exhibits a NM that is a syntactic head in the clausal spine must also be an NC language, a prediction that appears to be borne out. Also, I have pointed out that every language learner must start with the hypothesis that the target language is a DN language, unless there is evidence to the contrary, again a prediction that appears to have been correct. Finally, and relatedly, I have argued that the emergence of NC and/or particular kinds of NC systems must always be the consequence of additional syntactic changes in the domain of negation.

In Chapter 6, I have explained how variation among NC systems may have emerged diachronically, most notably along the lines of Jespersen's famous Cycle. When additional NMs become part of the negative system, this can lead to the emergence of NC, as has happened in and been illustrated for French. All of a sudden, the 1:1 mapping between negative form and negative meaning got disrupted, and NC emerged. In the same way, if NMs disappear, become optional, or have their syntactic properties changed, NC systems may disappear or change their type. This has been the case for the change from Strict to Non-strict NC languages (shown for Italian and Portuguese), for the NC system of Afrikaans (where its particular type of NC changed into the more general type of Strict NC), and for the emergence of the partial NC systems of French and English.

Conversely, I have also shown that the disappearance of a NM, as happened in most Germanic languages, may lead to the disappearance of NC and the emergence of DN, as I have illustrated for Dutch; here, suddenly, the 1:1 mapping between negative form and meaning re-emerged. Where the proposed learnability algorithm constitutes the space of variation with respect to the presence and types of NC, diachronic developments indeed determine which types of NC languages may actually emerge.

16.2.2 Negative quantifiers and their internal complexity

In Chapter 6, I have also shown how the emergence of NIs / neg-words as well as the exclusion of their universal counterparts can be accounted for, thus, among other things, providing a solution for the so-called *nall*-problem. Again, we see that, where grammar allows for various instances of variation in the domain of negation, diachronic effects may further limit this range of variation. The reason why negative existential quantifiers/indefinites like *no* or *nobody* in English can be abundantly attested, whereas their negative universal counterparts (non-existing *nall* or *neverything*) cannot, is not because grammars cannot allow a merger between a NM and a universal quantifier per se. Rather, it is that the conditions under which such a merger may take place are much rarer for universals than for existentials/indefinites.

This brings us to the syntax and semantics of such negative existential quantifiers/indefinites. I have argued in Chapter 7 that NIs, as I refer to them, in languages like Dutch, German, and English are not NQs in the Montegovian sense, but pieces of syntactic structure that consist of a negation and an indefinite, which are postsyntactically spelled out as a single morphological word. The reason for that is the existence of split-scope readings involving such NIs—readings where the negative part of a NI seems to outscope a scope-taking element under which the existential part of the NI takes scope. Split-scope effects, I have argued, are derived as a result of the Copy Theory of Movement. Concretely, I have proposed that, in split-scope constructions, after QR, the negative element is interpreted in a higher copy and the indefinite in a lower copy of the NI. Furthermore, I have demonstrated that alternative analyses that take NIs in Dutch and German to be NQs, neg-words, or to be resulting from amalgamation or incorporation processes face problems that the analysis presented here does not encounter.

A crucial ingredient of the analysis, necessary to rule out partial reconstruction of the negation below the indefinite in split-scope constructions, is that negation, once raised, does not reconstruct. While such a constraint seems empirically well-founded, it is at odds with certain approaches to Neg-Raising, the phenomenon where matrix negation is felt to be interpreted in the embedded clause.

The standard analysis for Neg-Raising, which aims at solving this question in pragma-semantic terms and not in terms of syntactic movement, goes back to Bartsch (1973) and has been elaborated in Horn (1978, 1989); Gajewski (2005, 2007); Romoli (2013), and many others. This standard approach takes negation to take scope from its surface position, and not to reconstruct. As such, this standard approach is fully compatible with what I have argued for NIs. Recently, however, this standard approach has been challenged by Collins and Postal (2014), who claim, after providing various novel arguments, that Neg-Raising does involve syntactic movement of the negation from the embedded clause into the matrix clause. The syntactic structure of *I don't think you're right* would then be: I do[n't]$_i$ think you're t$_i$ right, and the Neg-Raising reading would result from the interpretation of the lower copy of the negation.

In Chapter 8, I have assessed the major arguments put forward by Collins and Postal (2014). I have concluded that not only does this syntactic approach suffer from various problems, but also that it is not the case that the arguments presented in favour of it form an argument against the standard, pragma-semantic approach. It turns out that the standard, pragma-semantic approach is equally able to account for the relevant distribution of strict NPIs and Horn-clauses as well as the behaviour of negative parentheticals, the three major empirical arguments presented by Collins and Postal against this approach. Hence, there are no (non-theory-internal) reasons to maintain Collins and Postal's syntactic approach to Neg-Raising to explain why negation sometimes seems to take scope from a position inside an embedded clause.

16.3 Conclusions and open questions concerning the landscapes of Negative Polarity Items and Positive Polarity Items

In this section, I spell out the conclusions of the second main part of this study (Part III). Subsection 16.3.1 focuses on the landscape of NPIs, and Subsection 16.3.2 on the landscape of PPIs.

16.3.1 The landscape of Negative Polarity Items

This part started out by introducing two approaches to the nature of NPI: convergence and divergence. The convergence approach takes the cross-linguistic and language-internal variation attested with respect to the distribution of NPIs as a starting point and argues that the best way to approach the landscape of NPIs is by assuming that different elements, with completely different distributional restrictions, share the property that they need to appear in contexts that, in one way or another, count as negative. By contrast, a divergent approach starts out with the assumption that all NPIs share a common core, and that more superficial restrictions may result in differences in strength between NPIs. In Chapter 9, I have motivated why I start out investigating the landscape of NPIs (and also of PPIs) in terms of convergence and not of divergence.

In Chapter 10, I discussed a well-known distinction between NPIs, namely that between weak NPIs and strong NPIs. I have argued that only a modified version of the approaches by Chierchia and Gajewski to account for this distinction gets the facts right. Gajewski (2011) and Chierchia (2013), following Krifka (1995), take the strong–weak distinction to lie in the distinction between the exhaustifier either looking only at the semantics of the NPI licenser, or looking at its overall meaning contribution, including its presuppositions and implicatures. Weak NPIs want the exhaustifier to look at the semantics of the licenser only; strong NPIs want the exhaustifier to also look at the licenser's pragmatically enriched meaning contribution.

As has been demonstrated by Collins and Postal (2014), strong NPIs are sensitive to syntactic locality conditions, whereas weak NPIs are not. In this connection, I have argued that exhaustification of strong NPIs takes place in the syntax, but exhaustification of weak NPIs in pragmatics. Apart from the fact that this explains the differences between strong- and weak-NPI licensing in terms of syntactic locality, it also leads us to a better understanding of these NPIs in the first place. What makes an NPI an element that must appear in DE contexts is simply the obligatory introduction of domain alternatives, and does not necessitate the existence of particular syntactic features—the latter only play a role in the licensing of strong NPIs.

This, of course, does not entail that weak and strong NPIs are the only type of NPIs possible. In fact, I have raised the question whether NPIs that are always domain-wideners, such as *in years*, should be treated as a special class or not. Even though strong arguments have been provided for why domain-widening as such cannot be solely responsible for weak NPIs like *any* or *ever*, it is not the case, again against the background of the convergence approach, that no NPI whose NPI-hood (solely) depends on domain-widening can exist.

Differences between NPI strength exceed the strong–weak distinction, though. In Chapter 11, three other types of NPIs than strong and weak ones have been introduced. I have argued that superstrong NPIs are idiomatic and stored as such with their licensers. Strong/weak NPIs are lexically connected with a negation that needs to be spelled out higher in the structure, either as a NM or incorporated in another expression, along the lines of Collins and Postal's (2014) analysis of unary NPIs. Superweak NPIs, I have argued, following Lin et al. (2015, 2021), are referentially deficient and, therefore, only fine in non-veridical contexts; they may not entail the existence of a referent satisfying their description (cf. Lin 1996, 1998; Giannakidou 2011; Lin 2015, 2017). In addition, I have shown that acquisitional data appear to confirm these analyses, and also that (strong and) weak NPIs like *any* indeed form a different type of NPI from superstrong, strong/weak, and superweak NPIs.

This suggests that NPIs of different strengths are indeed NPIs for different reasons. But does the reverse also hold? Are all NPIs of the same strength also NPIs for the same reason? In Chapter 12, I have taken one step further, arguing that certain elements that are taken to be NPIs of the same strength can still be NPIs for different reasons. Concretely, I argue that a special construction that has been analysed as a weak NPI is not a weak NPI for the reasons spelled out in Chapter 10. Instead, it is an NPI for purely pragmatic reasons, in the sense that it gives rise to a blocking implicature that is suppressed in DE contexts: in languages like Dutch and German, certain cases of negation, such as negated indefinites, are ruled out in out-of-the-blue contexts with a reading where negation outscopes the indefinite. However, this reading becomes available again when the sentence is embedded in a DE context. In Chapter 12, I have argued that, by contrast, this phenomenon is best explained by adopting standard pragmatic assumptions. In short, I argue that the absence of such readings results from the existence of some alternative expression that conveys the intended reading only. Uttering a less simple construction will give rise to an implicature that states that the speaker does not intend to convey a reading that could have been expressed in a simpler fashion. The fact that this implicature is suppressed in NPI licensing contexts gives rise to the illusion that some 'real' NPI is involved in these constructions.

16.3.2 The landscape of Positive Polarity Items

Apart from NPIs, another type of negative dependency is formed by PPIs, elements that may not appear in the scope of negative, AA, and/or DE contexts. Naturally, the question emerges why particular elements cannot be embedded by negation, just as earlier the question emerged why certain elements must appear in negative contexts (or the like). The fact that NPIs form not a homogenous, but rather a heterogeneous class, with different types of NPIs resulting from different types of sources for NPI-hood, naturally extends to PPIs. Given the convergence approach, PPIs do not form a homogeneous class either, and PPI-hood has different sources too.

Earlier, it was discussed that NPIs that denote lower scalar end points, such as *any* or *ever*, are said to be only fine in DE contexts, since, outside such contexts, their semantics would give rise to a contradiction. Under Chierchia's (2006, 2013) approach, this contradiction arises as such NPIs both obligatorily introduce domain alternatives and trigger the presence of a covert exhaustifier. In Chapter 10, we saw that the nature of this trigger further constitutes the distinction between weak and strong NPIs.

Following this line of reasoning, it should be expected that elements with the same properties that denote the highest end point of a scale, such as universal quantifiers, are PPIs. Indeed, universal quantifier PPIs have been attested in the domain of modals (quantifiers over possible worlds)—English *must* and *should* are good examples of such universal quantifier PPIs (cf. Iatridou and Zeijlstra 2010, 2013; Homer 2015)—but not in the domain of quantifiers over individuals. However, I have argued that this absence is only an absence in disguise. Universal quantifier PPIs do exist, both in the domain of quantifiers over individuals and in the domain of quantifiers over possible worlds, as is predicted by Chierchia's (2006, 2013) approach to NPI-hood.

However, since the exhaustifier that is induced by these PPIs can act as an intervener between the PPI and its anti-licenser (at least for weak PPIs), universal quantifier PPIs may appear in disguise and take scope below their anti-licenser. Their PPI-like behaviour becomes visible only once they morphosyntactically precede their anti-licenser.

This still leads to several open questions. These questions especially address the potential types of PPIs that this approach predicts to be possible and to be impossible. For instance, what is the difference between *must* and *should*? One is a weak PPI and the other a strong one. But what underlies these differences? Is the mechanism behind strong and weak NPIs the same as the one that underlies strong and weak PPIs?

Second, whether something is an NPI or a PPI depends on whether its domain alternatives are weaker or stronger in an upward-entailing context. This also predicts that elements whose domain of quantification can give rise to both types of domain alternatives should be ambiguous between NPIs and PPIs. The question thus arises whether such elements can indeed be attested.

Third, not every PPI is a universal quantifier. *Some*, maybe the best known PPI, is existential, and the standard approach can therefore not account for its PPI-hood. The same holds for certain existential modals. *May* is polarity-insensitive in its deontic usage, but PPI-like when it is used epistemically.

A full theory of PPI-hood should also provide answers to these (and other) questions. In Chapter 14, an attempt in that direction has been made. I conjecture that both Chierchia's approach to NPI-hood and Lin's approach in terms of the Non-Entailment-of-Existence Condition can be naturally applied to account for PPI-hood as well. Chierchia's approach, with its predecessors in Kadmon and Landman (1993) and Krifka (1995), naturally accounts for both strong and weak universal PPIs, and also predicts hybrid PIs to be possible, as shown for *until*. The mirror image of Lin's Non-Entailment-of-Existence Condition, the Non-Entailment-of-Non-Existence Condition, predicts that there are weak existential PPIs, which can be attested among both quantifiers over individuals and quantifiers over possible worlds. In fact, it even predicts that existential modal PPIs of this kind only exhibit PPI-behaviour in an epistemic construal. Strong existential PPIs, to the best of my knowledge, have not been attested. What Chapter 14 has tried to show is that what underlies the landscape of NPIs also partially underlies the landscape of PPIs. Naturally, this does not mean that these are the only kinds of PPIs possible in this sense.

One particular question that arises in this respect is whether PPIs that lack any kind of NPI-counterpart can be attested, just as other types of NPIs lack PPI-counterparts. In Chapter 15, I have argued that this is indeed the case. Features encoding illocutionary force are such PPIs. Chapter 15 exploits the PPI-hood of features encoding illocutionary force for a unified explanation for two puzzling phenomena concerning the syntax and semantics of sentence-initial negation: the ban on TNIs that is attested in many languages, and the ban on sole NMs in sentence-initial position in V-to-C languages.

I have argued that both phenomena can be explained on the basis of the following three well-motivated assumptions: (i) features that encode the illocutionary force of a speech act are hosted on V_{fin} in C°, and, therefore, speech-act operators take scope from C° (Han 2001); (ii) operators that encode illocutionary force may not be operated on by a semantic negation (Frege 1892), i.e., they are essentially PPIs; and (iii) the Head Movement Constraint (HMC) (cf. Travis 1984), an instance of relativized minimality (cf. Rizzi 1989). I have argued that the explanation provided in this chapter correctly predicts that all languages where a NM is both semantically negative and non-phrasal ban TNIs, and that it also correctly predicts that every language that bans TNIs exhibits a NM that occupies some head position Neg°. I have also shown that, on the basis of these assumptions, it also follows that no negative material may outscope any illocutionary features present in C°, and that, for this reason, negative constituents may only appear in Spec, CP if they can be reconstructed at LF. This explains why sole NMs in V-to-C languages may not appear in Spec, CP, unless they involve instances of partial topicalization.

Finally, it shows that the landscape of PPIs is not a mirror image of (parts of) the landscape of NPIs, but that there are also elements that are PPI-like, such as the illocutionary features discussed in this chapter, that lack an NPI-like counterpart.

16.4 Open questions

In the following subsections, I will spell out a selection of questions that are still open. Naturally, this list is far from exhaustive, and the selection is, of course, subjective and, to some extent, also based on ongoing research. In any event, answers to these questions will hopefully further corroborate the empirical and theoretical claims made in this study, and provide better understandings of the described phenomena.

16.4.1 Open questions concerning Negative Concord

Naturally, various questions remain open when analysing NC. One of them concerns the taxonomy of NC types. The types of NC systems discussed in

Chapter 4 do not form an exhaustive list. There are NC languages that, even though they look like Strict NC languages in the sense that NMs can follow neg-words and still yield NC readings, forbid these NMs to precede them in NC constructions. West Flemish and Bavarian are good examples of such languages (cf. Stelling 2019).

(1) a. ... da Valère niemand (nie) gezien oat   (West Flemish)
       ... that Valère nobody not seen had
       '... that Valère had not seen anybody'

   b. ... das keine Unanstendlikeit (nichd) bassirt isd   (Upper Bavarian)
       ... that no indecency not happened is
       '... that no indecency has occurred'

(2) a. ... da Valère nie niemand gezien oat   (West Flemish)
       ... that Valère not nobody seen had
       '... that Valère hadn't seen nobody'

   b. ... das nichd keine Unanstendlichkeid bassirt ist   (Upper Bavarian)
       ... that not no indecency happened is
       '... that not no indecency occurred'

There is no straightforward way in which a [uNEG]–[iNEG] analysis may account for these facts. Since both neg-words and NMs may yield NC readings with preceding neg-words, both should be assigned a feature [uNEG]. But then the facts in (1)–(2) do not follow.

Haegeman and Lohndal (2010) argue that negative elements in West Flemish do not involve only [uNEG]–[iNEG] but also quantificational features ([uQ]–[iQ]). They use this to account for certain intricate NC patterns in West Flemish involving expressions like *not many*. But as Stelling (2019) has shown, the addition of such features does not solve the problem that has been raised. Moreover, the pattern is not restricted to West Flemish, but also appears in other Germanic NC varieties, such as many Bavarian varieties.[1]

Another area where further research is called for concerns the acquisition (and learnability) of NC systems, especially in the light of the FFFH. One prediction that the FFFH makes is that children should first take their target language as a DN language, before they can unlearn that and acquire that the target language as an NC language. The reason is that, given the absence of frequently occurring DN constructions in the language input, children can acquire DN systems only

---

[1] Instead, Stelling argues that West Flemish *nie* is lexically ambiguous between a real negation and a semantically non-negative element, which he takes to be a so-called *expletive NM* (after Van der Wouden 1994, see Delfitto 2020 for discussion and overview). Even though this assumption gets the facts right, it still remains an open question why and how NMs, all of a sudden, can become homophonous NPIs (see Chapter 12).

by taking as a starting hypothesis that every negatively marked element is also a semantic negation.

Indeed, it has been shown for English that children start out taking the language to be a DN language and only later on converge to the more complex English invisible NC system (cf., among others, Klima and Bellugi 1966; Bellugi 1967; de Villiers and de Villiers 1985; Déprez and Pierce 1993; Drozd 1995; Thornton and Tesan 2013; Thornton et al. 2016). However, what also needs to be shown to confirm the HHHF from an acquisitional perspective is that other DN languages are acquired straightforwardly without any kind of NC upheaval in the children's production. Also, it is predicted that children acquiring regular NC systems, both Strict and Non-strict NC systems, go through a DN phase prior to acquiring their target NC system. And within these types, it is actually predicted that Non-strict NC is acquired earlier than Strict NC, the reason being that a NM's [uNEG] status can be acquired only if, before, it is taken to be semantically negative. Whether these predictions hold is an open question, and currently part of ongoing research (though see Nicolae and Yatsushiro 2020 for arguments that German children do undergo an NC stage when acquiring DN).

Finally, many questions concerning the domain of language change with respect to negation and NC also remain open. It has been shown how French Strict NC could emerge owing to developments coming from Jespersen's Cycle, as well as how it subsequently developed into a partial NC language. It has also been shown how Strict NC languages can change into Non-strict ones (e.g. Italian or Portuguese) or even into DN languages (e.g. Dutch). But that does not mean that these changes are the only ones attested.

Docekal (2009) shows, among others, that Slavic languages, which are canonical Strict NC languages, were Non-strict NC languages in earlier stages. Old Church Slavonic was largely a Non-strict NC language, although NMs could optionally be attached to the finite verb. This suggests that Old Church Slavonic was already on the way from Non-strict NC to Strict NC. Naturally, the question arises as what triggered that change. The answer to this question, I must leave open, though I would like to mention that, if the NM changed from a clitic-like element into a regular agreement affix, obligatory occurrences of the latter as opposed to the former is not an unexpected phenomenon. Whether this is indeed the case, again, I leave open for future research.

16.4.2 Open questions concerning negative quantifiers and their internal complexity

Naturally, also in this domain, questions remain open. For instance, all analyses of split scope discussed thus far have been designed to account for split-scope readings yielded by NIs. However, it has also been observed that split-scope readings may be triggered by other quantifiers that are not upward monotonic. Take the following examples by Hackl (2000) and Rullmann (1995), quoted in Abels and Marti (2010):

(3) At MIT one must publish fewer than three books in order to get tenure
'At MIT one must publish at least n books in order to get tenure, and n is less than three'[2]
How many books does Chris want to buy?
'What is the number n such that Chris wants it to be the case that there are n books that he buys?'[3]

That split-scope readings may emerge in comparatives and comparative quantifiers is well known since Hackl (2000); De Swart (2000); and Heim (2001) (see also Alrenga and Kennedy 2014). The question that arises is whether these two types of split-scope phenomena, i.e., split-scope phenomena with respect to negation and with respect to other non-monotonic operators, such as comparative quantifiers, reflect different grammatical phenomena or can be said to follow from a single, unified analysis of split-scope phenomena.

One reason, put forward by Jacobs (1980) and Penka (2011), for a non-unified approach to split scope is that NIs can also give rise to split-scope readings across universal quantifiers with a particular hat contour (cf. Büring 1995). For many speakers of German, (4) receives a reading where not every doctor has a car.

(4) /JEDER Arzt hat KEIN\ Auto   (German)
    every doctor has no car
    'Not every doctor has a car'

Crucially, however, such split-scope readings do not emerge with other non-upward monotonic quantifiers:

(5) ??/JEDER Arzt hat weniger als DREI\ Autos   (German)
    every doctor has fewer than three cars
    'Every doctor has at least n cars, and n is less than three'

(6) */JEDER Arzt hat GENAU\ drei Autos   (German)
    every doctor has less three cars
    'Every doctor has at least three cars'

Since examples like (4) are not available for every speaker of German (unlike the examples of split scope involving NIs and modals and intentional operators discussed in Chapter 7), Abels and Marti (2010) take split scope involving the hat

---

[2] Example from Hackl 2000
[3] Example from Rullman 1995

contour to be a phenomenon that is independent from other types of split scope, thus paving the way for a unified approach for split scope involving negative and other non-monotone increasing quantifiers, such as comparative quantifiers and numerals. For them, a NQ like German *kein* is a NQ over choice functions, which scopes from its raised position. The noun phrase is interpreted below where the trace of the quantifier leaves a choice function variable that takes the denotation of the noun as its argument. Since Abels and Marti take common noun denotations to be indexed by a world, which can be bound by a higher intensional operator, the impression of a split-scope reading is the result. The split-scope reading of (7a) results from the LF in (8b) (where @ stands for the actual world).

(7) a. Du musst keine Krawatte anziehen (German)
 you must no tie wear
 'It is not required that you wear a tie' ¬ > must > ∃
 b. ¬∃f CF(f) & ∀w'R@, you wear f(tiew') in w'

However, it remains unclear why speakers who accept split-scope readings with the hat contour systematically accept split-scope readings across intensional operators, something that is not immediately clear if the two phenomena are truly independent. Hence, more research is called for.

Finally, in the discussion on Neg-Raising, it was mentioned that all examples provided by Collins and Postal (2014) for a syntactic approach could not be upheld, except for Horn-clauses. Given the fact that negative inversion must be licensed locally, the question emerges of how subject-auxiliary inversion can be licensed in (9) if negation does not start out in the embedded clause and consequently raise into the matrix clause.

(8) I don't think that ever before have the media played such a major role in a kidnapping

One way to potentially circumvent this problem for pragmatic/semantic approaches to Neg-Raising is by assuming that parasitic licensing underlies Horn-clauses. Parasitic licensing involves cases where a strict NPI can be licensed non-locally if it stands in a local relation with a non-strict NPI, as shown for the strict NPI *meer* ('any more') and the non-strict NPI *ooit* ('ever') in Dutch.

(9) a. Ik hoop dat je niet meer van mening verandert (Dutch)
 I hope that you not any more of opinion change.
 'I hope you will not change your opinion any more'

 b. *Ik hoop niet dat je meer van mening verandert
 I hope not that you any more of opinion change
 Int.: 'I hope you won't change your opinion any more'

c. Ik hoop niet dat je ooit meer van mening verandert
   I hope not that you ever any more of opinion change
   'I hope that you will never change your opinion any more'

If the subject-auxiliary inversion in (8) is indeed a strict NPI, maybe even a super-strict NPI, as the licensing relation requires a spec-head configuration, (8) might indeed reflect an instance of parasitic licensing, and this does not require a local negation.

Naturally, the question arises then of how such parasitic licensing works. Why is it that subject-auxiliary inversion is NPI-like in (8), and why can an NPI in the specifier satisfy its needs? There is no clear answer here, but recent ongoing work suggests that subject-auxiliary inversion may require some emphasis. It is licensed if there is no previous expectation of the assertion. To show this, they provide the following data:

(11) Context 1: We expect a reputable journal to correct its data for inflation. *The Finance Chronicle* did not correct its data for inflation.
   a. *And nowhere did it mention this omission*
   Context 2: We expect that dishonest Dr. N. will not correct his data for inflation and will not mention this omission in his article.
   b. #*And nowhere did he mention it*

This suggests that this emphasis arises as a result of covert *even*-exhaustification (see Chapter 10), which requires a DE context. The only way to ensure that this is the case is by including a DE element in the specifier of the raised auxiliary (yielding negative inversion) or by including an (emphatic) NPI in it. Since the latter must be licensed by a negation (or another proper licenser) in such a way that nothing intervenes between the negation and the NPI, such licensing relations are restricted to a number of predicates only, including Neg-Raising predicates.

16.4.3 Open questions concerning the landscape of Negative Polarity Items

The list of types of NPIs discussed in Part III is not exhaustive. Even though I primarily focused on different NPI strengths, NPIs may also differ in other directions, such as the kind of entities that constitute their domain of quantification. For instance, we saw that *any* is an NPI that quantifies over individuals, but *need* quantifies over possible worlds.

There are also existential NPI modals. English *can* is a good example:

(12) She can*('t) be in her office

Clearly, (12) shows that *can* is an NPI. But it is only an NPI when used epistemically. Deontic or root usages of *can* are not polarity-sensitive:

(13) a. She can('t) leave right now
    b. She can('t) swim very well

The question is thus why only epistemic *can* is an NPI. Of course, it could be that epistemic *can* is a separate lexical item, homophonous with the other *can*. But such a solution is not very satisfactory, not least because it does not seem like a coincidence that only epistemic *can* is an NPI.

Outside the domain of epistemic modals, no other existential NPI has been attested, at least not to my knowledge. The only potential example I know of is the short-lived Middle Dutch NPI *dorven* ('may') (cf. Meijer 2014).

(14) a. Ganse ne darftu niit vermiden   (Middle Dutch)
    health NEG may.you NEG avoid
    'You may not forget about your health'

    b. Maar dat ne darf hi clagen niet
    but that NEG may he complain NEG
    'But he doesn't have to / may not complain'

However, it is far from clear that this is an existential NPI, as the data seem to suggest that *dorven* ('may') may have an unspecified modal force: in certain contexts, it appears to have an existential interpretation, in other contexts rather a universal one. Hence, it may even be the case that non-epistemic existential NPI-hood may be more systematically ruled out. Alternatively, it may just be very rare, perhaps for functional reasons (as modals generally reconstruct below negation; see Chapter 13). Naturally, this calls for further research.

Another question that has emerged concerns the acquisition of weak NPIs like *any*. Following earlier work by Tieu (2011), Lin et al. (2021) showed that *any* starts out only under the direct scope of the NM or in negatively biased polar questions, before children start to use it in all kinds of DE contexts. In Chapter 11, young children's *any* was considered a superstrong NPI; it may only appear in anti-morphic contexts (taking biased polar questions to have a meaning like $\{\neg p, \neg\neg p\}$). However, it is unclear how children make the acquisitional step from something that must be directly outscoped by negation into an element that must have its stronger domain alternatives exhaustified.

One observation that was already presented in Lin at al. (2021) is that, although the children's initial analysis of *any* allows only the indefinite to appear in the immediate scope of *not*, the employment of *any* in this environment is not the only option in early child English. As indicated by the child utterances in (15), besides *any* (15a), bare NPs, (15b), and NPs selected by a plain indefinite article, (15c), are also good in negative clauses introduced by *not* in early child language.

(15) a. They don't have any chairs, that's why!   (3;02.23)[4]
     b. I don't want bubbles   (2;10.18)[5]
     c. Haven't got a racing car   (3;00.00)[6]

The pattern illustrated in (15) is far from unfamiliar in adult language. What is it that determines whether *any* is used in the environments where *any* can be used? Kadmon and Landman (1993) observed the (possible) semantic difference between using an *any*-NP and an *a/an/ø* NP in the utterances such as (15), and showed, based on this pattern, that *any* is a domain-widener, whereas *a/an/ø* are not, implemented by Chierchia (2006, 2013) in terms of obligatory introduction of domain alternatives (see Chapter 10). On the basis of these distinctions, Lin et al. suggest that the pattern in (15), observed in early child language, does not manifest itself at random, but mirrors adult-language usage of *any*, namely that children employ an *any*-NP only in those contexts where all stronger domain alternatives are false.

By experimentally examining the domain-widening effect of *any*, which is absent with plain indefinite articles *a* or *an*, Tieu and Lidz (2016) show that English children, at least those four- and five-year-olds, are aware of the interpretational difference with respect to domain-widening between *any* and its plain counterparts. Hence the question arises whether younger children may also be sensitive to the domain-widening effect of *any*. A further qualitative analysis of the context of the utterance of *any chairs* in the scope of the sentential negation, (15a), and that of the utterance containing *a racing car* in the scope of the sentential negation, (15c), seems to suggest a positive answer.

When uttering (15a), the child expressed the reason why James and his sister, two cartoon figures from a storybook, could not reach the biscuits on the kitchen table: They did not have chairs on which they could stand to reach the biscuits, not even a chair-like thing that could fulfil the same function. However, after uttering (15c) as an answer to the question of the adult *Have you got a racing car?*, the child continued their conversation by telling the adult that he actually has a little racing car, somewhere downstairs in his house. Given the difference observed between the contexts in which English three-year-olds employ an *any*-NP and those in which they utter an NP modified by a plain indefinite, it may not be implausible to assume that children have already acquired the knowledge that *any* is a domain-widening indefinite before the age of four. Again, this calls for further research.

A final question related to those constructions which were traditionally analysed as involving a light negation and which I analysed in terms of pragmatic competition concerns the differences between the licensing of these constructions

---

[4] Example from Fletcher and Garman (1988: spdav.cha: line 2016).
[5] Example from Theakston et al. (2001: liz34b.cha: line 682).
[6] Example from Fletcher and Garman (1988: spkev.cha: line 2139).

and weak NPIs. For example, as (16) shows, this utterance may only receive the unmarked reading if it is interpreted counterfactually.

(16) Wenn Fritz nicht eine Fremdsprache könnte, wäre er
if Fritz not a foreign.language knew, were he
durchgefallen (German)
failed
'If Fritz hadn't known a foreign language, he would have failed'

The question why such negated indefinites, definites, and disjunction may not appear in a non-counterfactual conditional is not accounted for yet. In Chapter 12, I suggested that there might be a way of understanding this fact by assuming that conditionals, to the extent that they license NPIs (cf. Heim 1984), still impose additional restrictions on their interpretation. Under this view, such constructions are fine, even with their unmarked reasons, but still, in NPI licensing contexts, subtle pragmatic competition may take place between a sentence with a conditional containing a negated indefinite and one with a NI. In other words, under this view, the primary implicature that rejects the unmarked readings for negated indefinites is suppressed, but, as a secondary or local implicature, it may still play a role (albeit a much weaker one, as is generally the case with secondary implicatures; cf. Panizza et al. 2009 for recent discussion).

An alternative option might be to assume that what underlies the suppression of the relevant (primary) implicature is not DE itself, but rather the presence of a negative antecedent in the discourse. Bar-Asher Siegal (2017) has argued that Jewish Babylonian Aramaic exploited two different negators, *lā* and *lāw*, which differed exactly with respect to previously uttered positive or negative assertions in the contexts. Whether such an analysis is extendable to the construction discussed in Chapter 12 needs to be further investigated.

16.4.4 Open questions concerning the landscape of Positive Polarity Items

One of the results presented in Chapter 13 is that *must* is a weak PPI and *should* a strong one. One might wonder why these two modals differ in this way. It might be a 'just so' matter, opening up the possibility that, in other languages, the patterns might be different. However, there are reasons to think that it may not be random. First, in Greek and Dutch (and many other languages; see von Fintel and Iatridou 2007), the weak necessity modal (which translates as *should / ought to*) is a regular, strong necessity modal (like *must* or its translations) combined with counterfactual morphology. However, it is unclear what the principle might be that makes the quantificationally weaker modal (*tha eprepe / zouden moeten*) be a strong PPI, even though the strong modal it contains (*prepi / moeten*) is a weak PPI. Note, though, that this may not be a general pattern. In Hungarian and Croatian, the metamorphosis of *must* to *should/ought* does not change the PPI-strength of the resulting modal. However, I know of no language where the PPI-hood of the weak necessity modal is stronger than that of the strong necessity modal. So, again, further investigation is needed.

A second question concerns the PPI-hood of universal quantifiers over individuals. I have argued that Dutch *iedereen* ('everybody') is a PPI, as it cannot reconstruct below negation:

(17) Iedereen vertrok niet (Dutch)
 everybody left not $\forall > \neg; *\neg > \forall$
 'Nobody left'

Evidence for this came from examples like (18), which show that this PPI can be reconstructed below negation if it appears under another NPI-licenser.

(18) Het verbaast me dat iedereen niet blijft (Dutch)
 it surprises me that everybody not stays
 'It surprises me that not everybody stays'

However, as discussed in Chapter 14, this only holds for weak PPIs. The question thus arises whether other universal PPIs that quantify over individuals can be attested that are strong PPIs. I do not know of any such examples, but the range of languages investigated is too small to draw any substantive conclusions on that.

In Chapter 14, it was shown that certain elements are polarity-sensitive, but are rather underspecified for the kind of polarity they are sensitive to. English *until* behaves NPI-like when combined with perfective morphology, and PPI-like when combined with imperfective morphology. A question that comes to mind is whether elements can even be both NPIs and PPIs at the same time. Arguably, if the source of the NPI- and PPI-hood were the same, this would not be possible, as its licensing requirements would be contradictory. But given the convergence approach, different NPI- and PPI-sources might coexist on the same element. Van der Wouden (1994) refers to such elements as bipolar PIs.

In this light, I would like to refer to Shimoyama (2011), who argues that neg-words (or other kinds of NPIs) could either be perceived as existentials that take obligatory scope under negation or universals that obligatory outscope negation (see also Szabolcsi 1981; Giannakidou 2000). She argues that Korean and Japanese neg-words are examples of that (though she incorrectly takes them to be plain NPIs). Such proposals have often been criticized for a lack of understanding of what properties could make a particular item obligatorily outscope negation. However, nothing would forbid a (weak) universal quantifier PPI of the type discussed

16.4 OPEN QUESTIONS 399

in Chapters 13–14 to be equipped with a [uNEG]-feature. Then, it would have its [uNEG]-feature first checked below negation, subsequently raise across it, and not be reconstructable below it. Naturally, this would trigger parsing questions, as these languages are Strict NC languages, where the semantic negation is only covertly present; but those questions may very well be answerable. Whether such universal neg-words exist in the above-mentioned or other languages is something that will have to be investigated.

Finally, it should be mentioned that a currently hotly debated topic in semantic and pragmatic theory concerns the illocutionary contribution of imperatives. Imperatives like *Sit down!* trigger various readings, such as obligations, permissions, and, in the right context (for instance when followed by something like *and you'll relax*), even conditional interpretations (cf. von Fintel and Iatridou 2017).

Theories that assign a rich meaning to imperatives (e.g. Han 2000; Kaufmann 2012) have a hard time accounting for these multiple meaning contributions. By contrast, theories that assign a much poorer meaning to imperatives appear more apt for that, such as Portner (2007), who argues that imperatives simply denote properties that, via some pragmatic procedure, get added to a hearer's to-do list. Under such approaches, there is simply no illocutionary feature present, neither in the semantics nor in the syntax. Other approaches, such as Condoravdi and Lauer's (2012) account in terms of speakers' effective preferences, take intermediate positions.

The relatively poor or underspecified meaning contribution that imperatives make is, however, at odds with the account in the previous chapter, which takes illocutionary properties to be encoded in high functional heads. The PPI-hood of such illocutionary features cannot be understood otherwise.

One way to resolve these apparently conflicting constraints is assuming that (i) the illocutionary meaning contribution of imperatives is the same as that of other sentence types (at least declaratives, leaving interrogatives out of the discussion here); (ii) this meaning contribution is still encoded in some syntactic head, at least in the case of imperatives; and (iii) all other syntactic and semantic differences between imperatives and declaratives reduce to differences in the rest of their syntax. Let us discuss each assumption in turn, focusing on the distinction between declaratives and imperatives.

While, semantically, they appear quite different, in both declaratives and imperatives, there is a shared illocutionary effect where, in the case of a declarative, the speaker wants to inform the hearer about something. In other words, by uttering a declarative, the speaker invites the hearer to update their information stage accordingly. In the case of an imperative, the speaker enforces or invites the hearer to contemplate a particular action. Rather than attributing these differences to different illocutionary properties of declaratives vs imperatives, one could say that, in both cases, the illocutionary properties are the same and can be informally paraphrased as 'the speaker invites the hearer to consider doing something with ….'

The result of this is that, to the extent that declaratives and imperatives require a particular dedicated head (as the C-head in mainland Germanic languages), there is one and the same head present in declaratives and imperatives. The crucial innovation is that there are no two different heads for declaratives and imperatives.

The question then arises of what differentiates imperatives from declaratives. This involves two different, but related questions: how are imperatives different from declaratives syntactically, and how are imperatives different from declaratives semantically?

Here, one may assume, following standard analyses, that declaratives involve a full-fledged finite TP and that this TP is interpreted as a proposition, i.e., a set of possible worlds. This accounts for the fact that declaratives are always tensed and marked for finiteness. It also accounts for the fact that, as propositions constitute pieces of knowledge, the hearer, when addressed, can only decide to accept this piece of knowledge, consider it, or reject it. Hence, a declarative indeed involves the speaker inviting the hearer to consider accepting or rejecting the proposition, or keeping it open.

By contrast, imperatives are known to be syntactically deprived. Concretely, we assume that imperatives lack the TP layer and are vPs/VPs directly embedded under the illocutionary head (see Zanuttini, Pak, and Portner 2012 for related discussion). Syntactically, this accounts for the fact that imperatives are formed either by bare stems or by very poorly marked inflection. Semantically, if vPs/VPs denote events or properties, uttering an imperative results in the speaker inviting the hearer to consider doing something with that event/property, i.e., carrying it out, or at least consider carrying it out and considering its consequences. That is compatible with all attested usages of the imperative. Pragmatic considerations may further narrow down the usage of an imperative in a particular social and conversational situation. Such a view could potentially reconcile the morphosyntactic poverty of imperatives and their unspecified semantics with the fact that an illocutionary feature still needs to be syntactically encoded.

16.5 Final remarks

All conclusions and open questions so far have concerned the study of negation and negative dependencies. However, these conclusions also have repercussions for other areas of syntax, semantics, and the interface between them. For instance, the way feature-checking works here (where the checker c-commands the checkee) is different from more standard versions of Agree. Also, the way grammaticalization works from the perspective of the FFFH should not only apply to negation.

And, finally, if NC is an example of a grammaticalized semantic dependency, more instances of such dependencies should be attested.

In the next chapter, I will discuss certain avenues for further research from this perspective: What are the consequences of this study for other areas of syntax, semantics, and the syntax–semantics interface? It turns out that the above-mentioned predictions are indeed all borne out.

17
Avenues for further research

17.1 Outline

In this chapter, I concentrate on the syntactic and semantic repercussion of the theories presented in this monograph. One area in which the theory made a number of non-trivial predictions is the nature of syntactic agree(ment) in general: while, for NC, it is clear that negative features must probe upwards, this has not been the standard assumption in the literature (Chomsky 2000, 2001), leading to an intensive debate (cf. Wurmbrand 2012a, b; Zeijlstra 2012a; Preminger 2013; Preminger and Polinsky 2015; Bjorkman and Zeijlstra 2019). Also, the FFFH applies much more generally than just for the acquisition of negative features. In fact, it makes universal predictions for all (kinds of) formal features. The consequences, both for the nature of formal features and for the role they play in syntactic structure, will be addressed in Section 17.2. For one, this will include an attempt to derive Upward Agree from the FFFH.

It turns out that two existing puzzles in the domain of verb movement can be readily explained by the outcomes of this study. These are discussed in in Section 17.3. One concerns the so-called Rich Agreement Hypothesis (RAH), which I argue, basing myself on Koeneman and Zeijlstra (2014), follows directly from the FFFH. The other concerns a long-standing puzzle in the syntax of head movement: Is rightward, string-adjacent head movement possible or not? I show that what has been presented as the strongest piece of evidence for this position no longer holds, given the existence of universal quantifier PPIs.

Finally, the fact that syntactic feature-checking underlies NC also entails that it should be possible that such feature-checking configurations also underlie other grammatical dependencies. In Section 17.4, I show how this works for the phenomenon of Sequence of Tense (SoT) and for the relation between φ-agreement and pro-drop. I will also show, though, that this mechanism cannot underlie every syntactic/semantic dependency for which this has been proposed; for Modal Concord (MC), for instance, other mechanisms should be at stake.

Section 17.5 spells out some final conclusions.

17.2 Upward Agree, the FFFH, and the derivational behaviour of formal features

In this section, I first discuss to what extent the presented feature-checking mechanism may apply universally (i.e., for other syntactic agree(ment) phenomena as well). I argue in Subsection 17.2.1, basing myself on Zeijlstra (2012a) and Bjorkman and Zeijlstra (2019), who I largely follow here, that this is indeed possible, though only if structure-building mechanisms (feature-checking) are formally and operationally disentangled from structure-enrichment mechanisms (feature valuation). Naturally, this leads to the question of why upward probing should take place in the first place, and how feature-checking results in structure-building, a question I address in Subsection 17.2.2.

17.2.1 Upward Agree

The idea that NC involves an instance of feature-checking where the checker c-commands the checkee has serious consequences for the nature of agreement and the syntactic operation Agree. This version of Agree, generally dubbed 'Upward Agree' (UA), works in the opposite direction from the standard, Chomskyan version of Agree, referred to as 'Downward Agree' (DA). The definitions of the two versions of Agree are listed below:

(1) UA: α Agrees with β iff:
   a. α carries at least one uninterpretable feature and β carries a matching interpretable feature;
   b. β c-commands α;
   c. β is the closest goal to α.

(2) DA: α Agrees with β iff:[1]
   a. α carries at least one uninterpretable feature and β carries a matching interpretable feature;
   b. α c-commands β;
   c. β is the closest goal to α.

As discussed in Bjorkman and Zeijlstra (2019), the motivation for UA has come indeed from phenomena such as NC (see Chapters 3–4), (Strict) NPI licensing (Chapter 10), SoT (Subsection 17.4.1), and also binding (Hicks 2009; Reuland 2006; etc.), semantic agreement (Smith 2015), and inflection-doubling (Wurmbrand 2012a, b, 2014; Bjorkman 2016). The central motivation for DA

---

[1] After Chomsky (2000, 2001). For the sake of exposition, I did not include the so-called *Activation Condition* in the definition, which states that the goal should also carry an additional uninterpretable feature (see Zeijlstra 2012a for more discussion).

has arisen primarily from patterns of φ-agreement with lower arguments, often collectively referred to as 'long-distance agreement'. For instance, as shown by Polinsky and Potsdam (2001), in Tsez, embedded absolutive topical arguments control agreement on the matrix verb. Clearly, and discussed in detail in Polinsky and Potsdam (2001), there is no derivational stage in which the embedded topic is structurally higher than the matrix verb.

(3) Enir [užā magalu b-āc'rułi] b-iyxo (Tsez)
mother [boy bread.ABS(**III**) III-ate] **III**-know
'The mother knows [(that) (as for the bread) the boy ate it]'

In this context, the question arises of whether either DA or UA can provide a unified account of featural relations in syntax or not. As for the latter, there is an increasing body of work that argues that the direction of probing should be flexible, across languages and potentially across features (Baker 2008; Béjar and Rezac 2009; Merchant 2006b, 2011). However, Bjorkman and Zeijlstra (2019) have argued that a unification of feature-checking in the direction of UA is to be preferred.

The argument goes as follows. While long-distance agreement under DA should be the core case of agreement given (2), long-distance agreement is, in fact, less robust than agreement with higher arguments in several ways, casting doubt on the universal validity of DA. Downward φ-agreement (i.e., morphological agreement between a φ-probe and a goal c-commanded by this probe) appears to always be parasitic on pre-existing UA-relations between such probes and goals. This can already be seen in (3), where the embedded DP that can control agreement must itself be marked for special information-structural status, a phenomenon that can also be attested in various Algonquian languages (cf. Branigan and MacKenzie 2002; Hamilton and Fry 2014). Baker (2008) has made similar observations for languages with so-called case-linked φ-agreement where long-distance φ-agreement must be licensed by case-Agree.

Bjorkman and Zeijlstra argue that this asymmetry arises because downward φ-agreement in all cases amounts to instances of (possibly incomplete) upward valuation dependent on a separate, independently established UA relation, often based on case-agreement, but sometimes based on other features as well. This move unifies downward φ-agreement with canonical instances of UA (spec–head agreement, but also NC and its kin).

A necessary ingredient for Bjorkman and Zeijlstra is the distinction between feature-checking and valuation, as has already been proposed in Pesetsky and Torrego (2007); Arregui and Nevins (2012); and Bhatt and Walkow (2013). This enables them to conclude that long-distance agreement is not incompatible with UA, because UA is a mechanism of feature-checking which, in some cases, is compatible with the checker of a probe's being distinct from the element that values it.

17.2 UPWARD AGREE, THE FFFH, AND FORMAL FEATURES

For this, Bjorkman and Zeijlstra state that (1) only applies to feature-checking. Furthermore, they propose that feature-checking is a necessary precondition for valuation, which, therefore, must always precede it. In other words, an uninterpretable and unvalued feature [uF:] can only be valued after it has been checked via UA by a matching c-commanding interpretable feature. Because checking is only possible in UA configurations, the checker must c-command the checkee at some point in the derivation.

At the same time, long-distance agreement shows that there are cases of φ-agreement where the valuer never c-commands the valuee. The disentanglement of checking from valuation prevents the apparent contradiction between these two claims, opening up the possibility that the checker and the valuer of a particular [uF:] are distinct. For Bjorkman and Zeijlstra, if a checker for independent reasons cannot value its checkee (or can only partially value it), some other feature may act as an alternative source of valuation.

The question is, then, how to allow lower elements to value higher features without reintroducing downward probing; after all, if a probe could search in its c-command domain to find a valuer, one would expect it to be able to find a checker by the same means. To do so, Bjorkman and Zeijlstra suggest that Agree (which is always upward probing) establishes a relation of accessibility between syntactic elements, defined as in (4):

(4) α and β are accessible to each other iff a [uF] on α has been checked (via UA) by a corresponding interpretable feature ([iF]) on β.

For Bjorkman and Zeijlstra, it is the combination of (1) and (4) that captures not only cases of NC and similar instances of UA, but also the other two types of agreement configurations: spec–head agreement and long-distance agreement.

Under spec–head agreement, a probe, when there is no immediate goal available, does not just 'search down', but rather searches for any element it already stands in a UA relation with that is a suitable candidate to raise to its immediately c-commanding position (i.e., its specifier) to be checked and, if possible, to be valued by it. This is, for instance, the case if (finite) T has an unchecked and (φ-)unvalued [uD]-feature. Since the closest DP with nominative case, i.e., a DP with an uninterpretable finite Tense feature [uT] having been checked against T earlier, this DP, given (4), is accessible to T, and can thus raise to Spec, TP and value its [uD]-feature for φ.

If, however, for whatever reason, the checker of a probe, say T, lacks φ-values of itself, T cannot be fully valued by this checker. This is, for instance, the case in Icelandic quirky case constructions, when a dative DP is in Spec, TP. Assuming with Anagnastopoulou (2005) that datives are encapsulated by a dative shell that only contains a 3rd-person feature but no number feature, such a dative can only value the φ-probe on T for person, but not for number. If, however, T still stands in a UA relation with a lower DP, *in casu* a nominative, it should be possible for this nominative to complete valuation for number. The structure of (5a) is thus as in (5b):

(5) a. Jóni líkuðu Tessir sokkar (Icelandic)
 Jon.DAT like.3PL these socks.NOM
 'Jon likes these socks'
 b. [Jóni_{[iφ: 3RD]} líkuðu_{[iT][uφ: 3RD, PL]} Tessir sokkar_{[uT][i3.PL]}]

The fact that both the dative subject and the nominative object stand in a UA relation with T ensures that both φ-value T. Further evidence for this comes from the fact that, in Icelandic, nominative objects valued for 1st or 2nd person cannot appear in such quirky case constructions, as, then, valuation would end up being conflicting:

(6) *Einhverjum hafið alltaf líkað thið[2] (Icelandic)
 Someone has all liked you
 Int.: 'Someone likes y'all'

The above thus shows that cases of long-distance agreement are not incompatible with UA (pace Preminger 2013; Preminger and Polinsky 2015). The feature-checking mechanism behind NC may indeed apply universally, including instances of long-distance agreement, provided that feature-checking and feature valuation are formally and operationally disentangled, and that previously established Agree relationships remain visible for further derivational computations.

Naturally, many questions are open at this stage. For one, in many cases of long-distance agreement, downward φ-agreement is licensed (through accessibility) by upward case agreement, whereas it is far from clear that what underlies case assignment is actually feature-checking (cf. Marantz 1991; McFadden 2004; Baker 2015; Preminger 2014). Second, UA appears to work in a countercyclic fashion, something that is unexpected or even disallowed under certain minimalist perspectives (cf. Chomsky 1995a et seq.). But, perhaps even more importantly, it is not clear why there should be a c-command relation between a higher goal and a lower probe in the first place. Irrespective of the directionality of agree(ment), the question arises as to why it is c-command that constitutes the proper configurations for the operation to take place to begin with. Only if these questions (along with various others) can be satisfactorily explained can UA be said to be a better replacement of DA.

---

[2] Taken from Boeckx (2008).

17.2.2 The FFFH and the derivational behaviour of formal features

One of the major outcomes of Chapter 5 was the conclusion, based on the FFFH, that not only uninterpretable but also interpretable formal features lack semantic content. The fact that those features are visible only in the syntactic component and nowhere else ensures that such formal features only determine the syntactic behaviour of the elements that they are part of. But if those features determine the syntactic distribution of the elements that carry them, such formal features are actually identical to categorial features, which also lack semantic content and also only determine the syntactic behaviour of the elements that they are part of.

In this sense, so-called interpretable formal features (or better: independent formal features) are no different from better-known categorial features, such as [N] or [V], which determine the categorial status of lexical categories (a verb has a feature [V], a noun [N], etc.). Such categorial features also only determine the syntactic distribution of lexical elements, but are not transparently mapped onto a particular meaning: Even though every verb clearly carries a feature [V], not every verb has a meaning denoting an action or a state.

Much in the same vein, there is no principled distinction between uninterpretable formal features (or better: dependent formal features) and selectional features either: a selectional feature encodes the requirement to be merged with an element that carries a particular independent feature; and that is exactly what a dependent feature does: dependent features encode dependencies on other features. For instance, a feature [uD] encodes the dependency on an element carrying [D]. Hence, the full syntactic distribution, and, therefore, all categorial information of a particular syntactic element comes from both its independent and its dependent features. By disentangling formal features from semantic features, all so-called interpretable, uninterpretable, selectional, and categorial features reduce to two types of categorial features: independent and dependent features.

This opens up ways to understand why Agree should work in an upward fashion. Given the above, every lexical item can be said to contain three sets of features: a set of phonological features (if vocabulary insertion does not take place postsyntactically, an assumption on which nothing crucial hinges here), a set of semantic features, and a set of formal features, where the latter come about in two types— dependent and independent formal features. A lexical item like the preposition *on* would then consist of the following formal feature set: {[P], [uD]}. The independent feature [P] determines the syntactic behaviour of a preposition; [uD] is a dependent feature that requires (or 'selects') an element with feature [D] (*in casu*, a DP). Both types of formal features ([P] and [uD]) thus determine the lexical item's syntactic behaviour. Now, let us see what happens when two elements merge and this merger fulfils a featural dependency.

Suppose some element α that carries the formal features [F] and [uG] merges with an element β that carries the formal feature [G]. Then, α (minimally) contains a feature set {[F], [uG]}, and β a feature set {[G]}. The categorial status of α is that of an element of type F that needs an element of type G to survive. For instance, if F is P and G is D, α would be a preposition that needs to merge with a DP. Now, the result of merging a preposition that needs a DP-complement with just such a DP is a prepositional element that has this D-complement requirement satisfied (and, therefore, has the syntactic behaviour of a prepositional phrase). Thus, after merger, both the dependent feature ([uD]) and the element that satisfies the dependency ([D]) should no longer be present.

This should not come as a surprise. In fact, the hallmark of Categorial Grammar, a grammar that has syntactic operations fully driven by the categorial properties of lexical items and their combinations, is that the combination of the elements a/b and b yields an element of category a, just as, in semantic type theory, the mother of a daughter with type e and a daughter with type <e, t> is of type t, or the way unification works in frameworks like HPSG. Let us therefore formulate the following rule:

(7) Let A and B be two sets of formal features. If A merges with B, for any pair [F]-[uF], such that [F]∈A and [uF]∈B, or [F]∈B and [uF]∈, A neither [uF] nor [F] percolates; all features that do not stand in such pairs, percolate up.

Given (7), the merger of [F] and [G] then immediately yields the required result, as is shown in (8).

(8)
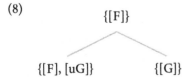

Note that, under this proposal, even though the leftmost daughter is clearly the head, headedness itself is not pregiven. It is just a result of the choice of feature sets that the merger of {[F], [uG]}, and {[G]} is {[F]}. Indeed, if the rightmost daughter contained an additional feature [uK], features from both daughters would percolate:

(9)
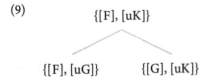

This way, UA can be derived. Given that all features have been reduced to categorial features, what look like traditional projection lines are nothing but percolations of independent(/interpretable) features. Now, by definition, independent features are not able to percolate beyond their maximal projection as maximal projections are defined in terms of feature percolation of independent

17.2 UPWARD AGREE, THE FFFH, AND FORMAL FEATURES

features: a [V]-feature cannot percolate beyond the VP it projects. However, such restrictions do not hold for dependent(/uninterpretable) features. No such feature is blocked from percolating at XP-level. In fact, if an element carrying [uF] does not merge with an element carrying [F], [uF] will percolate to the top node, irrespective of its original position.

This derives the asymmetry that underlies UA. What happens is that every uninterpretable feature will percolate upward until it stands in a sisterhood relation with a matching interpretable feature. Note that this also reduces feature-checking to a sisterhood relation, which thus solves the above-mentioned cyclicity problem.

This is illustrated in (10) for Agree between an interrogative C-head and a *Wh*-term. Under the assumption that the interrogative C-head carries an interpretable [Q]-feature and an uninterpretable *Wh*-feature [uWh], and that the *Wh*-term carries an interpretable *Wh*-feature [iWh] and an uninterpretable [uQ]-feature, it follows that the [uQ]-feature on the *Wh*-term can be checked in situ. The [uQ]-feature percolates all the way up to TP, where it is the sister of C. Neither [Q] on C nor [uQ] on TP percolate further. See (10) for an illustration (ignoring the vP-layer), where it should be noted that the [uWh]-feature on the top node should be checked by a raised *Wh*-term in Spec, CP later on.

(10)

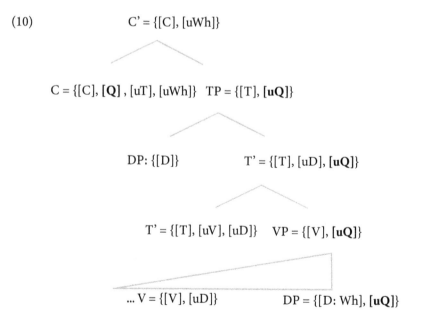

In this sense, Agree (or, rather, feature-checking) and selection amount to the same underlying relation. What looks like a non-local long-distance checking relation is nothing but postponed selection under sisterhood.

NC can be analysed very similarly. Take the following Strict NC example from Czech:

(11) a. Milan   nevolá   nikomu   (Czech)
        Milan   NEG.calls   NEG-body
        'Milan doesn't call anybody'

   b. [TP Op¬[NEG] Milan nevolá[uNEG] nikoho[uNEG]]

As discussed earlier, the NM in a Strict NC language like Czech carries [uNEG]. However, this cannot be the only feature it contains. If it did, the structure would be as in (12) (ignoring subject movement to Spec, TP):

(12)

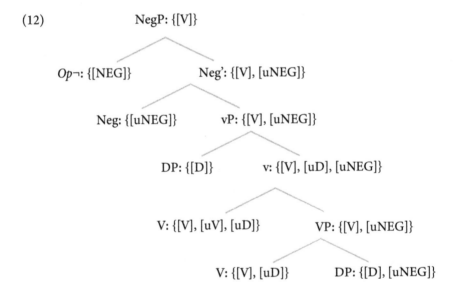

But such a structure cannot be correct. First, the NM would be an element that lacks any kind of independent feature. Second, even to the extent that this were possible (essentially by rendering negative particles acategorial; see Sheehan 2017; Biberauer 2017 for a discussion on such acategorial particles), under such an analysis, the observation that the NM is a head that is part of the verbal spine would no longer be captured. The NM is not a head, but, at best, an element selected by the verbal head. However, all diagnostics for phrasality of NMs indicate that the Czech NM *ne* clearly is a head, as shown in Chapter 1.

The problems just listed can easily be overcome if the NM is assigned a feature set {[V], [uV], [uNEG]}. Then, as the NM does carry an independent feature, it acts as a head, since its verbal feature projects and it selects the maximal projection VP, as can be seen in the structure in (13):

(13)

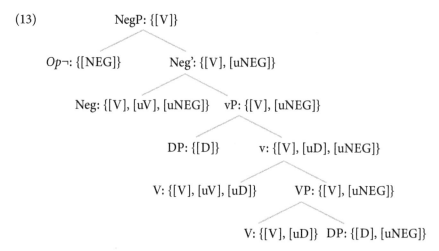

Note that, for Non-strict NC languages, things work in the same way. The only relevant difference between the Italian and the Czech construction is the absence of a covert negative operator and the presence of [NEG] instead of [uNEG] on the NM in the Italian. Everything else is similar.

(14) a. Gianno non ha detto niente   (Italian)
    Gianno NEG has said NEG-thing
    'Gianni didn't say anything'

b. [TP Gianni non[NEG] ha detto niente[uNEG]]

Even though the above-sketched view on Merge and feature percolation has started out as a way of understanding the directionality of Agree, it should be mentioned that it forms a more general feature architecture that aims at solving some other general problems as well.

One of them concerns the question of labelling. While the question of what provides the label upon merger has occupied a central position in minimalist theorizing (cf. Chomsky 1995a,b, 2008, 2013, 2015; Collins 2002, 2017; Adger 2003; Boeckx 2008; Cecchetto and Donati 2010, 2015; Adger 2013), up to this point, no fully satisfactory and uncontroversial labelling algorithm has been provided. In Zeijlstra (2020b), I argue that this is due to the fact that it is generally assumed that the operation Merge itself does not yield a label and that, therefore, an additional labelling algorithm is derived. However, given (7), labelling is an epiphenomenon of Merge, since it predicts what features form its output set. Hence, labelling results from the way Merge applies to the kind of formal features that the FFFH renders possible.

An additional outcome of this featural architecture is that selection and Agree are unified in the sense that both require pairs of matching independent and dependent features in a sisterhood relation. Given that selection triggers building of syntactic structures, it also follows that probes and goals are not only connected to each other by means of an UA relation (along the lines of Subsection 17.2.1), but also stand in a number of additional selectional/agreement pathways. This is especially relevant for long-distance agreement: A higher probing head selects a phrase, whose head, in turn, selects another phrase, and so on until a lower goal is reached. This means that, even if case features are not checked in narrow syntax, it is still the case that lower goals and higher probes stand in an accessibility relation, thus removing one potential problem for the UA proposal spelled out in Bjorkman and Zeijlstra (2019).

17.3 Uninterpretable features, Positive Polarity Items, and the nature of V-to-I movement

One of the outcomes of this study is that only in NC languages can NMs be heads in the clausal spine, and, consequently, affixal in nature. This has been shown to be the case for both Romance and Slavic languages. While NMs in Romance languages can be taken to be clitic-like (cf. Zanuttini 1997), and thus not part of the verbal inflectional morphology, NMs in Slavic languages (as well as various other Strict NC languages) are generally affixal in nature (see Chapter 1). As discussed in Chapter 5 in detail, such affixal heads may only emerge in NC languages. The FFFH renders formal features that project heads unlearnable if there is no agreement with respect to these features.

One of the consequences of these heads being affixes (or syntactic clitics) is that the verb must undergo syntactic head movement to be able to phonologically attach to them. What we thus see here is that NC, i.e., negative agreement, triggers V-to-Neg movement. If, however, the mechanism from which this follows is not specific for negation, but applies to formal features in general, it is expected that the existence of agreement with respect to particular features will trigger verb movement in other domains as well. This is indeed the case.

17.3.1 The Rich Agreement Hypothesis

One area where strong generalizations have been formulated concerning the relation between agreement and verb movement is the relation between (rich) φ-morphology and V-to-I movement. The generalization that V-to-I movement is conditioned by rich subject agreement on the finite verb, generally referred to as the *Rich Agreement Hypothesis* (RAH), has, ever since the 1980s, been an

17.3 UNINTERPRETABLE FEATURES, PPIS, V-TO-I MOVEMENT

important argument in favour of a direct connection between syntax and morphology (Kosmeijer 1986; Pollock 1989; Platzack and Holmberg 1989; Holmberg and Platzack 1991, 1995; Roberts 1993; Rohrbacher 1994; Vikner 1995, 1997; Bobaljik 1995; Bobaljik and Thráinsson 1998; Koeneman 2000; and others). In more recent years, the RAH has been disputed on both empirical and theoretical grounds. Empirically, data have been put forward that seem to suggest the existence of language varieties that are poorly inflected but still display V-to-I movement (e.g. Jonas 1995 for Faroese; Rohrbacher 1994 for French; and Bentzen et al. 2007 for Regional Northern Norwegian varieties), as well as varieties that do not display obligatory V-to-I movement despite being richly inflected (e.g. Bailyn 2005 for Russian; Bentzen et al. 2007 for Icelandic; Garbacz 2010 for Älvdalen Swedish).

Theoretically, under lexicalist approaches (cf. Chomsky 1995a), the tight connection between rich agreement and V-to-I movement has been taken as a strong argument in favour of the idea that morphology drives syntax (cf. Rohrbacher 1994; Vikner 1995; Koeneman 2000). However, in current generative models of grammar, morphological insertion is assumed to take place after the syntactic computation (cf. Bonet 1991; Marantz 1991; Noyer 1992; Bobaljik 2008), suggesting that morphology can have no direct influence on the syntactic derivation. This is also what has been proposed in Section 17.2: structure-building drives structure enrichment, not the other way round.

Two lines of response have been formulated to the empirical problems. One is to abandon the RAH altogether (cf., for instance, Bentzen et al. 2007). The other has been to weaken the generalization by assuming that the RAH only applies in a uni-directional fashion (cf. Bobaljik and Thráinsson 1998, among others). Generally speaking, examples showing that V-to-I may take place in the absence of rich agreement have always appeared stronger than examples suggesting that languages with rich agreement lack V-to-I movement. If so, this allows one to at least maintain a weak version of the RAH: if the language has rich agreement, it must have V-to-I movement, but no prediction is made for languages without rich agreement (cf. also Rohrbacher 1994; Vikner 1995; Bobaljik 1995; Thráinsson 1996; Bobaljik and Thráinsson 1998; Koeneman 2000).

The abandonment of the RAH no longer presupposes any correlation between morphology and syntax, and is thus in line with recent ideas on postsyntactic spellout of morphology. However, as Bobaljik (1995), Thráinsson (1996), and Bobaljik and Thráinsson (1998) have pointed out, the idea that morphological insertion takes place after syntax does not entail that any correlation between morphology and syntax becomes unstatable. For them, rich inflection may motivate the presence of more functional projections, and it is this extra structure that triggers verb movement.

In Koeneman and Zeijlstra (2014), novel arguments have been provided that show that both of these approaches are on the wrong track, and that, contrary to current ideas, the RAH should be reinstalled in its strongest, bi-directional form. The reasons for this are twofold.

First, Koeneman and Zeijlstra argue that the empirical arguments hitherto provided with the aim of showing that the RAH is (at least partially) incorrect are, at best, incomplete and quite often just false. It is shown that all presented counterexamples to the RAH are actually fully compatible with it.

Second, Bobaljik and Thráinsson's conjecture that morphological richness reflects a rich(er) functional structure should be extended, in that it does not just reflect but also determines functional structure. Given the FFFH, rich morphology forms the only possible cue for language learners to postulate those formal features that can project this richer functional structure in the first place. In this way, even though morphology does not drive syntax in the linguistic model, where structure enrichment is parasitic on structure-building, as argued for in Section 17.2, morphology does determine syntax through acquisition, thus establishing a tight connection between the two.

Koeneman and Zeijlstra (2014) start by pointing out that, in terms of the featural system, all languages in the world show at least featural distinctions with respect to [speaker], [participant], and [plural] in their pronominal systems (cf. Greenberg 1963; Harley and Ritter 2002; Cysouw 2003, see also Zeijlstra 2015b). For them, every subject paradigm is constituted by these three features.

Here, it should be noted that Harbour (2016) argued against this observation by stating that there are subject paradigms that are smaller than this, in the sense that some systems may lack a 1st–2nd person distinction, other systems a participant–non-participant distinction, and, again, other systems a number distinction.

However, Tvica (2017) has shown that Harbour's opposition does not hold strong. Strikingly, every language that does not distinguish between 1st- and 2nd-person subject persons disambiguates between them by means of verbal agreement. This is shown for Winnebago (Helmbrecht and Lehmann 2010: 11, taken from Tvica 2017: 56) in (15), where, as a result of verbal agreement, *nee* in (15a) must be interpreted as a 1st-person subject and *nee* in (15b) as a 2nd-person.

(15) a. Nee   ha-šgác   (Winnebago)
      1/2   1.SG-play
      'I play'

    b. Nee   ra–šgác
      1/2   2.SG-play
      'You play'

It turns out that every language checked for this indeed makes a distinction between the three persons, with the notable exception of Sanapana, where 2nd and 3rd person are indeed syncretic. Given that this is the only known counterexample, it might be the case that, here, sheer accidental homophony is involved. This attested syncretism is not in any way systematic.

In the domain of number, things are slightly less straightforward. Even though a significant number of languages that lack a number distinction in the pronoun system compensate for that in their agreement system, most languages still distinguish (particular) number-specific from number-unspecific pronouns. For instance, in Classical Chinese, certain pronouns can only have a singular interpretation, whereas others can be used for both singular and plural. *Yú, yu, yí*, and *zhèn* only mean 'I', whereas *wú, wo*, and *àng* can mean 'I' or 'we'. There is only one language known to Tvica (2017) that does not make any number distinction among pronouns, namely Jarawa.

Now, Koeneman and Zeijlstra (2014) observe that, in every language where the verbal-agreement paradigm is equally rich, i.e., where both at least [±speaker], [±participant], and number distinctions are being made, the verb moves to a vP-external position; and in languages where this is not the case, the verb stays in situ, unless it has to raise for other reasons (e.g., to C^0 in languages with V-to-C movement). Icelandic and Yiddish, which count as rich-agreement languages in this sense, indeed have the verb raised across vP-boundary adverbs (such as *ekki/nit* 'not') ((16)–(17)), whereas poor-agreement languages do not have their verbs raised across such adverbs, as shown for Danish and English (using adverbs like *ofte/often* 'often' and *ikke* 'not') ((18)–(19)).

(16) a. Ég spurði hvort Jón {sæi} **ekki** {*sæi} myndina (Icelandic)
I asked if John saw NEG saw the.movie
'I asked if John didn't see the movie'

b. Ég spurði hvort Jón {hefði} **ekki** {*hefði} séð myndina
I asked if John had NEG seen the.movie
'I asked if John had not seen the movie'

(17) Ikh veys nit ven di ku {iz} **nit** {*iz} geshtanen
I know NEG when the cow is NEG stood
in tsimer (Yiddish)
in.the room
'I do not know when the cow didn't stand in the room'

(18) a. Gad vide om John {*fik} ikke {fik} set filmen (Danish)
I wonder if John saw NEG the movie
'I wonder if John did not see the movie'

b. Gad vide om John fik {*fik} ofte {fik} set filmen
I wonder if John saw often the movie
'I wonder if John often saw the movie'

(19) I wonder if John {saw} **often** {saw} the movie.

The reason for this, they argue, is that, jointly, these feature distinctions constitute grammatical argumenthood. That is, the formal feature [Argument] is a composite of these three features. Given the FFFH, only if there is evidence in terms of agreement with respect to the three above-mentioned features can the feature [Argument] be acquired. By contrast, if, in a verbal paradigm, these featural distinctions are not represented, there is no evidence for the language learner that a feature [Argument] exists in the target language.

Consequently, only in a language with rich verbal agreement can agreement features be seen as an instantiation of a feature [Argument]. In fact, those features then form the head of a functional projection Arg(ument)P that is taken to be immediately above vP.

The structural difference between languages with rich agreement and those with poor agreement is that only the former, not the latter, have a functional position. This position is standardly referred to as I°, but, actually, it is a projection of the feature [Argument]. Movement to this position can then simply be taken to result from application of the Stray-Affix Filter (Lasnik 1981, 1995; Baker 1988) or any implementation of it. In languages with rich agreement, the semantic notion of argumenthood gets grammaticalized, triggering movement into the head of ArgP, whereas, in poor-agreement languages (20b), argumenthood is only a semantic notion and not part of syntax (20a).

(20) a. Poor-agreement languages:

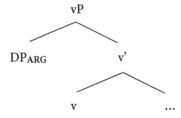

b. Rich-agreement languages:

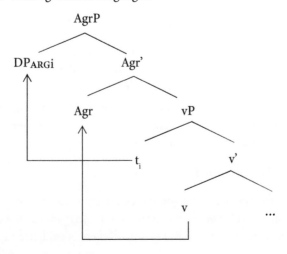

The RAH is thus another prediction that can be derived from the FFFH, and thus be used to prove its correctness. And, as Koeneman and Zeijlstra (2014) and Tvica (2017) have shown, various apparent counterexamples have indeed turned out not to hold under closer scrutiny. The study by Tvica (2017), which has a much stronger empirical basis, also typologically confirms the RAH.

17.3.2 Alleged V-to-I movement in Korean

One possible caveat must be made, though. In testing the validity of the RAH, Koeneman and Zeijlstra (2014), Tvica (2017), and their predecessors only focused on head-initial languages, the reason being that V-to-I (or V-to-Arg) movement is hard to diagnose in head-final languages, given that such movement would be string-adjacent.

In fact, it is questionable in the first place whether rightward string-adjacent head movement can take place at all. If something like the Stray-Affix Filter is what is behind V-to-I/Arg movement, rightward V-to-I/Arg movement should not be expected, given that the conditions under which the Stray-Affix Filter applies are already trivially met.

Whether rightward string-adjacent head movement exists or not has been an issue of debate for a long time. Otani and Whitman (1991), Yoon (1994), Koizumi (1995, 2000), and Choi (1999), among others, have argued that, in Japanese, verbs must raise out of the VP for reasons involving ellipsis, scrambling, coordination, and NPI licensing. By contrast, Kim (1995), Kim (1999), Chung and Park (1997), Hoji (1998), and Fukui and Sakai (2003) have shown that all these facts can also be accounted for by approaches that do not allude to rightward head movement, and thus do not provide any evidence in favour of it.

The argument in favour of rightward (string-adjacent) head movement that is often considered the strongest comes from language-internal variation in Korean. Han et al. (2007, 2016) have shown that there are two varieties of Korean: a variety where universal quantifier objects outscope sentential negation, and a variety where such universal quantifier objects take scope below sentential negation:

(21) John-i motun chayk-ul an ilk-ess ta (Korean)
 John-NOM every book-ACC NEG read-PST-DECL
 Variety I: 'John didn't read every book' $\neg > \forall$
 Variety II: 'John read no book' $\forall > \neg$

As Han et al. (2016) show, this variability is attested between speakers, but not within the language of any one speaker, which suggests that the two varieties of Korean have different grammars. Moreover, they show that this variation appears to be rather arbitrary; for instance, it cannot be predicted on the basis of the variety of the parents what variety the child has.

Han et al. (2007) base themselves on the following three assumptions. First, they follow Hagstrom (2000, 2002), who argues that objects in Korean always raise from a VP-internal position to a VP-external position. Second, they assume that Korean is scope-rigid (Joo 1989; Ahn 1990; Sohn 1995; Hagstrom 2000). And, third, they argue that, morphosyntactically, the NM needs to attach to the finite verb.

Then, Han et al. (2007) argue that, in Variety I, the verb raises from V to T and the negation raises along, whereas, in Variety II, the verb stays in situ, and the tense marker lowers down to V. Since, in Variety I, negation raises along with the verb to a position (T) higher than the object, negation outscopes the object (22a). In Variety II, negation is in a position that is structurally lower than the (raised) object, such that the object outscopes negation (22b).

(22) a. Variety I:

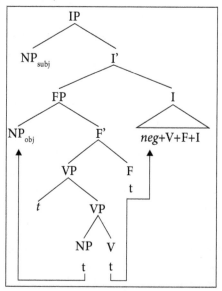

17.3 UNINTERPRETABLE FEATURES, PPIS, V-TO-I MOVEMENT

b. Variety II:

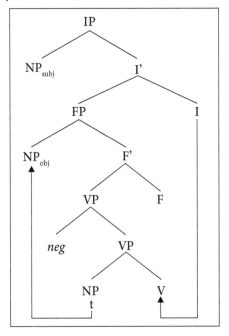

However, it is far from clear that Korean provides evidence for rightward string-adjacent head movement and that the presence or absence of rightward verb raising explains the difference between the two varieties. In fact, we will see that the two varieties are only different in terms of the polarity-sensitivity of universal quantifiers. Consequently, what is perhaps the strongest argument in favour of rightward (string-adjacent) head movement vanishes.

First of all, Korean indeed appears to be scope-rigid with respect to quantifiers that surface in their base position; only scrambling gives rise to ambiguity, as shown below.

(23) a. Nwukwunka-ka   motun salam-ul   piphanhay-ss-ta.   (Korean)
     someone-NOM   every person-ACC   criticize-PST-DECL
     'Someone criticized every person' (∃ >∀; *∀> ∃)

  b. [Motun salam-ul]ᵢ   nwukwunka-ka tᵢ piphanhay-ss-ta
     every person-ACC   someone-NOM   criticize-PST-DECL
     'Someone criticized every person' (∃ > ∀; ∀>∃)

But such scope-rigidity does not inform us about the scopal relation between quantifiers and other scope-taking elements, such as negation, as can be shown for German (cf. Fanselow 2001; Fanselow and Cavar 2002; Bobaljik and Wurmbrand 2012). German quantifiers behave in the same way in terms of scope-rigidity with respect to each other (24), but, as discussed in Chapters 13–14, German quantifiers and modals are not scope-rigid with respect to negation (25).

(24) a. ... dass fast jeder Mann mindestens eine Frau kennt   (German)
    ... that nearly every.NOM man at least one.ACC woman knows
    '... that nearly every man knows at least one woman'(∀> ∃; *∃ >∀)

  b. ... dass [mindestens eine Frau] fast jeder Mann t_i kennt
    ... that at least one.ACC woman every.NOM man knows
    '... that nearly every man knows at least one woman' (∀>∃; ∃ > ∀)

(25) a. Marie hat nicht eine Frau gesehen   (German)
    Marie has NEG a woman seen   (¬ > ∃; ∃ > ¬)

  b. Jeder hat nicht gearbeitet
    everybody has NEG worked   (∀ > ¬; ¬ > ∀)

  c. Marie soll nicht gehen
    Marie should NEG leave   (should>¬; *¬>should)

  d. Marie darf nicht gehen
    Marie may NEG leave   (¬>may; #may>¬)

Hence, quantifier scope-rigidity does not extend to other scopal construals. Also, Korean appears to not be fully scope-rigid with respect to subject quantifiers and negation. While universal subject quantifiers take wide scope with respect to negation (26a), NPI subjects take narrow scope (26b).[3]

(26) a. Ta an o-ass-ta   (Korean)
    all NEG come-PST-DECL
    'All didn't come'   (∀ > ¬)

  b. Amwuto khwukhi-lul an mek-ess-ta
    anyone cookie-ACC neg eat-PST-DECL
    'Nobody ate the cookies'   (¬ > ∃)

So, nothing would forbid quantifier reconstruction below negation in sentences like (21). Consequently, Variety II should display ambiguity for such sentences, contrary to fact.

A second problem, as acknowledged by Han et al., is that Korean speakers of Variety I also take sentences like (21) to be true in scenarios where John read no book. Under the view that neither negation nor objects may reconstruct in Korean, this is a problem for their analysis. To circumvent this problem, Han et al. argue that, since the ∀>¬ reading entails the ¬>∀ reading, the participants in their experiments who accepted the ¬>∀ reading also accepted the ∀>¬ reading (since the ¬>∀ reading is still true in a ∀>¬ scenario). However, for speakers of a language where a universal quantifier object takes scope below negation (as in English *Mary didn't eat all the cookies*), such sentences are generally not felicitous when uttered

---

[3] Though see Shimoyama (2011), who argues that NPI in Korean must outscope negation irrespective of their surface position (see also Section 16.4.4).

in a scenario where ∀>¬ is true, the reason being that such sentences also trigger an existential implicature (e.g. that Mary ate at least one cookie). Hence, Variety II shows an ambiguity that is predicted to not arise.

Folloqing Zeijlstra (2022), these problems call for an alternative analysis of the Korean facts. And, given the discussion in Chapter 13, one alternative suggests itself almost immediately. Universal quantifiers which are PPIs are elements that are fine under negation, but that may not reconstruct below negation if they appear above it at surface structure. The reason why *everybody* in (27a) can scope below negation, but Dutch *iedereen* ('everybody') cannot is that the latter, unlike the former, is such a PPI.

(27) a. Everybody didn't walk   (∀ > ¬; ¬ > ∀)
     b. Iedereen liep niet   (∀ > ¬; *¬ > ∀)
        everybody walked not

The circumstances under which subject *every/ieder(een)* may or may not reconstruct are virtually identical to the circumstances under which negated universal quantifier objects in Korean appear: in their surface position, they are in a position higher than the negation. Assuming, then, that, in Variety I, the universal quantifier is polarity-neutral, whereas, in Variety II, it is a PPI (of the kind discussed in Chapter 13) explains the full pattern. In Variety I, the object raises to a position outside negation, but can reconstruct in its base position. Therefore, these sentences are fine with both a ¬>∀ and a ∀>¬ construal. In Variety II, the object raises as well, but since the object is a PPI, the object can no longer reconstruct, and the only available reading is ∀>¬. In (28a), the analysis of Variety I, reconstruction is possible, whereas this is forbidden in (28b), the analysis of Variety II.

(28) Variety I   [$_{TP}$ [$_{FP}$ OB$_i$ [[<OB$_i$> V] NEG]] T]
     Variety II [$_{TP}$ [$_{FP}$ OB$_i$ [[<OB$_i$> V] NEG]] T]

The Korean facts can thus be better explained by simply reducing the difference between the two varieties to the polarity-sensitivity of the universal quantifier: In Variety II, it is a PPI; in Variety I, it is not. Variation with respect to polarity-sensitivity is widely attested in other languages as well, as we have already seen for universal quantifier subjects. And even within a single language, such variation can be found. As discussed in Chapter 13, Dutch modal *moeten* 'must' is a PPI in most western varieties of the language, but not in most eastern varieties (see also Iatridou and Zeijlstra 2013). Finally, Dutch *ooit* 'ever' is an NPI in the northern varieties, but not in the southern varieties (Hoeksema 1999a). Consequently, the type of variation attested in Korean is not in any way exceptional. It belongs to the kind of semantic variation that is well-known and provides evidence neither for the existence of rightward (string-adjacent) head movement in syntax, nor for arbitrary variation with respect to it, at least in Korean.

17.4 Other types of syntactic dependencies

The final avenue to be taken in this chapter involves a comparison with other syntactic dependencies where some semantic property appears to be spread over multiple items in a sentence. After all, there is nothing negation-specific about the NC analysis; so, such dependencies are predicted to manifest themselves in other domains too. One such domain is tense, and I briefly sketch in Subsection 17.4.1 how a particular phenomenon in the semantics of embedded tense, SoT, can be naturally analysed in the same way as NC. In Subsection 17.4.2, I discuss the phenomenon of pro-drop, where it also appears to be the case that overt elements with some uninterpretable features can be checked by a covert element. An analysis of pro-drop in the same vein as NC is especially striking given the discussion in Subsection 17.2.1, where the question arose whether φ-agreement should be taken to be different from other types of 'agreement', such as NC. However, I would also like to emphasize that not every grammatical dependency can receive such an analysis. In Subsection 17.4.3, I demonstrate that the phenomenon of MC, despite previous attempts, should not be analysed on a par with NC.

17.4.1 Sequence of Tense

It has long been known that sentences in which a past tense is embedded under a matrix past have two readings: a simultaneous (sim) one and a backward-shifted (b-s) one, where the former constitutes the most salient interpretation.

(29) John said Mary was ill
 Sim: John, at some time earlier than the utterance time: 'Mary is ill'
 B-s: John, at some time earlier than the utterance time: 'Mary was ill'

The availability of the sim reading for past-under-past embeddings is commonly referred to as *Sequence of Tense* (SoT), and has been a prevalent topic of research for an extensive period of time. One reason for the continuing interest is that, intuitively, there are two ways to think about past tense, and each of them fails to predict the two-fold meaning distinction observed in (29).

Under an absolute view on past tense, each instance of past tense is taken to place the event time of the predicate it scopes over prior to the sentence's utterance time (cf. Reichenbach 1947; Prior 1967; Comrie 1985; Declerck 1995b, 2015). In cases in which a past-tense morpheme is embedded under a matrix past, two such prior-to-utterance-time relations are established, but their internal order is not further specified. Such a view correctly predicts the availability of the sim and the b-s readings for past-under-past sentences. At the same time, however, it also, incorrectly, predicts a forward-shifted (f-s) interpretation to be available, falsely supporting the following paraphrase for (29):

(30) John, at some time earlier than the utterance time: 'Mary will be ill'

The second intuitive way to look at past tense is to regard it as a relative tense. Under such a view, each instance of past tense is assumed to place the event time of the predicate it scopes over prior to the predicate's local evaluation time, which is provided by its closest c-commanding tense, or, in the absence of such a tense, the utterance time (cf., e.g., Prior 1967).

In contrast to an absolute view on past tense, adopting a relative view correctly rules out an f-s interpretation of (29), since the matrix tense provides the local evaluation time of the embedded tense. At the same time, however, such a proposal fails to predict the availability of the sim reading. The only reading it predicts correctly is the b-s one.

Hence, neither of the two intuitive views on past tense explains the systematic two-fold meaning distinction of English past-under-past constructions. To solve this problem, it has become received wisdom in most SoT literature that there exists some mechanism by means of which the embedded past tense may lose (some of) its semantic contribution in SoT contexts. Implementations of this insight vary, among others, from the assumption of a void tense in SoT languages (cf. Partee 1973; Heim 1994; Kratzer 1998), to a past tense which is, in fact, a present-in-disguise (Ross 1967; Abusch 1988, 1997), an optional tense-deletion mechanism constrained by syntax (Ogihara 1995; Stowell 1995, 2007), and hybrid approaches (Kusumoto 1999; von Stechow 2009). Irrespective of the different manners of implementation, however, an assumption shared by all of these proposals is LF-ambiguity between the sim and b-s readings. A notable exception to this assumption is provided by pragmatic approaches such as Altshuler (2016) and Altshuler and Schwarzschild (2012), who explore the presence or absence of cessation implicatures. However, as proposed in Kauf and Zeijlstra (2018, 2021), SoT can be analysed fully on a par with NC, and thus does not require any semantic or pragmatic tense-deletion mechanism.

The idea that SoT and NC can be analysed in similar terms is not new; already Stowell (1995, 2007) posed the idea. Intuitively, one could argue that that past-tense markers carry some feature [uPAST], checked by a covert past-tense operator (carrying [iPAST]). Then, the meaning contribution of any second past-tense marker would be redundant, as is the case with the negative marking of multiple elements in NC constructions. However, one point where NC and SoT diverge is that SoT constructions are always ambiguous between a sim and a b-s reading, whereas NC constructions are generally not ambiguous between NC and DN readings (French NC constructions being a notable exception).

Kauf and Zeijlstra (2018, 2020) argue that SoT constructions should be split into two components. Indeed, past-tense markers carry a feature [uPAST], to be checked by a higher covert past-tense operator. But, in addition, every past-tense morpheme should be assigned the semantics of a relative non-future, roughly meaning something like 'no later than the local evaluation time'. With these assumptions, formalized in (31) and (32), both single-past sentences and past-under-past embeddings receive the proper readings.

(31) $[[Op_{PAST[iPAST]} (P)]] = \lambda t^* \exists t. t < t^* \& P$ at t.

(32) $[[\text{-ed}(P)_{[uPAST]}]] = \lambda t'. \exists t. t \leq t' \& P$ at t.

To see this, take (33a). (33a) has an LF as in (33b) and a corresponding reading as in (33c). Given that the local evaluation time of Op_{PAST}, t^*, will, by default, be set to t^u, it means that, at some point in the past, Susan loved her mother.

(33) a. Susan loved her mother
 b. $[Op_{PAST[iPAST]}$ [love-ed$_{[uPAST]}$ her mother]]
 c. $\exists t'. t' < t^u \& \exists t^2. t^2 \leq t' \&$ love(Susan, her mother) at t^2
 There is a time t' strictly before the utterance time t^u and Susan's loving her mother starts at a time t^2 no later than t'.

This proposal deviates from standard analyses in that it introduces vagueness with respect to the ordering of t' and t^2 in (33). Either they refer to the same point in time, or the latter precedes the former. In this sense, a clause containing a single past-tense morpheme should be able to yield both a regular past-tense interpretation and an interpretation very close to that of a past perfect. At first sight, this seems like a counter-intuitive complication of the meaning of past tense. However, this additional relative non-future semantics of the past-tense morpheme is empirically well-supported. If t' and t^2 are taken to refer to the same point in time, the most prominent interpretation of the sentence, a simple past reading, is derived. The b-s reading usually remains unnoted in unembedded sentences, most likely owing to pragmatic blocking effects, as the same information can, more transparently, be expressed via a past-perfect construction. Crucially, though, there are contexts in which a speaker may choose to use a simple past-tensed sentence even though the interpretation she wants to trigger is actually more comparable to a past-perfect one, and, thus, t^2 is to be interpreted to precede t'. One such context is the following:

(34) Q. Did Susan go to today's 4 pm class?
 A. No, she left for Spain.

The intended interpretation of (34) is one that places Susan's leaving for Spain prior to 4 pm today, i.e., prior to a past reference time in the sense of Reichenbach (1947).

The payback of this underspecification approach is that it provides single LFs for SoT constructions. Given that a covert operator may only be included when grammatically necessary (see Chapter 3), a single covert past-tense operator can, in principle, check off all of the uninterpretable past-tense features in its syntactic domain via multiple agree, just like any other covert operator. Consequently, a sentence with both a past-tense morpheme in the matrix and in an embedded clause, in principle, requires the presence of only one past-tense operator. In (35), one Op_{PAST} will check all present [uPAST]-features, and no further Op_{PAST} may be included.[4] Together with the relative non-future semantics we attribute to past tense, this yields the proper readings for sentences like (35).

(35) a. John said Mary was ill
   b. [$Op_{PAST[iPAST]}$ [John say-ed$_{[uPAST]}$ that Mary be-ed$_{[uPAST]}$ ill]]
   c. $\exists t'.t' < t^u$ & $\exists t^2.t^2 \leq t'$ & say(John, [$\exists t^3.t^3 \leq t^2$ & Ill(Mary) at t^3]) at t^2
   There is a time t' strictly before the utterance time t^u and John's saying starts at a time t^2 no later than t' and Mary's illness start at a time t^3 no later than t^2.

This way, both the sim and b-s readings of (35) are captured without alluding to any kind of tense-deletion or other (pragmatic) mechanism. Moreover, the fact that SoT readings are underspecified rather than the result of different LFs also follows from the following examples:

(36) *At breakfast (earlier this morning), John said, 'Mary was ill a month ago', and Bill said, 'Mary is ill now'.*
   a. During breakfast, John said that Mary was ill, and Bill did so, too
   b. Therefore, during breakfast, both John and Bill said that Mary was ill (at some point)

Since ellipsis or distributive quantification require the same LF, under an LF-ambiguity approach, the two examples should be illicit. However, informants generally like them, albeit with a preference for adding *at some point* in (36b).

Naturally, much more needs to be said about SoT, such as discussing certain f-s readings that are allowed in SoT constructions, past tense in relative clauses, the relation between past tense and present tense, and whether tense semantics should be implemented quantificationally or presuppositionally. I refer the reader to Kauf and Zeijlstra (2018, 2021) for a full assessment of these facts and the details of an SoT analysis of feature-checking fully analogous to that in NC constructions. However, all this already shows that SoT and NC can indeed be analysed on a par with each other.

---

[4] However, there is one possible caveat, in the sense that it must be ensured that the Agree relations do not violate any locality relation. If the embedded clause is a CP, the question arises why the phase edge does not forbid Agree to apply across it. This potential problem, however, can be circumvented by assuming that Agree, in general, may apply across phase boundaries, provided that the phase edge itself also participates in the Agree relation, a corollary of phase theory (cf. Chomsky 2001). For the SoT analysis, this would mean that the C-head should contain some tense or finiteness feature, an assumption that is well-supported by the fact that complementizers are generally marked for (in)finiteness.

17.4.2 Pro-drop

Another syntactic dependency that can potentially be analysed on a par with NC is pro-drop. As outlined in Subsection 17.2.1, the question arises as to whether φ-agreement can be taken to be a syntactic dependency similar to NC or not. Preminger (2013) and Preminger and Polinsky (2015) have strongly argued that this should not be the case. For them, φ-agreement is the result of (unfailed) valuation from above, whereas NC is a grammatical phenomenon where overt elements carrying uninterpretable features are to be checked by higher, potentially covert, operators. It is indeed the case that φ-agreement can be analysed in different terms from those used for NC, but, as argued for in Subsection 17.2.1, it does not have to be.

In this section, I address the question of whether pro-drop, the phenomenon where a subject pronoun does not have to be overtly present, is a case where, similarly to NC, a lower checkee is overt, but a higher checker may be overt. If that is indeed the case, pro-drop forms a strong argument for a unified analysis of φ-agreement and NC in terms of UA.

As is well-known, in a language like Italian, it is possible to leave out the subject. This is in contrast to English, as the following examples show.

(37) a. (Io) parlo (Italian)
 I speak.1SG
 'I speak'
 b. *(I) speak

Italian is therefore called a pro-drop ('pronoun drop')—or null-subject— language, whereas English is not. A straightforward and plausible intuition that formed the starting point for a theoretical investigation of the phenomenon is that leaving out or not expressing the subject is made possible, in Italian, by the fact that it has rich subject agreement encoded on the verb (cf. Perlmutter 1971; Taraldsen, 1978; Rizzi 1982). The agreement affixes, then, allow speakers to reconstruct the missing subject. As a consequence, languages with poor agreement, like English, have to overtly express the subject in order to create a grammatical sentence.

Under the assumption that, in a sentence displaying pro-drop, the argument has been 'left out', several options arise as to what 'leaving out' means exactly. The following positions have been defended in the literature (following the overview in Koeneman and Zeijlstra 2019):

(38) a. The empty constituent is a separate lexical entry, known as *pro*
 b. There is no empty constituent
 c. The empty category is a regular pronoun phonologically unexpressed

Position (38a) allows the existence of an empty subject pronoun that syntactically takes the same position as an overt one. The difference between Italian and English is then minimal: both have subjects agreeing with the verb but, in Italian, this subject can be covert *pro*. The appeal is in the syntactic uniformity that can be upheld between these two languages.

Position (38b) holds that *pro* does not exist. Under the assumption that clauses generally need a subject in the functional domain of the clause (known as the Extended Projection Principle (EPP); cf. Chomsky 1981), it could be argued that, in a pro-drop language, agreement on the verb—which, after all, is 'pronominal'—satisfies this requirement (cf. Borer 1986; Alexiadou and Anagnostopoulou 1998; and others). The uniformity achieved under position (38a) is then lost, because what counts as the subject is distinct between languages. The gain, however, is in not having to postulate an invisible subject.

Under position (38c), the empty subject is just a regular pronoun, the only difference being that it does not receive phonological content at the relevant level (Perlmutter 1971). Especially in a grammatical model in which insertion of morphophonological forms follows after the creation of morphosyntactic representations (Halle and Marantz 1993; Embick and Noyer 2007), this can be naturally stated.

Omitting a lot of details, the different positions can be displayed as follows:

(39) a.

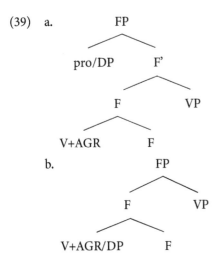

b.

Positions (38a/c) argue that the presence of some constituent is required as the specifier of FP to ensure grammaticality, as in (39a), whereas position (38b) argues that the structure without a specifier is grammatical as is (cf. (39b)). Empirically, arguments have gone both ways. Barbosa (2009) argues on the basis of a comparison between European and Brazilian Portuguese that the former (a consistent pro-drop language) has no obligation to move a constituent to Spec, FP, in line with (39b). Pinto (1997) and Sheehan (2010), on the other hand, argue that an investigation into wide and narrow focus in a number of Romance pro-drop languages leads to the conclusion that there must be an empty constituent in Spec, FP (see the references for further details).

For Holmberg (2005, 2010) and Roberts (2010), who both offer an analysis along the lines of (38c), the impetus of this proposal is conceptual. In their approach to agreement relations, agreement features are not only uninterpretable, but their values have to be provided by a constituent carrying interpretable features (cf. Chomsky 2000, 2001 for details). Hence, a subject provides values (say, 1st person and singular) to the agreement feature on some functional head in the clausal spine. Under the assumption that *pro* is an empty subject, however, pro-drop cannot be treated along the same lines: in the traditional conception, *pro* needs to be identified by rich agreement, and not the other way around. Only interpretable elements can value uninterpretable features, such as the ones underlying agreement morphology, and *pro*, by definition, is unvalued. One can, of course, assume that the grammar of Italian contains different *pro*s, one for every person/number context, thereby enriching the lexicon with at least six additional pronouns. This, however, is conceptually awkward. Under the assumption that an empty subject is a regular, fully specified pronoun that is just not pronounced, it can value the uninterpretable agreement features just like in English, and no additional lexical items have to be assumed.

The idea that pro-drop and NC are two sides of the same coin only upholds under position (38a), which, according to Holmberg and Roberts, is unmaintainable. However, under current minimalist views, nothing forbids valuation in the other direction. Given the idea that valuation and checking should be disentangled (see Subsection 17.2.1), nothing would prevent an uninterpretable valued feature from valuing an interpretable unvalued feature. Hence, (38a) is still a viable position. In fact, (38a) is to be preferred over (38b–c).

Position (38b) takes agreement morphology to be inherently pronominal, i.e., in a pro-drop language, the agreement marker is a weak pronoun, and cases where both a 'real subject' and an agreement marker are present involve subject-doubling. There are at least two conceptual problems with this approach.

First, agreement morphology does not always behave on a par with other pronouns. To see this, take Gujarati, which is a clear pro-drop language (cf. Mistry 2000). Gujarati is also a language that adheres to Baker's (2008) principle, called *Scopa*, that states that person agreement can only be local (for Baker, under spec–head agreement of a T probe), whereas number or gender agreement can apply either locally or at a distance. Baker points out that, in perfective aspect, Gujarati verbs agree with the object (40a). However, such objects can never trigger person agreement on an (auxiliary) verb (40b), even though auxiliary verbs can agree in person when agreement is with the subject in Spec, TP (40c).

(40) a. mEN tehmahri behEn-one bolawi (Gujarati[5,6,7])
    I.ERG your sisters.F-ACC invited.F
    'I invited your sisters'
  b. Mãi tam-ne mar-yãche
    I.ERG you.PL-ACC strike-PRF.M.PL be.PRES.3SG
    'I have struck you'
  c. tEhme ãw-ya cho
    you.PL come-PRF.M.PL be.PRES.2SG
    'You have come'

If the agreement marker in (40b) were indeed a weak pronoun, it would create a semantic mismatch between the object and the agreement marker, whereas such mismatches are generally ruled out. Note that, since 2nd-person agreement markers do exist in the language, one cannot argue that the weak subjects form a 2nd–3rd-person syncretism.

But even if that were the case, a second problem pops up. Given the discussion in Subsection 17.3.1, pronominal paradigms always, directly or indirectly, make 1st–2nd–3rd person distinctions. However, various agreement paradigms in pro-drop languages exhibit person syncretisms. To see this, take the Romanian agreement paradigm.

(41) Romanian agreement paradigm

	Romanian
1SG	cânt-Ø
2SG	cânț-i
3SG	**cânt-ă**
1PL	cânt-ăm
2PL	cânt-ați
3PL	**cânt-ă**

Romanian exhibits a syncretism between 3rd-person singular and plural. Still, it is a pro-drop language. Such syncretisms, especially in tenses outside the present tense, occur very often in the agreement paradigms of pro-drop languages. If those agreement markers were real pronouns themselves, this would be hard to explain. If, however, these agreement markers are the result of spell-out rules of valued agreement features, such syncretisms are very natural.

The fact that richness is not always what is behind pro-drop also forms a strong argument against position (38c). It turns out that richness of agreement is not

---

[5] Bhatt 2005: 774, cit. in Baker 2008: 92.
[6] Bhatt 2005: 801, cit. in Baker 2008: 92.
[7] Bhatt 2005: 801, cit. in Baker 2008: 92.

a sufficient condition for pro-drop. The agreement paradigms of Icelandic and German are as rich (or poor) as that of Romanian.

(42) German and Icelandic agreement paradigms

	German	Modern Icelandic
1SG	spazier-e	heyr-i
2SG	spazier-st	heyr-ir
3SG	spazier-t	heyr-ir
1PL	spazier-en	heyr-jum
2PL	spazier-t	heyr-ið
3PL	spazier-en	heyr-a

Following Koeneman and Zeijlstra (2021), the reason why Icelandic and German do not license pro-drop, whereas Romanian does, is that, in the latter, the agreement marker is morphosyntactically separate from the tense marker, whereas, in the former languages, this is not the case. In Icelandic and German, the agreement morphology forms the realization of a single head, which contains both φ- and T-features, whereas, in Romanian/Italian, there are two distinguished heads (T° and Arg°).

Under a PF perspective on pro-drop, this would be hard to understand, as DP-deletion can be purely contextually and not in such a way syntactically motivated. However, under position (38a), this would follow quite naturally. If the agreement marker were to value *pro*, it should not have additional tense or other inflectional features, as pronominal subjects crucially lack those: it should only be valued by Arg°.

Hence, in the current landscape of pro-drop analyses (of which there are many), only the 'real-pro analysis' upholds. Since that has exactly the same footprint as NC, pro-drop forms an additional argument for having a unified UA analysis for both.

17.4.3 Modal Concord

Even though various grammatical dependencies can be analysed in terms of UA (next to the ones previously mentioned, case assignment, binding, and various others come to mind), it is not the case that this can be done for every grammatical dependency. An example of such a dependency, for which attempts to analyse it on a par with NC turned out unsuccessful (cf. Zeijlstra 2007), is Modal Concord (MC).

If two modal elements are of the same modal type (epistemic/deontic/...) and have similar quantificational force (universal/existential), the most salient reading is mostly not a cumulative one but a concord reading, where the semantics seems to contain only one modal operator. This phenomenon, MC, has first been observed by Halliday (1970) and Lyons (1977), and has first been analysed by Geurts and Huitink (2006), who coined the term. Examples are in (43) and (44) for existential, epistemic MC, and universal, deontic MC, respectively.

(43) You may possibly have read my little monograph upon the subject
'The speaker thinks that it is possible that you read his little monograph'
?'The speaker thinks that it is possible that it is possible that you read his little monograph'

(44) Power carts must mandatorily be used on cart paths where provided
'It is obligatory that power carts are used on cart paths where provided'
?'It is obligatory that it is obligatory that power carts are used on cart paths where provided'

An immediate question that arises is whether MC is a grammatical phenomenon or whether the concord readings can be derived by entailment. An argument that shows that the latter cannot be fully correct comes from Geurts and Huitink (2006), who have argued that, if MC readings can be semantically derived via entailment, this entailment is restricted to the domain of epistemic modality and does not apply to the domain of deontic modality. The fact that epistemic modality may allow for concord readings is due to the fact that the Principles of Veridicality (45) and Positive Introspection (46) apply.

(45) Veridicality:
$\Box \varphi \to \varphi$ (knowledge is factive)

(46) Positive Introspection:
$\Box \varphi \to \Box \Box \varphi$ ($\equiv \Diamond \Diamond \varphi \to \Diamond \varphi$)

Thus, the concord reading of (43) can be taken to be a result of the application of the Principle of Positive Introspection. However, (45) and (46) do not hold for deontic modality. If something is obligatory or desirable, its truth is not guaranteed, and, likewise, if something is obligatory, it is not necessarily the case that it is obligatory that it is obligatory. Hence, the instances of deontic MC as in (44) demonstrate that MC readings, at least for deontic modality, cannot be explained by entailment as a consequence of (45) and (46).[8]

---

[8] Moreover, it is even doubtful whether Veridicality always applies to epistemic modality in natural language (cf. Karttunen 1972; von Fintel and Gillies 2010; Giannakidou and Mari 2018). Take, for instance, the following examples:

(i) This must be Alesia
(ii) This is Alesia

Clearly, (i) does not entail (ii). Therefore, the principles of Veridicality and Positive Introspection may not be the cause of the existence of MC readings in a straightforward way.

Zeijlstra (2008c) explores the hypothesis that MC is an instance of syntactic agreement, just like NC. As a starting point, the fact that (in languages like English) the quantificational force of modal elements is lexically encoded, it would be natural to assume that modal features are only specified for quantificational force. Modal type flavour is generally determined by the context of the utterance. Therefore, the featural decomposition of modal elements should not exceed the distinction with respect to the modal quantificational force, and the following four modal features can be postulated:

(47)   [i∃-MOD]
      [u∃-MOD]
      [i∀-MOD]
      [u∀-MOD]

Then, both existential and deontic MC constructions can be naturally analysed in terms of syntactic feature-checking (48), (49). And cases where the auxiliary is the only overt modal element are then taken to involve a covert modal operator (50), (51).

(48)   You may perhaps have read the book
      [$_{CP}$ You perhaps$_{[i∃\text{-MOD}]i}$ may$_{[u∃\text{-MOD}]}$ [t$_i$ have read the book]]

(49)   The students must obligatorily register themselves
      [$_{CP}$ The students obligatorily$_{[i∀\text{-MOD}]i}$ must$_{[u∀\text{-MOD}]}$ [t$_i$ register themselves]]

(50)   John may be home
      [John *OP*$_{∃\text{-MOD}[i∃\text{-MOD}]}$ may$_{[u∀\text{-MOD}]}$ [$_{VP}$ be home]]

(51)   John must go home
      [John *OP*$_{∀\text{-MOD}[i∀\text{-MOD}]}$ must$_{[u∀\text{-MOD}]}$ [$_{VP}$ go home]]

Of course, many questions arise, e.g., how the restriction on the same type of modal flavour can be explained, or why the auxiliary, carrying the uninterpretable modal feature, may raise across the adverb. However, it turns out that the analysis I have provided is already untenable. Grosz (2012) has presented examples, such as (52), involving MC where the quantificational force of the adverb and the auxiliary are different, but where negation still ensures that the overall quantificational status of the negated auxiliary and the adverb are the same. In (52), an MC reading appears, even though *mandatorily* is a universal modal and *may* an existential one. Grosz also shows that a negated auxiliary (that takes scope below this negation) of the same quantificational force can no longer give rise to an MC reading, as shown in (53).

(52) *You are now entering a secure area of this public facility. We would now like to specify the rules that make up our special security standards. Nothing forces us to have these security standards, yet we have them, as we are special.*
In view of our special security standards, you mandatorily may not cross the yellow line without a special permit issued by the facility headquarters.

(53) #You mandatorily need not stay in this area

These facts are predicted to be impossible under the syntactic agreement approach I have sketched. Naturally, the question arises of how MC must then be analysed. This is not clear yet, though Anand and Brasoveanu (2012) present a promising account. In short, they suggest that modal force is introduced by modal auxiliaries, and modal flavour by modal adverbs. For auxiliaries, this is quite clear: *must* always has a universal modal reading, but is ambiguous between an epistemic and a deontic interpretation, even though other modals, such as *might*, do not reflect this ambiguity. For modal adverbs, this is harder to show: is *obligatorily* a quantificationally underspecified deontic adverb, or does it also have universal force? Only if the former is the case do MC readings not violate compositionality: the universal deontic modal reading in (49) then transparently comes from the deontic adverb and the universal auxiliary. If modal adverbs induce modal force as well, compositionality appears to be violated, and other explanations for the phenomenon should be called for.

17.5 Finally

In this final chapter, I have presented several avenues for further research that I have carried out, which are based on the previous 16 chapters. In short, I have argued that the somewhat unorthodox agreement mechanism invoked for NC turns out to be universally applicable, unlike its more standard alternatives, and may even open up the way to understand the nature of Merge, selection, and labelling more generally.

I have also argued that the syntactic and semantic findings of this book (concretely, the FFFH, and the existence and workings of universal quantifier PPIs) provide a better understanding of verb movement. I have shown that the so-called RAH can be reinstalled (along the lines of Koeneman and Zeijlstra 2014) and that the arguments presented by Han et al. concerning rightward movement in strictly head-final languages do not uphold under empirical scrutiny.

Finally, I have shown how this analysis compares with other syntactically encoded semantic dependencies, such as SoT, and φ-agreement (focusing on pro-drop). These case studies are not exhaustive; many more phenomena lend themselves for a similar treatment. However, it must be noted that not all grammatical dependencies can be treated in this way. In the final section, I have shown that MC must receive a different kind of explanation. After all, it would not be good to close a book like this without a negative end.

References

Abels, K. and L. Marti. 2010. 'A unified approach to split scope.' *Natural Language Semantics* 18: 435–47.

Abels, K. and A. Neeleman. 2012. 'Linear Asymmetries and the LCA.' *Syntax 15*: 25–74.

Abusch, D. 1988. 'Sequence of tense, intensionality and scope.' In: H. Borer (ed.), *Proceedings of the 7th West Coast Conference on Formal Linguistics*. Stanford, CA: CSLI. 1–14.

Abusch, D. 1997. 'Sequence of tense and temporal de re.' *Linguistics and Philosophy 20*: 1–50.

Abusch, D. 2002. 'Lexical alternatives as a source of pragmatic presupposition.' In: B. Jackson (ed.), *Proceedings of Semantics and Linguistic Theory (SALT) Conference*, Washington, DC: LSA, *12*. 1–19.

Abusch, D. 2010. 'Presupposition triggering from alternatives.' *Journal of Semantics 27*: 1–44.

Ackema, P. and A Neeleman. 2002. 'Effects of Short-Term Storage in Processing Rightward Movement.' In: S. Nooteboom, F. Weerman, and F. Wijnen (eds), *Storage and Computation in the Language Faculty*. Dordrecht: Kluwer. 219–56.

Ackema, P. and A. Neeleman. 2004. *Beyond Morphology: Interface Conditions on Word Formation*. Oxford: Oxford University Press.

Acquaviva, P. 1997. *The Logical Form of Negation: A Study of Operator-Variable Structures in Syntax*. New York: Garland.

Adger, D. 2003. *Core Syntax: A Minimalist Approach*. Oxford: Oxford University Press.

Adger, D. 2013. *A Syntax of Substance*. Cambridge, MA: The MIT Press.

Ahn, S.-H. 1990. *Korean quantification and Universal Grammar*. PhD dissertation, University of Connecticut.

Alboiu, G. 2002. *The Features of Movement in Romanian*. Bucharest: University of Bucharest Press.

Alexiadou, A. and E. Anagnostopoulou. 1998. 'Parametrizing Agr: Word Order, V-Movement, and EPP-Checking.' *Natural Language and Linguistic Theory 16*: 491–539.

Aloni, M. (2007). 'Free choice, modals and imperatives.' *Natural Language Semantics 15*: 65–94.

Aloni, M. and R. van Rooij. 2007. 'Free choice items and alternatives.' In: G. Bouma, I. Kraemer, and J. Zwarts (eds), *Proceedings of the KNAW Academy Colloquium: Cognitive Foundations of Interpretation*. Amsterdam: Edita KNAW. 5–26.

Alonso-Ovalle, Luis and Paula Menéndez-Benito. To appear. 'Free Choice and Modal Indefinites.' In Lisa Matthewson, Cecile Meier, Hotze Rullmann and Thomas Ede Zimmermann (eds.), *Companion to Semantics*, Blackwell.

Alrenga, P. and C. Kennedy. 2014. 'No more shall we part: quantifiers in English comparatives.' *Natural Language Semantics 22*: 1–53.

Altshuler, D. 2016. *Events, States and Times: An Essay on Narrative Discourse in English*. Berlin: De Gruyter.

Altshuler, D. and R. Schwarzschild. 2012. 'Moment of change, cessation implicatures and simultaneous readings.' In: E. Chemla, V. Homer, and G. Winterstein (eds), *Proceedings of Sinn und Bedeutung 17*. Paris: École Normale Supérieure. 45–62.

Anagnostopoulou, E. 2005. 'Strong and Weak Person Restrictions. A Feature Checking Analysis.' In: L. Heggie and F. Ordoñez (eds), *Clitics and Affix Combinations: Theoretical Perspectives*. Amsterdam: Benjamins. 199–235.

Anand, P. and A. Brasoveanu. 2012. 'Modal concord as modal modification.' In: M. Prinzhorn, V. Schmitt, and S. Zobel (eds), *Proceedings of Sinn and Bedeutung 14*. Vienna: Institute for Linguistics. 19–36.

Anderwald, L. 2002. *Negation in Non-Standard British English*. London: Routledge.

Arregui, K. and A. Nevins. 2012. *Morphotactics: Basque Auxiliaries and the Structure of Spellout*. Dordrecht: Springer.

Asher, N. and B. Reese. 2005. 'Negative bias in polar questions.' In: E. Maier, C. Bary & J. Huitink (eds), *Proceedings of Sinn und Bedeutung 9*. Nijmegen: KUN. 30–43.

Bailyn, J. 2005. *Free Word Oder and Minimalism*. St. Petersburg: St. Petersburg State University Linguistics Papers.

Baker, C. 1970. 'Double negatives.' *Linguistic Inquiry 1*: 169–86.

Baker, M. 1985. 'The Mirror Principle and morphosyntactic explanation.' *Linguistic Inquiry 16*: 373–415.

Baker, M. 1988. *Incorporation. A Theory of Grammatical Function Changing*. Chicago/London: The University of Chicago Press.

Baker, M. 2008. *The Syntax of Agreement and Concord*. Cambridge: Cambridge University Press.

Baker, M. 2015. *Case: Its Principles and its Parameters*. Cambridge: Cambridge University Press.

Bar-Asher Siegal, E. 2017. 'Notes concerning the emergence of negation words in the Semitic languages.' *Leshonenu 79*: 44–63.

Barbiers, S. 2002. 'Microvariation in negation in varieties of Dutch.' In: S. Barbiers, L. Cornips, and S. van der Kleij (eds), *Syntactic Microvariation*. Amsterdam: Meertens Institute Electronic Publications in Linguistics. 10–34.

Barbiers, S., O. Koeneman, and M. Lekakou. 2010. 'Syntactic doubling and the structure of wh-chains.' *Journal of Linguistics 46*: 1–46.

Barbiers, S., J. van der Auwera, H. Bennis, E. Boef, G. de Vogelaer, and M. van der Ham. 2008. *Syntactische Atlas van de Nederlandse Dialecten Deel II/Syntactic Atlas of the Dutch Dialects Volume II*. Amsterdam: Amsterdam University Press.

Barbosa, P. 2009. 'Two kinds of subject pro.' *Studia Linguistica 63*: 2–58.

Barouni, M. 2018. *Topics in the syntax-semantics of Greek particles*. PhD dissertation, University of Crete.

Bartsch, R. 1973. '"Negative transportation" gibt es nicht.' *Linguistische Berichte 27*: 1–7.

Baunaz, L., L. Haegeman, K. de Clercq, and E. Lander. 2018. *Exploring Nanosyntax*. Oxford: Oxford University Press.

Bech, G. 1955/57. *Studien über das deutsche Verbum infinitum*. Copenhagen: Det Kongelige Danske Akademie av Videnskaberne.

Beghelli, F. and T. Stowell. 1997. '"Distributivity and Negation." The syntax of *each* and *every*.' In: A. Szabolcsi (ed.), *Ways of Scope Taking*. Dordrecht: Kluwer. 71–107.

Béjar, S. and M. Rezac. 2009. 'Cyclic Agree.' *Linguistic Inquiry 40*: 35–73.

Belletti, A. 1990. *Generalized Verb Movement*. Torino: Rosenberg & Sellier.

Bellugi, U. 1967. *The acquisition of the system of negation in children's speech*. PhD dissertation, Harvard University.

Benincà, P. 2006. 'A detailed map of the Left Periphery in Medieval Romance.' In: R. Zanuttini, H. Campos, E. Herburger, and P. Portner (eds), *Negation, Tense, and Clausal Architecture: Crosslinguistic Investigations*. Washington, DC: Georgetown University Press. 53–86.

Benincà, P. and L. Vanelli. 1982. 'Appunti di sinatassi veneta.' In: M. Cortelazzo (ed.), *Guida ai dialetti veneti. Vol. 4*. Padua: CLEUP. 7–38.

Bentzen, K. 2007. *Order and structure in embedded clauses in Northern Norwegian*. PhD dissertation, University of Tromsø.

Bentzen, K., G. Hrafn Hrafnbjargarson, Þ. Hróarsdóttir, and A.-L. Wiklund. 2007. 'Rethinking Scandinivian verb movement.' *Journal of Comparative Germanic Linguistics 10*: 203–33.

Berwick, R. and A. Weinberg. 1986. *The Grammatical Basis of Linguistic Performance: Language Use and Acquisition*. Cambridge, MA: The MIT Press.

Béziau, J.-Y. and G. Basti (eds). 2017. *The Square of Opposition: A Cornerstone of Thought*. Basel: Birkhäuser.

Bhatt, Rajesh. 2005. 'Long distance agreement in Hindi-Urdu.' *Natural Language and Linguistic Theory 23*: 757–807.

Bhatt, R. and M. Walkow. 2013. 'Locating agreement in grammar: An argument from agreement in conjunctions.' *Natural Language and Linguistic Theory 31*: 951–1013.

Biberauer, T. 2008. 'Doubling vs. Omission: Insights from Afrikaans Negation.' In: S. Barbiers, O. Koeneman, M. Lekakou, and M. van der Ham (eds), *Microvariation in Syntactic Doubling*. Bingley: Emerald Publishers. 103–40.

Biberauer, T. 2009. 'Jespersen off course? The case of contemporary Afrikaans negation.' In: E. van Gelderen (ed.), *Linguistic Cycles*. Amsterdam: Benjamins. 91–130.

Biberauer, T. 2017. 'The Final-over Final Condition and partciles.' In: M. Sheehan, T. Biberauer, A. Holmberg, and I. Roberts (eds), *The Final-over Final Condition. A Syntactic Universal*. Cambridge, MA: The MIT Press. 187–297.

Biberauer, T. and I. Roberts. 2011. 'Negative words and related expressions: a new perspective on some familiar puzzles.' In: R. Ingham and Pierre L'Arrivée (eds), *The Evolution of Negation: Beyond the Jespersen Cycle*. Berlin: De Gruyter. 23–60.

Biberauer, T. and I. Roberts. 2015. 'Rethinking formal hierarchies: a proposed unification.' *Cambridge Occasional Papers in Linguistics 7*: 1–31.

Biberauer, T., I. Roberts, and M. Sheehan. 2014. 'No-choice Parameters and the Limits of Syntactic Variation' In: R. Santana-LaBarge (ed.), *Proceedings of the 31st West Coast Conference on Formal Linguistics (WCCFL 31)*. Sommerville, MA: Cascadilla. 46–55.

Biberauer, T. and H. Zeijlstra. 2011. 'Negation in Afrikaans: in search for the missing language.' In: S. Lima, K. Mullin, and B. Smith (eds), *Proceedings of NELS 39*. Amherst, MA: GLSA. 95–108.

Biberauer, T. and H. Zeijlstra. 2012a. 'Negative concord in Afrikaans: filling the typological gap.' *Journal of Semantics 29*: 345–71.

Biberauer, T. and H. Zeijlstra. 2012b. 'Negative changes: three factors and the diachrony of Afrikaans negation.' In: C. Galves, S. Cyrino, R. Lopes, F. Sandalo, and J. Avelar (eds). *Diachronic Syntax. Parameter Theory and Dynamics of Change*. Oxford: Oxford University Press. 238–64.

Bjorkman, B. 2016. 'Go get, come see: motion verbs, morphological restrictions, and syncretism.' *Natural Language and Linguistic Theory 34*: 53–91.

Bjorkman, B. and H. Zeijlstra. 2019. 'Checking up on (Φ-)Agree.' *Linguistic Inquiry 50*: 527–69.

Blanchett, F. 2015. *English negative concord, negative polarity, and double negation*. PhD dissertation, CUNY.
Bobaljik, J. 1995. *Morphosyntax: the syntax of verbal inflection*. PhD dissertation, MIT.
Bobaljik, J. 2008. 'Where's Phi? Agreement as a Post-Syntactic Operation.' In: D. Harbour, D. Adger, and S. Béjar (eds), *Phi-Theory: Phi Features across Interfaces and Modules*. Oxford: Oxford University Press. 295–328.
Bobaljik, J. and H. Thráinsson. 1998. 'Two heads aren't always better than one.' *Syntax 1*: 37–71.
Bobaljik, J. and S. Wurmbrand. 2012. 'Word order and scope: transparent interfaces and the 3/4 signature.' *Linguistic Inquiry 43*: 371–421.
Boeckx, C. 2008. *Aspects of the Syntax of Agreement*. London: Routledge.
Boeckx, C. and S. Stjepanović. 2001. 'Head-ing toward PF.' *Linguistic Inquiry 32*: 345–55.
Bonet, E. 1991. *Morphology after syntax: pronominal clitics in Romance*. PhD dissertation, MIT.
Borer, H. 1984. *Parametric Syntax*. Dordrecht: Foris.
Borer, H. 1986. 'I-Subjects.' *Linguistic Inquiry 17*: 375–416.
Bošković, Ž. 2007. 'On the locality and motivation of Move and Agree: An even more minimal theory.' *Linguistic Inquiry 38*: 589–644.
Boyd, J. and A. Goldberg. 2011. 'Learning what NOT to say: The role of statistical preemption and categorization in A-adjective production.' *Language 87*: 55–83.
Brabantsche yeesten – Jean-Henri Bormans (ed.). 1869. 'De Brabantsche yeesten, of Rijmkronijk van Braband, zevende boek.' In: F. Van Oostrom (ed.), *1998. CD-ROM Middelnederlands*. Den Haag: SDU.
Braine, Martin. 1971. 'On two types of models of the internalization of grammars.' In: D. Slobin (ed.), *The Ontogenesis of Grammar: A Theoretical Symposium*. New York: Academic Press. 153–186.
Brandtler, J. 2006. 'On Aristotle and baldness-topic, reference, presupposition of existence and negation.' *Working Papers in Scandinavian Syntax 77*: 177–204.
Branigan, P. and M. MacKenzie. 2002. 'Altruism, A-bar-movement, and object agreement in Innu-aimûn.' *Linguistic Inquiry 33*: 385–407.
Breitbarth, A. 2009. 'A hybrid approach to Jespersen's Cycle in West Germanic.' *Journal of Comparative Germanic Linguistics 12*: 81–114.
Breitbarth, A. 2013. 'The development of negation in Low German and Dutch.' In: D. Willis, C. Lucas, and A. Breitbarth (eds), *The History of Negation in the Languages of Europe and the Mediterranean*. Oxford: Oxford University Press. 190–238.
Breitbarth, A. 2014. *The History of Low German Negation*. Oxford: Oxford University Press.
Breitbarth, A. 2017. 'Studies on negation: syntax, semantics, and variation.' *Wiener Arbeiten zur Linguistik 3*: 21–47.
Breitbarth, A. and L. Haegeman. 2014. 'The distribution of preverbal *en* in (West) Flemish: Syntactic and interpretive properties.' *Lingua 147*: 69–86.
Brody, M. 1995. *Lexico-logical Form: A Radically Minimalist Theory*. Cambridge, MA: The MIT Press.
Brown, R. and C. Hanlon. 1970. *Derivational Complexity and Order of Acquisition in Child Speech. Cognition and the Development of Language*. New York: Wiley.
Brown, S. 1999. *The Syntax of Negation in Russian*. Stanford, CA: CSLI Publications.
Büring, D. 1995. *The 59th Street Bridge accent. On the meaning of topic and focus*. PhD dissertation, Tübingen University.
Büring, D. 2004. 'Negative inversion.' In: L. Bateman and C. Ussery (eds), *Proceedings of NELS 35*. Amherst, MA: GSLA, 1–20.

Burridge, K. 1993. *Syntactic Change in Germanic. Aspects of Language Change in Germanic.* Amsterdam: Benjamins.
Caha, P. 2009. *The nanosyntax of case.* PhD dissertation, University of Tromsø.
Carlson, G. 1977. *Reference to kinds in English.* PhD dissertation, UMass Amherst.
Cartwright, T. A., & Brent, M. R. (1997). Syntactic categorization in early language acquisition: Formalizing the role of distributional analysis. *Cognition, 63*(2), 121–170.
Cecchetto, C. and C. Donati. 2010. 'On labeling: principle C and head movement.' *Syntax* 13: 241–78.
Cecchetto, C. and C. Donati. 2015. *(Re)labeling.* Cambridge, MA: The MIT Press.
Chatzopoulou, K. 2012. *Negation and nonveridicality in the history of Greek.* PhD dissertation, University of Chicago.
Cheng, L. 1991. *On the typology of wh-questions.* PhD dissertation, MIT.
Cheng, L. 1994. 'Wh-words as polarity items.' *Chinese Languages and Linguistics 2*: 615–40.
Cheng, L. 1995. 'On *dou*-quantification.' *Journal of East Asian Linguistics* 4: 197–234.
Chierchia, G. 2004. 'Scalar implicatures, polarity phenomena, and the syntax/pragmatics interface.' In: A. Belletti (ed.), *Structures and Beyond, vol. 3.* Oxford: Oxford University Press. 39–103.
Chierchia, G. 2006. 'Broaden your views. Implicatures of domain widening and the "Logicality" of language.' *Linguistic Inquiry 37*: 535–90.
Chierchia, G. 2013. *Logic in Grammar: Polarity, Free Choice, and Intervention.* Oxford: Oxford University Press.
Chierchia, G. and H. Liao. 2015. 'Where do Chinese *wh*-items fit.' In: L. Alonso-Ovalle, P. Menéndez-Benito, C. Baker, and J. McCarthy (eds), *Epistemic Indefinites: Exploring Modality beyond the Verbal Domain.* Oxford: Oxford University Press. 31–59.
Choi, Y.-S. 1999. 'Negation, its scope and NPI licensing in Korean.' In: R. Daly and A. Riehl (eds), *The Eastern States Conference on Linguistics '99.* Ithaca, NY: Cornell Linguistic Circle. 25–36.
Chomsky, N. 1957. *Syntactic Structures.* The Hague: Mouton.
Chomsky, N. 1973. 'Conditions on transformations.' In: S. Anderson and P. Kiparsky (eds), *A Festschrift for Morris Halle.* New York: Holt, Rinehart, and Winston. 232–86.
Chomsky, N. 1981. *Lectures on Government and Binding.* Dordrecht: Foris.
Chomsky, N. 1995a. *The Minimalist Program.* Cambridge, MA: The MIT Press.
Chomsky, N. 1995b. 'Bare phrase structure.' In: G. Webelhuth (ed.), *Government and Binding Theory and the Minimalist Program.* Oxford: Blackwell. 383–439.
Chomsky, N. 2000. 'Minimalist inquiries: the framework.' In: R. Martin, D. Michael, and J. Uriagereka, (eds), *Step by Step. Essays in Honor of Howard Lasnik.* Cambridge, MA: The MIT Press. 89–155.
Chomsky, N. 2001. 'Derivation by phase.' In: M. Kenstovicz (ed.), *Ken Hale: A Life in Language.* Cambridge, MA: The MIT Press. 1–54.
Chomsky, N. 2005. 'Three factors in language design.' *Linguistic Inquiry 36*: 1–22.
Chomsky, N. 2008. 'On phases.' In: R. Freiden, C. Otero, and M.-L. Zubizarreta (eds), *Foundational Issues in Linguistic Theory: Essays in Honor of Jean-Roger Vergnaud.* Cambridge, MA: The MIT Press. 133–166.
Chomsky, N. 2013. 'Problems of projection.' *Lingua 130*: 33–49.
Chomsky, N. 2015. 'Problems of projection: extensions.' In: E. Di Domenico, C. Hamann, and S. Matteini (eds), *Structures, Strategies and Beyond. Studies in Honour of Adriana Belletti.* Amsterdam: Benjamins. 1–16.
Chung, D. and H.-K. Park. 1997. 'NPIs outside of negation scope.' In: H.-M. Sohn and J. Haig (eds), *Japanese/Korean Linguistics, vol. 6.* Stanford, CA: CSLI Publications. 415–35.

Cinque, G. 1999. *Adverbs and Functional Heads*. Oxford: Oxford University Press.
Cinque, G. (ed.). 2002. *Functional Structure in DP and IP. The Cartography of Syntactic Structures (vol. 1)*. Oxford: Oxford University Press.
Cinque, G. (ed.). 2006. *Restructuring and Functional Heads. The Cartography of Syntactic Structures (vol. 4)*. Oxford: Oxford University Press.
Cirillo, R. 2009. *The syntax of floating quantifiers: stranding revisited*. PhD dissertation, University of Amsterdam.
Clark, E. 1987. 'The principle of contrast: a constraint on language acquisition.' In: B. MacWhinney (ed.), *Mechanisms of Language Acquisition*. Hillsdale, NJ: Lawrence Erlbaum. 1–33.
Collins, C. 2002. 'Eliminating labels.' In S. Epstein and T. Seely (eds), *Derivation and Explanation in the Minimalist Program*. Oxford: Blackwell. 42–64.
Collins, C. 2017. 'Merge(X/Y) = {X, Y}.' In: L. Bauke, A. Blümel, and E. Groat (eds), *Labels and Roots*. Berlin: De Gruyter. 47–68.
Collins, C. and P. Postal. 2014. *Classical NEG Raising*. Cambridge, MA: The MIT Press.
Collins, C. and P. Postal. 2017. 'Interclausal NEG raising and the scope of negation.' *Glossa* 2: 29.
Collins, C. and P. Postal. 2018a. 'Dispelling the cloud of unknowing.' In: K. Turner and L. Horn (eds), *Pragmatics, Truth and Underspecification. Towards an Atlas of Meaning*. Leiden: Brill. 54, 81.
Collins, C. and P. Postal. 2018b. 'Disentangling two distinct notions of NEG raising.' *Semantics and Pragmatics* 11: 5.
Comrie, B. 1985. *Tense*. Cambridge: Cambridge University Press.
Condoravdi, C. 2008. 'Punctual until as a scalar NPI.' In: K. Hanson and S. Inkelas (eds), *The Nature of the Word*. Cambridge, MA: The MIT Press. 631–53.
Condoravdi, C. and S. Lauer. 2012. 'Imperatives: meaning and illocutionary force.' *Empirical Issues in Syntax and Semantics* 9: 37–58.
Corbett, G. 2006. *Agreement*. Cambridge: Cambridge University Press.
Corblin, F., V. Déprez, H. de Swart, and L. Tovena. 2004. 'Negative concord.' In: F. Corblin and H. de Swart (eds), *Handbook of French Semantics*. Stanford, CA: CSLI Publications. 417–52.
Cowie, F. 1997. 'The logical problem of language acquisition.' *Synthese* 111: 17–51.
Cysouw, M. 2003. *The Paradigmatic Structure of Person Marking*. Oxford: Oxford University Press.
Dahl, Ö. 1979. 'Typology of sentence negation.' *Linguistics* 17: 79–106.
Dahl, Ö. 2001. 'Inflationary effects in language and elsewhere.' In: J. Bybee and P. Hopper (eds), *Frequency and the Emergence of Linguistic Structure*. Amsterdam: Benjamins. 471–80.
Davidson, D. 1967. 'The logical form of action sentences.' In: N. Resher (ed.), *The Logic of Decision and Action*. Pittsburgh, PA: University of Pittsburgh Press. 81–95. Reprinted in: D. Davidson (ed.). 1980. *Essays on Actions and Events*. Oxford: Clarendon Press. 105–22.
Dayal, V. 1998. '*Any* as inherently modal.' *Linguistics and Philosophy* 21: 433–76.
Dayal, V. 2004. 'The universal force of free choice "any".' *Linguistic Variation Yearbook* 4: 5–40.
Dayal, V. 2009. 'Variation in English free choice items.' In: R. Mohanty and M. Menon (eds), *Universals and Variation: Proceedings of GLOW in Asia VII*. Hyderabad: English and Foreign Languages Press. 37–256.
Dayal, V. 2013. 'A viability constraint on alternatives for free choice.' In: A. Fălăuş (ed.), *Alternatives in Semantics*. London: Palgrave MacMillan. 88–123.

de Swart, Henriette and Arie Molendijk. 1999. Negation and the temporal structure of narrative discourse. *Journal of Semantics 16*: 1–43.
Declerck, R. 1995a. 'The problem of *not...until*.' *Linguistics 33*: 51–98.
Declerck, R. 1995b. 'Is there a relative past tense in English?' *Lingua 97*: 1–36.
Declerck, R. 2015. *Tense in English: Its Structure and Use in Discourse.* London: Routledge.
de Haan, F. 1997. *The Interaction of Modality and Negation: A Typological Study.* New York: Garland.
De Morgan, Augustus. 1858; On the Syllogism, No. Ill, and on Logic in general; Transactions of the Cambridge Philosophical Society; Cambridge Philosophical Society 10. 173–230. Cambridge University Press
Dekker, P. and H. Zeijlstra. 2012. 'Concord and doubling phenomena: an introduction.' *Journal of Semantics 29*: 295–303.
Delfitto, D. 2020. 'Expletive negation.' In: V. Déprez and M.-Th. Espinal (eds), *The Oxford Handbook of Negation.* Oxford: Oxford University Press. 443–64.
den Besten, H. 1983. 'On the interaction of root transformations and lexical deletive rules.' In: W. Abraham (ed.), *On the Formal Syntax of the Westgermania.* Amsterdam: Benjamins. 47–131.
den Besten, H. 1986. 'Double Negation and the Genesis of Afrikaans.' In: P. Muysken and N. Smith (eds), *Substrata Versus Universals in Creole Genesis.* Amsterdam: Benjamins. 185–230.
den Besten, H. 1989. *Studies in West Germanic Syntax.* Amsterdam/Atlanta, GA: Rodopi.
den Dikken, M. 2002. 'Direct and indirect polarity item licensing.' *Journal of Comparative Germanic Linguistics 5*: 35–66.
den Dikken, M. 2006. 'Parasitism, secondary triggering and depth of embedding.' In: R. Zanuttini, H. Campos, E. Herburger, and P. Portner (eds), *Crosslinguistic Research in Syntax and Semantics: Negation, Tense, and Clausal Architecture.* Washington, DC: Georgetown University Press. 151–74.
den Dikken, M. 2016. 'Negation topicalisation.' In: M. Newson and P. Szigetvári (eds), *The Even Yearbook 2016.* Budapest: ELTE Department of English Linguistics. http://seas3.elte.hu/even
Déprez, V. 1997. 'Two types of negative concord.' *Probus 9*: 103–42.
Déprez, V. and A. Pierce. 1993. 'Negation and functional projections in early grammar.' *Linguistic Inquiry 24*: 25–647.
Déprez, V., S. Tubau, A. Cheylus, and M.-T. Espinal. 2015. 'Double negation in a negative concord language: an experimental approach.' *Lingua 163*: 75–107.
Despic, M. 2020. 'On negative imperatives, aspect and Agree.' In: P. Kosta and T. Radeva-Bork (eds), *Current Developments in Slavic Linguistics. Twenty Years After (based on selected papers from FDSL 11).* Berlin: Peter Lang. 173–84.
de Swart, H. 1996. 'Meaning and use of *not... until*.' *Journal of Semantics 13*: 221–63.
de Swart, H. 2000. 'Scope ambiguities with negative quantifiers.' In: K. von Heusinger and U. Egli (eds), *Reference and Anaphoric Relations.* Dordrecht: Springer. 109–32.
De Swart, H. 2006. Marking and interpretation of negation: A bi-directional OT approach. In *Comparative and cross-linguistic research in syntax, semantics and computational linguistics, GURT 2004*, eds. R. Zanuttini, H. Campos, E. Herburger, and P. Portner, 199–218. Washington: Georgetown University Press.
de Swart, H. 2010. *Expression and Interpretation of Negation.* Dordrecht: Springer.
de Swart, H. and I. Sag. 2002. Negative concord in Romance. *Linguistics and Philosophy 25*: 373–417.

Deumert, A. 2004. *Language Standardization and Language Change. The Dynamics of Cape Dutch*. Amsterdam/Philadelphia, PA: Benjamins.

Deurloo, R. 2009. *Het Nederlands van negative concord naar double negation taal*. MA thesis, University of Amsterdam.

de Villiers, J. and P. de Villiers. 1985. 'The acquisition of English.' In: D. Slobin (ed.), *The Crosslinguistic Study of Language Acquisition, vol. 1: The Data*. Hillsdale, NJ: Lawrence Erlbaum. 27–140.

Devos, M. and J. van der Auwera. 2013. 'Jespersen Cycles in Bantu: double and triple negation.' *Journal of African Languages and Linguistics 34*: 205–74.

Devos, M., M. Kasombo Tshibanda, and J. van der Auwera. 2010. 'Jespersen Cycles in Kanincin: double, triple and maybe even quadruple negation.' *Africana Linguistica 16*: 155–82.

de Vries, Wobbe. 1910. *Dysmelie. Opmerkingen over Syntaxis*. Verhandeling behoorende bij het programma van het gymnasium der gemeente Groningen voor het jaar 1910–1911.

Diesing, M. 1992. *Indefinites*. Cambridge, MA: The MIT Press.

Di Sciullo, A.-M. and E. Williams. 1987. *On the Definition of Word*. Cambridge, MA: The MIT Press.

Dočekal, M. 2009. 'Negative concord: from Old Church Slavonic to contemporary Czech.' In: B. Hansen and J. Grković-Major (eds), *Diachronic Slavonic Syntax: Gradual Changes in Focus*. Munich/Berlin/Vienna: Sagner. 29–40.

Dowty, D. 1979. *Word Meaning and Montague Grammar*. Dordrecht: Reidel.

Dressler, W. 1987. 'Word formation (WF) as part of natural morphology.' In: W. Dressler, W. Mayerthaler, O. Panagl, and W. Wurzel (eds), *Leitmotifs in Natural Morphology*. Amsterdam: Benjamins. 99–126.

Drozd, K. 1995. 'Child English pre-sentential negation as metalinguistic exclamatory sentence negation.' *Journal of Child Language 22*: 583–610.

Dwivedi, V. 1991. 'Negation as a functional projection in Hindi.' In: K. Hunt, T. Perry, and V. Samiian (eds), *Proceedings of WECOL 4*. Fresno, CA: CSU Department of Linguistics. 88–100.

Eckardt, R. 2003. *Eine Runde im Jespersen-Zyklus: Negation, emphatische Negation und negativ-polare Elemente im Altfranzösischen*. Ms. ZAS, Berlin.

Eckardt, R. 2006. *Meaning Change in Grammaticalization: An Enquiry into Semantic Reanalysis*. Oxford: Oxford University Press.

Eckardt, R. 2012. 'The many careers of negative polarity items.' In: K. Davidse, T. Breban, L. Brems, and T. Mortelmans (eds), *Grammaticalization and Language Change: New Reflections*. Amsterdam/Philadelphia, PA: Benjamins. 299–326.

Embick, D. and R. Noyer. 2007. 'Distributed morphology and the syntax-morphology interface.' In: G. Ramchand and C. Reiss (eds), *The Oxford Handbook of Linguistic Interfaces*. Oxford: Oxford University Press. 289–324.

Epstein, S., E. Groat, R. Kawashima, and H. Kitahara. 1998. *A Derivational Approach to Syntactic Relations*. Oxford: Oxford University Press.

Epstein, S. and D. Seely. 2002. *Derivation and Explanation in the Minimalist Program*. Oxford: Blackwell Publishers.

Ernst, T. 2001. *The Syntax of Adjuncts*. Cambridge: Cambridge University Press.

Ernst, T. 2009. 'Speaker oriented adverbs.' *Natural Language and Linguistic Theory 27*: 497–544.

Espinal, M. Teresa, 2007. Licensing expletive negation and negative concord in Romance languages. In: Floricick, F. (Ed.), *La Né gation Dans les Langues Romanes*. John Benjamins, Linguisticae Investigationes Supplementa 26, Amsterdam, pp. 49–74.

Espinal, M. T. and S. Tubau. 2016. 'Interpreting argumental n-words as answers to negative questions.' *Lingua 177*: 41–59.

Espinal, M. T., S. Tubau, J. Borràs-Comes, and P. Prieto. 2016. 'Double negation in Catalan and Spanish: interaction between syntax and prosody.' In: P. Larrivée and C. Lee (eds), *Negation and Polarity: Experimental Perspectives.* Cham: Springer. 145–76.

Etxeberria, U., S. Tubau, V. Déprez, J. Borràs-Comes, and M.T. Espinal. 2018. 'Relating (un)acceptability to interpretation: experimental investigations in negation.' *Frontiers in Psychology 8*: Article 2370.

Fălăuş, A. 2009. *Polarity items and dependent indefinites in Romanian.* PhD dissertation, University of Nantes.

Fălăuş, A. and A. Nicolae. 2016. 'Fragment answers and double negation in strict negative concord languages.' In: M. Moroney, C. Little, J. Collard, and D. Burgdorf (eds), *Proceedings of SALT 28.* Washington, DC: LSA. 584–600.

Fanselow, G. 2001. 'Features, theta-roles, and free constituent order.' *Linguistic Inquiry 32*: 405–37.

Fanselow, G. and D. Cavar. 2001. 'Remarks on the economy of pronunciation.' In: G. Müller and W. Sternefeldt (eds), *Competition in Syntax.* Berlin: De Gruyter. 107–50.

Fanselow, G. and D. Cavar. 2002. 'Partial deletion.' In: A. Alexiadou (ed.), *Theoretical Approaches to Universals.* Amsterdam: Benjamins. 65–97.

Fauconnier, G. 1979. 'Implication reversal in a natural language.' In: F. Guenther and S. Schmidt (eds), *Formal Semantics and Pragmatics for Natural Languages.* Dordrecht: Reidel. 289–301.

Fernald, T. and E. Perkins. 2007. 'Negative polarity items in Navajo.' In: S. Tuttle (ed.), *Athabaskan Languages Conference Papers.* Fairbanks, AK: Alaska Native Language Center Working Papers. 19–48.

Fillmore, C. 1963. 'The position of embedding transformations in a grammar.' *Word 19*: 208–31.

von Fintel, K. 1989. 'Theticity in generative grammar.' In E. Bach, A. Kratzer, and B. Partee (eds), *Papers on Quantification: Report on NSF Grant BNS 8719999.* Amherst, MA: UMass Department of Linguistics. 85–100.

von Fintel, K. 1999. 'NPI-licensing, Strawson-entailment, and context-dependency.' *Journal of Semantics 16*: 97–148.

von Fintel, K. and A. Gillies. 2010. 'Must ... stay ... strong!' *Natural Language Semantics 18*: 351–83.

von Fintel, K. and S. Iatridou. 2007. 'Anatomy of a modal construction.' *Linguistic Inquiry 38*: 445–83.

von Fintel, K. and S. Iatridou. 2017. 'A modest proposal for the meaning of imperatives.' In: A. Arregui, M. Rivero, and A. Salanova (eds), *Modality Across Syntactic Categories.* Oxford: Oxford University Press. 288–319.

von Fintel, K. and S. Iatridou. 2019. *Since since.* In: D. Altshuler and J. Rett (eds), *The Semantics of Plurals, Focus, Degrees, and Times: Essays in Honor of Roger Schwarzschild.* Cham: Springer. 305–33.

Fletcher, P. and M. Garman. 1988. 'Normal language development and language impairment: Syntax and beyond.' *Clinical Linguistics & Phonetics 2*: 97–113.

Fox, Danny. 2000. *Economy and Semantic Interpretation.* Cambridge, MA: The MIT Press.

Fox, Danny and Benjamin Spector. 2018. 'Economy and embedded exhaustification.' *Natural Language Semantics 26*: 1–50.

Frege, G. 1892. 'Über Sinn und Bedeutung.' *Zeitschrift für Philosophie und philosophische Kritik 100*: 25–50.
Fukui, N. and H. Sakai. 2003. 'The visibility guideline for functional categories: Verb-raising in Japanese and related issues.' *Lingua 113*: 321–75.
Gajewski, J. 2002. *L-analyticity and natural language*. Ms. MIT.
Gajewski, J. 2005. *Neg raising: presupposition and polarity*. PhD dissertation, MIT.
Gajewski, J. 2007. 'Neg-raising and polarity.' *Linguistics and Philosophy 30*: 298–328.
Gajewski, J. 2011. 'Licensing strong NPIs.' *Natural Language Semantics 19*: 109–48.
Gajewski, J. and Y. Sharvit. 2008. 'On the calculation of local implicatures.' In: C. Chang and H. Haynie (eds), *Proceedings of the 26th West Coast Conference on Formal Linguistics*. Somerville, MA: Cascadilla Press. 411–19.
Gajewski, J. and Y. Sharvit. 2012. 'In defense of the grammatical approach to local implicatures.' *Natural Language Semantics 20*: 31–57.
Gajic, J. 2020. *Negative coordination*. PhD dissertation, University of Göttingen.
Garbacz, P. 2010. *Word order in Övdalian: a study in variation and change*. PhD dissertation, Lund University.
Gärtner, H.-M. 2002. 'Are there V2 relative clauses in German?' *Journal of Comparative Germanic Linguistics 3*: 97–141.
Gazdar, G. 1979. *Pragmatics: Implicature, Presupposition, and Logical Form*. New York: Academic.
Gazdar, G., E. Klein, G. Pullum, and I. Sag. 1985. *Generalised Phrase Structure Grammar*. Oxford: Blackwell.
Geurts, B. 1996. 'On no.' *Journal of Semantics 13*: 67–86.
Geurts, B. and J. Huitink. 2006. 'Modal concord.' In: P. Dekker and H. Zeijlstra (eds), *Concord Phenomena and the Syntax Semantics Interface*. Malaga: ESSLLI. 15–20.
Giannakidou, A. 1998. *Polarity Sensitivity as (Non)veridical Dependency*. Amsterdam: Benjamins.
Giannakidou, A. 1999. 'Affective dependencies.' *Linguistics and Philosophy 22*: 367–421.
Giannakidou, A. 2000. 'Negative ... concord?' *Natural Language and Linguistic Theory 18*: 457–523.
Giannakidou, A. 2001. 'The meaning of free choice.' *Linguistics and Philosophy 24*: 659–735.
Giannakidou, A. 2002. 'Until, aspect, and negation: a novel argument for two *untils*.' In: B. Jackson (ed.), *Proceedings of SALT 12*. Ithaca, NY: Cornell. 84–103.
Giannakidou, A. 2006a. '*Only*, emotive factive verbs, and the dual nature of polarity dependency.' *Language 82*: 575–603.
Giannakidou, A. 2006b. 'N-words and negative concord.' In: M. Everaert, R. Goedemans, and H. van Riemsdijk (eds), *The Syntax Companian*, 327–91. London: Blackwell.
Giannakidou, A. 2007. 'The landscape of EVEN.' *Natural Language and Linguistic Theory 25*: 39–81.
Giannakidou, A. 2011. 'Negative and positive polarity items: Licensing, compositionality and variation.' In: C. Maienborn, K. von Heusinger, and P. Portner (eds), *Semantics: An International Handbook of Natural Language Meaning*. Berlin: De Gruyter. 1660–712.
Giannakidou, A. 2018. 'A critical assessment of exhaustivity for NPIs: the view from Greek, Korean, Mandarin, and English.' *Acta Linguistics Academia 65*: 503–45.
Giannakidou, A. and A. Mari. 2018. 'The semantic roots of positive polarity: epistemic modal verbs and adverbs in English, Greek and Italian.' *Linguistics and Philosophy 41*: 623–64.

Giannakidou, A. and H. Zeijlstra. 2017. 'The landscape of negative dependencies: negative concord and n-words.' In: M. Evaerert and H. van Riemsdijk (eds), *The Blackwell Companion to Syntax, 2nd Edition*. Oxford: Blackwell.

Giorgi, A. 2004. 'From temporal anchoring to long distance anaphor binding.' Paper presented at the 23rd *West Coast Conference in Formal Linguistics*. April 23-25, University of California at Davis, Davis, CA.

Giorgi, A. and F. Pianesi. 1997. *Tense and Aspect. From Semantics to Morphosyntax*. New York/ Oxford: Oxford University Press.

Godard, D. 2004. 'French negative dependency.' In: F. Corblin and H. de Swart (eds) *Handbook of French Semantics*, Stanford, CA: CSLI Publications. 351-90.

Goldberg, A. 2011. 'Corpus evidence of the viability of statistical preemption.' *Cognitive Linguistics* 22: 131-53.

Greenberg, J. 1963. 'Some universals of grammar with particular reference to the order of meaningful elements.' In: J. Greenberg (ed.), *Universals of Grammar*. Cambridge, MA: The MIT Press. 73-113.

Grimshaw, K. 1997. 'Projections, heads and optimality.' *Linguistic Inquiry* 28: 373-442.

Gropen, J., S. Pinker, M. Hollander, and R. Goldberg. 1991. 'Affectedness and direct objects: the role of lexical semantics in the acquisition of verb argument structure.' *Cognition* 41: 153-95.

Grosz, P. 2012. 'Grading modality, a new approach to modal concord and its relatives.' In: M. Prinzhorn, V. Schmitt, and S. Zobel (eds), *Proceedings of Sinn and Bedeutung 14*. Vienna: Institute for Linguistics. 185-201.

Gruber, B. 2013. *The spatiotemporal dimensions of person: a morphosyntactic account of indexical pronouns*. PhD dissertation, Utrecht University.

Guerzoni, E. 2003. *Why even ask?: on the pragmatics of questions and the semantics of answers*. PhD dissertation, MIT.

Gyuris, B. 2009. 'Quantificational contrastive topics with verum/falsum focus.' *Lingua* 199: 625-49.

Hackl, M. 2000. *Comparative quantifiers*. PhD dissertation, MIT.

Hacquard, V. 2011. 'Modality.' In: C. Maienborn, K. Von Heusinger, and P. Portner (eds), *Semantics: An International Handbook of Natural Language Meaning*. Berlin: De Gruyter. 1484-515.

Haegeman, L. 1995. *The Syntax of Negation*. Cambridge: Cambridge University Press.

Haegeman, L. 2000. In: L. Horn and Y. Kato (eds), *Negation and Polarity*. New York: Oxford University Press. 21-61.

Haegeman, L. and T. Lohndahl. 2010. 'A new approach to negative concord and multiple agree: a case study of West Flemish.' *Linguistic Inquiry* 41: 181-211.

Haegeman, L. and R. Zanuttini. 1991. 'Negative heads and the neg-criterion.' *The Linguistic Review* 8: 233-51.

Haegeman, L. and R. Zanuttini. 1996. 'Negative concord in West Flemish.' In: A. Belletti and L. Rizzi (eds), *Parameters and Functional Heads*. Oxford: Oxford University Press. 117-79.

Haeseryn, W., K. Romijn, G. Geerts, J. de Rooij, and M. van den Toorn. 1997. *ANS, Algemene Nederlandse Spraakkunst*. Groningen: Martinus Nijhoff.

Hagstrom, P. 2000. 'Phrasal movement in Korean negation.' In: L. Veselinova, S. Robinson, and L. Antieau (eds), *Proceedings of the 9th Student Conference in Linguistics (SCIL 9)*. Cambridge, MA: MITWPL. 127-42.

Hagstrom, P. 2002. 'Implications of Child Error for the Syntax of Negation in Korean.' *Journal of East Asian Linguistics* 11: 211-42.

Halle, M. and A. Marantz. 1993. 'Distributed morphology and the pieces of inflection.' In: K. Hale and S. Keyser (eds), *The View from Building 20*. Cambridge, MA: The MIT Press. 111–76.

Halliday, M. 1970. 'Functional diversity in language as seen from a consideration of mood and modality in English.' *Foundations of Language* 6: 322–61.

Hamblin, C. 1973. 'Questions in Montague English.' *Foundations of Language* 10: 41–53.

Hamilton, M. and B. Fry. 2014. 'Long-distance agreement in Algonquian: accounting for syntactic variation.' In: R. Burkholder, C. Cisneros, and E. Coppess (eds), *Proceedings of the 50th Annual Meeting of the Chicago Linguistic Society*. Chicago, IL: Chicago Linguistic Society. 159–73.

Han, C.-H. 2000. *The Structure and Interpretation of Imperatives: Mood and Force in Universal Grammar*. New York: Garland.

Han, C.-H. 2001. 'Force, negation and imperatives.' *The Linguistic Review* 18: 289–325.

Han, C.-H., J. Lidz, and J. Musolino. 2007. 'V-raising and grammar competition in Korean: Evidence from negation and quantifier scope.' *Linguistic Inquiry* 38: 1–47.

Han, C.-H., J. Musolino, and J. Lidz. 2016. 'Endogenous sources of variation in language acquisition.' *Proceedings of the National Academy of Sciences* 113: 942–7.

Harbour D. 2016. 'Parameters of poor pronoun systems.' *Linguistic Inquiry* 47: 706–22.

Harley, H. 2004. 'Merge, conflation, and head movement: the first sister principle revisited.' In: K. Moulton and M. Wolf (eds), *Proceedings of NELS 34*. Amherst, MA: GLSA. 239–54.

Harley, H. and E. Ritter. 2002. 'A feature-geometric analysis of person and number.' *Language* 78: 482–526.

Haspelmath, M. 1997. *Indefinite Pronouns*. Oxford: Oxford University Press.

Heim, I. 1984. 'A note on negative polarity and downward entailingness.' In: C. Jones and P. Sells (eds), *Proceedings of NELS 14*. Amherst, MA: GLSA. 98–107.

Heim, I. 1994. 'Comments on Abusch's theory of tense.' In: H. Kamp (ed.), *Ellipsis, Tense and Questions*. Amsterdam: University of Amsterdam. 143–70.

Heim, I. 2001. 'Degree operators and scope.' In: C. Féry and W. Sternefeld (eds), *Audiatur Vox Sapientiae: A Festschrift for Arnim von Stechow*. Berlin: Akademie Verlag. 214–39.

Heim, I. 2006. 'Little.' In: M. Gibson and J. Howell (eds), *Proceedings of the 16th SALT Conference*. Washington, DC: LSA. 35–58.

Helmbrecht, J. and C. Lehmann. 2010. *Hocąk Teaching Materials, Volume 1: Elements of Grammar/Learner's Dictionary*. Vol. 1. New York: SUNY Press.

Herburger, E. 2001. 'The negative concord puzzle revisited.' *Natural Language Semantics* 9: 289–333.

Herburger, E. and S. Mauck. 2007. 'A new look at Ladusaw's puzzle.' In: H. Zeijlstra and J.-P. Soehn (eds), *Proceedings of the Workshop on Negation and Polarity*. Tübingen: Collaborative Research Centre 441. 64–70.

Hicks, G. 2009. *The Derivation of Anaphoric Relations*. Amsterdam: Benjamins.

Higginbotham, J. and R. May. 1981. 'Questions, quantifiers and crossing.' *Linguistic Review* 1: 41–79.

Hiraiwa, K. 2001. 'Multiple agreement and the defective intervention effect.' In O. Matsushansky (ed.), *The Proceedings of the MIT-Harvard Joint Conference (HUMIT 2000)*. Cambridge, MA: MITWPL. 67–80.

Hoeksema, J. 1997. 'Negation and negative concord in Middle Dutch.' In: D. Forget, P. Hirschbühler, F. Martineau, and M.-L. Rivero (eds), *Negation and Polarity: Syntax and Semantics*. Amsterdam/ Philadelphia, PA: Benjamins. 139–56.

Hoeksema, J. 1999a. 'Aantekeningen bij *ooit*, deel 2: de opkomst van niet polair "ooit".' *Tabu* 29: 147-72.
Hoeksema, J. 1999b. 'Blocking effects and polarity sensitivity.' In: J. Gerbrandy, M. Marx, M. de Rijke, and Y. Venema (eds), *JFAK. Essays Dedicated to Johan van Benthem on the Occasion of his 50th Birthday*. Amsterdam: Vossiuspers AUP. 1-13.
Hoeksema, J. 2007. 'Parasitic licensing of negative polarity items.' *Journal of Comparative Germanic Linguistics 10*: 163-82.
Höhle, T. 1992. 'Über verum-Fokus im Deutschen.' In: J. Jacobs (ed.), *Informationsstruktur und Grammatik*. Opladen: Westdeutscher Verlag. 112-41.
Hoji, H. 1998. 'Null object and sloppy identity in Japanese.' *Linguistic Inquiry* 29: 127-52.
Holmberg, A. 2005. 'Is there a little pro? Evidence from Finnish.' *Linguistic Inquiry* 36: 533-64.
Holmberg, A. 2010. 'Null subject parameters.' In: T. Biberauer, A. Holmberg, I. Roberts, and M. Sheehan (eds), *Parametric Variation: Null Subjects in Minimalist Theory*. Cambridge: Cambridge University Press. 88-124.
Holmberg, A. and C. Platzack. 1991. 'On the role of inflection in Scandinavian syntax.' In: W. Abraham, W. Kosmeijer, and E. Reuland (eds), *Issues in Germanic Syntax*. Berlin/New York: De Gruyter. 93-118.
Holmberg, A. and C. Platzack. 1995. *The Role of Inflection in Scandinavian Syntax*. Oxford: Oxford University Press.
Homer, V. 2008. 'Presuppositions can be disruptors too: a case against Strawson-entailment.' In: N. Abner and J. Bishop (eds), *Proceedings of the 27th WCCFL*. Somerville, MA: Cascadilla. 220-8.
Homer, V. 2009. 'Disruption of NPI licensing: the case of presuppositions.' In: T. Friedman and S. Ito (eds), *Proceedings of SALT 18*. Ithaca, NY: Cornell Linguistic Circle. 429-46.
Homer, V. 2015. 'Neg-raising and positive polarity: The view from modals.' *Semantics and Pragmatics* 8: 1-88.
Homer, V. 2021. 'Domains of polarity items.' *Journal of Semantics 38, 1*: 1-48.
Hopper, P. and E. Traugott. 1993. *Grammaticalization*. Cambridge: Cambridge University Press.
Horn, L. 1969. 'A presuppositional analysis of *only* and *even*.' In: R. Binnick, A. Davidson, G. Green, and J. Morgan (eds), *Papers from the Fifth Regional Meeting of the Chicago Linguistic Society*. Chicago, IL: University of Chicago. 98-107.
Horn, L. 1971. 'Negative transportation: unsafe at any speed?' In: P. Peranteau, J. Levi, and G. Phares (eds), *Papers from the Seventh Regional Meeting of the Chicago Linguistic Society*. Chicago: University of Chicago. 120-33.
Horn, L. 1972. *On the semantic properties of logical operators in English*. PhD dissertation, UCLA.
Horn, L. 1978. 'Remarks on neg-raising.' In: P. Cole (ed.), *Pragmatics*. New York: Academic Press. 129-220.
Horn, L. 1984. 'Towards a new taxonomy of pragmatic reference: Q-based and R-based Implicature.' In: D. Schiffrin (ed.), *Meaning, Form, and Use in Context: Linguistic Applications*. Washington, DC: Georgetown University Press. 11-42.
Horn, L. 1985. 'Metalinguistic negation and pragmatic ambiguity.' *Language* 61: 121-74.
Horn, L. 1989. *A Natural History of Negation*. Chicago, IL: The University of Chicago Press.
Horn, L. 2005. 'Airport '86 revisited: toward a unified indefinite any.' In: G. Carlson and F. Pelletier (eds), *The Partee Effect*. Stanford, CA: CSLI. 179-205.

Horn, L. 2007. 'Histoire d'*O: lexical pragmatics and the geometry of opposition.' In: J.-Y. Béziau and G. Payette (eds), *New Perspectives on the Square of Opposition*. New York: Peter Lang. 393–426.

Horn, L. 2014. 'The cloud of unknowing.' In: J. Hoeksema and D. Gilbers (eds), *Black Book: A Festschrift in Honor of Frans Zwarts*. Groningen: University of Groningen. 178–96.

Horn. L. and S. Bayer. 1984. 'Short-circuited implicature: a negative contribution.' *Linguistics and Philosophy 7*: 397–414.

Huang, J. 1982. *Logical relations in Chinese and the theory of grammar*. PhD dissertation, MIT.

Huddleston, K. 2010. *Negative indefinites in Afrikaans*. PhD dissertation, Utrecht University.

von Humboldt, A. 1836. *Über die Verschiedenheit des menschlichen Sprachbaues und ihren Einfluss auf die geistige Entwickelung des Menschengeschlechts*. Berlin: F. Dümmler.

Iatridou, S. 1990. 'About AgrP.' *Linguistic Inquiry 21*: 421–59.

Iatridou, S. 2000. 'The grammatical ingredients of counterfactuality.' *Linguistic Inquiry 31*: 231–70.

Iatridou, S., E. Anagnostopoulou, and R. Izvorski. 2001. 'Observations about the form and meaning of the perfect.' In: M. Kenstowicz (ed.), *Ken Hale: A Life in Language*. Cambridge, MA: The MIT Press. 189–238.

Iatridou, S. and T. Kroch. 1992. 'The licensing of CP-recursion and its relevance to the Germanic verb second phenomenon.' *Working Papers in Scandinavian Syntax 50*: 1–24.

Iatridou, S. and I. Sichel. 2011. 'Negative DPs, A-Movement, and Scope Diminishment.' *Linguistic Inquiry 42*: 595–629.

Iatridou, S. and S. Tatevosov. 2016. 'Our *even*.' *Linguistics and Philosophy 39*: 295–331.

Iatridou, S. and H. Zeijlstra. 2010. 'On the scopal interaction of negation and deontic modals.' In: M. Aloni, H. Bastiaanse, T. de Jager, and K. Schulz (eds), *Proceedings of the Amsterdam Colloquium 2009*. Berlin: Springer. 315–24.

Iatridou, S. and H. Zeijlstra. 2013. 'Negation, polarity and deontic modals.' *Linguistic Inquiry 44*: 529–68.

Iatridou, S. and H. Zeijlstra. 2017. 'Negated perfects and temporal *in*-adverbials.' In: C. Halpert, H. Kotek, and C. van Urk (eds), *A Pesky Set: Papers for David Pesetsky*. Cambridge, MA: MITWPL. 65–74.

Iatridou, S. and H. Zeijlstra. 2021. 'The complex beauty of boundary adverbials: *in years* and *until*.' *Linguistic Inquiry 52*: 89–142.

Ippolito, M. 2002. *On the semantic composition of subjunctive conditionals*. PhD dissertation, MIT.

Israel, M. 1996. 'Polarity Sensitivity as Lexical Semantics.' *Linguistics & Philosophy 19*: 619–66.

Israel, M. 2011. *The Grammar of Polarity: Pragmatics, Sensitivity, and the Logic of Scales*. Cambridge: Cambridge University Press.

Jackendoff, R. 1969. *Some rules of semantic interpretation for English*. PhD dissertation, MIT.

Jackendoff, R. 1972. *Semantic Interpretation in Generative Grammar*. Cambridge, MA: The MIT Press.

Jacobs, J. 1980. 'Lexical decomposition in Montague grammar.' *Theoretical Linguistics 7*: 121–36.

Jaeger, F. and M. Wagner. 2003. *Association with focus and linear order in German*. Ms. Stanford University.

Jäger, A. 2008. *A History of German Negation*. Amsterdam: Benjamins.
Jäger, A. 2010. 'Anything is nothing is something. On the diachrony of polarity types of indefinites.' *Natural Language and Linguistic Theory* 28: 787–822.
Janssen, T. 1997. 'Compositionality.' In: J. van Benthem and A. ter Meulen (eds), *Handbook of Logic and Language*. Amsterdam: Elsevier. 417–70.
Jaspers, D. 2005. *On the negative logic of natural language. Operators in the lexicon*. PhD dissertation, University of Leiden.
Jespersen, O. 1917. *Negation in English and Other Languages*. Copenhagen: A. F. Høst.
Jespersen, O. 1924. *Philosophy of Grammar*. London: Allen & Unwin.
Jonas, D. 1995. *Clausal structure and verbal syntax of Scandinavian and English*. PhD dissertation, Harvard University.
Joo, Y. 1989. *A cross-linguistic approach to quantification in syntax*. PhD dissertation, University of Wisconsin, Madison.
Kadmon, N. and F. Landman. 1993. 'Any.' *Linguistics and Philosophy* 16: 353–422.
Karawani, H. 2014. *The real, the fake, and the fake fake: in counterfactual conditionals, crosslinguistically*. PhD dissertation, University of Amsterdam.
Karttunen, L. 1971. 'Implicative verbs. *Language* 2: 340–58.
Karttunen, L. 1972. '*Possible* and *must*.' In: J. Kimball (ed.), *Syntax and Semantics, Volume 1*. New York: Academic Press. 1–20.
Karttunen, L. 1974. 'Until.' In: M. La Galy, R. Fox, and Anthony Bruck (eds), *Papers from the Tenth Regional Meeting of the Chicago Linguistic Society*. Chicago, IL: University of Chicago. 283–97.
Karttunen, L. 1977. 'Syntax and semantics of questions.' *Linguistics and Philosophy* 1: 3–44.
Kauf, C. and H. Zeijlstra. 2018. 'Towards a new explanation of sequence of tense.' In: S. Maspong, B. Stefánsdóttir, K. Blake, and F. Davis (eds), *Proceedings of the 28th Semantics and Linguistic Theory Conference*. Washington, DC: LSA. 59–77.
Kauf, C. and H. Zeijlstra. 2021. *Towards a new explanation of Sequence-of-Tense*. Ms. MIT/University of Göttingen.
Kaufmann, M. 2012. *Interpreting Imperatives*. Dordrecht: Springer.
Kayne, R. 1989. 'Notes on English Agreement.' *CIEFL* 1: 40–67.
Kayne, R. 1994. *The Antisymmetry of syntax*. Cambridge, MA: MIT Press.
Kayne, Richard. 2000. *Parameters and Universals*, Oxford University Press, New York.
Keenan, E. and D. Westerståhl. 1997. 'Generalised quantifiers in linguistics and logic.' In: J. van Benthem and A. ter Meulen (eds), *Handbook of Logic and Language*. Amsterdam: Elsevier. 837–893.
Kim, J.-B. 1995. 'On the existence of NegP in Korean.' In: S. Kuno (ed.), *Harvard Studies in Korean Linguistics VI. Proceedings of the 1995 Harvard International Symposium on Korean Linguistics*. Cambridge, MA: Harvard University. 267–82.
Kim, S. 1999. 'Sloppy/strict identity, empty objects, and NP ellipsis.' *Journal of East Asian Linguistics* 8: 255–84.
Kiparsky, P. and C. Condoravdi. 2006. 'Tracking Jespersen's Cycle.' In: M. Janse, B. Joseph, and A. Ralli (eds), *Proceedings of the 2nd International Conference of Modern Greek Dialects and Linguistic Theory*. Mytilene: Doukas. 172–97.
Klein, W. 1994. *Time in Language*. London: Routledge.
Klima, E. 1964. 'Negation in English.' In: J. Fodor and J. Katz (eds), *The Structure of Language. Readings in the Philosophy of Language*. Englewoods Cliffs, NJ: Prentice-Hall. 246–323.
Klima, E. and U. Bellugi. 1966. 'Syntactic regularities in the speech of children.' In: J. Lyons and R. Wales (eds), *Psycholinguistic Papers*. Edinburgh: Edinburgh University Press. 183–208.

Koeneman, O. 2000. *The flexible nature of verb movement*. PhD dissertation, Utrecht University.
Koeneman, O. and H. Zeijlstra. 2014. 'The rich agreement hypothesis rehabilitated.' *Linguistic Inquiry* 45: 571–615.
Koeneman O. and H. Zeijlstra. 2019. 'Morphology and pro-drop.' In: M. Aronoff (ed.), *Oxford Research Encyclopedias of Linguistics*. Oxford: Oxford University Press. https://www.oxfordreference.com/view/10.1093/acref/9780190682361.001.0001/acref-9780190682361-e-610
Koeneman, O. and H. Zeijlstra. 2021. *Null subjects*. Ms. Radboud University of Nijmegen/University of Göttingen.
Koizumi, M. 1995. *Phrase structure in minimalist syntax*. PhD dissertation, MIT.
Koizumi, M. 2000. 'String vacuous overt verb raising.' *Journal of East Asian Linguistics* 9: 227–85.
Kosmeijer, W. 1986. 'The status of the finite inflection in Icelandic and Swedish.' *Working Papers in Scandinavian Syntax* 26: 1–41.
Koster, C. and S. van der Wal. 1996. 'Acquisition of negative polarity items.' In: M. Aldridge (ed.), *Child Language*. Clevedon, Avon: Multilingual Matters. 92–102.
Kratzer, A. 1981. 'The notional category of modality.' In: H.-J. Elkmeyer and H. Rieser (eds), *Worlds, Words, and Contexts*. Berlin/New York: De Gruyter. 38.74.
Kratzer, A. 1991. 'Modality.' In: A. von Stechow and D. Wunderlich (eds), *Semantics: An International Handbook of Contemporary Research*. Berlin/New York: De Gruyter. 639–50.
Kratzer, A. 1995. 'Stage-level and individual-level predicates.' In: G. Carlson and F. Pelletier (eds), *The Generic Book*. Chicago, IL: University of Chicago Press. 125–75.
Kratzer, A. 1998. 'More structural analogies between pronouns and tenses.' In: D. Strolovitch and A. Lawson (eds), *Proceedings of the Semantics and Linguistic Theory Conference 8*. Washington, DC: LSA. 92–110.
Krifka, M. 1989. 'Nominal reference, temporal constitution, and quantification in event semantics.' In: J. van Benthem, R. Bartsch, and P. van Emde-Boas (eds), *Semantics and Contextual Expressions*. Dordrecht: Foris. 75–115.
Krifka, M. 1992. 'Some remarks on polarity items.' In: D. Zäfferer (ed.), *Semantic Universals in Universal Semantics*. Berlin: Foris. 150–89.
Krifka, M. 1995. 'The semantics and pragmatics of polarity items in assertion.' *Linguistic Analysis* 15: 209–57.
Krifka, M. 2001a. 'For a structured meaning account of questions and answers.' In: C. Féry and W. Sternefeld (eds), *Audiatur Vox Sapientia. A Festschrift for Arnim von Stechow*. Berlin: Akademie Verlag. 287–319.
Krifka, M. 2001b. 'Quantifying into question acts.' *Natural Language Semantics* 9: 1–40.
Kroch, A. 1979. *The Semantics of Scope in English*. New York: Garland.
Kumar, R. 2006. *Negation and Licensing of Negative Polarity Items in Hindi Syntax*. New York: Routledge.
Kusumoto, K. 1999. *Tense in embedded contexts*. PhD dissertation, UMass Amherst.
Labov, W. 1972. *Sociolinguistic Patterns*. Philadelphia, PA: University of Pennsylvania Press.
Ladusaw, W. 1979. *Polarity Sensitivity as Inherent Scope Relations*. NY: Garland Publishing.
Ladusaw, W. 1992. 'Expressing negation.' In: C. Barker and D. Dowty. *Proceedings of SALT II*. Ithaca, NY: Cornell Linguistic Circle. 237–59.
Ladusaw, W. 1996. 'Negation and Polarity Items.' In: S. Lappin, (ed.), *The Handbook of Contemporary Semantic Theory*. Oxford: Blackwell. 321–41.

Lahiri, U. 1998. 'Focus and negative polarity in Hindi.' *Natural Language Semantics* 6: 57–123.
Laka, I. 1990. *Negation in syntax: on the nature of functional categories and projections*. PhD dissertation, MIT.
Lanceloet – Jonckbloet, Willem (ed.). 1846-1849. Roman van Lancelot, (XIIIe eeuw). 'Naar het (eenig-bekende) handschrift der Koninklijke Bibliotheek, op gezag van het gouvernement uitgegeven.' In: F. Van Oostrom (ed.), *1998. CD-ROM Middelnederlands*. Den Haag: SDU.
Lasnik, H. 1975. 'On the semantics of negation.' In: D. Hockney (ed.), *Contemporary Research in Philosophical Logic and Linguistic Semantics*. Dordrecht: Reidel. 279–311.
Lasnik, H. 1981. 'Restricting the theory of transformations: a case study.' In: N. Hornstein and D. Lightfoot (eds), *Explanation in Linguistics*. London: Longman. 152–73.
Lasnik, H. 1995. 'Verbal morphology: syntactic structure meets the Minimalist program.' In: H. Campos and P. Kempchinsky (eds), *Evolution and Revolution in Linguistic Theory: Essays in Honor of Carlos Otero*. Washington, DC.: Georgetown University Press. 251–75.
Lassiter, D. 2011. *Measurement and modality: the scalar basis of modal semantics*. PhD dissertation, NYU.
Lechner, W. 2004. 'An interpretive effect of Head Movement.' In: M. Frascarelli (ed.), *Phases of Interpretation*. Berlin/New York: De Gruyter. 45–69.
Lee, C. 1988. 'Speech act terms and mood indicators (in Korean).' *Acta Linguistica Hungarica 38*: 127–41.
Lee, T. 1986. *Studies on quantification in Chinese*. PhD dissertation, University of California, Irvine.
Levinson, S. 2000. *Presumptive Meanings: The Theory of Generalized Conversational Implicature*. Cambridge, MA: The MIT Press.
Li, Audrey Ye-Hui. 1992. Indefinite Wh in Mandarin Chinese. *Journal of East Asian Linguistics 1*: 125–55.
Lin J. 2017. 'Distributionally constrained items in child language: the acquisition of superweak NPI shenme 'a/some' in Mandarin Chinese.' *Glossa 2*: 15.
Lin, J., F. Weerman, and H. Zeijlstra. 2014. 'Mandarin SHENME as a superweak NPI.' In: J. Hoeksema and D. Gilbers (eds), *Black Book: A Festschrift in Honor of Frans Zwarts*. Groningen: University of Groningen. 229–51.
Lin, J., F. Weerman, and H. Zeijlstra. 2015. 'Emerging NPIs: the acquisition of Dutch *hoeven* ('need').' *The Linguistic Review 32*: 333–76.
Lin, J., F. Weerman, and H. Zeijlstra. 2018. 'Acquisition of the Dutch NPI hoeven 'need': From lexical frames to abstract knowledge.' *Language Acquisition 28*: 155–77.
Lin, J., F. Weerman, and H. Zeijlstra. 2021. 'NPIs of different strengths: acquisition and beyond.' *Language & Linguistic Theory 40*: 123–58.
Lin J.-W. 1996. *Polarity licensing and wh phrase quantification in Chinese*. PhD dissertation, UMass Amherst.
Lin, J.-W. 1998. 'On existential polarity wh-phrases.' *Journal of East Asian Linguistics 7*: 219–55.
Linebarger, M. 1980. *The grammar of negative polarity*. PhD dissertation, MIT.
Linebarger, M. 1987. 'Negative polarity and grammatical representation.' *Linguistics and Philosophy 10*: 325–87.
Löbner, S. 1987. 'Quantification as a major module of natural language semantics.' In: J. Groenendijk, D. de Jongh, and M. Stokhof (eds), *Studies in Discourse Representation Theory and the Theory of Generalized Quantifiers*. Dordrecht: Foris. 53–85.

Löbner, S. 1990. *Wahr neben Falsch: Duale Operatoren als die Quantoren naturlicher Sprache*. Tübingen: Max Niemeyer.

Lohnstein, H. 2000. *Satzmodus-kompositionell. Zur Parametrisierung der Modusphrase im Deutschen*. Berlin: Akademie Verlag.

Longobardi, G. 1991. 'Island Effects and Parasitic Constructions.' In: J. Huang and R. May (eds), *Logical Structure & Linguistic Structure*. Dordrecht: Kluwer. 149–96.

Ludlow, P. 2002. 'LF and natural logic.' In G. Peter and G. Preyer (eds), *Logical Form and Language*. Oxford: Oxford University Press. 132–68.

Lyons, J. 1977. *Semantics*. Cambridge: Cambridge University Press.

MacWhinney, B. 2000. *The CHILDES Project: Tools for Analyzing Talk. Third Edition*. Mahwah, NJ: Lawrence Erlbaum Associates.

Mahajan, A. 1990. *The A/A-bar distinction and movement theory*. PhD dissertation, MIT.

Manzini, R. and L. Savoia. 2005. *I dialetti italiani e romanci*. Alessandria: Edizioni dell' Orso.

Manzini, R. and K. Wexler. 1987. 'Parameters, binding theory, and learnability.' *Linguistic Inquiry 18*: 413–44.

Marantz, A. 1991. 'Case and licensing.' In: G. Westphal, B. Ao, and H.-R. Chae (eds), *Proceedings of the Eighth Eastern States Conference on Linguistics*. Columbus, OH: Ohio State University, Department of Linguistics. 234–53. Reprinted in: E. Reuland (ed.). 2000. *Arguments and Case: Explaining Burzio's Generalization*. Amsterdam: Benjamins. 11–30.

Marcus, G. 1993. 'Negative evidence in language acquisition.' *Cognition 46*: 53–85.

Marcus, G., S. Pinker, M. Ullman, M. Hollander, J. Rosen, and F. Xu. 1992. 'Overregularization in language acquisition.' *Monographs of the Society for Research in Child Development 57*: i–178.

Martins, A.-M. 2000. 'Polarity Items in Romance: underspecification and lexical change.' In: S. Pintzuk, G. Tsoulas, and A. Warner (eds), *Diachronic Syntax: Models and Mechanisms*. Oxford: Oxford University Press. 191–219.

Mathewson, L. 1998. *Determiner Systems and Quantificational Strategies. Evidence from Salish*. The Hague: Holland Academic Graphics.

May, R. 1985. *Logical Form: Its Structure and Derivation*. Cambridge, MA: The MIT Press.

May, R. 1989. 'Interpreting logical form.' *Linguistics and Philosophy 12*: 387–435.

May, R. 1977. *The grammar of quantification*. PhD dissertation, MIT.

Mayr, C. 2013. 'Downward monotonicity in questions.' In: E. Chemla, V. Homer, and G. Winterstein (eds), *Proceedings of Sinn und Bedeutung 17*. Paris: École Normale Supérieure. 345–62.

Mayr, C. and B. Spector. 2012. 'Generalized scope economy – not too strong!' In: M. Prinzhorn, V. Schmitt, and S. Zobel (eds), *Proceedings of Sinn und Bedeutung 14*. Vienna: Institute for Linguistics. 305–21.

McFadden, T. 2004. *The position of morphological case in the derivation: a study on the syntax-morphology interface*. PhD dissertation, UPenn.

Meijer, M. 2014. *A landslide in the field of deontic modals: the rise of polar moeten and hoeven in (Middle) Dutch*. MA thesis, University of Amsterdam.

Menéndez-Benito, P. 2005. *The grammar of choice*. PhD dissertation, UMass Amherst.

Menéndez-Benito, P. 2010. 'On universal free choice items.' *Natural Language Semantics 14*: 33–64.

Merchant, J. 2001. *The Syntax of Silence*. Oxford: Oxford University Press.

Merchant, J. 2004. 'Fragments and ellipsis.' *Linguistics and Philosophy 27*: 661–738.

Merchant, J. 2006a. 'Why no(t)?' *Style 20*: 20–3.
Merchant, J. 2006b. 'Polyvalent case, geometric hierarchies, and split ergativity.' In: J. Bunting, S. Desai, R. Peachey, C. Straughn, and Z. Tomkov (eds), *Proceedings from the Annual Meeting of the Chicago Linguistic Society 42*. Chicago: Chicago Linguistic Society. 57–76.
Merchant, J. 2011. 'Aleut case matters.' In: E. Yuasa, T. Bagchi, and K. Beals (eds), *Pragmatics and Autolexical Grammar: In Honor of Jerry Sadock*. Amsterdam: Benjamins. 382–411.
Middelnederlandsche gedichten en fragmenten –De Pauw, Napoleon (ed.), 1903. Middelnederlandsche gedichten en fragmenten Deel 2: Wereldlijke gedichten. Gent: Siffer.
Miestamo, M. 2005. *Standard Negation. The Negation of Declarative Verbal Main Clauses in a Typological Perspective*. Berlin: De Gruyter.
Mintz, T. 2002. 'Category induction from distributional cues in an artificial language.' *Memory & Cognition 30*: 678–86.
Mintz, T. 2003. 'Frequent frames as a cue for grammatical categories in child directed speech.' *Cognition 90*: 91–117.
Mintz, T., E. Newport, and T. Bever. 2002. 'The distributional structure of grammatical categories in speech to young children.' *Cognitive Science 26*: 393–424.
Mistry P. 2000. 'Lexical anaphors and pronouns in Gujarati.' In: B. C. Lust, K. Wali, J. Gair, and K. Subbarao (eds), *Lexical Pronouns and Anaphors in Selected South Asian Languages: A Principled Typology*. Berlin: De Gruyter. 397–470.
Mittwoch, A. 1977. 'Negative sentences with *until*.' In: W. Beach, S. Fox, and S. Philosoph (eds), *Papers from the Thirteenth Regional Meeting of the Chicago Linguistic Society*. Chicago: Chicago Linguistic Society. 410–17.
Miyagawa, S. 2010. *Why Agree? Why Move? Unifying Agreement-based and Discourse Configurational Languages*. Cambridge, MA: The MIT Press.
Miyagawa, S., N. Nishioka, and H. Zeijlstra. 2017. 'Negative sensitive items and the discourse-configurational nature of Japanese.' *Glossa 1*: 33.
Monachesi, P. 2001. 'Clitic placement on the Romanian verbal complex.' In: B. Gerlach and J. Grijzenhout (eds), *Clitics in Phonology, Morphology and Syntax*. Amsterdam: Benjamins. 255–93.
Müller, G. 2004. 'Verb-second as vP-first.' *Journal of Comparative Germanic Linguistics 7*: 197–234.
Neeleman, A. and K. Szendroi. 2007. 'Radical pro drop and the morphology of pronouns.' *Linguistic Inquiry 38*: 671–714.
Neeleman, A. and H. van de Koot. 2002. 'The configurational matrix.' *Linguistic Inquiry 33*: 529–74.
Nicolae, A. 2012. 'Negation-resistant polarity items.' *Empirical Issues in Syntax and Semantics 9*: 225–42.
Nicolae, A. 2015. 'Questions with NPIs.' *Natural Language Semantics 23*: 21–76.
Nicolae, A. and K. Yatsushiro. 2020. *Not eating kein veggies. Negative concord in child German*. Ms. Leibniz-ZAS, Berlin.
Nilsen, Ø. 2003. *Eliminating positions: syntax and semantics of sentential modification*. PhD dissertation. Utrecht University.
Noyer, R. 1992. *Features, positions, and affixes in autonomous morphological structure*. PhD dissertation, MIT.
Ogihara, T. 1995. 'The semantics of tense in embedded clauses.' *Linguistic Inquiry 26*: 663–79.
Oikonomou, D. 2016. *Covert modality in root contexts*. PhD dissertation, MIT.

Oosthuizen, J. 1998. 'The final nie in Afrikaans negative sentences.' In: *Stellenbosch Papers in Linguistics 31*: 61-93.
Otani, K. and J. Whitman. 1991. 'V-raising and VP-ellipsis.' *Linguistic Inquiry 22*: 345-58.
Ouali, H. 2005. 'Negation and negative polarity items in Berber.' In: M. Ettlinger, N. Fleisher, and M. Park-Doob (eds), *Proceedings of the Thirtieth Annual Meeting of the Berkeley Linguistics Society*. Berkeley, CA: Berkeley Linguistics Society. 330-40
Ouhalla, J. 1991. *Functional Categories and Parametric Variation*. London/New York: Routledge.
Pan, H. 2006. 'Focus, tripartite structure, and the semantic interpretation of Mandarin *dou*.' *Research and Exploration on Grammar 13*: 163-84.
Panizza, D., G. Chierchia, and C. Clifton Jr. 2009. 'On the role of entailment patterns and scalar implicatures in the processing of numerals.' *Journal of Memory and Language 61*: 503-18.
Parsons, T. 1990. *Events in the Semantics of English. A Study in Subatomic Semantics*. Cambridge, MA: The MIT Press.
Partee, B. 1973. 'Some structural analogies between tenses and pronouns in English.' *Journal of Philosophy 70*: 601-9.
Partee, B. 1975. 'Montague Grammar and Transformational Grammar.' *Linguistic Inquiry 6*: 203-300.
Partee, B. 1984. 'Compositionality.' In: F. Landman and F. Veltman (eds), *Varieties of Formal Semantics*. Dordrecht: Foris. 281-311.
Paul, I. 2005. 'Or, *wh*- and not: Free choice and polarity in Malagasy.' In: J. Heinz and D. Ntelitheos (eds), *UCLA Working Papers in Linguistics 12*. LA: UCLA. 359-367.
Payne, J. 1985. 'Negation.' In: T. Shopen (ed.), *Language Typology and Syntactic Description. Vol. I: Clause Structure*. Cambridge: Cambridge University Press. 197-242.
Penka, D. 2007. *Negative indefintes*. PhD dissertation, Tübingen University.
Penka, D. 2011. *Negative Indefinites*. Oxford: Oxford University Press.
Penka, D. and A. von Stechow. 2001. 'Negative Indefinita unter Modalverben.' In: R. Müller and M. Reis (eds), *Modalität und Modalverben im Deutschen, Linguistische Berichte, Sonderheft 9*. Hamburg: Helmut Buske. 263-86.
Penka, D. and H. Zeijlstra. 2010. 'Negation and polarity: an introduction.' *Natural Language and Linguistic Theory 28*: 771-86.
Perlmutter, D. 1971. *Deep and Surface Structure Constraints in Syntax*. New York: Holt, Rinehart & Winston.
Pesetsky, D. and E. Torrego. 2004. 'Tense, case, and the nature of syntactic categories.' In: J. Guéron and J. Lecarme (eds), *The Syntax of Time*. Cambridge, MA: The MIT Press. 495-537.
Pesetsky, D. and E. Torrego. 2007. 'The syntax of valuation and the interpretability of features.' In: S. Karimi, V. Samiian, and W. Wilkins (eds), *Phrasal and Clausal Architecture: Syntactic Derivation and Interpretation*. Amsterdam: Benjamins. 262-94.
Pinker, S. 1984. *Language Learnability and Language Development*. Cambridge, MA: Harvard University Press.
Pinker, S. 1995. 'Language acquisition.' In: L. Gleitman and M. Liberman (eds), *Language: An Invitation to Cognitive Science 1*. Cambridge, MA: The MIT Press. 135-82.
Pinker, S. 2013. *Learnability and Cognition: The Acquisition of Argument Structure*. Cambridge, MA: The MIT Press.
Pinto, M. 1997. *Licensing and interpretation of inverted subjects in Italian*. PhD dissertation, Utrecht University.

Platzack, C. and A. Holmberg. 1989. 'The role of AGR and finiteness.' *Working Papers in Scandinavian Syntax 44*: 101–17.
Poletto, C. 2000. *The Higher Functional Field in the Northern Italian Dialects*. Oxford/New York: Oxford University Press.
Poletto, C. 2008. 'On negative doubling.' *Quaderni di lavoro ASIT 8*: 57–84.
Poletto, C. and Jean-Yves Pollock. 2004. 'On the left periphery of some Romance WhQuestions.' In: Luigi Rizzi (ed.), *The Structure of CP and IP: The Cartography of Syntactic Structures 2*. Oxford: Oxford University Press. 251–96.
Polinsky, M. and E. Potsdam. 2001. 'Long-distance agreement and topic in Tsez.' *Natural Language and Linguistic Theory 19*: 583–646.
Polinsky, M. and O. Preminger. 2019. 'The agreement theta generalization.' *Glossa 4*: 102.
Pollock, J.-Y. 1989. 'Verb movement, universal grammar, and the structure of IP.' *Linguistic Inquiry 20*: 365–424.
Pollock, J.-Y. 1993. *Notes on clause structure*. Ms. Université de Picardie, Amiens.
Ponelis, F. 1993. *The Development of Afrikaans*. Frankfurt am Main: Peter Lang.
Portner, P. 2007. 'Imperatives and modals.' *Natural Language Semantics 15*: 351–83.
Postal, P. 2004. 'The structure of one type of American English vulgar minimizer.' In: P. Postal (ed.), *Skeptical Linguistic Essays*. New York: Oxford University Press. 159–72.
Postma, G.-J. 2002. 'De enkelvoudige clitische negatie in het Middelnederlands en de Jespersen-cyclus.' *Nederlandse Taalkunde 7*: 44–82.
Preminger, O. 2013. 'That's not how you agree: a reply to Zeijlstra.' *The Linguistic Review 30*: 491–500.
Preminger, O. 2014. *Agreement and its Failures*. Cambridge, MA: The MIT Press.
Preminger, I. and M. Polinsky. 2015. *Agreement and Semantic Concord: A Spurious Unification*. University of Tromsø: Lingbuzz/002363. https://ling.auf.net/lingbuzz/002363.
Prior, A. 1967. *Past, Present and Future*. Oxford: Clarendon Press.
Progovac, L. 1992. 'Negative polarity: a semantico-syntactic approach.' *Lingua 86*: 271–99.
Progovac, L. 1993. 'Negative polarity: downward entailment and binding.' *Linguistics and Philosophy 16*: 149–80.
Progovac, L. 1994. *Negative and Positive Polarity: A Binding Approach*. Cambridge: Cambridge University Press.
Ramchand, G. 2004. 'Two types of negation in Bengali.' In: V. Dayal and A. Mahajan (eds), *Clause Structure in South Asian Languages*. Dordrecht: Springer. 39–66.
Redington, M., N. Chater, and S. Finch. 1998. 'Distributional information: a powerful cue for acquiring syntactic categories.' *Cognitive Science 22*: 425–69.
Reichenbach, H. 1947. 'The tenses of verbs.' In: S. Davis and B. S. Gillon (eds), *Elements of Symbolic Logic*. New York: Macmillan. 526–34.
Reuland, E. 2006. 'Icelandic logophoric anaphora.' In: M. Everaert, R. Goedemans, and H. van Riemsdijk (eds), *The Syntax Companian*. London: Blackwell. 544–57.
Rivero, M. 1994. 'Negation, imperatives and Wackernagel effects.' *Rivista di Linguistica 6*: 91–118.
Rivero, M. and A. Terzi. 1995. 'Imperatives, V-movement, and logical mood.' *Journal of Linguistics 31*: 301–32.
Rizzi, L. 1982. *Issues in Italian Syntax*. Dordrecht/Cinnaminson, NJ: Foris Publications.
Rizzi, L. 1989. *Relativised Minimality*. Cambridge, MA: The MIT Press.
Rizzi, L. 1991. *Residual Verb Second and the Wh-Criterion*. Technical Reports in Formal and Computational Linguistics 2. Geneva: University of Geneva. Reprinted in: A. Belletti and L. Rizzi (eds). 2006. *Parameters and Functional Heads*. Oxford: Oxford University Press. 63–90.

Rizzi, L. 1997. 'The fine structure of the left periphery.' In: L. Haegeman (ed.), *Elements of Grammar: Handbook in Generative Syntax*. Dordrecht: Kluwer. 281–337.

Rizzi, L. 2004. *The structure of CP and IP. The Cartography of Syntactic Structures (volume 2)*. Oxford: Oxford University Press.

Robbers, K. 1992. 'Properties of negation in Afrikaans and Italian.' In: R. Bok-Bennema and R. van Hout (eds), *Linguistics in the Netherlands*. Amsterdam: Benjamins. 223–34.

Roberge, P. 1994. 'On detecting a prior linguistic continuum in Cape Dutch.' In: G. Olivier and A. Coetzee (eds), *Nuwe Perspektiewe op die Geskiedenis van Afrikaans*. Johannesburg: Southern Books. 153–65.

Roberge, P. 2000. 'Etymological opacity, hybridisation, and the Afrikaans brace negation.' *American Journal of Germanic Linguistics and Literatures* 12: 101–76.

Roberts, I. 1993. *Verbs and Diachronic Syntax*. Dordrecht: Kluwer.

Roberts, I. 2007. *Diachronic Syntax*. Oxford: Oxford University Press.

Roberts, I. 2010. 'Varieties of French and the null subject parameter.' In: T. Biberauer, A. Holmberg, I. Roberts, and M. Sheehan (eds), *Parametric Variation: Null Subjects in Minimalist Theory*. Cambridge: Cambridge University Press. 1–57.

Roberts, I. and A. Roussou. 2003. *Syntactic Change. A Minimalist Approach to Grammaticalisation*. Cambridge: Cambridge University Press.

Rohrbacher, B. 1994. *The Germanic languages and the full paradigm*. PhD dissertation, UMass Amherst.

Romero, M. and C.-H. Han. 2004. 'On Negative *Yes/No* Questions.' *Linguistics and Philosophy* 27: 609–58.

Romoli, J. 2013. 'A scalar implicature-based approach to neg-raising.' *Linguistics and Philosophy* 36: 291–353.

Rooryck, J. 2017. A compositional analysis of French negation. Ms. Leiden University.

Rooth, M. 1985. *Association with focus*. PhD dissertation, UMass Amherst.

Rooth, M. 1992. 'A theory of focus interpretation.' *Natural Language Semantics* 1: 75–116.

Ross, J. 1967. *Constraints on variables in syntax*. PhD dissertation, MIT.

Ross, J. 1973. 'Slifting.' In: M. Griss, M. Halle/ M.-P- Schützenberger (eds), *The Formal Analysis of Natural Languages*. The Hague: De Gruyter. 133–69.

Rowlett, P. 1998. *Sentential Negation in French*. Oxford: Oxford University Press.

Rullmann, H. 1995. 'Geen eenheid.' *Tabu* 25: 194–7.

Sadock, J. and A. Zwicky. 1985. 'Speech act distinctions in syntax.' In: T. Shopen (ed.), *Language Typology and Syntactic Description*. Cambridge: Cambridge University Press. 155–96.

Saebo, K.-J. 2001. 'The semantics of Scandinavian free choice items.' *Linguistics and Philosophy* 24: 737–88.

Sailer, M. 2006. 'Don't believe in underspecified semantics: Neg raising in lexical resource semantics.' *Empirical Issues in Syntax and Semantics* 6: 375–403.

Sauerland, U. 2004a. 'On embedded implicatures.' *Journal of Cognitive Science* 5: 107–37.

Sauerland, U. 2004b. 'Scalar implicatures in complex sentences.' *Linguistics and Philosophy* 27: 367–91.

Schlenker, P. 2005. 'The lazy Frenchman's approach to the subjunctive.' In: T. Geerts, I. van Ginneken, and H. Jacobs (eds), *Romance Languages and Linguistic Theory. Selected Papers from 'Going Romance' 2003*. Amsterdam: Benjamins. 269–309.

Schwarz, B. 2004. How to rescue negative polarity items. Ms. UTexas Austin.

Schwarz, B. and R. Bhatt. 2006. 'Light negation and polarity.' In: R. Zanuttini, H. Campos, E. Herburger, and P. Portner (eds), *Cross-Linguistic Research in Syntax and Semantics:*

Negation, Tense and Clausal Architecture. Washington, DC: Georgetown University Press. 175–98.

Seuren, P. 2006. 'The natural logic of language and cognition.' *Pragmatics 16*: 103–38.

Sheehan, M. 2010. '"Free" inversion in Romance and the null subject parameter.' In: T. Biberauer, A. Holmberg, I. Roberts, and M. Sheehan (eds), *Parametric Variation: Null Subjects in Minimalist Theory*. Cambridge: Cambridge University Press. 231–62.

Sheehan, M. 2017. 'The final-over final condition and processing.' In: M. Sheehan, T. Biberauer, A. Holmberg, and I. Roberts (eds), *The Final-over Final Condition. A Syntactic Universal*. Cambridge, MA. The MIT Press. 79–98.

Shimoyama, J. 2001. *Wh-constructions in Japanese*. PhD dissertation, UMass Amherst.

Shimoyama, J. 2006. 'Indeterminate phrase quantification in Japanese.' *Natural Language Semantics 14*: 139–73.

Shimoyama, J. 2011. 'Japanese indeterminate negative polarity items and their scope.' *Journal of Semantics 28*: 413–50.

Gysbreght – Smits-Veldt, Mieke (ed.). 1994. Joost van den Vondel, Gysbreght van Aemstel. Amsterdam: Amsterdam University Press.

Smith, P. 2015. *Feature mismatches: consequences for syntax, morphology and semantics*. PhD dissertation, University of Connecticut.

Snyder, W. 2008. 'Children's grammatical conservatism: implications for linguistic theory.' In: T. Sano, M. Endo, M. Isobe, K. Otaki, K. Sugisaki, and T. Suzuki (eds), *An Enterprise in the Cognitive Science of Language: A Festschrift for Yukio Otsu*. Tokyo: Hituzi Syobo. 41–51.

Sohn, K.-W. 1995. *Negative polarity items, scope and economy*. PhD dissertation, University of Connecticut.

Staniszewski, F. 2019. *Until phrases as obligatory free choice items*. Ms. MIT.

Starke, M. 2001. *Move dissolves into merge: a theory of locality*. PhD dissertation, University of Geneva.

Starke, M. 2004. 'On the inexistence of specifiers and the nature of heads.' In: A. Belletti (ed.), *Structures and Beyond. The Cartography of Syntactic Structures. (vol.3)*. Oxford: Oxford University Press. 252–68.

von Stechow, Arnim (1990), "Focusing and backgrounding operators", in Wer- ner Abraham (ed.), *Discourse particles*, John Benjamins, Amsterdam, 37–84.

von Stechow, A. 2009. 'Tenses in compositional semantics.' In: W. Klein and P. Li (eds), *The Expression of Time*. Berlin: De Gruyter. 129–66.

von Stechow, A. and E. Zimmermann. 1984. 'Term answers and contextual change.' *Linguistics 22*: 3–40.

Stelling, M. 2019. 'Never not a negative concord item: expletive negative concord in West Germanic.' In: A. vam Alem, A. Ionova, and C. Pots (eds), *ConSOLE XXVI: Proceedings of the 26th Conference of the Student Organization of Linguistics in Europe*. Leiden: Leiden University Centre for Linguistics. 279–92.

Stowell, T. 1995. 'What is the meaning of the present and past tenses.' In: P.-M. Bertinetto, V. Bianchi, and M. Squartini (eds), *Temporal Reference, Aspect, and Actionality, Vol. 1: Semantic and Syntactic Perspectives*. Torino: Rosenberg & Sellier. 381–96.

Stowell, T. 2007. 'The syntactic expression of tense.' *Lingua 117*: 437–63.

Suñer, M. 1995. 'Negative elements, island effects and resumptive *no*.' *The Linguistic Review 12*: 233–373.

Svenonius, P. 2001. 'Subject positions and the placement of adverbials.' In: P. Svenonius (ed.), *Subjects, Expletives, and the EPP*. Oxford/New York: Oxford University Press. 199–240.

Svenonius, P. 2006. 'Interpreting uninterpretable features.' *Linguistic Analysis 33*: 375–413.

Szabolcsi, A. 1981. 'The Semantics of Topic/Focus Articulation.' In: J. Groenendijk, T. Janssen, and M. Stokhof (eds), *Formal Methods in the Study of Language*. Amsterdam: Amsterdam Mathematical Center. 513–40.

Szabolcsi, A. 1984. 'From the definiteness effect to lexical integrity.' In: W. Abraham and S. de Meij (eds), *Topic, Focus, and Configurationality*. Amsterdam: Benjamins. 321–48.

Szabolcsi, A. 2004. 'Positive polarity-negative polarity.' *Natural Language and Linguistic Theory* 22: 409–52.

Taraldsen, T. 1978. *On the NIC, Vacuous Application and the That-Trace Filter*. Ms. MIT.

Temmermans, T. 2012. *Multidominance, ellipsis and quantifier scope*. PhD dissertation, Leiden University.

Temmermans, T. and J. Van Craenenbroeck. 2017. 'How (not) to elide negation.' *Syntax* 20: 41–76.

Theakston, A., E. Lieven, J. Pine, and C. Rowland. 2001. 'The role of performance limitations in the acquisition of verb-argument structure: An alternative account.' *Journal of Child Language* 28: 127–52.

Thornton, R. and G. Tesan. 2013. 'Sentential negation in early child English.' *Journal of Linguistics* 49: 367–411.

Thornton, R., A. Notley, V., Moscati, and S. Crain. 2016. 'Two negations for the price of one.' *Glossa 1*: 45.

Thráinsson, H. 1996. 'On the (non)-universality of functional projections.' In: W. Abraham, S. Epstein, H. Thráinsson, and J.- W. Zwart (eds), *Minimal Ideas: Syntactic Studies in the Minimalist Framework*. Amsterdam/Philadelphia, PA: Benjamins. 253–81.

Tieu, L. 2011. 'On the tri-ambiguous status of 'any': the view from child language.' In: L. David and N. Li (eds), *Proceedings of SALT 20*. Ithaca, NY: Cornell Linguistic Circle. 19–37.

Tieu, L. 2013. *Logic and grammar in child language: how children acquire the semantics of polarity sensitivity*. PhD dissertation, University of Connecticut.

Tieu, L. and J. Lidz. 2016. 'NPI licensing and beyond: children's knowledge of the semantics of *any*.' *Language Acquisition* 23: 311–32.

Travis, L. 1984. *Parameters and effects of word order variation*. PhD dissertation, MIT.

Truckenbrodt, H. 2006. 'On the semantic motivation of syntactic verb movement to C in German.' *Theoretical Linguistics* 32: 257–306.

Truswell, R. 2007. 'Extraction from adjuncts and the structure of events.' *Lingua 117*: 1355–77.

Truswell, R. 2011. *Events, Phrases, and Questions*. Oxford: Oxford University Press.

Tvica, S. 2017. *Agreement and verb movement*. PhD dissertation, University of Amsterdam.

Ura, H. 1996. *Multiple feature-checking: a theory of grammatical function splitting*. PhD dissertation, MIT.

Uribe-Etxebarria, M. 1996. 'Levels of representation and negative polarity item licensing.' In: J. Camacho, L. Choueiri, and M. Watanabe (eds), *Proceedings of WCCFL 14*. LA: USC Department of Linguistics. 571–86.

Vanden levene ons heren – Beuken, W. (ed.). 1968. 'Vanden levene ons heren. Zwolle.' In: Frits Van Oostrom (ed.), *1998. CD-ROM Middelnederlands*. Den Haag: SDU.

van der Auwera, J. 1996. 'Modality: The three-layered scalar square.' *Journal of Semantics* 13: 181–96.

van der Auwera, J. 2005. 'Prohibitives: why two thirds of the world's languages are unlike Dutch.' In: P. Dekker and M. Francke (eds), *Proceedings of the Fifteenth Amsterdam Colloquium*. Amsterdam: ILLC. 25–30.

Van der Auwera, J. 2010. 'On the diachrony of negation.' In: L. Horn (ed.), *The Expression of Negation*. Berlin/New York: De Gruyter. 73–101.

Van der Auwera, J. 2011. 'The Jespersen Cycles.' In: E. van Gelderen (ed.), *Cyclical Change*. Amsterdam: Benjamins. 35–71.

Van der Auwera, J. and O. Krasnoukhova. 2020. 'The typology of negation.' In: V. Déprez and M.-Th. Espinal (eds), *The Oxford Handbook of Negation*. Oxford: Oxford University Press. 91–118.

van der Wouden, T. 1994. *Negative contexts*. PhD dissertation, University of Groningen.

van der Wouden, T. and F. Zwarts. 1995. 'A semantic analysis of negative concord.' In: U. Lahiri and A. Wyner (eds), *Proceedings of SALT III*. Ithaca, NY: Cornell University Department of Modern Languages and Linguistics. 202–19.

van der Wal, S. 1996. *Negative polarity items and negation: tandem acquisition*. PhD dissertation, University of Groningen.

van Gelderen, E. 2008. 'The Negative Cycle.' *Linguistic Typology 12*: 195–243.

van Gelderen, E. 2009. *Cyclical Change*. Amsterdam: Benjamins.

van Gelderen, E. 2011. *The Linguistic Cycle: Language Change and the Language Faculty*. Oxford: Oxford University Press.

van Rooij, R. 2003. 'Negative polarity items in questions: strength as relevance.' *Journal of Semantics 20*: 239–73.

van Rooij, R. 2008. 'Towards a uniform analysis of *any*.' *Natural Language Semantics 16*: 297–315.

Verkuyl, H. 1993. *A Theory of Aspectuality: The Interaction Between Temporal and Atemporal Structure*. Cambridge: Cambridge University Press.

Vikner, S. 1995. *Verb Movement and Expletive Subjects in the Germanic Languages*. Oxford: Oxford University Press.

Vikner, S. 1997. 'V to I movement and inflection for person in all tenses.' In: L. Haegeman (ed.), *The New Comparative Syntax*. London: Longman. 187–213.

Vikner, S. and B. Schwartz. 1996. 'The verb always leaves IP in V2 clauses.' In: A. Belletti and L. Rizzi (eds), *Parameters and Functional Heads*. Oxford: Oxford University Press. 11–62.

Waher, H. 1978. *Die probleem van die bereik van die ontkenning met spesiale verwysing na Afrikaans*. PhD dissertation, University of Cape Town.

Watanabe, A. 2004. 'The genesis of negative concord.' *Linguistic Inquiry 35*: 559–612.

Wechsler, S. 1991. 'Verb second and illocutionary force.' In: K. Leffel and D. Bouchard (eds), *Views on Phrase Structure*. Dordrecht: Kluwer. 177–91.

Weerman, F. 1989. *The V2 conspiracy; a synchronic and a diachronic analysis*. PhD dissertation, Utrecht University.

Weerman, F. 2006. 'It's the economy, stupid! Een vergelijkende blik op *men* en *man*.' In: M. Hüning, U. Vogel, T. van der Wouden, and A. Verhagen (eds), *Nederlands tussen Duits en Engels*. Leiden: Stichting Neerlandistiek Leiden. 19–46.

Weerman, F. and J. Evers-Vermeul. 2002. 'Pronouns and Case.' *Lingua 112*: 301–38.

Weiss, H. 2002. 'Three types of negation: a case study in Bavarian.' In: S. Barbiers, L. Cornips, and S. van der Kleij (eds), *Syntactic Microvariation*. Amsterdam: Meertens Institute Electronic Publications in Linguistics. 305–32.

Wijnen, F. 1988. 'Spontaneous word fragmentations in children: evidence for the syllable as a unit in speech production.' *Journal of Phonetics 16*: 187–202.

Wijnen, F. and G. Bol. 1993. 'The escape from the optional infinitive stage.' *Language and Cognition 3*: 105–18.

Williams, E. 1981. 'On the notions "lexically related" and "head of a word".' *Linguistic Inquiry* 12: 245–74.

Willis, D., C. Lucas, and A. Breitbarth (eds). 2013. *The History of Negation in the Languages of Europe and the Mediterranean. Volume 1: Case Studies*. Oxford: Oxford University Press.

Wurmbrand, S. 2012a. 'Parasitic participles in Germanic: evidence for the theory of verb clusters.' *Taal en Tongval 64*: 129–56.

Wurmbrand, S. 2012b. 'The syntax of valuation in auxiliary–participle constructions.' In: J. Choi, A. Hogue, J. Punske, D. Tat, J. Schertz, and A. Trueman (eds), *Proceedings of the 29th West Coast Conference on Formal Linguistics (WCCFL 29)*. Tucson, AZ: Coyote Working Papers in Linguistics. 154–62.

Wurmbrand, S. 2014. 'The merge condition.' In: P. Kosta, S. Franks, T. Radeva-Bork, and L. Schürcks (eds), *Minimalism and Beyond: Radicalizing the Interfaces*. Amsterdam: Benjamins. 130–67.

Wurmbrand, S. 2018. 'The cost of raising quantifiers.' *Glossa 31*: 19.

Xie, Z. 2007. 'Nonveridicality and existential polarity wh-phrases in Mandarin.' In: M. Elliott, J. Kirby, O. Sawada, E. Staraki, and S. Yoon (eds), *Proceedings of Chicago Linguistic Society 43*. Chicago, IL: Chicago Linguistic Society. 121–35.

Yaeger-Dror, M. and L. Hall-Lew. 2002. 'Presidential use of negation.' *Texas Linguistic Forum 45*: 187–94.

Yoon, J. 1994. 'Korean verbal inflection and checking theory.' In: H. Harley and C. Phillips (eds), *The Morphology-Syntax Connection*. Cambridge, MA: MITWPL. 251–70.

Zanuttini, R. 1991. *Syntactic properties of sentential negation*. PhD dissertation, University of Pennsylvania.

Zanuttini, R. 1994. 'Speculations on negative imperatives.' *Rivista di linguistica 6*: 119–142.

Zanuttini, R. 1997. *Negation and Clausal Structure. A Comparative Study of Romance Languages*. Oxford/New York: Oxford University Press.

Zanuttini, R. 2001. 'Sentential negation.' In: M. Baltin and C. Collins (eds), *The Handbook of Contemporary Syntactic Theory*. London: Blackwell. 511–35.

Zanuttini, R., M. Pak, and P. Portner. 2012. 'A syntactic analysis of interpretive restrictions on imperative, promissive, and exhortative subjects.' *Natural Language and Linguistic Theory 30*: 1231–74.

Zeijlstra, H. 2004. *Sentential negation and negative concord*. PhD dissertation, University of Amsterdam.

Zeijlstra, H. 2006. 'The ban on true negative imperatives.' *Empirical Issues in Syntax and Semantics 6*: 405–25.

Zeijlstra, H. 2007. 'Negation in natural language: on the form and meaning of negative elements.' *Language and Linguistics Compass 1*: 498–518.

Zeijlstra, H. 2008a. *Negative Concord is Syntactic Agreement*. LingBuzz/000645. https://ling.auf.net/lingbuzz/000645.

Zeijlstra, H. 2008b. 'On the syntactic flexibility of formal features.' In: T. Biberauer (ed.), *The Limits of Syntactic Variation*. Amsterdam: Benjamins. 143–74.

Zeijlstra, H. 2008c. 'Modal concord.' In: M. Gibson and T. Friedman (eds), *Proceedings of SALT XVII*. Ithaca, NY: CLS Publications. 317–32.

Zeijlstra, H. 2009. 'Functional structure, formal features and parametric variation: consequences of conflicting interface conditions.' In: K. Grohmann (ed.), *InterPhases*. Oxford: Oxford University Press. 82–113.

Zeijlstra, H. 2010a. 'On French negation.' In: I. Kwon. H. Pritchett and J. Spence (eds), *Proceedings of the 35th Annual Meeting of the Berkeley Linguistics Society*. Berkeley, CA: BLS. 447–58.

Zeijlstra, H. 2010b. 'Emphatic multiple negative expressions in Dutch.' *The Linguistic Review* 27: 37–73.
Zeijlstra, H. 2011. 'On the syntactically complex status of negative indefinites.' *Journal of Comparative Germanic Linguistics* 14: 111–38.
Zeijlstra, H. 2012a. 'There is only one way to agree.' *The Linguistic Review* 29: 491–539.
Zeijlstra, H. 2012b. 'Not a light negation.' In: A. Chereches (ed.), *Proceedings of SALT 22*. Elanguage. 545–64. https://ling.auf.net/lingbuzz/000645
Zeijlstra, H. 2012c. *NALL. Paper presented at the 3rd World Conference on the Square of Opposition, American University Beirut, Lebanon, 26–30 June, 2012.
Zeijlstra, H. 2013a. 'Not in the first place.' *Natural Language and Linguistic Theory* 31: 865–900.
Zeijlstra, H. 2013b. 'Negation and polarity.' In: M. Den Dikken (ed.), *The Cambridge Handbook of Generative Syntax*. Cambridge: Cambridge University Press. 793–826.
Zeijlstra, H. 2014. 'On the uninterpretability of interpretable features.' In: P. Kosta, S. Franks, T. Radeva-Bork, and L. Schürcks (eds), *Minimalism and Beyond*. Amsterdam: Benjamins. 109–29.
Zeijlstra, H. 2015a. 'The morpho-syntactic realization of sentential negation.' In: A. Alexiadou and T. Kiss (eds), *The International Syntax Handbook*. Berlin: De Gruyter. 275–310.
Zeijlstra, H. 2015b. 'Let's talk about you and me.' *Journal of Linguistics* 51: 465–500.
Zeijlstra, H. 2016a. 'Negation and negative dependencies.' *Annual Review of Linguistics* 2: 233–54.
Zeijlstra, H. 2016b. 'Diachronic developments in the domain of negation.' *Language & Linguistics Compass* 10: 284–95.
Zeijlstra, H. 2017a. 'Universal positive polarity items.' *Glossa* 2: 91.
Zeijlstra, H. 2017b. 'Does neg-raising involve neg-raising?' *Topoi: An International Review of Philosophy* 37: 417–33.
Zeijlstra, H. 2020a. 'Negative quantifiers.' In: Déprez, V. and M.-T. Espinal (eds), *The Oxford Handbook of Negation*. Oxford: Oxford University Press. 426–40.
Zeijlstra, H. 2020b. 'Labeling, selection, and feature checking.' In: P. Smith, J. Mursell, and K. Hartmann (eds), *Agree to Agree: Agreement in the Minimalist Programme*. Berlin: Language Science Press. 137–74.
Zeijlstra 2022. *Two varieties of Korean: Rightward Head Movement or Polarity Sensitivity?*. Linguistic Inquiry: Just accepted.
Zimmermann, E. 1993. 'On the proper treatment of opacity in certain verbs.' *Natural Language Semantics* 1: 149–79.
Zuber, R. (1984). 'Semantic restrictions on certain complementizers.' In: S. Hattori and K. Inoue (eds), *Proceedings of the 13th International Congress of Linguists*. Tokyo: Proceedings Publications Committee. 434–6.
Zwart, J.-W. 1993. *Dutch syntax: A minimalist approach*. PhD dissertation, Groningen University.
Zwarts, F. 1981. 'Negatief polaire uitdrukkingen I.' *Glot* 4: 35–132.
Zwarts, F. 1986. *Categoriale grammatica en algebraïsche semantiek: een onderzoek naar negatie en polariteit in het Nederlands*. PhD dissertation, University of Groningen.
Zwarts, F. 1995. 'Three types of polarity.' In: F. Hamm and E. Hinrichs (eds), *Plural Quantification*. Dordrecht: Kluwer. 177–238.
Zwicky, A. and G. Pullum. 1983. 'Cliticization vs. inflection: English *n't*.' *Language* 59: 502–13.

Index

Acquisition 40, 111–21, 134–9, 156, 197, 264–7, 275–9, 390–1, 395, 414, *see also* language acquisition
Adverb 5, 8–9, 12–17, 31–2, 38–9, 111, 127, 130, 135–8, 153, 251, 258, 275, 318, 350, 358, 373, 415, 432–3
Adverbial 15–16, 135, 136, 182, 240–1, 250–2, 335, 371
Afrikaans 16, 29–30, 77–9, 88–95, 124–5, 149–50, 382–3
  Afrikaans A 88–95, 124–5, 149–50, 382–3
  Afrikaans B 88–95, 382–3
Agree 14, 67–70, 80, 91–3, 114–21, 129–32, 218, 243–7, 400–12, 425
  Downward Agree 68, 403–6
  Upward Agree 68, 403–12, 426, 430
Amalgamation 172, 189–90, 260, 291, 384
Anti-additive 19–21, 34–5, 52–5, 63, 66, 131, 234–9, 254–6, 262–7, 275–7, 308–14, 326–31, 346–9
Anti-morphic 19–21, 34–5, 229, 264, 308
Anti-veridical 346, 387
Arabic 141, 325, 387

Bavarian 30, 156–7, 162, 366–8, 390
Berber 9, 14
brauchen 256–63

C-command 26, 61–3, 68–71, 82–4, 102–9, 114, 133, 154, 201, 204, 262, 302, 309, 320–5, 358–67, 373, 400, 403–6, 423
Catalan 9, 46, 88, 94, 109, 125–8, 148, 382
Chinese 21–2, 228, 255, 268, 271–8, 345–6, 415, *see also* Mandarin Chinese
Choice functions 194–6, 260, 291, 393
Clitic 8–10, 322, 356–60, 365–6, 391, 412
Cloud-of-Unknowing 211–14, 219–24
Conjunction 168–9, 236, 302
Contradiction 24–5, 57, 72, 119–20, 164, 234–9, 246–52, 276, 301–4, 316–24, 331, 334, 338–48, 387, 405
Convergence 226–8, 345, 386–7, 398
Criterion 50–1
  Neg 51, *see also* Neg-Criterion
  Wh 50–1, *see also* Wh-Criterion

Czech 8, 12, 29, 30, 46–7, 57, 61, 74, 79–83, 89, 123–4, 133, 364, 368, 410–11

Danish 382, 415
Definite 280, 285, 295–300
Degree 196, 216–17
Denial 92, 98, 128, 218
Directionality 406, 411
Disjunction 65, 167–9, 280, 285, 297–300, 397
Divergence 226–8, 385–6
Domain alternatives 227, 235–52, 269, 276–8
Domain widening 23, 229, 249–53, 342–3, 386, 396
Double Negation 30, 45, 121, 197, 218, 263, *see also* Negation
Doubt 55, 75, 98, 111–12, 128, 138, 146, 210–11, 383, 404
Dutch 9–13, 16, 19–20, 29, 45–54, 65, 89, 101, 121, 149, 154–63, 171–98, 207, 254, 256–68, 280–300, 307–16, 321–6, 332–4, 351–3, 361, 366, 368, 370–7, 384, 387, 391–8, 421
  Middle Dutch 154–63, 395
  Old Dutch 155

Ellipsis 64, 73, 85
Emphasis 167, 187–8, 417
Emphatic Multiple Negative Expressions 158–62
En/ne-deletion 154–8
English 7–13, 17–23, 29–31, 38, 49, 54–6, 61–5, 77–9, 93–5, 100–11, 129–30, 135–8, 141–4, 151–4, 162–4, 171–98, 228–30, 255–61, 268–78, 294, 301, 306–16, 321–5, 329–34, 343, 376, 382–98, 415, 420, 423, 426–8, 432
  Middle English 152–3
    Early Middle English 152
  Modern English 153
    Early Modern English 153
  Old English 151–2
    Late Old English 152
Evenki 7
Event 6, 17, 57, 60, 62, 71–2, 251–2, 338–42, 400, 422–3
Excluded middle 199–201, 210, 224

INDEX   463

Exhaustification 24, 228, 234–53, 269, 276, 301–5, 316–23, 330–2, 338–46, 386, 394
  Pragmatic exhaustification 245–8, 330–3
  Syntactic exhaustification 245–8, 330–3

Factive 212, 224, 267, 431
Feature checking 68, 70, 74, 119, 243, 248, 262, 319, 338, 400–9, 425, 432
Feature valuation 115, 403, 406
Flexible Formal Feature Hypothesis 41, 111–39, 381, 383, 390, 407–17, 433
Focus 37, 87, 92–5, 98, 128, 146, 152, 169–70, 191, 246–53, 284–5, 292–9, 309, 330, 342–3, 358
  Contrastive focus 152, 250, 253, 309, 342–3
Focus-sensitive operator 246–8, 330, 358
Free Choice 268–70
Free Choice Items 268–70
French 9–11, 16, 30, 41, 52–8, 95–100, 105, 112, 127–9, 131, 141–7, 150–1, 162, 166, 215–19, 358, 382–3, 391, 413, 423
  Middle French 141, 145–7, 150–1
  Old French 141–5, 150, 215
Frysian 161
Full Interpretation 114

German 8–13, 36–7, 68, 89, 158–63, 171–98, 216–17, 256–9, 280–300, 307, 321, 325, 332–4, 353–4, 368, 391–3, 397, 419–20, 430
  Old High German 89, 94, 162, 382
Grammaticalization 400
Greek 11–12, 20, 29, 46, 59–64, 74, 81, 85–6, 89, 142–4, 201, 228, 260, 268, 308–15, 321–2, 360–8, 397

Haitian Creole 141–2
Head movement 11–13, 102–3, 356, 389, 402, 412–21
Hindi 24, 77, 79, 106–9, 129–31, 134, 382
hoeven 20, 28, 256–68, 307, 328
Horn clauses 205–8, 211–14, 219–24, 385, 393
Hungarian 46, 54, 79, 364–8, 398

Icelandic 370, 405–6, 415, 430
Idioms 20, 34, 176–7, 185–6, 192–4, 215, 229, 254–5, 276–8
Illocution 230, 350–77, 381, 389, 399–400
Imperfective 313, 334–43, 352, 398
in weeks/in years 211, 233, 239–42, 245, 249–53, 262, 329–30, 342–3, 386
Incorporation 172, 189–90, 208, 260, 291, 384
Inference 38, 169, 199–200, 221, 237–9, 246–53, 296, 299–300, 303, 338–42

Actuality Inference 250–2, 334–43
Beyond expectation Inference 252, 334–43
Intervention 93, 191, 310–11, 326
Italian 8, 11–12, 15, 28–36, 45–63, 68–76, 77–80, 86–9, 122–4, 145–8, 158–60, 356–63, 368–9, 382–3, 391, 411, 426–30
  Old Italian 147–8, 360–1, 369

Japanese 46, 68, 79, 201, 325, 398, 417
Jespersen's cycle 9, 88, 139–56, 162, 170, 383, 391
Judgement 24, 236, 287–8, 303, 334

Klima tests 5, 218, 376
Korean 79, 228, 398, 417–21

Language acquisition 40, 111–21, 134–9, 156, 197, 264–7, 275–9, 390–1, 395, 414
Language change 138, 140–70, 381, 391
Language variation 134–5, 383
Latin 9, 57, 94, 141–2, 163
  Old Latin 141–2
  Proto Latin 141
Lexicalization 162–70
Licensee question 23–6
Licenser question 18–23
Licensing question 26–8
Locality 53, 63, 68, 73, 111, 203–5, 223–4, 228, 243–7, 262, 330, 386, 425

Mandarin Chinese 21–2, 228, 255, 268, 271–8, 345–6, 415, *see also* Chinese
Markedness 375
Minimizer 141–6, 150, 215–17, 253
Modal
  Deontic modal 25, 31, 260, 306, 318, 327, 347–9, 388, 395, 430–3
  Epistemic modal 21, 271, 275–6, 318, 327
  Existential modal 292, 306, 327, 347–9, 388
  Modal Concord 430–3
  Modal flavour 347–9, 430–3
  Modal force 395, 430–3
  Universal modal 228, 263, 305–7, 313, 316–19, 332, 432–3
Mood 10, 13, 359–69, 365

Nall 162–9, 305, 384
need 17, 20, 25, 174–5, 184, 228, 255–63, 306–7
Negation
  Constituent negation 3–6, 374–6
  Contrastive negation 308–13
  Double Negation 30, 45, 121, 197, 218, 263
  Embracing Negation 96, 150
  Emphatic negation 142–7, 152

Negation (*Continued*)
  Light negation 280–300, 396
  Metalinguistic negation 308, 326
  Sentential negation 4–9, 14–17, 30, 56–7, 71, 94–5, 148–55, 217, 265–7, 306, 358, 376, 396, 417
Negative
  Negative absorption 49–50
  Negative adverb 5, 9, 12–13, 17, 130, 141, 153, 258, 371
  Negative affix 14, 153, 169
  Negative auxiliary 136
  Negative Concord
    Invisible Negative Concord 105–9, 129–34, 138–40, 151–4, 391
    Optional Negative Concord 74, 78, 87, 95, 125–8
    Partial Negative Concord 77, 100, 105–9, 134, 150–1, 383, 391
  Negative doubling 156–7
  Negative factorization 51
  Negative head 14, 16, 25, 102–5, 134–6, 155, 197, 261, 360–6
  Negative imperative 81–2, 104, 351–2, 355–69
    Surrogate negative imperative 82, 352, 369
    True negative imperative 81, 351–2, 355–69
  Negative inversion 205–7, 222, 312, 393–4
  Negative parenthetical 208–11, 385
  Negative particle 8–14, 410
  Negative spread 94, 157
Neg-Criterion 51
Neg-raising 38–40, 199–225, 262, 384–5, 393–4
Non-Entailment-of-Existence Condition 274–5, 345–6, 388
Non-Entailment-of-Non-Existence Condition 346–9, 388
Non-veridicality 21, 267–70, 274–5, 346
Norwegian 156, 368, 413

Object intensional verbs 175, 183–5
Old Saxonian 89, 94

Paduan 11
Pejorative 216–17
Perfective 230, 336–42
Polarity Items
  Hybrid polarity items 334–43
  Negative Polarity Items (NPIs)
    Non-strict NPIs 63, 203, 207, 247, 331, 393
    Strict NPIs 63, 202–11, 218–25, 245–7, 330–1, 385, 393, 403
    Strong/weak NPIs 28, 34, 228–9, 254–67, 276–8, 386

Superstrong NPIs 20, 28, 34, 229, 254, 276–8, 395
Superweak NPIs 21, 22, 25, 28, 34, 228–30, 271–6, 328, 345
Positive Polarity Items (PPIs)
  Strong PPIs 308–14, 329–34, 349, 398
  Weak PPIs 308–14, 326–34, 343, 349, 388
Polarity sensitivity 17–28, 31–2, 40, 230, 261, 344, 419–21
Polish 46, 351–6, 360–4, 368
Presupposition 199–201, 210, 220–7, 235–42, 278, 299, 318, 330, 350, 386, 425
Pro-drop 68, 402, 426–30
Punjabi 77, 79, 106–9, 129–31, 134

Quantification 50–2, 55–7, 62, 96, 143, 163–70, 191–8, 236, 241, 249–52, 261, 291, 302, 318, 327–8, 342–8, 358, 388–90, 394, 397, 425, 430–3
  Higher-order quantification 193–4
  Quantification over abstract individuals 191–3
Quantifier Raising (QR) 53, 56–7, 63, 121, 171–2, 180–90, 291, 384
Quebecois 141, 366–8

Reanalysis 162, 166–7, 265, 276
Reconstruction 28, 104–8, 131, 168, 172, 180–2, 187, 198, 221–2, 256, 301, 305, 317–26, 338, 373–7, 384–9, 395–9, 420–1, 426
Referential 25, 228–9, 254–5, 274–6, 328, 346, 386
  Referential deficiency 25, 228–9, 254–5, 274–6, 328, 346, 386
Rich Agreement Hypothesis 412–17
Romanian 30, 54, 268, 364–9, 429–30
Russian 133, 413

Sequence of Tense 422–5
Serbian/Croatian 89, 93, 208, 364, 398
Shenme 21–2, 255, 271–8, 345–6
Spanish 12, 54–60, 72–6, 82–5, 89, 111–12, 132–3, 147–8, 268, 321–2, 352–63, 368
Speech act 15, 38, 82, 230, 351–76, 389
Split scope 37–40, 171–98, 259–67, 290–2, 384, 391–3
Square of opposition 163–70
Swedish 12–13, 89, 101, 156, 353–4, 368, 376, 413

Tongan 7
Tsez 244, 404
Turkish 7, 13–14

Underspecification 363, 398–9, 424–5
Until 203–4, 227, 230–4, 239–41, 245, 334–43, 388–9
  Until-d (durative until) 334–43
  Until-p (punctual until) 241, 334–43

V-to-C movement 11, 322, 332–3, 354, 370, 372, 415
V-to-I movement 370, 412–21
Veridicality 227, 267, 431

V2 12, 156, 180, 353, 370

West Flemish 9, 15–16, 29–30, 48–51, 78–87, 109, 125–8, 161, 382–3, 390
Wh-Criterion 50–1
Winnebago 414

Yiddish 29, 156–7, 366–70, 415

Zero quantifier 57, 96

OXFORD STUDIES IN THEORETICAL LINGUISTICS

PUBLISHED

1 **The Syntax of Silence**
Sluicing, Islands, and the Theory of Ellipsis
by Jason Merchant

2 **Questions and Answers in Embedded Contexts**
by Utpal Lahiri

3 **Phonetics, Phonology, and Cognition**
edited by Jacques Durand and Bernard Laks

4 **At the Syntax-Pragmatics Interface**
Concept Formation and Verbal Underspecification in Dynamic Syntax
by Lutz Marten

5 **The Unaccusativity Puzzle**
Explorations of the Syntax-Lexicon Interface
edited by Artemis Alexiadou, Elena Anagnostopoulou, and Martin Everaert

6 **Beyond Morphology**
Interface Conditions on Word Formation
by Peter Ackema and Ad Neeleman

7 **The Logic of Conventional Implicatures**
by Christopher Potts

8 **Paradigms of Phonological Theory**
edited by Laura Downing, T. Alan Hall, and Renate Raffelsiefen

9 **The Verbal Complex in Romance**
by Paola Monachesi

10 **The Syntax of Aspect**
Deriving Thematic and Aspectual Interpretation
Edited by Nomi Erteschik-Shir and Tova Rapoport

11 **Aspects of the Theory of Clitics**
by Stephen Anderson

12 **Canonical Forms in Prosodic Morphology**
by Laura J. Downing

13 **Aspect and Reference Time**
by Olga Borik

14 **Direct Compositionality**
edited by Chris Barker and Pauline Jacobson

15 **A Natural History of Infixation**
by Alan C. L. Yu

16 **Phi-Theory**
Phi-Features Across Interfaces and Modules
edited by Daniel Harbour, David Adger, and Susana Béjar

17 **French Dislocation**
Interpretation, Syntax, Acquisition
by Cécile De Cat

18 **Inflectional Identity**
edited by Asaf Bachrach and Andrew Nevins

19 **Lexical Plurals**
by Paolo Acquaviva

20 **Adjectives and Adverbs**
Syntax, Semantics, and Discourse
Edited by Louise McNally and Christopher Kennedy

21 **InterPhases**
Phase-Theoretic Investigations of Linguistic Interfaces
edited by Kleanthes Grohmann

22 **Negation in Gapping**
by Sophie Repp

23 **A Derivational Syntax for Information Structure**
by Luis López

24 **Quantification, Definiteness, and Nominalization**
edited by Anastasia Giannakidou and Monika Rathert

25 **The Syntax of Sentential Stress**
by Arsalan Kahnemuyipour

26 **Tense, Aspect, and Indexicality**
by James Higginbotham

27 **Lexical Semantics, Syntax, and Event Structure**
edited by Malka Rappaport Hovav, Edit Doron, and Ivy Sichel

28 **About the Speaker**
Towards a Syntax of Indexicality
by Alessandra Giorgi

29 **The Sound Patterns of Syntax**
edited by Nomi Erteschik-Shir and Lisa Rochman

30 **The Complementizer Phase**
edited by Phoevos Panagiotidis

31 **Interfaces in Linguistics**
New Research Perspectives
edited by Raffaella Folli and Christiane Ulbrich

32 **Negative Indefinites**
by Doris Penka

33 **Events, Phrases, and Questions**
by Robert Truswell

34 **Dissolving Binding Theory**
by Johan Rooryck and Guido Vanden Wyngaerd

35 **The Logic of Pronominal Resumption**
by Ash Asudeh

36 **Modals and Conditionals**
by Angelika Kratzer

37 **The Theta System**
Argument Structure at the Interface
edited by Martin Everaert, Marijana Marelj, and Tal Siloni

38 **Sluicing**
Cross-Linguistic Perspectives
edited by Jason Merchant and Andrew Simpson

39 **Telicity, Change, and State**
A Cross-Categorial View of Event Structure
edited by Violeta Demonte and Louise McNally

40 Ways of Structure Building
edited by Myriam Uribe-Etxebarria and Vidal Valmala

41 The Morphology and Phonology of Exponence
edited by Jochen Trommer

42 Count and Mass Across Languages
edited by Diane Massam

43 Genericity
edited by Alda Mari, Claire Beyssade, and Fabio Del Prete

44 Strategies of Quantification
edited by Kook-Hee Gil, Steve Harlow, and George Tsoulas

45 Nonverbal Predication
Copular Sentences at the Syntax-Semantics Interface
by Isabelle Roy

46 Diagnosing Syntax
edited by Lisa Lai-Shen Cheng and Norbert Corver

47 Pseudogapping and Ellipsis
by Kirsten Gengel

48 Syntax and its Limits
edited by Raffaella Folli, Christina Sevdali, and Robert Truswell

49 Phrase Structure and Argument Structure
A Case Study of the Syntax-Semantics Interface
by Terje Lohndal

50 Edges in Syntax
Scrambling and Cyclic Linearization
by Heejeong Ko

51 The Syntax of Roots and the Roots of Syntax
edited by Artemis Alexiadou, Hagit Borer, and Florian Schäfer

52 Causation in Grammatical Structures
edited by Bridget Copley and Fabienne Martin

53 Continuations and Natural Language
by Chris Barker and Chung-chieh Shan

54 The Semantics of Evaluativity
by Jessica Rett

55 External Arguments in Transitivity Alternations
A Layering Approach
by Artemis Alexiadou, Elena Anagnostopoulou, and Florian Schäfer

56 Control and Restructuring
by Thomas Grano

57 The Interaction of Focus, Givenness, and Prosody
A Study of Italian Clause Structure
by Vieri Samek-Lodovici

58 The Morphosyntax of Gender
by Ruth Kramer

59 The Morphosyntax of Imperatives
by Daniela Isac

60 Sentence and Discourse
edited by Jacqueline Guéron

61 Optimality-Theoretic Syntax, Semantics, and Pragmatics
From Uni- to Bidirectional Optimization
edited by Géraldine Legendre, Michael T. Putnam, Henriëtte de Swart, and Erin Zaroukian

62 The Morphosyntax of Transitions
A Case Study in Latin and Other Languages
by Víctor Acedo-Matellán

63 Modality Across Syntactic Categories
edited by Ana Arregui, María Luisa Rivero, and Andrés Salanova

64 The Verbal Domain
edited by Roberta D'Alessandro, Irene Franco, and Ángel J. Gallego

65 Concealed Questions
by Ilaria Frana

66 Parts of a Whole
Distributivity as a Bridge between Aspect and Measurement
by Lucas Champollion

67 Semantics and Morphosyntactic Variation
Qualities and the Grammar of Property Concepts
by Itamar Francez and Andrew Koontz-Garboden

68 The Structure of Words at the Interfaces
edited by Heather Newell, Máire Noonan, Glyne Piggott, and Lisa deMenaTravis

69 Pragmatic Aspects of Scalar Modifiers
The Semantics-Pragmatics Interface
by Osamu Sawada

70 Encoding Events
Functional Structure and Variation
by Xuhui Hu

71 Gender and Noun Classification
edited by Éric Mathieu, Myriam Dali, and Gita Zareikar

72 The Grammar of Expressivity
by Daniel Gutzmann

73 The Grammar of Copulas Across Language
edited by María J. Arche, Antonio Fábregas, and Rafael Marín

74 The Roots of Verbal Meaning
by John Beavers and Andrew Koontz-Garboden

75 Contrast and Representations in Syntax
edited by Bronwyn M. Bjorkman and Daniel Currie Hall

76 Nominalization
50 Years on from Chomsky's *Remarks*
edited by Artemis Alexiadou and Hagit Borer

77 Majority Quantification and Quantity Superlatives
A Crosslinguistic Analysis of *Most*
by Carmen Dobrovie-Sorin and Ion Giurgea

78 The Grammar of the Utterance
How to Do Things with Ibero-Romance
by Alice Corr

79 The Derivational Timing of Ellipsis
edited by Güliz Güneş and Anikó Lipták

80 Negation and Negative Dependencies
by Hedde Zeijlstra

PUBLISHED IN ASSOCIATION WITH
THE SERIES

The Oxford Handbook of Linguistic Interfaces
edited by Gillian Ramchand and Charles Reiss

IN PREPARATION

The Place of Case in Grammar
edited by Elena Anagnostopoulou, Dionysios Mertyris, and Christina Sevdali

Phi Syntax
A Theory of Agreement
by Susana Béjar

Stratal Optimality Theory
by Ricardo Bermúdez Otero

Phonology in Phonetics
by Abigail Cohn

Generality and Exception
by Ivan Garcia-Alvarez

Computing Optimality
by Jason Riggle

Gradience in Split Intransitivity
by Antonella Sorace

Syntactic Reconstruction in Minimalism
by Dominique Sportiche

The Syntax of Perspectival Anaphora
by Sandhya Sundaresan